Guide to
the New York Real
Estate
Salespersons'
Course

Third Edition

Guide to
the New York Real
Estate
Salespersons'
Course

Third Edition

Norman Weinberg

Director, The Real Estate Institute, New York University
Editor, *Real Estate Review*

Paul J. Colletti

The Real Estate Institute, New York University
Principal and General Counsel, Preferred Land Services, Inc.

William A. Colavito

The Real Estate Institute, New York University
Vice President and Regional Counsel, Chicago Title Insurance Company

Frank A. Melchior

The Real Estate Institute, New York University
Vice President and Associate Eastern Regional Counsel,
First American Title Insurance Company

JOHN WILEY & SONS

New York   Chichester   Brisbane
Toronto   Singapore

Portions of this book are based on material from GUIDE TO REAL ESTATE LICENSING EXAMINATIONS FOR SALESPERSONS AND BROKERS by William B. French, Stephen J. Martin, and Thomas E. Battle, III, published by John Wiley & Sons, Inc. Some of the chapters have been modeled after the French/Martin/Battle text and have been rewritten to meet the needs of the New York State law. Permission to use the copyrighted material has been granted.

ISBN 0-471-82644-8

Printed in the United States of America

10 9 8 7 6

Preface

New York State law specifies that the prospective real estate salesperson must complete a state-approved course. Actually, many literate adults are able to pass the required examination before they complete the course. They are prepared by studying from a Department of State pamphlet on the New York Real Estate Salesperson's License. Most individuals, however, choose to complete an approved course before undertaking the examination.

This text has been prepared to meet the needs of students who are taking the best of the courses that are offered by universities and colleges in New York, by selected proprietary schools, and by certain real estate boards. These quality courses are designed to turn laymen into first-rate real estate professionals. They prepare students in various areas of real estate law, title, finance, valuation, human rights, and land use regulations. In additon the courses recognize that to bring a transaction to fruition, the professional must develop a high level of negotiating skill and a sound understanding of human psychology. The authors are grateful to all those who have made suggestions and criticisms and particularly to members of the Real Estate Institute of New York University who have made comments based on classroom use of the text.

State Law requires that a state-approved real estate salespersons' course total 45 hours of instruction, and it specifies the content of each of these courses. The chart below lists the number of hours that must be devoted to each topic and designates the chapters in which the topics appear.

The format of the book is designed to be helpful to those students who are preparing for licensing examinations. It is also designed to remain useful to readers who want to retain the book as a

SUBJECT	HOURS	CHAPTERS
Real estate instruments	6	3, 4, 5
Law of contracts	5	6
Real estate financing	5	7, 8
Closing and closing costs	4	9, 10
Law of agency	5	11
License law and ethics	5	12
Valuation and listing procedures	5	13, 14
Human rights and fair housing	4	15
Land use regulations	3	16
Mathematics	3	17

working reference. Thus, each chapter contains a vocabulary list of key terms and a series of review questions. The book also includes Appendices, which contain relevant sections of the Real Estate Salespersons' License Law, Real Property Law, and Law of Agency.

The authors are aware that women are assuming important roles as real estate professionals. However, most of the terms that are used to acknowledge the growing presence of women in the industry make text material harder to read and make complex arguments hard to follow. In most places, therefore, we have used the pronouns *he*, *his*, and *him* to refer to both men and women.

Norman Weinberg
Paul J. Colletti
William A. Colavito
Frank A. Melchior

Contents

Part I

Introduction and Overview

Chapter 1
Use of the Guide

THIS BOOK covers the major topics in the field of real estate in a format designed to prepare students for the New York Real Estate Sales License Examination.

The text in each chapter is the key to your understanding of the material and contains the information you will need to prepare for and pass the examination. To help you understand the material, most of the chapters also provide a vocabulary list of key terms and concepts and end-of-chapter review questions.

As does any discipline, real estate has its own vocabulary, and success or failure in real estate and in the licensing examination depends in part on your mastery of the vocabulary. Therefore, each of the chapters covering real estate topics opens with a list of key terms and concepts. You should pay particular attention to the vocabulary. You will gain a basic understanding of the vocabulary by reading the chapter carefully. In addition, each term is defined in the glossary at the end of the book.

The review questions at the end of most chapters are designed to give you feedback on the material you have just studied and also help you prepare for the examination. After you read each chapter, you should answer all the questions. Then, as part of your final preparation for the examination, you should again attempt to answer all the questions. The answers to all the questions are in Appendix A.

As a further review, Chapter 17 of this text covers real estate mathematics and contains various real estate math problems and instructions on how to perform them. The solutions to the math practice problems are also in the appendix.

REAL ESTATE LICENSING RULES

Who can become a real estate salesperson? What are the educational requirements? How does one go about taking the Real Estate Sales License Examination? Although these questions are examined in Chapter 12, License Law and Ethics, we review the pertinent questions here so that you will know how to get started.

Are You Eligible to Be a Real Estate Salesperson?

In order to understand who needs a real estate salesperson's license, you must first understand the definition of a real estate broker. A real estate broker is a person (or a corporation) who sells an owner's real estate and who charges the owner a fee for the service. The law actually defines the service that the broker performs quite broadly. If a person sells, buys, rents, exchanges, or negotiates to do any of these things, he is engaging in brokerage activity. He is also engaging in brokerage if he collects rents, negotiates a mortgage loan for a buyer, or is a "tenant relocator."

A real estate salesperson is anyone employed by a licensed real estate broker to undertake any of the activities that were just described.

There are many more qualifications for becoming a broker than there are for becoming a salesperson. The law says that a broker must be 19 years old, a U.S. citizen (or legal resident alien of the U.S.), and may not have been convicted of a felony. (The latter disability may be removed by special action.)

Regarding salespersons, the law requires only that the salesperson be at least 18 years old. However, any successful salesperson will eventually want to become a broker and thus will be concerned that he will be able to qualify as a broker.

Licensing and Educational Requirements for Salespersons and Brokers

Every person wishing to become a real estate salesperson must file an application with the New York State Department of State, Division of Licensing Services. The applicant must pass a written examination that satisfies the department as to character and general intelligence. Within one year of receiving a salesperson's license, the applicant has to submit to the department proof that a state-approved real estate salesperson's course has been successfully completed. Since all the material in the examination is covered in the course, most persons elect to complete the course before they file their applications to take the salesperson's examination.

The salesperson's course is 45 hours long. Both the school that offers it and the faculty must be approved by the Department of State. The salesperson candidate should, however, check carefully that he is taking an approved course. The topics of the approved course form the basis for the organization of this book.

The candidate for a broker's license must complete a second 45-hour course, must show that he has participated in the general real estate brokerage business as a licensed real estate salesperson for at least one year, and must pass a broker's license examination.

License Renewal

The license that the new real estate salesperson receives must be regularly renewed. The initial license that the salesperson receives expires on October 31 for the next odd-numbered year. Thereafter, licenses are issued for terms of two years, ~~effective on November 1 of the odd-numbered year, and expiring on October 31, two years later.~~

effective for 3 years from date of issue.

APPLYING FOR THE LICENSE

Persons who wish to apply for a real estate salesperson's license may obtain application forms from the Division of Licensing Services, Department of State, at any of the offices listed below. A copy of the current application form is reproduced in Figure 12-1.

Albany
  162 Washington Avenue
  Albany, New York 12231
Binghamton
  State Office Building
  Binghamton, New York 13901
Buffalo
  65 Court Street
  Buffalo, New York 14202
Hauppauge
  NYS Office Building
  Veterans Hwy., Hauppauge
  New York 11787
Mineola
  114 Old Country Road
  Mineola, New York 11501
New York City
  270 Broadway, New York
  New York 10007

Rochester
  One Marine Midland Plaza
  Rochester, New York 14604
Syracuse
  Hughes State Office Building
  Syracuse, New York 13202
Utica
  State Office Building
  Utica, New York 13501

Any specific or particularly troublesome questions should be directed to the Secretary of State, Division of Licensing Services, at the Albany address.

Applications must be returned with a $20 licensing fee (this includes the testing charge). Each applicant must supply the following information:

☐ His name and address.
☐ Describe his occupation for two preceding years in some detail.
☐ Indicate how long (if at all) he has been in the real estate business.
☐ Indicate the name and address of a broker who has promised to employ him as salesperson.

The last requirement means that the potential salesperson must find a broker-sponsor who promises to employ him once the license is issued. When you study the details of license law in Chapter 12, the reasons why the state requires a sponsoring broker will become self-evident.

If, after you have received your assignment, you wish to change your test location, contact the local office of the Secretary of State.

Examination Dates

The real estate salesperson's examination is conducted every Monday in New York City, Albany, Buffalo, Hauppauge, Mineola, Poughkeepsie, Rochester, and Syracuse. The examination is usually given on alternate Mondays (twice a month) in Binghamton, Newburgh, Utica, and Yonkers. The examination is also given once a month in Plattsburgh and Watertown.

Upon applying for a license, the candidate will be given a copy of "Real Estate Salespersons' License Law" to study. The relevant portions of that pamphlet are reproduced as Appendix B of this book.

TAKING THE EXAMINATION

When you report to the examination center to

which you have been assigned, you must have with you a proper admission ticket or authorization. In addition you should bring with you at least three no. 2 pencils and an eraser. You must also have a photograph of yourself.

Examination Center Regulations

All the examination centers follow the same set of guidelines and rules so as to ensure equality in the examination process. The basic rules are as follows:

☐ No books, dictionaries, or papers of any kind (including scratch paper) are permitted in the examination room. Any candidate found with any of these items will not be allowed to continue the examination.
☐ Candidates are not permitted to work beyond the prescribed time.
☐ Eating, smoking, and drinking are not permitted in the examination room.
☐ If a candidate desires to leave the room for any purpose, permission must be obtained from the test supervisor.
☐ Any candidate engaging in any form of misconduct will be reported to the licensing agency. Disciplinary action is the responsibility of the licensing agency.

Calculators

New York State permits the use of a calculator. The rules concerning the use and types of instruments permitted are:

☐ The candidate may use only hand-held, silent, battery-operated instruments that do not have a paper-tape printing capacity. If the testing supervisor determines prior to admission to the examination that the instrument does not meet the described standards, the candidate will be permitted to take the examination upon surrender of the instrument to the supervisor for the duration of the examination.
☐ If the candidate's instrument should not function during the examination, this will not be grounds for challenging examination results or demanding extended time for completion of the examination.

Note: It is the opinion of the authors that calculators are really not necessary to complete the calculations needed for the examination questions. Any figuring can be done by pencil and paper in the time allotted.

The Answer Sheet

Answers are written on a separate answer sheet, which is numbered and lettered to correspond to the questions in the examination booklet. To record your answer, you must choose the one *best* response from the four choices listed and mark the appropriate letter on the answer sheet. If you mark more than one answer for a single question, the question may be scored as incorrect. Therefore, if you change an answer, be sure the erasure is complete.

How the Examination Is Scored

Your score is based on the number of questions you answer correctly. Do not be overly concerned if there are a few questions you cannot answer. However, since there is no penalty for an incorrect answer, don't be afraid to guess.

Guidelines to Better Test Taking

☐ When you receive your examination booklet, read the directions carefully so as not to miss anything that might be of importance to the examination and cause you to lose credit.
☐ Try to use your allotted time carefully and economically. Take the questions in order and do not waste time on any one question.
☐ Sometimes in a multiple-choice examination "distractors" are used. A math problem, for example, may contain information that is not needed for the solution. Or in a vocabulary-based question, more than one answer may appear to be correct. However, there is always only one *best* answer. If you are not properly prepared, these types of questions may appear to be tricky or unfair. However, if you know the material, you will not be fooled by these distractors.
☐ Read each question thoroughly and completely, and then read *all* the possible choices before selecting the one *best* answer.
☐ Beware of negatives, both in the use of negative prefixes on words or the placement of the word *not*. If you understand the vocabulary, you will not be fooled by the various prefixes and how they are used.

☐ Eliminate the wrong answers from the possible selections. Certain choices will be recognizable immediately as being wrong. This will help you narrow down your possible choices. You can usually eliminate two or even three answers if you read the question carefully and understand the material. In other questions there may be two answers that are possibly correct, but one will be slightly better than the other. At this point your knowledge and reasoning power will help you decide.

☐ If you are not sure of an answer, guess at what you feel the correct response should be. You are not penalized for guessing; if it is a wrong guess, it will not lower your score any more than if it were left blank.

☐ Do not let questions bog you down. If a question takes more than a minute or so, go on to the next question and come back later if you have time. Budget your time proportionately among the questions and sections on the test. Do the questions that are easy for you and get them out of the way quickly; then return to the more difficult questions.

☐ When you are unsure of an answer, put a question mark next to the question on the answer sheet and return to it when you are reviewing the questions at the end of the examination to see if that is still the response you desire. Some other question may have given you a clue to what the correct response is.

Solving Math Problems

☐ Read the problem carefully and decide what is being asked.

☐ Reread the problem for the pertinent information given.

☐ Decide what principle or principles of math need to be applied to the problem.

☐ See how to apply the required principles.

☐ Carefully apply each principle and reach a solution.

☐ Check your work for errors in both computation and methodology.

☐ If you use a calculator, make a note of the various calculations on some scrap paper. (Do not ever write on the test booklet or exam.) This will facilitate review and allow you to see where errors are made and which other calculations are affected by such errors.

☐ Look carefully at your answers to see if they make sense and answer the questions.

In summary, you will do your best on the examination if you have adequately prepared prior to the examination, read the questions carefully, think before you answer, and allow time to check your work.

Chapter 2
The Real Estate Business

REAL ESTATE could easily be considered the most important factor in today's world. No everyday activity goes unaffected by real estate. It allows the production of food and provides the natural resources of domestic and commercial shelters. The study of real estate therefore involves all the aspects of land and structures which might be built on it.

THE RIGHT TO OWN LAND

Real estate, being both unique and valuable, has developed its own body of laws. In feudal England, title (or ownership) of all land was in the king. He granted to certain lords the right to use the king's land (hence the term *landlord*). Initially, lords were tenants of the king and did not own the land.

The "landlord," in turn, granted a lease (more properly a sublease) to his own subjects. They had the right to use the land at the pleasure of their landlord, who, in turn, held the right to use the land at the pleasure of the king.

At first, the lords' right to land lasted for their lifetime only. Late in the thirteenth century, the lords were granted the right to pass their interest in the lands on to their heirs.

Social relations changed gradually. After a long period of time, the subtenants' rights came to include the right to pass their land interests on to their heirs, and ultimately they acquired title, or ownership, as opposed to a mere *possessory* interest in the land.

UNIQUENESS OF LAND

Real estate has become the subject of a particular body of law because it has special and unique characteristics. Every parcel or lot of land is unique in character. It differs from every other parcel of land by reason of many characteristics. The following are some of the obvious differences:

☐ Location
☐ Size
☐ Topography
☐ Water supply
☐ Drainage
☐ Vegetation
☐ View
☐ "Improvements" (if any)
☐ Nature of adjacent property

Because each parcel of real estate is unique, it is impossible to duplicate any given piece of land exactly. By contrast, personal property, whether an automobile or a can of soup, is rarely unique and is generally replaceable in kind.

VALUE

Real estate is generally and consistently a possession of high value compared to the value of other assets that individuals or legal entities may own. It is frequently the largest single investment that individuals make during their lifetime. This is usually true even if the individuals buy real estate more than once.

Corporations, likewise, whether they own it for production, distribution or marketing purposes, frequently find that real estate is the single largest item of capital expense they are likely to incur.

TRANSFERABILITY

Because land is immovable, there arises a special need for laws that apply uniquely to real estate. Ownership cannot be established by the physical possession of a lot. (An individual cannot carry his lot with him or put it in a safe.) Nor can the ownership be transferred by the physical delivery of a real estate parcel, unlike a refrigerator or a stock certificate that can be given into the possession of a new owner.

RESULTING CONCEPTS

Because of all these special characteristics of real estate, several important concepts have evolved.

Contracts

Generally, the courts will enforce contracts involving title to, or an interest in, land only if they are in writing. Although verbal contracts concerning most matters are generally enforceable, it is extremely rare that a verbal contract concerning an interest in real estate is enforced.

Taxes

Since we have developed a system for recording notices of real property ownership, that ownership is reasonably and readily ascertainable; and since property ownership usually involves substantial assets, it has become a special, readily available, object of taxation and an instrument in the collection of debts. Real estate taxes have become a major source of funding for governmental and school operations.

Land Records

Because it is physically impossible to possess a parcel of land, transfers of possession may be difficult to establish and must be demonstrated in some way. Therefore, because of the uniqueness and value of property, it became necessary to have a system of keeping records that were both readily accessible to the public and showed the various interests (ownership rights) in land. In New York, documents that give evidence about, and protect an owner's rights to, real property are filed in the County Clerk's office. These documents are instruments called deeds, mortgages, releases, assignments, subordinations, modifications, satisfactions, leases and subleases, boundary line agreements, easements, licenses, and numerous other names. We shall study these documents in Chapter 5.

REAL ESTATE ELEMENTS

Individuals interested in the real estate business must start by learning about the basic elements of the business itself. Obviously, the most important resource is raw land. The primary use of land has always been for the cultivation of crops or for pasturing livestock.

Second only to its use for food production is the use of land for shelter, more commonly called housing. Housing can take many forms, ranging from luxury single-family homes to the most modest low-income apartments. In addition, many commercial structures are built on land: retail stores, shopping centers, factories, warehouses, and office buildings. Our everyday lives also bring us into structures like schools, churches, hospitals, and recreational facilities. The generalized term for any structure built on land is *improvement*.

The basic definition of real estate is simple and must be mastered by all who enter the business. *Real estate* is defined as land and all improvements permanently attached to it. The term *real property* is often used interchangeably with real estate, although it has a slightly different meaning. Real property commonly refers to the legal rights to land and its improvements. We shall discuss these legal rights to real estate in Chapters 3 and 4.

CHARACTERISTICS OF REAL ESTATE
Land

We have already noted that each individual plot of land is unique. It has its own special physical characteristics. Its location is fixed. No two plots are identical. It is indestructible.

These three points must be considered for all plots of land. But land, as a category of assets, differs economically from all other assets:

☐ There is only a limited quantity of land. With infinitesimally small exceptions the quantity of land cannot be increased. Usable land is thus relatively scarce.

☐ All usable land can be improved or have its value increased when structures are built on it.

☐ The location of the land determines its value to a great extent.

Improvements

Over one-half of the national wealth is represented by real estate resources—that is, land and improvements. The real estate business consists primarily of individuals utilizing such resources to meet the demands of the marketplace. The greatest demand for improved real estate is for housing. Residential property includes single-family residences, duplexes, triplexes, quadriplexes, apartment buildings, cooperatives, condominiums, and mobile homes. The existing supply of residential structures is great, but the demand for more housing keeps the residential construction business expanding at a rapid pace. Today it is through the residential market that most individuals enter the real estate industry. But this industry was not always so active. It might be helpful for you to have a basic historical perspective of what has made the industry what it is today.

THE MODERN REAL ESTATE MARKET

The real estate market is influenced by many factors, but supply and demand are responsible for its existence. This market is somewhat different from the markets for other goods. Since real estate is immovable, its market must be a local one. If houses are selling well in Rockland County, the demand there may exceed the supply, yet Nassau County may have an oversupply of housing. However, housing cannot be moved about the state from an area of low demand to an area where greater demand exists. There are even greater discrepancies in the national market. In the period 1974–1976, housing markets in California boomed while New York markets were depressed. During the upswing from 1976 through the spring of 1982, Manhattan

real estate boomed, activity in the Bronx remained depressed, and activity in the other New York City boroughs and in the various counties of the state remained moderate.

It must also be noted that building new structures to meet rising housing demand takes time. Supply cannot respond quickly to increased demand for real estate. Furthermore, large sums of money are needed to initiate real estate construction. Such funds invested in real estate are called *capital*. The availability or lack of such capital also limits the market for real estate by controlling the effective supply of new structures.

Human Resources

The sophistication of the modern real estate market has created a need for different specialists to become involved in the marketplace. Perhaps one of the most difficult choices the newcomer to real estate must make involves deciding which area of the business is the most interesting.

Because of the high cost of purchasing real estate and the complexity involved in transferring ownership from one party to another, the most commonly found specialist in real estate is the broker or salesperson who markets residential or commercial real estate. The real estate *broker* is the specialist who brings the parties together and negotiates the transaction, whether it be buying, selling, renting, or exchanging real estate. A *salesperson* is a licensed individual who engages in these activities under the supervision of a responsible broker.

The broker's or salesperson's compensation for this service is a fee known as *commission*. The relationship between the broker (or salesperson) and the real estate buyer and seller is governed by the law of agency and by New York State real property law. The broker (or salesperson) is the *agent* of the seller (with responsibilities to the buyer) or he is the agent of the buyer (with responsibilities to the seller).

New York real property law requires that the candidate for the real estate salesperson's license devote five classroom hours to license law and ethics and five additional hours to the law of agency.

The topics of the above two paragraphs are examined in detail in Chapters 11 and 12. However, in the following paragraphs, we briefly examine the business aspects of the broker-client relationship.

In New York, as in most states, the real estate business operates with a two-tier system of licensing. The broker is the individual responsible for the transaction. On the second tier is the salesperson, who must be affiliated with a particular broker who holds the salesperson's license. Also found on this tier are brokers who are not principals in real estate firms and who perform the same sales role as salesperson. Such brokers may be called *broker associates*.

Types of Real Estate Service

Many areas of expertise exist in the real estate business. The following is a listing of the major categories of the business with a description of the function, compensation, and opportunities in each area:

Brokerage (a service function)

☐ *Function.* The primary function of brokers and salespersons is to bring buyers and sellers together. The most common function that an agent performs is to list a seller's residence for sale. Commercial and industrial brokers perform this service for commercial sellers.

☐ *Compensation.* Brokers' compensation is a commission that is a percentage of the gross selling price of the property.

☐ *Opportunities.* Since compensation is a percentage of the sales results, it can be virtually unlimited. Commission rates vary greatly from community to community, as does the division of an earned commission between the broker and salesperson.

Property Management (a service function)

☐ *Function.* The property manager attempts to manage the owner's real estate resources in such a way as to produce for the owner the desired objectives. The manager handles the day-to-day problems of the real property, collects rent, arranges for repairs, pays bills, supervises custodial help, rents vacant space, renders a periodic accounting to the owner, and conserves the property and surroundings.

☐ *Compensation.* Managers are compensated in two ways. They receive a fee for managing the property and a commission for leasing or renting —for example, the manager of an office building usually earns a set fee for management services. Plus, they receive a percentage of the value of each new tenant's lease.

☐ *Opportunities.* Opportunities in this field are expanding as a result of the increase in absentee

ownership and the need for specialists in operating complex properties.

Financing (a service function)

☐ *Function.* This service function brings together a lender and a purchaser who must borrow money. Individuals in real estate finance must understand policies that determine what loans lenders will make. Considerations involve the borrower's creditworthiness, the value of the property as security for the loan, and economic trends affecting the property.

☐ *Compensation.* There are many positions for people involved in lending. Individuals who work for a lending institution such as a bank, savings and loan association, or insurance company, are usually salaried. A mortgage broker, who acts in an agency capacity between the lender and borrower, earns a commission. The mortgage broker may also receive a fee for "servicing" the loan. Most mortgage brokers are independent agents and place loans with financial institutions as the representative of the borrower.

☐ *Opportunities.* With financial arrangements becoming more and more complex, opportunities for skilled specialists are growing. In many respects, financing today is the determining factor in planning a new development, marketing existing property, or determining the future use of real property.

Appraising (a service function)

☐ *Function.* This is generally the most respected professional area in real estate. An appraiser is employed by a client to render an opinion about the value of a property. The buyer wants to know if the seller's asking price is reasonable; the seller wants to know if the buyer's offer is fair; the lender wants to know if the property is adequate collateral for the loan.

☐ *Compensation.* The outside appraiser is paid on the basis of time, knowledge, and skill, and usually receives a predetermined fee. In no event is the fee based on a percentage of the appraised value because that might bias the appraiser's conclusion.

☐ *Opportunities.* Many appraisers are independent fee appraisers and their opportunities are limited only by their development of a professional standing in the community. Other appraisers are staff appraisers employed by financial institutions, insurance companies, or corporations. They receive "middle management" salaries.

Development (a production function)

☐ *Function.* A developer is an entrepreneur who plans and produces "improvements" of land or structures. Whether the developer builds an industrial park or creates a subdivision or an apartment complex, he alters the character of the community for better or for worse.

☐ *Compensation.* Since the developer is an entrepreneur, his compensation is largely profit, and the profit depends on the developer's ability to market the completed package at a price over and above his land acquisition and developing costs.

☐ *Opportunities.* In a dynamic economy where the need for housing, commercial, and industrial construction is accelerated by an expanding population, the opportunities are good and profits are related primarily to the developer's resourcefulness and ability to finance within the current market.

Building and Construction (a production function)

☐ *Function.* Some building contractors are developers. Others merely offer services to developers. This productive function creates new units or rehabilitates old structures, altering the character of the community. The contractor is a businessman seeking a profit.

☐ *Compensation.* The contractor may accept a job on a fixed-fee basis or for a percentage of the final cost of the project. When the builder is also the developer, his profit is the difference between the builder's cost and selling price on a speculative ("spec") house or structure.

☐ *Opportunities.* Opportunities are good for the builder who has access to financing and who can plan and organize his operation within the framework of the local market.

Active Real Estate Investing and Operation (service and production functions)

☐ *Function.* Real estate investors and operators act for themselves and not as agents for others. They buy, sell, rent, and renovate their own real estate holdings. (In some parts of New York, the word *operator* is derogatory. An operator is thought of as an investor who is excessively conniving and uninterested in the public welfare.)

☐ *Compensation.* Their remuneration is the profit they derive from the operation of their own business.

☐ *Opportunities.* Fortunes have been built in real estate through the operation of a business in which an individual's own energy and initiative can create a very great profit.

Special Services (advisers)

Other experts involved in the private sector of the real estate business include the following:

☐ *Consultants.* Trained persons who advise individuals, industry, business, and governmental units on real estate matters.

☐ *Land use planners.* Specialists, such as metropolitan and city planners, involved in planning for the use of real estate resources.

☐ *Engineers.* Specialists who concentrate in an area of real estate, such as engineers who design structural features of buildings and civil engineers responsible for utility design and layout of subdivisions and other major projects.

☐ *Lawyers.* Many attorneys are involved in the demanding but rewarding category of real estate specialization.

☐ *Title abstractors and insurers.* Companies involved in bringing abstracts (summaries of real estate records—see Chapters 4 and 8) up to date and issuing title insurance. These are vital services in assisting the transfer of real property.

☐ *Architects.* Design and plan the physical aspects of new structures and may also provide inspection and construction supervision for new buildings.

☐ *Tax and accounting experts.* Advise investors and others about the impact and growing importance of taxes (especially federal income taxes) on real property.

Public (governmental) Real Estate Specialists

☐ *Federal employees.* The federal government is directly involved in the real estate business through such agencies as the Veterans Administration (VA), U.S. Department of Housing and Urban Development (HUD), and the General Services Administration (GSA).

☐ *State employees.* The state is responsible for protecting the health, safety, and welfare of its citizens and their property. This is important to the maintenance of stable real estate values. The state also participates in the planning of real estate resources and governs the real estate industry through regulatory agencies. In New York, the regulatory agency is the Division of Licensing of the Department of State.

☐ *Local officials.* Local government affects real estate activity through the administration of zoning ordinances, building codes, and planning regulation. Local governments also own substantial blocks of real estate, such as streets, parks, playgrounds, and municipal buildings.

Real Estate as a Profession

The general public views real estate practitioners as business people rather than as professionals. Even though real estate practitioners do not have the same standing as doctors or lawyers, they must nevertheless conduct their client's business in a responsible, professional manner. Although each broker (and the salesperson responsible to the broker) competes with other brokers for new properties to list and sell, all brokers in a community should work together to establish and maintain ethical standards for dealings with clients, with fellow brokers and salespersons, and with the general public.

High standards of ethical conduct are very important because in the real estate business clients often do not have a good understanding of the services they are entitled to receive. In a typical real estate transaction, the broker may be required to perform a number of services with which clients are generally unfamiliar. Clients rely on the broker (or the salesperson) to guide them through the complicated maze of activities involved in buying or selling a home. It is most important, therefore, that the client be able to have the utmost confidence in the individual performing this critical service. Chapter

12 is devoted to the ethical responsibilities of the real estate broker and salesperson.

Real Estate Organizations

The real estate industry is organized into several associations that operate on national, state, and local levels. They promote the general interest of the real estate community, and they advocate the high standards of ethical conduct desired by those in the industry.

By far the largest of the real estate trade associations is the National Association of Realtors® (NAR®). The NAR® functions at local, state, and national levels. To be eligible to use the designation REALTOR®, a broker must be a member of NAR.®

Most brokers join a local real estate board, which, in turn, is affiliated with a state association and the national association. Brokers and salespersons associated with principal brokers who are members of a local board join the board as associate members for a small additional fee assessed to the principal.

There are many other national associations of real estate professionals. Each is usually related to a real estate specialty and offers membership in both the national organization and in local chapters. Some publish distinguished professional publications. Many offer specialized training, either through self-study or through organized classes. They usually urge real estate professionals to become candidates for their professional designations and certifications. Since many of these designations cannot be earned merely by the completion of courses and examinations, but require an experience component, new professionals are advised to examine association's literature carefully.

Appendix D lists the names and addresses of the major national real estate associations. It examines the purpose of each, the designations they confer, and the requirements for earning each designation.

Part II
Basic Concepts

Chapter 3
Estates and Interests

VOCABULARY

You will find it important to have a complete working knowledge of the following concepts and words found in this chapter:

ad valorem taxes
affirmative easement
allodial ownership
assessment
commercial easement in gross
condemnation
consequential damages
dominant tenement
easement
easement appurtenant
easement in gross
eminent domain
encroachment
encumbrance
escheat
estate in land

estate in possession
fee on condition
fee on limitation
fee simple absolute
fee simple determinable
feudal tenure
freehold estates
future estate
grantor
homestead exemption
leasehold estate
license
lien
life estate
limited access highway

mechanic's lien
municipal improvements
negative easement
nonconforming use
nuisance
police powers
possibility of reverter
profit à prendre
remainder
reversion
right of reacquisition
servient tenement
trespass
variance
zoning

IN THE UNITED STATES TODAY true and absolute ownership of land is recognized. Of course, there have always been some limitations on the "absoluteness" of an owner's rights to his property, but there are strong indications that the trend is growing to place even greater limitations on ownership rights. As you read this chapter you will come to your own conclusion as to the completeness of ownership rights even as they are recognized today.

FEUDAL SYSTEMS OF LAND TENURE

Feudal land tenure had its origins in English law as it developed after the Norman Conquest in A.D. 1066. Under this system no one except the ruling monarch—the king—really owned real estate. Instead of granting outright ownership, the king created feuds, which were the equivalent of today's leases of real estate. The holder of the feud held it so long as he enjoyed the king's favor and performed the duties imposed by the king. The most important duties involved the maintenance of a military force loyal to and available to support the king (the government). This system of ownership rights in land subject to the whim of a monarch is commonly referred to as *feudal tenure* because continued ownership depended upon continuous performance of the duties imposed by the king. Even though feudal rights to land and property were ultimately recognized as inheritable, such inheritance was surrounded with so many restrictions that the feudal owner never achieved absolute ownership; ownership was always conditional.

Although this system of ownership had changed dramatically by the time of the American Revolution, the remnants of the system of royal prerogatives and landowner obligations were, nevertheless, an important cause of the Revolution, because the dream of Americans was absolute ownership of land. This goal is approachable but may be impossible to achieve absolutely in a society of laws.

ALLODIAL SYSTEM OF LAND TENURE

Under the *allodial* system of land ownership which prevails today in the United States, property rights are vested in the person possessing title to the land. The owner owns the real estate absolutely; ownership is not subject to the whims of a ruling monarch nor must the owner perform the burdensome duties that existed under the feudal system. But since the owners' rights are granted by the government, and since occasionally government rights or needs or policy conflict with private goals, individual owners must make significant concessions and limit their rights of absolute ownership.

Although the basic definition of allodial rights implies that the property owner has an absolute right to use or dispose of the real property as he wishes, in practice there are many restrictions on that right. The state (government) can use its powers to assert certain rights over private property; it can also delegate those rights. However, the state's power to restrict private property rights is balanced by its obligation to compensate owners for any "taking." Another way in which the state restricts allodial rights is by taxing or assessing a landowner on the value of his property. Lastly, common law restricts the allodial rights of individual owners under the doctrines of trespass and nuisance.

The principal restrictions on absolute allodial rights are discussed below.

Eminent Domain

The power of *eminent domain* is inherent in government. It is the power of governmental units to take private property when the government concludes that such action is in the public interest. The method by which this power is exercised is called *condemnation*. Privately owned property may be taken by condemning it, thus making it available for public use. In the United States condemnation is subject to four general rules:

☐ The taking or condemning of private property must be done in accordance with specific legislative authority, and that legislation must recognize the protection of property rights that both federal and state constitutions give to property owners.

☐ The governmental body that does the taking

must pay the property owner for the fair value of the property taken. In New York, when part but not all of a tract of land is taken, the owner can collect damages not only for the value of the land taken but also for any resulting reduction in the value of the remainder of the parcel. Damages to the remaining parcel or tract are often referred to as *consequential damages.*

For example, consider the taking of land for a new highway. Figure 3-1 indicates that when the government condemns land on the 80-acre Jones farm to create the right of way for a limited-access highway, it leaves four acres of land separate from the rest of the farm, surrounded by neighboring properties and effectively landlocked.

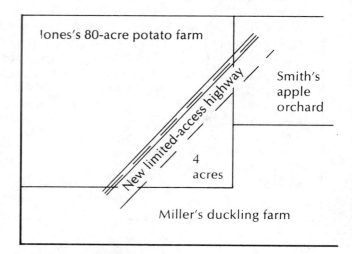

FIG. 3-1   Consequential damage caused by new highway.

Clearly, Jones is entitled to be paid for the strip taken. But what is the impact on the four acres that are landlocked with no access? This acreage has been substantially diminished in value, and perhaps so has the value of the rest of the farm. Under these circumstances, Jones should receive compensation for the diminution in value of the remaining acreage. Perhaps he should receive full value for the four acres.

☐ The government can delegate the power of eminent domain to nongovernmental entities like power companies, water companies, and other public utilities, and to housing and redevelopment corporations, allowing these organizations to condemn property that they need to extend their services. Generally, these organizations seek easements (discussed later in the chapter) as opposed to outright takings. Nevertheless, even an easement (for power lines, for example) carries with it the right to enter the property in order to install and maintain the utility. Extensive damage to the real estate may be caused if, for instance, heavy equipment is brought through a field to repair a power or gas line.

☐ Once a governmental body, acting in accordance with the enabling legislation, has determined that private property is needed for a public purpose (i.e., the taking has not been arbitrary or capricious), the property owner has no choice but to accept the taking. An owner may argue about the value of the property being taken, but such litigation may take years to resolve. The taking, however, may be as immediate as is necessary for the public purpose to be served.

Real Estate Taxation

It is obviously necessary to generate funds to pay for the governmental system that makes it possible to have absolute ownership of real estate. Both federal and state governments rely heavily on income taxes to support their activities. In addition, most state and local governmental units impose taxes upon real estate, upon the land, upon residences and commercial property, indeed upon almost all privately owned real estate and improvements. These taxes pay for a wide variety of local services, such as police protection, fire departments, schools, and libraries.

Reasoning that all these services, in one way or another, protect the institution of private property, and recognizing that ability to pay is an important practical criterion of tax policy, almost all local governments impose *ad valorem* real estate taxes. That is, real estate taxes are usually based on the value of the property as appraised or assessed. Although there are some built-in inequities in this system, proponents argue that the system is reasonably fair, is easy to administer and avoids high administrative costs. Under this system all property in a given tax jurisdiction is periodically revalued and a uniform tax rate is applied equally to all properties. If a property owner fails to pay real estate taxes, the taxing authority has the right to seize and sell the property (tax sale) and retain the proceeds to pay for the delinquent taxes.

Assessments for Governmental Improvements

Very often, improvements made by municipalities or other governmental bodies benefit all property owners in a specific area and presumably increase the value of their property. For example, the homeowners on a specific street may benefit because the municipality improves the street, puts in sidewalks, installs street lamps, or extends sewers for connection to those properties.

The municipality usually charges the cost of these improvements using some sort of equitable basis to each property owner who benefits from them. Charges may be levied according to feet or frontage or amount of acreage. As a general rule, affected property owners are first notified that the proposed improvement is planned, and are informed of its anticipated cost and the method of prorating this expense. They then have the opportunity, by majority vote, to decide whether or not they want the improvement.

Of course, an improvement may be forced upon property owners because it is essential to the health or safety of the entire community. In such a case, the government must exercise its *police powers*. For example, the population density and the soil conditions in a particular subdivision may make it mandatory that city water and sewage disposal facilities be installed because of a threatened water pollution problem. Property owners in that subdivision may be given no choice in deciding whether they want the improvements, but are nevertheless compelled to pay for them.

Zoning

The inherent power of government to regulate the conduct of its citizens is so well established that it does not merit full discussion in this book. However, the government's use of its police power frequently affects the use of privately owned real estate.

Perhaps the most important governmental exercise of police power as it affects privately owned real estate is in zoning. *Zoning*, whether exercised by a zoning board, an area planning board, or a commission, determines the uses to which real estate in a particular area may be put. Obviously, the decisions of such boards and commissions may have a dramatic impact upon the value of specific pieces of real estate.

For example, a five-acre tract that may be used only for family residence may have a value of $40,000. However, if the tract were rezoned to permit the construction of a high-rise office building, it might be worth $200,000. Clearly, the zoning powers of government are very important to everyone in real estate. Three specific zoning concepts merit discussion:

☐ *The preexisting nonconforming use.* Suppose that a legally constituted zoning board designates that a particular area may now be used only for single-family residences with a maximum height of 40 feet. Assume further that in the middle of this zone there already exists a six-story hotel. Must the hotel be demolished? Normally, the answer is no, because it was already in existence when the new zoning ordinance was adopted and presumably it did not violate earlier laws or zoning ordinances. If the new zoning ordinance were to require the hotel's demolition, the ordinance would be considered an act of condemnation and the owner would be entitled to be paid for the market value of the property that the government was taking. Vacant lots in the area, however, would be subject to the ordinance. In most cases, lot owners would not be entitled to compensation for loss suffered.

☐ *The variance.* Even though an area of a zone may be for one purpose (say, single-family residences), there may be reasons to permit another real estate use in the area. A convenience shopping center might benefit all local residents. A developer wishing to build such a shopping center could apply to the appropriate zoning body and request permission to vary the use from the existing zoning ordinance. Normally, the zoning body would convene a public hearing after giving proper notice to all property owners whose property values might be affected by the developer's proposal. Subsequently, the zoning body would decide to permit or deny the proposed variance.

☐ *Rezoning.* Sometimes so many violations of existing zoning rules have occurred in an area (either because residents do not object or governmental agencies are not vigilant) that for all practical purposes the general usage of property in the area differs from that specified in the zoning regulations. Older neighborhoods that are zoned for single-family residential use sometimes have been transformed into multifamily, commercial, or even light industrial areas. When this occurs, it is possible to seek rezoning of the entire area so that remaining single-family residential properties can be sold or used for a purpose that actually is more appropriate. There are, of course, many positive planning reasons that persuade a locality to alter zoning in a particular area.

Urban Planning

In recent years, in addition to the well-recognized power to zone areas for particular uses, urban or area planning programs, which also have an important impact on land values, have evolved. Still another exercise of governmental power is exhibited in such planning, which may be completely at odds with the planning of the owners of property in the affected areas.

Escheat

The law of the State of New York asserts that if an owner of real estate dies without a valid will (intestate) by means of which the owner disposes of the real estate, and if there are no legal heirs entitled to inherit the property, then the real estate *escheats* to the state to be utilized for the benefit of all the people of the state. Thus, the state is the potential "heir" of all owners of real estate and inherits their property unless someone else succeeds to its ownership either by virtue of disposition by a valid will or by the state rules of inheritance.

The doctrine of escheat has been part of real property law for centuries. The basic concept has not changed, although its application has been modified.

Even after early English common law recognized the right to inherit real estate by the survivors of owners, only close family members could acquire real estate by inheritance. Today, an owner who has no legal heirs who have a statutory right to inherit the property, may leave the property to others simply by executing a valid will. As a result, although the doctrine of escheat still exists, it is seldom seen in action.

Other Limitations to Absolute Ownership

All the above limitations on rights of individual owners either to use or to dispose of individually owned real estate may cast some doubt on the validity of the concept of absolute or allodial ownership today. In addition to the foregoing restrictions on the use and ownership of one's own property, there also exist the classic common law doctrines of trespass and nuisance, which limit owners because they provide private remedies for adjoining property owners in cases of conflict. These two concepts are discussed briefly below.

Trespass

Any property owner is entitled to initiate a civil suit against a neighbor or stranger who enters upon his property without permission. This is true whether the trespass is occasional or continuous, and the law presumes that some damage that can be measured in dollars always occurs when there has been a trespass. For example, regardless of whether an individual occasionally trespasses by driving across a neighbor's property or does it as a matter of habit, the trespasser may be assessed for money damages and/or enjoined (ordered) to refrain from doing so again.

Nuisance

A real estate owner is entitled to insist that the owner of neighboring property refrain from using it in a way that injures his property. This is true even if the offending use or action violates no law.

For example, even though no law prohibits it, an owner of a residential lot can be sued for damages or prohibited from using the lot as an open trash dump. There is evidence that the concept of nuisance was in existence as early as the year 200 B.C. While the doctrine protects the rights of individual property owners against their neighbors' undesirable acts, it obviously also restricts their own property rights in the same manner.

ESTATES IN LAND

An *estate in land*, or an estate in real property, describes the nature, quantity, quality, and duration (or extent) of an individual's ownership interest in real property. Estates traditionally and historically have been classified as either freehold or nonfreehold. *Freehold* estates are of indefinite and uncertain duration, and are what we intuitively understand to be ownership. *Nonfreehold* estates are those of definite and certain duration and are often called *leaseholds*.

Current New York State statutes classifying and defining estates in real property have sought to modernize and simplify terminology by eliminating the use of terms like freehold and nonfreehold, which now have only historical significance. Instead, the New York statutes classify estates according to three characteristics:

- ☐ Duration
- ☐ Number of persons
- ☐ Time of enjoyment and creation

The important estates in property are summarized below and in Figure 3.2.

ESTATES CLASSIFIED AS TO DURATION

Fee simple ownership and *estates for life* are freehold estates; that is, ownership is for an uncertain and indefinite length of time. There are several categories of fee ownership.

Fee Simple Absolute

A *fee simple absolute* is the highest and most complete form of ownership designated under New York State laws. It endows the holder with the entire interest and all rights in the property recognized by law, including the right to create lesser estates or interests. Fee simple absolute rights may, however, be subordinated to rights of other members of society protected by the same law as the property owner. Thus, the owner may not maintain a nuisance; the property may be taken from the owner for public purposes; the owner's use of the property may be restricted for the public benefit.

In England, there once existed a fee simple absolute interest known as *fee tail* estate. This was a fee simple absolute restricted for inheritance to direct descendants of the holder. The fee tail interest has been held to be an unreasonable restraint on the owner's right to transfer the property (the right of *alienation*). It is, in fact, outlawed by statute in New York and in most other states; these states have converted this interest to a fee simple absolute.

Fee on Condition

The *fee on condition* contains all the elements of the fee simple absolute, except that the interest may be terminated if a violation of a specified condition occurs. Since it is possible that the condition will never be broken or violated and the time at which a violation may occur cannot be determined at the time the interest is created, the fee on condition is potentially a fee absolute. When (or if) the condition is broken, the fee reverts as a fee simple absolute to its creator (grantor), or to the creator's heirs, or to whomever else might be named in the deed that created the fee on condition. The breach of the condition does not automatically divest the interest of the person holding this estate. The grantor, or the grantor's heirs or designee, must terminate the fee on condition by physical reentry or by a legal action.

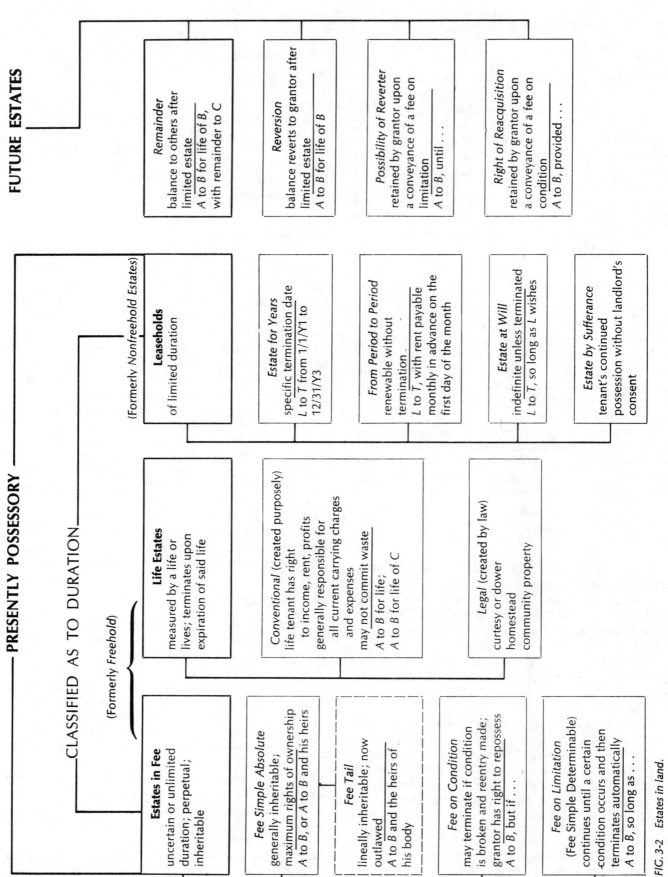

FIG. 3-2 *Estates in land.*

Example: A conveys [certain property] to Hometown College on the condition that the property be used for educational purposes. If the property is not used for educational purposes, then A has the right to reenter and repossess the property.

Example: B conveys [certain property] to X provided that if alcoholic beverages are sold on the premises, then B or his heirs have the right to reenter and repossess the property.

Fee on Limitation

The *fee on limitation* is an estate that is sometimes called a *fee simple determinable*. Like the fee on condition, it contains all the elements of the fee simple absolute, except that the interest is subject to possible termination in the event the specified condition is breached. But in the case of a fee on limitation, the breach *automatically* reverts the estate to the grantor or his heirs or designee.

Example: A conveys [certain property] to the Isaac Walton League of America for so long as the property is used as a conservation club. In the event such use ceases, the property is to go to the State of New York for use as a public park.

Here, since the transfer expresses no limitation on the scope of the interest being conveyed, that interest may be presumed to be in the nature of a fee simple absolute. However, the transfer is clearly conditional upon its continued use for a specific purpose. When the condition is broken, the fee simple interest is "determined" (terminated). Hence, the name fee simple determinable.

It is evident that prior to the breach of the limiting condition the grantee holding either a fee on condition or a fee on limitation, enjoys the same *quantity* of estate as the grantee holding a fee simple absolute. However, such a grantee does not possess the same *quality* of estate as the owner of the fee simple absolute. Because such a grantee does not hold the right to unrestricted use of the property, the quality or value of the fee on condition or the fee on limitation is clearly less than that of a fee simple absolute.

It can also be said that the quality of interest of the grantee of a fee on condition is better than that of the grantee of a fee on limitation. In the former case, the grantee's property does not revert to another until action is taken by the grantor or his heirs, while in the latter case the reversion is automatic.

Because some deeds use imprecise language, it is sometimes difficult to determine whether a deed is intended to create a fee on condition or a fee on limitation. Generally, a fee on condition is created by the use of conditional words such as "but if," "on condition that," and "provided." A fee on limitation is generally created using words relating to the running of time, such as "until," "so long as," and "during."

Example: A conveys [certain property] to B and his heirs *provided that* if Gloversville becomes an incorporated village, A has the right to reenter and repossess the land.

Example: A conveys [certain property] to B and his heirs *until* Gloversville becomes an incorporated village.

In practice, the clarity with which such interests are created frequently leaves something to be desired, so that caution should be exercised in dealing with them.

Estates for Life

A *life estate* is an estate in land that is limited to the lifetime of the holder, or, occasionally, to the lifetime of another. The life tenant in possession holds the property as a trustee for a *remainderman*. The life tenant is ordinarily entitled to use the land just as if he were an owner in fee simple absolute. He is entitled to the rents and profits from the property but cannot lawfully commit any act that would harm the interests of the remainderman; that is, commit any waste of the property.

Example: A conveys [certain property] to B for B's life.

Example: A conveys [certain property] to B for the life of C, with the remainder to D.

In the first case, B's life estate is measured by his own life, in the second case B's life estate is measured by the life of another, C. In the first case, the grantor and his heirs are the holders of a *reversionary interest* upon the termination of B's life estate. In the second example, D and his heirs receive the remainder interest when the death of C terminates B's life estate.

Dower and Curtesy

The life estates described above were created in the conventional way by deed or grant. In some states there is a form of life estate that is created by statute and runs in favor of a surviving spouse. This form of estate no longer exists in New York. Dower is a life estate that a surviving wife receives in one-third of the real estate that her deceased husband owned during the continuance of the marriage. Curtesy is the life estate that a husband receives in real estate that his wife owned during the marriage.

In those states in which the traditional legal life estates of dower and curtesy are still recognized, the holder of the life estate (through dower or curtesy) has the same limited rights in the property as any holder of a conventional life estate. New York and many other states have abolished the rights of dower and curtesy. In their stead, a surviving spouse is given a right of "election" against the will of the deceased spouse. If a deceased spouse has willed real property to other than the surviving spouse, the survivor can demand the equivalent of what he or she would have received if the deceased had died intestate under the state's intestate distribution statute.

Homestead Exemption

The public policy motive that was responsible for the creation of the interests of dower and curtesy was the belief that a spouse should be protected against disposition of real estate by the other spouse without the concurrence of the first spouse. In addition, public policy in the United States seeks to protect the family (at least the physical integrity of the home) from exercise of the rights of creditors acting against the head of the household.

The *homestead exemption*, as the name implies, makes the home exempt from creditors' claims for debts incurred solely by the head of the household (traditionally, the husband) without the concurrence of his wife. In the absence of such concurrence, the typical homestead exemption in most cases protects the homestead. There is one generally well-recognized exception—the debt that the householder incurred for the initial purchase of the homestead.

If a judgment is assessed against a householder in New York State, his principal residence is exempt from attachment to satisfy that judgment for an amount up to $10,000, unless the judgment was recovered wholly for the purchase price of the residence. The exempt property may be a traditional dwelling on its own plot of land, the householder's shares of stock in a cooperative apartment corporation, a unit in a condominium, or a mobile home. The householder need not make a formal declaration or designation of what property is his principal residence or homestead.

Community Property

Some states (most notably California and Texas) recognize a concept of community property, a concept that originated in Spain. In these states all property owned by a husband or a wife at the time of the marriage or acquired during the marriage by inheritance, will, gift, or use of separate funds is considered separate property free from any interest or claim of the other spouse. All other property acquired during the marriage, presumably through their joint efforts, vests as community property in both husband and wife.

New York does *not* recognize the community property concept of ownership as such. However, New York has enacted an act determining the uniform disposition of community property rights at death. This act deals with the disposition, at the death of a married person, of community property acquired in a jurisdiction that recognizes community property, of property acquired through the use of such community property, or of the proceeds thereof.

Leasehold Estates

Estates for Years

An estate for years is customarily called a *leasehold estate*. A leasehold estate is an estate in land created by a contract called a lease, where the owner (the landlord) for a consideration (rent) grants the right of possession to an individual (the tenant) who is entitled to the possession of the real property, usually for a specific period of time. Although we do not discuss contracts and conveyances until later chapters, your intuitive understanding of these terms should be adequate for this discussion.

A lease has aspects of both a contract and a conveyance. The landlord (the lessor) conveys to the tenant (the lessee) the right to occupy or possess the property for the term of years specified in the lease. In addition, the lease contains a contract or covenant by the tenant to pay rent to the landlord. Invariably it also contains numerous other covenants and undertakings, both by the tenant and the landlord.

Example   A (the landlord) *demises* (leases) the premises to B (the tenant) for a period of three years, commencing on January 1, 1981 and terminating on December 31, 1983, at an annual rental of $3,000 payable. . . .

The essentials for the creation of a valid lease are as follows:

☐ The parties must be competent (sane adults).
☐ The lease must contain a definite demising clause whereby the lessor (landlord) leases and the lessee (tenant) takes the property leased.
☐ The lease must contain a reasonably definite description of the property leased.
☐ There must be a clear statement of the term or duration of the letting (the verb *to let* is equivalent to the words *to lease*).
☐ The lease must indicate the rent payable and how it is to be paid.
☐ If the term of the lease is for more than one year it must be in writing, signed by all parties thereto, and duly delivered.

In addition, if the lease is to be recorded (filed in the public land records), it must be for a term of three years, or more, and must be duly signed and acknowledged by the parties thereto.

Estates from Period to Period

An estate from period to period is also a form of leasehold estate. However, it is a lease of indefinite duration. Such an estate continues for successive periods (from year to year or other period to period) until (pursuant to the contract) one of the parties terminates the estate by giving due and proper notice of termination to the other party. This is unlike the automatic termination of a lessee's estate under an estate for years at the time that the specified term expires.

Example A (landlord) hereby demises the premises to B (tenant) at a monthly rental of $300, payable on the first day of the month. . . .

Estates at Will

An *estate at will*, or a tenancy at will, is a third form of leasehold estate. This estate is also of indeterminate duration. At common law such an estate can be terminated by either part at will at any time.

Example A (landlord) hereby demises premises to tenant during the will and pleasure of A.

A statute in New York provides that in order for a landlord to terminate a tenancy at will, the landlord must give the tenant thirty days' written notice.

Estate by Sufferance

An *estate by sufferance* is a form of leasehold estate enjoyed by an individual who comes into possession of the real property lawfully, but who holds over or continues in possession of the premises after the termination of the estate and without the consent of the individual then entitled to possession. For example, when an individual with a written lease (an estate for years) remains in possession of the premises after the term of the lease expires but does not sign a new lease, that is an estate by sufferance.

At common law such tenancy, which is similar to a tenancy at will, could be terminated by either party without notice. However, here, too, according to New York State law the landlord must give thirty days' written notice to the tenant.

Modern Trend to Greater Tenant Protection

In addition to general and statewide applicable law governing the landlord-tenant relationship, there exist various local laws that relate to said relationship and generally afford a residential tenant protection. Thus, some cities, including New York City, have enacted emergency housing, rent control, and rent stabilization laws. Some counties have enacted similar legislation.

These local laws impose guidelines and limits regarding the amount of rent that may be charged, and they further govern the rights and obligations of the landlord and tenant. They are, of course, applicable only to those apartment units that come under their purview. These relatively modern statewide and local laws and the judicial decisions interpreting them are generally aimed at giving the tenant a better bargaining position and greater protection. This is particularly so in the case of residential leases, in which the greatest degree of inequity formerly existed and the landlord enjoyed a substantial advantage in bargaining power.

ESTATES CLASSIFIED AS TO NUMBER OF PERSONS

Another way in which the New York statutes classify estates in real property is according to the number and relationship of their owners. There are estates in severalty, joint tenancies, tenancies in common, and tenancy by the entirety. The nature of these interests is discussed in detail in Chapter 4.

ESTATES CLASSIFIED AS TO TIME OF ENJOYMENT AND CREATION

We tend to think of estates in real estate as present facts. But the last two sections have repeatedly introduced the factor of time into our discussion of estates. A fee on condition or an estate for life both imply that the estates of certain individuals will change after a specified time. As we indicated, a clear statement of term (time) is a requisite of a valid lease. So it is also useful to classify estates in property in terms of the time during which the estate owner "enjoys" the property. An estate may be an *estate in possession* or a *future estate*.

An estate in possession is an estate that entitles the owner to the immediate possession of the property. A future estate is one in which possession starts at a future time. Although the future estate is presently "owned," the use, possession, and enjoyment of it is postponed to the future time.

> Example: S conveys [certain property] to his partner B for the life of B, with the remainder in fee to S's son, J.

This conveyance gives B a life estate. The life estate is an estate in possession because B is immediately entitled to the possesion of the property. J, the holder of the remainder interest, possesses a future estate, because during the lifetime of B he is not entitled to possession. But J will become entitled to possession upon the termination of B's life estate. At that point, J's estate becomes an estate in possession.

Future Estates

In the example above, J's future estate is a remainder. There are several types of future estates.

Remainder

A remainder is a future estate that is created in favor of a person other than the creator (grantor). As indicated in the preceding example, J's interest is a remainder interest. In the discussion of the fee on limitation, we described a conveyance that specified that if certain property were no longer used as a conservation club, the property would go to the State of New York. The interest of the State of New York in that case would be a remainder interest.

Reversion

A reversion is a future estate that is retained by the creator (or by his successors in interest) at the time the estate is conveyed. For example suppose A owns a property in fee simple absolute and conveys a life estate to B. Obviously, A has himself retained a reversion interest in fee simple. A has conveyed the property to B for B's life, but upon the death of B, the property reverts once again to A (or his heirs), and is thus a future estate upon reversion for A.

The definition of reversion must be amended to include two other circumstances: the possibility of reverter and the right of reacquisition.

Possibility of Reverter

The possibility of reverter is best illustrated by example. In the example of the fee on limitation, the grantor conveyed property to the Isaac Walton League for so long as the property were used as a conservation club. If such use were to cease, the property would be returned to the grantor (or his successors in interest). Thus, even after conveying the property, the grantor retains an estate called a possibility of reverter. This possibility of reverter is a future estate that is left in the creator or his successors in interest upon the simultaneous creation of an estate that will terminate automatically upon the occurrence of a specified event.

Right of Reacquisition

A right of reacquisition is a future estate remaining in the creator (or his successors in interest) when an estate is created on a condition subsequent. In our discussion of fee on condition, we cited the example of an individual who conveyed property to Hometown College, provided that the property were used for educational purposes. If Hometown College discontinued using the property for such purposes, the grantor retained the right of reacquisition—that is, retained a future interest.

OTHER INTERESTS, LESS THAN ESTATES

We have been classifying estates in land and other real property according to their quantity and quality. We now turn to a category of interests in land that are less than those normally thought of as estates. The most important of these interests are

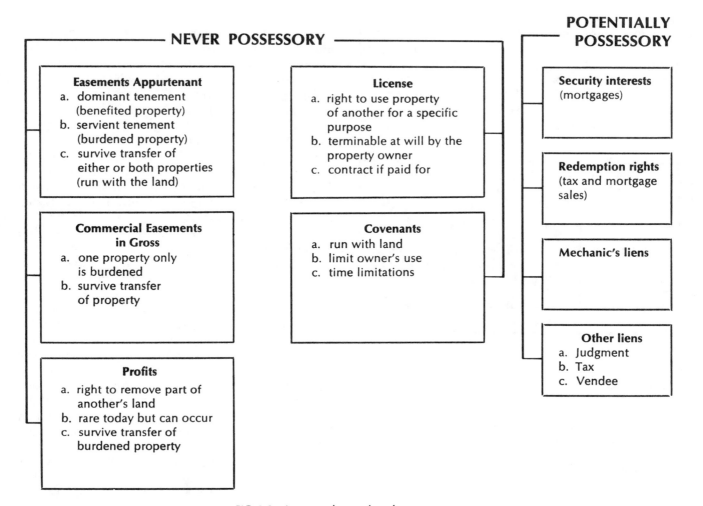

FIG. 3-3   Interests that are less than estates.

easements, profits, and licenses, described below and shown in Figure 3-3.

Easements

An *easement* is a nonpossessory interest that an entity (like a public utility) may hold in land owned by another—that is, it has a right in the land of another that is less than the right of possession. An easement is an intangible right and creates no right of ownership in the land itself. Easements benefit the holder and restrict the rights of the owner of the property subject to the easement. They therefore affect the value of property either upward or downward.

Easement Appurtenant

Under an *easement appurtenant* the owner of one piece of land has the right to certain uses of or

to restrictions on the use of land owned by another. The land that is benefited by the easement is called the *dominant tenement*. The land encumbered by the easement is called the *servient tenement*. In Figure 3-4, *B* owns a dominant tenement that permits the use of a right of way across the servient tenement owned by *S.*

The easement appurtenant is not merely *B*'s personal right; it is a right that attaches to the dominant tenement and passes with it to a new owner. The servient tenement is encumbered or restricted by the easement, and when *S* transfers the land to a new owner, the easement will also be transferred. Such an easement is said to *run with the land*. It enhances the value of the dominant tenement and decreases the value of the servient tenement.

An easement appurtenant may be either affirmative or negative. Under an *affirmative easement*, a portion of the servient tenement may be subject to use by the owner of the dominant tenement (as *S*'s property is subject to *B*'s use). Under a *negative easement*, the owner of the servient tenement may be required to refrain from making certain uses of his own land for the benefit of the owner of the dominant tenement. There may be restrictions on the height or locations of building structures on *M*'s property that would cut off light and air to the dominant tenements of *S* and *B*. (See Figure 3-4.)

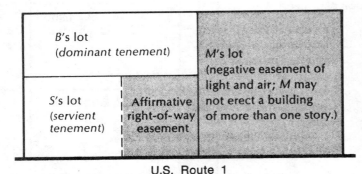

| B's lot (dominant tenement) | | M's lot (negative easement of light and air; M may not erect a building of more than one story.) |
| S's lot (servient tenement) | Affirmative right-of-way easement | |

U.S. Route 1

FIG. 3-4

Easements in Gross

An easement in gross also grants the holder the right to use the property of another. However, an easement in gross does not benefit any adjoining property. Easements in gross are generally regarded as personal to the grantee and therefore, unlike easements appurtenant, are not transferable or inheritable.

For example, if *S* were to grant an easement in gross to *J* (who is not an adjoining landowner) the easement would be personal to *J*. It would not run with the land so as to benefit those succeeding *J*'s interests.

Commercial easements in gross are an important variation of easements in gross. A commercial easement in gross is given a special status; it is assignable, can be both conveyed and inherited, and runs with the land so as to burden the servient tenement.

In the past, this type of easement was used for railroad rights of way, for pipelines, and for electrical and telephone lines. Such easements often pose serious title problems because it is difficult to determine the scope of the easement that may have been granted by an earlier owner of the property. Two common problems are described below.

In the early days of the expansion of the power industry, electrical power line easements were often broadly written. It is not unusual to find broad clauses in a grant of a commercial easement in gross, using such terms as "the right to install electrical power lines over, under, or through any and all property which I presently own in any County, this State." At the time that such easements were taken, much of the land to which they applied was farmland, but today, this land may be urban, residential, industrial, or commercial property. The existence of such broad easements is frequently a problem, simply because the easement holders have the legal right to place power lines wherever they choose. Obviously, a landowner runs the risk that the power company may choose to install electrical lines "over, under, or through" the luxury apartment building that the owner plans to construct. The practical solution to this problem is to obtain from the utility involved a deed that releases from the easement the land that the utility does not actually need and that limits what the utility may use.

Railroad rights of way abandoned by companies that have long since gone out of business pose a similar problem. Generally, case law indicates that when a company abandons such a commercial easement in gross, the easement is terminated and the owner of the fee simple then owns the property free of the encumbrance of the easement. Unfortunately, many of these easements were created by deeds that are so ambiguous that it is sometimes difficult to tell whether they were intended to convey a fee interest or an easement. Occasionally, the owner of such an easement has made a conveyance of it under the false belief that he owned the fee rather than having only an easement. Clearing the title to such a piece of property and proving ownership can be difficult and costly.

Profits

A *profit* in land is the right to take part of the soil or product of land owned by someone else. The term includes the right to take soil, gravel, minerals, oil, gas, crops, and the like, from the land of another. It is not an important interest in land today but, like the overly broad commercial easement in gross, its existence in the chain of title to a piece of real estate can be troublesome. The precise legal term of this interest is *profit à prendre*.

Licenses

A *license* is the privilege to enter property owned by another for a specific purpose. It does not give the holder of the license any interest in the property. It may be revoked at any time by the property owner without rendering the owner liable for damages to the license holder, unless the license was created by contract and was paid for by the licensee. The difference between a purchased license and one granted without a fee is readily explained by example.

Example A, a landowner, permits J to hunt upon A's property without receiving payment from J. A may revoke this license at any time.

Example The management of a ball team sells a ticket to a spectator for a game at a stadium, thus granting the spectator the right to be present for the game. The stadium arbitrarily ejects the spectator before the event is complete. The spectator has paid for the license and is entitled to be compensated for this breach of contract.

Encroachments

It frequently occurs that buildings on a piece of real estate extend beyond the property line. In most cases, this is the result of an honest error and the encroachment was not deliberate action. Regardless of the intent of the encroaching party, however, the resulting problem can be quite troublesome. In some cases, the encroaching party may acquire title to part of the adjoining property under the doctrine of adverse possession (to be discussed in Chapter 5), but in other cases, the encroacher may be compelled to remove the encroaching structure. In either situation, it may take expensive litigation to resolve the matter.

Sometimes, limited encroachments and projections of structures over or onto streets are expressly permitted by statute. These generally remain valid for only as long as the encroaching building remains standing. The most notable examples of such permissive provisions are found in the Village Law, the Town Law, the General City Law, and the New York City Administrative Code.

Security Interests

A *mortgage lien* or a deed of trust creates potentially possessory interests in real estate in both the lender and the borrower.

A mortgage may provide a lender with a lien on a debtor's property to secure repayment of the debt evidenced by the mortgage note. However, a mortgagee's (lender's) rights to a property are contingent upon a default by the mortgagor (the borrower). In general, when there is a default by the borrower, the mortgagee has the right to bring legal proceedings to compel the sale of the property in order to satisfy the debt. This is the right to foreclose on the lien. The defaulting borrower has a limited period of time within which the property may be redeemed, the *equity of redemption*. This grace period permits the defaulting borrower to remain in possession of the property for a limited period of time in order to pay the debt and thus redeem the property from the possibility of foreclosure. This equity of redemption is "cut off" or foreclosed on the sale of the premises pursuant to the judgment of foreclosure.

The nature of notes and mortgages and other security interests are discussed more fully in Chapter 7.

Mechanic's Liens

Mechanics and materialmen who furnish labor or materials for the improvement of real property with the consent of the owner have a lien on the property for the value of the labor or materials. The lien may be established by the filing of a notice of lien in the office of the clerk of the county in which the property is situated. The notice must be filed no later than eight months (four months if the property involved is a single-family dwelling) after the work is completed or the materials supplied. During a period starting when the improvement begins and ending four or eight months after the improvement is completed, the property owner should not record a conveyance or mortgage of the property unless the property owner (as conveyor-grantor or borrower-mortgagor) *covenants* that any monies received from these transactions will be used as a trust fund to pay the mechanics and materialmen who created the improvement. The property owner promises to make those payments before using any part of the sale or mortgage money for any other purpose. The only mechanic's liens to which the property owner's obligations apply are those filed prior to or within four or eight months after the property owner records the sale or mortgage transaction. The statute provides that a statement in substantially the following form contained in the instrument of conveyance or mortgage shall be deemed to comply with the law: "Subject to the trust fund provisions of Section 13 of the Lien Law."

If the lien law covenant or its equivalent is not present in a deed, mortgage, or other instrument of conveyance, the grantee, purchaser, or mortgage lender runs the risk of having his interest subject to a mechanic's lien about which he was not informed at the time of the conveyance and which was subsequently filed within the applicable period. Mechanic's liens may be foreclosed in substantially the same manner as mortgages.

Broker's Affidavit, Broker's Lien

Of particular interest to brokers and salespersons are some current legislative changes. Effective March 21, 1983, pursuant to the addition of a new Section 294-b of the Real Property Law, a real estate broker may file an affidavit on the land records as evidence of his entitlement to commission for completed brokerage services. The law provides that such affidavit does not constitute a lien, shall not invalidate any transfer or lease of real property, and shall be discharged one year after filing. The affidavit will nonetheless be on the record and will thus provide notice to those dealing with the property. Perhaps it will facilitate the collection of earned commissions.

In addition, sections 2 and 10 of the Lien Law have been amended effective March 21, 1983. Section 2 now includes as an item of "improvement" the performance of real estate brokerage services in obtaining a lessee for a term in excess of three years, for real property to be used for other than residential purposes, pursuant to a written contract. Section 10 has been amended to provide for the filing of the notice of lien, together with a copy of the contract, in the county clerk's office where the property is situated. Note that this somewhat baffling lien provision is apparently applicable only in the case of nonresidential leases in excess of three years. Furthermore, since this new law restates Section 10, it may have inadvertently repealed the rather recent prior amendment of the section providing for an eight-month filing period, as discussed under "Mechanic's Liens" above. Ob-

viously, some legislative revision clarifying all provisions is required.

Other Liens and Encumbrances

An *encumbrance* is any right or interest in land that exists in someone other than the owner and so diminishes the value of the owner's estate. An encumbrance may be a claim, a lien, or a charge of liability attached to and affecting and binding the estate in real property.

Thus far we have discussed several encumbrances, namely, easements, encroachments, profits and licenses, mortgages, and mechanic's liens. In addition, there are also:

☐ Judgment liens, which result from the successful outcome of a lawsuit and the docketing of the judgment by the plaintiff (judgment creditor) in the county where the defendant's (judgment debtor) real property is found.
☐ Federal and New York estate tax liens that attach to the real property of an individual upon his death.
☐ Federal gift taxes liens and other federal and Internal Revenue Code liens.
☐ Corporate franchise tax liens.

In addition, covenants or restrictions that limit the use of land may be created in instruments of conveyance, declaration, or subdivision plot. These also constitute encumbrances on land.

The interest of a contract vendee (purchaser) under a contract of sale and that of a purchaser under an installment contract are also encumbrances.

REVIEW QUESTIONS

√ 1. The most complete form of ownership our law recognizes today is the

(a) Easement.
(b) Fee simple conditional.
(c) Life estate.
(d) Fee simple absolute.

√ 2. The holder of a life estate measured by his own life

A. Has a duty to refrain from committing waste to the property.
B. Is entitled to the net income the property produces.

(a) A only.
(b) B only.
(c) Both A and B.
(d) Neither A nor B.

3. The owner of a fee simple absolute interest in real estate can legally

A. Create a life estate in *A* with the remainder in fee to *B*.
B. Sell the property on a land contract to *A* and mortgage it to *B*.

(a) A only.
(b) B only.
(c) Both A and B.
(d) Neither A nor B.

4. To determine whether the property is subject to an encroachment, the purchaser should obtain

(a) An abstract.
(b) An appraisal.
(c) A survey.
(d) None of the above.

5. Fee simple ownership for the individual is held under

(a) The feudal system of tenure.
(b) The allodial system of tenure.
(c) Both a and b.
(d) Neither a nor b.

6. If a person dies intestate with no heirs with the capacity to inherit his real property, the property will

(a) Be foreclosed and sold at public auction.
(b) Be condemned and sold under eminent domain.
(c) Escheat to the state.
(d) None of the above.

7. A deed, "*A* to *B* for life, then to *C* in fee," creates in *C* the following interest:

(a) A determinable fee.
(b) A remainder.
(c) A reversion.
(d) A fee tail.

8. The estate known as a fee on limitation

(a) Is sometimes called a fee simple determinable.
(b) Automatically reverts to the grantor, his heir, or designee at the time of the breach of the condition upon which it is limited.

(c) Is generally created utilizing words relating to the running of time, such as "so long as."
(d) All of the above.

9. A license is an interest in land which is

(a) Less than an estate in land.
(b) Assignable.
(c) Inheritable.
(d) None of the above.

10. A fee on condition is an estate which

A. Is automatically divested upon breach of the condition.
B. Is generally created utilizing conditional words such as "provided' or "but if."

(a) A only.
(b) B only.
(c) Both A and B.
(d) Neither A nor B.

11. The power of government to absolutely take private property for a public purpose is called

A. Eminent domain.
B. Escheat.

(a) A only.
(b) B only.
(c) Both A and B.
(d) Neither A nor B.

12. Even though an area is zoned for single-family dwelling units only, some commercial use may be permitted if

A. The commercial use was a preexisting nonconforming use.
B. A variance is authorized by the zoning board for a new nonconforming use.

(a) A only.
(b) B only.
(c) Both A and B.
(d) Neither A nor B.

13. When the owner of real estate erects improvements on his property which extend over onto adjoining property, there exists a(an)

(a) License.
(b) Profit.
(c) Nuisance.
(d) Encroachment.

14. In order to protect the family from the financial irresponsibility of the head of the household, most states provide some form of relief from creditors called

(a) Credit insurance.

(b) Homestead exemption.

(c) Moratorium on all debt repayment.

(d) Low interest rate debt consolidation loans.

15. The right to enter upon the property of another and to take from it sand, gravel, or the like, is called a

(a) Trespass.

(b) Nuisance.

(c) License.

(d) Profit à prendre.

16. An easement of light and air which restricts the building of structures on one lot in favor of another lot is

A. A negative easement.

B. An easement appurtenant.

(a) A only.   (c) Both A and B.

(b) B only.   (d) Neither A nor B.

17. A mortgagee's interest in the mortgaged property is

(a) Presently possessory.

(b) A freehold estate.

(c) Potentially possessory.

(d) None of the above.

18. An estate from period to period

(a) Is a form of leasehold estate.

(b) Automatically terminates at the expiration of the period.

(c) Is an estate of greater quality and quantity than that of a fee on limitation.

(d) Both a and b.

19. The current New York statutes

A. Have eliminated the use of terms such as "freehold" or "nonfreehold."

B. Have eliminated or outlawed the "fee tail" estate.

(a) A only.   (c) Both A and B.

(b) B only.   (d) Neither A nor B.

20. A true easement appurtenant

A. Involves two pieces of property, one of which is benefited and the other burdened.

B. Is extinguished when either piece of prop is sold to a third party.

(a) A only.   (c) Both A and B.

(b) B only.   (d) Neither A nor B.

Chapter 4
Forms of Ownership

VOCABULARY

You will find it important to have a complete working knowledge of the following words and concepts found in this chapter:

beneficiary
bundle of rights
condominium
cooperative
corporation
deed restriction
equitable title
fixture
Horizontal Property
   Act, *or* Condominium
   Act

joint tenancy
partition
partnership
planned unit
   development (PUD)
real estate
real property
regime
severalty
stockholder
survivorship

tenancy in common
tenancy by the entirety
tenancy in partnership
trade fixtures
trust
trustee
trustor
trust *res*
undivided interest
unities of time, title,
   possession, and interest

OWNERSHIP

BROADLY DEFINED, ownership of real property is the holding of rights or interests in real estate. However, certain clear-cut limitations exist. These limitations on absolute ownership were extensively examined in the last chapter. The exercise of the exclusive right of ownership of private property is subject to at least four governmental limitations. Additionally, certain other reservations may be placed on property through both public and private action. Salespersons must be aware of these reservations, since they significantly affect the use, marketability, and value of real property. To review these limitations are:

☐ Public control through the use of
Eminent domain enables government to take private property for public use.

Property taxation affects the value of property (nonpayment can affect the ownership).

Zoning and building codes limit an owner's use of property.

Escheat makes possible the reversion of private property to the state at the death of an owner without heirs.

☐ Nonpublic (private) controls
Deed restrictions are limitations placed upon the use of real property in the deed by which ownership is transferred. They were the basis of our extended discussion of various estates in real property.

Easements are the right to make limited use of real property owned by another without taking actual possession of it.

Profit is the right to take part of the soil or product of land owned by someone else.

License is the privilege of going upon the land of another for some specific purpose.

Real Property

We have earlier alluded to the fact that there is a difference between the terms *real estate* and *real property*. Before we amplify upon this difference, we must bring more detail to the definition of real estate. The term real estate includes land and all things permanently attached to it. It also includes fixtures. *Fixtures* are items of personal property that would normally be governed by the laws relating to personal property ownership. Their legal status, however, changes when they are permanently attached to land. From that point on they are governed by the laws of real estate ownership and are no longer personal property.

If any owner constructs a residence upon a plot of land and brings to the structure various components that are to be permanently attached to the land, they become, legally, a part of the land. They are known in the law as fixtures in order to distinguish them from the land itself. This transformation in character is important, because from the time of permanent attachment to the land, ownership of the land includes ownership of the fixtures. Once permanently attached, they may not be removed without following the laws relating to ownership of the underlying real estate. The lumber, nails, windows, furnace, etc., which were personal property before they became essential elements of a structure, become real estate by virtue of the permanent attachment intended.

One clear-cut exception to the law of fixtures exists. *Trade fixtures* used in commercial or industrial activity do not become part of the real estate. When trade fixtures, such as commercial refrigerators, necessary to the business purposes for which the real estate is used are attached to the property, they do not become part of the real estate, and their ownership does not pass with the transfer of ownership of the underlying real estate. Such trade fixtures can generally be separated and removed from the property provided their removal does no structural damage to the building.

We have now defined real estate as the land and all things permanently attached to it, both structures and fixtures. The term real property includes real estate in that it also implies the legal rights that flow from the ownership of real estate. These ownership rights may be the all-inclusive rights of fee simple absolute ownership or they may be the limited rights, for example, of a short-term lease. In order to sort out the various elements of real property ownership the law has developed a concept of ownership called a *bundle of rights*.

Bundle of Rights

We have seen that a wide variety of interests or rights can exist in the same piece of real estate. If O holds the fee simple absolute title to a piece of real estate, and there are no outstanding mortgages and others do not hold life estates, leases, licenses, or any other lesser interests, he owns all the possible rights our law recognizes. Since O owns the whole "bundle," he has the power to "unbundle" this package of rights within limitations imposed by our

legal system. He can create and convey to others any or all of the following interests in the same property:

☐ A mortgage on the property to secure a debt.
☐ An easement of right of way to a neighbor.
☐ A license to another to hunt upon the property.
☐ A life estate in the property to *J* with the remainder to *S*.
☐ A lease of the property to *P* for a period of years.

The order in which O unbundles or transfers the bundle of rights contained in the fee simple absolute estate that he originally held makes a great deal of difference, because an owner can never transfer more than he owns. For example, should O mortgage the property and then convey a life estate to *J* with the remainder to *S*, the interests of *J* and *S* would be subject to the rights of the mortgagee. By the same token, if the property were leased prior to conveying, the rights of the leasing tenant would not be cut off and the conveyance would be subject to the tenant's rights.

Ownership in Severalty

Even though the term *severalty* seems to indicate that some form of ownership is shared by two or more persons, this is not the case. The term *severalty* is a technical term meaning sole ownership. Therefore, when we say that *B* owns an estate in land "in severalty" we mean that he owns it outright and in his own name alone without a co-owner. An owner can be a natural person like *B*, a trust, a corporation or other entity.

✳ CO-OWNERSHIP

Most people are familiar with joint bank accounts and joint ownership of stocks, which are forms of personal property co-ownership. Co-ownership of real estate, however, is much more sophisticated. Several different forms are recognized, and the rights of the co-owners and their creditors vary depending upon the type of co-ownership that exists.

Individuals enter into co-ownership relationships for a wide variety of reasons: to control the transfer from one owner to the other upon the death of one; to pool their resources in order to buy real estate that no single one of them could afford individually; etc. Co-ownership can occur even if the co-owners did not intend it to happen. Co-ownership is the result when several heirs inherit real estate from a person who dies intestate. The form of co-ownership may be changed, by law, as occurs when the tenancy by the entireties of a husband and wife is converted upon divorce to a tenancy in common.

The owner of real estate may not really be aware of the types of consequences of co-ownership with another; however, any one active in the real estate business must be aware of the differences between the forms of co-ownership and the rights of a co-owner of real estate.

The three common forms of co-ownership (sometimes called *co-tenancies*) widely recognized are:

☐ Tenancy in common.
☐ Joint tenancy with right of survivorship.
☐ Tenancy by the entirety.

Each of these is discussed in detail below, but first certain basic differences and characteristics should be pointed out.

In each of these three co-tenancies, each co-tenant has an undivided right to possession of the whole of the property. In addition, each of the co-owners is ratably (proportionately) responsible for the payment of taxes, mortgages, maintenance, and other expenses relating to the property; and each is ratably entitled to the rents and profits derived from the property.

The law prefers tenancies in common to joint tenancies. Because of this, joint tenancies must be specifically created—that is, a deed must clearly express the party's intent to create a joint tenancy. The co-owners in a joint tenancy each own an *undivided interest* in the whole property. The interest to each is necessarily equal. When one joint tenant dies, his or her interest terminates and passes automatically to the surviving tenant or tenants.

Tenants in common each own an undivided fractional interest in the real estate. These fractions are not necessarily equal, and there is no survivorship feature—that is, when one tenant dies, his interest is retained by his heirs.

A tenancy by the entirety is created automatically by a conveyance to a husband and wife; to avoid the tenancy, the deed must express a contrary intent. Neither the husband nor the wife can convey or encumber any part of the real property so as to affect the right of survivorship in the other.

The discussions below and Figure 4-1 summarize the characteristics of these forms of co-ownership.

Joint Tenancy *with right of survivorship*

The creation of a joint tenancy never happens by accident. Before a joint tenancy (that special relationship that gives each tenant the right of survivorship) is created, the parties to the tenancy must demonstrate a clearly expressed intent to create such a tenancy and certain coinciding circumstances must be present. Each joint tenant must have acquired an equal interest at the same time, with the same degree of ownership or title, as well as the same right to possession of the whole property in question. These coinciding events are called the four *unities* of time, title, possession, and interest. Only then can the true joint tenancy with the right of survivorship arise. As has been indicated, the intent to create a joint tenancy must be clearly expressed or the tenancy may be deemed (pursuant to statute) to have been intended as a tenancy in common.

The highly technical common-law rules for creating a joint tenancy are met in a deceptively simple fashion. A deed that simply recites that the real estate is "hereby conveyed to S, J, and B, equally, as joint tenants with right of survivorship and not as tenants in common" leaves no room for doubt. A conveyance by such a deed assures that the four unities, because they are not limited in any fashion, will necessarily follow. Pursuant to statute, a disposition of property to two or more persons as executors, trustees, or guardians, creates in them a joint tenancy.

Survivorship

The right of *survivorship* that exists under a true joint tenancy is one of its most important features. Upon the death of one joint tenant, the entire interest passes to the surviving tenant(s). The deceased tenant has no estate to survive him and the property does not go to his heirs. However, when one tenant severs the joint tenancy by selling his interest to an outsider, the outsider purchases the seller's share of the property as a tenant in common. *The buyer does not purchase the right of survivorship.*

Partition and Creditors

A joint tenant can legally terminate his interest by means of a partition action. Partition actions are discussed below in the section for tenancy in common. A creditor of a joint tenant can proceed

FORMS OF CO-OWNERSHIP

partnership w/survivorship   *partnership w/not survivorship*

	Joint Tenancy With Rights of Survivorship	Tenancy in Common	Tenancy by the Entirety
Characteristics	Always equal interests ☐ each has right to possession of the whole ☐ this is the tenancy of co-executors, co-trustees, or co-guardians ☐ at death, interest of decedent passes to surviving tenants automatically ☐ necessary for each co-tenant to sign deed, mortgage, contract, lease, etc., to cover entire interest in property	Not necessarily equal interests ☐ each entitled to possession of the whole ☐ each interest inheritable ☐ a will may pass title to share owned by decedent ☐ necessary for each co-tenant to sign deed, mortgage, contract, lease, etc., to cover entire interest in property	Equal interests of husband and wife ☐ each spouse entitled to possession of the whole ☐ divorce converts to a tenancy in common ☐ on death, interest of decedent passes automatically to surviving tenant ☐ necessary for each co-tenant to sign deed, mortgage, contract, lease, etc., to cover entire interest in property
Creation	Must be created on purpose except where individuals not married are described in deed as husband and wife ☐ one deed ☐ equal interests ☐ survivorship must be specified ☐ four unities—time, title, possession, and interest—must exist	May happen accidentally ☐ inheritance by more than one heir ☐ purchase in shares which may or may not be equal ☐ failure to specify joint tenancy with rights of survivorship	Created automatically by a deed to a husband and wife ☐ fact of marriage critical ☐ description as husband and wife not necessary ☐ other tenancy to avoid entirety must be specified

	Tenancy in Common	Joint Tenancy	Tenancy by the Entirety
Rights and obligations	Each tenant has an undivided share in the whole property, is ratably responsible for expenses and ratably entitled to rents and profits	Each tenant has an undivided share in the whole property, is ratably responsible for expenses and ratably entitled to rents and profits	Each tenant has an undivided share in the whole property, is ratably responsible for expenses and ratably entitled to rents and profits
Termination	Terminated by sale of one co-tenant □ unities destroyed □ new owner is tenant in common □ partition available	Sale by one co-tenant does not terminate □ buyer succeeds to interest □ substitution is result □ partition available	One member can sell his interest □ right of survivorship not defeated □ divorce converts to tenancy in common □ partition not available
Creditors Rights	□ debtor's rights limited □ creditor can become tenant in common	□ debtor's rights survive him □ creditor can become tenant in common	□ creditor can levy against husband or wife singly □ creditor takes subject to right of survivorship

FIG. 4-1 Forms of co-ownership.

against that tenant-debtor's joint interest, force a sale, and use the proceeds to satisfy the debt. If the creditor or other purchaser acquires title at the sale, he becomes a tenant in common with the remaining co-tenants. *who owns property then? Previous joint tenants + creditor who forced the sale? Does creditor get only proceeds that would have belonged to tenant debtor? Yes, the he is a co-owner...*

Tenancy in Common *goes to heirs*

We indicated that the creation of a tenancy in common frequently happens by inadvertence. If an owner dies without a will, his several descendants may become tenants in common of the property. In the case of real estate held by a husband and wife during the marriage as tenants by the entirety, a divorce destroys the tenancy by the entirety and creates a tenancy in common. It must be repeated that the statutory preference in favor of a tenancy in common is such that a transfer of property to two or more persons (who are not a husband and wife) creates in them a tenancy in common, unless they expressly and appropriately declare it to be a joint tenancy.

Nature of Co-tenants' Interest

The tenants in such a tenancy each own an undivided interest in the real estate that can be sold, mortgaged, or left to heirs without affecting the tenancy or the rights of other tenants. Each co-tenant has an undivided right to the possession of the whole of the property. As in the case of the joint tenancy, a creditor of the tenant in common can proceed against that tenant's interest and the creditor or other purchaser at a forced sale can succeed to that interest.

Partition

The tenant in common has an interest that can be legally terminated individually by partition. This is the tenant's absolute right. If the tenant takes appropriate action, the court will divide the property physically or sell it and divide the proceeds. The partition of real estate held by tenants in common occurs when one or more of them desires to have the undivided interest of each tenant specifically segregated and set off in severalty. If the property can be easily divided on a fair and equitable basis, the court will order such division and the tenants will thereafter own their shares (which are now divided as opposed to undivided) individually and free of the rights of the other tenants to possession and use of the whole property. It frequently happens,

however, that an equitable physical segregation of shares is not practicable; in such cases the court will order a sale of the whole property and then order a division of the net proceeds of sale among the tenants in accordance with the fractional interests that each owned prior to the sale.

Tenancy by the Entirety *- Husband + Wife*
of the debtor *goes to survivor*

This tenancy arises from any disposition (transfer) of real property to a man and woman who are husband and wife at the time of conveyance, unless the transfer documents declare that their ownership will be a joint tenancy or a tenancy in common. Generally, the deed need not express an intent to create a tenancy by the entirety for the married couple. However, a disposition of real property to persons who are *not* legally married to one another but who are described in the disposition as husband and wife creates in them a joint tenancy, unless the deed expressly declares it to be a tenancy in common.

Characteristics

The tenancy by the entirety, while it has some of the characteristics of a joint tenancy, is not a joint tenancy in all respects. In New York, unlike many states, either one of the tenants by the entirety can individually convey, mortgage, or otherwise encumber his or her interest and his or her credtors can reach this interest. However, the rights obtained by such a grantee (buyer), mortgagee, creditor, or other party nonetheless remain subject to the right of survivorship of the other tenant. *? means what?*

Termination

Unlike the situation in joint tenancy and the tenancy in common, one tenant by the entirety may not maintain an action in partition against the other. The tenancy by the entirety can be terminated by sale if (and only if) both husband and wife consent to the sale. Upon the death of either the husband or the wife, the survivor succeeds to the entire interest held by the entirety. To this extent, this tenancy is similar to the joint tenancy. In the event of divorce the real estate is subsequently held by the divorced couple as tenants in common. This frequently poses serious problems for the real estate broker or salesperson. In the most usual case, the salesperson is trying to sell the divorced couple's house. But all the rules applicable to tenancy in common apply. Each divorced spouse owns an undivided half of the property, and both must agree to every part of the sale or transfer terms of ownership.

CO-OWNERSHIP BY PARTNERSHIPS, TRUSTS, AND CORPORATIONS

There are other forms of concurrent or co-ownership of real property most notably ownership by partnership, trust, or corporation.

A *partnership* is an association of two or more persons to carry on (as co-owners) a business for profit. In the partnership agreement the partners agree to contribute their capital, labor, and skills in pursuance of a lawful business, and they agree to share the profits and to bear the losses in agreed proportions.

Real property may be acquired and transferred in the partnership name. The partners are said to be co-owners with one another of the real property, holding the same as *tenants in partnership*. Each partner has a right, together with the other partners, to possess the specific partnership property for partnership purposes. The individual partner has no separate and distinct right in the partnership property. Thus, no individual partner may assign or transfer his interest in such property without assigning the rights of all the partners. The partner's interest in specific property cannot be transferred at his death by will or intestacy. The creditor of a specific partner cannot place a lien on partnership property if the debt is the individual's debt alone. In a sense, the partnership entity is the holder of the title to the real property. *I don't understand this!*

A trust can be created by deed, will, or trust agreement. Each of these documents may represent a transaction whereby one called a *trustor*, or *settlor*, transfers property "in trust to an individual or entity that is designated as a *trustee*." The trustee is given the duty to administer the property (a *trust res*) for the benefit of a designated person or *beneficiary*. If real property is involved, the trustee receives the title to the property by deed or will. The legal title to the property is in the trustee and the *equitable title* is lodged in the beneficiaries.

A *corporation* may be described as a fictitious legal person or legal entity created pursuant to statute. It is an entity that is separate and distinct from its individual shareholders or stockholders. The business of a corporation is conducted by its board of directors. The corporate entity may hold title to real property. The stockholders have ownership interests represented by their stock in the corporation. But the ownership of stock is considered personal property.

CONDOMINIUMS

The condominium is a modern form of real estate ownership. Unlike other estates and interests in real estate, the condominium has no basis in common law. The estates and interests in land and the varieties of co-ownership that we have discussed are simply not flexible enough to permit the creation of a true condominium. Consequently, the condominium form of ownership was recently created by statute as a recognized form of tenancy in real estate. In many states, the laws are known as horizontal property acts; in New York, it is known as the Condominium Act.

A condominium is a parcel of real estate, and the building(s) thereon, owned by more than one person. Each person owns his unit or apartment individually in fee simple, and each person also owns an undivided interest in common with the others in and to all common areas or common elements. The underlying land, recreation areas, lobbies, hall, etc. are common areas. The boiler, plumbing, foundation, etc., are common elements. A developer or owner, or other interested group, creates a condominium by the recording of a declaration that submits the property to the provisions of the act. Bylaws governing the operation of the property must be annexed to this declaration and a set of project floor plans must be recorded in the office of the recording officer. Initially, each unit is conveyed by the original declarant; subsequently, it is conveyed to individual owners by separate and individual deeds.

The Condominium Declaration

The declaration of a condominium *regime* on certain real estate must be made by all the owners who have an interest in the property. A condominium regime is the set of rules for ownership of the property; it replaces, for instance, the fee simple rules that previously governed the ownership of the property. The declaration must include a detailed description of the land, a complete description of the proposed building, and a set of floor plans indicating the dimensions of each apartment. In addition, the declaration must describe the common areas that may be used by all the apartment owners, as well as other limited common areas, and must list the percentage of common area ownership belonging to each apartment owner. This percentage of ownership is the basis upon which each owner will be entitled to vote on matters relating to the whole property. The bylaws that must accompany the declaration must specify the procedure for election of officers who will run the condominium and indicate how the condominium will be managed. The declaration, bylaws, and plans must be recorded with the recorder of the county in which the land is situated. The declaration is not valid unless it has been properly recorded. The establishment of a condominium is similar in many respects to the formation of a corporation.

The establishment of a condominium is not absolutely irrevocable, and a New York statute specifically provides that the property on which a condominium property regime has been declared may be removed from the regime. When the property is removed from the regime, the apartment owners, in effect, become tenants in common with a right to partition. Their share is determined by the percentage of the common areas and facilities of the condominium they previously owned. However, while the condominium regime is intact, the common elements must remain undivided and tenants have no right of partition, except under special circumstances (such as substantial destruction).

Rights of Unit Owners

Each unit owner in the condominium has a fee simple title to his unit and the right to exclusive ownership and possession of the unit. The owner also has a proportionate undivided interest in common areas and facilities. Since the owner has, by statute, an estate in land, the New York State Real Property Law gives him the right to deal with it as with any other estate. The owner can sell, mortgage, give away, or leave the unit to heirs. In addition, any form of co-ownership of land recognized by state law may be applied to the unit. It may be held in tenancy by the entirety, joint tenancy with right of survivorship, or tenancy in common.

The rights and duties of each apartment owner concerning property operation and maintenance are specified in the condominium bylaws. The Real Property Law specifies that bylaws must provide for the following:

☐ The election of a board of directors; a method for perpetuating the board, the duties of the board, and its compensation.

☐ The election of a president, secretary, and treasurer.

☐ Meetings of the apartment owners; how they are to be called, the necessary quorum for such meetings, and the percentage of votes required to amend the bylaws.

☐ The method of collection of expenses paid by apartment owners.

☐ The method of adopting and amending administrative rules and regulations governing the operation and use of the common areas and facilities; the maintenance and repair of common areas.

The rights of unit owners concerning common areas and maintenance and repair may be complex and may change from time to time in accordance with the bylaws. Therefore, a buyer of such an interest should be thoroughly familiar with the bylaws before purchasing an apartment.

Rights of Creditors

Each apartment is an estate characterized as real property. The owner therefore has a distinct interest that may be used as security for a loan and can mortgage the interest to secure a creditor.

If the mortgage is foreclosed because the unit owner defaults, the mortgagee generally has a lien that is prior to the lien for the common charges that the unit owner owes to the condominium association. It therefore appears that the purchaser who now buys the unit at a foreclosure sale does not become liable for any common expenses or assessments against the apartment that were incurred by the old owner. If the defaulting owner owes the condominium association for common charges and assessments, this unpaid sum becomes the common liability of all of the apartment owners. The new purchaser will be liable also, but only for his proportionate share.

Real estate taxes and assessments by local government units are assessed against each condominium unit individually. That is, each apartment is taxed as though it were a separate parcel of real estate; each is carried separately on the tax rolls. If the owner is delinquent in paying taxes, the lien of taxes and assessments can only be enforced against the unit to which it applies.

When the condominium association levys charges or assessments against members' units, each charge becomes a lien against the unit. This lien is generally given priority over all other lines, except those for real estate taxes and unpaid first mortgages.

The statute, however, provides that the declaration of an *exclusive nonresidential* condominium, such as an office building or industrial park, may provide that the lien for common charges be superior (prior) to any mortgage liens. The common charges lien is enforceable as though it were a mortgage lien.

When an individual purchases a condominium unit from a previous owner (not at a foreclosure sale), the new owner-purchaser takes title subject to any existing liens, including the lien for unpaid charges or assessments by the apartment owners' association. The new purchaser is entitled to a statement from the association that specifies the amounts of the association's claims against the unit, and the purchaser cannot be held liable for charges not on that statement. The purchaser should obtain this statement separately, because it is not a matter of public record, as are real estate taxes and the existing mortgage.

√ When each condominium unit is *first* conveyed, the Condominium Act allows a mortgage-tax credit with respect to a purchase money mortgage. The credit is calculated by multiplying the purchaser's pro rata percentage of interest in the common elements by the mortgage tax previously paid on the prior construction or blanket mortgage.

Note that in the case of a residential condominium, the land, the building, and all improvements must be owned in fee simple absolute. A special legislative exception has been provided for the Battery Park City complex in New York City, in which a residential condominium is founded in part upon a leasehold interest. Condominiums devoted exclusively to nonresidential purposes may be based on lease or sublease interests of not less than 30 years.

For the most part we have discussed condominiums from the viewpoint of a residential regime. The same basic structure and legal principles apply to a commercial condominium regime. Although not nearly as numerous as residential regimes, commercial condominium regimes do exist and are becoming more popular. One of the most notable commercial condominiums is the land and building known as 1166 Avenue of the Americas in the borough of Manhattan in the City of New York. In that condominium one commercial entity owns units in excess of half the building and another entity holds title to the remaining units.

COOPERATIVES

Creation of the Cooperative

Cooperative ownership may be generally described as ownership of a multiunit apartment dwelling by its tenant-residents as a group. As an initial example, we will assume this group is a corporation. The corporation owns the land and building. Each tenant has a stock ownership interest in the corporation. Each tenant also has a lease or occupancy agreement entitling the tenant to possess his particular apartment. While the typical cooperative ownership vehicle is a corporation, a cooperative may be owned by a partnership or a trust or by any of the co-ownership forms that we have discussed. In New York, the cooperative vehicle is almost always a corporation. However, the obligations of the cooperative stockholders differ quite drastically from those of stockholders in a normal corporation. Typically, the risk undertaken by the owner of a share of corporate stock is limited to the purchase price. Usually, the stock certificate is freely transferable and can be bought or sold readily, assuming there is an active market for it. Stock in a cooperative corporation may have severe restrictions upon its transferability. And the owner may obligate himself to repeated assessments.

Ownership of the stock certificate does not normally give the owner the right to occupy a particular apartment in the building. The right to possession of an apartment and the conditions of occupancy are established by long-term apartment lease from the building corporation to its shareholder. The lease agreement (called a *proprietary lease*) usually has unique terms. Typically, the tenant may not sell (or, more accurately, assign) his rights under the lease without the prior approval of the corporation-landlord. This restriction protects the other owner-tenants. The corporation wants to assure itself that new tenants are financially responsible, since there is a definite risk that all tenants may be assessed to help pay the share of expenses left by a defaulting tenant.

Rights of Owners

The rights of the owner of a cooperative apartment are found in the stock certificate (which indicates the extent to which the owner can affect the management of the property) and in the lease (which describes the owner's rights and obligations). These rights and duties vary from one building to another.

The lease is usually long term. After all, the owner-tenant has actually paid for the apartment and wants to be assured of continuous occupancy. Because the lease is long term, the owner-tenant can be given a wide degree of latitude with regard to apartment modifications and is allowed to customize the apartment.

The cooperative apartment owner-tenant pays no rent as such. Instead, the owner-tenant pays a monthly assessment, representing costs of maintenance, real estate taxes, and debt service on the corporation mortgage (unless there is none). No landlord profit is involved. The costs may be offset by any rental income earned from whatever commercial space is included in the building. Tenancy in a cooperative apartment building tends to be stable. This is due, in part, to the fact that each tenant is a shareholder in the corporation. It is also due to the fact that the shareholders control the policies established with regard to the acceptability of new tenants.

The advantages of cooperative ownership are partially offset by certain disadvantages. The cooperative shareholder does not, in fact, own real estate, and even though the lease creates an estate under New York State law, the tenant does not have an interest acceptable to lenders as traditional loan security. The result is that the cooperative shareholder, in order to raise the funds to obtain an apartment, must borrow on personal credit or by using the cooperative stock as security. Interest rates are generally higher than for normal mortgage loans. The corporation's right to approve new purchasers creates problems of marketability for individual tenants. The tenant-owners may have difficulty in finding an acceptable replacement purchaser and, because of the lease or bylaws, may not be permitted to sublet the apartment. There is also always the danger that some owner-tenants will default in their obligations to maintain the building, with the other tenants then called upon to bear proportionate shares of this unpaid expense.

Rights of Creditors

As indicated, the typical cooperative apartment venture is a corporation that owns and operates the building. The shareholders are the tenants, not by virtue of their stock ownership but by virtue of their leases for individual apartments. As a result, creditors may be creditors of the corporation itself or creditors of individual tenants.

Creditors of the corporation have the normal rights they would have against any corporation. The major creditor of the corporation is probably the mortgage lender who holds a long-term mortgage loan on the building. This lender wants sound tenant leases because it is their quality that is the underlying security for the repayment of the mortgage loan. Because the security of the major creditor is a

mortgage on the whole building, individual apartment purchasers may have difficulty in obtaining additional long-term financing, because their creditor's interest will be subordinate to the underlying mortgage interest.

PLANNED UNIT DEVELOPMENT

A planned unit development, or PUD, is a form of development generally consisting of individually owned units contiguous to common areas or facilities that are owned proportionally by the individual owners or by an association whose members consist of such individual-unit owners. It is characterized by the clustering of buildings, common open areas, and mixed land uses and buildings. Although a PUD may be utilized for industrial and commercial properties, it is most frequently employed for residential developments. The development may consist of detached or attached single-family residences and town houses. It may also consist of rental apartments, cooperatives, condominiums, and commercial shopping areas. The essential identifying characteristic of the PUD is the inclusion and use of the common areas.

Since PUDs depart from customary zoning requirements, state or municipal legislation generally governs them. The municipality often will issue special permits for such developments or will utilize a rezoning process.

The PUD is usually created by the recording of a subdivision map or plat that delineates the various building lots and common areas or facilities. In addition, a declaration of covenants, conditions, restrictions, and easements is recorded. The declaration sets forth the rights and obligations of the parties and the rules for operating the property.

Among the advantages of the PUD are the following:

☐ The developer is permitted a higher density, enabling him to construct more units per acre than is allowed under a standard subdivision.

☐ The municipality is relieved of the obligation and expense of maintaining the streets and utilities that are located in the common areas and are thus privately owned.

☐ The individual-unit owners are able to enjoy the environs of open space and recreational facilities and are freed from the labor and worry of outside maintenance.

REVIEW QUESTIONS

1. To transfer title to property owned in a true joint tenancy,

   A. The signature of any tenant is sufficient since all true joint tenants are agents of the others.
   B. All tenants must join in the transfer.

   (a) A only.
   (b) B only.
   (c) Both A and B.
   (d) Neither A nor B.

2. If tenants in common cannot agree upon the division of their interests, they can request the court to

   (a) Condemn the property.
   (b) Escheat the property.
   (c) Partition the property.
   (d) None of the above.

3. Under tenancy in common ownership, each owner

   A. Has undivided interest in the property.
   B. Has unity of title.

   (a) A only.
   (b) B only.
   (c) Both A and B.
   (d) Neither A nor B.

4. Among the limitations on absolute ownership of land as we know it today is

   A. The power of eminent domain under which private property can be taken for public use.
   B. The police power, under which the use to which private property may be put is controlled by governmental agencies. (zoning)

   (a) A only.
   (b) B only.
   (c) Both A and B.
   (d) Neither A nor B.

5. To mortgage property held in a tenancy by the entirety it is necessary to have the mortgage signed by

   A. The husband only, because he is head of the household under law.
   B. Both the husband and wife, because neither one alone has the power to deal with all of the property.

   (a) A only.
   (b) B only.
   (c) Both A and B.
   (d) Neither A nor B.

6. When two individuals own real estate as joint tenants with right of survivorship,

   A. Each has the right to use of the entire property for life.
   B. The share of each descends to his heirs at death.

   (a) A only.
   (b) B only.
   (c) Both A and B.
   (d) Neither A nor B.

7. Tenants in common

   (a) Always have identical shares in the property.
   (b) All have the right to use of the whole property.
   (c) Lose their interest at death to the surviving tenants.
   (d) Have interests which may not be reached by creditors.

8. Under tenancy by the entirety, the interest of the deceased spouse

   A. Goes to the surviving spouse by law.
   B. Passes by will or intestate succession to descendants or heirs.

   (a) A only.
   (b) B only.
   (c) Both A and B.
   (d) Neither A nor B.

9. When owners of a tenancy by the entirety are divorced, they

   (a) Become tenants at sufferance.
   (b) Become joint tenants with right of survivorship.
   (c) Become tenants in common.
   (d) Remain tenants by the entirety.

10. The owner of an apartment in a condominium may

    A. Sell the interest to another.
    B. Mortgage the interest to secure a debt.

    (a) A only.
    (b) B only.
    (c) Both A and B.
    (d) Neither A nor B.

11. Creditors of an owner of an undivided interest as a tenant in common

    A. May pursue that interest and force the sale of it to apply against the debt.
    B. Cannot pursue that interest unless the debt is that of all the tenants.

    (a) A only.
    (b) B only.
    (c) Both A and B.
    (d) Neither A nor B.

12. When the individual owns property in his name alone, he has

    (a) A sole estate.
    (b) An estate in severalty.
    (c) An estate in common.
    (d) None of the above.

13. The apartment owner-tenant in a cooperative apartment building

    A. Owns a fractional share of the land and building.
    B. Owns stock in a corporation which owns the land and building and leases apartment space from that corporation.

    (a) A only.   (c) Both A and B.
    (b) B only.   (d) Neither A nor B.

14. The interests of tenants in common

    (a) Are always equal.
    (b) Are never equal.
    (c) May be equal.
    (d) Both (a) and (c).

15. When the interest of one tenant under a true joint tenancy is transferred to a third party, the new owner

    A. Succeeds to all the rights of the original tenant including the right of survivorship.
    B. Becomes a tenant in common with the other joint tenants.

    (a) A only.   (c) Both A and B.
    (b) B only.   (d) Neither A nor B.

16. The cooperative apartment tenant

    (a) Pays rent as do customary apartment tenants.
    (b) Receives right to occupy a particular apartment solely by virtue of his ownership of the stock certificate.
    (c) Is responsible for a monthly assessment representing his fractional share of maintenance costs, real estate taxes, mortgage debt service, and other carrying charges.
    (d) Both (a) and (c).

17. To transfer full ownership by deed, it is necessary to obtain the signature of all the owners when they hold title as

    (a) Joint tenants with right of survivorship.
    (b) Tenants in common.
    (c) Tenants by the entirety.
    (d) All of the above.

18. When the owner of a condominium apartment fails to pay local real estate taxes,

    A. The delinquent taxes become a lien on all the other apartments on a pro rata basis.
    B. The tax lien applies only against the apartment of the defaulting taxpayer.

    (a) A only.   (c) Both A and B.
    (b) B only.   (d) Neither A nor B.

19. The creation of true joint tenancy

    A. Frequently happens by accident, such as inheritance in equal shares.
    B. Must be intentionally created and include the unities of time, title, possession, and interest.

    (a) A only.   (c) Both A and B.
    (b) B only.   (d) Neither A nor B.

20. Under the bundle of rights concept, the owner of the fee simple has the power to

    A. Create a life estate in A with a remainder interest in B.
    B. Mortgage the property and then sell the fee simple subject to the mortgage.

    (a) A only.   (c) Both A and B.
    (b) B only.   (d) Neither A nor B.

Chapter 5
Real Estate Instruments and the Transfer of Real Property

VOCABULARY

You will find it important to have a complete working knowledge of the following words and concepts found in this chapter:

acceptance of deed	escrow	notary public
acknowledgment	execution	quiet title action
administrator	executor	quitclaim deed
adverse possession	executor's, *or* fiduciary,	real estate transfer tax
bargain and sale deed	deed	recital of consideration
with covenant	full covenant and	recording
bargain and sale deed	warranty deed	record plat
without covenant	grantee	rectangular, *or* governmental grid
certificate of acknowledgment	granting clause	referee's deed
consideration	grantor	spouse's right of election
conveyance	habendum clause	statute of frauds
decedent's estate	intestate	survey
deed	legal capacity	testate
delivery	legal description	void
descent	metes and bounds	voidable
devise	monument	will

TRANSFERS OF OWNERSHIP

Now THAT we have studied the various interests in land recognized by modern law and the various forms of ownership by which these interests may be held, it is appropriate to discuss the various methods by which ownership can be transferred. In addition, we will take up the question of the *quality* of each ownership interest transferred and how this quality is ascertained.

One rule must be kept in mind: An owner of real estate cannot transfer more than he owns. If, for example, the owner of real estate has only a conditional fee, he cannot transfer, by sale or otherwise, more than the conditional fee. Even though he executes a *deed* that warrants or guarantees that he owns the fee simple absolute and that degree of

ownership is assured by an attorney's opinion or title insurance, he has not transferred absolute title to the buyer, and the buyer does not hold absolute title.

A deed should not be confused with a contract. A contract is a document that outlines an agreement between two parties to a transaction. If the contract is an agreement to transfer land, the deed is the document that makes the transfer.

By far the most common method of transferring ownership of real estate is by execution of a deed. However, it is not the only method. Title (ownership) of real estate may be transferred in other ways. Inheritance, right of survivorship, mortgage or trust deed foreclosure, or even a legal form of theft (adverse possession) all result in real estate transfers.

Property that is transferred by deed is said to be *conveyed.* Several types of deeds are commonly used as conveyances. They range from the general or *full covenant and warranty deed,* which guarantees the transferor's ownership and the quality of the title that is being transferred, down to the *quitclaim deed,* which transfers only what the seller has, and does not include any guarantees concerning the quantity or quality of the title that is being sold. It is therefore quite important that the real estate professional be aware of the wide range of "products" and the wide variety of the accompanying "guarantees."

FORMS OF LEGAL DESCRIPTION

Since the logical and orderly process of deeding, mortgaging, leasing or other transfer of interests in real property and the soundness and reliability of the system that records these transfers depend on an accurate means of identifying real property, it is important to understand the basic ways in which real property may be legally described. Before proceeding to our discussion of the various ways in which interests in real property may be transferred, we should consider the various forms of legal descriptions in common use.

The purpose of a legal description is to identify, with reasonable certainty, the precise property that is intended to be conveyed, mortgaged, or leased. Generally, there are three basic types of legal description:

☐ Metes and bounds descriptions.
☐ Rectangular or governmental grid system descriptions.
☐ Record plat descriptions.

When reading any form of legal description one must keep in mind that the description is based upon information supplied by some person, usually a land surveyor, who has visited and physically located the boundaries of the property. The written description of the boundaries prepared by such a surveyor or other individual is generally referred to as the legal description of the real property.

Metes and Bounds Descriptions

The metes and bounds form of description is the oldest known method of describing real property. This form of description was followed by the colonists who settled this country. Literally, metes are measures of length (such as inches and feet), and bounds are the physical boundaries, whether natural or artificial (such as streams or streets).

The metes and bounds description sets forth the measurements and boundaries of a tract or parcel of land. It begins at some known point in the boundary of the tract to be described. Such a point could be a surveyor's "mere-stone," or *monument;* it could be a corner formed by the intersection of the sides of two streets; it may be a specified distance from such an intersection. The description starts at the point of beginning, then continues reciting the directions (courses) and the distances from point to point, moving entirely around the tract of land described and ending at the beginning point. If any or all of the courses, directions, and distances run along or terminate at a monument, natural or artificial, that monumentation is included in the description. In the event of error either in direction or distance, the actual location of the physical monument controls the description. For example, assume that one of the courses in a description runs from a fixed and correct point easterly a distance of 120 feet to *the westerly side of Broadway in New York City.* (In this description the westerly side of the street is the monument.) Later measurement shows that the actual physical distance from the fixed point to the westerly side of Broadway is 150 feet. Then, the course that we are describing, by virtue of the monumentation, will "carry" 150 feet.

The early metes and bounds descriptions usually run from a beginning point at the head or mouth of a stream or from a tree or other natural monument. The more modern metes and bounds descriptions run from beginning points that are generally fixed from street locations or, on occasion, from artificial monuments which are physically located on the land by surveyors. For purposes of illustration, Figure 5-1 is an example of a survey and the metes and bounds description based on that survey.

Rectangular, or Governmental Grid, System

At the end of the American Revolution vast areas of land, much of which was sheer wilderness, became the property of the federal government. It was determined that a new method was necessary to describe these large and undeveloped tracts of land. In 1785, Congress adopted the governmental, or rectangular, system of land description. Thirty of the present 50 states utilize this form of description. The other 20 states, including the original 13 colonies and other states carved out of them, do not

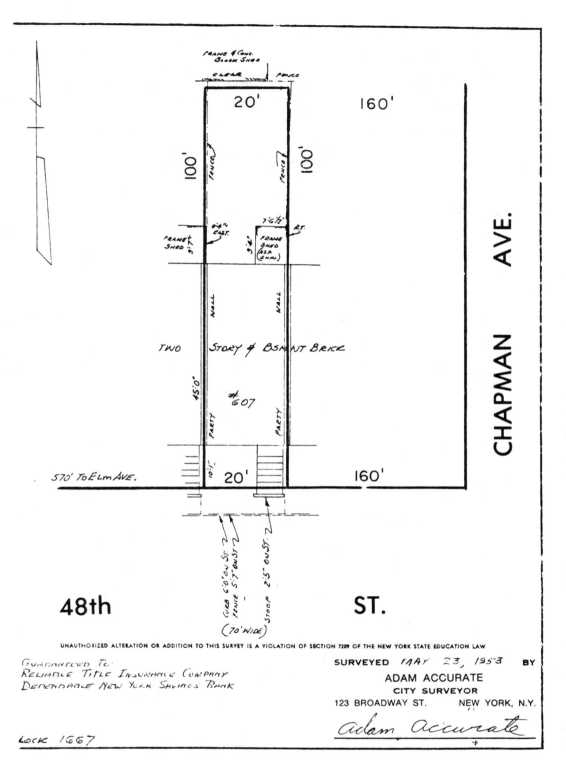

GUARANTEED To:
RELIABLE TITLE INSURANCE COMPANY
DEPENDABLE NEW YORK SAVINGS BANK

SURVEYED MAY 23, 1953 BY
ADAM ACCURATE
CITY SURVEYOR
123 BROADWAY ST.   NEW YORK, N.Y.

Adam Accurate

BLOCK 1667

ALL that certain lot, piece or parcel of land, situate, lying and being in the Borough of
Brooklyn, County of Kings, City and State of New York, bounded and described as follows:
BEGINNING at a point on the northerly side of 48th Street, distant 160 feet westerly from the
intersection formed by the northerly side of 48th Street and the westerly side of Chapman Avenue;
RUNNING THENCE northerly parallel with Chapman Avenue and part of the distance through a party
wall a distance of 100 feet;
THENCE westerly parallel with 48th Street for a distance of 20 feet;
THENCE southerly parallel with Chapman Avenue and part of the distance through a party wall a
distance of 100 feet to the northerly side of 48th Street,
and THENCE easterly along the northerly side of 48th Street a distance of 20 feet to the point
or place BEGINNING.

FIG. 5-1   Survey with metes and bounds description.

utilize this rectangular system. The State of New York does *not* use this system.

The governmental or rectangular survey refers to a grid of north- and south-running lines known as *meridians*, and east- and west-running lines known as *parallels*, or base lines. The vertical rows of the grid are known as *checks*, and the horizontal rows are called *tiers*. In each area, the government surveyed and designated certain meridians, called *principal meridians,* and certain parallels, known as *base lines*. The distance between a principal meridian and the next standard, or guide, meridian is 24 miles; the distance between a base line and the next standard parallel is also 24 miles. A single square in the grid, known as a tract, is 24 miles on each side, or 576 square miles.

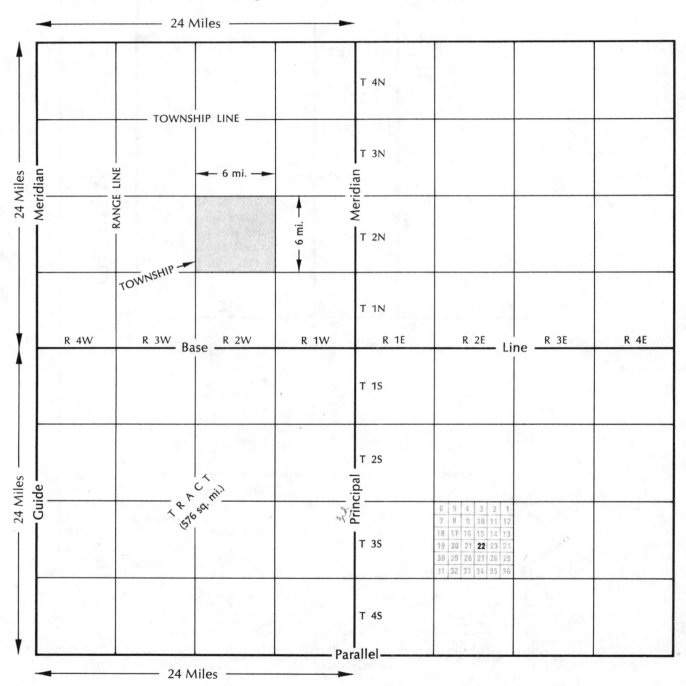

FIG. 5-2   *Rectangular, or governmental grid, system.*

East and west lines, called *township lines,* run at 6-mile intervals parallel to the base line. North and south lines, called *range lines,* run parallel to the principal meridian at regular 6-mile intervals. This cross-hatching results in the establishment of 16 grid squares, or townships, each approximately six miles square. To locate a particular square in that grid the government assigns a township number and a range number to each square. Figure 5-2 illustrates the utilization of the system and the method of division. Note that in the upper left quadrant of the figure, the shaded square six miles on a side could be described as Township 2 North, Range 2 West of the principal meridian. (Each principal meridian is identified. For example, this may be the Third Principal Meridian.)

The 36-square-mile township is further subdivided into 36 sections. Each section is 1 mile square and can be divided easily for platting purposes. Note that the 1 mile square section in the lower right quadrant of Figure 5-2 may be described as Section **22,** Township 3 South, Range 2 East of the Third Principal Meridian.

Figure 5-3 shows how the land within a section is identified. Each section is divided into quarters (northeast quarter, southeast quarter, etc.), and each quarter is again divided into quarters. In Figure 5-3, for example, the shaded area is the northwest quarter of the southeast quarter of the section, etc. Figure 5-4 indicates the linear size of various fractional parts of a section.

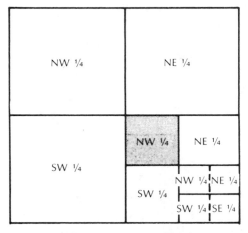

FIG. 5-3   A section of land.

Record Plat Descriptions

Many residential properties are situated in subdivisions which are legally described by means of a *record plat* (sometimes called a description by lot

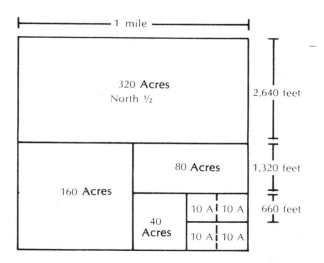

FIG. 5-4   Linear measurement of a section.

and block). It is important, therefore, that the real estate salesperson become familiar with this type of legal description. An example of a record plat is shown in Figure 5-5.

The record plat typically utilizes several means of describing real estate. First of all, if the property is in an area that uses the rectangular, or government, system as a base system of reference, the record plat incorporates that system. Section corners and section lines are sometimes referred to in the record plat. In areas like New York State, some other identifiable and monumented beginning point, such as a street intersection, may be utilized as the basic point of reference. Secondly, the record plat typically utilizes the metes and bounds (measures and direction) technique to describe the outer boundary of the land included in the record plat. Finally, the record plat includes a pictorial representation of the several lots (the parcels of land that are being conveyed) and a description of streets, easements, rectangular system references, metes and bounds, calls, and other information. Once the detailed surveying, calculation, and drafting have been done, the pictorial illustration that is a major part of the record plat makes the subsequent description of a parcel of real property relatively simple.

While the technical work associated with preparation of a record plat is indeed important, it is equally important that the record plat be recorded and thus made part of the land records in the county in which the land is situated. It is from this recorded information and the representations made in the record plat that a legal description for a particular lot can be generated. For example, Lot 8, as

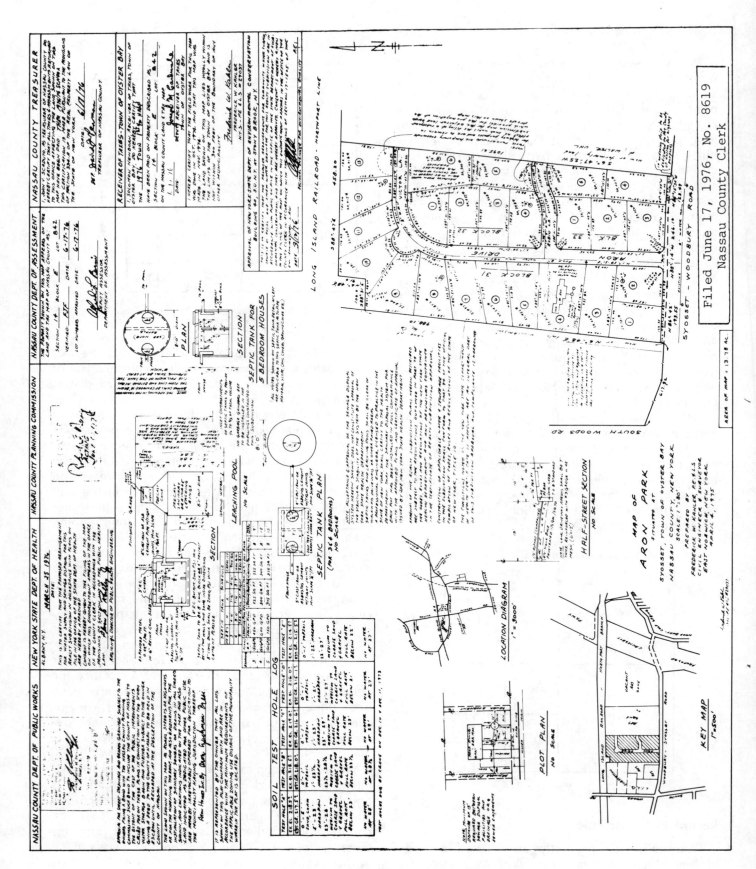

FIG. 5-5 Example of a record plat.

shown in Figure 5-5, would be described as follows:

Lot 8, in Block 31, of Map of Aron Park,
which map was filed June 17, 1976, file number 8619, in the Office of the County Clerk,
County of Nassau, State of New York.

As can be surmised, a metes and bounds description of this same Lot 8 would be a difficult, time-
consuming effort.

Information typically shown on a record plat, as
illustrated in Figure 5-5, includes:

☐ Name of the subdivision.
☐ Lot lines (including directions and distances).
☐ Lot numbers.
☐ Block numbers (a block usually is defined as con-
  tiguous lots bounded by streets).
☐ Area of the lot.
☐ Easements, such as utility, sewer, and drainage.
☐ Street names, and width and longitudinal dimen-
  sions of rights-of-way.
☐ North arrow and scale of drawing.
☐ Location and description of monuments and
  markers.
☐ Beginning point.
☐ Adjoining property references.
☐ Recording information, including time and date
  of recording, instrument number, book and page
  number, where recorded, and name of recorder.
☐ Statements and signatures of approval of the
  County Planning Commission and other state,
  county, or municipal agencies.
☐ Location diagram and key map.
☐ Soil test, septic tank, and leaching pool data.
☐ Landowner's dedication of the platted ground as
  shown on the plat or map for lots, streets, ease-
  ments, etc.
☐ Name of person preparing plat and date of preparation.

Other information which is sometimes included
as part of the record plat, but is not shown in Figure
5-5, includes:

☐ Legal description of the perimeter boundary of
  the record plat.
☐ Land surveyor's certification of plat accuracy.
☐ Private restrictions attached to use of land.
☐ Reference to other pertinent recorded instruments
  made a part of the plat.
☐ Building lines, illustrating required setback of all
  structures from the street or right-of-way.
☐ Execution of the record plat by the owners of
  lands to be platted.

While the record plat is a highly detailed, technical representation of a particular parcel of real
property, it does not offer any comment as to the
quality of an owner's title. It therefore does not relieve the buyer of the need for a thorough search
and opinion of title or a title policy. For example,
an easement may exist on the real property which
does not appear on the record plat; an owner may
convey a portion of a lot to another person, and
thus the ownership of a particular lot may be different from what is represented on the record plat.

However, while the record plat does not solve all
the problems associated with transfer of title, it
makes the job of transfer much simpler for the salesperson, lender, attorney, abstractor, title insurance
company, land surveyor, owner, prospective purchaser, and other persons involved with the transfer
of real property.

Occasionally a legal description may describe the
land with reference to a record plat or map as well
as by metes and bounds. If there is a conflict between the metes and bounds description and the
lot as shown on the map or plat, the description as
set forth on the map will generally control.

In the City of New York property is generally described by a metes and bounds description based
upon and derived from a physical survey of the
premises. In areas of New York State outside of the
City of New York, and particularly in rural areas and
those which have been more recently developed,
legal descriptions are often made utilizing the record plat or map form of description.

TYPES OF DEEDS — on final exam

Now that we understand how a plot of land may
be identified and described, we can discuss the
techniques of transferring or conveying interests in
described properties by means of a deed. To re-
peat, a deed is an instrument or written document
by means of which a landowner transfers or conveys the ownership or title to real property. In New
York State, there are six forms or types of deeds in
general use.

☐ Deed with full covenants, or a full covenant and
  warranty deed.
☐ Bargain and sale deed with covenant against
  grantor's acts.
☐ Bargain and sale deed without covenant against
  grantor's acts.
☐ Quitclaim deed (no covenants).

☐ Executor's, or other fiduciary, deed (includes covenant as to grantor's acts).

☐ Referee's deed (no covenants).

Specimen forms of these deeds, as well as some of the other instruments discussed in this chapter, are found in Appendix F.

The Full Covenant and Warranty Deed

As the name indicates, the full covenant and warranty deed contains several warranties and covenants on the part of the seller. In many states, a so-called *short-form warranty deed* is used. This short-form deed includes the word *warrant*, which, in effect, makes it a general warranty deed.

In New York State short forms of the full covenant and warranty deed, as well as the other deeds listed, are prescribed by statute. However, the law does not prevent or invalidate the use of other forms. The state does not authorize the use of specific words or phrases that must appear if a deed is to carry the full warrants. Instead, it concisely sets forth the warranties that the grantor (seller) must make. The statute refers to the seller (grantor) as the party of the first part and to the buyer (grantee) as the party of the second part. The five specific warranties are as follows:

First, that the party of the first [seller] part is seized of the said premises in fee simple, and has good right to convey the same;

Second, that the party of the second [buyer] part shall quietly enjoy the said premises;

Third, that the said premises are free from incumbrances;

Fourth, that the party of the first [seller] part will execute or procure any further necessary assurance of the title to said premises;

Fifth, that the party of the first [seller] part will forever warrant the title to said premises.

In general the full covenant and warranty deed offers the following five types of protection and warranty, or guarantees:

(1) The *covenant of seisin* is a guarantee to the purchaser (grantee) that the seller (grantor) is the owner in fee simple of the interest in the land being conveyed and has full power, right, and authority to convey such title.

(2) The *covenant of quiet enjoyment* warrants or guarantees that the grantor will be responsible for losses resulting from a disturbance or interference with the grantee's possession by someone else claiming an interest in the property.

(3) The *covenant against incumbrances* assures the grantee that the premises are conveyed free and clear of all outstanding interests and liens.

(4) The *covenant of further assurance* guarantees the grantee that should any additional documents be necessary to perfect the title conveyed to the grantee, they will be so provided by the grantor.

(5) The *covenant of warranty of title* assures the grantee that the grantor or his successors will defend the title conveyed against all persons lawfully claiming an interest therein.

If a grantor conveys a property with a full covenant and warrant deed and all the previous transfers make an unbroken chain of general warranty deeds, each grantor in the chain may be liable to all subsequent grantees for any claim arising prior to the date that a particular grantor made his conveyance. However, the measure of damages for breach of warranty is limited to the value of the real property at the time of the conveyance, which value is conclusively presumed to be the consideration received by the grantor.

When the chain is broken because a grantor executes a deed other than a general warranty, subsequent grantees may not look for redress to any grantors who may have executed warranty deeds prior to the date when the chain was broken. However, the covenants of "quiet enjoyment," "further assurance," and "warranty of title" run with the land and inure to the benefit of remote grantees, even though these grantees may have acquired their title by deeds other than the full covenant and warranty deeds. Perhaps some examples may be helpful:

Example A conveys Greenacre to B by means of a full covenant and warranty deed. A does not actually own either all or part of the title conveyed. This is an obvious breach of the covenant of seisin. B may sue A for damages suffered.

Example A conveys Greenacre, consisting of 20 acres, to B by means of a full covenant and warranty deed. Two of said acres are in the possession of G, who excludes B from possession of said acres. The grantee's (B's) possession has certainly been disturbed with respect to these two acres. A breach of the covenant of quiet enjoyment has arisen and B may sue A for damages. In addition, if G asserts a claim of title for the two acres, a breach of the covenant of seisin may be involved as well.

Example A conveys Greenacre to B by means of a full covenant and warranty deed. In fact, it appears there are one or more mortgages or tax liens which affect the property conveyed. This is an obvious breach of the covenant against incumbrances, and B may sue A for the cost of removing any such incumbrance.

A, the grantor or covenantor, could have avoided liability for breach of the covenants in each of these examples if he had made the conveyance specifically subject to the outstanding interests of which he was aware by inserting appropriate recitals in the deed.

Bargain and Sale Deed With Covenant

limited to any claim coming from the period of ownership of the party executing the deed.

This deed is in all respects identical to the bargain and sale deed without covenant, except that it contains the following single covenant: "And the party of the first part covenants that he has not done or suffered anything whereby the said premises have been incumbered in any way whatever." The warranty contained in this deed is limited to any claim arising out of the period of ownership of the grantor executing the deed. Thus, if an owner held title from January 1 to October 31, his bargain and sale deed warrants only against any claims arising out of that particular period. The owner's warranty would not extend back to the beginning of time. Here again, the implications are demonstrated by an example:

Example A conveys Greenacre to B by executing and delivering to B a bargain and sale deed with covenant against grantor's act. B subsequently discovers that Greenacre is subject to a Utopia Savings Bank mortgage which was recorded against the property before A acquired it, and a mortgage for a loan by Quickbuck Finance Co. which was recorded against the property after A acquired it. B may successfully sue A for breach of the covenant and recover the cost of removing the Quickbuck mortgage *but not* the earlier Utopia Savings Bank mortgage.

Bargain and Sale Deed Without Covenant

Doesn't guarantee title isn't defective.

This is perhaps the simplest form of deed. It conveys all the right, title, and interest of the owner of the real property described in the document, but it contains no covenants by the grantor. Being without covenant, it has the practical effect of a quitclaim deed, except that the use of the language "grant and release" implies that the grantor owns the property described in the deed. (The quitclaim deed does not have even this implication.) An example of the implications of a bargain and sale deed without covenant follows:

Example A conveys Greenacre to B by means of a bargain and sale deed without covenant against the grantor. Subsequently, B discovers that Greenacre is subject to a judgment lien, a mortgage, an easement, or other interest in the property conveyed. Since A has made no covenant with respect to such matters and has conveyed to B whatever interest he owned at the time of conveyance, B has no recourse against A.

Quitclaim Deed

usually used by government agencies – nothing guaranteed

As previously indicated, this form of deed has the same practical effect as the bargain and sale deed without covenant. However, in this deed, the conveyor uses the following conveyancing language: "remise, release and quitclaim." These words do not imply that the grantor owns the title to the property that he is conveying. The grantee of the quitclaim deed acquires only whatever interest the grantor may have in the property at the time of the conveyance. If the grantor has no interest at all, the grantee gets nothing; if the grantor has good and full title or a partial interest, then the grantee receives that full or that partial interest. As in the case of the bargain and sale deed without covenant, if the title is defective, the grantee has no recourse against the grantor. In both of these types of deeds, all risks of title are borne by the grantee.

Quitclaim deeds are sometimes used to convey lesser interests in real estate, such as life estates or other minor interests. They also are widely used to correct prior conveyances that have been improperly executed or are otherwise defective. They are utilized to remove a cloud from title to the real property by grantors who are uncertain of the extent or value of their interest in that particular real property.

Executor's Deed

A person who dies and leaves a properly executed will is said to have died *testate*. A properly executed will appoints an executor to administer the assets of the estate. The executor's deed is used by an executor to transfer real property owned by the decedent (deceased person) at the time of the decedent's death. The statutory form of such a deed contains a covenant that the executor "has not done or suffered anything whereby the said premises have been incumbered in any way whatever." This covenant as applied to the acts of the executor makes the executor's deed similar to the bargain and sale deed with covenant against grantor's act.

Similar types of deeds are utilized by other fiduciaries, such as the administrator of an *intestate* (a person who dies without leaving a will), the guardian of an infant, or the committee or conservator of an incompetent. These fiduciary deeds should and generally do contain recitals indicating the source of authority under which such fiduciaries are appointed and under which they have acted. Since these fiduciaries are required to act in the best interest of the parties whom they represent, all such deeds should contain a recital of the full *consideration* that the grantee gave to the grantor, lest a question exist as to whether or not the fiduciary acted properly and within the scope of his authority.

Referee's Deed

The referee's deed is generally utilized for the conveyance of real property that is sold as the result of a judicial order in an action for the foreclosure of a mortgage or in a partition action. This form of deed (like the bargain and sale deed without covenant against grantor's act, and the quitclaim deed) contains *no* covenants. Similar deeds are utilized whenever property is conveyed by a public official (such as a sheriff or treasurer) pursuant to court order (as a result of a judgment execution, tax enforcement proceeding, or otherwise). This type of deed, like the executor's or fiduciary deed, also contains recitals as to the source and authority of the grantor-official.

Summary

The protection, guarantee, or warranty of title that the purchaser or grantee receives varies with the form of deed executed by the grantor. The grantee must be aware of the different protections afforded by the various deed forms, particularly at that earlier time period when he is negotiating or executing the agreement or contract of purchase and sale that ultimately leads to the deed.

In New York State, if the purchaser has not contracted for a full covenant and warranty deed, he may not be entitled to receive such a deed. If the contract is silent, local custom concerning deed forms will prevail, and the custom varies within different localities in this state. In New York City and in other large metropolitan areas, the bargain and sale deed with the one covenant against grantor's act is customary. In the upstate area and in the more rural areas the full covenant and warranty deed is likely to be the norm.

BASIC REQUIREMENTS OF A VALID DEED

When there is a transfer of title to real estate by conveyance (by a deed from the seller to the buyer), certain minimum legal requirements must be met to make the transfer of ownership effective.

The Grantor Must Have Legal Capacity

The grantor (seller or owner) must have the legal power to make a deed or transfer ownership. Now, a grantor may be an individual, a partnership, a trust, a corporation, a unit of government, or any other legally recognizable entity. The requirements that establish legal capacity are different for each type of grantor.

Individuals

Individuals must be competent in terms of age and mental capacity. In New York, the term *infant* or *minor* designates a person who has not attained the age of 18 years. Generally, one must have attained the age of 18 years in order to convey real property in New York. An exception exists in that married minors may hold and convey real property which they occupy or are to occupy as a home. Married minors may convey, mortgage, and otherwise deal with such property as if they had attained their majority. Neither spouse may later disaffirm any action taken on the basis of either spouse's minority.

In all other cases the deed of a minor is voidable and the minor may set it aside when he or she reaches the age of majority. The deed of one who is, in fact, mentally incompetent may also be set aside. Such deeds are not void (meaningless) at the outset. The courts assume that each party to a deed is competent until a complainant offers proof of one party's incompetency and takes affirmative action to set the deed aside. There is therefore an element of risk in dealing with young persons and those who seem to be unstable at the time of the transaction.

A different rule applies if a grantor has already been adjudged incompetent by a local court. In such cases the finding of incompetency is a matter of record, and all persons are assumed to know what the public records reveal even though they may not, in fact, have this knowledge. Once there has been a formal adjudication that finds an individual to be incompetent, and once a guardian (or conservator) has been appointed by the court, deeds signed by that individual are void. Only the legally appointed guardian can deal with the incompetent's property.

Partnerships

Under the Uniform Partnership Act (UPA) and the Uniform Limited Partnership Act (ULPA), both of which have been adopted in the State of New York, partnerships may hold title to real estate in the partnership name, and any general partner may transfer the partnership's property by executing a deed. The purchaser should seek proof of the fact that the person executing the deed is a general partner. The wise purchaser always seeks an attorney's opinion before accepting the validity of a partner's deed.

The attorney must examine the provisions of the partnership agreement (and the certificate of limited partnership) and any modifications thereto to determine (1) whether a valid partnership has been formed, (2) that the partner executing the instrument of conveyance is duly authorized under the agreement, and (3) that any special conditions set forth in the partnership agreement regarding the conveyance of the real property have been complied with in the present transaction.

Corporations

Corporations are legal entities created by statutes that permit their formation and permit them to conduct business, including the ownership and sale of real estate. A corporation may conduct business only through its authorized officers, and evidence of the authority of particular officers to convey the corporation's real estate is of crucial importance in determining the validity of the deed. This is especially true if the deed transfers real estate that represents all or substantially all of the corporation's assets. In such cases it may be necessary to show not only that the board of directors has authorized the sale but also that the shareholders have approved the transaction.

In New York, the consent of two-thirds of the shareholders voting at a duly called meeting, or the unanimous written consent of all shareholders, without a meeting, is required if all or substantially all of the assets of the corporation are to be sold and such sale is not in the usual or regular course of business actually conducted by such corporation. There is obviously no substitute for legal counsel in such situations.

Government Units

Government units have no inherent power or capacity to sell real estate, and they must therefore follow very strictly the statutes and necessary public proceedings to permit the sale of public property. In the absence of statutory authority appropriately exercised, the deeds of government units may be absolutely void. Again, legal counsel should pass upon the validity of such deeds.

Fiduciaries

There are severe limitations on the authority of fiduciaries (trustees, administrators, executors, agents, guardians) to convey title to real estate. These limitations may be imposed by the agreements under which they operate or by the courts that appoint them. A safe rule to follow is the following: If an individual attempts to convey title to real property and the records show that he does not own the property, the buyer should insist on strict proof of the conveyor's authority to sell. This evidence may be a written and recorded agreement or a court order. The conveyor's authority must be actual (as opposed to apparent) authority, and there must be recorded (or recordable) evidence of such authority. The limitations on the authority of fiduciaries can hardly be overemphasized.

The Grantee Must Be Named With Reasonable Certainty

The second basic requirement of a valid deed is that the buyer must be named with reasonable certainty. More than just good business practice dictates that the grantee (buyer) be named with accuracy. It is important to the effectiveness of the recording systems by which the validity of titles to land is determined.

It is also important that the deed specify the form of ownership being conveyed to the grantee. For example, as discussed previously, it is essential to create clearly a joint tenancy with right of survivorship. Such a deed should read, "to John Jones and Mary Jones, as joint tenants with right of survivorship and not as tenants in common." If the creation of a tenancy in common were desired, the deed should read, "to John Jones and Mary Jones as tenants in common in the following shares: as to an undivided one-third to John Jones and as to the remaining two-thirds to Mary Jones."

In New York, a deed to two people who are husband and wife automatically creates a tenancy by the entirety, even though the parties are not identified as husband and wife. Once again, a careful attorney describes the relationship and may even go further and specify the tenancy intended. Such a deed might read, "to John Jones and Mary Jones, husband and wife, as tenants by the entirety."

It should be noted in connection with the naming of the grantees who are today's buyers that they may be tomorrow's sellers. At that point, the certainty of their identity and their interests in the real estate becomes important in determining the quality of their title and the effectiveness of their deed to pass good title.

The addresses of the grantor and the grantee should be stated in the deed. The statute provides that no conveyance of real property shall be recorded unless the residence of the seller and of the purchaser are stated in such conveyance. The addresses help future investigators attempting to determine whether or not certain judgments or other liens against individuals with names similar to those of the parties to the deed or in the chain of title are in fact against those parties. The addresses are also needed if a defect in the title makes it necessary to find one of the parties in order to dispose of the defect.

There Must Be Words of Conveyance

Unless the deed clearly expresses intent to transfer the ownership of real estate, it may be ineffective in accomplishing its purpose, or at least it may create ambiguity as to just what its purpose is. The standard form deeds in use today utilize standard terms like the following:

Full covenant and warranty deeds—"grant and release . . . , and covenants."

Bargain and sale deeds with covenant—"grant and release . . . and covenants."

Bargain and sale deeds without covenant—"grant and release."

Quitclaim deeds that imply no warranties of any kind—"release and quitclaim."

While the use of such words of conveyance are customary, the exact words are not necessary. What is essential is that the language manifest a clear intent to convey or transfer the property.

Care must be exercised whenever something less than the entire fee simple absolute is being transferred. The presumption is that the entire fee (or

whatever other interest is being transferred) is being conveyed, unless the deed clearly states a contrary intent. If the owner of the fee simple wishes, for example, to reserve a life estate to himself, the deed must clearly say so: " . . . convey and warrant all of my right, title, and interest in and to [the property described] reserving, however, to myself a life estate in said property. . . ."

The *granting clause*, the clause in the deed or instrument of conveyance that contains the operative conveyance words, may be said to show the quantity or extent of the estate conveyed. The deed should also contain a *habendum clause*. This clause is usually found near the end of the deed and may read as follows: "To have and to hold the premises herein granted unto the party of the second part forever." This clause was used in early conveyancing to limit or qualify the interest granted. It rarely serves that purpose in modern conveyancing, although it may do so. Nonetheless, limitations or qualifications contained in either the granting clause or habendum clause must be considered carefully in the examination of any deeds. If the granting clause and habendum clause are inconsistent or repugnant to one another, the courts have held that the granting clause controls.

There Should Be a Recital of Consideration

When we discuss the elements of a valid contract in Chapter 6, we will discover that one of those elements is *consideration*. Consideration is something of legal value that each party to the contract commits to pay or to do. Since the definitions of considerations are complex, we will, for the moment, define consideration merely as what the buyer pays the seller.

Most deeds do not show the full purchase price paid because the parties wish the price to remain private and not be a matter of public record. To meet the requirement of consideration, the deed usually includes a statement to the effect that there was paid "$10 and other valuable consideration, the receipt of which is hereby acknowledged by the seller." One might argue that a seller would not sign and deliver a deed to valuable real estate without payment and that it is unnecessary to include such a statement. Its inclusion is, however, crucial as evidence that there was payment and the buyer will need it if he ever must bring suit against the seller upon any warranties made in the deed. It is far easier to introduce the deed as evidence than to attempt to prove payment by other evidence.

The use of a nominal sum in the recital of consideration satisfies the technical requirement of contract law that there be some consideration. It is not necessary to the validity of the deed that the amount stated be the fair value of the property. In the absence of fraud on the rights of creditors, the amount of the actual consideration is inconsequential and, indeed, the property may be transferred as a gift or in consideration of love and affection.

Despite a recital of nominal consideration, a good estimate of the actual consideration paid may often be gleaned from close examination of the instrument. In order to record the deed, New York State Real Estate Transfer Tax stamps must be affixed to the deed. Effective May 1, 1983 the rate of this transfer tax has been increased to $2 (formerly 55¢) per $500 of consideration or any fractional part thereof. The value of any lien or encumbrance (that is, an existing mortgage) is excluded when (1) the conveyance or transfer involves a one-, two-, or three-family house or individual residential condominium unit or (2) the consideration is less than $500,000. The deduction for existing liens and encumbrances was formerly available with respect to all transactions. Thus, an examination of the revenue stamps on the deed and a determination of the amount of any existing liens would enable an individual to estimate the actual selling price.

In addition to the New York State transfer tax, the City of New York has a conveyancing tax. The rate of the city tax is either 1 percent or 2 percent of the new consideration, depending upon the amount of the consideration and the nature of the property conveyed. No deduction is allowed for preexisting mortgages or other liens. Generally, the 1 percent rate is applicable to transfers involving consideration of more than $25,000 and less than $500,000 or transfers involving a one-, two-, or three-family house or an individual residential condominium unit irrespective of a greater amount of consideration. The 2 percent rate is generally applicable to all other transactions involving consideration of $500,000 or more.

In the City of New York, the real property transfer tax return reflecting the computation of this city tax and signed by both the grantor and grantee, or their respective representatives, is filed with the City Register or with the County Clerk of Richmond. This return (NYC–RPT) must accompany the deed if it is to be accepted for recording. In order to record a deed in the City of New York, a Multiple Dwelling Registration Application or Affidavit as to Non-Multiple Dwelling must also accompany the deed. Copies of these forms are found in Appendix F of this book.

Outside the City of New York, in lieu of the trans-

fer tax return, a State Board of Equalization and Assessment Real Property Transfer Report (see Appendix F) must accompany the deed for recording by the respective county clerk. This is so even when the real property is located in the City of Yonkers or in the City of Mount Vernon, which have transfer taxes and returns of their own.

Article 31-B of the New York State Tax Law imposes a 10 percent tax on the gain realized from the transfer of real property occurring on or after March 29, 1983. The definition of transfer under the Real Property Transfer Gains Tax Law includes the acquisition of a controlling interest in an entity that owns real property. Certain transactions are exempt from the tax, most significantly (1) transactions involving gross consideration of less than $1,000,000 and (2) transfers of real property occupied by the transferor as his residence (but only with respect to that portion of the premises actually occupied and used for such purposes). In addition, Section 333 of the Real Property Law now includes a new subdivision 1-f prohibiting a recording officer from recording any conveyance of real property unless accompanied by (1) a State Department of Taxation and Finance Statement of Tentative Assessment or Statement of No Tax Due or (2) an affidavit affirming the existence of certain exceptions (most notably the residential exemption set forth above), or that the consideration is less than $500,000.

The New York State Department of Taxation and Finance has issued forms and instructions to assist in the compliance with the pretransfer audit procedure mandated by the law. Such forms and instructions may be obtained at the various Department of Finance offices and from title companies. In Appendix F of this text you will find copies of the affidavit forms issued for use by individuals and by corporations, partnerships, estates, or trusts. If the transaction is such that an affidavit may be properly utilized, then no pretransfer filings with the Department of Finance are necessary.

The Deed Must Be Executed by the Grantor

To effectively transfer title by a deed, it must be executed by the grantor. This means that it must be signed by the grantor who intends that ownership of some interest in land be transferred to the grantee. If there are co-owners of the property and the agreement is to transfer the interests of each of them, all the owners must sign the deed. Married couples generally hold title to their residential property in some form of joint tenancy with right of survivorship. Clearly, both the husband and wife who intend to transfer their property must sign the deed, so that their entire interest will be effectively conveyed. Even where it is apparent that only one of them owns the property, in many states it is still necessary that both the husband and wife sign the deed to cut off the rights of dower and curtesy or their statutory substitutes. The prudent buyer requires the signatures of both husband and wife on any deed to property owned by only one of them, unless legal counsel indicates that this precaution may be omitted. Dower and curtesy have been abolished in New York State, and the state has developed applicable law that permits a spouse who owns property individually to convey his or her interest without the necessity that the other spouse join in signing the deed.

The execution of a deed to property owned by a partnership generally can be accomplished by any general partner's signature on the deed. It is, of course, necessary to verify that the signer is a general partner, and an attorney's review of the partnership agreement and related documents and his approval of the effectiveness of the execution should be obtained. Much the same is true for the execution of deeds by a corporation, and a resolution of the board of directors which authorizes certain officers to execute deeds should be obtained. Again, an attorney's opinion should be sought.

The Deed Must Be in Writing and Should Be Acknowledged

The requirement that the deed be in writing is obvious from the nature of the discussion thus far. A New York statute, similar to the statutes in other states, requires that estates or interest in real property (other than leases for a term not exceeding one year) cannot be created or granted, except by act or operation of law, or by a deed or conveyance in *writing*, subscribed by the person creating or granting such estate or by his lawful agent authorized in writing. Contracts for the purchase and sale of real property must also be in writing in order to be enforceable. Contracts are discussed in detail in Chapter 6. The statutes that require conveyances and contracts for real property to be in writing are generally referred to as the *statute of frauds*.

Notice that the heading of this section reads, "The deed *must* be in writing and *should* be acknowledged." This implies that while there are important reasons for "acknowledgment" of the deed, acknowledgment is not required to make the deed effective between the parties.

As a practical matter, without acknowledgment the deed cannot be recorded and thus provide notice of the transfer to the general public. The ac-

knowledgment of a deed is more than a mere witnessing of the signatures, and only certain publicly appointed officials (usually notaries public) can take acknowledgments. The acknowledgment of a deed involves the appearance before the notary public by the signers and their declaration to the notary that their signatures were free and willful. The notary then countersigns and seals or stamps the deed after stating upon it the above facts. Typically, this statement reads as follows:

STATE OF NEW YORK
COUNTY OF _____ } ss.

On this _____ day of _____ before me came _____, to me known to be the individual described in, and who executed the foregoing instrument, and acknowledged that he executed the same.

_____
Notary Public
County _____ No. _____
My commission expires _____, 19__

For the forms of acknowledgment utilized in New York State, both individual and corporate, see the forms of instruments and the form of acknowledgments in those instruments in Appendix F.

As indicated above, the acknowledgment is the formal declaration by the person who has signed the deed or other instrument that the signed document is that person's voluntary act and deed. Sometimes the word *acknowledgment* is also used to refer to the notary's certificate (or the certificate of the officer who recites that the individual appeared before him and acknowledged that he executed the instrument as his free and voluntary act and deed). This latter recital is more properly referred to as a *certificate of acknowledgment*.

In addition to the requirements for recording discussed in this chapter, no deed or other real estate instrument may be recorded in New York State unless the residences of the parties are set forth in the instrument. In New York City there is another requirement that any deed or lease of a multiple dwelling must be accompanied by a multiple dwelling registration statement and appropriate fees. If the property transferred is not improved by a multiple dwelling and registration is not required, an affidavit to that effect must be submitted (see Appendix F).

When the deed has been properly acknowledged and is otherwise in recordable form, it may be recorded in the public records. Recording the deed constitutes notice of its contents to all persons who may subsequently deal with the property conveyed.

The Deed Must Be Delivered to and Accepted by the Grantee

The final legal steps necessary to transfer title to real estate are the delivery of the deed by the grantor to the grantee and its acceptance by the grantee. In the majority of cases these steps are quite straightforward. They are accomplished by a simple exchange of the deed for payment of the purchase price. However, while the grantee's acceptance of the deed is presumed in all but the most unusual circumstances, occasionally, delivery of the deed, an act crucial to its legal effectiveness, is not clear and in some circumstances is legally ineffective. A few illustrations of appropriate and inappropriate delivery follow:

The *intent* of the grantor to transfer title by delivery of the deed is a crucial element. Therefore, if the grantor hands the deed to the grantee (or to his lawyer, broker, or other agent) so that the grantee can examine its adequacy and accuracy, this does not constitute delivery, even though the grantee or his agent has physical possession of the deed.

If the grantor places the deed in *escrow*, that is, delivers it to an independent third party to be held until all the conditions of the sale are met (the most significant condition being payment), the grantor has not made a legally effective delivery, because the escrowee is not the agent of either party. Even though the grantor has parted with the deed, there has been no delivery because of the missing element of intent.

The delivery and acceptance of the deed can be accomplished with *intent* to transfer title to the grantee by delivery of the deed to a third party who is the agent of the grantee. This agent may be the grantee's attorney, lender, or even his broker.

Frequently, in order to avoid the expense of probating a will, an ill-advised individual will execute deeds to transfer real estate to various relatives and then place the deeds in a safe deposit box where they are found after the grantor's death. It is almost universally found that because these deeds never left the control of the grantor, they are ineffective for lack of delivery. And, of course, the grantees could hardly accept them if they did not even know of their existence.

As a general rule, the fact that a deed has been executed, acknowledged, and recorded creates a presumption that the deed has been delivered and accepted. This presumption may be rebutted upon proof that neither delivery nor acceptance was actually intended by the party so claiming; however, legal action would be required to set the record straight.

TRANSFER BY DESCENT OR DEVISE

While real estate is most commonly transferred as the result of a sale, it often happens that the title to real estate is transferred as a result of the owner's death.

Certain interests in land do not survive the owner at death. Each of these interests expires or is automatically transferred when the holder of the interest dies.

The interests of the holder of a life estate, or of the holder of a license, or of a tenant in a tenancy at will, expire at death, and they therefore may not be transferred. Certain other interests pass by law to survivors, as, for example, in joint tenancy with the right of survivorship and tenancy by the entirety.

However, generally speaking, all other interests in land, along with some obligations attached to ownership, descend or survive the death of the owner. For example, if the decedent (the one who died) owned the entire fee simple absolute, this interest is theoretically perpetual; it survives the death of the owner, and is therefore inheritable. We will review the rules that apply to interests that are inheritable, what happens to them at the owner's death, and how they may be sold during the administration of the estate.

Alternative Dispositions of Real Property Upon the Owner's Death

If a real estate owner dies and has made a valid will which disposes of the real estate, the property will go to the *devisees* (those named as recipients by the will). If no will, the property will *descend* to the legal heirs in accordance with local state laws of descent and distribution. It is frequently said that if an individual makes no will, the state makes one for him. Generally speaking, state statutes result in inheritance of real estate by immediate family members—spouse, children, grandchildren. If no such relatives have survived the property owner, the property is inherited by other close family members (parents, brothers, sisters), and, failing their survival, by even more remote relatives. *why?*

The right to make a will is really a privilege, and it is subject to limitations imposed by state law that restrict the individual's freedom to leave his property to whomever he chooses. As a general rule, these limitations favor the surviving spouse and children whom the decedent had a legal obligation to support. As might be expected, the decedent's creditors (including inheritance tax collectors) occupy a favored position.

Limitations on Title Transfer

Generally, the title to any interest in land vests immediately in a decedent's heirs or in the devisees named in the will. If a person dies intestate (without a will), his interest passes immediately to the heirs. If a person dies testate (with a valid will), his interest passes immediately to the named devisees. However, this transfer of title is subject to the following limitations:

☐ *Rights of the personal representative.* The transfer is subject to the right of the personal representative (the executor or administrator) to take possession of the real estate. The personal representative not only has the right to take possession of the decedent's property but frequently has a positive duty to take possession for the benefit of the estate. This possession may be "constructive" rather than physical; that is, the representative, in effect, maintains ownership control of the property. If there is a tenant in possession under a valid lease, for example, the personal representative of the estate is entitled to receive the rents. The rights of the personal representative are not personal rights; the personal representative exercises them only for the benefit of the decedent's estate.

☐ *Creditors' rights.* The title which passes to the heirs or devisees is subject to all valid claims against the decedent. The primary purpose of estate administration is to protect creditors. That is, an individual's debts must be paid before gifts can be made after death to heirs or beneficiaries. The benefits that may flow to the heirs or devisees are therefore subject to the possibility that creditors' claims may compel sale of the property and application of the proceeds to payment of the decedent's debts.

☐ *Spouse's rights.* The title of the heirs or devisees is also subject to the surviving spouse's rights. The surviving spouse is generally entitled by statute to a specified share of the estate. This share depends upon who else survives the decedent, but it is usually at least one-third of the net estate. The surviving spouse is normally entitled to this share absolutely as a matter of right, and this right may not be superseded if the decedent's will makes a different disposition of the estate.

☐ *Existing liens and encumbrances.* The title of the heirs or devisees is subject to all liens and encumbrances on the real estate that exist at the time of the decedent's death. As a result, any mortgages or other liens pass with the property. The decedent's will may specify that debts are to be paid from some other source, such as other assets of the estate, but if the will makes no such provision, then title passes subject to all liens and encumbrances.

☐ *Rights of claimants omitted from the will.* Even if the decedent makes a will that devises the property to named devisees, there is always the possibility that the will may be attacked. The validity of a will may be questioned for several reasons. A claim may be made that the decedent was mentally incompetent to make a will at the time it was executed; or that the decedent was subjected to fraud, duress, or undue influence at the time of its execution. It may be claimed that the will was not executed and witnessed according to law. If any of these grounds can be sustained, the will is set aside and is ineffective to pass title to the named devisees. If a court finds that the will is invalid, the estate normally is treated as if the decedent had died intestate. Then, only the legal heirs can take any interest in the decedent's real estate and other property. An attack on a will is most likely when the decedent makes a property disposition to persons outside the immediate family.

☐ *Death and estate taxes.* The title of the heirs and devisees is subject to federal and state death, or estate, taxes that are imposed upon the decedent's estate. The estate and inheritance tax liens attach to all property, including real estate, owned by the decedent at the time of death. The death tax lien represents a serious defect in the title of the heirs or devisees until the actual tax liability is determined and paid by the estate's personal representative.

It is apparent from the foregoing that although title to inherited property vests instantly in the heirs and devisees, that title is tenuous at best and specific action must be undertaken to make the property salable. This action is the final decree of distribution by which the court having jurisdiction over the estate enters its judgment that all debts, taxes, and expenses of administration have been paid, that the claims of all parties have been settled or the time for filing them has passed without action being taken to perfect them, and that title is confirmed in the heirs or devisees.

The quality of the decedent's title at the time of death generally is unaffected by estate administration. The title that descends to the heirs or devisees is only as good as the title the decedent had during his lifetime. Since the passage of title through a decedent's estate is essentially a gift, the personal representative makes no warranty about the quality of the title. If not directed to do so by the will, the personal representative need not clear any liens or encumbrances on the property. If they are not cleared during administration of the estate, the heirs or devisees take the real estate subject to them.

The personal representative is authorized to begin a *quiet title action* to clear defects or adverse claims to the title. It may be necessary to do this if the property is to be sold during administration, since a buyer is entitled to insist upon a merchantable, or marketable, title (free from defect and doubt —discussed in Chapter 9). Heirs and devisees are not entitled to a merchantable title because they are not parting with consideration. They are receiving a gift; thus they take it with whatever defects exist.

Buying Real Property from a Decedent's Estate

The general public frequently assumes that the personal representative of a decedent's estate has complete authority to sell any of the decedent's assets, including his real estate. This may not be the case. With regard to real estate in particular, the personal representative must find authority from one of three sources: the will itself, statutes granting general powers to the personal representative, or the court having jurisdiction over the estate.

OTHER METHODS BY WHICH OWNERSHIP CAN BE TRANSFERRED

Adverse Possession

The doctrine of *adverse possession* is an antique of the Middle Ages that continues even today to be very useful. In a later discussion of proof of ownership by establishing an unbroken chain of title, it will be noted that prior to the advent of recording systems it was essential that the owner of real estate carefully preserve each and every document that evidenced claim of ownership to land. Inevitably, an important document would be lost. If the individual who was in possession and claimed ownership lost his deed, he was, of course, unable to prove ownership when he wanted to sell the property. To solve this problem, the common law developed the doctrine of adverse possession.

In its simplest terms the doctrine of adverse possession provides that if the purported owner had been in complete, absolute possession of the property, with an obvious claim of ownership for a very lengthy period of time and could prove these essential points, the court would conclude that he was the owner even though he lacked the necessary documentary evidence to prove it.

In New York and in many other states, the doctrine of adverse possession still exists. One who has possessed real property *adversely* for *ten* years acquires ownership of the title to that real property against the record owner and all other persons. If the state is the owner of record of the property, the individual in adverse possession must hold the property for *twenty* years. The periods of time indicated are, in effect, statutes of limitation; that is, they set forth the period of time in which an individual or the state must bring an action to recover the real property that is being adversely possessed. In order to acquire ownership by application of this doctrine, a person must possess the property for the period prescribed by the statute

- ☐ Actually,
- ☐ Openly and notoriously,
- ☐ Hostilely and under claim of right,
- ☐ Exclusively, and
- ☐ Continuously.

When the adverse possession is based upon *color of title*—that is, upon a written instrument such as a deed, judicial decree, or judgment—the adverse possessor may claim the entire property described in the written document, decree, or judgment. When such possession is not based on color of title, then the adverse possessor's claim is limited to only that area actually possessed, enclosed, improved, or cultivated by him.

Quiet Title Proceedings

Whenever title to real estate depends upon a claim by virtue of adverse possession, it may be necessary to obtain a judicial determination that acquisition of title has, in fact, occurred. The common name of such a proceeding is a quiet title suit, in which the individual who claims title brings legal action in a local court against anyone and everyone who may have or may ever have had any claim against the property, no matter how remote, to prove the validity of his title. Such suits typically name everyone even remotely connected with the property and "the rest of the world" as defendants. A lengthy public notice of the hearing is generally required, and the suit is a legal determination that the claimant (plaintiff) in the proceeding is the true owner of the property. Even though expensive and time consuming, such a suit may be the only way in which good legal title may be established so that the property can be sold. Thus, such a suit is utilized to establish the marketability of the title to the real property involved.

Eminent Domain or Condemnation

As discussed in Chapter 3, the state or other governmental subdivision may acquire ownership of real property for public use by the exercise of its power of condemnation or eminent domain.

Escheat

As also discussed in Chapter 3, real property may be acquired by the state for the benefit of all the people of the state when the owner of real estate dies without a valid will and there are no legal heirs entitled to inherit the property. Said real property reverts to the state by application of the doctrine of escheat.

Foreclosure

Mortgages are discussed in detail in Chapter 7. A mortgage is a written instrument that provides a lender with a lien on the debtor's property to secure repayment of a particular debt. When the debtor fails to meet the payments specified or required by the debt that is evidenced by a note signed by the debtor, he is in default. Upon default, the lender may bring legal proceedings to compel the sale of the property in satisfaction of the debt. As a result of these proceedings the lender or another purchaser at the sale may acquire title to the property.

Other liens on property, such as mechanic's liens, judgment liens, real property taxes, and estate tax liens may similarly be foreclosed or executed upon, forcing a sale of the property to satisfy the lien. As discussed previously in this chapter, a referee's deed or deed of other public official will be executed to reflect or evidence the transfer of ownership brought about by the foreclosure or other enforcement of these liens.

OTHER REAL ESTATE INSTRUMENTS AFFECTING REAL PROPERTY

In addition to the various forms of deeds there are many other instruments or documents which af-fect real property. In this section we will briefly identify some of the more common instruments.

A sale, mortgage, or other transfer of land is concluded upon the execution of the deed, mortgage, or other instrument evidencing the transfer in return for consideration. Some time prior to the conclusion of the sale, or closing, the parties involved have entered into an agreement, or *contract*, setting forth the rights and obligations of the respective parties and the conditions for the contemplated transaction. In the case of a sale, this contract states that the present owner agrees to sell and the prospective purchaser agrees to buy the property at a stipulated price and according to the other terms and conditions that are set forth in the agreement. If the transaction is a loan, the agreement sets forth the borrower's obligation to borrow a stipulated sum of money at a particular interest rate and subject to the other terms and conditions set forth in the agreement. The lender agrees to make the loan on that basis. The agreement to make the loan is generally referred to as a *loan commitment*.

An *option* is simply a written contract by which an owner of real property (optionor) gives to someone (optionee) the right to purchase the property within a specified time at a designated price and upon other specified terms. The execution of the option does not mean that the owner has sold his property. It does not give the optionee any interest in the property. The optionee has contracted for the right, upon notice, to purchase the property if he so desires. Only upon the exercise of the option does the option become a contract of purchase and sale.

As discussed previously, an individual may transfer property in trust with the transfer to be effective at his death and pursuant to the terms in his will, or he may transfer property by deed in trust to an individual or entity designated as trustee. When such a transfer is by deed, the terms and conditions under which the trustee holds the property for the benefit of the beneficiaries are generally set forth in a document called a *trust agreement*.

Leases are written instruments or agreements or contracts whereby the owner (landlord) grants the right of possession to his real property to another person (the tenant) for a period of time pursuant to the terms and conditions as contained in the lease.

Mortgages will be discussed in some detail in Chapter 7. They are written instruments providing a creditor security by means of a lien on the debtor's real property. By means of a document called a *release*, a portion of the mortgaged property may be released or set free from the lien. A written document called an *assignment* transfers the interest of the creditor or mortgagee to another person. A written document called a *satisfaction* evidences the payment of the debt and the satisfaction or elimination of the mortgage lien. A *subordination* is a written document whereby one who holds a lien, usually a mortgage, of higher rank and priority agrees that his lien will be junior or subordinate to a lien which would otherwise be of lesser rank and priority.

A *power of attorney* is a written instrument whereby one person, the principal, authorizes another person, the agent or attorney-in-fact, to act in his stead or on his behalf. Thus, an owner of real property may execute a power of attorney to authorize another individual to convey, mortgage, lease, or otherwise deal with the property of that owner.

There are other written documents that are utilized to file notices of mechanic's liens, real estate tax liens, and estate tax liens. All these instruments must be in writing in order to comply with the Statute of Frauds and to otherwise manifest the intent of the parties involved. With some variations, the other basic requirements previously set forth for a valid deed are applicable. Certainly to the extent that the instrument is designed to affect specific real property, such real property must be properly described; the parties in the transaction must be identified; the parties creating the interest must execute the instrument; and the transaction should be supported by consideration. In addition, the instrument must be acknowledged if it is to be recorded so as to provide notice of its contents to the public at large.

REVIEW QUESTIONS

1. The most protection afforded a purchaser in terms of warranty of title is that provided by a

   (a) Full covenant and warranty deed.
   (b) Bargain and sale deed.
   (c) Quitclaim deed.
   (d) Executor's deed.

2. A deed which is voidable because the grantor is in fact mentally incompetent

   A. May not be recorded.
   B. May be set aside later by legal proceedings.

   (a) A only.   (c) Both A and B.
   (b) B only.   (d) Neither A nor B.

3. "Lot 452 of Rolling Hills subdivision of the City of Anytown" would be part of what type of legal description?

   (a) Governmental survey.
   (b) Metes and bounds.
   (c) Platted subdivision.
   (d) None of the above.

4. A deed of property for a price of $40,000 meets the consideration test if it states that the consideration was

   A. $10 and other good and valuable consideration, the receipt of which is acknowledged.
   B. $40,000, the receipt of which is acknowledged.

   (a) A only.   (c) Both A and B.
   (b) B only.   (d) Neither A nor B.

5. To be valid, the deed must be

   (a) Executed by the grantor.
   (b) Accepted by the grantee.
   (c) Both A and B.
   (d) Neither A nor B.

6. Generally, a deed which is not acknowledged

   A. Is effective between the parties to transfer title.
   B. May not be recorded.

   (a) A only.   (c) Both A and B.
   (b) B only.   (d) Neither A nor B.

7. When a deed does not specify the estate being conveyed, it is presumed to transfer

   (a) A fee simple absolute.
   (b) A life estate.
   (c) A determinable fee.
   (d) An estate for years.

8. The deed form which may convey no rights in real property is a(n)

    (a) Sheriff's deed.
    (b) Full covenant and warranty deed.
    (c) Executor's deed.
    (d) Quitclaim deed.

9. An interest in land which can be inherited is the

    (a) Fee simple absolute.
    (b) Decedent's life estate.
    (c) Decedent's personal license.
    (d) Decedent's interest held with another as joint tenants with right of survivorship.

10. In the execution of a deed by an individual there is a presumption that

    A. He or she is of legal age.
    B. He or she is mentally competent.

    (a) A only.   (c) Both A and B.
    (b) B only.   (d) Neither A nor B.

11. When title to real estate is transferred by inheritance,

    (a) All title defects are cured by probating the will.
    (b) the heirs take the title subject to all defects and liens which existed at the time of the decedent's death.
    (c) The heirs or devisees are entitled to immediate possession at the time of the decedent's death.
    (d) Both b and c.

12. Which items would appear on a subdivision plat?

    (a) Sanitary sewer easement.
    (b) Storm sewer easement.
    (c) Electrical service lines.
    (d) All of the above.

13. Which form of description is not utilized in New York?

    (a) Metes and bounds.
    (b) Record plat.
    (c) Rectangular or governmental grid.
    (d) None of the above.

14. The doctrine of adverse possession enables one to acquire ownership by the required possession

A. For ten years against the record owner and all other persons other than the state.
B. For twenty years against the state.

    (a) A only.   (c) Both A and B.
    (b) B only.   (d) Neither A nor B.

15. A person who has real property devised to him through a will is said to have acquired title by

    (a) Adverse possession.
    (b) Escheat.
    (c) Reversion.
    (d) Inheritance.

16. A quiet title proceeding develops when

    (a) Questions arise regarding the validity of the title.
    (b) The purchaser buys a property with land tenants.
    (c) Family members purchase a property.
    (d) None of the above.

17. The maximum number of grantees which can be named in a deed is

    (a) Two.
    (b) Three.
    (c) Four.
    (d) Any number.

18. One who acquires property under a deed is a

    (a) Vendee.
    (b) Lessee.
    (c) Trustee. ans.
    (d) Grantee.

19. Title to real property passes to the grantee at the time the deed is

    (a) Delivered.
    (b) Written.
    (c) Signed.
    (d) Acknowledged.

20. The form of deed that is customarily utilized in New York City and other large metropolitan areas in New York State is

    (a) Quitclaim deed.
    (b) Bargain and sale deed without covenant.
    (c) Bargain and sale deed with covenant.
    (d) Full covenant and warranty deed.

Chapter 6
Contracts

VOCABULARY

You will find it important to have a complete working knowledge of the following concepts and words in this chapter:

acceptance
bilateral contract— *2 parties agree*
binder— *show good faith*
consideration
damages
duress
earnest money— *money paid to show good faith*
equitable title
execution
express contract
fraud

illegality
implied contract
impossibility of performance
incompetent
infant
legal capacity
legality
liquidated damages
majority age
marketable title
minor

mistake of fact
mistake of law
offer
specific performance
Statute of Frauds
undue influence
unilateral contract— *one sided*
valid contracts
void
voidable

THE BASIS for all relationships in the real estate brokerage business is found in the law. Since almost all real estate dealings originate with an agreement known as a contract, it is essential that real estate salespersons understand the basic elements of contracts. A discussion of general principles of contract law and of the real estate contract in particular follows.

THE CONTRACT DEFINED

A *contract* is an agreement that is recognized and enforced by law, involving either an exchange of promises, or the exchange of a promise for an act resulting in a binding and legally recognized obligation. The concept of "contract" is narrower than that of "agreement," since the latter includes promises that the law will not enforce as well as those that the law will enforce. It should also be noted that except in a limited number of circumstances a "naked" promise, or a promise standing alone (with no exchange), is not legally enforceable.

Binder

Before proceeding with a discussion of contracts, it would be appropriate to discuss a document, known as a *binder*, which is often involved in a typical real estate transaction.

A binder is generally viewed by the seller as a means of securing the sale, by the purchaser as a means of preserving the purchase, and by the broker as a means of guaranteeing the commission. The problem with binders, which are usually prepared by brokers, is that their legal effect is often in doubt. If a binder is complete enough in setting forth the details of the proposed sale, a court will enforce it as a contract. In other instances, if the binder does not contain the essential characteristics of a contract, in effect it binds no one. Even where a binder is legally enforceable, it almost never covers all the terms and provisions that an attorney for a seller or a buyer would prefer to have in a properly prepared contract of sale.

Because of the problems associated with binders, it is often advisable not to sign one but to proceed as quickly as possible to the actual contract of sale.

TYPES OF CONTRACTS

In order to understand the obligations of parties to contracts, it is useful to classify contracts into the following categories (these classifications are not mutually exclusive):

☐ Bilateral contract.
☐ Unilateral contract.
☐ Express contract.
☐ Implied contract.

A *bilateral contract* is a contract in which both parties make promises to each other. For example, A writes to B, "I will pay you $10,000 if you will promise to sell me this land." If B agrees, A has promised the payment of $10,000 and B has promised to sell him the land.

A *unilateral contract* is a contract in which one party gives a promise to another party in exchange for some actual performance by the second party. The promise made by the first party is not legally binding until the actual performance by the second party. For example, A says to B, "I will pay you $100 if you plow this field." If B plows the field, B has both accepted A's offer and performed his part of the contract. At this point, A's promise to pay B $100 is legally binding.

An *express contract* is a contract in which the agreement is stated in words, either oral or written. For example, A says to B, "I will pay you $100 if you promise me to plow this field." B says, "It's a deal."

An *implied contract* is a contract in which, even though there are no spoken or written words, the agreement between the parties can be inferred from their conduct alone. For example, A says to B, "I will pay you $100 if you promise me to plow this field." B says nothing, but walks over to the barn, starts up the plow, and begins plowing. The contract has been established.

Validity of Contracts

Since the validity and enforceability of contracts can vary greatly from situation to situation, it is necessary to be aware of several definitions that indicate the legal status of particular contracts. Legally, contracts may be

☐ Valid
☐ Void
☐ Voidable

A *valid contract* possesses all the required elements of a legal contract and legally binds all the parties involved to the agreement.

A *void contract* is any agreement that has no legal status. It never met the requirements for a legal contract and was therefore never binding on the parties. For example, an agreement made with a person who had been adjudicated incompetent is void from the outset.

A *voidable contract* is a contract in which one party or the other may take action to have the agreement declared void. A contract made with an *infant* is voidable at the option of the infant.

Is there a time limit on this?

State of Execution

The state of execution of a contract also is subject to special legal terminology. If all the provisions of a contract have been fulfilled, it is said to be *executed*. If something in the contract remains to be performed, it is said to be *executory*. The typical real estate contract is executory up to the time of the closing of title.

BASIC ELEMENTS OF A CONTRACT

All of the following elements must be present for a contract to be valid:

☐ *Offer*. One party must make an offer.
☐ *Acceptance*. The other party must accept the offer.
☐ *Consideration*. Each party must give up something of legal value.
☐ *Legal capacity*. Both parties must be legally competent to enter into contracts.
☐ *Validity*. The contract must be free of duress, fraud, undue influence, or mutual mistakes.
☐ *Illegality and impossibility*. The purpose of the contract must be legal, and it must be possible to perform.

The Statute of Frauds

The U.S. legal system established prior to the Revolutionary War and based on English common law has been altered by individual states from time to time, but many basic principles of property law hold true throughout the United States. Under common law, writing was usually not a necessary element to the formation of a contract, and an oral contract was as enforceable as a written one. Today a statute, known as the Statute of Frauds, requires most forms of contracts, including real estate contracts, to be in writing. Its purpose is to produce certainty in the obligation and to remove the possibility of proving a nonexistent undertaking by the use of perjured evidence.

In real estate, the statute of frauds has the following practical consequences with respect to contracts:

☐ All contracts for the sale and purchase of real estate must be in writing and signed by each party to be charged (or by an individual designated in writing to be the agent of the party to be charged).

☐ Any contract for the leasing of real estate for a period of more than one year must be in writing and signed by each party to be charged (or by an individual designated in writing to be the agent of the party to be charged).

Usually a contract of sale or a lease is signed by both principal parties to the agreement.

In order for the requirements of the statute of frauds to be satisfied, the written memorandum of contract must contain the following information:

☐ The identity of the contracting parties either by name or description.

☐ The identification of the subject matter of the contract.

☐ The consideration.

Oral Agreements

There is room in the law for considerable flexibility in determining what constitutes a sufficient memorandum. For example, a binding contract for the purchase and sale of realty may be made by an oral acceptance of a satisfactory written offer. In addition, if an oral agreement is made and action of sufficient scope is undertaken to implement the oral contract, there may be sufficient part-performance to make the contract legally enforceable.

However, certain exceptions aside, an oral agreement to buy and sell real property, regardless of how firm the initial resolve of the parties to the transaction may have been, is not legally enforceable until the agreement has been reduced to a written contract.

Offer

In any contract there must be a meeting of the minds—or in legal terminology, an offer and acceptance.

The *offer* is the initial step in formation of a contract. In the absence of an offer there can be no contract. To be effective, an offer must be unqualified and definite.

The law requires that to be valid, the offer must be clearly intelligible to a reasonable person. The reason that the law insists upon the standard of the so-called reasonable person is that, unless the meaning of the offer is reasonably certain, any re-

sulting agreement cannot be an agreement at all because of the basic inability to define the terms of the agreement.

The offeror is in complete command of the terms of the offer. The offer is a free and voluntary act on the part of the one who makes it, and the offeror is free to make the offer on any terms or conditions he chooses. One of the most important features of this element of control of the offer is that it may be withdrawn at any time before it is acted upon. The offeree is not injured by the withdrawal unless and until he acts upon the offer. This rule is true even though the offer, by its terms, specifies that it will be available for a stated period of time. It may be arbitrarily withdrawn before the specified time, as long as the offeree has not responded.

The offer must of course be communicated to the offeree.

Options

An offer should be distinguished from an option. An option is a right, for which a consideration (as hereinafter defined) has been paid, to buy, lease, or sell a particular piece of real estate to or from another at a specified price and within a designated period.

An option may itself be a contract if all of the essential elements of a contract exist. Where the option constitutes a contract, it cannot be withdrawn or revoked during the period specified therein. Today, however, there is a statute that makes any offer irrevocable if in writing, signed by the offeror or his agent, and stating that the offer is irrevocable. If the period of irrevocability is stated in the writing, the offer cannot be revoked for that period; otherwise it may be revoked after a reasonable time. In New York State an option is deemed to be a recordable interest in real estate and is entitled to the protection of the recording act.

Acceptance

The next essential step in the formation of a contract is the acceptance of the offer. The offer by itself is meaningless unless and until the offeree indicates that it is satisfactory. The acceptance consists of a simple assent to the terms of the offer and an expression of intent to be bound by the terms of the resulting agreement. Legally, it must be just that and nothing more. If the offeree adds to or alters the terms of the offer, he has not accepted it. The acceptance must be absolute, unequivocal, and without any change in the terms of the offer. If not, it is not an acceptance; it is something less and a contract has not been made. There is no such thing as a conditional acceptance of an offer. The addition of any terms to the offer in the acceptance destroys the acceptance and by necessary implication rejects the offer. Such a response is, in legal effect, a counter-offer or new offer; it cannot operate as an acceptance.

The acceptance of the offer must be communicated to the offeror. The offeree may not simply decide that he accepts the offer; the law requires that the offeree take positive action to bind the offeror to the terms of the offer. In most cases, the offer will have dictated the method by which it must be accepted. For example, the offer might provide that written acceptance must be received by the offeror by a specified time. In such a case, it is the responsibility of the offeree to deliver the acceptance to the offeror by the stated time. If an offer is mailed to the offeree, then the offeree is entitled to assume that mailing of his acceptance by the time specified will result in a binding contract. (The offeror has by implication indicated that the mails are an acceptable agency for communication.)

In real estate sales transactions in most areas of New York State, an offer is set forth in a "proposed contract" prepared by the seller's attorney. The proposed contract is submitted to the purchaser's attorney. If the purchaser accepts it in the form in which it was submitted, it becomes a contract upon proper subscription (when it is properly signed). If the purchaser modifies the offer, the purchaser's response becomes a counter-offer to be accepted by the original offeror (the seller). Usually the mail is used to transmit both offer and acceptance, especially when the property being sold consists of vacant land or a one- or two-family dwelling. When commercial or industrial property is involved, the execution of the offer and acceptance often takes place at a meeting (contract signing) in the presence of all the parties including, on occasion, the real estate broker who may have brought about the sale.

Consideration

Consideration is the third major element that is necessary to make a contract valid and enforceable. The concept of consideration is not only one of the most difficult notions of contract law to define, it is also one of the most difficult to justify. It would seem to be sufficient that the parties to a contract intend for it to be legally enforceable, without imposing the technical requirement that there be

some consideration to make their commitments binding.

Simply defined, *consideration* is something of legal value that each party commits to a contract. The commitment *to pay* or *to do something* of value constitutes consideration and makes the promises of the parties enforceable.

In most real estate contracts, the element of consideration is so obvious that it is seldom necessary to look for it. Assume a typical offer and acceptance for the purchase of real estate:

☐ The buyer offers (promises to pay) $10,000 for the seller's property.
☐ The seller accepts and agrees (promises) to convey the property for $10,000.
☐ A binding contract results because there is consideration to support each promise—the promise of the other party.

It should be noted that the buyer did not tender or hand over $10,000 at the time of the offer, nor did the seller tender the property or surrender it to the purchaser. Each one merely promised to perform an act of substantial value. Consideration need not be money paid. A promise to perform an act of value to the other side is sufficient. Two aspects of consideration are important from a practical standpoint in the real estate business.

The value that a buyer promises to give may be legally adequate consideration even though it has little relationship to the actual value of the property purchased. Unless the inadequacy of the consideration shocks the conscience of the court, the sufficiency of the consideration usually cannot be successfully attacked by someone seeking to void a contract. The courts do scrutinize the adequacy of consideration carefully when they must make a judgment about a contract involving an infant, an incompetent, an insolvency, or a fiduciary relationship.

While contracts recite the actual consideration that the parties have agreed to, deeds usually contain a recital only of *nominal* consideration (such as, one dollar and other valuable consideration) so that the public record does not reflect the sales price of the subject premises. Although the recital of only nominal consideration in the deed attempts to conceal the purchase price, that attempt is usually thwarted by the existence of transfer tax stamps on the deed from which an outsider may usually ascertain the property's sales price.

The foregoing discussion has not mentioned the traditional down payment or *earnest money* deposit (usually 10 percent of the purchase price). The reason is that a down payment is not essential to make a contract for the sale of real estate legal or binding on the parties. The contract is made enforceable by the mutual promises of the parties, and the deposit does not increase its binding nature. The true function of the down payment is that it serves as a possible source for the payment of damages to the seller in the event that the purchaser changes his mind and breaches the contract.

Legal Capacity

Each party to a contract must have the *legal capacity* or power to make a legal contract and to agree to its terms. The law defining who is and who is not competent to enter into a contract is quite technical. It is designed to protect the incompetent from his or her own improvident acts and to protect a business entity from the unauthorized acts of one of its members. If the court concludes that one party to a contract was insane, a minor (sometimes referred to as an "infant"), or intoxicated at the time of the agreement, it will usually consider the contract not binding. Contracts entered into by such persons are either void or voidable by the incompetent individuals; they are not voidable by the other party to the contract.

The real estate salesperson or broker must be aware of the legal capacity of the parties brought to a contract. He must recognize the limitations of the parties in the negotiation and execution of the contract of sale. In order to be competent to enter into a binding contract, individuals must be of age and must be mentally competent. Minors (those less than eighteen years of age) may enter into contracts prior to reaching majority, but they have an option to void them if they choose to do so when they reach majority. To protect the interests of the minor, the law requires a court proceeding authorizing the sale of an infant's real property.

Because it may be impossible for a party to a contract to recognize that the other party is mentally incompetent, the threat of mental incapacity is hard to avoid. Each party and his agent must exercise good judgment. The law recognizes two categories of mental incompetence: The person who is actually incompetent at the time of the transaction but who has not been adjudged incompetent by a court; and the adjudged incompetent who has been placed under formal guardianship.

If an adjudged incompetent has been placed under a guardianship as a result of a court proceeding, this fact is often a matter of public record and the law expects a prudent individual to be aware of the facts. Once the guardianship has been established, the incompetent (the ward) has no capacity to enter into contracts. One may do business with such a person only through the guardian or a committee appointed by the court to handle his affairs. The incompetent's contracts are absolutely void and cannot be enforced. His property may be sold only through a court proceeding.

It is the actual but not adjudged incompetent who frequently poses a real problem, particularly since such a person does not always exhibit evidence of incompetence. There is a certain natural hesitancy on the part of the incompetent's relatives to take the action necessary to have a guardian appointed. The fact that the proceeding is a matter of public record and there is a stigma associated with incompetence make such a step distasteful. As a result, many incompetents are never adjudged as such. Contracts with such incompetents may be voidable if the individuals were incompetents at the time of the agreement. They are not automatically void, and it takes affirmative action to void them, but it is quite possible to void them.

Validity

Every contract must be free from undue influence, duress, fraud, and mistakes of fact or law, as these terms are defined below:

☐ *Duress.* If the contract is the result of force (such as, one party threatens the other with personal injury), and the threat has forced one party to act against his will, the forced party may void the contract.

☐ *Undue influence.* If one of the parties has taken unfair advantage of the other party to the contract because of a particular relationship that exists, the contract is voidable by the party who was unjustly treated.

☐ *Fraud.* If one of the parties used fraud to procure the contract, the aggrieved party may (among other remedies) bring an action to void and rescind the contract.

☐ *Mistakes.* Two general types of mistakes can occur in the formation of contracts—*mistakes of fact* and *mistakes of law.*

☐ A *mistake of fact* occurs when a person assumes something to be a fact which is incorrect and this error is included in the agreement. If there was a mistake of a material fact, the party injured by the mistake may bring action to rescind the contract. If the mistake was minor, the contract can be corrected by the process known as *reformation.*

☐ A *mistake of law* occurs when one party has an erroneous notion of the legal obligations he has assumed by entering into the contract. For example, the purchaser of a home may believe that he is not obligated to complete payment for the property if he changes his mind about occupying the property at a later date. Until recently, parties could not be relieved of their obligation under contracts that they had entered into with full knowledge of the facts but with erroneous assumptions about the law. A statute now provides that when a party seeks relief because of a mistake of law, relief shall not be denied merely because the mistake is one of law rather than one of fact. The court is empowered to grant such relief in appropriate cases, even if the mistake was a mistake of law.

Illegality of Purpose

A valid contract should be both legal and possible of performance. Clearly, if a contract requires the performance of a criminal act by one of the parties, it cannot be enforced by law. Such a contract would be in violation of the law at the outset, and no court would entertain a lawsuit to compel performance by either party. A contract to commit a criminal act, however, is not the only possible illegal contract. A wide variety of contracts are illegal in the sense that they violate public policy, are in restraint of trade, would be injurious to third persons, would violate usury statutes, would constitute gambling contracts, etc. An illegal purpose that is not criminal in nature makes the contract voidable (unenforceable) as to the illegal condition, but a contract for a criminal purpose is totally void.

A few examples of illegal purposes illustrate this element of contracts, as it applies to real estate transactions and may serve to illustrate the impact of the general contract law rule:

Example J enters into a contract to lease property from L specifying that he will use the property for the purpose of operating a gambling casino in a state where gambling is illegal. Since the purpose of the lease violates a criminal statute, the contract to lease is void and cannot be enforced by either party.

Example J deeds real estate to his son, J, Jr., on the condition that J, Jr., never marry. The deed is not void; but since the condition violates public policy, the courts will treat the deed as an absolute transfer of title and will disregard the condition.

Impossibility of Performance

Occasionally, parties enter into otherwise binding contracts that for one reason or another prove to be impossible to perform. The question then arises as to whether there is relief available to the party who promised to do the impossible and who usually seeks relief. Whether that party receives relief hinges upon the definition of *impossible* that has developed under contract law. The law recognizes two types of impossibilities that are best illustrated by an example.

Example F promises to sell a building to B, but it is impossible for F to do so because he does not own the building. Is F excused under the doctrine of impossibility? No. It may be impossible for F to deed this building, but it is not impossible for someone to deed it to B. F is liable for breach of contract to B. To have the benefit of the defense of impossibility of performance, F would have to prove that no one could have deeded the property. The court could compel F to buy the property at whatever price he had to pay in order to carry out his promise. As an alternative, F could be found liable to B for money damages for the difference between the agreed purchase price and the price B must pay for a comparable building plus other damages.

A problem closely related to impossibility of performance is that of difficulty or unanticipated expense of performance. Suppose a contractor agrees to dig a basement for a house in an area that he believes to be sand and gravel and has priced the job at $1,000. Upon performing the excavation work, he discovers there is pure granite below the topsoil and that the excavation will cost more than $10,000. Is he relieved from performing his contract? No. Extreme or extraordinary difficulty of performance does not relieve him from his obligation. It is not impossible to perform the contract; it is merely costly and difficult.

PURPOSE OF THE CONTRACT IN THE REAL ESTATE TRANSACTION

Although it is not absolutely necessary to use a contract to transfer title to real property, contracts are used by the parties because they serve several important functions:

☐ A contract can serve to legally obligate the parties.

□ A contract may provide for financing requisites.

□ A contract makes possible the performance of numerous acts on which the transfer may be conditioned.

Legal Obligation

The contract legally binds the seller and purchaser to the transaction. The real estate contract is customarily prepared by the seller's attorney and mailed to the purchaser's attorney for review and execution by his client. Neither party may arbitrarily default or withdraw from an executed contract without incurring certain legally enforceable penalties. The specific rights and obligations set forth in the contract are usually valid right up to the date of title closing. At that time they are merged into the deed that transfers the title. However, the contract may provide expressly for rights and obligations between the parties that survive the closing of title. For example, the contract may contain warranties of construction by a builder.

Financing Requisite

The contract provides an opportunity for the purchaser to secure necessary financing. Most real estate contracts are contingent upon the buyer being able to obtain a commitment from a mortgage lender within a stated period of time (usually two to three weeks after the execution of the contract). The contract usually specifies the basic mortgage terms that the purchaser must accept if the lending institution offers the purchaser a loan. It specifies the term and the amount of the loan and the maximum interest rate that the purchaser must accept. With the variety of mortgage forms that have been developed recently, this clause takes on added significance and must be carefully considered, especially by the attorney for the purchaser.

Physical Inspection

The contract enables the purchaser to make a more detailed physical inspection of the property. After the buyer and seller agree upon a price and other basic terms, the seller usually pressures the buyer to execute a purchase contract. But the buyer must remember that the warning *caveat emptor*, "Let the buyer beware," applies most particularly to real estate transfers. The purchaser should satisfy himself about the physical condition of the property before he goes to a closing. In the absence of fraud or of a survival provision in the contract, any physical defects that he discovers subsequent to the closing of title are his responsibility. If the purchaser has not completed the necessary inspections before he executes the contract, he must insert into the contract conditions that limit his obligation if an inspection of the property discloses infestation and structural defects.

The contract may provide that if such defects are discovered, depending on the nature of the problem, one of the following actions must be taken:

□ The seller must make repairs prior to closing.

□ The purchase price may be reduced.

□ The purchaser may have the right to withdraw from the sale contract.

Title Verification

The contract enables the purchaser to research the legal status of the property prior to the closing of title. In most transactions, a purchaser of real property is entitled to a marketable title. A *marketable title* is one that is free of material legal defects, free of liens and encumbrances, and reasonably free of the possibility of litigation against it. The "implied warranty of marketability" that exists in all contracts for the sale of such real property continues until it is merged into the deed of conveyance thereafter.

The purchaser can usually establish the legal status of the property that he is buying from a title company report or commitment. In certain areas of the state, the purchaser orders an abstract of title.

We will discuss in a later chapter how a purchaser assures himself of the quality of the title (ownership) that he is buying. For the present, the following definitions are sufficient:

□ An abstract of title is a digest of relevant public documents.

□ A title company report reflects the legal status of the title by a company that is prepared to insure the quality of the title to the buyer.

A copy of the title company's "exception sheet" is usually forwarded to the seller's attorney who must clear the title of any defects or persuade the purchaser to take subject to the defects.

Common Real Property Contract Provisions

Most real estate contracts will contain specific provisions about the following matters:

□ *Date of the agreement.* Although it is not essential to the validity of the agreement, a contract should be dated.

□ *Names and signatures of the parties.* In order to satisfy the Statute of Frauds, both the seller and *who is this?*

buyer must be identified by name in the contract of sale. The statute also requires that the (party to be charged) must subscribe the contract. The word *subscribe* means that the signature of the buyer (the party to be charged) must appear at the end of the contract. Usually, the contract for the sale of real property is subscribed by both the buyer and the seller.

☐ *Legal description of the property.* A contract for the sale of realty must describe the property with reasonable definiteness. Usually, the description of the property is the same as that appearing in the deed to the seller. If a change in the property description occurs, that change should be reflected in a revised contract description. In Chapter 5, we discussed three standard ways of describing real property that is being conveyed or transferred.

  Metes and bounds description
  Record plat or filed map description
  Governmental grid description

☐ *Consideration.* The Statute of Frauds requires that the consideration for the conveyance of real property be set forth in the contract. Customarily, a 10 percent down payment, or earnest money payment, is paid by the buyer's personal check drawn to the seller and dated at the time of the execution of the contract Because circumstances may arise in which it may be necessary to try to get these funds back, the buyer should request that the seller's attorney hold the down payment in escrow, either until the title is closed or until the buyer obtains the mortgage commitment as provided for in the contract.

In New York, the purchaser of a newly constructed residential condominium unit, or any other residential structure designed for the occupancy of not more than two families, has the option of requiring that the down payment funds be deposited in an interest-bearing escrow account. Alternatively, the seller may post a bond with the purchaser, issued by a licensed security company, that guarantees the return of the monies if that becomes necessary under the contract or other provisions of law.

☐ *Terms of payment.* A contract for the sale of real property should describe the payment terms in detail. The contract should set forth how much is being paid in cash and when it is to be paid. If the buyer is taking over an existing mortgage, obtaining a new mortgage from a lending institution, or receiving partial financing from the seller, the terms of financing (such as, interest rates, amount to be borrowed, the repayment

schedule) should also be specified in the contract.

☐ *Apportionment clause.* The contract should specify who pays what portions of claims like taxes, insurance, outstanding fuel bills, etc.

☐ *Encumbrances.* The contract should specify those encumbrances subject to which the property will be sold. Title may be subject to covenants, restrictions, easements, tenancies, or defects that can be shown by a survey.

☐ *Zoning regulations.* The contract usually contains a provision that the property is being sold subject to zoning regulations that are not violated by existing structures. The limiting effect of both encumbrances and zoning regulations on the use of the premises must be carefully considered by the purchaser and his attorney.

☐ *Date and place of closing.* The contract should specify the date and place of closing. By custom and practice the closing usually takes place at the office of either the seller's attorney or the lender's attorney. If the contract states that "time is of the essence," the closing must take place on the agreed date or the defaulting party may be liable in damages. Unless time is stated to be of the essence, either party may obtain an adjournment of the closing by showing reasonable cause.

A copy of a standard form contract is found in Appendix F.

CONTRACTS WITH ENTITIES OTHER THAN PERSONS

Partnerships

Any "general partner" of a partnership may make a contract for the partnership. Under the New York Partnership Act, it is usually not necessary that all partners join in the execution of documents relating to real estate.

A partnership may acquire real estate in the partnership's name. The real estate so acquired can be sold (conveyed) only in the partnership's name. The partnership law makes each partner the agent of the partnership. It validates their actions for the partnership unless the person acting had no actual authority to act in the particular matter, and the person whom he was dealing with knew about the limitation of authority. Good practice dictates that the person who wants to purchase real estate from a partnership review the partnership agreement in order to determine if any such limitations of authority exist with respect to the sale of real property. Although it is usually not necessary that all partners join in the execution of documents relating to real estate transactions, if the sale of the real property were to make it impossible for the partnership to carry out its ordinary business, the partnership act requires that all the partners consent to the sale. *Does this mean they all have to sign the documents?*

Corporations

A contract for the sale of corporate real property must be executed in the name of the corporation. It is not valid if it merely uses the name of the principal stockholder or officer. The contract must be signed in the corporate name by a properly authorized officer, who, in addition to entering the corporate name, subscribes his own name and his official capacity. An example would be, "*ABC* Realty Inc. by *JJ*, president." For someone who wishes to engage in a real estate transaction with a corporation, the safest course to follow is to obtain a resolution of the board of directors authorizing a specific officer to buy or sell the real estate. If the transaction involves a sale of all, or substantially all, of the corporate assets, the buyer should obtain stockholder approval.

People doing business with corporations should review the certificate of incorporation and corporate bylaws in order to determine whether there are any limitations on the authority of officers or specific provisions that relate to the purchase or sale of real property.

Other Organizations

Associations that are neither formal partnerships nor corporations often do not have a clearly recognized status as legal entities. The only safe way to deal with them, as far as real estate transactions are concerned, is to treat them as a group of individuals selling individual interests in the property, that is, as though they were tenants in common. Each one of the members of the association (or syndicate, or other designation) must have the capacity to deal with his own property. *If one is incapacitated is deal void?*

Governmental units are strictly controlled by statutes or ordinances and have no capacity to conduct business of any kind unless they are specifically authorized by the governing statutes to do so. It is very important in dealing with any governmental unit to verify its authority to buy or sell or to enter into a contract to do either.

Court officers such as receivers, commissioners, etc., must have specific court authority to enter into contracts that will be binding upon the property being dealt with. Court officers do not have authority to buy or sell real estate simply because they have been appointed court officers. Formal approval of the court is always essential. An attorney should always be consulted in connection with transactions with court officers to be sure of their authority and to be sure that the necessary documentation is preserved as a matter of record to avoid later complications so far as the title to the real estate is concerned.

Fiduciaries generally have specific statutory authority to deal with real estate. The term *fiduciary* includes executors, administrators, trustees, and agents. However, the cautious businessman always verifies that this authority exists.

ENFORCEMENT OF CONTRACTS FOR REAL ESTATE

While this remedy is not always available, generally the enforcement of contracts is limited to the collection of money damages for any breach of contract that may occur. That is, contracts are enforced by the implied threat of a suit for damages. The parties know that if they fail to keep a promise that is enforceable under contract law principles, the injured party may maintain a lawsuit for the breach and can obtain a judgment entitling that person to recover whatever damages he can show have resulted from the breach.

Specific Performance

While this remedy is always available, the law recognized early that in certain situations an award of money damages is not a really satisfactory remedy and that in certain situations the injured party can receive real justice only by the performance for which he had bargained. This is the doctrine known as *specific performance*. It is not a usual remedy. It is an extraordinary remedy that is reserved for unique situations in which money damages are clearly insufficient. Although the doctrine of specific performance is applicable to real estate transactions, the occasions for its use are quite rare.

The law today still considers each parcel of real estate to be absolutely unique and different from any other parcel of real estate. This is true even though the parcel may be a lot in a subdivision in which there are hundreds of other lots with precisely the same dimensions, facing the same street, and alike as two peas in a pod to anyone who might inspect them. In many cases, the buyer of such a lot may in fact be quite easily satisfied with another lot or money damages for the loss of the bargain. However, legally, a buyer does not have to be satisfied with anything other than the lot or parcel for which he bargained. If the buyer pursues the remedy of specific performance, he is favored with a presumption that nothing else will be satisfactory.

There is a basic difference between a judgment for damages and one for specific performance. A judgment for money damages is simply a conclusion of the court that the plaintiff is entitled to so many dollars from the defendant. The court does not in any way compel the defendant to pay the money. Payment is accomplished by formal execution of the judgment under which the sheriff may seize assets and sell them if the defendant fails to pay the judgment. There may be small satisfaction to the plaintiff if the sheriff can find no assets to seize. Further action to enforce the judgment may be cumbersome and expensive.

A decree of specific performance, however, constitutes an order from the court to the defendant to perform. This is a different matter entirely, because failure to obey is contempt of court for which the defendant is subject to severe penalties.

Potential Results of Nonperformance

Every breach of contract entitles the injured party to sue for damages. The theory behind compensatory damages is to put the injured party in as good a position, so far as money damages can do so, as he would have occupied had the party who breached the contract fully performed.

The contract itself may stipulate that a certain sum will have to be paid by the party who breaches the contract. This stipulation is called a liquidated damages clause. A liquidated damage clause must meet two requirements if it is to be enforceable:

☐ The harm caused by the breach must be very difficult to estimate accurately, and
☐ The amount so fixed must be a reasonable forecast of just compensation for the harm caused by the breach.

In many jurisdictions, if the buyer has made installment payments (say for an automobile), and then is unable to complete payments and therefore breaches the contract, he may have to forfeit the money he has already paid to the seller. This forfeiture is often based on a contract provision that states that in the event of the buyer's default, all payments are to be retained by the seller as liquidated damages.

In real estate, such a forfeiture of monetary consideration could also take place if the contract were a long-term land contract. Long-term land contracts allow the seller of the property to cancel the contract if the buyer defaults, to retake possession, and to retain all prior payments. Some states believe that these contractual provisions ought to be enforced as written. In other states, a trend toward consumerism has expanded the buyer's rights and has made these clauses more difficult to enforce.

Equitable Title

Equitable title is a concept used in certain circumstances that permits the courts to enforce specifically a seller's contractual obligation to sell land. The courts ~~may~~ *must* hold that at the moment that a contract to convey an interest in land is signed, equitable title becomes vested in the purchaser. Although legal title remains in the seller during the period from contract signing to closing, equitable title passed when the contract was formed. An obligation was created that the courts will enforce. The obligations may be created by contract, court order, or will. *Equitable title carries more weight than legal title? No*

ASSIGNMENT OF CONTRACTS

Most real estate contracts can be assigned. This means that a party to a contract can assign (turn over) his rights to someone else. In order to demonstrate the concept of assignment by example, we must define the terms *assignor* and *assignee*.

Example Assume that C and J had a contract in which C provided services for J. After C performed his part, J owed him $100 for services performed. C assigns his contractual right to the $100 for services performed to M. C is the assignor, M is the assignee. Once an effective assignment is completed, the assignor's right against the other party to the contract is extinguished, and a similar right is created in the assignee. In the above example, after C assigns his contractual right against J to M, C no longer has any claim to the $100 in question and M now has a contractual right against J for $100. J's responsibility remains unchanged, as he still owes $100.

If the assignment is in writing and signed by the assignor (or an agent that he has authorized in writing), no consideration need be given to support the assignment. The parties to the original contract (J and C above) may put a clause in that contract to prohibit its assignment to a third party provided that this arrangement is not made in order to circumvent the nondiscrimination laws effective in New York.

REVIEW QUESTIONS

1. The usual contract for the sale of real property contains the signature of

    A. The buyer.
    B. The seller.

    (a) A only.
    (b) B only.
    (c) Both A and B.
    (d) Neither A nor B.

2. A contract subscribed by a judicially declared incompetent is

    (a) Void.
    (b) Voidable.
    (c) Valid.
    (d) Illegal.

3. A counteroffer

    A. Results in a new contract if accepted.
    B. Invalidates the original offer.

    (a) A only.
    (b) B only.
    (c) Both A and B.
    (d) Neither A nor B.

4. The concept of duress is based on

    (a) Deception.
    (b) Fear.
    (c) Abuse of power.
    (d) The commission of a crime.

5. Consideration in a contract is

    (a) Not essential.
    (b) An exchange of promises.
    (c) More than 10 percent of the purchase price.
    (d) All of the above.

6. The statute of frauds requires contracts for the sale of real estate to be

    (a) In writing to be enforceable.
    (b) In outline forms.
    (c) Reviewed by the county recorder.
    (d) All of the above.

7. If a purchaser has signed a contract under duress, it is generally

    (a) Voidable by the seller.
    (b) Voidable by the buyer.
    (c) Valid.
    (d) Void.

8. Which of the following terms does not terminate an offer to sell real estate?

    (a) Lapse of reasonable time.
    (b) Rejection of the offer by the offeree.
    (c) Death of the sales agent.
    (d) A revocation of the offer.

9. Once the contract for the sale of real property has been signed, the purchaser has

    (a) Legal title to the real estate.
    (b) The right to possess the real estate.
    (c) Nothing until he receives the deed.
    (d) Equitable title in the real estate.

10. Which of the following may be a contract?

    (a) A deed.
    (b) An option.
    (c) A mortgage.
    (d) None of the above.

11. An express contract can be

    (a) Oral.
    (b) Written.
    (c) Both a and b.
    (d) Neither a nor b.

12. A contract may be assigned *if not prohibited then it automatically can be assigned to a 3rd party.*

    A. Unless prohibited in the agreement.
    B. To a third party.

    (a) A only.
    (b) B only.
    (c) Both A and B.
    (d) Neither A nor B.

13. Consideration is

    (a) Not required to have a binding contract.
    (b) Something that makes promises enforceable.
    (c) Both a and b.
    (d) Neither a nor b.

14. Down payment deposits

    A. Are essential to the contract for the sale of real property.
    B. Serve as a source of payment of damages to the seller in case of a breach by the buyer.

    (a) A only.
    (b) B only.
    (c) Both A and B.
    (d) Neither A nor B.

15. Under the Partnership Act

   A. All partners must be dealt with in the execution of documents relating to real estate transactions.
   B. Third parties may usually rely upon a partner's representation of capacity to contract.

   (a) A only.   (c) Both A and B.
   (b) B only.   (d) Neither A nor B.

16. A contract is generally void if it

   A. Was entered into with a minor.
   B. Requires an illegal act for performance.

   (a) A only.   (c) Both A and B.
   (b) B only.   (d) Neither A nor B.

an illegal act is not always a criminal act.

17. A contract involving an exchange of promises between the parties is

   (a) A unilateral contract.
   (b) A bilateral contract.
   (c) Neither a nor b.
   (d) Both a and b.

18. The acceptance of an offer must be

   (a) Communicated to the offeror.
   (b) Received by the time specified in the offer.
   (c) Both a and b.
   (d) Neither a nor b.

19. The contract provides the purchaser with the opportunity to

   (a) Obtain financing when necessary.
   (b) Ascertain the legal status of the property prior to closing.
   (c) Both a and b.
   (d) Neither a nor b.

20. Where the contract provides as to the closing date that time is of the essence

   (a) Only the seller may postpone the closing without incurring a penalty.
   (b) Only the purchaser may postpone the closing without incurring a penalty.
   (c) Both the seller and purchaser must agree to the postponement of the closing date so as to avoid the imposition of penalties.
   (d) Neither of the above.

Chapter 7
Mortgages

VOCABULARY

You will find it important to have a complete working knowledge of the following words and concepts found in this chapter:

acceleration clause	foreclosure	priorities of mortgages
alienation clause	free and clear	promissory note
assignment	grace period	right of redemption
assumption of mortgage	judicial action and sale	satisfaction of mortgage
collateral	junior mortgage	second mortgage
deed of trust	mortgage	security interest
default	mortgage bond	senior mortgage
deficiency judgment	mortgage note	statutory foreclosure
due-on-sale clause	mortgagee	subject to mortgage
equity of redemption	mortgagor	trust deed
estoppel certificate	personal liability	trustee
first mortgage	prepayment penalty	

A MORTGAGE is a *security interest* upon real estate and real estate improvements. The concept of security interest was merely mentioned in Chapter 3, which examined estates and interests in real estate. A security interest is a creditor's interest in the debtor's property. Depending on the type of debt and the type of property that the debtor pledges as security, the interest may be called a mortgage, a pledge, an equipment trust, etc. The security interest is a lien (a charge or claim) on the property that endures until the specific debt that is shown in a bond or note is paid. Thus, the borrower, or *mortgagor*, has pledged his property to secure his debt to the lender, or *mortgagee*. If the borrower does not repay his debt as promised, the lender can exercise his interest, force the sale of the property, and apply the proceeds against the amount due on the loan.

Historical Development

When the concept of land ownership by ordinary people developed, mortgages were unknown to the legal system. Land had to be purchased for cash, although it was possible to make installment payments to the seller until the purchase price was paid. Since most people did not have the money to buy land outright, and since many landowners needed money, lenders had many opportunities to enter into real estate transactions. To assure themselves of repayment, the lenders took title to the land being purchased by the borrowers. The borrower and the lender usually entered into an agreement that conveyed a total fee interest to the lender, but their agreement also stipulated that the lender would reconvey the land and improvements to the borrower if and when the debt was paid according to the terms of the contract.

This procedure, delivering full ownership to the lender, left much to be desired. Some lenders, being greedy, managed to secrete themselves so that the borrower could not make payment on the due date. A tempting offer from another buyer caused some lenders to "forget" their duty to return the land to the borrower. When the new buyer searched the title, the records would show the lender to be the owner. Consequently, a new buyer could purchase from the lender and defeat the true owner's interest in the land. Even if the lender were honest, a borrower might, through misfortune and no fault of his own, be detained and prevented from making the payment when it was due, thus losing his entire investment in the property.

To prevent this type of unfairness, the courts developed the theory of redemption. This theory is also known as the *equity of redemption* because the courts of equity created this right. The right exists today in modified form. The equity of redemption is a right given to an owner (borrower) to buy back the land within a reasonable time after the due date of the mortgage obligation. In order to fix the time limit, it was necessary to go to court and ask the chancellor (judge) to fix the rights between the parties and to set the time limit during which the money had to be finally paid in order for the property to be redeemed.

Once lenders lost the advantage of being able to sell the land unrestrained by the borrower's rights, the borrower-lender agreements and the instruments that conveyed title made the title that was conveyed *subject to the redemptive rights* that were agreed upon between the parties. These instruments became known as mortgages. The mortgage puts the person dealing with the mortgagee (lender) on notice that the title is subject to the rights of the borrower (mortgagor). With the passage of time, a number of states, including New York, have changed the legal meaning of the mortgage further. These states now view the mortgage only as being a lien or security interest. This security is for the performance of an obligation. The performance secured by the mortgage is usually a promise to pay.

BONDS AND NOTES

Bonds and notes are essentially the same. A bond or note is a promise to pay the borrowed amount, with interest at a fixed or ascertainable rate, at fixed times and places. The bond or note spells out in detail the agreement to repay, and often states that the loan is being secured by the mortgage. As a practical matter, the lender usually dictates the form of the written promise to pay. Unless the borrower is a very substantial customer of the lender, he usually has no bargaining power over the form or language of the promise to pay.

A mortgage note, such as the one shown in Figure 7-1, includes the following essential elements:

☐ It identifies the institution (or individual) to whom the debt is owed. This institution is sometimes called the "obligee" (local savings bank).
☐ It identifies the borrower, "the obligor" (John and Mary Homeowner).
☐ It facilitates the sale of the note by the lender. (John and Mary Homeowner are directed to pay local savings banks, *or order*.)

☐ It states the amount of the obligation (the principal) and the interest rate that is to be paid from the date of the note.
☐ It indicates that the obligor has made further agreements that are to be found in a mortgage securing the note.
☐ It includes an "acceleration" clause, a clause that makes the principal due at the option of the noteholder if the obligor violates the mortgage terms.
☐ It may identify the property on which the mortgage is a lien, even though this duplicates information in the mortgage.

ESSENTIALS OF A MORTGAGE

To be valid and enforceable against the secured property owner, a mortgage must be in writing and must be signed by all parties that have any ownership interest in the property. They must acknowledge their signatures before a notary public or other appropriate official if the mortgage is to be recorded. All persons signing the mortgage must be of legal age and mentally competent.

(Since the standard form mortgage used in New York State is a lengthy document, that form is not shown in this chapter. It is reproduced in Appendix E, and readers should examine it in connection with the following description.) *P. 299, 301*

☐ The mortgage must identify the specific note or bond or other collateral obligation for which it serves as the security interest.
☐ There must be an appropriate mortgaging clause. The standard mortgage in Appendix E includes the words "the mortgagor hereby mortgages to the mortgagee all that certain plot, piece or parcel of land, with buildings thereon erected. . . ."
☐ The property must be described by a sufficient legal description so that it can be clearly identified.
☐ A mortgage generally contains the following statutory short-form mortgage covenants:
  1. That the mortgagor will pay the indebtedness in accordance with terms specified in the mortgage.
  2. That the mortgagor will maintain insurance on buildings on the premises against loss by fire for the benefit of the mortgagee. (This insurance covenant protects the value of the collateral. If the property were damaged or destroyed in the absence of insurance, its value as collateral might fall below the amount of the loan.)

Standard N.Y.B.T.U. Form 8011-**10M**   Mortgage Note. Individual or Corporation. (Straight or Instalment.)

CONSULT YOUR LAWYER BEFORE SIGNING THIS INSTRUMENT — THIS INSTRUMENT SHOULD BE USED BY LAWYERS ONLY

MORTGAGE NOTE

$50,000.00   **New York,** June 1st,   19xl

FOR VALUE RECEIVED, JOHN HOMEOWNER and MARY HOMEOWNER, husband and wife

promise   **to pay to**   Local Savings Bank

or order, at 123 Main Street, Anytown, New York

or at such other place as may be designated in writing by the holder of this note, the principal sum of

fifty thousand and 00 00 ....   **Dollars on**

with interest thereon to be computed from the date hereof, at the rate of   12   **per centum per annum**
and to be paid on the   1st   **day of**   July   19xl, **next ensuing and**

IT IS HEREBY EXPRESSLY AGREED, that the said principal sum secured by this note shall become due at the option of the holder thereof on the happening of any default or event by which, under the terms of the mortgage securing this note, said principal sum may or shall become due and payable; also, that all of the covenants, conditions and agreements contained in said mortgage are hereby made part of this instrument.

Presentment for payment, notice of dishonor, protest and notice of protest are hereby waived.

This note is secured by a mortgage made by the maker to the payee of even date herewith, on property situate in the

This note may not be changed or terminated orally.

_____

STATE OF NEW YORK, COUNTY OF   SS:

On the 1st day of June   19xl, before me
personally came
John Homeowner and
Mary Homeowner, his wife
to me known to be the individuals described in and who
executed the foregoing instrument, and acknowledged that
they   executed the same.

[SEAL]

                                        Notary Public

STATE OF NEW YORK, COUNTY OF   SS:

On the   day of   19 , before me
personally came

to me known to be the individual described in and who
executed the foregoing instrument, and acknowledged that
        executed the same.

STATE OF NEW YORK, COUNTY OF   SS:

On the   day of   19 , before me
personally came
to me known, who, being by me duly sworn, did depose and
say that   he resides at No.

that   he is the
of
                              , the corporation described
in and which executed the foregoing instrument; that   he
knows the seal of said corporation; that the seal affixed
to said instrument is such corporate seal; that it was so
affixed by order of the board of directors of said corporation, and that   he signed h   name thereto by like order.

STATE OF NEW YORK, COUNTY OF   SS:

On the   day of   19 , before me
personally came
the subscribing witness to the foregoing instrument, with
whom I am personally acquainted, who, being by me duly
sworn, did depose and say that   he resides at No.

that   he knows

                                to be the individual
described in and who executed the foregoing instrument;
that   he, said subscribing witness, was present and saw
        execute the same; and that   he, said witness,
at the same time subscribed h   name as witness thereto.

𝔐ortgage 𝔑ote

TITLE NO.

                    WITH

┌───┐
│ STANDARD FORM OF NEW YORK BOARD OF TITLE UNDERWRITERS │
│   Distributed by   │
│   CHICAGO TITLE   │
│   INSURANCE COMPANY   │
└───┘

SECTION

BLOCK

LOT

COUNTY OR TOWN

                Recorded at Request of
          CHICAGO TITLE INSURANCE COMPANY

              Return by Mail to

┌───┐
│   │
│   │
│   │
│   │
│   Zip No.   │
└───┘

FIG. 7-1   Plain English form mortgage note.

3. That no building on the premises will be removed or demolished without the consent of the mortgagee. (This is a covenant against removal that also protects the value of the property.)
4. That the whole of the principal sum of the loan will become due after the borrower "defaults in the payment of any installment of principal or interest for . . . days, or after default in the payment of any tax, water rate or assessment for . . . days after notice and demand."
5. That the holder of the mortgage, in any action to foreclose it, shall be entitled to the appointment of a receiver.
6. That the mortgagor will pay all taxes, assessments, or water rates. If the borrower is in default of these obligations, the mortgagee may pay them. (The lender requires a covenant to pay taxes because unpaid taxes become a lien against the collateral that is superior to the lender's.)
7. That the mortgagor within . . . days upon request in person or within . . . days upon request by mail," will furnish a statement of the amount due on this mortgage. *Certificate of Estoppel*
8. That the mortgagee may serve notice and demand or request on the mortgagor in writing either in person or by mail.
9. That the mortgagor warrants the title to the premises.

New York State and Local Mortgage Recording Taxes

New York is one of the few states that require the payment of a tax for the recording of a mortgage. *It figures!*

The imposition of a state tax in conjunction with varying local taxes results in different mortgage taxes for recording mortgages, depending on the locality within the state. In most areas the tax rate as combined is 1 percent of the principal amount secured ($1 for each $100 and major fraction thereof). Where property is improved or to be improved by a one- or two-family dwelling only (and the mortgage so recites), the tax rate is 75¢ for each $100 on the first $10,000 of principal debt. In cases in which this exemption is applicable, the calculation is easily made by applying the full 1 percent rate and then deducting $25. Note that a portion of the mortgage tax—1/4 of 1 percent, to be precise—must be paid by the lender when the property is

improved by a structure containing six residential units or less.

In New York City the combined mortgage tax is 1-1/2 percent of the prinicipal amount secured on mortgages under $500,000; 1-5/8 percent on mortgages of $500,000 or more on one-, two-, or three-family houses, residential condominium units, or individual cooperative apartments; and 2-1/4 percent on mortgages affecting all other kinds of property securing $500,000 or more. The $25 residential exemption and the lender-pay provision discussed in the preceding paragraph are also applicable.

Sales of Mortgaged Property

Because, under the prevailing theory of mortgages, the mortgagor of the real estate has title to the property and the mortgagee has a security interest that can be exercised only if the mortgagor defaults his loan obligations, it is clear that the owner of mortgaged property may sell it. It is also clear, however, that the rights of the mortgagee cannot be defeated by such a conveyance. The owner's title is subject to the lender's security interest, and the owner may sell only what he owns. There are four ways in which the mortgagor may sell his property, and the results of each are discussed here.

Free and Clear

The sale may be free and clear of the existing mortgage because one of the following events occurs:

☐ The owner satisfies the old mortgage at the time of the sale. The buyer provides sufficient cash to permit the seller-mortgagor to pay the debt. The mortgagor pays the debt, and the mortgagee relinquishes its security interest in the property. Once the seller has paid the debt and the lender has released the mortgage, the original mortgagor has no further liability, and the property is free and clear of the encumbrance of the mortgage.
☐ The buyer executes a new mortgage with the mortgagee or with some other lender. In many cases, the buyer simultaneously borrows money and executes a new mortgage as the seller pays off and extinguishes the old mortgage. The property is actually free and clear for only an instant, and it is difficult to recognize legally what has occurrred. From a practical standpoint, the property remains subject to a mortgage, but

there is a new debt, a new mortgage, and a new mortgagor-owner.

Subject to the Mortgage

Lenders want the existing mortgage pd. before or at closing.

When the seller does not satisfy the existing mortgage at the time of sale, the sale is not made free and clear. The sale is therefore subject to the existing mortgage with the following results:

☐ The seller remains personally liable for the debt. His mortgagee's note is unpaid and his obligation to pay it remains.
☐ The buyer is not legally liable for the debt, and the buyer has no *personal* obligation to pay the seller's debt, because he has not contracted to do so. However, he has purchased an interest in property that is subject to the mortgagee's security interest. If the original borrower defaults on the terms of the mortgage, and neither the buyer nor the seller has paid off the mortgage, the mortgagee may foreclose. As a practical matter, therefore, to protect his investment, the buyer must pay the debt or risk losing his interest in the property by foreclosure. But if he fails to pay the debt, he cannot be compelled to do so.
☐ The mortgagee's rights against the property are unchanged. Since the mortgage was an existing encumbrance, the property is still the security for the original borrower's debt. If the debt is unpaid, the mortgagee can foreclose against the property no matter who owns it. The mortgagee may then sue the original mortgagor for any balance still due, but it has no rights against the subsequent purchaser for any deficiency. Neither does the original mortgagor have any rights against the purchaser who bought "subject to" the mortgage.
☐ If, after the sale, there is a default and a deficiency, the seller is personally liable and the *new* buyer has no liability to either the seller or the mortgagee. It is very important that the reader understand that the seller remains personally liable and that the buyer does not become personally liable for the debt. The maximum risk that the buyer assumes is the loss of whatever payments he has made to the seller and the loss of payments he may have made against the mortgage debt.

Subject to the Mortgage With the Buyer Assuming and Agreeing to Pay the Mortgage Debt

The seller may not satisfy the existing mortgage at the time of sale, but the terms of the sale may require that the buyer affirmatively assume the debt (as opposed to merely buying "subject to" the mortgage). The following are the results of such a sale:

☐ The seller remains personally liable for the debt. The seller's underlying obligation to pay his personal debt is not affected by the fact that the buyer has assumed the obligation to pay the debt. The seller's note to the lender is unchanged and he is not relieved of the obligation.
☐ The buyer also becomes liable for the debt. The buyer (grantee) has become personally liable to pay the original debt because he obligated himself to do so.
☐ The mortgagee may collect from either or both parties to the extent of the debt. The original mortgagee now has two debtors against whom it can proceed. The mortgagee may collect from either or both of them for the amount of the debt and costs of collection to the extent that the proceeds from a foreclosure sale were insufficient to pay off the debt. However, the mortgagee is entitled to satisfaction only once, no matter how many assuming buyers (grantees) there are. If the assuming buyer is unable to pay the debt, the mortgagee will enforce the obligation against the original borrower. An owner who sells property that is subject to a mortgage and requires the buyer to assume the mortgage must determine whether or not the buyer is financially responsible.

In New York, a person assuming a mortgage debt must do so in writing and acknowledge same. This is customarily done by the grantee (in addition to the grantor) executing and acknowledging the deed.

Subject to the Mortgage With the Buyer Assuming and Agreeing to Pay the Mortgage Debt and the Maker of the Note Being Released from Liability

On occasion, a lender is willing to substitute the purchaser as the obligor (debtor) and release the original maker of the note from any personal liability for the payment of the loan. In order to accomplish this, both the buyer and the lender must execute a *release and assumption agreement*. The net effect of these actions by the buyer and the mortgagee is that the mortgage remains in effect but the buyer becomes the mortgagor. The property remains subject to a mortgage as if it were a new mortgage, just as it did in the free and clear sale

assumable mortgage

when the lender and buyer executed a new mortgage. This device can be utilized provided the purchaser's credit is at least as good or better than the original debtor's credit. If interest rates have risen, lenders frequently require an adjustment in the interest rate before they release the debtor.

Mortgage Clauses That Protect Lenders

A mortgage may include a *prepayment penalty clause* that increases the amount due to the lender if the mortgagor pays off the loan before it has matured. Lenders justify this penalty charge because, they say, it pays for the additional work required to reinvest the unexpectedly repaid capital. Lenders assert that if a loan is prepaid, the cost of originating it may not have been fully amortized. New York State law prohibits lenders from charging a penalty for prepayment after the first year of a residential mortgage.

Acceleration clauses permit the lender, under stated circumstances, to call for immediate payment of the balance of all principal and accrued interest without waiting for the due date on the note. Acceleration is not permitted unless provisions for it have been set forth in the note or mortgage. The most common reason for acceleration is default on any of the obligations under the note or mortgage. Bankruptcy of the debtor, condemnation of the property, or a transfer of title are other common reasons for acceleration. *Mortgagedue on sale*

Many mortgages contain a *due-on-sale*, or *alienation*, clause. These clauses accelerate the maturity of the mortgage if the property is sold, with the entire outstanding balance becoming due when the borrower transfers title. A due-on-sale clause would effectively prevent a sale or taking that is subject to the mortgage or that requires the buyer to assume the mortgage. If a property were sold to a buyer who was not creditworthy and the sale specified that the buyer was to assume the loan, this clause would permit the lender to call the loan.

During a period of rising interest rates, alienation clauses confer an even more important benefit on the lender, for they permit elimination of old, low-interest-rate loans whenever a property is sold. While a lender could waive the clause, generally it would do so only if a mortgage modification changed the interest rate to the current level.

Acceleration clauses enable lenders to demand payment in full at such times as they feel a loan is in jeopardy. These clauses are not covenants, but lenders assert that they need them in order to exercise control over who can become a mortgagor.

Failure to provide an acceleration clause would require that a lender wait until the due date on a note before attempting to recover all of the money due.

Because the ability to pass on a low-interest mortgage that has not been substantially amortized confers a substantial economic benefit on the owner of the land, much litigation has recently taken place regarding the enforceability of due-on-sale clauses. Western states have generally held such clauses to be unenforceable as unreasonable restraints on alienation. Eastern states, New York included, have generally upheld the enforcement of such clauses. The United States Supreme Court has recently held that as to federally chartered savings and loan institutions, state law could not prevent such enforcement. After this decision was announced, a trend developed wherein state-chartered thrift institutions, in those states that have not changed the law, began to convert to federal charters. Congress then further reinforced this view by enacting confirmatory legislation. Because of this, states are currently reviewing their positions on due-on-sale clauses so as to not lose the control of thrift institutions.

Estoppel Certificates

In any sales transaction in which the mortgage is not being paid off by the seller, *of the property* the buyer should obtain an *estoppel certificate*. This is a statement, in writing, signed by the mortgagee providing information about the principal and interest still due on the mortgage, indicating that there are no defaults thereunder and, frequently, specifying how much money is held in escrow for the payment of insurance and taxes.

In New York, when the mortgagee is an institution, a letter rather than a formal certificate is usually obtained.

Sales of Mortgages

A mortgagee may sell the mortgage, together with the note creating the obligation to pay. The buyer of the mortgage and note purchases the right to receive the remaining payments due. When a mortgage is sold, the mortgagee gives the mortgage buyer an *assignment of mortgage* that is recorded in the land records. It is advisable that the assignee (mortgage purchaser) require that the assignment contain a covenant that specifies the amount due. In addition, an estoppel certificate should be obtained from the property owner. If the property owner is not the original borrower, because the original owner-borrower sold the property subject to the mortgage, the mortgage purchaser should also obtain an estoppel certificate from both owner and borrower that states the amount of principal still owed and that asserts that the mortgage is still a valid obligation.

Priority of Mortgages

The same property may be pledged as collateral for more than one loan. That is to say, more than one security interest may be held against a single piece of property. The existence of multiple security interests obviously causes problems if the owner (borrower) defaults on one or more of the loans. Suppose there are three mortgages against a piece of property, and the owner (borrower) neglects to pay the periodic payments on the third. May the third mortgagee assert its lien on the property? Obviously this would interfere with the property rights of the other two lenders. Therefore, such assertion must be subject to the prior rights of the other lenders.

Suppose the borrower defaults against all the loans, and the property is sold in a foreclosure sale. In such circumstances, it is rare that a sale will produce sufficient funds to pay off all the borrower's obligations to all the lenders. How are the proceeds of foreclosure sale allocated? They are allocated in accordance with the "priority" of each loan.

Mortgages normally take priority in the order of their recording. The lender who records a mortgage against a property that is free and clear of mortgage debt is said to have a *first mortgage*. This mortgage is sometimes called the *senior mortgage*. A second lender who records a mortgage against the same property has a *second mortgage*, or a *junior mortgage*. It is possible to have third, fourth, and further mortgages, although some people call all junior mortgages (mortgages that are not first mortgages) second mortgages. Care should be taken to ascertain the meaning when the term "second mortgage" is used.

If a borrower has a first mortgage and a second mortgage and pays off the first mortgage, the junior mortgage moves up in priority and becomes the first mortgage.

A second mortgage involves a loan that is much more risky than a first mortgage. If the first mortgagee forecloses on a property and sells the property for less than the principal balance of the first mortgage, no monies are available to the junior mortgagee. The foreclosure sale extinguishes the security interest of the junior mortgagee but provides no funds for the junior mortgagee.

Satisfaction of a Mortgage

When the obligation secured by a mortgage has been met (the loan is paid), the property owner should obtain from the mortgagee a *satisfaction piece* or *satisfaction of mortgage*. This document must be promptly recorded in the land records to clear them of the mortgage, which no longer has validity. Any existing junior liens now move up in priority.

Sometimes borrower and lender agree to release part of the mortgaged property from the lien before the entire mortgage is satisfied. (Some of the acreage of a parcel of land may readily be identified for release from the mortgage.) In such a case, the borrower should obtain a *partial release* from the lender and place it on record.

DEEDS OF TRUST

A *deed of trust* or *trust deed* serves the same purpose as a mortgage. It makes it possible to use real property as security for a loan. However, it introduces a third party, *the trustee*, into the transaction. In a deed of trust the principal parties are sometimes renamed; the borrower is called *the trustor* and the lender is called the *beneficiary*.

Under this arrangement the borrower gives a promissory note to the lender, but instead of executing a mortgage, the borrower signs a trust deed. This document conveys title to a trustee who holds that title until the borrower fulfills the terms of the loan.

The trustee, of course, receives a limited title only. The borrower may still occupy and enjoy the property, and may sell it. But in the event that a borrower defaults and the beneficiary requests that the trustee act, the trustee has the right to foreclose and sell the pledged property.

Some states use trust deeds regularly instead of mortgages. They are common in the West and Southwest where states such as California and Texas use them regularly, but not exclusively. In still other states, including New York, the law considers the trust deed to be merely a lien. As such, it is much like a mortgage, with a clause that gives a third party the power of sale in certain circumstances. Thus, in New York State the trust deed is rarely used in standard real estate transactions.

FORECLOSURE

When a borrower defaults on the payments or any of the other covenants of the mortgage, or is in some way in noncompliance with the terms of the mortgage agreement, the mortgagee, or owner of the mortgage, may enforce its lien through foreclosure. The proximate cause of most foreclosures is the borrower's failure to make payments on time. But the lender does not automatically seek to foreclose the loan because the payments are late or delinquent.

Usually the lender tries to work things out. Foreclosure is a long and difficult legal process. The lender has no assurance that the property can be sold at a price that is sufficient to permit the lender to recoup the principal balance due. Often, the delinquent owner allows the property to deteriorate during the lengthy foreclosure process, and its value drops precipitously. The foreclosure of home mortgage loans is bad for the image of local savings banks, who are the typical home lenders. So, usually, lenders try to work with borrowers. They set up new stretched-out payment schedules or assist them in other ways.

But when other remedies are exhausted, the lender invokes its acceleration clause and starts proceedings to foreclose the borrower's rights in the property.

Judicial Action and Sale

By far the most common method of foreclosure in the State of New York is *judicial action and sale*. The mortgage holder institutes a lawsuit against the defaulting mortgagor and against all other parties that may be affected by the foreclosure (such as the junior mortgagees and other junior lienors.) After appropriate notice by summons and complaint, all parties whose rights can or will be affected are given an opportunity to be heard by a judge. At that time they may raise any defenses to the foreclosure.

The mortgagor may have a number of defenses against the complaint. He may claim that the loan is usurious or that full payment has been made or that payment is not due or that there is some defect in the mortgage as originally created. The court analyzes the evidence. If it concludes that the defenses are not valid, it enters a judgment that directs a sale of the mortgaged premises in order to pay the remaining principal and interest due on the loan, together with the costs and expenses of the sale. The foreclosed borrower can exercise his *right of re-demption* up to the time that the "hammer falls" at the auction sale. He does this by paying the full amount of the judgment including all costs and expenses. If no redemption is made within that time, the debtor loses all interest in the property.

The sale is an auction at which the highest bidder wins. Prior to the sale, the property is advertised to ensure that there will be public bidding. Of course, everyone hopes that someone will place a bid that is higher than the amount due on the defaulted obligation. Unfortunately, this is not a likely prospect. Otherwise, the borrower would have already sold the property to such a buyer and have come out ahead. (If there are junior mortgagees, the sale may produce enough to pay off some or all of the junior liens, but rarely is anything left over for the borrower.)

The lender itself may bid on the property. It may bid the amount of the mortgage, and it need put up no money beyond the costs of the sale. All other bidders must put up cash equal to the amount of their bids. The victorious bidder can pick up his deed immediately, although normally he will cause a title search to be made and then schedule a closing.

Statutory Foreclosure

While a judicial action and sale is by far the most common method of foreclosing mortgages in the State of New York, on occasion, a foreclosure by advertisement and sale may be had. This type of foreclosure is also called a *statutory foreclosure*. In order to have a foreclosure by advertisement and sale, it is essential that the mortgage contain a *power-of-sale clause* that gives the mortgagee that power, as a power of attorney, without going to court. The mortgagee's power may only be exercised on the mortgagor's default, and the mortgagee must comply strictly with the following requirements:

☐ A notice of foreclosure must be published in a newspaper published in the county where the property is located for 12 consecutive weeks immediately preceding the day of sale. The time and place of sale, as well as the condition of sale must be stated.
☐ A copy of the notice of sale must be given to the clerk of the county where the property is located no less than 84 days prior to the sale.
☐ A copy of the notice must also be posted at the entrance of the county court building, in the

county where the land is located, no less than 84 days before the sale.

☐ A copy of the notice must be served upon the mortgagor.

While a sale under the power of sale cuts off the owner's interest without redemption, the technique is seldom used because purchasers and their title insurers have difficulty in assuring themselves that all requirements of the sale have been properly met.

Strict Foreclosure

A strict foreclosure is a judicial proceeding similar to that in a foreclosure and sale. It differs in that the lender does not ask for a sale but asks, instead, that title be awarded directly to him. It is utilized in New York only as a corrective measure to cut off the rights of the holder of a subordinate interest who was inadvertently left out of the foreclosure action.

DEFICIENCY JUDGMENTS

In the event the proceeds of a foreclosure sale are inadequate to fully pay the obligation secured by the mortgage (including the cost of the proceedings of the sale and the attorney's fees), the lender may obtain a deficiency judgment for the remaining balance due. The deficiency judgment is a general lien against all the debtor's real estate in the county.

REVIEW QUESTIONS

1. Property encumbered by a mortgage may be sold

   A. Subject to the mortgage.
   B. Subject to the mortgage with the buyer assuming and agreeing to pay the debt.

   (a) A only.   (c) Both A and B.
   (b) B only.   (d) Neither A nor B.

2. A mortgage on real estate

   (a) Need not be recorded to be valid against all parties to the mortgage.
   (b) Must be in writing to be valid.
   (c) Must be executed by the owners to be valid.
   (d) All of the above.

3. During the equity of redemption period in a mortgage foreclosure proceeding, the defaulting buyer

   A. May cure that default by bringing the payments up to date.
   B. Must pay the entire balance due plus any expenses incurred by the mortgagee.

   (a) A only.   (c) Both A and B.
   (b) B only.   (d) Neither A nor B.

4. When property is sold subject to a mortgage

   A. The seller is relieved of all liability for the debt.
   B. The buyer becomes personally liable for the debt.

   (a) A only.   (c) Both A and B.
   (b) B only.   (d) Neither A nor B.

5. Where mortgaged property is sold and the buyer assumes and agrees to pay the mortgage debt

   A. The seller no longer has any liability for the debt.
   B. The lender can recover the balance from either the seller or the buyer or both.

   (a) A only.   (c) Both A and B.
   (b) B only.   (d) Neither A nor B.

6. When there are two mortgages against the same property and the borrower defaults, the proceeds of the sale of the property

   A. Are divided between the lenders on a pro rata basis.
   B. Are applied first to the satisfaction of the

first lender even if this exhausts the proceeds.

(a) A only.
(b) B only.
(c) Both A and B.
(d) Neither A nor B.

7. When the foreclosure sale of mortgaged property does not yield enough to pay off the mortgage(s), the lender(s)

A. May pursue other assets of the borrower for the deficiency.
B. Must be satisfied with the proceeds of the sale.

(a) A only.
(b) B only.
(c) Both A and B.
(d) Neither A nor B.

8. When there is a foreclosure sale under a mortgage and the sales price exceeds the amount of the debt, the expenses of collection are borne by the

(a) Attorney for the lender.
(b) Lender.
(c) Defaulting borrower.
(d) Sheriff who conducted the sale.

9. When the borrower has completely repaid a loan secured by a mortgage,

A. The borrower is entitled to a formal satisfaction to evidence the repayment.
B. The mortgage is no longer an enforceable lien on the property.

(a) A only.
(b) B only.
(c) Both A and B.
(d) Neither A nor B.

10. A strict foreclosure

A. May involve a judicial sale.
B. May involve no judicial sale.
C. Does not require service of process on junior creditors.

(a) A only.
(b) B only.
(c) A and C.
(d) B and C.

11. In New York a mortgage may contain statutory short-form covenants. There are

(a) Five covenants.
(b) Six covenants.
(c) Eight covenants.
(d) Nine covenants.

12. An acceleration clause is a clause in a mortgage note that

(a) Permits the lender to shorten the term of the mortgage and increase the periodic payments.
(b) Permits the borrower to pay off the mortgage whenever he wishes.
(c) Makes the principal due and payable if the borrower violates the mortgage terms.
(d) None of the above.

13. Which of the following clauses usually appears in a mortgage note?

(a) A mortgaging clause that identifies the collateral property.
(b) A statement that this is a first mortgage or a junior mortgage.
(c) A statement that the mortgagee will maintain insurance on the collateral.
(d) An acceleration clause.

14. Lenders like alienation causes because they permit the lender

A. To call the loan if the property is sold to an uncreditworthy buyer.
B. To eliminate old low-interest-rate loans whenever a property is sold.

(a) A only.
(b) B only.
(c) Both A and B.
(d) Neither A nor B.

15. Which of the following statements about the mortgage recording tax is true?

(a) Many states impose mortgage recording taxes.
(b) The tax rate differs for residential and commercial properties.
(c) Installment contracts are not subject to mortgage recording tax.
(d) Apartment buildings are taxed at the same rate per $100 of value as single- and two-family residences.

16. In which of these transactions does the purchaser not require an estoppel certificate?

(a) The property was sold free and clear.
(b) The property was sold subject to the mortgage.

(c) The property was sold subject to the mortgage with the buyer assuming the mortgage debt.

(d) The property was sold subject to the mortgage with the buyer assuming the mortgage but releasing the seller from his liability.

17. A deed of trust differs from a mortgage in the following manner.

A. It conveys title to the security property to a trustee.

B. In the event of the trustor/borrower's default, the right of foreclosure is in the trustee.

(a) A only.   (c) Both A and B.
(b) B only.   (d) Neither A nor B.

18. One of the following is not a valid legal defense against a foreclosure.

(a) The loan is usurious.

(b) The property is so deteriorated that it is uninhabitable.

(c) Payment is not due.

(d) Full payment has been made.

19. In order for a statutory foreclosure to be possible, the following condition(s) must exist.

A. The mortgage must contain a power-of-sale clause.

B. The mortgage must contain an acceleration clause.

(a) A only.   (c) Both A and B.
(b) B only.   (d) Neither A nor B.

20. Which of the following evidence of debt is not a security interest.

(a) The mortgage note.
(b) The mortgage.
(c) A pledge of goods.
(d) An equipment trust.

Chapter 8
Real Estate Finance

VOCABULARY

You will find it important to have a complete working knowledge of the following words and concepts found in this chapter:

amortization	interest rate	purchase-money mortgage
balloon mortgage	interim financing	Regulation Z
blanket mortgage	junior mortgage	RESPA
commercial bank	leverage	savings and loan association
conditional installment sale	loan discount	second mortgage
constant	mortgage	senior mortgage
construction loan	mortgage banker	straight-term mortgage
conventional loan	mortgagee	swing loan
escrow accounts	mortgagor	Truth in Lending Act
FHA loan	mutual savings bank	VA loan
flexible-payment mortgage	open-end mortgages	variable-rate mortgage
FNMA	points	wraparound mortgage
GNMA	principal	

LENDING

A MAJOR FACTOR contributing to the uniqueness of real estate as an economic commodity is the magnitude of the investment required in each real estate transaction. Due to this investment, the demand for credit and financing is continually growing. In most instances, the prospective purchaser does not have the required funds as outlined in the sales contract and consequently must obtain funds through some source of credit. While most purchasers will have *equity* funds invested in the property through a down payment, they will also have to rely on additional funding to be obtained through *debt financing*.

Salespersons and brokers have found that sales are directly related to the availability of debt financing. Most of the agent's customers have had little experience in real estate buying and therefore do not realize the credit options available to them. Since this is the major hurdle for most purchasers, it is to the advantage of the sales person to be familiar with the various forms of financing provided by lending institutions. An effective salesperson needs a knowledge of lending institutions, and their history, requirements, and current operations

to be able to advise buyers on the alternatives available to them. The most common form of financing is the use of a mortgage loan.

Even those purchasers who have sufficient funds to pay cash or trade in some other property when purchasing real estate will usually find it desirable to use as little of their own cash or other assets as possible to obtain the maximum benefit of leverage. *Leverage* is the use of other people's money—at a fixed cost, which is called interest and which is tax deductible—to maximize the return on the investor's capital by reason of any gain in value. Real estate values, although subject to downward fluctuation like any other asset, have traditionally increased in value at a rate equal to or faster than most, if not all, other assets. This presumed rate of increase can be enhanced by applying leverage. In a normal market a borrower may obtain up to 80 percent of the value of the real estate in the form of a conventional mortgage-secured loan. Under certain circumstances some borrowers may be able to obtain 97 percent or even 100 percent financing under certain government-insured lending programs. In the example of a conventional loan with a maximum 80 percent loan-to-value ratio, the benefit of leveraging is easily demonstrated. If we assume the purchase price to be $100,000 and assume, for illustration only, a 10 percent per-year compounded growth rate, the value of the property one year from purchase would be $110,000, or a 10 percent gain. If the borrower pays interest only on the loan, the borrower still owes $80,000 at the end of the first year, and the increase in value is added to the owner's equity for a total of $30,000. This represents a 50 percent gain, or return on equity, on the amount invested. Thus, the actual increase in value of 10 percent has become a 50 percent gain on the investment. After five years the value of the asset would be $161,051, or a 61 percent gain. The loan would still be $80,000, but the owner's $20,000 equity would now have grown to $81,051, or a return of 305 percent. Thus, in the example the leverage will multiply the working force of the investment five times. Although other investments may be leveraged, none may be leveraged as highly as real estate, with the exception of options, which are highly speculative and thus represent a substantial hazard to an investor.

THE MORTGAGE

Terms, rates, and conditions of mortgages are not uniform and vary from locale to locale. Many different factors influence mortgage costs. The supply of money offered by lending institutions, as well as the demand for this money, sets the basic interest rate for the mortgage. The degree of risk in a particular transaction and the general condition of the economy both affect the final interest rate charged on the mortgage.

At the time this book was written, the economy had just passed through a period of violent inflation. This inflation had been accompanied by a general shortage of money for mortgage lending, and mortgage interest rates had risen to record levels. The current easing of inflationary pressures has resulted in an easing of mortgage rates. Because the economic future is far from certain and because lenders have been hurt badly by rapid inflationary cost escalation in the recent past, a number of different types of mortgages have been experimented with, some more successfully than others. This experimentation is continuing, and so the list of types of mortgages that follows is not complete, but is designed to illustrate the number of variations that may exist.

TYPES OF MORTGAGES

Mortgages can be placed into categories based on several criteria:

☐ *The degree of priority is determined by the time of recording.* We recognize the following categories:

Senior mortgage (first mortgage). A mortgage giving the lender the first claim to the property if the borrower fails to repay the loan.

Junior mortgage. Any mortgage which is less than a first mortgage and junior or subordinate to the senior claim. Junior mortgages may be listed in order of priority as second, third, fourth, etc.

☐ *The method of repayment varies depending on the agreement made when the loan is granted.* We recognize the following categories:

Straight-term mortgage. A mortgage in which the principal is repaid in one lump sum at the date of maturity. Interest is paid on the principal during the term of the loan, but payments of principal are not actually made during the term.

Amortized (constant) mortgage. A mortgage in which a definite plan requires the repayment of certain amounts of both principal and interest at specified times, so that by the end of the term the entire debt, both principal and interest, is repaid or amortized.

Variable-payment mortgage. A mortgage with terms that enable borrowers to adjust their payments on a long-term schedule related to anticipated increases in income.

Variable-rate mortgage. A mortgage in which the interest rate fluctuates with changes in market conditions, thereby allowing the lender to better cover expenses.

Renegotiable-rate mortgage (RRM). A mortgage which, like a variable-rate mortgage, is subject to adjustment of interest rates at periodic intervals, but differs in that it has short-term notes secured by a long-term mortgage which requires new notes, or modification on notes and amortization rates, at fixed intervals.

Alternate mortgage instruments (AMI). Alternate mortgage instruments are variations of one or more of the above categories. They are designed to protect the lender against a loss of rate of return by reason of inflation and yet to be appealing to the borrower and within his financial ability to repay. Among AMIs are partially amortizing balloon mortgages, equity-participation mortgages, roll-over mortgages, renegotiable-rate mortgages, and adjustable-rate mortgages, to name just some examples.

Straight-Term Mortgage

Straight-term mortgages are usually not available to individual owners. In such mortgages there is no repayment of the principal until the end of the mortgage life. Payments are made on a regular basis to cover the interest only. The large payment, or *balloon*, is due at the end of the mortgage term. This balloon payment has curtailed the use of such loans for home buyers. Straight loans are, however, used to finance the purchase of commercial and investment properties.

Amortized Mortgage

Amortized mortgages require the borrower to make periodic, equal repayments that reduce the balance of the loan. These payments are usually due on a monthly basis and include the interest payment as well as a part of the principal amount. This payment is called the *constant*.

The interest accrued on the unpaid portion of the debt is deducted from the repayment, and then the balance of the repayment is applied toward reducing the outstanding principal balance. As the outstanding principal decreases, the amount of interest due on the outstanding balance drops. Because of this, larger and larger portions of the equal monthly payments can be used to reduce the remaining balance of the loan. The drop in interest payments and the rise in principal payments allow the monthly payment to remain the same. It is essential for the student to remember that the constant payment is exactly that; but the sum is allocated to principal and interest in a different ratio each month.

The lender may collect each month an amount over and above the constant amount for the principal and interest payments. These additional funds provide monies to pay property taxes and hazard insurance. The additional funds are placed in accounts called *escrow accounts*.

The escrow account is set up to benefit both the mortgagor and the mortgagee. The special insurance escrow account provides a safeguard to both in the event that the property is damaged by a hazard. The property is continually protected under the insurance, and thus, no loss is incurred by either party. The mortgagor is forced to put aside money for these two purposes (taxes and insurance) on a periodic basis and consequently is not overburdened financially when payments are due. With funds available for these two purposes, no tax liens or uninsured damage can result. The monthly payment then includes payment of the *principal, interest, taxes,* and *insurance,* and is often referred to as PITI payment.

Interest rates are, at the present time, somewhat higher for amortized mortgages than for most other forms of mortgage, because lenders fear being locked into below-market rates of return should inflation recur. Notwithstanding the interest-rate differential, amortized mortgages are by far the most popular with borrowers, since they can realistically plan their budgets and financial obligations with them.

Sample Amortization Calculations

Following are several examples that salespersons and brokers encounter. Only partial tables are presented here; more complete tables can be found for computing constant payments for an amortized loan.

Problem What are the monthly payments required to amortize a $60,000 loan at 12 percent interest for 30 years?

Solution Table 1 indicates the constant monthly payments required to amortize a $1,000 loan. Select the line for the 30-year term, read across to the 12 percent column. A monthly payment of $10.29 amortizes a 30-year, 12 percent loan of $1,000.

$60,000 ÷ $1,000 equals 60. Multiply 60 by 10.29, which equals $617.40. Thus, we find that $617.40 would be required for the monthly payment of such a loan under these terms.

TABLE 1   Constant Payment Table
Monthly Payments Required to Amortize a $1,000 Loan

Years	8%	10%	12%	14%	15%
1	86.99	87.92	88.85	89.79	90.26
5	20.28	21.25	22.25	23.27	23.79
10	12.14	13.22	14.35	15.53	16.14
15	9.56	10.75	12.01	13.32	14.00
20	8.37	9.66	11.02	12.44	13.17
25	7.72	9.09	10.54	12.04	12.81
30	7.34	8.78	10.29	11.85	12.65

In the course of doing business, the salesperson often must determine what is the remaining balance due for an amortized loan. There are tables that provide the necessary information. Table 2 is a

TABLE 2—Loan Progress Table—10%
Dollar Balance Remaining on a $1,000 Loan

Age of Loan	Original Term in Years				
	10	15	20	25	30
1	939	970	983	991	994
2	871	936	965	980	988
3	796	899	945	969	982
4	713	858	923	956	974
5	622	813	898	942	966
10	—	506	730	846	909
15	—	—	454	688	817
20	—	—	—	428	664
25	—	—	—	—	413
30	—	—	—	—	—

partial loan progress table showing the balances due on $1,000 loans. It is used in the following manner.

Problem For a 30-year loan of $40,000 at 10 percent interest with a remaining life of 25 years, what is the remaining balance?

Solution The loan is 5 years old. From Table 2 a $1,000 loan after 5 years has a remaining balance of $966. Multiply $966 by 40, and the answer is $38,640.

Variable-Payment Mortgages *Can be an ARM*

Advancing from straight-term loans through amortized mortgages leaves one final method of loan payment to be examined.

Realizing that the cost of housing was rising, the Federal Home Loan Bank on February 26, 1974, granted permission to federal savings and loan institutions to adopt variable-payment scheduling. In such mortgages the schedule of repayments is determined by the borrower's present and future financial position. The payment schedule allows for low payments in the beginning, followed by larger sums toward the middle and end of the term to satisfy the loan obligation. Two restrictions were placed on this method by the Federal Home Loan Bank board. The interest due on the loan for each period must be fully paid by the monthly payment.

Second, the loan must be on a fully amortizing basis by the end of the fifth year. Given these restrictions, the lowest payment that can be charged is one that merely covers the interest, and this low charge can continue only for a period of five years. A variable-payment loan may cover up to 95 percent of the value of the property if a form of mortgage insurance covers the top portion of the loan. An example is provided by the Federal Home Loan Bank Board:

Example On an 8 percent, $30,000 amortizing mortgage, the normal monthly payment of principal and interest would be $220. Using the variable-payment mortgage, the borrower could, instead, pay as little as $200 a month (a payment as low as the interest only) for the first five years and then pay $230 a month for the remaining term. This would enable a family with rising income expectations to purchase a home sooner than they otherwise could afford to.

Alternate Mortgage Instruments (AMI)

In the past few years of double-digit inflation, certain risks have developed for the mortgagee. Because of the uncertainty of economy, variable-rate mortgages have gained some popularity. Essentially, this method allows interest rates on the mortgage to fluctuate in accordance with market conditions. The rate can be raised or lowered, depending upon the supply of and demand for mortgage money. Variable-rate mortgages come in two varieties: renegotiable-rate and adjustable-rate mortgages.

Renegotiable-rate mortgages provide that at fixed intervals (typically from six months to five years), the lender may alter the interest rate at which the remaining payments become due. Usually, this will also result in a change in the size of the payment. The borrower may elect to accept the new rate or to prepay, without penalty, at this time. Although there are no limits on the amount of "renegotiation" that the lender may engage in, it is widely assumed that any such renegotiation will be within prevailing market-rate ranges, since the borrower would otherwise refinance the loan.

In the spring of 1980 the federal government authorized federally chartered savings and loan associations to begin making mortgages with amortization schedules of up to 30 years but with notes that mature in three, four, or five years. Instead of making a balloon payment at the end of the initial term, the loan must be renewed at a rate indexed to the change in the government's index of mortgage costs for used housing, with a maximum change of one-half percent times the number of years in the renewal period (1-1/2, 2, or 2-1/2 percent, respectively) up to a maximum change of 5 percent from the initial rate of interest for the life of the loan. No additional charges may be made at the time of renewal. Upward revisions of interest are optional with the lender; downward changes are mandatory.

Since the inception of the variable-rate mortgage program, other indexes have been utilized and some mortgages have been written without a cap on the amount of change. A further change in mortgage concept has developed in that notes have been written which mature in 30 years but which also provide for periodic adjustments of interest in accordance with the appropriate index.

Partially Amortizing Balloon Mortages

A further variation of the variable-rate mortgage is a mortgage which amortizes over 30 years, but which is due and payable after a short period, typically three to five years. Although the principal amount is amortized over a 30-year period, the amount outstanding at the maturity of the note is virtually the total indebtedness, creating a balloon mortgage. Partially amortizing balloon mortgages have been very popular in "creative financing," the term adopted for seller financing during tight money periods. Typically, the mortgage would amortize and would be subject to a normal level of payment, but would become due and payable, thus requiring a refinancing at a time when the borrower hoped interest rates would have dropped. Unfortunately for many parties in this situation, interest rates had not dropped at the time the first round of these mortgages became due, thus necessitating a refinance when purchasers (borrowers) could not obtain financing at institutional lenders' interest rates based on their income levels.

Roll-Over Mortgages — Bank will refinance for you.

A combination of some features of the partially amortizing balloon mortgage and the renegotiable-rate mortgage resulted in the roll-over mortgage, which requires, as in the partially amortizing balloon mortgage, that the loan become due in a relatively short time (typically from three to five years), but which obligates the lender to renew the

loan, at the option of the borrower, at rates to be negotiated. The principal difference between the roll-over mortgage and the renegotiable mortgage is that in the case of the former a new loan must be created at the expiration of the roll-over period, when the debt becomes due.

Equity-Participation Mortgages — not good — not used anymore —

Lenders have perceived a relationship between inflation and the increase in value of securities. As a result, to lower interest rates and payments, lenders have proposed that as additional interest they take a share of the appreciation in the value of the real estate upon the sale thereof or upon the expiration of a fixed time period (typically 10 years), whichever occurs first. In the typical scenario the lender charges 2/3 of the prevailing interest rate for conventional mortgages in return for a 1/3 share of any enhancement value. Although there is a resulting drop in the interest rate and therefore in the size of the monthly payment, this program has not been popular with purchasers. One of the reasons may be that after 10 years the home owner may have to buy out the lender's interest, which would be 1/3 of the property's increase in value. This would probably force the home owner to refinance the property in order to raise the necessary cash.

There is also some fear among lenders that the provision for added interest may be judged by some courts as oppressive and overreaching.

OTHER TYPES OF MORTGAGES

Blanket Mortgages

The term *blanket mortgage* indicates that more than one piece of real estate is utilized to provide the necessary security for a loan. Typically, such a mortgage is used by developers of a subdivision. The developers must make large expenditures to make the lots saleable. These include costs for engineering, for surveying and platting, for streets and utilities, and the like. The mortgage is structured so that as each lot is sold all or most of the proceeds from the sale of the lot is paid to the mortgage lender, who then releases the mortgage only on the particular lot. The "blanket" is lifted so that one lot is released, but the mortgage continues to be effective for the remaining lots. This process continues until all the lots are sold or until the entire loan has been paid off.

Open-End Mortgages

In an *open-end mortgage*, the lender agrees to advance additional funds to the borrower, using the original mortgage as security for these latter borrowings. This type of mortgage was devised to avoid the expenses involved in writing a new mortgage whenever later advances were made. Theoretically, the first lien of the mortgage lender is sufficient to protect the total advances made to the borrower, even if they exceed the amount of the original loan. However, legal authorities are not in accord as to whether or not the lender is protected by the first mortgage if the total amount loaned exceeds the amount of the original mortgage loan. Since the record shows the original amount of the mortgage loan, subsequent bona fide lenders may assume that no additional amount is owed when this is not, in fact, the case. To the extent that the outstanding loan exceeds the recorded amount, the original mortgage lender may be unsecured. Because of this possibility, careful lenders usually limit later advances up to the amount of the original mortgage balance and require a new mortgage if the amount loaned exceeds the amount of the original loan.

Package Mortgage

A *package mortgage* is a security interest in real estate as well as on personal property used in conjunction therewith. A good example is the security taken on a loan secured by a motel. To make the security meaningful, the lender needs to secure furniture, linens, and china in addition to the real estate. To perfect the security, a Uniform Commercial Code (UCC) Financing Statement should always be filed in addition to the mortgage.

Wraparound Mortgages *This is a baddie*

This type of mortgage is aimed at preserving for the borrower the benefit of an existing mortgage on real estate that has a lower interest rate than is currently available. While the wraparound mortgage is generally reserved for significant commercial transactions, the concept may gain popularity in the residential area in the future.

A *wraparound mortgage* is a relatively new type of second mortgage under which the second mortgage lender steps into the shoes of the mortgagor and makes the payments on the first mortgage. Assume that a property justifies a new loan of $100,000, but there is an existing first mortgage of $50,000 at a rate of 6 percent. The second mortgagee may agree to lend the owner an additional $50,000 under a wraparound mortgage at 8 percent, even though current rates are 9 percent. Under the wraparound, the mortgagor owes the second mortgagee $100,000 at 8 percent. The second mortgagee (after collecting payments on the full $100,000) pays the first mortgage debt service on the $50,000 loan. In effect, the wraparound lender is "assuming" the $50,000 loan at 6 percent, but is collecting 8 percent on the same loan *without* laying out $50,000.

The rate of return is dramatically high for the wraparound mortgagee, even though it is lending $50,000 at a preferential rate. To the borrower, the combination is more attractive than borrowing the whole $100,000 at 9 percent as opposed to 8 percent. Caution is urged in the use of this device. Not only is a skilled attorney needed but also a knowledgeable CPA with tax skills to be sure that the tax consequences do not destroy the economic advantages of the wraparound.

It should be apparent that the potential for flexibility in mortgage financing is limited only by the goals to be achieved and the ingenuity of the parties involved. For those in the real estate brokerage field, it is important to be aware of the fact that there are many ways to structure the financing of a particular transaction.

SPECIAL FORMS OF FINANCING

Second Mortgage

We have already discussed the legal implications of a second mortgage. We now wish to examine its economic implications.

Prospective purchasers of real estate, particularly purchasers of homes, have always been short of capital with which to make substantial down payments. To bridge the gap between required and available capital, the second mortgage has become popular as a means of providing money for the down payment.

If property that is sold for $40,000 has a $34,000 first mortgage against it, and the purchaser has only $2,000 cash to make a down payment, he needs a $4,000 *second*, or *junior, mortgage* to bridge the gap.

Second mortgages are usually short-term, and they carry a higher rate of interest than first mortgages. They are usually repaid in a series of large paybacks rather than following a form of amortization.

The second mortgage reads like the first mortgage, except that it is expected to make reference to and accept the priority of the first mortgage. Even if it does not, however, it is junior in priority to the first mortgage.

Swing Loans (Bridge Loan)

So-called *swing loans* generally are not secured by a mortgage. They are usually based upon the borrower's credit reputation and the equity he has in an existing house, which is then used to borrow money for a down payment on a new house.

An example illustrates its use:

Example The buyer owns property A, which is valued at $50,000 and which has a mortgage balance of $25,000. He has an "equity" of $25,000.

The buyer needs $20,000 to make a down payment on property B. A bank lends $20,000 on an unsecured basis, but looking to the equity in the old house as the source of repayment.

The buyer purchases property B. When property A is sold, the buyer repays the loan, which "swings" upon the equity she had in the property.

As noted above, the borrower in this case must have a very good credit reputation to qualify for such a loan and usually must be well known to the lender. If one or the other condition is lacking, the swing loan may still be made, but the lender may require an *indemnifying mortgage*, which is, in substance, the same as the second mortgage we have already discussed.

Sale and Leaseback

This is a technique that has developed in recent years to permit business and industry to free up capital that would otherwise be tied down in real estate and apply it to their own business or manufacturing operations. The user of the real estate sells it to an investor and then, simultaneously, leases the property for a desired period of time. The user may also have an option to repurchase the property at the end of the lease.

Thus, the former owner has the use of substantial capital and can also claim the full rent payments as an expense on his income tax, while the buyer (lessor) gains a tax shelter in the form of long-term capital gains upon the resale of the property.

Construction Loan

This form of interim financing is required by a developer during the construction of a property. The lender pays out funds in installments during the construction period, thus providing temporary financing until the house or project is ready for permanent financing. At that time, a traditional type of mortgage replaces the construction loan. This permanent mortgage is usually arranged for at the time the construction loan is negotiated. In the case of a single-family dwelling, the permanent mortgagor is the homeowner; in the case of commercial property, whoever will be the permanent owner assumes the mortgage.

This arrangement is necessary because of the reversal of cash flow and the chance of risk. In a construction loan, the money flows from the lender to the borrower over the life of the mortgage to pay for the costs of construction as they are incurred. The rate of interest is high because the risk of incomplete security is high. In permanent loans payments flow to the lender to amortize a loan that is secured by completed improvements.

A construction loan presents other special risks to the lender because of the possibility of mechanics' liens obtaining priority of lien over the mortgage. This risk may be minimized by strict compliance with the lien law including, but not limited to, the filing of Building Loan Agreements including borrower's affidavit as provided in Section 22 of the Lien Law.

Purchase-Money Mortgages

In some cases the seller is also the mortgage lender. A seller may elect to hold a *purchase-money* mortgage because the buyer cannot obtain favorable financing through normal sources, because the seller may view the mortgage as a good investment, because of the income tax consequences of the sale, or for other reasons. A purchase-money mortgage has priorities over certain other claims against the buyer-mortgagor, such as other liens against the property created by the mortgagor, particularly preexisting judgments against the buyer which become a lien against all property owned or acquired by such buyer. It is also exempt from usury ceilings, the interest being treated as part of the purchase price.

Any person or institution may furnish money, secured by a mortgage, for the purpose of purchasing the property and obtain all of the benefits of the "true," or seller's purchase money mortgage *except* the insulation from usury ceiling.

Conditional Installment Sale (Land Contract)

Another available form of financing is the *land contract*, which allows the seller to retain title to the property while entering into an installment contract for its sale. The contract entered into states that the seller will deliver title to the purchaser upon completion of the installment contract.

CONCERNS AND CONSIDERATIONS OF THE LENDER

The concerns of the lender go beyond the repayment plans mentioned earlier in this chapter. The terms and the borrower's qualifications are also of great importance in determining the attractiveness of a loan. By definition, the term of a mortgage is the time period extending from the original date of the mortgage to the date of its maturity. The majority of mortgages are long-term loans ranging from 20 to 30 years. Terms vary from mortgage to mortgage and depend on the type and characteristics of the property and the borrower's qualifications, which are contingent upon such items as his age and income. Mortgage institutions usually have their own lending guidelines, as well as following state and federal regulations imposed upon them.

Upon receiving a request for a loan from a potential home buyer, the mortgagee must give some consideration to the request. Institutions usually look at the suitability of both the property (that is, the physical security for the loan) and the applicant (that is, the borrower's ability to repay the loan).

Usury

Usury is the charging of excessive interest, and a lender found guilty of usury may be subject to severe loss. New York has both a civil and a criminal usury limit. In these inflationary times, the civil rate has changed quite frequently, while the criminal rate has remained at 25 percent. The civil rate, however, has never applied to corporate borrowers, and in early 1980 the federal government superseded state usury limits as to residential mortgages securing loans made by most commercial lenders.

The Property as Security

When deciding on an application for a loan, the lending institution must examine the property being acquired by the borrower to determine its suitability as security for the loan. In deciding the property's value, the lender looks at the economic life of the property. This is determined by the location of the property, its age, physical condition, structural soundness, and future marketability. On some types of loans, the mortgagee must also look at the income-producing ability of the property. Therefore, the use of the property is one of the major considerations of the lender.

Appraisals

All lending institutions require appraisals before considering loan applications. Appraisals are estimates of the value of property. The amount of the loan is based on either the sales price or the appraised amount, whichever is lower.

Borrower Qualifications

Having examined the quality of the property, lenders turn to the potential buyer and consider his ability to pay. Consequently, a credit analysis follows. The credit analysis considers the borrower's net worth, income, job stability and the type of employment, future economic status, number of dependents, age, and other obligations and expenses. All these factors are examined to determine the applicant's financial and personal stability. Lending institutions are most concerned with the borrower's income, which can come from various sources.

Primary Income of Borrower

The institution usually examines a buyer's monthly net income. From this amount various expenses are deducted for food, clothing, medical bills, house maintenance costs, and automobile payments. After deducting these items, the lender looks at the primary income remaining for the borrower to spend on housing. Lending institutions vary, but most lenders require that only a certain percentage of the applicant's gross income be spent on loan payments. Due to inflation and rising construction and housing costs these figures are constantly changing, and some institutions may permit borrowers to spend as much as 30 percent or more of income on mortgage payments.

Secondary Income

Although primary income is of major importance to lenders, secondary income is also considered—particularly if it is stable. This added income can come from several sources including stocks, other real estate, or part-time jobs. In the past, lenders have not relied on the total amount of the secondary income but have used only a percentage of it in order to allow for fluctuations in it.

Lending institutions are now paying more attention to the income of working women. In the case of married couples, lenders are currently using incomes of both spouses to determine loan applicant acceptability. The combined incomes have made it possible for more families to qualify for housing loans than ever before. In addition, nonemployment income such as alimony and child support payments is also considered in credit evaluations. These trends have opened credit opportunities both to married and single women.

LENDING INSTITUTIONS Not on Test

Buyers can obtain the necessary financing from various places. Mortgage loans can be obtained from the following institutions: mutual savings banks, savings and loan associations, commercial banks, life insurance companies, loan correspondents, individuals and organizations, pension funds, and real estate investment trusts.

In the State of New York, most home mortgages were obtained from savings banks. Savings and loan associations, commercial banks, and life insurance companies are also important mortgage sources.

The effect of the recent federal Depository Institutions Deregulatory Act (which permits a much wider range of activities by most lenders) on the source of mortgage money has not yet been fully determined. The former lines of lending activity and orientation of mutual savings banks, savings and loan associations, and commercial banks have begun to overlap and to blur. Mortgage brokers and bankers are also becoming a more significant source of loans.

Mutual Savings Banks

The mutual savings bank's main objective is thrift. Starting in 1816 with the Philadelphia Savings Fund Society, mutual savings banks have grown to become important lending institutions in eighteen states. Unlike savings and loan associations, which are spread out across the United States, the mutual savings banks are heavily concentrated in the industrialized Northeast. Three-fourths of the total assets of all mutual savings banks are concentrated in two states—New York and Massachusetts. This is due to the original intent of the savings banks, which was to encourage factory workers to save. All mutual savings banks are state chartered and must follow regulations established by the individual states.

Mutual savings banks are similar to savings and loan associations in that they are operated for the benefit of the depositors and are managed by a board of trustees. Their basic objective is to pool deposits to provide mortgage funds for potential owners of single-family homes.

Savings and Loan Associations

Savings and loan associations specialize in home loans, receiving most of their funds from local deposits in time savings accounts or certificates. Savings and loan associations are privately managed and owned financing institutions that are governed by state and federal regulations. They supply the greatest amount of single-family mortgage loans in the United States, although not in New York State. In the past, savings and loan associations concentrated their efforts on mortgage loans, but recently they have begun to diversify into home repair, construction, and multifamily housing projects. The goals of these associations are thrift and home ownership.

The basic function of the savings and loan association is to provide mortgages for the community. The funds are obtained from the institution's own time deposits, and interest earned on the mortgages goes to pay for the interest paid on the time deposits. State statutes and federal regulations affect the level of interest, as does market competition. The regulations affecting federally chartered institutions are set by the Federal Home Loan Bank Board.

Under the Federal Home Loan Bank system, the associations need not rely on local funds. The system was devised in 1932 to help solve the problems caused by dependency on local funds. The major element of the system is the ability to transfer funds from one institution to another. The system provides for 12 regional banks that assist local savings and loans in times of tight money situations. The main idea behind federal involvement in savings and loan associations was to develop a national mortgage market. Savings and loan associations are also subject to the statutes of a particular state, and state-chartered associations come under the auspices of the state commissioner of banking.

Savings and loan associations concentrate their efforts on residential construction, usually keeping away from larger commercial projects. Principally lending to people who want to purchase single-family residences, the down payment required by the savings and loan association fluctuates, depending on the economic conditions and the degree of risk involved. The maximum loan-to-value ratio is .95, thus allowing a down payment as small as 5 percent.

Savings and loan associations offer three major types of loans: new home construction loans, home purchase loans, and home improvement loans.

Commercial Banks

Of major importance to the lending of mortgage money is the commercial bank. If they are interested in this type of investment, banks often have special departments to handle home mortgages. Most commercial banks, however, concentrate on other types of loans, such as short-term loans for construction. Banks are regulated by federal and/or state authorities, depending upon the nature of the charter. Regulations are placed on the ratio of the loan to the appraised value of property and/or the term of the loan. Requirements are also enforced concerning shorter mortgage terms and interest-rate ceilings. Because of these federal and state restrictions, commercial banks find it difficult to compete with other lending institutions for long-term residential loans.

Commercial banks do, however, have a significant role in real estate financing, concentrating their major financing operations in the short-term area of building operations—the builder's construction loan. Upon completion of the project, the loan is transferred to a permanent mortgage financed by another lending institution. Commercial banks also provide loans for home improvements.

Real estate mortgage portfolios have tended to increase in commercial banks across the nation, and these institutions have moved from third to second place in the holding of mortgages.

Life Insurance Companies

Life insurance companies offer another major source of real estate mortgage financing. The major source of their investment dollars is from policyholders. In the past they have been conservative investors because of government regulations. These regulations govern the percentage of total assets that life insurance companies can invest in mortgages because of their limited liquidity and relative risk. All insurance companies are constrained also by the regulations of the state in which they are chartered. Usually they specialize in large, long-term loans on major real estate projects such as shopping centers, office buildings, and large multi-family projects.

Because of the nature of the life insurance companies' funds, there is usually less fluctuation in the availability of monies to lend for real estate projects. The placement of a loan with a life insurance company is usually accomplished through a *mortgage banker* or *mortgage broker*. Very few loans are made by a life insurance company directly to a borrower.

Loan Correspondents

Many times the larger lending institutions do not have the facilities needed to make the different mortgage loans. Instead of establishing loan departments in the individual institution—in an insurance company, for example—the company has a local agent or *loan correspondent* to make the mortgage loan for it. In other circumstances, if the company does not have a branch office in the area, it may utilize a loan correspondent in order to take advantage of his knowledge of the local real estate market, neighborhood characteristics, and economic conditions. Loan correspondents are either mortgage brokers or mortgage bankers, depending upon the type of job required.

Mortgage Brokers

The purpose of mortgage brokers is to channel mortgage funds from larger investors to real estate developers and owners. The broker serves as an intermediary between the lender and the borrower and receives a fee for the services performed. Lending institutions ask the mortgage broker to find and screen property and applicants for their mortgage dollars. The closing is done in the name of the lending institution and the mortgage broker receives a fee based on a percentage of the mortgage value.

Mortgage Bankers

Although mortgage bankers and mortgage brokers provide the same basic service of finding and matching applicants and mortgages, there is one basic distinction. Mortgage bankers use their own funds to make mortgage loans. After they originate a number of mortgages, which are closed in their name, a package of mortgages is then sold to a large financial institution and transferred to that institution. However, unlike the mortgage broker, the banker continues to service the loan for the investor. Servicing includes collecting monthly payments, paying taxes, and maintaining escrow accounts. For this service, the banker charges the institution a fee in addition to an origination fee.

METHODS OF FINANCE

Having learned about the different sources of financing available, the potential homeowner must be aware of the alternative types of financing available. One of the jobs of the broker or salesperson is to familiarize the buyer with the principal types of financing. The three major areas include conventional loans, government-backed loans, and assumption of loans already in existence.

Conventional Loans

Conventional loans are loans made by a lending institution directly to the buyer without governmental guarantees or insurance. The conventional mortgage has very few regulations governing it, so the terms and conditions of the mortgage fluctuate in accordance with market conditions. As the demand for money increases, the yield on the conventional mortgage loans may be increased by increasing interest rates.

Today most loans of this nature are for up to 80 percent of the sale price with terms of 25 or 30 years.

Government-Backed Loans

doesn't give out cash — just guarantees Lender no loss up to a certain amt

There are two major types of government-backed loans: the Federal Housing Administration (FHA) insures loans and the Veterans Administration (VA) guarantees loans. Each agency places tight restrictions on the type and conditions of the mortgage. (There are several other government loan or guarantee programs, such as those funded by the Small Business Administration (SBA) or the Farmers Home Administration (FHA), but these do not represent a substantial segment of market activity.)

The FHA and Its Programs

The FHA was developed under the National Housing Act of 1934. The agency's main function is to insure home mortgage loans made by private lending institutions.

The FHA insures loans; it does not lend money. The objective of the FHA is to encourage lenders to make loans by insuring them. Lenders are then more willing to accept lower down payments. To

finance its operation, the FHA charges a one-half of 1 percent mortgage insurance premium (MIP). The FHA has insured over ten million loans since its beginning.

The FHA places restrictions upon the type of mortgage it will insure. These restrictions are on the terms and amount of the mortgage loan. The physical property must meet FHA minimum property standards (MPS). To ensure that such standards have been met, each property must be appraised by an FHA-approved appraiser before the loan can be made. The term of the loan under FHA insurance may be any multiple of five years, up to a maximum of 30 years. In New York City the top limit varies depending on the number of dwelling units. For one-family units it is $90,000, two-family units $101,300, three-family units $122,650 and four-family units $142,650. These limits may vary geographically. Amounts must be in multiples of $50. Mortgages must be paid utilizing an amortization schedule, and escrow accounts must be established for collection of taxes and all insurance premiums. Interest rates charged on FHA residential loans are at a rate set by the marketplace.

The agency has established guidelines pertaining to loan-to-value ratios. The guidelines for single-family residences vary depending upon the age of the property, but generally specify ratios of 97 percent of the first $25,000 of value and 95 percent of the balance up to the foregoing limits.

Following are examples of approved loan amounts using the FHA guidelines. The percentages are computed on the *appraisal* or *sale* value of the property, whichever is lower, and the final product is adjusted downward to be a multiple of $50.

Example   What can the loan amount be on a property selling for $32,500 if it is FHA-insured?

Solution
97 percent of the first $25,000   = $24,250
95 percent of the $7,500 balance = $ 7,125
total   = $31,375

The loan amount of $31,375 must be adjusted downward to a multiple of $50. Therefore, the FHA-insured loan would amount to $31,350. The required down payment for this property would be $1,150 ($32,500 − $31,350).

Example   Determine the amount of an FHA-insured loan on a property selling for $45,000.

Solution
97 percent of the first $25,000 = $24,250
95 percent of $20,000 = $19,000

The total loan would be $43,250. No adjustment is necessary. Consequently the down payment required by the loan is $1,750.

Given an example in which the required loan totals over $67,500, the down payment would be the difference between the sales price and the maximum loan. The down payment must be provided by the assets of the purchaser. FHA requirements prevent the use of a second mortgage to provide the down payment.

The VA and Its Guaranteed Loans

After World War II the government recognized the need of returning veterans to obtain housing. Consequently, included in the Servicemen's Readjustment Act of 1944 was a stipulation authorizing the VA to *guarantee* veterans' loans. The act has been updated several times to include veterans of more recent American conflicts.

Under the guarantee program, lending institutions are guaranteed against loss on loans to veterans. Unlike the FHA-backed loans, the VA loans provide for the full amount of the guarantee to be refunded after reasonable efforts are made to collect upon default by a veteran. Obviously, the financial institution must attempt to satisfy its claim through foreclosure proceedings prior to applying to the VA for any deficiency.

The following groups of veterans are eligible for VA loans; eligibility does not expire until the privilege is used.

☐ Any veteran who served for 90 days or more in World War II between September 16, 1940 and July 25, 1947.
☐ Any veteran of the Korean conflict who served for 90 days or more, any part of which fell between June 17, 1950 and January 31, 1955.
☐ Any veteran of the Vietnam era who served on active duty for 90 days or more between August 5, 1964 and May 7, 1975.
☐ Any veteran who has served on active duty 181 days or more after January 31, 1955.
☐ Unremarried widows, and wives of veterans missing in action or captured, and those meeting certain other conditions.
☐ Those who qualify for restoration of previously used eligibility.

Under the current law, eligibility for VA benefits can be reestablished after an initial property mortgage under a VA loan has been paid in full and no other liabilities exist on the property. The law also allows eligibility to be restored if another veteran willingly assumes the obligations associated with that mortgage by using his eligibility. Effective October 1, 1978, the law limits the maximum percentage of a guarantee at 60 percent of the loan, or $25,000, whichever is less. As in the case of the FHA, a VA-approved appraiser must appraise the property prior to the loan.

Private Mortgage Insurance

Privately insured mortgages (PMI), commonly called "magic" (MGIC) because the first company in the field was Mortgage Guarantee Insurance Corporation, are similar in function to FHA-insured mortgages. However, while these mortgages can be processed more quickly, they tend to be more selective as to who is insured. The monthly insurance premium, one-half of 1 percent of the principal amount, is payable until the principal has been amortized so that the loan represents no more than 80 percent of the purchase price or the appraisal, whichever is lower. The usual minimum down payment for MGIC-insured loans is 5 percent.

Loan Discounts or Discount Points

Often lenders cannot charge mortgage interest rates that are competitive with other types of investments on the market. In some states usury laws place upper limits on mortgage interest rates and therefore limit the rate that mortgagees can obtain on their mortgage investment. In other instances, properties cannot be sold to buyers who can obtain conventional credit. They can obtain credit only if the loan is insured by the FHA or guaranteed by the VA. The interest rates on VA loans are set by Congress, and they may not allow the mortgagee to obtain a yield that is competitive with other investments, such as mortgages made at conventional rates.

Points are a *rate adjustment factor* that increase the yield of the mortgage to a level that persuades the mortgagee to make the loan. They may also be called a rate *equalization* factor. Having established the rate of interest that could be obtained on conventional loans, the lender then determines the number of "points" needed to equalize the yield between conventional and government-assisted loans. (A point is 1 percent of the loan amount.)

Using a general rule of thumb, lenders have decided that each one-eighth percent difference between the rate for a conventional mortgage and the rate obtainable under a VA guaranteed loan is equal to one discount point.

Assume the lender decides that it can obtain a yield of 12.5 percent on a regular mortgage not affected by VA requirements. Then it will charge eight discount points to accept the loan at 11.5 percent. Upon closing, the lender will disburse the face amount of the loan minus the eight discount points. For example, if a mortgage is being acquired for $20,000, with eight discount points being charged, the actual disbursement to the seller will be $20,000 minus 8 percent of the $20,000, or $18,400. However, the lender will hold a mortgage note for the full sum of $20,000, thereby obtaining a yield of 12.5 percent.

Under VA regulations, only the seller can pay the points. In most circumstances, the purchaser must pay 1 percent of the loan amount to the lender as a *loan origination fee.* This fee is not a discount point, but a fee for placing the loan on the books of the lender. *In this case the borrower must pay $1,600 + $1,000 = $2,600 just to get the loan?*

Prepayment Penalties

Some lending institutions impose a special charge (provided for in the mortgage contract) that may be collected from the borrower in the event the borrower repays all or part of the loan in advance of the maturity date. If there is no prepayment clause and the mortgagor desires prepayment, he bargains with the mortgagee as to the terms of prepayment. The penalty under these circumstances could range from all to part of the unearned interest on the remaining balance of the loan.

Prepayment penalties vary from lender to lender, but typically the charges are a certain percentage if the loan is prepaid in the first five years and a lesser percentage if the loan is prepaid after five years. The prepayment clause states on what balance this percentage is to be based. Other penalties include payment of one- to three-months' interest in exchange for the privilege of prepaying. The rationale behind prepayment penalties rests on the fact that prepayment interrupts the investment plans of the mortgagee; therefore the penalty is imposed on the mortgagor to reimburse the lending institution for the expense incurred in originating the loan.

Currently, FHA-insured and VA-guaranteed loans do not allow prepayment penalty clauses in the mortgage, and consequently no charge can be placed upon the prepaying borrower for single-family housing. New York State law provides for a one-year limit for prepayment penalties on residential mortgages.

FEDERAL INVOLVEMENT IN REAL ESTATE FINANCE

In times of tight money and credit crunches, the federal government has felt an obligation to help the lending institutions and the public. To do this, a *secondary mortgage market* has been created in which federal agencies and others buy primary mortgages from the various lending institutions, thus generating funds that permit lenders to make further loans. The primary secondary market purchasers are the Federal National Mortgage Association, the Government National Mortgage Association, and the Federal Home Loan Morgage Corporation. These institutions comprise the major part of the secondary market and often counteract monetary policies of the Federal Reserve that might be detrimental to the well-being of the mortgage lending institutions.

Federal National Mortgage Association (FNMA)

Commonly referred to as "Fannie Mae," this association was originally government-sponsored and is now a private corporation. Established in 1938, its main purpose is to establish a secondary mortgage market. FNMA buys existing FHA, VA, and conventional mortgages and allows the seller to continue to service the mortgage. FNMA provides a great service by attracting private capital into the housing market.

Government National Mortgage Association (GNMA)

This association, commonly referred to as "Ginnie Mae," purchases, services, and sells mortgages insured or guaranteed by the FHA or VA. Under Section 305 of the National Housing Act, GNMA is authorized to provide financing for selected types of mortgages. The association also provides assistance through the purchase of home mortgages, generally as a means of retarding or stopping a decline in mortgage lending and home-building activities which may threaten the stability of the national economy. GNMA got it start as a part of FNMA and was split off in 1968.

GNMA has specific guidelines to follow when purchasing mortgages, and these are similar to those for FHA- and VA-approved mortgages. When buying mortgages, GNMA stipulates that payment of the mortgage must be current. One of the primary goals of GNMA is to provide a secondary market for loans that otherwise would not be bought because of their high risks. The activities of GNMA are conducted through the sale of securities by the U.S. Treasury.

Federal Home Loan Mortgage Corporation (FHLMC)

This corporation's goals are similar to those of FNMA and GNMA. The corporation began by buying mortgages in September 1970 and follows the general criteria of the other two. Like GNMA, the Federal Home Loan Mortgage Corporation ("Freddie Mac") is required by law to buy only mortgages that do not exceed the 80 percent loan-to-value ratio. One stipulation this corporation places on its purchases is that the funds the seller obtains must be circulated back into the mortgage market within 180 days after a purchase is made by the corporation. In this manner the corporation makes sure the funds it provides are available for their intended use—which is to create a market for conventional mortgage loans by buying them from savings and loan associations, pooling them, and then selling bonds, holding the mortgages as security for the bonds.

Truth in Lending

Consumer concern over underlying mortgage terms and conditions spurred passage of the Consumer Credit Protection Act in July 1969. Included in the act was the Truth-in-Lending Act, which granted the Federal Reserve Board the power to implement the regulations. The board, using this power, established Regulation Z. The regulation applies to anyone who grants credit in any form. While it does not regulate interest rates, the board ensures consumers that the cost of the credit will be explicitly stated in printed form for their information. Another major purpose of Regulation Z was to standardize credit procedures, allowing consumers to shop around for the cheapest form of credit. The main emphasis of the act is on complete and full disclosure.

Effects of Regulation Z on Real Estate Transactions

The purpose of Regulation Z is not to set or regulate interest rates but to standardize the procedures involved in credit transactions. It requires that the consumer be fully aware of all the aspects of a credit transaction. It also applies to all advertising in which the seller engages.

All credit for real estate is covered under Regulation Z when it is for an individual consumer.

Disclosure

The lender must disclose what the borrower is paying for credit and what it will cost in terms of the total annual percentage rate. (The total finance charge in dollars paid by the parties in the transaction need not be stated.) This is done only for the sale of first mortgages on single-family dwellings. The finance charge includes interest, loan fees, inspection fees, FHA mortgage insurance fees, and discount points. Other fees are not included. A broker or real estate salesperson may not prepare or assist in the preparation of such an instrument as a loan application without full disclosure.

Right to Rescind

Regulation Z provides that the borrower shall have the right to rescind or cancel the transaction if it involves placing a lien against real estate which is his principal residence. This right must be exercised before midnight of the third business day following the transaction, allowing a three-day "thinking" period during which the borrower can reassess the transaction. (Note: The act specifically states that transactions to finance the construction of a new home or the purchase of a dwelling to be used as a home are not included in the right of rescission.)

Advertising

Real estate advertising is greatly affected by Regulation Z. It allows general terms describing financing available to be used. But if any details are given, they must comply with the regulations. Any finance charge mentioned must be stated as an annual percentage rate. If any other credit terms are mentioned, such as the monthly payment, term of loan, or down payment required, then the following information must be given: cash price, annual percentage rate required, down payment, amount and due date of all payments.

Effect on Real Estate Personnel

Regulation Z does not indicate that licensees should refrain from making direct contact with lenders on behalf of prospective purchasers. Of will lend to the borrower(s) in this transaction the amount below indicated. Interest computations on this amount will be at the contractual rate of _____ % on the outstanding balance. The **ANNUAL PERCENTAGE RATE** which includes with the contractual rate those costs listed below as **PREPAID FINANCE CHARGE** is _____ % and will begin to accure on _____. Beginning on the _____ day of _____ 19_____ and due the _____ day of the month thereafter payments for Principal and Finance Charge, will be due in _____ monthly installments of _____.

A. **AMOUNT OF LOAN** committed in this transaction .... $_____

B. Less **PREPAID FINANCE CHARGE** costs due at time of closing

    1. Loan Discount.. $_____

    2. Loan Processing Fee.. $_____

    3. Interest Thru .... $_____

    4. Private or F.H.A. Mortgage Insurance............................... $_____

    5. _____ $_____

    6. _____ $_____

    7. _____ $_____

                          Total **PREPAID FINANCE CHARGE** $_____

C. Equals **AMOUNT FINANCED** in this transaction... $_____

D. Other costs not included in **FINANCE CHARGE:**

	PAID BY CASH	PAID FROM LOAN PROCEEDS
1. Title Insurance or Abstract	$_____	$_____
2. Opinion on Title	$_____	$_____
3. Appraisal	$_____	$_____
4. Credit Report	$_____	$_____
5. Survey	$_____	$_____
6. Tax Escrow	$_____	$_____
7. Insurance Escrow	$_____	$_____
8. Hazard Insurance Premium	$_____	$_____
9. Recording Fee	$_____	$_____
10. _____	$_____	$_____
11. _____	$_____	$_____

                          Total Charges Paid From Loan Proceeds $_____

E. **NET PROCEEDS** .... $_____

F. This Institution's security interest in this transaction is a _____ on property located at_____ _____ also specifically described in the documents furnished for this loan. The documents executed in connection with this transaction cover all after-acquired property and also stand as security for future advances, the terms for which are described in the documents.

G. Late payment formula:
    In event of default a late charge of 5% of the Principal and Interest payment will be charged for each installment not received by the Association within 15 days after the installment is due.

H. Prepayment formula:
    When amount prepaid equals or exceeds 20% of the original loan, not more than 90 days interest on the amount prepaid may be charged beyond the date of payment.

I. Rebate formula:
    None

J. Miscellaneous disclosures:
    This Mortgage also secures the payment of any additional loans up to but not exceeding $5000.00 at the Mortgagee's option.

*K. **FINANCE CHARGE** includes:

    1. Total Prepaid Finance Charge (from B)................................ $_____

    2. Total Interest to be Earned over life of Loan........................ $_____

    3. _____ $_____

    4. _____ $_____

    5. _____ $_____

                          Total **FINANCE CHARGE** $_____

    TOTAL PAYMENTS on this transaction (Principal and Interest) will be .... $_____

INSURANCE

PROPERTY INSURANCE: Property insurance, if written in connection with this loan, may be obtained by borrower through any person of his choice, provided however, the creditor reserves the right to refuse, for reasonable cause, to accept an insurer offered by the borrower. If borrower desires property insurance to be obtained from or through the creditor, the cost will be $_____ for the_____ year term of the initial policy.   **OTHER INSURANCE:** Credit life, accident, health or loss of income insurance is not required to obtain this loan. No charge is made for such insurance and No such insurance may be provided unless the borrower signs the appropriate statement below. _____ is available at a cost of $_____ for the _____ year term of the initial policy.

(TYPE OF INSURANCE)

I desire _____ insurance coverage   I DO NOT desire such insurance coverage.

_____ _____   _____ _____
DATE   SIGNATURE   DATE   SIGNATURE

I hereby acknowledge receipt of the disclosures made in this notice.

                      _____ _____
                      BORROWER   DATE

BY _____   _____ _____
                      BORROWER   DATE

* Not required for 1st mortgage purchase loans.

FIG. 8-1   Notice to customer as required by Regulation Z.

prime importance, however, is that the lender must be the one who decides if the loan should be made. The licensee may not prepare or assist in the preparation of such an instrument as a loan application, note, mortgage, or land contract.

Enforcement of Regulation Z

A lender who fails to disclose any of the required credit information can be sued for a specified portion of the finance charge. The lender, under some circumstances, may be fined up to $5,000 or sentenced to a year in jail, or both.

Figure 8-1 illustrates a notice to the customer required by Regulation Z.

The Real Estate Settlement Procedures Act of 1974 (RESPA)

Few pieces of federal legislation in recent years have stirred as much controversy within the mortgage banking industry as RESPA. The law was intended to aid the consumer in obtaining residential mortgage financing and to minimize closing costs to the borrower by regulating the lending practices of the mortgage banking community. Even though the act was passed in 1974, to be effective June 20, 1975, it generated so much confusion and controversy that Congress made significant changes effective in January 1976 and June 1976. The comments here are related to the act as amended and effective June 30, 1976.

RESPA applies to all settlements on loans for residential properties that are "federally related." The most important aspect of this statement is that the act applies to all loans secured by a first mortgage on single- to four-family residential properties by any lender regulated by the federal government and even to those whose deposits are insured by an agency of the federal government. Some other lenders are also covered by the act, but the above broad category includes the vast majority of residential mortgages made throughout the United States today. In all such mortgage settlements, the uniform settlement statement prescribed by HUD (or an equivalent one) must be used. The form is complex by comparison with the closing statements previously used and, in practice, brokers usually prepare their own closing statements to clarify the transaction for their clients.

Provisions of RESPA

□ The lender must permit the borrower to inspect the closing statement one day prior to the closing. This statement must disclose the anticipated closing costs to the extent that they are known at that time; the costs are precisely determined at the time of closing.

□ The lender must provide to the borrower a booklet entitled "Settlement Costs" within three days after taking an application for a mortgage loan which is federally related, and the lender must also provide a good-faith estimate of the anticipated closing costs.

□ Limitations upon escrow account requirements by the lender are also regulated by the act. Generally, the maximum which may be required is the sum of the amount which normally would be required to maintain the account for the current month, plus one-sixth of the total estimated expenses for real estate taxes and insurance for the following 12-month period.

□ Kickbacks and unearned fees are also prohibited by RESPA.

□ The identity of the true borrower must be obtained by the lender, and the lender must make this information available to the Federal Home Loan Bank Board upon demand.

□ No fee may be charged by the lender for preparation of all of the forms required by RESPA.

□ The act requires the Secretary of Housing and Urban Development to establish model land-recording systems in selected areas of the country, with the ultimate goal of establishing a uniform system that, presumably, will be less expensive than the systems now in operation.

□ Sellers are prohibited from requiring buyers, as a condition of sale, from having to buy title insurance from a company designated by the seller unless the seller pays for the title insurance.

While RESPA is directed at mortgage lenders, it obviously has an impact on those engaged in the real estate brokerage business because of the industry's dependence on the easy availability of mortgage funds. Familiarity with the specified closing statements seems to be essential, if only for the purpose of being able to explain it to the buyer.

Figure 8-2 on pages 104-105 illustrates the basic RESPA settlement statement necessary for a loan closing. Pay special attention to Sections J and K on page 1 of the form; these sections summarize the funds to be transferred among buyer, seller, and lender. Page 2 of the form is a summary of all the settlement charges and should also be studied carefully. These forms are normally prepared in quadruplicate; there is a worksheet copy, a lender's copy, a borrower's copy, and a seller's copy. (A completed copy of the RESPA Settlement statement is shown in Chapter 10.)

INCOME TAXES

An integral part of every financing decision is the rate of return on the investment being made. The income-tax effect on the owner will materially affect the financing and investment decisions to be made. The consequences of ownership as it affects income taxes differ substantially among property that is the principal residence of the owner, vacation homes, and income property. The discussion below is, of necessity, an overview and should not be relied on, because of changes in the law and applicable regulations that may have occurred since this writing and the nuances that may affect a particular transaction. The advice of an attorney or CPA should be obtained in the matter of income taxes.

PRINCIPAL RESIDENCE

When the owner of real estate acquires and uses it as his principal residence, he is entitled to deduct from his gross income, among other items, the amount of money paid for real estate taxes and interest on the mortgage. The 30-year amortized mortgage in fairly common use today consists almost entirely of interest payments during the initial years of the term. At 12 percent per year for a 30-year amortizing payment, a mortgage in the amount of $80,000—the maximum conventional amount—on a $100,000 purchase would require a monthly payment of $822.90. The first month's interest payment on that mortgage would be $800, leaving a principal payment of slightly under $23. The total amount of interest paid during the first 12 months would be $9,584.38. If we assume the house to have a real estate tax bill of $2,400 per year, the ownership of the house would generate almost $12,000 in itemized deductions, which, if we also assume a combined federal, state, and city income-tax rate of 40 percent, would yield a reduction in income taxes of almost $4,800. In addition to these deductions, additional deductions may be utilized that otherwise would not take the taxpayer over the threshold in the tax tables.

In addition to the savings it generates on the income-tax return for each year of ownership, property builds equity as its value increases and the amount of outstanding indebtedness is gradually reduced.

When a principal residence is sold, the gain, like any other income, is taxable. If the property has been owned for more than one year, the gain is treated as a long-term capital gain. Property acquired after June 22, 1984, qualifies as a long-term capital gain when held for more than six months.

This special six-months provision reverts to one year at the end of 1987. A long-term capital gain is taxed at only 40 percent of the gain at the normal tax rate of the taxpayer. The gain is measured by deducting from the net proceeds of the sales price (after deducting all sales expenses, including the expense of fixing the property up for sale) the amount of money originally paid for the property and the cost of any capital improvements (as opposed to repairs) that have been made on the property. For example, on property acquired for $100,000 the owner made capital improvements consisting of a new roof, central air conditioning, and new carpeting. These added an additional cost factor of $15,000. The basis, or cost price, of the house would then be $115,000. The house sold for $160,000, from which was deducted a commission of $9,600, and $400 was spent on minor repairs in preparation for the sale. The net selling price of $150,000 would then be reduced by the $115,000 adjusted acquisition cost for a profit of $35,000. This, taxed at long-term capital gains, would be multiplied by 40 percent to arrive at a taxable income of $14,000, which would then be taxed at ordinary income-tax rates.

Since the addition of a substantial sum of money to the ordinary income flow would presumably qualify the taxpayer for income-averaging, the net taxable income would be reduced still further.

If the seller replaces the principal residence with another principal residence within 24 months before or after the date of sale, the entire gain is tax-deferred if the new principal residence costs at least as much as the prior one sold for. In that event the taxpayer must file an informational schedule, Form 2119 (see Appendix F), with his tax return and adjust the acquisition cost (basis) of the new house by subtracting the amount of the deferred gain from the new basis. This deferral may be used repeatedly as principal residences are exchanged, provided that gains are not deferred more than once per year unless the change is due to a change in employment.

In the event that the purchase price of the new house is less than the sales price of the prior residence, a portion of the gain is taxable. The amount of tax due should be determined by a tax accountant or attorney.

If the seller of a principal residence is 55 or older and has lived in the residence for at least three of the last five years, he may shield, as a once-in-a-lifetime exclusion, up to $125,000 of gain accrued through that and prior residences. If the gain is not

A.

♜ Chicago Title Insurance Company

SETTLEMENT STATEMENT
U.S. DEPARTMENT OF HOUSING AND URBAN DEVELOPMENT

B. TYPE OF LOAN		
1. ☐ FHA	2. ☐ FMHA	3. ☐ CONV. UNINS.
4. ☐ VA	5. ☐ CONV. INS.	
6. File Number:		7. Loan Number:
8. Mortgage Insurance Case Number:		

C. NOTE: *This form is furnished to give you a statement of actual settlement costs. Amounts paid to and by the settlement agent are shown. Items marked "(p.o.c.)" were paid outside the closing; they are shown here for informational purposes and are not included in the totals.*

D. NAME OF BORROWER:
    ADDRESS:

E. NAME OF SELLER:
    ADDRESS:

F. NAME OF LENDER:
    ADDRESS:

G. PROPERTY LOCATION:

H. SETTLEMENT AGENT: CHICAGO TITLE INSURANCE COMPANY
    ADDRESS:

PLACE OF SETTLEMENT:
    ADDRESS:

I. SETTLEMENT DATE:

J. SUMMARY OF BORROWER'S TRANSACTION		K. SUMMARY OF SELLER'S TRANSACTION	
100. GROSS AMOUNT DUE FROM BORROWER:		*400. GROSS AMOUNT DUE TO SELLER:*	
101. Contract sales price		401. Contract sales price	
102. Personal property		402. Personal property	
103. Settlement charges to borrower (line 1400)		403.	
104.		404.	
105.		405.	
Adjustments for items paid by seller in advance		*Adjustments for items paid by seller in advance*	
106. City/town taxes to		406. City/town taxes to	
107. County taxes to		407. County taxes to	
108. Assessments to		408. Assessments to	
109.		409.	
110.		410.	
111.		411.	
112.		412.	
120. GROSS AMOUNT DUE FROM BORROWER		420. GROSS AMOUNT DUE TO SELLER	
200. AMOUNTS PAID BY OR IN BEHALF OF BORROWER:		*500. REDUCTIONS IN AMOUNT DUE TO SELLER:*	
201. Deposit or earnest money		501. Excess deposit (see instructions)	
202. Principal amount of new loan(s)		502. Settlement charges to seller (line 1400)	
203. Existing loan(s) taken subject to		503. Existing loan(s) taken subject to	
204.		504. Payoff of first mortgage loan	
205.			
206.		505. Payoff of second mortgage loan	
207.			
208.		506.	
209.		507.	
Adjustments for items unpaid by seller		508.	
210. City/town taxes to		509.	
211. County taxes to		*Adjustments for items unpaid by seller*	
212. Assessments to		510. City/town taxes to	
213.		511. County taxes to	
214.		512. Assessments to	
215.		513.	
216.		514.	
217.		515.	
218.		516.	
219.		517.	
220. TOTAL PAID BY/FOR BORROWER		518.	
		519.	
300. CASH AT SETTLEMENT FROM/TO BORROWER		520. TOTAL REDUCTIONS AMOUNT DUE SELLER	
301. Gross amount due from borrower (line 120)		*600. CASH AT SETTLEMENT TO/FROM SELLER*	
302. Less amounts paid by/for borrower (line 220)	( )	601. Gross amount due to seller (line 420)	
		602. Less reductions in amount due seller (line 520)	( )
303. CASH (☐ FROM) (☐ TO) BORROWER		603. CASH (☐ TO) (☐ FROM) SELLER	

HUD-1 Rev. (5/76)

FIG. 8-2(a)   *RESPA settlement statement: summary of funds to be transferred.*

L. SETTLEMENT CHARGES

		PAID FROM BORROWER'S FUNDS AT SETTLEMENT	PAID FROM SELLER'S FUNDS AT SETTLEMENT
700.	TOTAL SALES/BROKER'S COMMISSION based on price $ @ %=		
	Division of Commission (line 700) as follows:		
701.	$ to		
702.	$ to		
703.	Commission paid at Settlement		
	(Money retained by broker applied to commission $ _____)		
704.	Other sales agent charges		
705.	Additional commission		
	800. ITEMS PAYABLE IN CONNECTION WITH LOAN		
801.	Loan Origination Fee %		
802.	Loan Discount %		
803.	Appraisal Fee to		
804.	Credit Report to		
805.	Lender's Inspection Fee		
806.	Mortgage Insurance Application Fee to		
807.	Assumption Fee		
808.			
809.			
810.			
811.			
	900. ITEMS REQUIRED BY LENDER TO BE PAID IN ADVANCE		
901.	Interest from to @ $ /day		
902.	Mortgage Insurance Premium for months to		
903.	Hazard Insurance Premium for years to		
904.	years to		
905.			
	1000. RESERVES DEPOSITED WITH LENDER		
1001.	Hazard insurance month @ $ per month		
1002.	Mortgage insurance month @ $ per month		
1003.	City property taxes month @ $ per month		
1004.	County property taxes month @ $ per month		
1005.	Annual assessments month @ $ per month		
1006.	month @ $ per month		
1007.	month @ $ per month		
1008.	month @ $ per month		
	1100. TITLE CHARGES		
1101.	Settlement or closing fee to		
1102.	Abstract or title search to		
1103.	Title examination to		
1104.	Title insurance binder to		
1105.	Document preparation to		
1106.	Notary fees to		
1107.	Attorney's fee to		
	(includes above items numbers;		
1108.	Title insurance to		
	(includes above items numbers;		
1109.	Lender's coverage $		
1110.	Owner's coverage $		
1111.			
1112.			
1113.			
	1200. GOVERNMENT RECORDING AND TRANSFER CHARGES		
1201.	Recording fees: Deed $; Mortgage $; Release $		
1202.	City/county tax/stamps: Deed $; Mortgage $		
1203.	State tax/stamps: Deed $; Mortgage $		
1204.			
1205.			
	1300. ADDITIONAL SETTLEMENT CHARGES		
1301.	Survey to		
1302.	Pest inspection to		
1303.			
1304.			
1305.			
1306.			
1307.			
1400.	TOTAL SETTLEMENT CHARGES (enter on lines 103, Section J and 502, Section K)		

The above settlement statement is hereby approved, the disbursements indicated are authorized, and settlement may be completed by settlement agent.

Borrower _____   Seller _____

HUD-1 Rev. (5/76)

FIG. 8-2(b)   RESPA settlement statement: summary of settlement charges.

fully taken, the unused balance is lost forever. If the sellers are husband and wife, the exclusion may be utilized for both of them and for any future spouse of either of theirs. The excess, if any, over the $125,000 exclusion is taxable in accordance with the rules noted above.

Second Homes

Second homes do not qualify for the tax deferral noted above, but do qualify for tax and interest deductions from income tax. If a second home is used to generate income, the owner may not use the property himself or lease it to friends and relatives at less than market value for more than two weeks out of each year. If that limitation is observed, the income property provisions noted below will apply.

INCOME PROPERTY

Income-producing property creates the same deduction in interest and taxes as any other property. The provisions of the principal-residence-replacement rule noted above do not apply.

Income-producing property is entitled to the benefit of depreciation even though the property may be increasing in value. Depreciation is the decline in value due to physical wear or technical obsolescence. Under The Economic Recovery Tax Act of 1981 (ERTA), as modified by the 1984 Tax Reform Act, the rules governing depreciation have been modified. Prior to ERTA, each component of a structure was given its own useful life and was depreciated accordingly. Now all real estate is to be depreciated over 18 years, except for low-income housing, which remains at 15 years.

Since land does not wear out or become obsolete, the value of land must be subtracted from the purchase price of the property to determine the amount of the investment that is subject to depreciation.

There are basically three types of depreciation: straight-line depreciation, double declining balance, and sum of the digits. The latter two are known as accelerated depreciation.

Straight-line depreciation spreads the depreciation equally over the life of the building. For example, the depreciable asset on property purchased for $250,000 whose land is valued at $70,000 is $180,000, which, divided by 18 years, yields a $10,000 per year depreciation deduction.

The other form of depreciation is accelerated depreciation, which creates a larger deduction early in the life of the asset in return for a reduced reduction toward the end of the asset's useful life. Accelerated deduction has become hazardous to the investor because it changes gain, upon a premature sale, from a long-term capital gain to ordinary income. Accordingly, any further explanation of accelerated depreciation should come from a tax professional, and such depreciation should be used only with his advice.

The depreciation amount computed in accordance with the above formula is a deduction from income even though no money has actually been spent and the value of the property has possibly gone up. This deduction, which frequently exceeds the net income from the property, will shield other income of the taxpayer, since the amount is deductible from that also. This is called a tax shelter. High-income individuals, such as doctors, can thus shield some of their ordinary income by buying income property and utilizing the depreciation to create a tax shelter. Tax shelter created by depreciation may be used only by persons owning the property and not by those deriving the income through an intermediate taxpayer. Limited partnerships have become a popular means of pooling investment funds, without risk beyond the amount contributed, and passing the tax shelter through the passive investor. This is feasible because partnerships do not pay income taxes; they file information returns only. The taxes of a partnership are presumed to be owned, pro rata, by the various partners.

When depreciation is taken, the basis of the asset is reduced by the amount of depreciation. When the property is sold, the tax will become due under the capital-gains rules previously explained. If the owner or partner has held the asset for more than one year, the sheltered income, together with any gain in value of the building, is now taxed as a long-term capital gain, thus shielding 60 percent of the income (100 percent less the 40 percent taxed as a long-term capital gain) from any income tax whatever.

The taxable gain may be deferred, provided that the sale is not for cash but is a swap for like property. In this case the basis of the swapped property would be adjusted to reflect the gain. A swap must consist of other income-producing real property. To shield the proceeds of the sale from tax, the seller may not obtain the money realized from the sale or the use of such money at any time. If the buyer does not have a similar asset to swap, a value may be agreed upon, the sales proceeds placed in escrow beyond the reach of the seller, and the seller may buy another piece of property with the proceeds. This process may continue through any number of parties until all parties to the transaction have satisfactorily disposed of their assets and acquired satisfactory replacement assets. Having acquired a new asset, the seller begins a new depreciation schedule, adjusted for the deferred gain. If the seller realizes any cash benefit out of the swap or is forgiven any mortgage indebtedness, such cash or mortgage forgiveness will be taxable.

Both investment property and principal residence thus qualify for tax deferrals upon sale, the only difference being in the rules governing the deferral. In both cases, the ultimate tax exemption is available. If the property is still held by the owner at the time of his or her death, no income tax will be required no matter how often gains have been deferred. An inheritance tax, based on the date of death or alternative valuation-date values, will be due on property as on any other asset the decedent owned. The heir or devisee taking the property will start his basis with the date-of-death valuation.

REVIEW QUESTIONS

1. A mortgage is a first mortgage (or senior mortgage) only if the following conditions exist.

    (a) There are no mortgages junior to it.
    (b) There are one or more junior mortgages.
    (c) There is a mortgage note.
    (d) There are no mortgages that have prior claims to the property.

2. Which of the following conditions does *not* apply to the straight-term mortgage. *baloon*

    (a) There are periodic payments of interest due.
    (b) These mortgages are usually unavailable to homebuyers.
    (c) Their terms must be 30 years or longer.
    (d) Principal is repaid in a single payment at the end of the term. *- baloon*

3. The periodic payment of principal and interest that is due on an amortized loan is called the

    (a) Debt reduction.
    (b) Constant.
    (c) Increasing amortization.
    (d) Escrow amount.

4. What is the monthly payment required to amortize a 20-year 12 percent loan of $75,000?

    (a) $826.50.
    (b) $900.75.   *See table p. 89*
    (c) $312.50.
    (d) $942.83.

5. A mortgage loan that requires the interest rate to fluctuate in accordance with some market indicator is called

    (a) A blanket mortgage.
    (b) A variable-payment mortgage.
    (c) A variable amortization mortgage.
    (d) A variable-rate mortgage.

6. All but one of these statements describe the wraparound mortgage. Which is incorrect?

    (a) It is a junior mortgage.
    (b) More than one piece of real estate serves as a security for the loan.
    (c) The wraparound rate is higher than the first mortgage rate.
    (d) The wraparound rate is usually less than the current market rate.

7. Which of the following is *not* characteristic of a second mortgage?

    (a) Usually short term.
    (b) Higher in interest rate than first mortgages.
    (c) Always self-amortizing.
    (d) Subordinate to first mortgage.

8. The lender of a "true" purchase money mortgage may be

    (a) A savings bank.
    (b) Any financial institution.
    (c) The seller.
    (d) Any private individual.

9. Part of the security for a mortgage is the value of the borrower's property. Value is *not* affected by

    (a) The property's location and age.
    (b) The term of the mortgage.
    (c) Marketability.
    (d) Structural soundness.

10. The instrument that creates a lien on the real property to secure the repayment of the indebtedness owed to the mortgagee is known as

   (a) The bond.
   (b) The escrow.
   (c) The mortgage.
   (d) None of the above.

11. The largest savings institutions in New York are

   (a) The mutual savings banks.
   (b) The savings and loan associations.
   (c) Commercial banks.
   (d) Mortgage banks.

12. Federally chartered savings and loan associations are regulated by the

   (a) Federal Reserve Board.
   (b) Federal Deposit Insurance Corp.
   (c) Federal Savings and Loan Regulatory Board.
   (d) Federal Home Loan Bank Board.

13. Mortgage bankers perform three of the following four activities. (Identify the inappropriate activity.)

   (a) Make and hold long-term mortgage loans.
   (b) Service mortgage loans.
   (c) Find and match mortgage investors and borrowers.
   (d) Hold mortgage loans for short time periods.

14. The FHA encourages home mortgage lending by

   (a) Lending to homeowners at low rates.
   (b) Subsidiary banks that lend to homeowners.
   (c) Insuring lenders against loss arising from the borrower's default.
   (d) Placing restrictions on the type of mortgage that a bank can make.

15. Points are defined as

   (a) The interest rate on mortgages.
   (b) A charge made to the borrower that increases the return to the lender and makes the mortgage rate equal the market rate.
   (c) A charge made by the bank that pays for the bank's cost of investigating the borrower.
   (d) A charge equal to one-eighth of the interest rate of the mortgage that must be held in escrow.

16. A point equals

   (a) 1 percent of the loan amount.
   (b) .1 percent of the loan amount.
   (c) .01 percent of the loan amount.
   (d) ⅛ percent of the loan amount.

17. As a rate equalization factor, each point charged makes up for what percent of the difference between the mortgage rate and the conventional market rate?

   (a) 1 percent.
   (b) .1 percent.
   (c) .01 percent.
   (d) ⅛ percent.

18. An organization that buys existing government-insured and conventional mortgages and thus creates a secondary mortgage market is the

   (a) FHA—the Federal Housing Administration.
   (b) VA—the Veterans Administration.
   (c) FDIC—the Federal Deposit Insurance Corporation.
   (d) FNMA—the Federal National Mortgage Association.

19. Regulation Z, which the Federal Reserve Board uses to implement the Truth-in-Lending Act of 1969, includes all the following controls except

   (a) Requirements for disclosure.
   (b) Consumer rights of rescission.
   (c) The right to revoke real estate salesperson's or broker's licenses.
   (d) Controls over real estate advertising.

20. The Real Estate Settlement and Procedures Act (RESPA) does not include the following regulation:

   (a) The lender must permit the borrower the right to cancel the mortgage within 30 days of closing.
   (b) The lender must provide the borrower with a booklet entitled "Settlement Costs."
   (c) The lender must permit the borrower to inspect the closing statement.
   (d) The lender must fill out a uniform mortgage settlement statement that meets federal requirements.

Chapter 9
Evidence of Title and Recording Systems

VOCABULARY

You will find it important to have a complete working knowledge of the following concepts and words found in this chapter:

abstract of title	closing	patent
bona fide mortgagee	commitment or binder to insure	recording system
bona fide purchaser	constructive notice	subrogation
certificate of title	marketable title	title insurance
chain of title	opinion of title	

MARKETABLE TITLE

PRIOR TO THE CLOSING, or finalizing of the transaction, the purchaser or lender or other transferee (recipient of title or lien) wants to satisfy himself that the transferor has a good and marketable title.

The contract, of course, usually specifies the nature of the title which the transferor is to convey. The parties may have agreed that title will be conveyed subject to certain liens and encumbrances, such as outstanding mortgages, real estate taxes, easements, or other defects in title, such as encroachments. However, in the absence of any such specification, the transferee is entitled to receive a *marketable* title.

The concept of a *marketable title* is difficult to define. The texts and judicial decisions have variously defined it as a title free from reasonable doubt; a title that can be readily sold to a reasonably prudent purchaser or mortgaged to a reasonably prudent lender; and a title that is reasonably free from the threat of litigation. We will use the following practical and easily understood definition:

A marketable title is a title that is free from any defects that would permit a transferee (buyer, lessee, lender, etc.) to reject the title legally when it is tendered to him and thereby to avoid a previously agreed-to contract to purchase, to lease, or to make a mortgage loan.

This is the concept of marketability in the ab-stract. But as we just pointed out, the parties may have by mutual agreement altered the nature of the transferor's obligation to convey a marketable title.

Before discussing the various forms of title evidence and assurance that may be provided to a purchaser, mortgage lender, or other transferee, it is necessary to examine the recording systems that collect and make available evidence concerning the rights of the parties to a real estate transaction, and the title examination process that searches these records.

CHAIN OF TITLE

To understand recording systems and how they work, and to appreciate their value, it is helpful to consider first the *chain of title* concept. This term means simply that the various transfers of ownership of a particular piece of real estate down through the years each constitute a link between each two successive owners so that a "chain" is formed. To determine who owns the property today, we examine the chain to see that it is unbroken and that there are no missing links. Before purchasing real estate, we expect and demand that the seller demonstrate that he is the owner by proving that the chain of title is unbroken from the time the first private owner received title from the government.

This initial transfer from the government or sovereign to the first private owner may have been a unique form of conveyance called a patent, although in many areas, property was transferred to the first private owner through a grant.

In some areas the federal government made initial transfers of title to new state governments as the latter were formed, and the states then conveyed to private owners.

Although a complete examination and chain of title should commence with the date that ownership was derived from the sovereign, in practice, in many areas the search is limited to the last forty to sixty years. In these areas the experience of those engaged in the examination of real property titles has established that the title to all local real property emanated properly from the sovereign, and that given local circumstances (improved property, established community) and the effect of legal doctrines (such as adverse possession and statutes of limitation), a transferee may safely assume that he has established good title if he can trace an unbroken chain for the forty to sixty years.

Since buyers demand proof of the chain of title extending back through such a lengthy period of time, present owners would have to have literally hundreds of documents in their possession to prove a chain of title. In fact, under early common law in England, this was exactly what was required. The seller had to produce the documents that formed the chain of title to prove his ownership to the buyer. Fortunately, in the United States, this potential problem was anticipated and dealt with by the establishment of a system for recording important documents as well as by maintaining public records of laws, legal proceedings, and other governmental action having an impact on property rights. Our modern recording systems arose from the need for reliable records that were available to the general public.

RECORDING SYSTEMS

There are really two different types of records that must be consulted in constructing the complete chain of title: those that are *governmental*, or mandatory, in nature, and those that are *private*, or voluntary, in nature. The distinction is discussed below.

Public Records

Certain matters become *public record* regardless of whether the individuals affected by them desire it. All state laws and local ordinances are matters of public record. In addition, so are court decisions in-

cluding such matters as formal appointments of guardians or conservators; the administration of decedents' estates, including wills; divorce decrees; judgments in civil cases for damages that may create judgment liens on the defendant's property; assessments for municipal improvements that create liens on the property benefited; proceedings of local zoning boards or commissions; liens for federal estate taxes that may exist even though unrecorded; and others. This entire body of public records exists and has an impact on the chain of title.

Records of Private Transactions

In addition to these public records, each state has established a separate system for recording documents that represent private transactions between parties. While there are minor variations among the states, there is essential uniformity in the purposes and general workings of all recording systems. Under these systems, properly prepared and acknowledged instruments are entitled to be recorded with the county recorder (or registrar) who is charged with the duty of preserving them, indexing them, and making them available to the general public. When we say that a document is *entitled* to be recorded, we mean that it may be recorded but need not be if the parties choose not to record it. Generally, all documents that affect the title to real estate may be recorded, such as deeds, mortgages, deeds of trust, land contracts, leases, mechanic's liens, *lis pendens* (notice that a lawsuit is pending against the present owner of the real estate), powers of attorney, declarations of trust, etc.

In New York State, the recording officer is the county clerk of the county except in counties having a register, in which case the register is the recording officer. The place of recording is the Office of the County Clerk or the Register of that county. In New York City, the counties of the Bronx, New York, Kings, and Queens are all part of the Office of the City Register, which has offices in each of these counties. Staten Island has its own County Clerk's Office independent of the City Register. In counties having both a County Clerk and a Register, mechanic's liens, *lis pendens,* judgments, and certain other documents are filed in the County Clerk's office. Thus, in such counties, one who is searching or examining the records affecting real property must search both the County Clerk's office and the Register's Office.

The process of recording does not affect the rights between the parties. For example, even though a deed is unrecorded, it is still effective to convey title in this state and in most states. What the recording process does is to make the transaction a matter of public record.

Once the document is recorded and becomes part of the public records, all persons dealing with the property are *bound* to know of its contents. Whether or not they actually do know that there has been a deed of property from *A* to *B*, they are legally *obligated* to know of it. By recording the document, the parties have given all members of the public what is called *constructive notice*. Once the document is recorded, it becomes a permanent part of the chain of title.

In addition to receiving the constructive notice imparted from the public land records, every purchaser, mortgagee, or transferee of land is charged with taking the notice that a reasonable inspection of the premises would impart. Thus, a transferee (buyer or lender) must inquire into the nature of the rights of those in possession of the property to be transferred, lest he remain in ignorance and nonetheless be charged with knowledge of those rights.

Example D conveys to *E* his fee or ownership interest in a six-family dwelling on July 10. *E* takes possession of one of the apartments, but he fails to record his deed. On August 24, *D* conveys the same premises to *B*. *B* causes a due and proper search of the records to be made, and it establishes *D* as the record owner. (*E*'s deed was never recorded.) *B* pays consideration to *D* and records his deed. In the controversy that ensues between *E* and *B*, *E* will win. *B* will be charged with the knowledge of *E*'s rights. The fact that *E* was in possession imparts constructive notice to *B* of *E*'s deed and his ownership thereunder. On the other hand, *E* won out only *because* his possession imparted constructive notice. The following section shows that one who records, such as *B*, also has some protection.

Who Is Protected by the Recording System?

In addition to having constructive notice of everything that is a matter of public record, persons dealing with property are entitled to rely upon the accuracy and completeness of these records. They are protected in dealing with the property after consulting these records. This protection, e.g., that the status of title as shown by the records in the recording system is correct, does not extend to everyone. The protection generally is available only to a *bona fide purchaser or mortgage lender for value.* This means that the purchaser or mortgage lender may rely upon the recording system if he (1) gives value (money) in reliance on the record, (2) acts in good faith, and (3) has no actual or constructive knowledge of any unrecorded instrument that affects the title.

Example Assume that the owner of record, *D*, deeds the property to purchaser, *E*, on July 10, this year, but *E* fails to record the deed. On August 24, this year, *D* deeds the same property to purchaser *B* who records the deed on that date. Who now owns the legal title? *B* was entitled to rely upon the record, and it showed that the seller had legal title. Assuming that *E* is not in possession and that *B* gave value (and here we mean a reasonable price, not just nominal consideration) for the property and that he did not actually know of the earlier deed, then *B* is the new owner. Earlier purchaser, *E*, is of course entitled to sue the defrauding seller, but he has lost the right to legal title by failing to record promptly. This rule is admittedly arbitrary, but it is justified by the notion that the law helps those who help themselves.

FORMS OF TITLE EVIDENCE AND ASSURANCE

We have already mentioned that the seller or transferor is obligated to transfer marketable title, or at least title in the condition specified in the contract. The purchaser-transferee or his attorney must satisfy himself that the seller's title is in the form to which the purchaser is entitled under the contract. In the New York City metropolitan area, it is generally the purchaser's obligation to obtain such evidence and assurance of title. In many areas in upstate New York, it is customary for the seller to provide such evidence. In any event, the matter may be directly treated in the contract. It is most significant to note that since the purchaser or other transferee will be charged, pursuant to the recording acts with knowledge of any defect in the title or interest of record and with such facts that an inspection of the premises would disclose, it is absolutely essential that he or his agent examine both the record title and the premises and that he inquire about the rights of all those in possession.

There are four basic kinds of title evidence: the abstract and opinion; the certificate of title; the registered title system (Torrens system); and title insurance.

The Abstract and Opinion Method

Although the law imposes upon all those who deal with real estate an obligation to investigate public records and charges them with the responsibility of knowing the information that such an investigation would yield, the individual purchaser, borrower, or lessee seldom undertakes this task himself. He usually employs others to accomplish this task.

One type of specialist in public records investigation is called an abstractor. The abstractor prepares a digest of all the relevant documents and facts that are in the public record, and then an attorney's opinion, based upon these facts, is obtained as to where title is currently vested and what defects in its quality may exist. This approach to title assurance is called the abstract and opinion method.

The use of an abstractor is essential because of the tremendous volume of records that must be checked and the complexity of the public records system. Nevertheless, the abstractor's function, even though critically important, is only that of accumulating information. Interpreting the meaning or legal significance of the public record is the province of the attorney. The attorney must review the abstract, the history of the title, and reach a decision as to the quality of the present owner's title. Each of these functions, its protective features and its limitations, is discussed below.

The abstract itself is a digest of the history of the title to a given parcel of real estate. It is not a compilation of all the recorded documents. That is, the abstractor does not make a copy of each and every document found in the chain of title. To do so would result, in many cases, in a very imposing book. The trained abstractor knows what portions of each document are significant in terms of ownership. He therefore abstracts each document and records only the essential facts in the abstract. For example, rather than copy an entire deed, the abstractor simply lists the following information in the abstract:

☐ The location of the deed in the records (the book and page where it can be found).
☐ The date of the deed and the date of its recording.
☐ The names of the grantor and grantee.
☐ A description of the property.
☐ The type of deed.
☐ Any conditions or restrictions included in the deed.

Whenever it is necessary to have the entire contents of the document included in the abstract to understand the transaction fully, the abstractor includes the entire document.

Extent and Limitations of Coverage

The time period covered by an abstract varies. A complete abstract includes the history of the title from the earliest known record. As a practical matter, however, most abstracts start with the first private ownership of the property—the patent from the United States to the first individual purchaser or from such later starting point as is considered safe by real estate attorneys and examiners in the area.

From that point forward the abstract shows all recorded facts that affect the title. It should be understood that, in addition to the deed and mortgage records, a wide variety of records is consulted. For example, the public records of all judgments, marriages, estate proceedings, and tax records are searched by the abstractor to be sure that all recorded facts and documents that might affect the quality of title are included in the abstract. It must be emphasized that the abstractor's search is restricted to the public records and does not report facts not in these records.

The abstractor does not investigate those areas that the purchaser is expected to investigate personally and that are not required to be a matter of record. The abstractor does not view or inspect the property to determine whether or not there are parties other than the seller who are in possession and who claim an interest in the property (such as under an unrecorded short-term lease). The abstractor does not undertake to determine if the physical condition and layout of the property are as represented by the seller.

The abstractor does not investigate whether there are encroachments, unrecorded easements, or violations of restrictive covenants. Since these are matters not in the public record, the abstractor has no knowledge of them and will not be willing to certify with respect to them. The purchaser who has to be satisfied about these facts must obtain his own survey of the premises.

Mechanic's liens may have a drastic effect upon the title to real estate. But as we have seen in Chapter 3, a mechanic's lien may be filed up to eight months (four months if the property involved is a single-family dwelling) after the completion of the work or the furnishing of material. Thus, a lien may not be recorded or filed at the time the abstractor examines the title. As a result, the abstract cannot preclude the possibility that such liens may be recorded for some period after the abstract is brought up to date, and the abstractor cannot, of course, accept responsibility for such liens.

The abstractor's certificate limits his liability for the quality of his work. It indicates that he is liable for any errors and omissions included in his work. However, if someone other than the person who has paid for the abstractor's work suffers a loss because of an error in the work, there is serious doubt that such a person can hold the abstractor liable.

Attorney's Opinion on the Abstract

An attorney's opinion rendered upon the abstract is the second important step of the abstract and opinion method of title assurance. The abstract is, after all, simply a compilation and summary of the documents and facts that affect the title to the real estate being investigated. It is the function of the attorney to determine how good the title is on the basis of the recorded facts. The attorney renders a professional opinion based on his detailed review that the title has, in fact, passed from each party who has owned it to the next party in the chain of title. The attorney also determines whether liens or encumbrances against the property have been satisfied so that there are no potential interests in anyone other than the apparent record title holder.

The abstract and opinion method is generally used in farm areas. In the midwest it is used in many areas outside of urban areas. In New York State it is utilized in some rural upstate areas.

The Certificate of Title Method

Under this method of title assurance, an opinion of title is issued by an attorney who has examined the public land records. However, unlike the practice in the abstract and opinion method, the attorney delivers no abstract of the chain of title to the purchaser or transferee. Sometimes the attorney may search and examine the records, making on-the-spot notations, but he does not prepare any formal abstract. The certificate of title method of title evidence is generally used in the southern United States and in rural areas of the northeast, including New York State.

Limits to Protection

It is important to understand both the extent of the protection and the limits to the protection that the abstract and opinion and the certificate of title methods of assurance give to a transferee. Both methods are based on public records, and they in-

vestigate the effect these records have upon the quality of the title of the present owner. The abstract reports only on matters that are in the public records and that can be found by a competent and reasonable search of those records. Anything that is not in the records does not go into the abstract.

Since the abstract is the basis of the attorney's opinion, that opinion is limited to the "record title" only. If the attorney is furnished additional information, he can expand his opinion to include the implications of the additional information.

The abstractor or attorney is not responsible for information that would be revealed by an inspection of the property. While the buyer is not obligated to have a survey performed, the courts have held that the buyer is bound by what the survey would have shown had it been performed.

The buyer's need to obtain information about the physical characteristics of the property plus two other limitations of both the abstract and opinion method and the certificate of title method of title assurance make it essential for the buyer to inspect the property.

☐ *Limitation 1—Absence of facts relating to physical possession.* The record does not necessarily show the rights of parties other than the owner. The fact that someone other than the owner is in possession of the property can be established only by inspecting the property. The law assumes that the purchaser has made such an inspection on the theory that a reasonable person would do so before parting with value. Any purchase of the property is subject to the rights of the parties who are in actual possession. If someone other than the owner is in possession, the buyer must determine what rights that person claims.

☐ *Limitation 2—Absence of information on liens.* Certain matters affecting the marketability of title may not be recorded at the time of the sale of the property. Particularly troublesome are mechanic's liens. If the work done by a mechanic was completed shortly before the sale, it may be that he will file a lien after the sale of the property. Once again, inspection of the property by the buyer just before the closing of the sale may reveal that work has been recently performed. If so, the buyer may be protected from later assertion of a lien by requiring evidence that the work has been paid for. It is also quite possible, of course, that even the most careful inspection will not reveal any evidence of repair work.

The abstract and opinion method of title assurance does not provide any protection against the possibility of liens that may result from work done or materials supplied shortly before the time the record is checked and the abstract brought up to date.

As was indicated in Chapter 3, the transferee (buyer or lender) may in most cases avoid problems with mechanic's liens if the deed (or mortgage) includes the lien law provision that this instrument or mortgage is subject to the trust fund provisions of Section 13 of the Lien Law.

Both the abstractor and the opining attorney involved in the two methods of title assurance may be held liable for negligence or malpractice if either has not performed his responsibilities competently and prudently. They have the duty to exercise that degree of care and skill and knowledge which reasonable abstractors or attorneys would exercise in the examination and certification of title to real estate. In the absence of fraud, a transferee who has used the services of an abstractor or attorney must undertake any actions for damages incurred as a result of errors, omissions, or defects in the abstract or opinion within three years if the claim is based upon negligence and within six years if it is based upon breach of contract.

Registered Title Systems

Several states including New York have, in addition to maintaining recording systems, adopted the Torrens system of registration of titles to land. Generally, under this system the title to real estate does not pass until the deed is registered with the registrar pursuant to the controlling statute. As with the other recording systems, registration under the Torrens system is not compulsory by law but is a practical necessity to obtain the benefits of registration.

The initial registration of property under the Torrens system is accomplished by an examination of the title to the real property, which is validated by a court proceeding similar to a quiet title action (discussed in Chapter 5) in which the individual who claims title to a piece of real estate files a claim with the court in the county in which the property is located. Notice to all possible interested parties is given, either by personal direct notice or by publication in local newspapers. If no one disputes the claimant's right to ownership within the statutory period specified, then the court will order the title to be registered.

After the registration, the owner receives a certificate which he transfers to the new owner when the property is sold. The certificate is in addition to the deed. The new owner presents these documents to the registrar, and a new certificate is then issued to the new owner of the property. There is also a limited form of title insurance under this system. When the registrar erroneously issues a new certificate, any damages suffered by the injured party are paid from the fund accumulated from the fees charged for registration. Under the Torrens system, the responsibilities of the registrar are much greater than are those of the county recorder under the standard recording system. The county recorder usually does not have the responsibility or duty of determining the accuracy or validity of deeds that are recorded. He simply checks to see that they are in recordable form and then records and indexes them. Any error made in the recording process which causes damage to anyone is borne by that person without financial relief from the recorder.

COMMERCIAL TITLE INSURANCE

The title insuring business was a natural outgrowth of the abstracting business. Title insurance is a single premium insurance policy that insures the condition of the title to a specified piece of real estate at a single precise point in time. It does not insure that the title will not be affected by actions that occur after the date the policy is issued.

While most title insurance companies have developed from an expansion of an abstract business, title insurance is also made available by attorneys who have formed such companies to insure titles on the basis of their opinions. The phenomenal growth in the use of title insurance, in metropolitan areas particularly, is due in no small part to the demands of institutional lenders (banks, insurance companies, etc.). Mortgage lenders almost universally require title insurance to cover their own interest in the property as a condition for making the loan. The lender's emphasis on the insurance of its interest in the property has also made purchasers more aware of title insurance and has tended to foster the growth of the title insurance business.

Like other insurance policies, the title insurance policy is a contract. Specifically, it is a contract of indemnity in which the insurer agrees to make good any loss sustained by the insured that arises out of defects in the title covered under the terms of the policy. The title insurer is obligated to defend at its own expense any lawsuit that attacks the title because of a defect not noted in the policy. Thus, title policies insure property owners against loss of title and the cost of satisfying a claim or encumbrance against it. Policies are also available that protect lenders to the extent of the balance owed to them by their borrower. As the loan is amortized, the amount of coverage is correspondingly reduced. Lessee (tenant) policies are also available; they are used particularly by tenants who intend to make substantial improvements to the property.

In most states, forms of owner's, loan, and leasehold policies developed by the American Land Title Association (ALTA) are available. In New York State, the New York Board of Title Underwriters' (NYBTU) standard policy, Form 100D (see Appendix F), is generally utilized to insure all interests. The form of policy and rates or premium charges are filed with the New York State Insurance Department.

The preparation and issuance of a title insurance policy is similar in many respects to the preparation of an abstract and opinion of title assurance. But there are certain important differences. The primary function of most types of insurance is risk assumption or casualty. The insurer offers the insured financial indemnity for a specific occurrence by pooling the risks and losses arising from the occurrence of an entire class of unforeseen *future* events. By contrast, the primary function of title insurance is to eliminate risk and prevent the losses and damages that may arise from defects in title. These defects generally arise out of events that have transpired in the *past*, prior to the issuance of the policy. Certainly the company assumes risks when it extends coverage to the insured. But the basic function of the insurer is to minimize risks and to eliminate losses.

The insurer's obvious first step is to inspect the real property records, to determine the chain of title, and to find any title defects that may exist. It may or may not prepare an abstract. The title insurer relies upon skilled personnel to trace the title and to recognize the transactions or facts which may result in a title defect. Rather than digesting every document, the title insurer digests only those that seem to pose a problem. The personnel who perform this function then report their findings to the company's title examiner, or reader, who usually is a real estate attorney. The company must then decide whether the defects found are so significant that the title cannot be insured, that it can be insured only with certain exceptions, or that it is insurable without exception because the defects found do not represent serious risk of loss.

The insurer then issues a preliminary binder or *commitment* that indicates its willingness to insure the title when it is acquired by the proposed new owner from the present owner. This preliminary binder or commitment is not an abstract and does not show any of the facts upon which the insurer has relied. It does list any significant defects for which the proposed policy does not provide any coverage. If there are serious defects, the parties to the transaction can then take corrective action to cure the defects so that the ultimate policy will be issued without exceptions.

In some areas, the final policy is issued after the transaction is completed and the documents have been recorded, so that the title insurer has the opportunity to see that the record reflects the transfer to the insured.

In New York City and some other areas, the title company's coverage is effective upon the consummation of the closing. Closing occurs at a meeting of the parties at which the instruments of conveyance are delivered to the transferee (buyer or lender) in return for the consideration that the transferee gives to the transferor. The title company's indemnity is in effect from the time of closing, and the insurer assumes the risk for any matters that relate to title and which occur between the time of closing and the time that the documents involved in the transaction are recorded.

Protected Parties

The parties protected or insured by the title insurance policy are specified in the policy. This is a matter of contract between the insurance company and the purchaser of the coverage. A lender's policy, for example, protects only the lender's interest in the property; the owner's interest is not covered. If the lender suffers a loss that is covered by the policy, the insurer pays to the lender the balance then due on the loan, and the owner is relieved from making further payment. However, the owner may suffer the loss of the property and whatever investment he made in it. If the owner wants to obtain protection of the owner's interest, he must purchase an owner's policy. The owner's policy protects only the owner named in the contract. If the property is once again sold, the protection of the owner's policy does not transfer to the new owner. Each subsequent purchaser of insured property must obtain a separate policy to cover his interests.

One person definitely not protected by the title insurance policy is the seller of the real estate. The mere fact that a buyer has purchased title insurance does not relieve the seller from liability for any defects in the title, if he has made the owner's warranties to the purchaser in the deed. It is not unheard of for the title insurer to bring suit against the seller upon his warranties when there has been a loss under a policy of title insurance, particularly if the defect in the title was known or should have been known to the seller.

When the insurer is required to pay a claim under the policy, the insurer acquires the *right of subrogation*. That is, the insurer acquires whatever rights the insured party would have had against the seller under his warranties. Assume that the seller knew of an assessment for sewers that he had not paid, but that this fact was not found by the title insurer and the seller did not mention it at the closing. When the assessment must be paid, the purchaser may look either to the seller or to the title insurer for reimbursement. The simplest procedure for the purchaser is to demand that the insurer pay the assessment under the terms of the insurance policy. The title insurer, when paying the claim, succeeds to the insured party's rights and may maintain suit against the seller upon his warranties. Such suits have been successfully maintained by title insurance companies.

However, if the seller had acquired a title insurance policy when he took title to the property, he would be protected by his own title insurer from defects covered by his policy. The NYBTU policy and the NYBTU rate manual imposes on the insurer continuing liability to the insured if the insured maintains an interest in the property. For example, if the insured is a seller who conveys the property by a warranty deed or if he conveys the property taking back a purchase money mortgage, his coverage remains in effect to protect him against any losses that he may sustain from the emergence of unsuspected title defects existing at the date of his policy.

Advantages of Title Insurance

As was indicated, the obligation and liability of the abstractor or the attorney certifier of title is based upon negligence. While in exceptional circumstances courts have sought to impose liability on a title insurer based upon negligence, the liability of the title insurer is based upon the agreements, terms, and conditions contained in the policy or contract of insurance. This liability is based upon contract law not upon negligence law. Also, this liability of the insurer is not limited by any statute of limitations. Thus, so long as the insured has an interest in the property and sustains a loss covered by the policy he will be able to recover from his insurer.

Another advantage exists by virtue of the nature of a title insurance company as opposed to an abstractor or an attorney. For example, an owner would gain little if he attempted to recover a loss from an individual abstractor or attorney who has died and whose estate has been closed. He would gain little from recovering a judgment against an individual abstractor or attorney who was insolvent, bankrupt, or otherwise unable to respond to the payment of the claim. By contrast, the title insurance company is usually a corporation having a perpetual existence. Because insurance law requires an insurer to maintain a capital base as well as policy and loss reserves, it is likely that any insurer will be able to respond by paying damages when losses are incurred and claims asserted. The assets of many title insurers are also substantially greater than the funds available under the title registration systems.

We have already indicated that the responsibility of the abstractor or attorney is limited to liability for failure to properly search and consider real property instruments that are in the record. Unlike the title insurer, an abstractor or attorney is not responsible for any information that does not appear or is not apparent in the record, that is, for such hidden defects as forgery, undisclosed heirs, misfiled instruments, infancy, incompetency, etc. The title insurer may, under appropriate circumstances, also give additional coverages concerning matters arising from the inspection of the premises and the possession thereof. We will examine two such special coverages for purposes of illustration.

☐ *Title insurance,* in effect, insures the accuracy of the recording system. If a document affecting the title has been improperly indexed and cannot be found by the most diligent and competent search, and if there is a resulting loss to the policy holder, a typical title insurance policy would cover that loss, while an abstractor or attorney could not be held liable for failure to find the document.

☐ *If the title insurer is furnished with an adequate survey,* the title insurance policy will cover matters that would be revealed by a survey. The title insurance companies have established minimum standards for surveys which they recognize and accept for purposes of insuring titles. Before recommending the procurement of a survey, the broker or salesperson should determine just what kind of survey the title insurer requires to induce it to insure survey matters such as, for example, compliance with restrictive covenants.

The utilization of title insurance is growing rapidly because the advantages for it are readily apparent. Title insurance is particularly advantageous to the many banks and institutions that are involved in real estate transactions on a national basis and package and sell their loans to one another. With the increase of litigation and the cost of attorney fees, the obligation of the insurer to defend takes on more and more significance. If a particularly cantankerous neighbor institutes a concededly unfounded suit against a homeowner that attacks either his title proper or asserts some interest therein, the defense of the action can be tendered to the homeowner's title insurer. The title insurer would be required to defend this suit at its own cost and expense pursuant to the terms of the policy.

REVIEW QUESTIONS

1. The summary of the recorded documents pertaining to the title to a parcel of real property is called

   (a) A recorder's digest.
   (b) A binder for title insurance.
   (c) An abstract.
   (d) A settlement statement.

2. Both the abstract and opinion method of assuring title and title insurance

   (a) Protect the buyer against encroachments by adjoining property owners.
   (b) Protect the buyer against the claim of another buyer under an unrecorded land contract.
   (c) Protect the buyer against defects of record.
   (d) Protect the buyer against unrecorded mechanic's liens.

3. The form of title evidence or assurance which generally provides the greatest degree of protection is

   (a) Commercial title insurance.
   (b) Torren's registration.
   (c) Abstract and opinion.
   (d) Certificate of title.

4. The recording system

   A. Cures all defects in title.
   B. Insures title against loss due to third party claims.

   (a) A only.   (c) Both A and B.
   (b) B only.   (d) Neither A nor B.

5. Instruments or documents which affect title to real estate are recorded

   A. In the office of the County Clerk or Register of the county in which the land is located.
   B. By indexing and photocopying them for the public land records.

   (a) A only.   (c) Both A and B.
   (b) B only.   (d) Neither A nor B.

6. Title insurance is a contract of indemnity which

   (a) Protects the seller.
   (b) Protects the grantor.
   (c) Insures the policy holder against financial loss.
   (d) All of the above.

7. The premiums on a title insurance policy are paid

   (a) At the time of the listing.
   (b) Annually with the taxes.
   (c) Once, upon issue of the policy.
   (d) None of the above.

8. In New York State the form of title policy which is generally utilized is

   (a) The ALTA policy.
   (b) The NYBTU policy. — *New York Board of Title Underwriters*
   (c) The Standard Fire Underwriters policy.
   (d) None of the above.

9. Under a Torrens system

   A. The registrar carefully determines that the deed presented is from the registered owner.
   B. A fund is available to pay claims arising from the registrar's errors.

   (a) A only.   (c) Both A and B.
   (b) B only.   (d) Neither A nor B.

10. The recording process provides the public with

    (a) Title insurance.
    (b) Constructive notice.
    (c) Building permits.
    (d) None of the above.

11. In investigating the history of the title to a given piece of real estate, the abstractor checks

    A. Public records relating to judgments, estate proceedings, tax records, and the like.
    B. Records maintained by the county recorder of deeds, mortgages, mechanic's liens, and the like.

    (a) A only.   (c) Both A and B.
    (b) B only.   (d) Neither A nor B.

12. The recording system protects a bona fide purchaser or mortgagee for value if he

    A. Gives value in reliance upon the record.
    B. Is acting in good faith and has no actual knowledge of unrecorded documents which affect the title.

    (a) A only.   (c) Both A and B.
    (b) B only.   (d) Neither A nor B.

13. To qualify for recordation a deed must be

    (a) In writing.
    (b) Signed by the grantor.
    (c) Acknowledged.
    (d) All of the above.

14. The county recorder's duty with regard to documents submitted for recordation includes

    A. A careful examination to verify that the document correctly describes the parties, the property, and the interest being created or transferred.
    B. Checking the document to see that it meets the eligibility requirements including the fact of acknowledgment.

    (a) A only.   (c) Both A and B.
    (b) B only.   (d) Neither A nor B.

15. Title insurance protects the insured for hidden defects not apparent in the public record, including

    (a) Forgery.
    (b) Misindexing.
    (c) Incompetency.
    (d) All of the above.

16. The general warranty given by an abstractor is that

    A. The abstract is complete and that all properly recorded instruments are digested correctly.
    B. The current owner of record has clear and marketable title.

    (a) A only.   (c) Both A and B.
    (b) B only.   (d) Neither A nor B.

17. The purchaser of real estate today is entitled to receive

    A. A perfect title with no defects except those included in the contract of sale.
    B. A merchantable or marketable title as determined by local standards.

    (a) A only.   (c) Both A and B.
    (b) B only.   (d) Neither A nor B.

18. The abstract and opinion method and the certificate of title method

    (a) Afford protection against hidden defects.
    (b) Provide for the cost of defense against adverse claims.
    (c) Afford protection against survey matters, mechanic's liens, and rights of parties in possession of the land.
    (d) None of the above.

19. Every purchaser, mortgagee, or transferee is charged with the constructive notice

    A. Imparted by the public records.
    B. That a reasonable inspection of the premises would impart.

    (a) A only.   (c) Both A and B.
    (b) B only.   (d) Neither A nor B.

20. G conveys land to B who fails to record his deed. G then conveys the same land to H who does record.

    A. B would be considered the owner if he were in possession at the time of the conveyance to H.
    B. H would be considered the owner if he is found to be a bona fide purchaser for value.

    (a) A only.   (c) Both A and B.
    (b) B only.   (d) Neither A nor B.

Chapter 10
Closing and Closing Costs

VOCABULARY

You will find it important to have a complete working knowledge of the following concepts and words found in this chapter:

adjustments   deposit   escrow closing
closing   earnest money   proration
                        RESPA

PREPARATION FOR closing may be said to begin immediately after the contract for purchase and sale or the loan agreement has been executed. If both a sale and a loan are contemplated, preparation for closing begins as soon as both agreements are executed. You no doubt recall that the contract sets forth the rights and obligations of the respective parties and the terms and conditions of the contemplated transaction. The closing is the time when that transaction is consummated. It is the time for the full and final performance of the obligations that the parties have previously set forth in their contract. At the closing, the sale, mortgaging, or other transfer of land is concluded by executing the instruments evidencing the transfer in return for the payment of the consideration. The *closing* may also be generally described as a "meeting" of all parties involved in a real estate transaction, at which time the actual transfer of title and mortgaging of title occurs and all contractually agreed upon payments and adjustments between the parties are made.

There is usually a period of time between the date of contract and the date of closing. In the usual residential transaction, this period may be thirty to sixty days. In commercial transactions and in unusual residential transactions, the period between contract and closing varies widely, depending upon the particular circumstances involved. The passage of this time interval is necessary so that the various conditions set forth in the contract can be fulfilled.

One of the more important conditions in a sale of property is that the purchaser be satisfied that the seller's title is as represented in the agreement. (In a mortgage transaction the lender wants the same assurance about the borrower's title.) Another important condition in most contracts is that the purchaser obtain any necessary financing that may be specified in the agreement. A contract may include many other and varied conditions: It may call for an engineering or termite inspection and report, or a boring test report of the condition of the soil; it may require the seller to furnish satisfactory evidence that the property is zoned as represented, and, indeed, in some instances it may require that a zoning change be effective; the seller may be required to furnish satisfactory evidence of leases; the sale may be conditioned on the issuance of various forms of governmental permits, such as building permits, fire underwriter's certificates, and certificates of occupancy. If the contract is for the purchase and sale of land upon which the seller is to construct a new building, then obviously the satisfactory completion of that construction is a condition that must be fulfilled.

THE CLOSING MEETING

The following represents a typical sequence of events leading up to a closing and the conduct of that closing. Of course, the events in any specific closing may vary as to the circumstances, nature, and the complexity of the particular transaction.

The parties have previously entered into their agreement of purchase and sale or into their mortgage loan agreement or into some other agreement involving the conveyance of an interest in real property. The purchaser has obtained a commitment for and has satisfied all preliminary conditions of any necessary financing. The lender is prepared to make the loan at the closing. The transferee and mortgagee have ordered title searches and examinations and have received commitments to insure from a title company. Exceptions have been cleared up so that the purchaser's attorney and mortgage-lender's attorney are satisfied with the status of title. Any other conditions previously referred to have been fulfilled or arrangements have been made to satisfy them at the closing meeting.

To the extent that the circumstances permit, drafts of the necessary instruments and other documents have been prepared and approved by the attorneys for all interested parties. Preliminary adjustments have been agreed to. Whatever matters, documents, and adjustments have not been reviewed prior to closing, must be approved and agreed upon at closing.

All interested parties eventually convene at the time and the place that either was designated in the contract or agreement, or was subsequently agreed upon. This place may be in the broker's office or the title insurer's office, but the closing meeting is most often held in the office of the lender's attorney.

Who is present at this closing conference? The cast of characters includes all interested parties: the purchaser and his attorney; the seller and his attorney; the lender and its attorney; the title insurance company representative; and the broker or its representative.

What transpires at this meeting? All documents relating to the property, such as certificates of occupancy, fire underwriting certificates, leases, and the keys to the premises are delivered by the seller to the purchaser. The delivery of the keys is sometimes forgotten in the rash of activity and concern, and this may cause considerable embarrassment and inconvenience.

Final adjustments that prorate real estate taxes, fuel, insurance, rent, mortgage interest, water and sewer charges, and other items between the parties are agreed upon. The settlement statement, which sets forth which parties have paid what sums for the various items listed, is prepared. The lender produces the net proceeds of the loan, usually in the form of a certified or other acceptable check. (The net loan amount is the total loan amount less loan expenses and less other items for which the buyer has directed the lender to draw checks.) Having struck a balance on a settlement sheet which in-

dicates what additional sums are due to seller, the purchaser delivers the lender's net check and produces a certified check or other agreed upon money equivalents which, when added to lender's funds, equal the balance due. Most contracts provide that the seller may utilize these funds to satisfy outstanding liens, thereby eliminating objections to title.

The instruments of conveyance are finally approved, executed, acknowledged, delivered, and accepted for recording by the title insurer's representative. The deed, mortgage, or other instruments of conveyance are reviewed and approved by the purchaser's, the seller's, and the lender's counsel, and by title closer or title company representative. The seller executes and acknowledges the deed before a notary, usually the title closer. The purchaser signs the note and signs and acknowledges the mortgage. The mortgage note is delivered to the lender (mortgagee). The deed and mortgage are delivered to the title closer for recording. They will be returned from the recorder's office to the purchaser and mortgagee respectively. The title closer amends the owner's commitment of insurance to indicate that the insurance is properly effective, insuring title in the purchaser. He similarly amends the mortgage loan commitment reflecting due insurance of the new mortgage. He signs both such commitments, giving a copy of each to the purchaser's attorney and the mortgagee's attorney. The closer will bring conformed copies back to the title company office so that a final policy may be issued.

At or subsequent to the closing, each attorney prepares a closing report for his client. These reports reflect what transpired at the closing and include a financial accounting of the transaction. When the parties are represented by counsel, their respective counsel attend to the adjustments, prepare the settlement sheets, conduct the closing, and furnish the report of closing. This is the usual situation in the metropolitan areas and is always true when substantial transactions are involved.

Sometimes a transaction that involves a purchase and sale but has no institutional mortgage is consummated without using attorneys. If a broker is involved in such a transaction, he may supervise the general conduct of the closing and furnish all the required documentation to both the purchaser and the seller. It is important to note that a broker may not prepare the documents of conveyance or otherwise give legal advice, lest he engage in the unlawful and unauthorized practice of law. One so engaged is guilty of a crime. For this reason, at least one attorney is usually involved to some degree in even the smallest transaction.

An Escrow Closing

The type of closing described above is sometimes called a *cash closing.* The instruments of conveyance were conveyed in exchange for the consideration at a face-to-face meeting of the parties to the transaction. This type of closing is prevalent in most areas of New York State, particularly in New York City. Under special circumstances and in certain other areas within the state and in other parts of the United States, real estate may be transferred through a process known as an *escrow closing.* In such a closing, the parties do not meet face to face. Rather, the purchaser deposits with an independent third party, called an escrow agent (often the title company), the agreed purchase price as well as such other documents as may be required, while the seller deposits with the escrow agent the executed deeds to the property and all other related documents. If financing by a lender is to be provided, the mortgage or deed of trust and related instruments are also duly executed and acknowledged and deposited with the escrow agent.

The duties of the escrow agent are set forth in an agreement (the escrow agreement) between the agent and the parties. The escrow agent must follow the instructions he receives in the agreement, and he is liable for the loss that any party may suffer as a result of his failure to fulfill his responsibilities under the agreement. The escrow agent receives a fee for his services. When the conditions specified in the agreement have been fulfilled, the escrow agent consummates the transaction. He delivers the deposited items to the appropriate parties, the transaction becomes effective, and title passes to the purchaser. While the items deposited by the parties are in the hands of the escrow agent they are considered to be "in escrow."

ADJUSTMENTS AND SETTLEMENT STATEMENTS

Our description of a typical closing indicated that it is most desirable that the documents, adjustments, and statements be prepared at least in preliminary fashion and reviewed by all parties prior to the closing. This is particularly important for the purchaser. Many inadequately advised purchasers are often quite dismayed when they realize that they will have to come up with substantial additional funds as a result of unanticipated costs and adjustment prorations.

RESPA

Any discussion of adjustments and settlement statements must include a reference to the *Real Estate Settlement Procedures Act (RESPA).* RESPA is an act of Congress enacted in 1975. As amended, RESPA and the regulations issued pursuant to said act apply (1) to all first-mortgage loan transactions (2) which are secured by a one- to four-family residential property (3) made by a federally regulated or insured lender where (4) the proceeds of loan are utilized to finance the borrower's purchase of the mortgaged property. Analysis of the four elements of this statement of application will lead to the conclusion that the act applies to most residential transactions within the United States in which a purchaser buys a residence and obtains financing for the purchase from a lender.

Among other things, the act requires the lender to provide each loan applicant with a special information booklet at the time of application or by mail within three business days after the loan application. In addition to the booklet, the lender must provide a good-faith written estimate of charges the borrower is likely to incur at settlement or closing. Whoever conducts the settlement or closing must allow a home buyer to inspect the settlement statement on the business day prior to settlement or closing. The settlement statement need be completed only to the extent that the person conducting the settlement has information at that time. The uniform settlement statement form prepared by the U.S. Department of Housing and Urban Development (HUD) must be used as the settlement statement.

Example fact sheets and completed statements appear as Figures 10-1 and 10-2. Figure 10-1 involves new financing by the purchaser. In Figure 10-2, the purchaser assumes a first mortgage and the seller takes back a second mortgage. RESPA does not generally apply to an assumption transaction. Figure 10-2 is provided to furnish an example for such transactions when the settlement-statement form is nonetheless voluntarily utilized by the parties. The forms list all adjustments and all charges due to and from both seller and purchaser. Note that the calculation of the charges in said examples is based on the rates in effect on the specified dates. The current rates for mortgage taxes, conveyancing taxes, and transfer taxes are as set forth in Chapters 5 and 7.

Prorating Charges

Many areas follow the title closings recommendations of the Real Estate Board of New York, Inc.

Most notable of these is that adjustments be computed by the 360-day method. This means that each month represents, 1/12 of an annual charge, and each day represents 1/30 of a monthly charge. Adjustments are made as of the day immediately preceding the day on which title is closed. To the uninitiated, the manner of arriving at adjustments of items which are to be prorated between the purchaser and seller appears complex. However, a simple example that considers the items involved and the prevailing customs reveals that adjustments are based upon simple logic and fairness.

Example S sells W his real property which consists of a parcel of land and a building which has been leased to G. G's annual rent under the lease is $12,000 payable in advance in January. The closing takes place on July 1. At the closing an adjustment must be made with respect to rent. S has collected a full year's rent of $12,000, yet W will be the owner of the property for the last six months of that year. It is appropriate that six months rent or $6,000 be transferred to purchaser, W.

The simple example with convenient figures effectively illustrates the problem and the method of solution. Let us try another example:

Example Real estate taxes on J's property amount to $1,800 annually and are payable in May of the year to which they apply. If the closing were held October 1 and seller, J, has indeed paid the taxes in May, then J would be entitled to a credit of $450. This is so because the purchaser will be the owner and enjoying the benefits of the property for three months of the year. The calculation is 1/12 (one month) times 3 times $1,800.

Additional examples of prorating closing charges may be found in Chapter 17.

In addition to the usual items which require proration, such as rent, taxes, sewer and water charges, and fuel, other costs involved in the closing must also be reflected in the closing or settlement statement. These costs include attorney's fees, title insurance premium, conveyancing taxes, mortgaging taxes, and recording fees. The figures that follow indicate how these matters are generally handled. Custom dictates whether the seller or purchaser is responsible for the payment of some of these charges. However, custom differs from location to location. In addition, one must realize that the parties in their agreements can specify the precise manner of handling adjustments, prorations, and the allocation of costs.

A SETTLEMENT, OR CLOSING, GUIDE

Figure 10-3 is a guide that helps the participants in a closing total up the various settlement costs. It consists of a *buyer's statement* and a *seller's statement*. It does not include every item that might possibly be encountered during a closing, but it does list the items that are usually found in a settlement.

Some elementary bookkeeping terms are commonly used in a settlement guide. The term *debit* means something that is owed. A debit on the buyer's statement is something that the buyer owes. A debit on the seller's statement is something that the seller owes. The term *credit* is something that is receivable. A credit may also mean a deduction from a previously listed debit. (The purchase price is listed as a buyer's debit. Any down payment that he had already made is a credit, not something receivable, but something that reduces the previously

FACT SHEET

Sales Contract Date: June 20, 1980
Closing on or before: July 20, 1980
Buyers: Harold A. Davis and Margaret A. Davis, husband and wife
Sellers: Gerald Y. Price and Rita I. Price, husband and wife
Property Location: 543 Sunset Drive, Elmwood, New York
Sales Price: $38,900
Personal Property: $750
Earnest Money Deposit: $2,000

Buyers New Loan:

Principal	$35,000
Loan fee	1%
Appraisal fee	25
Credit report	15
Inspection fee	15
Pest inspection	20
Survey	150

Tax reserve: seven months at $80 per month
Insurance reserve: one month: $20.00
Prepaid interest: $5.75 per day from settlement to 7/31/80 = $63.25

1980 property taxes of $960 are due and payable February 1, 1981, and are to be prorated to closing.

Settlement Charges	Buyer	Seller
Title Insurance	$ 75	$ 250
	(loan policy)	(owner policy)
Recording Deed	13	13
		(release)
Recording Mortgage	15	
New York State Transfer Tax ($1.10/thousand)		42.90
Elmwood Conveyancing Tax (1%)		389
Mortgage Tax (1¼%)	437.50	
Sales Commission (6% on $38,900)		2,334
1979 Real Estate Taxes		900
Special Assessment		400
Hazard Insurance	240	
Prior Mortgage Principal		33,474
Interest (from 7/1 at $5.50 per day)		110
Settlement Fee	50	50

Loan application date: June 21, 1980
Loan commitment date: June 30, 1980
Actual settlement date: July 20, 1980

Attorneys' fees	400	300

Comment: The settlement statement shows all the figures as gross amounts. The settlement agent may not actually handle all the funds. In such a case, a separate reconciliation will be needed to reflect the funds actually received and disbursed.

FIG. 10-1(a)   *Fact sheet for new financing by purchaser.*

listed debit. Debits also appear on the seller's statement.)

A principle of double-entry bookkeeping is that on any statement, debits must equal credits. The sum of everything that the buyer owes is equal to everything that the buyer receives. The same is true for the seller's debits and credits. However, the buyer's and seller's statements are unrelated. They must be treated individually even though they may appear on the same form.

The order in which the items appear on the settlement statement is a matter of choice. In Figure 10-3 they appear in the following order:

1. *Purchase price.* The amount to be paid by the purchaser at settlement for the property is entered as a debit to the buyer. (The buyer owes this

FACT SHEET

Sales Contract Date: August 2, 1980
Closing on or before: September 10, 1980
Buyers: Harold A. Davis and Margaret A. Davis, husband and wife
Sellers: Gerald Y. Price and Rita I. Price, husband and wife
Property Location: 1020 High Drive, Englewood, New York
Sales Price: $45,000
Personal Property: $5,340
Earnest Money Deposit: $3,000

Property is a four unit residence with owner living in one unit. The other three units are leased as follows:

	Rent Deposit	Rent Paid in Advance
Unit A	$150	$200 (9/1/80)
Unit B	175	225 (9/1/80)
Unit C	175	225 (9/1/80)

Buyer will assume the first mortgage. Seller will take back a second mortgage for $5,000
City taxes are paid in advance for the year on November 1. 1980 taxes paid were $150. Prorate to closing date.
County taxes are paid in arrears on February 1. 1979 taxes were $1,500 and will be the basis of prorations. Prorate to closing date.

First mortgage of Mayflower Mortgage Co. assumption figures as of September 1, 1980:

Principal balance with 9/1/80 payment made	$32,434.00
Collect September 1 payment	310.00

Interest paid in arrears at rate of 8.5% per annum
Reserve (impound) accounts with 9/1 payment made:

City Taxes	$ 137
County Taxes	1,125
Insurance Reserve	93

Loan Assumption Fee is $150
Hazard insurance $280 paid to 12/15/80 (assigned to buyer)

Settlement charges	Buyer	Seller
Settlement Fee	$ 50	$ 50
Title Insurance (owner)	425	
Recording Deed	13	
Recording Mortgage	15	
Englewood Conveyance Tax		125.66
(1% on new consideration:		
$45,000 minus $32,434 = $12,566)		
New York State Transfer Tax ($1.10 thousand)		49.50
Mortgage Tax (1¼%)	62.50	
Sales Commission (6% on $45,000)		2,700
Attorneys' Fees	450	400

Loan assumption date: August 10, 1980
Loan assumption commitment date: August 20, 1980
Actual settlement date: September 10, 1980

FIG. 10-2(a)   *Fact sheet, with buyer assuming first mortgage and seller taking back second mortgage.*

amount.) Since it is received by the seller, it is entered as a credit on the seller's statement.

2. *Deposit.* The earnest money amount paid by the purchaser which is to be used as part of the purchase price is entered as a credit to the buyer. (It reduces his debit, the amount he owes.) There is no entry for the seller.

3. *Sales commission* (broker's fee). The fee charged by the broker for the sale of the property is an expense to the seller and should be debited. There is no entry for the buyer unless the buyer has agreed to pay the broker a fee to find a property.

4. *New first mortgage.* If the buyer is obtaining a new loan to purchase the property, he treats the loan amount as a credit (a receivable). There is no entry on the seller's statement.

5. *Assumed mortgage.* If the seller's existing mortgage is being assumed by the buyer, the amount of that mortgage is entered as a credit to the buyer and a debit to the seller. The amount is being used by the buyer to pay for the property to reduce the debit of the purchase price. The seller must treat this amount as a reduction of the cost he is to receive. It is a reduction of the seller's credit in line 1.

6. *Existing mortgage.* The amount of the existing mortgage is debited to the seller. It is something that the seller owes. If it is assumed by the buyer (item 5), it reduces the credit due the seller in item 1. Of course, the seller can pay off the existing mortgage and transfer the property free and clear. The cash received for item 1 is reduced by the payment made for item 6.

7. *Second mortgage.* If the buyer needs a second loan to meet the purchase price, this loan, like the first mortgage, is a credit, a receivable that reduces the amount he must pay at the settlement. Thus, no entry to the seller.

8. *Purchase money mortgage.* When the seller takes a purchase money mortgage for part of the sales price, he extends a loan to the buyer. This is treated just like item 5, in which the buyer assumes the seller's existing mortgage. Enter the amount as a credit to the buyer against the sales price and a debit to the seller against his cash receivable.

9. *Taxes in arrears, prorated.* If the taxes have not yet been paid, prorate the annual amount of taxes including the day of settlement. Credit the purchaser and debit the seller for the amount that should have been paid to that day.

10. *Taxes in advance, prorated.* If the taxes have been paid in advance, determine the amount that applies for the portion of the year to date, including the day of settlement, and subtract it from the prepaid amount. The remainder should be debited to the buyer and credited to the seller.

F. 2853 R 7/76   Form Approved OMB No. 63-R-1501   Page 1

A.

♖ Chicago Title Insurance Company

SETTLEMENT STATEMENT
U.S. DEPARTMENT OF HOUSING AND URBAN DEVELOPMENT

B. TYPE OF LOAN		
1. ☐ FHA	2. ☐ FMHA	3. ☒ CONV. UNINS.
4. ☐ VA	5. ☐ CONV. INS.	
6. File Number: 36717457		7. Loan Number: 7-4056
8. Mortgage Insurance Case Number:		

C. NOTE: *This form is furnished to give you a statement of actual settlement costs. Amounts paid to and by the settlement agent are shown. Items marked "(p.o.c.)" were paid outside the closing; they are shown here for informational purposes and are not included in the totals.*

D. NAME OF BORROWER:	Harold A. Davis and Margaret A. Davis
ADDRESS:	3409 So. Prince Elmwood, New York 10317
E. NAME OF SELLER:	Gerald Y. Price and Rita I. Price
ADDRESS:	543 Sunset Drive Elmwood, New York 10317
F. NAME OF LENDER:	First Federal Savings & Loan
ADDRESS:	3201 So. Broadway Elmwood, New York 10317
G. PROPERTY LOCATION:	543 Sunset Drive Elmwood, New York 10317

H. SETTLEMENT AGENT:	CHICAGO TITLE INSURANCE COMPANY	I. SETTLEMENT DATE:
ADDRESS:		
PLACE OF SETTLEMENT:	909 17th Street	July 20, 1980
ADDRESS:	Elmwood, New York 10317	

J. SUMMARY OF BORROWER'S TRANSACTION		K. SUMMARY OF SELLER'S TRANSACTION	
100. GROSS AMOUNT DUE FROM BORROWER:		**400. GROSS AMOUNT DUE TO SELLER:**	
101. Contract sales price	38,900.00	401. Contract sales price	$38,900.00
102. Personal property	750.00	402. Personal property	750.00
103. Settlement charges to borrower (line 1400)	2,448.75	403.	
104.		404.	
105.		405.	
Adjustments for items paid by seller in advance		*Adjustments for items paid by seller in advance*	
106. City/town taxes to		406. City/town taxes to	
107. County taxes to		407. County taxes to	
108. Assessments to		408. Assessments to	
109.		409.	
110.		410.	
111.		411.	
112.		412.	
120. **GROSS AMOUNT DUE FROM BORROWER**	42,098.75	420. **GROSS AMOUNT DUE TO SELLER**	39,650.00
200. AMOUNTS PAID BY OR IN BEHALF OF BORROWER:		**500. REDUCTIONS IN AMOUNT DUE TO SELLER:**	
201. Deposit or earnest money	2,000.00	501. Excess deposit (see instructions)	
202. Principal amount of new loan(s)	35,000.00	502. Settlement charges to seller (line 1400)	3,378.90
203. Existing loan(s) taken subject to		503. Existing loan(s) taken subject to	
204.		504. Payoff of first mortgage loan	
205.			33,584.00
206.		505. Payoff of second mortgage loan	
207.			
208.		506. Payment 1979 City Taxes	900.00
209.		507. Payment Special Assessment	400.00
		508.	
Adjustments for items unpaid by seller		509.	
210. City/town taxes to		*Adjustments for items unpaid by seller*	
211. County taxes 1/1/80 to 7/20/80	533.33	510. City/town taxes to	
212. Assessments to		511. County taxes 1/1/80 to 7/20/80	533.33
213.		512. Assessments to	
214.		513.	
215.		514.	
216.		515.	
217.		516.	
218.		517.	
219.		518.	
220. **TOTAL PAID BY/FOR BORROWER**	37,533.33	519.	
300. CASH AT SETTLEMENT FROM/TO BORROWER		520. **TOTAL REDUCTIONS AMOUNT DUE SELLER**	38,796.23
301. Gross amount due from borrower (line 120)	42,098.75	**600. CASH AT SETTLEMENT TO/FROM SELLER**	
302. Less amounts paid by/for borrower (line 220)	(37,533.33)	601. Gross amount due to seller (line 420)	39,650.00
		602. Less reductions in amount due seller (line 520)	(38,796.23)
303. CASH (☒ FROM) (☐ TO) BORROWER	$ 4,565.42	603. CASH (☒ TO) (☐ FROM) SELLER	$ 853.77

HUD-1 Rev. (5/76)

FIG. 10-1(b)   Settlement statement for FIG. 10-1(a).

L. SETTLEMENT CHARGES

700. TOTAL SALES/BROKER'S COMMISSION based on price	PAID FROM BORROWER'S FUNDS AT SETTLEMENT	PAID FROM SELLER'S FUNDS AT SETTLEMENT
$ 38,900 @ 6 %= $2,334		
Division of Commission (line 700) as follows:		
701. $ 2,334 to JOE BROKER REALTORS		
702. $ to		
703. Commission paid at Settlement		
(Money retained by broker applied to commission $ _____)		2,334.00
704. Other sales agent charges		
705. Additional commission		
800. ITEMS PAYABLE IN CONNECTION WITH LOAN		
801. Loan Origination Fee %	$ 350.00	
802. Loan Discount %		
803. Appraisal Fee to JOHN MURRAY	25.00	
804. Credit Report to ACE CREDIT BUREAU	15.00	
805. Lender's Inspection Fee	15.00	
806. Mortgage Insurance Application Fee to		
807. Assumption Fee		
808.		
809.		
810.		
811.		
900. ITEMS REQUIRED BY LENDER TO BE PAID IN ADVANCE		
901. Interest from 7/20/80 to 7/31/80 @ $ 5.75 /day	63.25	
902. Mortgage Insurance Premium for months to		
903. Hazard Insurance Premium for 1 years to LINCOLN FIRE & CASUALTY	240.00	
904. years to		
905.		
1000. RESERVES DEPOSITED WITH LENDER		
1001. Hazard insurance 1 month @ $ 20 per month	20.00	
1002. Mortgage insurance month @ $ per month		
1003. City property taxes month @ $ per month		
1004. County property taxes 7 month @ $ 80 per month	560.00	
1005. Annual assessments month @ $ per month		
1006. month @ $ per month		
1007. month @ $ per month		
1008. month @ $ per month		
1100. TITLE CHARGES		
1101. Settlement or closing fee to CHICAGO TITLE INSURANCE CO.	50.00	50.00
1102. Abstract or title search to		
1103. Title examination to		
1104. Title insurance binder to		
1105. Document preparation to		
1106. Notary fees to		
1107. Attorney's fee to		
(includes above items numbers:		
1108. Title insurance to CHICAGO TITLE INSURANCE CO.	75.00	250.00
(includes above items numbers: 1102, 1103, 1104		
1109. Lender's coverage $ 35,000 (75)		
1110. Owner's coverage $ 38,900 (250)		
1111.		
1112.		
1113.		
1200. GOVERNMENT RECORDING AND TRANSFER CHARGES		
1201. Recording fees: Deed $13 ; Mortgage $ 15 ; Release $ 13	28.00	13.00
1202. City/county tax/stamps: Deed $ 389 ; Mortgage $		389.00
1203. State tax/stamps: Deed $ 42.90 ; Mortgage $ 437.50	437.50	42.90
1204.		
1205.		
1300. ADDITIONAL SETTLEMENT CHARGES		
1301. Survey to SHORT SURVEY CO.	150.00	
1302. Pest inspection to BUGGER CO.	20.00	
1303. ATTORNEYS' FEES TO GOLD & GOLD		300.00
1304. ATTORNEYS' FEES TO SILVER & SILVER	400.00	
1305.		
1306.		
1307.		
1400. TOTAL SETTLEMENT CHARGES (enter on lines 103, Section J and 502, Section K)	2,448.75	3,378.90

The above settlement statement is hereby approved, the disbursements indicated are authorized, and settlement may be completed by settlement agent.

Borrower _____   Seller _____

_____   _____

HUD-1 Rev. (5/76)

FIG. 10-1(c)   Settlement statement for FIG. 10-1(a).

F. 2853 R 7/76   Form Approved OMB No. 63-R-1501   Page 1

A. ![Chicago Title logo] **Chicago Title Insurance Company**	B. TYPE OF LOAN
	1. ☐ FHA 2. ☐ FMHA 3. ☒ CONV. UNINS.
	4. ☐ VA 5. ☐ CONV. INS.
	6. File Number: G-42351 7. Loan Number: 645-79
SETTLEMENT STATEMENT U.S. DEPARTMENT OF HOUSING AND URBAN DEVELOPMENT	8. Mortgage Insurance Case Number:

C. NOTE: This form is furnished to give you a statement of actual settlement costs. Amounts paid to and by the settlement agent are shown. Items marked "(p.o.c.)" were paid outside the closing; they are shown here for informational purposes and are not included in the totals.

D. NAME OF BORROWER: Harold A. Davis and Margaret A. Davis
    ADDRESS: 914 Poplar Road
    Englewood, New York 10318

E. NAME OF SELLER: Gerald Y. Price and Rita I Price
    ADDRESS: 1020 High Drive
    Englewood, New York 10318

F. NAME OF LENDER: Mayflower Mortgage Co.
    ADDRESS: 717 17th Street
    Englewood, New York 10318

G. PROPERTY LOCATION: 1020 High Drive
    Englewood, New York 10318

H. SETTLEMENT AGENT: CHICAGO TITLE INSURANCE COMPANY
    ADDRESS:

I. SETTLEMENT DATE: September 10, 1980

PLACE OF SETTLEMENT:
    ADDRESS: 909 17th Street
    Englewood, New York 10318

J. SUMMARY OF BORROWER'S TRANSACTION		K. SUMMARY OF SELLER'S TRANSACTION	
100. GROSS AMOUNT DUE FROM BORROWER:		**400. GROSS AMOUNT DUE TO SELLER:**	
101. Contract sales price	45,000.00	401. Contract sales price	45,000.00
102. Personal property	5,340.00	402. Personal property	5,340.00
103. Settlement charges to borrower (line 1400)	1,165.50	403. City Tax Reserve	137.00
104. City(137)-County(1,125) Tax Reserve	1,262.00	404. County Tax Reserve	1,125.00
105. Insurance Reserve	93.00	405. Insurance Reserve	93.00
Adjustments for items paid by seller in advance		Adjustments for items paid by seller in advance	
106. City/town taxes 9/10/80 to 12/31/80	46.00	406. City/town taxes 9/10/80 to 12/31/80	46.00
107. County taxes to		407. County taxes to	
108. Assessments to		408. Assessments to	
109. Hazard Ins. 9/10 to 12/15/80	74.00	409. Hazard Ins. 9/10 to 12/15/80	74.00
110.		410.	
111.		411.	
112.		412.	
120. GROSS AMOUNT DUE FROM BORROWER	52,980.50	420. GROSS AMOUNT DUE TO SELLER	51,815.00
200. AMOUNTS PAID BY OR IN BEHALF OF BORROWER:		**500. REDUCTIONS IN AMOUNT DUE TO SELLER:**	
201. Deposit or earnest money	3,000.00	501. Excess deposit (see instructions)	
202. Principal amount of new loan(s) to Seller	5,000.00	502. Settlement charges to seller (line 1400)	3,635.16
203. Existing loan(s) taken subject to	32,434.00	503. Existing loan(s) taken subject to	32,434.00
204. Rent Deposits	500.00	504. Payoff of first mortgage loan	
205. Prepaid Rents	455.00	505. Payoff of second mortgage loan	
206.			
207.			
208.		506. Rent Deposits	500.00
209.		507. Prepaid Rents	455.00
Adjustments for items unpaid by seller		508. Note from Buyer	5,000.00
210. City/town taxes to		509.	
211. County taxes 1/1/80 to 9/10/80	1,037.50	Adjustments for items unpaid by seller	
212. Assessments to		510. City/town taxes to	
213. Int. on existing mortgages 9/1 to 9/10/80	69.00	511. County taxes 1/1/80 to 9/10/80	1,037.50
214.		512. Assessments to	
215.		513. Interest on existing mortgage 9/1 to 9/10/80	69.00
216.		514.	
217.		515.	
218.		516.	
219.		517.	
220. TOTAL PAID BY/FOR BORROWER	42,495.50	518.	
		519.	
300. CASH AT SETTLEMENT FROM/TO BORROWER		520. TOTAL REDUCTIONS AMOUNT DUE SELLER	43,130.66
301. Gross amount due from borrower (line 120)	52,980.50	**600. CASH AT SETTLEMENT TO/FROM SELLER**	
302. Less amounts paid by/for borrower (line 220)	(42,495.50	601. Gross amount due to seller (line 420)	51,815.00
		602. Less reductions in amount due seller (line 520)	(43,130.66)
303. CASH (☒ FROM) (☐ TO) BORROWER	10,485.00	603. CASH (☒ TO) (☐ FROM) SELLER	8,684.34

HUD-1 Rev. (5/76)

FIG. 10-2(b) Settlement statement for FIG. 10-2(a).

		PAID FROM BORROWER'S FUNDS AT SETTLEMENT	PAID FROM SELLER'S FUNDS AT SETTLEMENT
L. SETTLEMENT CHARGES			
700.	TOTAL SALES/BROKER'S COMMISSION based on price $ 45,000.00 @ 6 %= 2,700		
	Division of Commission (line 700) as follows:		
701.	$ 2,700 to JOE BROKER REALTY		
702.	$ to		
703.	Commission paid at Settlement (Money retained by broker applied to commission $ _____)		2,700.00
704.	Other sales agent charges		
705.	Additional commission		
	800. ITEMS PAYABLE IN CONNECTION WITH LOAN		
801.	Loan Origination Fee %		
802.	Loan Discount %		
803.	Appraisal Fee to		
804.	Credit Report to		
805.	Lender's Inspection Fee		
806.	Mortgage Insurance Application Fee to		
807.	Assumption Fee	150.00	
808.			
809.			
810.			
811.			
	900. ITEMS REQUIRED BY LENDER TO BE PAID IN ADVANCE		
901.	Interest from to @ $ /day		
902.	Mortgage Insurance Premium for months to		
903.	Hazard Insurance Premium for years to		
904.	years to		
905.			
	1000. RESERVES DEPOSITED WITH LENDER		
1001.	Hazard insurance month @ $ per month		
1002.	Mortgage insurance month @ $ per month		
1003.	City property taxes month @ $ per month		
1004.	County property taxes month @ $ per month		
1005.	Annual assessments month @ $ per month		
1006.	month @ $ per month		
1007.	month @ $ per month		
1008.	month @ $ per month		
	1100. TITLE CHARGES		
1101.	Settlement or closing fee to CHICAGO TITLE INSURANCE CO.	50.00	50.00
1102.	Abstract or title search to		
1103.	Title examination to		
1104.	Title insurance binder to		
1105.	Document preparation to		
1106.	Notary fees to		
1107.	Attorney's fee to		
	(includes above items numbers;		
1108.	Title insurance to CHICAGO TITLE INSURANCE CO.	425.00	
	(includes above items numbers; 1102,1103,1104		
1109.	Lender's coverage $		
1110.	Owner's coverage $ 45,000		
1111.			
1112.			
1113.			
	1200. GOVERNMENT RECORDING AND TRANSFER CHARGES		
1201.	Recording fees: Deed $ 13 ; Mortgage $ 15 ; Release $	28.00	
1202.	City/county tax/stamps: Deed $ 125.66 ; Mortgage $		125.66
1203.	State tax/stamps: Deed $ 49.50 ; Mortgage $ 62.50	62.50	49.50
1204.			
1205.			
	1300. ADDITIONAL SETTLEMENT CHARGES		
1301.	Survey to		
1302.	Pest inspection to		
1303.	September Loan Payment		310.00
1304.	Attorneys' Fees to Gold & Gold		400.00
1305.	Attorneys' Fees to Silver & Silver	450.00	
1306.			
1307.			
1400.	TOTAL SETTLEMENT CHARGES (enter on lines 103, Section J and 502, Section K)	1,165.50	3,635.16

The above settlement statement is hereby approved, the disbursements indicated are authorized, and settlement may be completed by settlement agent.

Borrower _____ Seller _____

_____ _____

HUD-1 Rev. (5/76)

FIG. 10-2(c)   Settlement statement for FIG. 10-2(a).

SETTLEMENT STATEMENT WORKSHEET

	BUYER'S STATEMENT		SELLER'S STATEMENT	
	DEBIT	CREDIT	DEBIT	CREDIT
1. Purchase Price or Sales Price	XX			XX
2. Deposit		XX		
3. Sales Commission (Broker's Fee)			XX	
Financing:				
4. New 1st Mortgage (Trust)		XX		
5. Assumed Mortgage (Trust)		XX	XX	
6. Pay Existing Mortgage (Trust)			XX	
7. 2nd Mortgage (Trust)		XX		
8. 2nd Purchase Money Mortgage		XX	XX	
9. Taxes in Arrears—Prorated		XX	XX	
10. Taxes in Advance—Prorated	XX			XX
11. Delinquent Taxes			XX	
12. Fire Insurance—Cancelled				XX
13. Fire Insurance—New Policy	XX			
14. Fire Insurance—Assigned Policy	XX			XX
15. Interest in Arrears		XX	XX	
16. Interest in Advance	XX			XX
17. Interest on New Loan	XX			
18. Rent in Advance		XX	XX	
19. Rent in Arrears	XX			XX
20. Title Insurance—Owner's	XX			
21. Title Insurance—Mortgagee's	XX			
22. Deed Preparation			XX	
23. Abstract Continuation			XX	
24. Opinion of Abstract (Examination)	XX			
25. Appraisal Fee	Negotiable			
26. Attorney's Fee—Purchaser	XX			
27. Attorney's Fee–Seller			XX	

FIG. 10-3(a)   A typical settlement or closing statement worksheet. Entries will vary depending on the details of a particular transaction.

SETTLEMENT STATEMENT WORKSHEET
(Continued)

	BUYER'S STATEMENT		SELLER'S STATEMENT	
	DEBIT	CREDIT	DEBIT	CREDIT
28. Loan Origination Fee	XX			
Loan Discount—Points				
29. FHA			XX	
30. VA			XX	
31. Conventional	Negotiable			
32. Recording Deed	XX			
33. Recording Mortgage	XX			
34. Escrow Balances Assumed	XX			XX
35. Payoff Existing Loan				XX
36. Survey	XX			
37. Prepayment Penalty			XX	
38. Conveyance Tax			XX	
39. Mortgage Tax	XX			
40. Special Assessments	Negotiable			
41. Settlement Fee	Negotiable			
42. Credit Report	XX			
43. Photo Fee	XX			
44. Sale of Chattels	XX			XX
45. Balance Due from Purchaser		XX		
46. Balance Due Seller			XX	
	XXX	XXX	XXX	XXX

FIG. 10-3(b)

11. *Delinquent taxes.* If the taxes are delinquent, the amount of taxes owed should be charged to the seller. There is no entry to the buyer.

12. *Fire insurance, cancelled.* If the seller is cancelling his insurance coverage, credit the remaining premium balance to the seller.

13. *Fire insurance, new policy.* Enter the cost of the new policy as a debit to the purchaser.

14. *Fire insurance, assigned policy.* If the seller assigns the existing policy to the purchaser, prorate the premium and enter the amount of prepaid premium as a debit to the purchaser and a credit to the seller.

15. *Interest in arrears.* If the seller pays out the existing loan and interest is calculated in arrears, prorate to the date of closing the monthly interest due and enter it as a debit to the seller. If the buyer assumes the loan, enter the prorated amount as a debit to the seller *and* credit to the buyer.

16. *Interest in advance.* If the seller pays out the existing loan and the interest on a loan is paid in advance, enter a credit on the seller's statement. If the purchaser is assuming, then enter the prorated amount as a credit to the seller and a debit to the purchaser.

17. *Interest on new loan.* Interest may be charged on a newly originated loan. Enter the amount as a debit to the purchaser.

18. *Rent in advance.* Enter the prorated amount of tenant rents collected in advance as a credit to the purchaser and a debit to the seller.

19. *Rent in arrears.* If rent is collected in arrears, enter the prorated amount as a debit to the purchaser and a credit to the seller.

20. *Title insurance, purchaser's policy.* Enter as a debit to the purchaser.

21. *Title insurance, mortgagee's policy.* Enter as a debit to the purchaser.

22. *Deed preparation.* Enter this cost as a debit to the seller.

23. *Abstract continuation.* Enter as a debit to the seller.

24. *Opinion or examination of the abstract.* Enter as a debit to the purchaser.

25. *Appraisal fee.* A negotiable item. Whether the seller or the purchaser is debited for this cost depends on the relative bargaining strength of each.

26. *Attorney fees, purchaser.* Debit the purchaser.

27. *Attorney fees, seller.* Debit the seller.

28. *Loan origination fee.* Debit the purchaser for the cost of originating the new loan. If the purchaser has assumed the existing mortgages and the lender charges an assumption fee, debit that to the purchaser.

29. *FHA discount points.* By law these are debited to the seller.

30. *VA discount points.* By law these are debited to the seller.

31. *Conventional discount points.* The buyer and the seller may negotiate who pays discount points charged by the conventional lender.

32. *Recording of deed.* Debit to the purchaser.

33. *Recording of mortgage.* Debit to the purchaser.

34. *Escrow balance, assumed.* Debit to the purchaser and credit to the seller for the balance in any assumed escrow account.

35. *Escrow payoff, existing loan.* Credit to the seller as an offsetting item to the loan balance.

36. *Survey.* Payment of charges for a survey may be negotiable, but generally it is charged as a debit to the purchaser.

37. *Prepayment penalty.* Debit to the seller any penalty he was charged by his lender for prepaying loan balance.

38. *Conveyance tax.* This item is customarily paid by seller. (Debit to the seller.) The conveyance tax in New York State is $2 (formerly 55¢) per $500 of consideration or any fractional part thereof. In addition to the New York State tax, there may be local conveyancing taxes, such as in the City of New York. The New York City tax is 1 or 2 percent of the new consideration, depending upon the amount of the consideration and the nature of the property conveyed. See Chapter 5, page 55, for a more detailed discussion of these taxes.

39. *Mortgage tax.* Debit the purchaser. In the State of New York, there is a tax on mortgages when new mortgage funds are involved. This tax varies somewhat in amount depending upon the locality. In New York City the tax rate is 1-1/2 percent ($1.50 for each $100 or fraction thereof) of the principal amount secured by mortgages of less than $500,000; 1-5/8 percent secured by mortgages of $500,000 or more on one-, two-, or three-family houses, individual cooperative apartments, and residential condominium units; and 2-1/4 percent secured by mortgages of $500,000 or more on all other properties. However, when the mortgaged property is a one- or two-family dwelling (and the mortgage so recites), the tax rate is $1.25 for each $100 on the first $10,000 only of principal debt. (For additional details regarding the imposition of mortgage taxes, see Chapter 7.) A schedule of property recording fees and taxes for New York City is set forth in Appendix F.

40. *Special assessments.* The allocation of special assessments charged to the property is negotiable.

41. *Settlement fees.* Negotiable.

42. *Credit report.* Debit the purchaser.

43. *Photo fee.* Debit the purchaser.

44. *Sale of chattels.* If the purchaser has bought some personal property, as well as the real property, debit the cost of this "chattel" property to the purchaser and credit to the seller. Chattels need not be included in the closing. They may be sold under a separate bill of sale given by the seller to the buyer.

45. *Balance due from the purchaser.* This is the amount owed by the purchaser at settlement after subtracting all his credits from all his debits. Enter on the credit column of his statement, since this is the sum needed to balance the double-entry system (to make debits equal credits).

46. *Balance due seller.* This is the amount received by the seller at settlement after subtracting the debits from the credits. Enter as a debit if the credits exceed the debits as a balancing item. Enter as a credit if the debits exceed the credits.

Practice in Filling out the Settlement Statement

To familiarize salespersons with the computation of settlement costs, a hypothetical case is described below.

The Nickless Property

On August 22, this year, you as salesperson for Suburban Real Estate Company of Anytown, New York, listed the property owned by Mr. Jack Nickless and his wife, Margaret, at 2785 Nulsen Drive in Anytown. At the time you obtained a 90-day exclusive authorization to sell listing. The house is a frame Cape Cod with three bedrooms downstairs, two full baths, a full basement, and all built-in appliances in the kitchen, except an automatic dishwasher. The recreation room is 14' by 18' with a fireplace. The home was originally constructed in 1955. It has hardwood floors, with carpeting in the 18' by 22' living room, dining room, and all bedrooms. The house has city water and sewers, electricity, and is heated by natural gas. It also has aluminum storm windows and a two-car attached garage. The lot is 120' by 140' on the west side of the street.

The Nicklesses have an outstanding mortgage balance as of August 1 of $10,586. The payments are $125 per month, including principal and interest only, and are due the first of each month. The interest rate is 7 percent paid in advance. The loan is assumable, and the mortgagee is the Anytown Savings Bank. There is a fire and extended coverage insurance policy that expires April 30, next year, and has been paid in advance at $80 per year. The coverage is for $24,000. The taxes are $8.50 per $100, with the property having an assessed value for the land of $1,500 and the improvements of $6,500. The taxes are payable by December 31, this year, and have not yet been paid. The Nicklesses feel they can give possession on or before ten days after the final closing.

The terms are set at a listing price of $28,500 payable in cash, or cash plus the assumption of the existing mortgage. They will not accept an exchange. They also desire to have the house shown only by appointment between 10 a.m. and 7 p.m., Monday through Saturday. They can be reached for an appointment at 821-5168, and the key will be available at the Suburban Real Estate office. The Nicklesses also agree to the 6 percent brokerage fee.

The Offer

On September 3, this year, Mr. Charles Vance and his wife, Wilma, are shown the Nickless house. Both Mr. and Mrs. Vance like the house and make an offer of $28,000 that same day. They ask in the offer that the washer and dryer be included in the sales price. The offer is to run until midnight of the next day if it is not accepted prior. The offer is contingent upon the Vances' being able to obtain new financing in the amount of 80 percent of the purchase price for 25 years at a rate not to exceed 8 percent. They also tender $1,000 earnest money by check to you and ask that, if accepted, the closing take place at the Suburban Real Estate offices. You immediately submit the offer to the Nicklesses, and they accept the following afternoon.

Settlement (Closing)

With the terms of the contract being met, closing was set for September 30, this year, at the Suburban Real Estate offices. In addition to the purchase price, deposit, new mortgage and insurance proration, and brokerage fee, pursuant to the agreement of the parties the following will be charged at the closing:

☐ Title examination—one-half percent of the sales price will be charged to the purchaser.
☐ Recording fee for the new mortgage—$25 will be charged to the purchaser.

SETTLEMENT STATEMENT WORKSHEET

	BUYER'S STATEMENT		SELLER'S STATEMENT	
	DEBIT	CREDIT	DEBIT	CREDIT
Sales Price	28,000.00			28,000.00
Brokerage Fee			1,680.00	
New Mortgage		22,400.00		
Nickless Mortgage			10,522.75	
Deposit		1,000.00		
Taxes		510.03	510.03	
Insurance	46.69			46.69
Title Examination	140.00			
Recording New Mortgage	25.00			
Appraisal Fee			40.00	
Mortgage Title Insurance	75.00			
Deed Recording Fee			7.50	
Deed Preparation			50.00	
Loan Origination Fee	224.00			
Survey Fee			50.00	
Balance Due from Buyer		4,600.66		
Balance Due Seller			15,186.41	
	$28,510.69	$28,510.69	$28,046.69	$28,046.69

FIG. 10-4   A completed settlement statement worksheet.

Calculations

1. *Brokerage fee:*
   $28,000 × .06 = $1,680

2. *New mortgage:*
   $28,000 × .80 = $22,400

3. *Nickless mortgage:*
   $10,586 × .07 = $741.02
   $741.02/12 = $61.75
   $125.00 − $61.75 = $63.25
   $10,586.00 − $63.25
     = $10,522.75

4. *Taxes:*
   $1,500.00 + $6,500.00
     = $8,000.00
   $8,000.00 × $8.50/$100
     = $680.00
   $680/12 = $56.67
   $56.67 × 9 months
     = $510.03 to purchaser

5. *Title examination:*
   .005 × $28,000 = $140

6. *Loan origination fee:*
   .01 × $22,400 = $224

7. *Insurance:*
   $80.00/12 = $6.67/month

Expiration	Day	Month	Year
date	30	4	NY
Closing date	30	9	TY
Remaining	0	7	0

   $6.67 × 7 months prepaid
     = $46.69 to seller

☐ Appraisal fee—$40 will be charged to the sellers.
☐ Mortgagee's title insurance—$75 will be charged to the purchaser.
☐ Recording fee—$7.50, and
☐ Deed preparation fee—$50 will be charged to the sellers.

☐ Loan origination fee—1 percent of the amount financed will be charged to the purchaser.
☐ Survey fee—$50 will be charged to the sellers.

The completed settlement statement and the necessary calculations for the above transactions are shown in Figure 10-4.

REVIEW QUESTIONS

1. The meeting at which time all interested parties convene to complete a real estate transaction is called

    (a) The contract conference.
    (b) The title evidence conference.
    (c) The closing or settlement conference.
    (d) None of the above.

2. A homeowner's policy with a term of three years was taken out on June 1, 1979. The premium paid for three years was $720. The property was sold on January 1, 1981. Upon proration

    (a) Purchaser will receive a credit of $240.
    (b) Seller will receive a credit of $360.
    (c) Purchaser will be charged or debited $180.
    (d) None of the above.

3. A closing in which all relevant documents and consideration are delivered to a third party pending the satisfaction of specified conditions is called

    (a) An escrow closing.
    (b) A defunct closing.
    (c) A cash closing.
    (d) None of the above.

4. Seller conveys his property to purchaser on June 15, 1980. Seller is transferring the prepaid three-year insurance policy expiring on December 31, 1981. The premium was $540.

    (a) The policy has been in force one year, 5 months, 14 days.
    (b) The amount of unexpired premium is $278.
    (c) The unexpired premium is a debit to purchaser.
    (d) All of the above.

5. A federal statute which regulates disclosure and closing requirements relative to first mortgage loans on one- to four-family residential property is known as

    (a) The Truth-in-Lending Act.
    (b) The Interstate Land Sales Act.
    (c) Fair Credit Disclosure Act.
    (d) Real Estate Settlement Procedures Act.

6. A mortgage tax is imposed

    (a) Uniformly throughout New York State.
    (b) With some variation depending upon the locale in New York State.
    (c) In some states, but not in New York State.
    (d) Only on commercial transactions in New York State.

7. The fee or commission charged by the broker is usually paid by the

    (a) Purchaser.
    (b) Seller.
    (c) Lender.
    (d) None of the above.

8. If a closing is to take place on September 10, 1980 and the prepaid fire insurance policy, with an annual premium of $360, expires on June 20, 1981, what is the amount to be prorated and credited to seller?

    (a) $270.
    (b) $280.
    (c) $250.
    (d) $210.

9. Rent collected in arrears will be prorated

    A. As a credit to the seller.
    B. As a debit to the purchaser.

    (a) A only.
    (b) B only.
    (c) Both A and B.
    (d) Neither A nor B.

10. Interest paid in advance on an existing mortgage is prorated

   A. As a credit to the seller.
   B. As a debit to the purchaser.

   (a) A only.   (c) Both A and B.
   (b) B only.   (d) Neither A nor B.

11. Conveyancing or transfer taxes are imposed in New York

   A. As a uniform state tax.
   B. Independently by certain municipalities.

   (a) A only.   (c) Both A and B.
   (b) B only.   (d) Neither A nor B.

12. The 1980 real estate taxes on a residence were $1,260. Seller paid the taxes in February and sold the house to purchaser on September 15, 1980. Seller is entitled to a credit of:

   (a) $420.75.
   (b) $367.50.
   (c) $298.00.
   (d) None.

13. School taxes on a parcel of real property are $1,400 for a calendar year. The seller paid the first half of these taxes. Seller conveys to purchaser on December 20. Upon proration

   (a) Seller will receive a credit of $39.
   (b) Purchaser will receive a credit of $580.
   (c) Seller will be charged or debited $661.
   (d) None of the above.

14. At the closing

   (a) All relevant documents of conveyance are duly executed and delivered.
   (b) All adjustments and prorations are made or confirmed.
   (c) The consideration, purchase price or loan proceeds, is paid or disbursed.
   (d) All of the above.

15. Which of the following are generally closing expenses of the seller.

   (a) Conveyance or transfer taxes.
   (b) Preparation of deed.

   (c) FHA or VA discount points.
   (d) All of the above.

16. The Real Estate Settlement Procedures Act (RESPA) requires

   (a) The lender to furnish the borrower with a special information booklet and a good faith estimate of closing or settlement charges.
   (b) The utilization of a uniform settlement statement.
   (c) The obtaining of flood insurance.
   (d) a and b, but not c.

17. Property is sold on August 20, 1980 subject to an existing current mortgage. The monthly interest on that mortgage is $90 and is paid in arrears.

   (a) Seller will receive a debit of $57.
   (b) Purchaser will receive a credit of $57.
   (c) Purchaser will be charged $33.
   (d) Both a and b.

18. Which of the following are generally closing expenses of the purchaser?

   (a) Recording the deed.
   (b) Recording the new mortgage.
   (c) Payment of the mortgage tax.
   (d) All of the above.

19. Property is transferred on August 20, 1980 subject to an existing current mortgage. The monthly interest on that mortgage is $180 and is paid in advance.

   (a) Seller will receive a credit of $66.
   (b) Seller will receive a debit of $114.
   (c) Purchaser will be charged or debited $66.
   (d) Both a and c.

20. Whether the purchaser or seller is responsible for the payment of various closing charges

   A. May be dictated by local custom.
   B. May be specifically provided for in the contract between the parties.

   (a) A only.   (c) Both a and b.
   (b) B only.   (d) Neither a nor b.

Part III

The Business of Brokering and Selling

Chapter 11
Law of Agency

VOCABULARY

You will find it important to have a complete working knowledge of the following concepts and words found in this chapter:

agency
agent
attorney in fact
commission
fiduciary

independent contractor
general agency
master-servant relationship
power of attorney

principal
respondeat superior
special agency
universal agency

NATURE OF THE RELATIONSHIP

An AGENCY RELATIONSHIP usually results from a contract in which one party, the *agent*, agrees to act for the benefit of and under the direction of a second party, the *principal*.

In most agency relationships the principal compensates the agent for the services rendered. However, this is not always true. A principal and an agent may make an agreement that does not provide for compensation. The authority of the agent may be as broad or as narrow as the parties agree it should be. Various agreements confer different levels of responsibility upon the agent. The degree of authority that is conferred upon the agent may be classified into three basic categories:

☐ Universal agency
☐ General agency
☐ Special agency

Universal Agent

A *universal agent* may perform all lawful acts for the principal without any limitation. A universal agent is not restricted to a particular business, transaction, or sphere of activity. In real estate transactions principals rarely confer universal agencies upon their agents and grants of authority are usually quite narrow.

General Agent

A *general agent* has a wide range of authority. A person designated as a general agent may act in any lawful manner in the principal's interest relating to a particular line of business or to a specific objective. General agency is frequently used in the real estate business. For example, the agreement between a principal and a real estate broker instructing the broker to locate investment properties or to manage properties usually confers upon the broker the status of general agent.

Special Agent

A *special agent* is appointed to do a specified task or series of tasks. For example, a real estate broker who has been retained to find a purchaser or tenants for a specific piece of property, or who has been authorized to lease and operate a commercial piece of property, is a special agent. The difference between general and special agents is sometimes difficult to establish. Real estate brokers are usually special agents.

An *attorney in fact,* an indivdual who has been asked to execute a deed or mortgage and note, is also a special agent. The instrument creating an attorney in fact, commonly called a *power of attorney,* must specifically designate exactly which acts the special agent may perform, and the instrument must be acknowledged and recorded in the county land records. Purchasers, tenants, and others usually will not rely on any act by the attorney in fact that is not expressly authorized in the instrument nor will they accept an instrument that has not been recorded.

Reliance on a power of attorney, whether recorded or not, is dangerous and chancy. As a general rule, the death, incompetence, or revocation by the principal terminates the agent's powers, and a purchaser must assure himself that the power was valid at the time it was exercised. A recently enacted New York State statute provides that a power of attorney may, under certain circumstances, remain valid even though the principal becomes incompetent. However, this does not alter the fact that voluntary revocation or the death of the principal terminates an agency.

Master-Servant Relationship

The *master-servant relationship* must be distinguished from that of principal and agent. The difference, although sometimes subtle, may be extremely important. The master-servant relationship is essentially the relationship between employer and employee, and may be inferred from the master's right to control the activities of employees or servants. Because the master has the right to control his servants, he has a corollary duty to control properly. As a result, the master is legally responsible for the acts of the servant when those acts are related to the servant's performance during the course of business.

The master is responsible for the servant's acts even if the specific conduct is detrimental to the master's interest. This doctrine is known as *respondeat superior*. For example, the master may incur liability for the consequences of an automobile accident in which his employee was involved while engaged in the employer's business. Or, if the employee defames a party while engaged on the master's business, the employer may be liable. In both examples, it is obvious that the act giving rise to the liability was not an act performed at the master's direction or instigation, nor did it result in benefit to him. Nevertheless, the master is probably liable to the party injured by his servant.

The Independent Contractor

While the distinction between the master-servant relationship and the principal-agent relationship may in some cases be faint and blurred, it becomes readily apparent when the agent is an independent contractor who has been hired to achieve a specific

result and who functions without any direct control from the principal. Under these circumstances, it is unlikely that the relationship will be considered that of master-servant.

An independent contractor may be an agent. But he controls the use of his time. He may have employees, and he controls their compensation. He pays for furnishing and staffing his office. He makes decisions about methods of doing business and other independent determinations. Nevertheless, a contractor who has been retained to achieve a specific result is truly an agent. The scope of the agency is determined by the nature of the expected result.

A relationship with an independent contractor therefore frees the principal from certain of the legal liabilities the agent may incur. It also frees the principal from the responsibility for such items as worker's compensation or various types of employer taxes.

The relationship between the real estate broker and his principal, typically, is that of an independent contractor with his principal. The real estate salesperson may be either a servant of the broker or an independent contractor of the broker, depending on the agreement between them. In either case, however, the salesperson has no *direct* relationship with the broker's principal.

A person acting for another in the sale, financing, or renting of real estate must be licensed as a real estate broker or as a real estate salesperson working for a licensed broker. New York law provides for this requirement even if the property is located in another state. Certain individuals, such as attorneys and court officials, are exempt from this requirement. Failure to have a proper license may result in the inability to collect a commission and the imposition of penalties, which are discussed in Chapter 12.

AUTHORIZATION, DURATION, AND TERMINATION

The authorization issued by the principal to the agent may be either formal or informal. It may be a written contract that specifically outlines the scope of the agency, its duration, and the compensation that the agent is to receive. Or, it may be extremely informal, consisting of no more than a general understanding between the parties. For practical business considerations, the agency agreement between principal and agent in a real estate transaction should always be in writing. (See Chapter 14.)

An agency relationship may exist for only a short period of time, or it may endure for a long period, depending on the needs and understanding of the parties. In the real estate sales or management field, the agency relationship generally lasts for a period long enough to achieve the presumably desired results. When an agent agrees to attempt to sell a single-family residence, the relationship usually lasts from sixty days to half a year. On the other hand, when an agent agrees to manage a commercial property for a principal, the relationship may extend over a period of many years. The duration of the relationship is generally spelled out in the agreement. Despite the terms of any written agreement, the arrangement may be terminated by impossibility. An agency relationship may be ended by the sale of the property outside of the agency relationship, by operation of law, or by the death or incapacity of either the principal or agent.

The Secretary of State of New York, through the Division of Licensing Services, has described the authorization and employment of the broker by the principal in great detail. This description is reproduced in Appendix C. *pg. 261*

LIABILITIES OF PRINCIPAL AND AGENT

agent, principal + 3rd pty = disclosed agency

When an agent does business with a third party and the third party knows of the agency relationship and knows the identity of the principal, the relationship is known as a *disclosed agency*. In a disclosed agency it is assumed that any contract the third party makes with the agent is one that he intended to make with the principal and, consequently, the principal is liable on the contract. Provided the agent has not exceeded or abused the power given him, he does not have liability for the contract; all liability is with the principal. Of course, should the agent have abused or exceeded his powers, he is liable to the principal for any damage that may arise because of that excess and abuse.

There are situations in which the third party knows the agent is acting as an agent but does not know the identity of the principal. The agent may deliberately conceal the principal's identity. In that situation, the agent is liable to the third party for damages under any agreements he makes with the third party.

In the case of an *undisclosed agency*—that is, in the case in which the third party has no knowledge of the agency relationship and, of course, is unaware of the principal, the agent is liable for all his actions. The undisclosed principal, whether he was the hidden principal in a disclosed agency or the principal in an undisclosed agency, may identify himself and ratify or accept the contract, and thus become liable. In any event, if in the latter two situations the principal is discovered, the third party may elect to hold him liable along with the agent.

Fiduciary Relationship

The relationship between principal and agent is one of trust, and is known as a *fiduciary relationship*. A fiduciary relationship means that at all times the agent must put the interest of the principal ahead of his own interest.

Because of the fiduciary relationship, it is essential that the agent totally abstain from any dealings in which he has a personal interest, whether directly or indirectly, unless a full, complete, and understood disclosure has been made to the principal and the principal's consent to the personal involvement has been obtained. Money belonging to the principal or to third parties, such as earnest money or escrow deposits, coming into the agent's hands by reason of his fiduciary responsibilities must always be placed in a separate bank trust account. The money may under no circumstances be comingled with the agent's own funds.

Power of Attorney

It was indicated above that a power of attorney is a special agency for stated limited purposes. A principal may give an agent a power of attorney to make and deliver a deed, to execute a note and mortgage, or to perform some similar specific function. A power of attorney must always be in writing, must state the precise purpose for which it is to be used, and must be executed and acknowledged with sufficient formality to permit its recording in the County Clerk's office. Because a power of attorney for a special agency may be revoked, either expressly or by operation of law prior to the exercise thereof, a purchaser or lender should not normally rely on the agent's power of attorney unless an independent verification of its continuing validity is obtained at the time of the transactions.

AGENT'S COMPENSATION

The agency agreement generally spells out the compensation to be earned by the agent and the conditions upon which it is payable. However, the agent in real estate transactions may not collect any fees if he or his subagents (brokers and salespersons) are not properly licensed to do the business they have engaged in.

There are no fixed rates for agency services. In the past realty boards or trade associations have suggested "standard" commission rates. However, the federal government is now investigating the activities of such boards and organizations as possible violations of the antitrust laws, and agreements about standard commissions are not expected to continue. Prevailing custom and market pressures will dictate the rate to be charged.

In New York State, unless otherwise agreed, the broker-agent is entitled to a commission for the sale of real property when a ready, willing, and able buyer has been procured. There may be a further agreement between broker and salesperson to establish when the latter's commission is earned.

It is good practice for a principal to insist that an agent's compensation is not earned until settlement (the closing) takes place. This provision should be, if agreed upon, inserted into the agency agreement. The principal has the continuing expense of the property—of paying carrying charges on the mortgage, taxes, utilities, insurance—and, in addition, does not have available the equity capital. As a result, the principal often must seek high-cost temporary financing for a new property. The broker (agent), on the other hand, has incurred little additional expense in finding a buyer for the property. Brokers invest the same time and effort in all potential buyers, regardless of whether a deal is consummated or the buyers turn out to be just "lookers." In any event, the broker will find that it is good business to ask, at most, for reimbursement only for out-of-pocket expenses and to look to the future and the hope of being retained once again as agent. This practice builds goodwill in the community and buys the cheapest and most effective form of advertising—word-of-mouth praise from a satisfied client.

Commissions for renting income property, like other commissions, are subject to negotiation between the principal and agent. Commissions are calculated on an annual basis, and it is customary to pay them out of the first rent collected for the period for which the commission is being paid. For example, on a three-year lease, commission for the first year would be paid in the first month of the first year. Commission for the second year, would be paid in the first month of the second year, and

so on. As in other instances, the parties to the agency agreement may nevertheless make their own arrangements.

Salespersons' Compensation

Salespersons' compensation is not standardized or regulated by law. It is the subject of individual negotiation between the salesperson and the broker for whom such person works. The most common arrangement appears to be a split of the broker's commission with the salesperson on a percentage basis.

The percentage of commission a broker will pay to a salesperson depends on many factors, such as the commissions paid by other brokers in the area; the amount and value of the support services—for example, office space and services, telephones, leads—the broker furnishes; whether or not the broker furnishes group insurance, paid vacations, retirement plan, and other benefits; and the productivity of the salesperson. A salesperson who consistently produces a high volume of listings and sales will enable a broker to earn more money and to amortize the overhead over a larger volume. Accordingly, such a salesperson can normally negotiate an above-average commission.

Thus the salesperson's compensation is highly flexible. In areas where brokers split commissions, with half going to the listing broker and the other half to the selling broker, it is not uncommon for the brokers to again split with their salespersons. Under this arrangement, the listing salesperson and the selling salesperson may each realize approximately 25 percent of the commission for a specific sale. Should the same salesperson be responsible for both the listing and the sale, the resulting commission would be approximately half the broker's commission.

The value of the commission split may be further affected by arrangements permitting either a minimum salary against commissions earned or a "draw" against future commissions. In a drawing account, a minimum compensation, which is later adjusted between the parties for actual commissions earned, is paid. The relationship between the broker and salesperson, whether that of employer-employee or principal-independent contractor, also affects both the income tax and social security status of the parties.

REVIEW QUESTIONS

1. The agency relationship always

    (a) Requires the principal to compensate the agent.
    (b) Must be the result of a written agreement.
    (c) Makes the principal responsible for all acts of the agent.
    (d) None of the above.

2. The number of basic categories into which agency may customarily be classified is

    (a) One.
    (b) Two.
    (c) Three.
    (d) None of the above.

3. Most real estate brokers have the following type of agency relationship with their principals:

    (a) Special.
    (b) General.
    (c) Universal.
    (d) None of the above.

4. A person who attends a closing on behalf of the sellers and who executes and delivers the deed and other documents, as well as receives the proceeds of the sale, is

    (a) A universal agent.
    (b) A general agent.
    (c) A special agent.
    (d) None of the above.

5. An agency to sell real estate will be terminated by all of the following except

    (a) Death of the principal.
    (b) Death of the agent.
    (c) Prior sale of the property.
    (d) None of the above.

6. In New York, under certain circumstances, an agency to sell real estate will not be terminated by

    (a) Death of the principal.
    (b) Incompetency of the principal. —I say
    (c) Incompetency of the agent.
    (d) Death of the agent. — bk. says p. 138

7. The doctrine of *respondeat superior* applies to

    A. Principal–agent relationships.
    B. Employer–employee relationships.

    (a) A only.
    (b) B only.
    (c) Both A and B.
    (d) Neither A nor B.

8. Employers are not liable to third parties for the acts of their employees

    (a) In all events.
    (b) In those cases where the act was done at the direction of the employer.
    (c) Where the act was done in relationship to the employment, whether authorized or not.
    (d) Where the act was done in relationship to the employment, but only if authorized, directly or indirectly, by the employer.

9. The broker/salesperson relationships of employer–employee and of independent contractor can be distinguished by

    (a) The degree of control the principal has over when and how the act is performed.
    (b) The method of compensation.
    (c) The length of time the relationship exists.
    (d) None of the above.

10. The real estate broker who has a sales staff composed of independent contractors is responsible for

    A. Payment of unemployment compensation.
    B. Payment of social security taxes for the sales staff.

    (a) A only.
    (b) B only.
    (c) A and B.
    (d) Neither A nor B.

11. In New York State a power of attorney dealing with real property

    (a) Must be in writing to be effective.
    (b) Must be in writing because of the licensing laws.
    (c) Must recite that the broker is licensed and contain the license number as part of the agreement.
    (d) Does not have to be in writing.

12. An agency agreement is customarily for

   (a) An indefinite period.
   (b) A fixed period.
   (c) A fixed period with automatic extensions.
   (d) A period as set forth by law.

13. Compensation of the agent is customarily

   (a) A percentage of the sales price.
   (b) A flat fee.
   (c) A fee based on the hours of work expended, plus actual expenses incurred.
   (d) None of the above.

14. If compensation is paid to an agent who is not licensed in New York State, the person having paid the commission may sue to recover

   (a) $1,000.
   (b) The amount actually paid.
   (c) Four times the amount paid.
   (d) The difference between the amount paid and the value of the services rendered by the agent.

15. Unless otherwise stated and agreed, the commission for the sale of a property is due and payable

   (a) Upon the making of an offer by the buyer.
   (b) Upon the seller's acceptance of an offer, subject to the availability of a mortgage.
   (c) When the broker obtains a ready, willing, and able buyer.
   (d) None of the above.

16. The compensation for the broker usually

   A. Affects the compensation of the salesperson.
   B. Is not affected by the salesperson's not being licensed in New York.

   (a) A only.   (c) Both A and B.
   (b) B only.   (d) Neither A nor B.

17. The commission which has been earned by the broker may be lost if the listing contract provides that it is not due and payable until closing, if

   (a) The seller changes his mind and refuses to close.
   (b) The buyer changes his mind and refuses to close.
   (c) The buyer cannot get the financing needed to close.
   (d) None of the above.

18. Rental commissions for a period of three years are normally payable

   (a) At the signing of the lease.
   (b) Each month, as the rent is collected.
   (c) At the collection of the initial rent sufficient to pay the commission.
   (d) Each year, out of the first rents collected for the period.

19. A salesperson's compensation is

   (a) The same, regardless of which broker employs the salesperson.
   (b) Always the same for obtaining a listing agreement or a contract of sale.
   (c) Regulated by law.
   (d) None of the above.

20. An agent may receive an earnest money deposit with an offer to purchase and

   (a) Deposit the money in his office account.
   (b) Hold the check until closing takes place or a breach occurs.
   (c) Give the money to the seller upon his acceptance of the offer.
   (d) None of the above.

Chapter 12
License Law and Ethics

VOCABULARY

You will find it important to have a complete working knowledge of the following concepts and words found in this chapter:

assumed name	finder	nonresident broker
broker	license	pocket cards
business broker	license year	police powers
commission	misdemeanor	salesperson
fiduciary	net listing	temporary rent collector

ALL OF THE STATES, as well as the District of Columbia, have license laws that regulate the activities of real estate practitioners. In New York, most of these regulatory laws are found under Article 12A of the Real Property Law or consist of case law decisions interpreting portions of the Real Property Law. The purpose of the statute, which has been held to be a valid exercise of the state's police powers, is to protect the public against two types of problems:

☐ Dishonest practices of unscrupulous brokers and salespersons.
☐ Costly mistakes of incompetent real estate agents.

The enforcement of the law by the Department of State attempts to reduce fraudulent practices and to promote higher standards of efficiency and trustworthiness. By specifying licensing procedures, Article 12A controls the entry of brokers and salespersons into the real estate business. This chapter examines the obligations and restrictions that Article 12A imposes on the activities of real estate practitioners and discusses certain general principles of brokerage law.

The pamphlet entitled "Real Estate Salespersons' License Law" published by the Division of Licensing Services of the New York State Department of State and which contains copies of certain relevant provisions of Article 12A (administrative regulations promulgated by the Department of State, case law citations, and opinions of the Attorney General's office), is reprinted in Appendix B.

Although this chapter contains highlights of the material published in the pamphlet, students are encouraged to further review the subject of license law and ethics by reading the pamphlet contained in the appendix. p. 261

Definitions

A *real estate broker* may be generally defined as a person, firm, or corporation who, acting for another and for a valuable consideration, buys, sells, leases, or exchanges real estate; or who collects or attempts to collect rent for the use of real estate; or who negotiates or attempts to negotiate loans that will be secured by real estate. The definition also includes a person who performs any of the above stated functions with respect to the resale of most condominium property.

A *real estate salesperson* is one acting under the employment and direction of a broker to perform any of the aforementioned activities that the broker may perform with respect to real estate.

Though rarely used today, the term *finder* should be briefly defined. A finder is one who merely brings

together two or more persons for the consummation of a transaction. A finder is distinguished from a
broker in that the former merely introduces the
parties and has no further role in the transaction,
whereas a broker continues to be involved and
negotiates the agreement between the parties.
Courts are reluctant to award finder's fees unless the
limited role of the finder is specifically agreed to by
the parties at the time of his employment. With
respect to transactions that involve real estate, the
finder must be duly licensed in order to be entitled
to a commission.

Eligibility for License

All real estate brokers and salespersons must be
licensed before they can act or hold themselves out
as such. The mere filing of an application for a license does not authorize the applicant to engage in
the brokerage business.

QUALIFICATIONS FOR INDIVIDUALS

A person may obtain a *broker's license* provided
that he is over 19 years of age and is a citizen of the
United States or is an alien lawfully admitted for permanent residence in the United States.

To be licensed as a *real estate salesperson*, the
applicant must be 18 years of age or older. The license law sets forth no citizenship requirement for
a salesperson.

No one shall be entitled to a license as a broker
or salesperson who has been convicted of a felony
and who has not, subsequent to such conviction,
received an executive pardon or a certificate of
good conduct from the parole board in order to remove the disability.

A license may also be granted to a person operating under an assumed name if the licensing authorities are convinced that the applicant has
changed his name or is operating under the assumed name in good faith and for an honest purpose.

QUALIFICATIONS FOR ENTITIES
OTHER THAN INDIVIDUALS

A person may obtain a broker's license either as
an individual, an officer of a corporation, or a member of a partnership. If the licensee is a corporation,
the license issued to it shall entitle the president or
other designated officer to act as a broker in behalf

of the corporation. Additional licenses are required
for other officers desiring to serve as real estate
brokers in behalf of the corporation. A broker's license issued to an officer of a corporation does not
authorize him to act as a broker in his individual
capacity. If in such capacity he earns any commissions as a broker, they may be collected by the corporation.

Rules for Corporations

There is a full set of rules applicable to corporations that act as real estate brokers:

☐ All corporate officers who participate directly or
   indirectly in brokerage negotiations must be licensed as brokers.
☐ A corporate officer may not be licensed as a real
   estate salesperson in the employ of the corporation of which he is an officer.
☐ An employee who is not a corporate officer may
   be licensed only as a salesperson and not as a
   broker.

When a corporation wants to be licensed as a
real estate broker, it must first check with the Division of Licensing Services and with the Division of
Corporations and State Records (both are divisions
of the Department of State in Albany, New York) to
be sure its name is satisfactory and is not already
being used by some other corporate entity. A corporation would be unwise to incur expenses in
connection with the proposed name until it has received clearances from both divisions.

Rules for Partnerships

If the licensee is a co-partnership, the broker's license that it receives entitles one of the members
to act as a real estate broker. Each additional member of the firm who desires to act as a real estate
broker must obtain an additional license. The rules
for licensed partnerships follow:

☐ The partners who desire to act as real estate brokers must be so licensed.
☐ No salesperson license shall be issued to any of
   the partners.
☐ Employees of the firm who are not partners may
   be licensed only as salespersons.

APPLICATION FOR LICENSE

Applicants for the broker's or salesperson's license must file with the Department of State an application for the kind of license required in the

form prescribed by the Secretary of State of New York. The license application for salespersons is shown in Figure 12-1.

Educational Requirement

Effective November 1, 1979, additional educational requirements were established for new applicants for both the broker's and the salesperson's license.

These educational standards require that an applicant for a broker's license submit proof that he has attended and successfully completed 90 hours of courses approved by the office of the Secretary of State as to method, content, and supervision. Broker's license candidates who have successfully completed a 45-hour salesperson's course need only complete an additional 45-hour broker's course.

An applicant for a salesperson's license must complete the 45-hour salesperson's course mentioned above. But while an applicant for a broker's license must complete the educational requirement before applying for a license, the applicant for the salesperson's license need not have taken a course before taking the salesperson's examination to earn the license. The applicant for the salesperson's license is allowed one year subsequent to the issuance of the salesperson's license before he must submit proof that he has complied with the salesperson's educational requirements. If proof of such attendance is not timely submitted to the department, the license shall automatically terminate. Proof of such attendance may be submitted at any time within one year after the termination of the conditional license or the granting of an extension of such license. Upon acceptance of such proof, the license shall be restored, if not previously extended and made unconditional for the balance of the license period. However, since the educational requirement is a specially designed 45-hour course that helps the license candidate prepare for the official examinations, it is likely that most candidates will complete the course before sitting for the examination.

Continuing Education Requirement

Brokers who have held their broker's license for less than 15 years and all salespersons who wish to renew their licenses must complete a continuing education course every four years. At the license renewal date of November 1, 1983, and every four years thereafter, licensees seeking a renewal must submit proof of satisfactory attendance and successful completion of an approved real estate course during the preceding four years. If such proof is not submitted in a timely manner due to no fault of the licensee, the Department of State may, at its discretion, issue a temporary renewal license for such period of time as it deems necessary in order to permit the submission of the required proof of attendance.

Written Examination

The applicant for a salesperson's license must pass a written examination that shall satisfy the Department of State as to character and general intelligence.

The applicant for a broker's license must pass a written examination designed to determine the trustworthiness and competency of the prospective licensee. The department requires proof that the applicant has a fair knowledge of the English language, a fair understanding of the general purposes and general legal effect of deeds, mortgages, land contracts, and leases, a general and fair understanding of the obligations between principal and agent, and is familiar with the provisions of Article 12A of the Real Property Law.

A person who does not apply for renewal of either a broker's or salesperson's license within two years from expiration of a previously issued license must qualify by again passing a written examination.

Experience

There are no experience requirements for applicants for salesperson's licenses.

As a prerequisite for a brokerage license, the applicant must have actively participated in the general real estate brokerage business as a licensed real estate salesperson under the supervision of a licensed real estate broker for a period of not less than one year. Alternatively, the applicant may have had the equivalent experience in general real estate business for a period of at least two years. The required one-year participation in the brokerage business as a licensed real estate salesperson shall consist of active service under a broker's supervision for at least 35 hours per week for 50 weeks in each year required for qualification under the law.

STATE OF NEW YORK
DEPARTMENT OF STATE

DIVISION OF LICENSING SERVICES
162 WASHINGTON AVENUE
ALBANY, NY 12231

APPLICATION FOR LICENSE AS REAL ESTATE SALESPERSON   411201-554(3/83)

1. APPLICANT'S NAME

LAST NAME — FIRST NAME — MIDDLE INITIAL

2. HOME ADDRESS

NUMBER AND STREET

CITY

STATE   *ZIP CODE*   *COUNTY*

3. BROKER OR FIRM NAME
(exactly as it appears on Broker License)

CONTINUE ON NEXT LINE IF NECESSARY

4. BROKER OR FIRM PRINCIPAL OFFICE ADDRESS
(exactly as it appears on Brokers License)

NUMBER AND STREET — CONTINUE ON NEXT LINE IF NECESSARY

CITY

STATE   *ZIP CODE*   *COUNTY*

5. OFFICE ADDRESS AT WHICH APPLICANT WILL BE PERMANENTLY STATIONED

NUMBER AND STREET — CONTINUE ON NEXT LINE IF NECESSARY

(IF DIFFERENT FROM QUESTION 4)

CITY

STATE   *ZIP CODE*   *COUNTY*

6. DATE OF BIRTH OF APPLICANT

MONTH   DAY   YEAR

7. ALL NEW APPLICANTS MUST PASS A WRITTEN EXAMINATION.
Examinations are held weekly, except in Plattsburgh and Watertown, where they are held every other month. Please circle the city in which you wish to take your examination. You will be notified by mail of the date, time and location of the examination.

ALBANY   BINGHAMTON   BUFFALO   HAUPPAUGE   MINEOLA   NEWBURGH   NEW YORK CITY
PLATTSBURGH   ROCHESTER   SYRACUSE   UTICA   WATERTOWN   YONKERS

■ If a temporary rent collector's permit is required, please submit a written request.

PARTNERSHIP OR CORPORATION ONLY:
8.   Are you a member of the partnership or an officer of the corporation?   ☐ YES   ☐ NO
9.   If you are to be associated with a corporation, do you own any voting stock in the corporation?   ☐ YES   ☐ NO

FIG. 12-1(a)   Application for license as real estate salesperson.

IF YOU ARE ALREADY LICENSED:

10. Do you intend to represent any real estate broker(s) other than the one you named in Question 3? ☐ YES ☐ NO
    ▶ If YES, you must submit written acknowledgement by each broker/agency that the broker/agency is aware of your intention.

ALL APPLICANTS:

11. Has a real estate broker's or salesperson's license ever been issued to you by this State? ☐ YES ☐ NO
    ▶ If YES, in what year? _____

NOTICE: A claim of licensure prior to November 1, 1979 may form the basis for waiver of prelicensing school requirements, providing you are able to furnish proof. Please attach a copy of your expired license, pocket card, or other proof to substantiate your claim.

12. Have you previously filed an application for a real estate broker's or salesperson's license in this State? ☐ YES ☐ NO
    If YES, in what year? _____

13. Has a real estate broker's or salesperson's license issued to you ever been denied, suspended, or revoked by this State or any other governmental jurisdiction? ☐ YES ☐ NO

14. Are there presently charges pending against you brought or filed by any department, bureau, board, prosecuting officer, criminal court or any other governmental or regulatory body of this State or elsewhere? ☐ YES ☐ NO
    ▶ If YES, provide full details.

15. Have you ever been convicted of any crime or offense, other than minor traffic violations? If YES, submit a certified copy of each conviction. ☐ YES ☐ NO

16. In what occupation(s) and/or business(es) have you engaged during the two years previous to this application? State names of employers (if self, so state), addresses and dates of employment. Attach additional sheets if necessary.

. . . .

. . . .

■ I remit check or money order, payable to DEPARTMENT OF STATE, in the amount of $ ☐☐☐
    The fee is $20 for the term beginning November 1, of an odd numbered year and ending October 31, of an odd numbered year. For licenses effective after November 1, of an even numbered year, the fee is $10. **FEE IS NONREFUNDABLE.**
    Check the schedule below for the correct amount:

	Jan.	Feb.	Mar.	Apr.	May	June	July	Aug.	Sept.	Oct.	Nov.	Dec.
Odd number year	$10	$10	$10	$10	$10	$10	$10	$10	$10	**$10**	$20	$20
Even number year	$20	$20	$20	$20	$20	$20	$20	$20	$20	**$20**	$10	$10

■ I subscribe and affirm, under the penalties of perjury, that the statements made in this application (including statements made in any accompanying papers) have been examined by me and to the best of my knowledge and belief are true and correct.
    I have completed an approved course of study in Real Estate and the original school certificate is attached.
    I understand that if I have not completed an approved course, my license when issued will be a conditional one and will be voided one year from the effective date, unless I complete an approved course and send the original school certificate to the Albany office.

SIGNATURE OF APPLICANT ▶ . . . . DATE . . . .

EMPLOYER'S STATEMENT:

I hereby request that the application of the individual who signed above for a license as a Real Estate Salesperson be favorably acted upon. The applicant intends to be associated with my agency, and I believe that he/she is honest, truthful and trustworthy, and is competent to transact business as a Real Estate Salesperson. And I hereby express my willingness to stand responsible for the acts of the applicant in relation to his/her work as Real Estate Salesperson during the time the salesperson's license is in effect. I understand that if the applicant herein does not provide proof to the Department of State of successful completion of an approved course of study within one year from the issuance of the license, that such will be cancelled, and I agree to return same to the department when requested to do so. I hereby make the same representations in the event a temporary rent collector's permit is requested in this application and the same is issued to the applicant.

BROKER NAME ☐☐☐☐☐☐☐☐☐☐☐☐☐☐☐☐☐☐☐☐☐☐☐☐
(exactly as it appears Please Print Last Name — First Name — Middle Initial
on Brokers License)

SIGNATURE ▶ . . . .

FOR (NAME OF FIRM) . . . .

NOTICE TO APPLICANT:

The information given on your application is subject to verification and investigation. In order to prevent any unnecessary return of your application, and to help us to avoid unwarranted field travel for investigation, we request your cooperation by providing us with information that will help us to contact you by telephone, if needed.

Business _____   Residence _____   Alternate _____
Area Code   Number   Area Code   Number   Area Code   Number

FIG. 12-1(b)

The equivalent two-year experience must be similar to that of a salesperson working for a broker. For example, an employee of a construction firm who sells or rents the homes that the company erects, or an individual entrepreneur involved in the extensive purchase, sale, or leasing of his own investment properties may be considered to have equivalent experience.

Supervision of Salesperson

A licensed real estate broker must supervise the salesperson in his service. Supervision involves consistent personal guidance by the broker concerning the broker's general real estate brokerage business. The broker and salesperson must retain written records of the following transactions:

☐ All listings obtained by the salesperson.
☐ All sales made by the salesperson.
☐ All other transactions in which the salesperson participated.

The records must be maintained for the period of the salesperson's employment. They must include sufficient detail to identify the transactions and the dates thereof. These records must be submitted to the Department of State with the salesperson's application for a broker's license.

Temporary Rent Collectors Permit

An applicant for a real estate salesperson's license who has not yet received that license, may, upon express request, be issued a permit authorizing that applicant to act as a rent collector for a period not exceeding 90 days.

If the applicant's employment terminates before the permit expires, the broker must return the permit to the Department of State.

RETENTION OF SALESPERSON'S LICENSE

Although a salesperson's license is issued in the name of the salesperson, it is delivered by the Secretary of State to the broker employing the salesperson. The license must remain with the broker so long as the salesperson remains in his employ.

In order that licensees may identify themselves as licensed salespersons, the Department of State issues to each licensee a pocket card that he must show to any person whom he approaches in the course of business and who requests it.

EXEMPTIONS FROM LICENSING REQUIREMENTS

Certain individuals may engage in the sale of real estate interests in New York State without complying with the requirements of Article 12A. The list of such persons includes the following:

☐ Individuals selling or offering real estate for themselves.
☐ Attorneys at law duly admitted to practice in the courts of New York. However, should such an attorney employ a salesperson or salespersons or should he elect to obtain a broker's license, he subjects himself to all of the licensing provisions of Article 12A except the continuing-education requirements for license renewal.
☐ Receivers, referees, administrators, executors, guardians, or other persons appointed by or acting under the judgment or order of any court.
☐ Public officers, while performing their official duties.
☐ Business brokers who negotiate the sale of business establishments may sell the real estate that is part of the total business being transferred.
☐ A superintendent or janitor may, in addition to his regular duties, show space and collect rents from his employer's tenants.
☐ A person employed by an owner of real property on a salary basis exclusively to perform with respect to his property any of the activities of a broker or salesperson.

LICENSE PERIOD AND FEES

A broker's or a salesperson's license is valid for a term beginning November 1 of odd-numbered years and ending October 31 two years thereafter. Applicants earning their licenses in the middle of one of these two-year periods therefore receive initial licenses that are valid only until the end of the official license period.

The current fee for a license issued or being reissued to a real estate broker is $100 per license period (not per annum). The fee for a salesperson's license is $20 per license period. If either license is issued for a year or less, the fee is $50 for the broker's license and $10 for the salesperson's license.

Display of License

The broker's license must be conspicuously displayed in his principal place of business at all times.

The broker can obtain supplemental licenses for each branch office that he maintains upon payment of the full fee. Those licenses must be similarly displayed.

As indicated earlier, the salesperson's license is held by the broker. The salesperson can identify himself only by his pocket card.

COMMISSIONS (FEES)

As a prerequisite for claiming a commission, a broker must establish that he was duly licensed when he performed the services. A broker is not entitled to a commission on a transaction that was negotiated after his license expired and before a renewal license was issued. The commission is usually paid to the broker by his client (principal), the seller. However, a broker may be employed by either party and may, in fact, receive compensation from more than one party, as long as all the parties to the transaction have full knowledge and give their consent.

A real estate salesperson may receive compensation for services rendered only from a duly licensed broker who is his regular employer. He is prohibited from seeking a commission from his broker's customer. At the closing of title, when the broker's commission is *customarily* paid, the commission check must be made payable to the broker and not the salesperson. A real estate broker may not split his commission with any person for any service rendered unless that person is a duly licensed broker or salesperson.

Kickbacks

Payments made for referrals of clients, customers, or business are known as kickbacks.

The distinction between a kickback and a commission or fee is that the person who is being referred or whose business is being transferred is unaware of the payment.

The essential immorality of a kickback is that a referral or transfer of business may be made for reasons not in the client's best interest. In some but not all cases, kickbacks are illegal. In all instances they should be avoided as constituting unethical practice.

When the Commission Is Earned

To be entitled to a commission, as a matter of law, a real estate broker must do more than merely introduce the parties to one another or bring the property to the attention of the purchaser. The broker must obtain for the paying seller a prospect who is ready, willing, and able to proceed with the transaction on the terms set forth by the seller. The law also requires that the broker must have negotiated a meeting of the minds of the parties.

Sometimes an owner authorizes a number of different brokers to perform the same service. For example, he may instruct each to attempt to sell the same building. Unless otherwise provided in the listing agreement, only the broker whose services are the procuring cause of the sales transaction is entitled to compensation.

The broker must bring about a meeting of the minds between the buyer and seller not only as to price but as to certain other basic terms of the transaction. The terms about which the parties should agree include at least the following:

- [ ] Price of the property.   *PADRA*
- [ ] Amount of cash down payment.
- [ ] Duration of mortgage loan.
- [ ] Rate of interest.
- [ ] Amortization schedule (schedule of payment for loan principal).

Even though a broker is usually deemed by law to have earned his commission prior to closing, he may agree to waive the payment of commissions in the event the sale of the premises is not consummated. He may agree to do so in what is sometimes known as an *if, as and when* clause. An agreement with such a clause is also known as a *preclusive agreement*, because it precludes the broker from asserting a commission claim prior to completion of the title closing. To be effective between the parties, the agreement must be in writing. Even if the broker chooses to sign a preclusive agreement, he should require that it provide that a *willful default* by the seller (refusal to sell after the seller has signed the sales contract) will not deprive the broker of his commission, unless otherwise specifically provided. A broker must be aware that in signing such an agreement, he relinquishes certain rights to collect his commission.

The New York Department of State prohibits a compensation agreement between the seller and the broker that results in a *net listing*. In a net listing agreement, the seller agrees to pay the broker as a commission the amount of money by which the sales price exceeds some fixed sum. For example, an agreement that the seller will pay the broker all of the sales price in excess of $100,000 would be prohibited under the rules promulgated by the office of the Secretary of State. Under such a listing, the broker would be tempted to work for himself rather than his customer in obtaining a higher sales price, thereby breaching his duty of loyalty.

Broker's Lien for Services Rendered

[handwritten margin note: This means agreement must be in writing so it is enforceable]

A real estate broker is authorized to file a notice of lien for services rendered in connection with a leasehold transaction in which the lease exceeds three years and all or a portion of the leasehold premises are to be used for other than residential purposes.

The notice of lien may be filed only after the performance of brokerage services and the execution of the lease by both the lessor and lessee and provided that a copy of the alleged brokerage agreement is attached to the notice of lien.

Affidavit of Entitlement

A broker who asserts that he has procured a person ready, willing, and able to purchase or lease all or part of a parcel of real property may file an affidavit of entitlement for the commission in the recording office of any county in which the real property is located.

Such an affidavit shall include the following items:

☐ The name and license number of the broker claiming the commission.
☐ The name of the seller or person responsible for the commission.
☐ The name of the person authorizing the sale on behalf of the seller, if any, and the date of such authorization.
☐ A copy of the written agreement, if any.
☐ A description of the real property.
☐ The amount of commission claimed.
☐ A description of the brokerage services performed.
☐ The dates thereof.

The statute authorizing such filing provides that the recording of such an affidavit shall not invalidate the transfer or lease of real property affected by the filing, nor shall the notice constitute a lien on the real property. It appears that the filing of such an affidavit of entitlement would be of limited practical value to a broker.

The aforementioned material relating to a broker's lien and Affidavit of Entitlement is also considered in Chapter 3.

SANCTIONS AND PENALTIES FOR VIOLATING ARTICLE 12A

The Department of State may suspend the license of a broker or salesperson subject to a hearing. Subsequent to such a hearing, the department may impose any of the following penalties if the hearing concludes that the licensee has violated provisions of Article 12A.

☐ It may revoke the license of a broker or salesperson.
☐ It may suspend the license of a broker or salesperson.
☐ It may impose a fine not exceeding $1,000.
☐ It may issue a censure for the following offenses:
Any violation of Article 12A.
A material misstatement in the application for a license.
Conviction for fraud or dishonest or misleading advertisements.
Untrustworthiness or incompetency.

If the Department of State suspends a broker's license, it also automatically suspends the license of every real estate salesperson who was employed by that broker. Such a salesperson's license will be reinstated when the salesperson establishes a relationship with a new broker.

Before imposing any of these penalties, the Department of State must first have provided the licensee with at least ten days' prior written notice of a date for a hearing of the charges so that the party being charged, or his counsel, has the opportunity to be heard. The actions of the Department of State in imposing such penalties are subject to judicial review.

In addition to being subject to these penalties, a violation of any provision of Article 12A is also a misdemeanor that may be prosecuted by the attorney general's office. A misdemeanor is a crime punishable by a fine of not more than $1,000 or imprisonment for a term not exceeding one year or by both the fine and imprisonment.

The offender may also be civilly liable to an aggrieved party for a penalty of not less than the sum of money received by him as profit and not more than four times the sum so received.

Whenever the license of a real estate broker or salesperson is revoked by the Department of State, that individual becomes ineligible for relicensing for a period of one year from the date of revocation.

FIDUCIARY RELATIONSHIP BETWEEN THE BROKER AND SELLER

The broker is generally deemed to be the seller's agent. Consequently, the principles of agency law charge the broker with certain responsibilities in his business dealings with the seller. Not only is the broker bound to act in good faith but also with reasonable diligence and with the skill that is usually possessed by persons of ordinary capacity acting in the same business.

Many of the rules and regulations promulgated by the Department of State define and clarify this *good faith* obligation that the broker has towards his client. In the typical real estate transaction, the seller expects the broker to negotiate and obtain the highest possible price for the premises being sold. Accordingly, a broker's failure to disclose to all parties that the broker has a personal interest in the transaction would subject the broker to the penalties and disciplinary provisions under Article 12A (see also Sections 175.4, 175.5, 175.6 of Department of State Rules and Regulations). Examples of flagrant breaches of a broker's obligation to disclose a personal involvement would be the purchase of property by the broker in his wife's maiden name or the purchase of a property by a corporation in which the broker was a substantial stockholder.

As previously indicated, the good faith obligation does not prevent a broker from collecting commissions from more than one party, provided he obtains the consent of all parties and all parties have a full knowledge of the facts (see Section 175.7 of Department of State Rules and Regulations). If, however, the broker, without the knowledge and consent of the seller, receives additional compensation from the purchaser (whether that compensation is paid as a bribe or otherwise), the seller may recover from the broker not only the commission that the seller paid the broker but also the money that the purchaser paid the broker. The seller is entitled to the latter sum on the theory that the purchaser was willing to pay a higher price for the property equal to the amount of the monies he paid to the broker.

A broker is prohibited from commingling the money or property of the principal with his own money or assets. The broker must maintain a special account, in a federally insured bank, to be used exclusively for the deposit of such funds. Interest earned from such funds must be credited to the benefit of the depositor (Section 175.1 of Department of State Rules and Regulations).

The fiduciary duty that both the broker and the salesperson have toward their client does not permit them to draw legal documents or to otherwise act as attorney in the client's behalf. If either attempts to do so he may be subject to criminal penalties.

OTHER LICENSING REQUIREMENTS

Broker's Responsibility for Acts of the Salesperson

Violation of Article 12A by a real estate salesperson or other employee of a broker shall not be cause for the revocation or suspension of the broker's license unless it can be established that the broker knew of the violation and retained the benefits of a wrongfully negotiated transaction. A broker is guilty of a misdemeanor if he employs a salesperson who is not licensed.

Change of Salesperson's Employment

If a salesperson decides to change employers, the old employing broker returns the license to the salesperson. At the same time the broker sends in a Termination of Employment form (R113-403) to the Department of State (no fee required). The salesperson gives his license to the new employing broker who sends the Department of State a Salesperson Change of Employer form (R113-404), with a $1 fee.

Once the new broker has submitted this form and fee, the salesperson changes his own license by crossing out the old broker's name, number, and address and substituting the name, number, and address of the new employing broker. The salesperson makes similar changes on his pocket card. He gives the new employing broker the license and retains the pocket card.

Change of Address

Before a broker can move his principal or branch office, he must secure the approval of the Department of State. He must remit to the department a Broker Change of Address form (R113-401) and Salesperson Change of Address form (R113-402), accompanying each with the required $1.00 fee. Then, the broker must cross out the old address and write the new address on his own license as well as those of all his salespersons. Appropriate changes must also be made on the pocket cards of all the salespersons.

Death of the Broker

A license issued to an individual broker may be used after the death of such licensee by a duly appointed administrator or executor of the estate for not more than 120 days after the broker's death in order to complete unfinished transactions in the process of negotiation by the broker prior to his death. In order to have this privilege, the executor must have the authorization of the surrogate court. The 120-day period may be extended for cause. Without this provision it is doubtful as to whether the executor or administrator could complete pending negotiations without the consent of the broker's principals.

Licenses for Nonresidents

A nonresident real estate broker is (within the meaning of the statute) one who lives in another state and does not maintain an office in the State of New York. A nonresident broker regularly engaged in the real estate business as a vocation and who maintains a definite place of business in his state shall not be required to maintain a place of business in New York State provided that his state offers the same privilege to the licensed brokers and salespersons of New York. However, the nonresident broker must file a duly executed irrevocable consent that permits the service of legal process upon the Secretary of State of New York with the same force and effect as if served upon the broker personally. This guarantees the presence of a party who may be served in a legal proceeding against a nonresident broker.

Nonresident brokers may be licensed to conduct business in this state and obtain a New York license just like resident brokers. A nonresident broker must pass the New York licensing examination of this state unless there is a reciprocal agreement between his state and New York. Such agreements usually provide that each state will issue licenses to license holders in the other state without an examination requirement.

Apartment Information Vendors

Pursuant to Article 12C of the Real Property Law, apartment referral agents have been designated *apartment information vendors* and, as such, must be licensed by the Office of the Secretary of State. Apartment information vendors are persons who for a fee furnish information concerning the location and availability of real property, including apartment housing which may be leased, shared, or sublet, generally for purposes of a private dwelling. The definition of apartment information vendors also includes *apartment sharing agents*, who for a fee cause a meeting between customers and the current owners or occupants of legally occupied real property for the purpose of sharing that housing with one or more individuals as a private dwelling. Persons responsible for the relocation of commercial and residential tenants from buildings being demolished, rehabilitated, or structurally altered are excluded from the statute.

Applicants for apartment information vendor licenses must be 18 years or older, and must have established to the satisfaction of the Department of State that they are trustworthy and bear a reputation for good and fair dealings.

A license application fee of $250 must be submitted to the department (the operation of branch offices requires the issuance of supplemental licenses). All licenses are effective for a period of one year beginning November 1 and ending October 31 one year later. As a precondition to the issuance of licenses, applicants must establish and maintain an interest-bearing trust account in the minimum amount of $5,000, plus $2,500 for each additional branch office then in operation. Applicants whose business is limited to apartment sharing shall be required to maintain an account of only $2,500, plus $1,200 for each additional licensed office.

Every licensed apartment information vendor must furnish to customers a contract setting forth services to be performed on a form approved by the Secretary of State. Payments to the vendor of advance fees except as set forth below are prohibited. In no event shall the advance fee charged to the customer or legal occupant exceed one month's rent. The vendor shall be entitled to his fee where a customer has leased a privated dwelling or place of residence through the information provided by the vendor. The customer shall be entitled to a refund of the advance fee within ten days of written notification to the apartment information vendor that the customer has not secured a private dwelling or place of abode through information supplied by the vendor. The statue provides that an apartment information vendor may retain a maximum of $15 out of any advance fee for administrative services, with the balance of such fee being placed in an escrow account (not necessarily interest bearing) pending redelivery to the customer.

However, where the service rendered are those of an apartment sharing agent, the full advance fee may be retained regardless of whether the customer leases or rents the private dwelling through the information provided by the vendor.

Each apartment information vendor shall file a quarterly report with the Secretary of State containing such information as may be required.

A license issued under the statute shall be conspicuously displayed at all times at the place of business for which it was granted. The Secretary of State may revoke or suspend a license, impose a fine not to exceed $5,000, order refunds to aggrieved parties, and issue reprimands upon a finding that a licensee has violated any of the provisions of this article, made material misstatements in the application for such license, engaged in fraudulent practices or misleading advertisements, or has demonstrated untrustworthiness or incompetency to act as an apartment information vendor.

The licensee who is accused of wrongdoing is entitled to a hearing before the Secretary of State subject to the licensee receiving 10 days prior written notice of the nature of the charges against him as well as notice of the time and place set for the hearing. The determination made by the Secretary is subject to further judicial review.

A violation of this law constitutes a misdemeanor and may also subject the licensee to additional civil fines and penalties.

REVIEW QUESTIONS

1. A broker commission is usually determined by

   (a) Statutory law.
   (b) The local realty board.
   (c) Agreement between the broker and his client.
   (d) None of the above.

2. Upon conviction of a violation of Article 12A by a broker, the Department of State may

   (a) Revoke his license.
   (b) Suspend his license.
   (c) Censure the broker.
   (d) Any of the above.

3. A violation of Article 12A constitutes a crime known as a

   (a) Felony.
   (b) Misdemeanor.
   (c) Either of the above.
   (d) Both of the above.

4. A broker's license fee is payable

   (a) Once a year.
   (b) Twice a year.
   (c) Once every two years.
   (d) None of the above.

5. An employee of a corporation may be licensed

   (a) Only as a broker.
   (b) Only as a salesperson.
   (c) As either of the above.
   (d) As neither of the above.

6. For a broker to be entitled to a commission he must

   (a) Be licensed.
   (b) Have applied for a license.
   (c) Neither of the above.
   (d) Have consummated at least three prior closings.

7. A salesperson may collect his commission from

   (a) The seller.
   (b) The purchaser.
   (c) His broker.
   (d) None of the above.

8. A broker may agree to waive the receipt of his commission until the closing of title by an agreement known as

   (a) An option.
   (b) A preclusive agreement.
   (c) Neither of the above.
   (d) Both of the above.

9. The fiduciary relationship between the broker and his client prevents the broker from

   (a) Collecting a commission.
   (b) Self-dealing with his client's property.
   (c) Both of the above.
   (d) Neither of the above.

10. A broker may be paid a commission by

    (a) The seller.
    (b) The realty board.

(c) Either of the above.
(d) Neither of the above.

11. For a violation of a provision of Article 12A, a broker may

  (a) Have his license revoked.
  (b) Be fined up to $2,000.
  (c) Both a and b.
  (d) Neither a nor b.

12. Prior to applying for his broker's license, a salesperson must first have the following work experience with a broker:

  (a) One year.
  (b) Two years.
  (c) Three years.
  (d) None of the above.

13. The fee for a salesperson's license is

  (a) $10 per annum.
  (b) $20 per license term.
  (c) $5 per license term.
  (d) $25 per license term.

14. A broker may split his commission with

  (a) Another broker.
  (b) An unlicensed salesperson.
  (c) Both of the above.
  (d) Neither of the above.

15. A broker basically serves in a fiduciary capacity to

  (a) The seller.
  (b) The attorney.
  (c) The buyer.
  (d) None of the above.

16. Pocket cards are issued by the Secretary of State to

  (a) All brokers.
  (b) All salespersons.
  (c) Both of the above.
  (d) Neither of the above.

17. The statute in New York which regulates the activities of real estate brokers and salespersons is

  (a) Article 12A of the Real Property Law.
  (b) Article 3B of the Real Property Law.
  (c) Article 3A of the Real Property Law.
  (d) Both b and c.

18. A broker may be licensed as such if he is

  (a) 18 years or older.
  (b) 20 years old or older.
  (c) Age 21 or older.
  (d) Age 19 or older.

19. If a broker's license is revoked, he may apply for a new license

  (a) Immediately.
  (b) One year after revocation.
  (c) Two years after the revocation.
  (d) Five years after the revocation.

20. A broker's license may be issued to an individual under an assumed name

  (a) If he pays a special charge.
  (b) If the Secretary of State is satisfied as to the reason for the use of such name.
  (c) To conceal his identity from potential creditors.
  (d) None of the above.

Chapter 13
Real Estate Appraisal

ONE OF the most challenging aspects of the real estate business is the determination of price, or the value of the rights to real estate. With a relatively disorganized market and virtually no standardization of the commodity, it is difficult to estimate the exchange or market value of a property. In other types of markets, such as the stock market, the price of the commodities exchanged can be more easily determined. In real estate, buyers and sellers need guidance from experts before deciding on listing prices or preparing offers. Many other real estate professionals involved in the real estate decision making process also need such advice when making transactions.

Appraising is a specialty in the real estate business that requires professional qualifications. While real estate brokers and salespersons are constantly involved in making decisions regarding value, they usually do not perform on the same level as a professional appraiser. A typical broker or salesperson may use experience to estimate a probable sales price. The appraiser undertakes a full appraisal process that involves much more than estimating the sales price of the property.

REASONS FOR APPRAISALS

All real estate transactions involve determining the value of the land and any improvements which may be on it. The need for appraisals can typically be found in the different types of transactions that occur involving real property.

Appraisals may be required for any of the following reasons:

☐ To arrive at the value of the security that the property offers the mortgage lender.
☐ To provide a sound basis for the borrower's real estate decisions.
☐ To establish a basis for insuring the valued property.
☐ To aid prospective buyers in determining an offering price.
☐ To aid prospective sellers in determining a selling price.
☐ To establish the value of property being exchanged or merged through some form of reorganization.
☐ To establish just compensation in condemnation proceedings in order to
  Estimate the value before the act of condemnation.
  Estimate the value after the act of condemnation.
☐ To establish a basis for taxation in order to
  Estimate applicable depreciation rates on buildings and to value nondepreciable items such as land
  Determine gift or inheritance tax values
  Determine real estate taxes.

REAL ESTATE APPRAISAL DEFINITIONS

A student should approach the study of real estate like the study of a foreign language. Unless you know the terminology or vocabulary, you cannot communicate with others in the business. Included in the appraisal field are many definitions that must be mastered before a person can have a basic understanding of the topic.

An Appraisal

Simply defined, *an appraisal* is an estimate or opinion of value. The fundamental purpose of any appraisal is to estimate the value of a particular property as it is used for a defined purpose at a particular time.

Capitalization

Capitalization is a technique for converting all the future income that one expects from an investment into its present value. The flows of future income are often called the return on the investment. The return that an investor earns on the money invested in property is usually relatively high. Because real estate investment carries higher risks than a savings account or an investment in a government bond, the real estate investor expects to receive a higher rate of return.

The *capitalization rate* is the rate of return that a reasonable investor would want on an investment; it is a percentage used to convert income flow into present value.

Assume that an investor expects a property to produce a net income of $10,000 per year. If the annual income is divided by a *cap rate* of 10 percent, one arrives at a value of $100,000 for the property ($10,000 ÷ .10 = $100,000). Had the investor chosen a cap rate of 15 percent, the property would have been valued at $66,667 ($10,000 ÷ .15). If a cap rate of 20 percent were used, the property value would be $50,000 ($10,000 ÷ .20). The higher the capitalization rate at a given level of annual income, the lower the value of the property.

In this example, if the investor believes that 10 percent is a reasonable rate of return on his investment, he would be willing to pay $100,000 for the property; if he wants a 20 percent rate of return, he would be willing to pay only $50,000 for it.

Establishing the "Cap" Rate

As you can see, the capitalization rate is one of the most important variables in the appraiser's calculations. It is also one of the most difficult. To select a cap rate intelligently, an appraiser must be aware of the returns that are offered for all of the investments that are competing for investment funds. He must take into consideration the riskiness of the investment, the probable economic life of the property, and thus its depreciation. He must consider available financing and the stability and duration of the property's income flow. All these factors involve definitions and concepts that we explore below.

Three Investment Techniques

There are at least three popular techniques that appraisers use to calculate cap rates, or return on investment rates.

In the summation (or built-up) method, the appraiser starts with a rate for a safe investment (say Treasury bonds) and adds rates for the riskiness of the property, the illiquidity of the investment, and the problems of managing such an investment, until he arrives at a sum, which is the cap rate. Thus, at this writing, he would start with a Treasury bond rate of 12.5 percent, add (say) 5 percent for the other factors, and arrive at a 17.5 percent cap rate.

An important technique that the appraiser can use is to compare the rate he wishes to use with the rates that were used in recent sales of comparable property. To do this he must have data on the sale prices of these properties and their incomes. Above all, he must make sure that the investments are truly comparable (particularly in respect to their financing).

The band of investment technique of cap rate determination relies on the fact that most real estate investments have mortgage financing. (We will consider only fixed-rate mortgages, because today's complex alternative-rate mortgages raise theoretical and mathematical problems that are beyond the scope of this chapter.) The band of investment technique weighs the return to each capital source according to its contribution and to its risk, as we show in the following simplified example:

Source of Funds	% of Funds		Return	Weighted Return
First Mortgage	50%	×	12%	6.0%
Second Mortgage	30%	×	18%	5.4%
Equity	20%	×	20%	4.0%
			Total	**15.4%**

The return demanded by a financing band increases as its risk increases. When the property in the example is valued by a cap rate of 15.4 percent, each capital source receives a "market" rate of return.

Depreciation

The simple definition of capitalization in the preceding section assumed that an investor could resell the property for $100,000. This is not necessarily true. We must therefore consider the meaning of the word *depreciation*.

Depreciation is a loss in property value for any reason. The most obvious type of depreciation is *physical depreciation*, the reduction of property value because of simple deterioration or wearing away through use.

Properties also depreciate because they become obsolete. A property with electrical wiring that cannot deliver adequate current to modern appliances is *functionally obsolete*. An office building that does not offer the amenities and modern conveniences of its competitors may depreciate because of *functional obsolescence*.

The *economic life* of a property is the period during which it will yield the investor a return on investment over and above the rent attributable to the land. If it were not for price inflation, the appraiser could readily estimate the rate at which a building is being "used up" (depreciates). There was a time when we could estimate with reasonable accuracy that the "life" of a certain type of office building was, say, fifty years. If that were true today, an investor would know that his investment would depreciate at 2 percent a year.

Appraisers must consider depreciation rate when they estimate capitalization rate. It is safe and conservative to assume that a building will depreciate at a steady rate. This is so, even though we can point to buildings that, because of price inflation, are worth more today then they were ten years ago.

Does Land Depreciate?

An appraiser assumes that land does not depreciate. For the purposes of computing taxable income the federal government does not permit an investor to assume that land depreciates. On the other hand, we know that one of the most important factors in determining land values is *location*. Neighborhoods change. Land can become functionally obsolescent. Land can both depreciate and appreciate.

Present Value and Internal Rate of Return

Earlier in this chapter we described present-value computation as a technique for converting all the future income that one expects from an investment into its present value. But then we demonstrated a present-value computation by dividing only *one year's income* by a capitalization rate. We obviously have not considered *all* future income in this computation. We have instead substituted a rule of thumb that has severe limitations. In our example, a $10,000 income was capitalized at 10 percent to a $100,000 value. Suppose that in Year 3, because a restrictive lease expires and a much better lease is expected to be negotiated, income is expected to rise to $20,000. In Year 3 the building will be worth $200,000. What is it worth today? Or let's make another assumption. Suppose we can reasonably expect income to rise 8 percent per year for each of the next 10 years. What level of income should be capitalized?

There is another problem with the rule of thumb capitalization. It assumes that the investor will sell the building for exactly the same price that he paid. If the investor puts $100,000 in a savings account at 10 percent and every year draws out $10,000 interest, at the end of 10 years he still has $100,000 in the bank. But if he buys a building and sells it in 10 years, the value of the property may have depreciated to $75,000 or it may have increased with inflation to $150,000.

Lastly, the rule of thumb computation does not consider the time value of money. You will hear many complicated explanations of the time value of money in your real estate career, but the following is an adequate introduction: Money received this year is worth more than money received next year because this year's money can always be invested safely at a reasonable rate. For example, $10,000 received in Year 1 is worth more than $10,000 in Year 2. If it is invested at 10 percent, it will be worth $11,000 in Year 2. Conversely, $10,000 received in Year 2 is worth only $9,091 in Year 1.

The major implication of including the time value of money in the present-value calculation is that the present value of an investment is affected not only by the *amount* of future cash flows but by their *timing*. The calculation of present value that considers all possible future cash returns to the investor, including the flow from the sale of property, is most complex. It usually requires the use of an electronic calculator or a computer. It is beyond the scope of this introductory chapter.

Is it better than the rule of thumb calculations? That depends on how good the investor's guestimates are about future income and reversion (income from the sale of property). Investors who paid high prices for New York City office buildings in 1981, betting that income and building values would rise as the office boom continued, were paying for an optimistic future that did not quite materialize.

Internal Rate of Return

Real estate professionals who sell major investment properties must learn the term *internal rate of return*. A simple explanation will do to start. If a sophisticated real estate investor wishes to establish the value of a property, he discounts future income flows at his capitalization rate to arrive at a net present value. If the seller is adamant about the selling price of his building, the investor knows that there is some rate at which he can discount the income flows that will result in the price the seller wants. Thus, we have the definition of internal rate of return: the rate of return that equates the present value of expected future cash flows to the initial capital invested. If the internal rate of return is equal to or higher than his cap rate, the investor will seek to buy.

Highest and Best Use

The highest and best use to which a property may be put is that which will produce the greatest net income stream or intrinsic value over a period of time. Every property has a highest and best use as of a single point in time. It is not always reasonable to calculate the value of the property based on its actual current economic income. It may not be being put to its best use, and a calculation based on its current income may undervalue it. A property in transition from one use to another cannot be valued on the basis of one use for land and another for improvements. In other words, the current value of the land plus improvements may not be the highest and best use. If the improvements are obsolete, the land alone might be worth more based on highest and best use.

THREE APPROACHES TO VALUE

The appraiser may determine the value of a property by three routes. He may use a cost approach, a market data approach, or an income approach. In the majority of assignments, an appraiser utilizes all three. On occasion, he may believe the value indication from one approach is more significant than that from the other two. Nevertheless, the appraiser uses all three as checks against each other and as tests of his judgment.

Obviously, there are some appraisal problems in which certain approaches cannot be used. A value indication for vacant land cannot be obtained through use of the cost approach. One cannot value a specialized property like a municipal garden by the market data approach, nor can one establish the value of an owner-occupied home by the income approach. Generally, however, the use of all three approaches is pertinent to most appraisals.

Cost Approach

In the cost approach, the appraiser obtains a preliminary indication of value by adding to an estimate of the land's value an estimate of the depreciated reproduction cost of the building and other improvements. This approach assumes that the reproduction cost is the upper limit of value. If the subject building is not new, the cost approach assumes that its value is less than that of a newly constructed building by an amount of accumulated depreciation. The computation of simple depreciation was discussed earlier.

The cost approach consists of five steps:

1. Estimating the site's value as if it were vacant.
2. Estimating the current cost of reproducing the existing improvements.
3. Estimating depreciation from all causes.
4. Deducting depreciation from current reproduction costs.
5. Totaling the value of the site and the depreciated reproduction cost of improvements.

In discussing the cost approach, it is essential to understand the differences between replacement cost and reproduction cost. Reproduction cost is today's cost to produce an exact replica of a property using the identical design and materials. Replacement cost is today's cost of an equally desirable property in which, possibly, some of the functional obsolescence of the original structure might be cured.

Since step two of the cost approach requires the appraiser to estimate depreciation from all causes, it is necessary to be able to calculate the depreciation. The methods that appraisers commonly use are complex. The principal techniques include the market method, the capitalization method, the straight-line method, the engineering method, and the breakdown method. Information on how calculations are made by these methods can be found in standard appraisal texts.

Market Data Approach

The market data approach is essential in almost every appraisal of the value of real property. In this approach, the appraiser searches for market value. The value estimated by this approach frequently is defined as the price at which a willing seller would sell and a willing buyer would buy, neither being under abnormal pressure. This definition assumes that both the buyer and seller are fully informed about the property and about the state of the market for that type of property, and that the property has been exposed in the open market for a reasonable time.

The market data approach produces an estimate of the value of a property by comparing it with properties of the same type and class that have recently been sold or are currently being offered for sale in competing areas. The determination of the degree of comparability between two properties involves judgments as to their similarity with respect to factors such as location, construction, age and condition, layout, and equipment. The sales prices of the properties deemed most comparable tend to set the range in which the value of the subject property will fall. Further consideration of the comparative data indicates to the appraiser a figure representing the market value of the subject property.

Market Value

The word value has many meanings. In the case of real estate, market value is what lenders, buyers, and sellers of residential property are concerned with. Other types of value include assessed value, insurable value, loan value, and condemnation value.

Since market value is utilized the most, we shall study it in detail. A basic definition for real estate market value can be found in *Real Estate Appraisal Terminology*, by Byrl N. Boyce: "The highest price in terms of money which a property will bring in a competitive and open market under all conditions requisite to a fair sale, the buyer and seller, each acting prudently, knowledgeably and assuming the price is not affected by undue stimulus."*

* Byrl N. Boyce, *Real Estate Appraisal Terminology*, Cambridge, Mass.: Ballinger Publishing Company, 1975.

According to this definition market value is the price that would be paid at a current sale if the following conditions were true:

☐ Neither the buyer nor the seller have any unusual motivation.
☐ Both parties are well informed or well advised, and each acts in what is considered his own best interest.
☐ A reasonable time is allowed for exposure in the open market.
☐ Payment is made in cash or its equivalent.
☐ Financing, if any, is on terms generally available in the community at the specified date and typical for a property of this type in its locale.
☐ The price represents a normal consideration for the properties sold, unaffected by special financing amounts or terms, services, fees, costs, or credits incurred in the transaction.

Stated in simpler form, market value is the price at which a willing seller would sell and a willing buyer would buy, both being informed and knowledgeable and neither being under duress.

It is of great importance that the words *value*, *price*, and *cost* not be used interchangeably since they are not always the same. Price and value may, for example, appear to be the same if two similar properties in the same neighborhood are compared. However, if different financing plans are used to purchase each property, the actual prices may vary greatly. Usually the only time at which cost and value are likely to be the same is when the improvements are new and the property is being used for its highest and best use. Otherwise, many factors such as the location of the property and its relation to surroundings come into play and cause value and cost to differ.

Gross Rent Multiplier

The *gross rent multiplier* (GRM) is another variable that appraisers use in arriving at an estimation of real estate value. The GRM is obtained by dividing the known sales prices of comparable properties by the rental income of these properties. The appraiser can average the GRMs of several comparable properties, and can then multiply the gross rental income of the property being appraised by this factor.

Example The following data concerning nearby properties are utilized to arrive at the GRM:

Sales Price	Gross Monthly Rent	Multiplier
$17,500	$175	100
18,900	180	105
17,750	180	99[a]
18,000	185	97[a]

[a] rounded

Given the market data above, we might conclude that properties in a certain neighborhood are selling for 100 times their gross monthly rent. If the property we are appraising rents for $182.50, the $182.50 times 100 equals $18,250, which is the estimated value using the GRM.

Income Approach

In using the income approach, the appraiser attempts to establish the present worth of the future potential benefits of a property. The potential future benefits are usually assumed to be the net income that a fully informed person is warranted in assuming the property will produce during its remaining useful life. After the reasonableness of the income assumptions is verified by comparing them with the income from investments of similar type and class, this net income is capitalized into a value estimate.

Selecting the capitalization rate is one of the most important steps in the income approach. As previously indicated, a variation of only one-half of 1 percent in cap rate can make a difference of many thousands of dollars in the capitalized value of the income. If a building that earns $50,000 a year is capitalized at 10 percent and at 10½ percent, the lower cap rate produces a value that is almost $24,000 greater than the other rate.

The work to be done in assembling and processing income data is of four kinds:

1. The appraiser must obtain the rent schedules and the percentage of occupancy for the subject property and for comparable properties for the current year and for several years in the past. This information provides gross rental data and shows trends in rentals and occupancy. These data are then related and adjusted by the market data appraisers so that the appraiser can make an estimate of the gross income that the subject property should produce.
2. The appraiser must than obtain expense data such as taxes, insurance, and operating costs that are being paid by the subject property and by

comparable properties. He must also examine trends in these expenses.
3. The appraiser must estimate the remaining useful economic life of the building to establish the probable duration of its income.
4. The appraiser must select an appropriate capitalization rate and the applicable technique and method for processing the net income into present value.

Using the Three Approaches

The cost approach is most frequently used when a lack of data prevents use of the other approaches. It is commonly used for buildings such as post offices, libraries, and schools. The income approach is always used for properties for which information such as rent rolls and expense items is readily available.

Perhaps the most commonly used approach among brokers, the market approach is employed when recent information is available on comparable properties (comps). While this concept is relatively simple to use and can provide quick answers, the analyst must use this approach carefully. It can result in substantial error if the "comps" are not carefully selected. Real estate investors and others have been prone to misjudgments in the selections of "comps."

RECONCILIATION, FINAL ESTIMATE, AND THE APPRAISAL REPORT

The final step in the appraisal process is the correlation of the three indications of value derived by the cost, income, and market data approaches. In correlating the results of these three approaches into a final estimate of value, the appraiser takes into account the purpose of the appraisal, the type of property, and the adequacy of the data processed in each of the three approaches. These considerations influence the weight to be given the estimate produced by each approach.

The appraiser does not obtain a final estimate of value by averaging the individual indications of value arrived at by means of the three approaches. Instead, he examines the spread between minimum and maximum figures of the three preliminary value estimates, and gives the greatest weight to the estimate arising from the approach that appears to be the most reliable as an indication of the answer to the specific appraisal problem. He may then modify this estimate in accordance with his judgment about the degree of reliance he can place in the other two indications of value.

The final appraisal report may be a completed standardized form, a one-page letter, or a large volume containing statistics and narrative. But all appraisals must contain the date and purpose for which the appraisal was conducted, the final value estimate derived, a description of the property, any qualifying statements affecting the property, and a certificate by the appraiser with his signature.

An appraisal report is a word portrayal of the property, the facts concerning the property, and the reasoning by which the appraiser has developed the estimate of value. The best report is the one that, in the fewest number of words, permits the reader to follow intelligently the appraiser's reasoning and to concur with his conclusions. As every report is an answer to a question from a client, it should show the facts considered and clearly outline the reasoning employed by the appraiser in arriving at an answer.

VALUATION FOR LISTING PURPOSES

While appraising is an art and not a science, because of the number and the complexity of the approaches that the appraiser uses, his appraisal is substantially more precise than the estimates that most brokers and salespersons can make when they must value a property to be sold. When a salesperson or broker is approached by a potential seller to discuss a listing agreement in connection with the sale of the sellers' residence, the salesperson or broker needs to arrive at a quick answer. He must therefore use a less formal approach than the appraiser uses.

One of the immediate questions that arises is, "How much shall we list the house for?" A realistic answer to that question usually is related to the sales prices of similar units in the neighborhood. In smaller communities, brokers and salespeople are generally fully aware of every transaction in the community. In larger communities trade associations such as local real estate boards frequently publish summaries of all sales. Multiple listing boards are also useful for this purpose. If such a service is not available in a given community, a sales-

person can obtain this information by visiting the county clerk's office and looking at recorded deeds. Much price information can be obtained from the consideration recited in the deed and the tax payment disclosed by the instrument.

The broker who maintains records of sales in his community will be able to ascertain quickly what sales of similar properties have recently occurred. With this information and a copy of the listing sheets of the sold properties, the broker can quickly compare the property that his potential client wishes to sell with other properties. The broker can base the sales price of his new client's property on the comparable sales, adjusting the current price for differences in the properties, such as additional rooms, fireplaces, porches, etc. He may make further adjustments because he discerns upward or downward market trends in the community.

Having arrived at an approximate probable sales price, the broker or salesperson should candidly discuss with the client both the price and the method by which it was estimated. At this point, it is wise to remember that most householders selling their own homes have no valid basis for determining the value of their property. They are likely to have a grossly inflated concept of its value. Many home sellers arrive at a sales price by the following reasoning. They invested a certain sum of money in the property. They believe that as the result of inflation, it should have increased by a certain multiplier. Since they would like to receive a net amount from the sale, they add closing costs and broker's commission to their net expectation and thus arrive at a proposed sales price. This method of computation usually results in a price that has no market relevance.

The listing price that is established for the house should be somewhat higher than the sales price that the salesperson or broker and their client agree upon. The listing price should leave room for some negotiation, and it should be high enough to absorb any possible miscalculation by the salesperson or broker that may have made the price too low. However, the salesperson or broker should exercise caution in figuring this cushion because an unrealistically high sales price can prevent the property from selling. The amount of cushion depends on local market conditions and practices but in most areas is usually about 5 percent.

REVIEW QUESTIONS

1. In establishing the value of real estate for the sale of residential property the method commonly used is

   (a) Income approach.
   (b) Market data (comparable) approach.
   (c) Cost approach.
   (d) Average of all of above.

2. Depreciation can be attributed to

   (a) Economic obsolescence.
   (b) Functional obsolescence.
   (c) Physical deterioration.
   (d) All of the above.

3. An investor determines that a building is worth $480,000 and the land on which it sits is worth $70,000. He purchases the property for $550,000 and depreciates his investments over a 15-year period. At the end of four years he carries the property in his books at the following value:

   (a) $403,335.
   (b) $128,000.
   (c) $352,000.
   (d) None of the above.

4. The salesperson of residences usually uses which appraisal approach when a seller wants a quick answer?

   (a) Cost.
   (b) Income.
   (c) Market.
   (d) None of the above.

5. The most accurate approach in attempting to appraise an old public library building is

   A. Market.
   B. Income.

   (a) A only.   (c) Both A and B.
   (b) B only.   (d) Neither A nor B.

6. Use the cost approach to value the following property: The building was built 20 years ago for $300,000. It depreciated at 2 percent per year. The site is now worth $50,000.

   (a) $170,000.
   (b) $180,000.
   (c) $230,000.
   (d) $350,000.

7. Real estate appraisers are paid

   (a) Based on the value determined.
   (b) On a commission basis.
   (c) On a fee basis by the broker representing the seller.
   (d) None of the above.

8. Curable types of depreciation include:

   A. Economic obsolescence.
   B. Functional obsolescence.

   (a) A only.   (c) Both A and B.
   (b) B only.   (d) Neither A nor B.

9. The process of appraising properties is deemed to be

   (a) An exact science.
   (b) An art.
   (c) Neither of the above.
   (d) Both of the above.

10. In the majority of assignments an appraiser utilizes which approach to the appraisal process:

    (a) Cost.
    (b) Market data.
    (c) Income.
    (d) All of above.

11. A woman owns a building for which she paid $103,000. She desires a 12 percent return on this investment each year. What net annual income must the building generate to meet this requirement?

    (a) $858,333.
    (b) $12,360.
    (c) $90,640.
    (d) None of the above.

12. An investor is interested in purchasing a building that has a net income of $214,000. He knows he can get a 16 percent mortgage for 20 years for 80 percent of the property value, and he wants a 20 percent return on his equity invest-

88 people

ment. Using the band of investment technique, determine the capitalization rate that he will use to value the property.

(a) 18.0 percent.
(b) 17.6 percent.
(c) 17.4 percent.
(d) 16.8 percent.

13. The time value of money is best explained by the following factors:

(a) Investors prefer to be liquid.
(b) Investors must receive money to pay current debts.
(c) Investors feel that money flows received in the distant future are more risky than money received in the near future.
(d) Money received today can be invested at a profit.

14. In appraising a special-purpose structure, the most reliable approach to valuation is the

(a) Market data approach.
(b) Cost approach.
(c) Income approach.
(d) None of the above.

15. Define internal rate of return:

(a) The capitalization rate.
(b) The return that equates future income flows to the value of the invested capital (including reversion).
(c) The return that equates future income flows (excluding reversion) to the value of invested capital.
(d) All of the above.

16. Capitalization is a process for

(a) Disbursing present income.
(b) Converting future income into present value.

(c) Both a and b.
(d) Neither a nor b.

17. The income approach could best be applied to

(a) A church.
(b) A new single-family residence.
(c) An apartment complex.
(d) Two of the above.

18. The appraisal process consists of which of the following steps?

(a) Making a preliminary survey and planning the appraisal.
(b) Defining the problem and writing the appraisal report.
(c) Applying the approaches, correlating the data, and making a final estimate of value.
(d) All of the above.

19. Which of the following would yield a 10 percent capitalization rate?

(a) Gross income of $8,000; sales price of $80,000.
(b) Net expenses of $8,000; sales price of $80,000.
(c) Net income of $8,000; sales price of $80,000.
(d) Gross expenses of $8,000; sales price of $80,000.

gross rate multiplier

20. If the established monthly GRM is 105, and a property has a gross income of $6,000 annually and monthly expenses of $200, what is the estimated market value using the GRM method?

(a) $630,000.
(b) $73,500.
(c) $882,000.
(d) $52,500.

Chapter 14
Listing Agreements

VOCABULARY

You will find it important to have a complete working knowledge of the following concepts and words found in this chapter:

agency
agent
exclusive agency listing

exclusive authorization (right)
    to sell
exclusive listing
listing contract

multiple listing
open listing
principal
subagent

THE AGENT'S (broker's) right to compensation depends on being able to prove that he had been requested and authorized to do the work for which he seeks compensation. The object of this chapter is to familiarize you with some of the basic laws regulating listing agreements and some of the specific problems and mechanics involved in the preparation of the listing contract.

The forms used here have been designed to point out certain pertinent parts of a transaction; they are not suggested as forms that you should use in the business. Forms vary from firm to firm and from community to community, and you will become familiar with the format used in your own community.

LEGAL CHARACTERISTICS OF A LISTING AGREEMENT

A listing agreement essentially is a contract of employment between a broker and a property owner whereby the owner agrees to pay the broker a commission or fee upon the successful negotiation of the sale, lease, or exchange of a specified parcel of real property.

In order to be entitled to a commission, a broker must be able to establish that

☐ He was duly licensed at the time he negotiated the specific transaction.

☐ A contract of employment (listing agreement) existed between the broker and his client.
☐ The broker fulfilled his obligation under the contract.

Although customarily referred to as an agreement, the basic elements necessary to a contract, outlined in Chapter 6, must also be present in a valid and enforceable listing agreement. These include:

☐ *Mutual assent* to the listing.
☐ *Consideration* or something of legal value being exchanged.
☐ *Proper parties* who possess the requisite legal capacity.
☐ *Legality* of purpose.

Mutual Assent

An agreement or meeting of the minds must be proven whereby the broker is to procure a prospect ready, willing, and able to consummate the transaction upon terms agreed to or ultimately deemed to be satisfactory to the seller.

Consideration

In exchange for the broker's obtaining a satisfactory prospect, the seller agrees to pay the broker an agreed-upon commission. The commission payable is either a sum previously agreed upon or an

164

amount customarily payable for such services in the area.

Proper Parties

Both the client and the broker must have the legal capacity to enter into a contractual relationship. The parties must be of full age and sound mind in order to enter into a binding contract.

Legality of Purpose

The agreement must be one which is permitted by law. An agreement which is prohibited by the rules and regulations promulgated by the office of the Secretary of State (such as a net listing agreement) may not be enforceable in a court of law.

Significance of Contractual Aspects of the Listing Agreement

The contractual implications of listing agreements are recognized by courts of law.

In one instance a broker who was unable to find a prospect willing to pay the price requested by the seller agreed to reduce his commission on an offer so that the net price received by the seller would be the same as if his asking price had been met. The court held that the seller was not obligated to convey at the reduced price nor to pay the broker any commission, since the terms of the original contract or listing agreement had not been complied with.

ORAL OR WRITTEN CONTRACT

A listing contract may be oral or written. Although the Statute of Frauds in New York State provides that a contract for a sum in excess of $500 must be in writing, real estate listing agreements are expressly exempted from that requirement. However, brokerage agreements that will take more than one year to be completely performed must be in writing.

Although it is not legally required, all listing agreements should be in writing. An oral listing agreement is enforceable, but it is much easier to prove a written contract than a verbal one. More important, a written contract gives the broker a psychological advantage because the principal knows that he has made a firm agreement about payment. To expend time and energy on a verbal listing agreement is sheer folly.

There are three kinds of listing agreements, the difference between them being when commissions are payable. These categories are opening listings, exclusive agency listings, and exclusive right to sell listings.

OPEN LISTINGS

Open listings are listing agreements in which the principal retains the broker, as his agent, to sell the property. The seller (principal) makes no representations that the agent will be the only agent retained or authorized to do the work, and the seller promises to compensate the agent only if the sale comes about because of this particular agent having procured the ready, willing, and able purchaser. Should the principal find a purchaser independently of this agent's efforts, the purchaser will pay the agent no commission.

This type of listing, at first impression, would seem to be very desirable for a seller, because the seller may add additional agents and apparently multiply the sales effort without assuming liability for duplicated commissions. Additionally, he may sell the property himself and not have to pay commission to anyone . The presumed benefits are, however, illusory. Most brokers (particularly residential brokers) will not spend time and effort to advertise and show a property that is also being offered by many others, because any competition may deprive them of the commission and they would receive nothing for the efforts they have expended. As a result, if a broker accepts an open listing, he tends to take little, if any, initiative to sell the property. Certainly, if a buyer comes along looking for a property just like the one on the open listing and if the broker has no suitable substitute among his exclusive listings, the broker will show the open listing property. An open listing contract is shown in Figure 14-1.

EXCLUSIVE AGENCY

An exclusive agency contract, like an open listing agreement, provides that the principal will pay a commission to the agent when the agent procures a sale for the principal's property. The key distinction, the one that makes the exclusive agency contract more acceptable to the broker, is that the principal has agreed in the contract to pay a commission, if the property is sold, to the broker with whom he made the agreement, even if another broker's actions bring the seller and purchaser together. The owner does, however, reserve unto himself the right to make a direct sale (not using any broker) without paying a commission. If the owner is foolish enough to retain a second broker after he has signed an exclusive agency contract with an initial broker, he may be obligated to pay duplicate commissions.

The exclusive agency contract assures the broker of a commission if he, or any other broker, sells the property. Thus the broker will in all probability expend substantial efforts to bring about a sale. The owner, on the other hand, is protected from having to pay a commission if he is fortunate enough to negotiate a sale personally. Brokers holding exclusive agency contracts usually cooperate with other brokers (either through a multiple listing service or directly) to open the property to the largest number of interested parties. When a broker cooperates with another broker, he shares the commission earned with the broker whose actions result in the sale. Under the economic and competitive circumstances prevailing in New York, the exclusive agency contract is a fair and practical arrangement for both sellers and agents. An exclusive agency contract is shown in Figure 14-2.

Multiple Listing

When a broker belongs to a multiple listing service, he has the opportunity to sell properties listed by other brokers. When a broker in a multiple listing service sells such a property, he is acting as a subagent of the listing broker. Normally, the seller does not pay any extra commission if his property is sold through a multiple listing arrangement. The actual selling broker's commission is paid by the listing broker. All the broker-members of a multiple listing service are obligated to share their listings with the other members of the service. This device opens a substantially larger market for the seller and eliminates the need for open listings because the seller who lists with one broker is effectively listing with all brokers in the area.

EXCLUSIVE RIGHT TO SELL

An exclusive right to sell agreement (sometimes called an exclusive authorization to sell agreement) provides that a commission will be paid to the broker in the event that any sale is brought about, whether by the listing broker, by any other broker, or by the owner. It is thus similar to the exclusive agency contract, but it gives the broker the right to a commission even in the event the owner himself makes the sale. Under the exclusive authorization to sell, if the property sells, the agent gets paid. This is the form normally offered by brokers to principals,

and is the form required by many multiple listing services. Most principals do not object (or do not know enough to object). An example of an exclusive right to sell appears as Figure 14-3.

Subagent

The aforementioned listing agreements may involve the use of a subagent. A subagent is an agent of one already acting as an agent for a principal.

The original, or prime, agent may delegate authority given to him by the principal when the principal has consented or when such delegation of authority is customary. When a broker delegates his authority, the question of possible liability for the payment of the broker's commission to both the agent and subagent must be carefully considered by the principal, usually with the guidance of an attorney.

OTHER LISTING AGREEMENT PROVISIONS

When a real estate broker prepares a listing agreement he must immediately deliver a duplicate original of that contract to all the parties in the agreement. For purposes of this rule, a listing agreement is an instrument that relates to the employment of a broker for services pertaining to the consummation of a lease; the purchase, sale, or exchange of real property; or any other type of real estate transaction in which he may participate as a broker.

A listing agreement continues in force for such time as is agreed to between the parties. New York real property law provides that no real estate broker shall be a party to an exclusive listing contract that contains an automatic continuation of the period of his authority beyond the fixed termination date set forth in the agreement. If no time is agreed upon, a listing contract terminates after a reasonable time. When acting in good faith, the principal may cancel the authority after any length of time.

An agent's (broker's) authority will also terminate upon any of the following events:

☐ When the sale has not been performed during the specified period. Or, if the period of authority is unspecified, and the sale has not been performed within a reasonable time.
☐ Sale of the property by another broker.
☐ Death or insanity of a broker or principal.
☐ Bankruptcy of the broker or the principal.
☐ Destruction of the property.
☐ Broker's fraudulent conduct for his own benefit.

SALES PRICE __$73,500__ TYPE HOME __Ranch__ TOTAL BEDROOMS __2__ TOTAL BATHS __1__

ADDRESS __321 Rose Street, Anytown__ JURISDICTION OF __Brown County, New York__

AMT. OF LOAN TO BE ASSUMED $ __None__ AS OF WHAT DATE _____ TAXES & INS. INCLUDED _____ YEARS TO GO _____ AMOUNT PAYABLE MONTHLY $_____@____% TYPE LOAN

MORTGAGE COMPANY_____ 2nd MORTGAGE _____

OWNER'S NAME __Edward Smith and Mary Smith (H & W)__ PHONES (HOME) _____ (BUSINESS) _____

TENANT'S NAME _____ PHONES (HOME) _____ (BUSINESS) _____

POSSESSION __at closing__ DATE LISTED: __June 15, TY__ FOR (PERIOD) __120 days__ DATE OF EXPIRATION __Oct. 15, TY__

LISTING BROKER __ABC Realty__ PHONE _____ KEY AVAILABLE AT _____

LISTING SALESMAN __You as salesperson for ABC Realty__ HOME PHONE _____ HOW TO BE SHOWN: _____

ENTRANCE FOYER ☐	CENTER HALL ☐	AGE 22 yrs.	AIR CONDITIONING ☐	TYPE KITCHEN CABINETS	
LIVING ROOM SIZE 12' x 15'	FIREPLACE ☐	ROOFING Composition	TOOL HOUSE ☐	TYPE COUNTER TOPS	
DINING ROOM SIZE 10' x 12'		GARAGE SIZE	PATIO ☐	EAT-IN SIZE KITCHEN ☐	
BEDROOM TOTAL: 2 DOWN UP		SIDE DRIVE ☐	CIRCULAR DRIVE ☐	TYPE STOVE ☐	
BATHS TOTAL: 1 DOWN UP		PORCH ☐ SIDE ☐ REAR ☐	SCREENED ☐	BUILT-IN OVEN & RANGE ☐	
DEN SIZE	FIREPLACE ☐	FENCED YARD	OUTDOOR GRILL ☐	SEPARATE STOVE INCLUDED ☑	
FAMILY ROOM SIZE	FIREPLACE ☐	STORM WINDOWS ☑	STORM DOORS ☑	REFRIGERATOR INCLUDED ☑	
RECREATION ROOM SIZE	FIREPLACE ☐	CURBS & GUTTERS ☐	SIDEWALKS ☐	DISHWASHER INCLUDED portable	
BASEMENT SIZE 25' x 35'		STORM SEWERS ☐	ALLEY ☐	DISPOSAL INCLUDED ☐	
NONE ☐ 1/4 ☐ 1/3 ☐ 1/2 ☐ 3/4 ☐ FULL ☑		WATER SUPPLY well		DOUBLE SINK ☐ SINGLE SINK ☐	
UTILITY ROOM		SEWER ☐	SEPTIC ☑	STAINLESS STEEL ☐ PORCELAIN ☐	
TYPE HOT WATER SYSTEM: electric 30 gal.		TYPE GAS: NATURAL ☐	BOTTLED ☐	WASHER INCLUDED ☐ DRYER INCLUDED ☐	
TYPE HEAT electric		WHY SELLING		LAND ASSESSMENT $ 6,000	
EST. FUEL COST				IMPROVEMENTS $ 15,000	
ATTIC ☐		PROPERTY DESCRIPTION		TOTAL ASSESSMENTS $ 21,000	
PULL DOWN STAIRWAY ☐ REGULAR STAIRWAY ☐ TRAP DOOR ☐		Bloom Addition, Anytown, Brown County, Your State		TAX RATE $8.25/$100	
NAME OF BUILDER		LOT SIZE 150' x 200'		TOTAL ANNUAL TAXES $ 1,732.50	
SQUARE FOOTAGE		LOT NO. 6 BLOCK SECTION			
EXTERIOR OF HOUSE					

NAME OF SCHOOLS: ELEMENTARY: _____ JR. HIGH: _____

HIGH: _____ PAROCHIAL: _____

PUBLIC TRANSPORTATION: _____

NEAREST SHOPPING AREA: _____

REMARKS: ___Will take 15 yr. purchase money mortgage at 8%, 30% downpayment, 180 equal monthly payments including principal and interest only__ Air conditioner, washer, dryer, and lawn mower sold separately.

Date: __June 15, TY__

In consideration of the services of _____ABC Realty_____ (herein called "Broker") to be rendered to the undersigned (herein called "Owner"), and of the promise of Broker to make reasonable efforts to obtain a Purchaser therefor, Owner hereby lists with Broker the real estate and all improvements thereon which are described above, (all herein called "the property"), and the Owner hereby grants to Broker the right to sell subject to prior sale, such property from 12:00 Noon on __June 15__, 19 __TY__ until 12:00 Midnight on __Oct. 15__, 19 __TY__ (herein called "period of time"), for the price of __Seventy-three__ thousand five hundred and no/100 _____ Dollars ($__73,500.00__) or for such other price and upon such other terms (including exchange) as Owner may subsequently authorize during the period of time.

It is understood by Owner that the above sum or any other price subsequently authorized by Owner shall include a cash fee of __6__ per cent of such price or other price which shall be payable by Owner to Broker upon consummation by any Purchaser or Purchasers of a valid contract of sale of the property during the period of time when Broker was a procuring cause of any such contract of sale.

Broker is hereby authorized by Owner to place a "For Sale" sign on the property and Owner hereby agrees to make the property available to Broker at all reasonable hours for the purpose of showing it to prospective Purchasers.

Owner agrees to convey the property to the Purchaser by deed with the usual covenants of title and free and clear from all encumbrances, tenancies, liens (for taxes or otherwise), but subject to applicable restrictive covenants of record. Owner acknowledges receipt of copy of this agreement.

WITNESS the following signature(s) and seal(s):

Date Signed: __June 15, TY__ ___Edward Smith___ (Owner)

Listing Agent __ABC Realty, you as salesperson__

Address __321 Rose St.__ Telephone _____ ___Mary Smith___ (Owner)

FIG. 14-1 Real Estate Listing Contract (Open Listing).

SALES PRICE ___$81,000.00___   TYPE HOME ___Ranch___   TOTAL BEDROOMS __3__ TOTAL BATHS _1½_

ADDRESS _1516 Alta Drive, Anytown_   JURISDICTION OF __Madison County, New York__

AMT. OF LOAN
TO BE ASSUMED $ _9,650.00_   AS OF   WHAT DATE Sept. 15, TY   TAXES & INS. INCLUDED __no__   YEARS TO GO ____   AMOUNT PAYABLE MONTHLY $_96.00_ @ 6 %   TYPE LOAN Conv.

MORTGAGE COMPANY _Home Federal Savings and Loan_   2nd MORTGAGE ____

OWNER'S NAME ___Carolyn Turner (widow)___   PHONES (HOME)_334-3388_ ___(BUSINESS)____

TENANT'S NAME _____N/A_____   PHONES (HOME)____ ___(BUSINESS)____

POSSESSION Complete - 15 DAFC ___ DATE LISTED: Sept. 27, TY   EXCLUSIVE FOR _90 days_ DATE OF EXPIRATION Dec. 27, TY

LISTING BROKER Held Real Estate   PHONE ____   KEY AVAILABLE AT Held Real Estate

LISTING SALESMAN _You, as salesperson for Held Real Estate_   HOME PHONE____   HOW TO BE SHOWN: by appointment

ENTRANCE FOYER ☐	CENTER HALL ☐	AGE 14 yrs.	AIR CONDITIONING ☑	TYPE KITCHEN CABINETS wood
LIVING ROOM SIZE 16' x 18'	FIREPLACE ☑	ROOFING asphalt-shingle	TOOL HOUSE ☐	TYPE COUNTER TOPS Formica
DINING ROOM SIZE 14' x 16'		GARAGE SIZE 2-car attached	PATIO ☑	EAT-IN SIZE KITCHEN ☐
BEDROOM TOTAL: 3 DOWN UP		SIDE DRIVE ☑	CIRCULAR DRIVE ☐	TYPE STOVE ☐
BATHS TOTAL: 1½ DOWN UP		PORCH ☑ SIDE ☐ REAR ☑	SCREENED ☑	BUILT-IN OVEN & RANGE ☑ gas
DEN SIZE 12' x 12'	FIREPLACE ☑	FENCED YARD yes	OUTDOOR GRILL ☐	SEPARATE STOVE INCLUDED ☐
FAMILY ROOM SIZE	FIREPLACE ☐	STORM WINDOWS ☑	STORM DOORS ☑	REFRIGERATOR INCLUDED ☐
RECREATION ROOM SIZE	FIREPLACE ☐	CURBS & GUTTERS ☑	SIDEWALKS ☑	DISHWASHER INCLUDED yes
BASEMENT SIZE		STORM SEWERS ☑	ALLEY ☑	DISPOSAL INCLUDED ☑
NONE ☑ 1/4 ☐ 1/3 ☐ 1/2 ☐ 3/4 ☐ FULL ☐		WATER SUPPLY city		DOUBLE SINK ☑ SINGLE SINK ☐
UTILITY ROOM 6' x 8'		SEWER ☐	SEPTIC ☐	STAINLESS STEEL ☑ PORCELAIN ☐
TYPE HOT WATER SYSTEM: 40 gal. gas		TYPE GAS: NATURAL ☑	BOTTLED ☐	WASHER INCLUDED ☑ DRYER INCLUDED ☐
TYPE HEAT gas, forced air		WHY SELLING		LAND ASSESSMENT $ 6,000
EST. FUEL COST		moving to condominium		IMPROVEMENTS $ 21,000
ATTIC ☑ Unfinished		PROPERTY DESCRIPTION		TOTAL ASSESSMENTS $ 27,000
PULL DOWN ☑ REGULAR ☐ TRAP STAIRWAY STAIRWAY DOOR ☐		Plat Book 6, Page 31		TAX RATE $7.00/$100
NAME OF BUILDER John H. Hammer		LOT SIZE 100' x 120'		TOTAL ANNUAL TAXES $ 1,890.
SQUARE FOOTAGE 2400		LOT NO. 45 BLOCK SECTION		
EXTERIOR OF HOUSE Frame Lakewood Addition in the City of Anytown, County of Madison, Your State				

NAME OF SCHOOLS: ELEMENTARY: _P.S. 101_   JR. HIGH: _Binford Middle School_

HIGH: _Anytown High School_   PAROCHIAL: _St. Peter's Catholic, Elementary_ ____

PUBLIC TRANSPORTATION: _City bus – 1 block_

NEAREST SHOPPING AREA: _Monroe Mall 5 min._

REMARKS: _____No exchange_

Date: ____Sept. 27, TY____

In consideration of the services of _____Held Real Estate_____ (herein called "Broker") to be rendered to the undersigned (herein called 'Owner'), and of the promise of Broker to make reasonable efforts to obtain a Purchaser therefor, Owner hereby lists with Broker the real estate and all improvements thereon which are described above, (all herein called "the property"), and the Owner hereby grants to Broker the exclusive agency to sell such property from 12:00 Noon on ____Sept. 27____, 19_TY_ until 12:00 Midnight on ____Dec. 27____, 19 _TY_ (herein called "period of time"), for the price of ___Eighty-one thousand and no/100_____ Dollars ($ _81,000.00_)

or for such other price and upon such other terms (including exchange) as Owner may subsequently authorize during the period of time. Seller reserves the right to sell directly without incurring any obligations under this agreement.

It is understood by Owner that the above sum or any other price subsequently authorized by Owner shall include a cash fee of ____7____ per cent of such price or other price which shall be payable by Owner to Broker upon consummation by any Purchaser or Purchasers of a valid contract of sale of the property during the period of time provided Broker or any other Broker was the procuring cause of any such contract of sale, but expressly excepting any sale made directly by owner.

If the property is sold or exchanged by Broker or by any other person to any Purchaser to whom the property was shown by Broker or any representative of Broker within sixty (60) days after the expiration of the period of time mentioned above, Owner agrees to pay to Broker a cash fee which shall be the same percentage of the purchase price as the percentage mentioned above.

Broker is hereby authorized by Owner to place a "For Sale" sign on the property and to remove all signs of other brokers or salesmen during the period of time, and Owner hereby agrees to make the property available to Broker at all reasonable hours for the purpose of showing it to prospective Purchasers.

Owner agrees to convey the property to the Purchaser by deed with the usual covenants of title and free and clear from all encumbrances, tenancies, liens (for taxes or otherwise), but subject to applicable restrictive covenants of record. Owner acknowledges receipt of copy of this agreement.

WITNESS the following signature(s) and seal(s):

Date Signed: ____Sept. 27, TY____   _Carolyn Turner_ ____ (Owner)

Listing Agent ___Held Real Estate, You as salesperson___

Address ___1516 Alta Dr.___ Telephone _334-3388_   ____ (Owner)

FIG. 14-2 Real Estate Listing Contract (Exclusive Agency).

SALES PRICE __$158,700__ TYPE HOME __Duplex__ TOTAL BEDROOMS __3/unit__ TOTAL BATHS __1½/unit__

ADDRESS __125 West 3rd St., Anytown__ JURISDICTION OF __Blue County, New York__

AMT. OF LOAN
TO BE ASSUMED $ __28,500.00__ AS OF WHAT DATE __9/1/TY__ TAXES & INS. INCLUDED __yes__ YEARS TO GO ____ AMOUNT PAYABLE MONTHLY $ __450.00__ @ __8__ % TYPE LOAN __Conv.__

MORTGAGE COMPANY __Martin Savings and Loan__ 2nd MORTGAGE _____

OWNER'S NAME __John T. Murphy and Betty Murphy (H & W)__ PHONES (HOME) __478-5168__ (BUSINESS) _____

TENANT'S NAME _____ PHONES (HOME) _____ (BUSINESS) _____

POSSESSION __Complete/Landlord's__ DATE LISTED: __Sept. 15, TY__ EXCLUSIVE FOR __60 days__ DATE OF EXPIRATION __Nov. 15, TY__

LISTING BROKER __City Realty__ PHONE _____ KEY AVAILABLE AT __City Realty__

LISTING SALESMAN __You, as salesperson__ HOME PHONE _____ HOW TO BE SHOWN: __By appointment__

ENTRANCE FOYER ☐	CENTER HALL ☐	AGE 9 years	AIR CONDITIONING ☑	TYPE KITCHEN CABINETS
LIVING ROOM SIZE 16' x 18'	FIREPLACE ☐	ROOFING	TOOL HOUSE ☐	TYPE COUNTER TOPS
DINING ROOM SIZE 12' x 12'		GARAGE SIZE	PATIO ☐	EAT-IN SIZE KITCHEN ☐
BEDROOM TOTAL: 3/unit DOWN	UP	SIDE DRIVE ☐	CIRCULAR DRIVE ☐	TYPE STOVE ☐
BATHS TOTAL: 1½/unit DOWN	UP	PORCH ☐ SIDE ☐ REAR ☐	SCREENED ☐	BUILT-IN OVEN & RANGE ☑
DEN SIZE	FIREPLACE ☐	FENCED YARD	OUTDOOR GRILL ☐	SEPARATE STOVE INCLUDED ☐
FAMILY ROOM SIZE	FIREPLACE ☐	STORM WINDOWS ☐	STORM DOORS ☐	REFRIGERATOR INCLUDED ☑
RECREATION ROOM SIZE	FIREPLACE ☐	CURBS & GUTTERS ☐	SIDEWALKS ☐	DISHWASHER INCLUDED yes
BASEMENT SIZE		STORM SEWERS ☑	ALLEY ☐	DISPOSAL INCLUDED ☐
NONE ☑ 1/4 ☐ 1/3 ☐ 1/2 ☐ 3/4 ☐ FULL ☐		WATER SUPPLY city		DOUBLE SINK ☐ SINGLE SINK ☐
UTILITY ROOM		SEWER ☑ city	SEPTIC ☐	STAINLESS STEEL ☐ PORCELAIN ☐
TYPE HOT WATER SYSTEM: 30 gal. gas		TYPE GAS: NATURAL ☑	BOTTLED ☐	WASHER INCLUDED ☐ DRYER INCLUDED ☐
TYPE HEAT gas forced air		WHY SELLING		LAND ASSESSMENT $ 9,000
EST. FUEL COST				IMPROVEMENTS $ 36,000
ATTIC ☐		PROPERTY DESCRIPTION		TOTAL ASSESSMENTS $ 45,000
PULL DOWN STAIRWAY ☐	REGULAR STAIRWAY ☐ TRAP DOOR ☐	City of Anytown, County of Blue, Your State		TAX RATE $9.25/$100
NAME OF BUILDER		LOT SIZE 150' x 200'		TOTAL ANNUAL TAXES $ 4,162.50
SQUARE FOOTAGE		LOT NO. 104-105 BLOCK	SECTION	
EXTERIOR OF HOUSE Brick with wood trim.				

NAME OF SCHOOLS: ELEMENTARY: _____ JR. HIGH: _____

HIGH: _____ PAROCHIAL: _____

PUBLIC TRANSPORTATION: _____

NEAREST SHOPPING AREA: _____

REMARKS: _____ Garbage pick up, will not accept trade; 9 mos. remaining on lease; $180 rent monthly on rental unit; rental unit possession subject to tenants' rights.

Date: __Sept. 15, TY__

In consideration of the services of __City Realty__ (herein called "Broker") to be rendered to the undersigned (herein called "Owner"), and of the promise of Broker to make reasonable efforts to obtain a Purchaser therefor, Owner hereby lists with Broker the real estate and all improvements thereon which are described above, (all herein called "the property"), and the Owner hereby grants to Broker the exclusive and irrevocable right to sell such property from 12:00 Noon on __Sept. 15__, 19 __TY__ until 12:00 Midnight on __Nov. 15__, 19 __TY__ (herein called "period of time"), for the price of __One hundred fifty-eight thousand seven hundred and no/100__ Dollars ($ __158,700.00__) or for such other price and upon such other terms (including exchange) as Owner may subsequently authorize during the period of time.

It is understood by Owner that the above sum or any other price subsequently authorized by Owner shall include a cash fee of __6__ per cent of such price or other price which shall be payable by Owner to Broker upon consummation by any Purchaser or Purchasers of a valid contract of sale of the property during the period of time.

If the property is sold or exchanged by Owner, or by Broker or by any other person to any Purchaser to whom the property was shown by Broker or any representative of Broker within sixty (60) days after the expiration of the period of time mentioned above, Owner agrees to pay to Broker a cash fee which shall be the same percentage of the purchase price as the percentage mentioned above.

Broker is hereby authorized by Owner to place a "For Sale" sign on the property and to remove all signs of other brokers or salesmen during the period of time, and Owner hereby agrees to make the property available to Broker at all reasonable hours for the purpose of showing it to prospective Purchasers.

Owner agrees to convey the property to the Purchaser by deed with the usual covenants of title and free and clear from all encumbrances, tenancies, liens (for taxes or otherwise), but subject to applicable restrictive covenants of record. Owner acknowledges receipt of copy of this agreement.

WITNESS the following signature(s) and seal(s):

Date Signed: __Sept. 15, TY__

John T Murphy (Owner)

Listing Agent __City Realty, You as salesperson__

Address __125 W. 3rd St.__ Telephone __478-5168__

Betty Murphy (Owner)

FIG. 14-3   *Real Estate Listing Contract (Exclusive Right to Sell).*

Another provision sometimes included in all three forms of listing agreement provides that the seller shall not be obligated for any commission nor is the broker entitled to one unless and until the settlement (closing) is reached unless, of course, such failure to settle is due to the breach or fault of the sellers. The seller's attorney, or the sellers themselves if they have had prior real estate experience, will normally insist upon this clause. It should not cause any apprehension on the part of the broker because if the "sale" did not result in a closing, the commission would probably be contested. In such case the seller would undoubtedly claim that there was no closing because the buyer was either unwilling or unable to purchase, and that the buyer's failure to complete the transaction was evidence of that. If the broker were to try to collect under these circumstances, he would undoubtedly have to undergo the expense of litigation and, worse, risk the loss of good reputation among the seller and his friends. The prudent broker, even without such a provision, would relinquish all or a major portion of his commission in order to maintain community goodwill.

Corporate Relocations

With increasing frequency, homeowners must sell their houses because of a corporate transfer or change of employment. In many of these situations, the employer or corporate relocation company designated by the employer may subsidize the sale of the transferred employee's house. The employer or relocation company establishes a fair value for the property based on an appraisal, or on the average of a number of separate appraisals, and agrees to purchase the house at that price provided the householder agrees to sell promptly—typically within 30 to 60 days. During the 30- to 60-day period, the transferred householder is free to try to get a better price in the marketplace.

If the householder has made such an agreement, he is frequently instructed not to enter into any listing agreement unless it specifies that a sale to the employer or to the relocation company is excluded from the broker's commission. Such a seller wants to add the following clause to the exclusive agency listing contract: "Seller reserves the right to sell to [name of employer or relocation company], or its nominee, without incurring any liability for a commission thereby." This type of listing is generally acceptable to a broker because the relocation company or employer probably will continue to utilize the broker to resell the house to an ultimate user.

State Regulations

The Secretary of State of New York, through the Division of Licensing Services, has described the authorization and employment of the broker by the principal in great detail. This summary is reproduced in Appendix C.

THE LISTING AGREEMENT

A typical listing agreement appears in Figure 14-4. As you may have noticed in Figures 14-1 to 14-3, the format for all three types of listing agreement is essentially the same. However, for exclusive listings for one-, two-, or three-family dwellings (but not for condominiums or cooperatives), Regulation 175.24 (see also Appendix B) requires that the following paragraph be attached to the listing or be printed on the reverse side of the listing and signed by the homeowner's agent:

Explanation:
An "exclusive right to sell" listing means that if you, the owner of the property, find a buyer for your house, or if another broker finds a buyer, you must pay the agreed commission to the present broker.
An "exclusive agency" listing means that if you, the owner of the property, find a buyer, you will not have to pay a commission to the broker. However, if another broker finds a buyer, you will owe a commission to both the selling broker and your present broker.

For instruction purposes, we have divided this form into five major sections, and the numbers in the following summary are keyed to those in the figure.

REAL ESTATE LISTING CONTRACT (EXCLUSIVE RIGHT TO SELL)

SALES PRICE ___1___ TYPE HOME ___2___ TOTAL BEDROOMS ___3___ TOTAL BATHS ___4___

ADDRESS ___5___ JURISDICTION OF ___6___

AMT. OF LOAN TO BE ASSUMED $ ___7___ AS OF WHAT DATE ___8___ TAXES & INS. INCLUDED ___9___ YEARS TO GO ___10___ AMOUNT PAYABLE MONTHLY $ ___11___ @ ___% TYPE LOAN ___12___

MORTGAGE COMPANY ___13___ 2nd MORTGAGE ___14___

OWNER'S NAME ___15___ PHONES(HOME) ___16___ (BUSINESS) ___16___

TENANT'S NAME ___17___ PHONES (HOME) ___18___ (BUSINESS) ___18___

POSSESSION ___19___ DATE LISTED: ___20___ EXCLUSIVE FOR ___21___ DATE OF EXPIRATION ___22___

LISTING BROKER ___23___ PHONE ___24___ KEY AVAILABLE AT ___25___

LISTING SALESMAN ___26___ HOME PHONE ___27___ HOW TO BE SHOWN: ___28___

Section 1

ENTRANCE FOYER ☐	CENTER HALL ☐	AGE	AIR CONDITIONING ☐	TYPE KITCHEN CABINETS
LIVING ROOM SIZE	FIREPLACE ☐	ROOFING	TOOL HOUSE ☐	TYPE COUNTER TOPS
DINING ROOM SIZE		GARAGE SIZE	PATIO ☐	EAT-IN SIZE KITCHEN ☐
BEDROOM TOTAL: DOWN UP		SIDE DRIVE ☐	CIRCULAR DRIVE ☐	TYPE STOVE ☐
BATHS TOTAL: DOWN UP		PORCH ☐ SIDE ☐ REAR ☐	SCREENED ☐	BUILT-IN OVEN & RANGE ☐
DEN SIZE	FIREPLACE ☐	FENCED YARD	OUTDOOR GRILL ☐	SEPARATE STOVE INCLUDED ☐
FAMILY ROOM SIZE	FIREPLACE ☐	STORM WINDOWS ☐	STORM DOORS ☐	REFRIGERATOR INCLUDED ☐
RECREATION ROOM SIZE	FIREPLACE ☐	CURBS & GUTTERS ☐	SIDEWALKS ☐	DISHWASHER INCLUDED
BASEMENT SIZE		STORM SEWERS ☐	ALLEY ☐	DISPOSAL INCLUDED ☐
NONE ☐ 1/4 ☐ 1/3 ☐ 1/2 ☐ 3/4☐ FULL ☐		WATER SUPPLY		DOUBLE SINK ☐ SINGLE SINK☐
UTILITY ROOM		SEWER ☐	SEPTIC ☐	STAINLESS STEEL ☐ PORCELAIN ☐
TYPE HOT WATER SYSTEM:		TYPE GAS: NATURAL ☐	BOTTLED ☐	WASHER INCLUDED☐ DRYER INCLUDED☐

Section 2

TYPE HEAT	WHY SELLING	LAND ASSESSMENT $ ___1___
EST. FUEL COST		IMPROVEMENTS $ ___2___
ATTIC ☐	PROPERTY DESCRIPTION	TOTAL ASSESSMENTS $ ___3___
PULL DOWN STAIRWAY ☐ REGULAR STAIRWAY ☐ TRAP DOOR ☐		TAX RATE ___4___
NAME OF BUILDER	LOT SIZE	TOTAL ANNUAL TAXES $ ___5___
SQUARE FOOTAGE	LOT NO. BLOCK SECTION	
EXTERIOR OF HOUSE		

Section 3

NAME OF SCHOOLS: ELEMENTARY _____ JR. HIGH: _____

HIGH: _____ PAROCHIAL: _____

PUBLIC TRANSPORTATION: _____

NEAREST SHOPPING AREA: _____

REMARKS: _____

Section 4

Date: ___1___

In consideration of the services of ___2___ (herein called "Broker") to be rendered to the undersigned (herein called 'Owner"), and of the promise of Broker to make reasonable efforts to obtain a Purchaser therefor, Owner hereby lists with Broker the real estate and all improvements thereon which are described above, (all herein called "the property"), and the Owner hereby grants to Broker the exclusive and irrevocable right to sell such property from 12:00 Noon on ___3___, 19 _____ until 12:00 Midnight on ___4___, 19 _____ (herein called "period of time"), for the price of ___5___ Dollars ($ ___6___) or for such other price and upon such other terms (including exchange) as Owner may subsequently authorize during the period of time.

It is understood by Owner that the above sum or any other price subsequently authorized by Owner shall include a cash fee of ___7___ per cent of such price or other price which shall be payable by Owner to Broker upon consummation by any Purchaser or Purchasers of a valid contract of sale of the property during the period of time and whether or not Broker was a procuring cause of any such contract of sale.

Section 5

If the property is sold or exchanged by Owner, or by Broker or by any other person to any Purchaser to whom the property was shown by Broker or any representative of Broker within sixty (60) days after the expiration of the period of time mentioned above, Owner agrees to pay to Broker a cash fee which shall be the same percentage of the purchase price as the percentage mentioned above.

Broker is hereby authorized by Owner to place a "For Sale" sign on the property and to remove all signs of other brokers or salesmen during the period of time, and Owner hereby agrees to make the property available to Broker at all reasonable hours for the purpose of showing it to prospective Purchasers.

Owner agrees to convey the property to the Purchaser by deed with the usual covenants of title and free and clear from all encumbrances, tenancies, liens (for taxes or otherwise), but subject to applicable restrictive covenants of record. Owner acknowledges receipt of copy of this agreement.

WITNESS the following signature(s) and seal(s):

Date Signed: ___8___ ___12___

(Owner)

Listing Agent ___9___

Address ___10___ Telephone ___11___

(Owner)

FIG. 14-4 *Completing the listing agreement.*

Section 1

1   This is the selling price at which the broker and principal have agreed to list the house.
2   The architectural style of the house.
3   Total number of bedrooms.
4   Total number of bathrooms. Normally you would list full baths and half baths separately; that is, one full bath and two half baths do not add up to two full baths.
5   The street address of the property (and the town if the broker serves more than one community).
6   If necessary, enter the county in which the property is located.
7   If the seller has an assumable mortgage, enter the amount of the loan balance.
8   If the buyer assumes the mortgage, this date would normally be the same as the date of closing.
9   Are taxes and insurance included in the monthly amount noted in item 11?
10 How many years are there remaining in the assumable mortgage?
11 What is the current monthly mortgage payment? What is the current interest rate?
12 What kind of financing is the current mortgage? Is it an FHA or VA loan? A conventional one?
13 With whom is the current mortgage held? Give name and address.
14 If there is a second mortgage, enter the details here.
15 The name of the owner of the property would go here.
16 The owner's business and home telephone numbers should be included.
17 If there is a tenant, the tenant's name should be entered.
18 The tenant's phone number would go here.
19 This would be the date on which the seller would give possession of the property to the buyer, and the type of possession given.
20 This is the date on which the listing is taken.
21 This is the number of days for which the listing contract will be in effect.
22 This is the actual date on which the listing contract expires. For example, a 90-day listing beginning on April 3 would expire on July 3.
23 If the person taking the listing is the broker, the broker's name and the company name would be entered here; if the person taking the listing is a salesperson, only the company name would be entered here.
24 The phone number of the listing broker's office.
25 Note here where the key may be obtained in order to show the property.
26 If the person taking the listing is a salesperson, the name of the salesperson would go here.
27 This is the home phone number of a listing salesperson.
28 You will want to note here any specific instructions as to how and when the property may be shown.

Section 2

The items in this section describe the house and the property and are basically self-explanatory. Not all of the items would be applicable for every house.

Section 3

The items in this section cover tax and assessment information which many prospective buyers will want to know.
1   Land is assessed separately from the improvements.
2   Improvements, as you will recall, are the buildings and structures on a particular piece of property.
3   The total assessed value of the property is the sum of the assessed value of the land plus the assessed value of all the improvements. The assessed value and the market price of a piece of property are not necessarily related.
4   Tax rates are often expressed as dollars per $100 of total assessed value. Sometimes they are expressed in mills, which is fractions of a cent per $1 of assessed value.
5   What are the current total taxes on the property?

Section 4

This is general information about the schools and neighborhood in which a buyer would be interested.

The "remarks" section would be used for any information not otherwise noted in the listing form.

Section 5

This is the legal section of the form and it establishes the contractual agreement between the seller (the principal) and the broker (the agent).

1 This is the date on which the contract is entered into.
2 The name of the listing broker or firm would be inserted here.
3 The effective date on which the listing contract is to begin. This is not always the same as the date on which the contract is entered into. A listing could begin some time after the contract date.
4 This is the date on which the contract is to expire and it would be the same as the date in item 22, Section 1.
5 Write out the amount of the listing price, as you would on a check.
6 Write the amount of the listing price in numerals, as you would on a check.
7 What is the rate (as a percent) of the broker's fee or commission.
8 What is the date on which the parties to the contract have signed it.
9 This is the name of the brokerage firm, with the listing agent's name.
10 This is the broker's address.
11 This is the broker's phone number.
12 This is where the seller would sign the contract.

REVIEW QUESTIONS

1. The difference between exclusive right to sell and exclusive agency is

   (a) The agent's promise to pay all promotional expenses.
   (b) The principal's reservation of the right to sell his or her own home through another broker.
   (c) The principal's reservation of the right to pay the agent no commission.
   (d) The principal's reservation of the right to pay the agent no commission if the principal should sell the property.

2. When an agent has produced a buyer who is ready, willing, and able, the agent has generally

   (a) Consummated the sale.
   (b) Established his or her personal competence.
   (c) Earned a commission.
   (d) Accounted to the principal.

3. An agency agreement may be terminated by all of the following except

   (a) Revocation by the principal.
   (b) Reciprocity.
   (c) Renunciation by the agent.
   (d) Mutual consent.

4. Upon the death of a broker his or her listings will always be taken over by

   (a) A salesperson.
   (b) A spouse.
   (c) A trust company.
   (d) None of the above.

5. A real estate listing contract is

   (a) A list of all property owned by one person.
   (b) A list of all property for purposes of taxation.
   (c) The employment of a broker by the owner to sell real property.
   (d) None of the above.

6. The relationship of a licensed real estate broker to his principal is that of a

   (a) Salesperson.
   (b) Beneficiary.
   (c) Superior.
   (d) Fiduciary.

7. A broker may lawfully receive a commission from

   A. A co-broker.
   B. The owner.

   (a) A only.   (c) Both A and B.
   (b) B only.   (d) Neither A nor B.

8. An authorization to a person to act for and in behalf of another in a real estate transaction is called

   (a) A special agent.
   (b) An option.
   (c) Power of attorney.
   (d) An escrow.

9. An attorney-in-fact is the holder of

   (a) A power of attorney.
   (b) A law degree.
   (c) A listing.
   (d) A decree from a court.

10. When the buyer does not have sufficient money for an earnest money deposit .

    A. The broker may loan him money from his or her escrow account.
    B. The broker may take a personal check and hold it without depositing it in an escrow account.

    (a) A only.   (c) Both A and B.
    (b) B only.   (d) Neither A nor B.

11. A real estate broker, retained to find a purchaser for a single family house is

    (a) A universal agent.
    (b) A general agent.
    (c) A special agent.
    (d) None of the above.

12. A real estate salesperson who has obtained a listing from a potential seller of real estate is

    (a) A universal agent.
    (b) A general agent.
    (c) A special agent.
    (d) None of the above.

13. The relationship between broker and salesperson is one of:

    A. Principal-agent.
    B. Employer-employee.

    (a) A only.   (c) Either A or B.
    (b) B only.   (d) Neither A nor B.

14. In New York, a listing agreement for the sale of real estate

    (a) Must always be in writing because of the Statute of Frauds.
    (b) Must always be in writing because of laws other than the Statute of Frauds.
    (c) Should not be in writing.
    (d) Does not have to be in writing, but should be in writing for business reasons.

15. A broker with an exclusive right of sale listing does not earn a commission

    (a) When the owner sells by himself.
    (b) When the owner refuses an offer in accordance with the listing.
    (c) If he has no real estate license.
    (d) When the seller changes his mind and does not complete the sale.

16. A broker obtaining an exclusive right to sell listing of a residence in New York must explain the meaning of that type of listing

    (a) According to rules.
    (b) According to statutes.
    (c) Orally.
    (d) The above statement is false.

17. The employment of a real estate broker is terminated by

    (a) The sale of the listed property.
    (b) The death of the broker.
    (c) The death of the seller.
    (d) Any of the above.

18. A broker may represent the buyer and the seller

    (a) Whenever he can.
    (b) At no time.
    (c) If either seller or buyer consent.
    (d) If both buyer and seller consent.

19. The broker's commission rate is

    (a) Fixed by the Secretary of State.
    (b) Fixed by statute.
    (c) Fixed by the local real estate board.
    (d) Fixed between broker and principal.

20. A broker may not, in New York, accept

    (a) An exclusive right to sell listing.
    (b) An exclusive agency listing.
    (c) An open listing.
    (d) A net listing.

Chapter 15
Human Rights/Fair Housing

VOCABULARY

You will find it important to have a complete working knowledge of the following concepts and words found in this chapter:

blockbusting

Caucasian clause

Department of Housing and Urban Development (HUD)

discrimination

Federal Deposit Insurance Corporation (FDIC)

flood-prone area

intrastate transaction

kickback

National Association of Realtors® (NAR)®

nonsolicitation order

panic selling

racial steering

redlining

right of rescission—*cancellation of agreement*

Truth-in-Lending Act

FEDERAL AND NATIONAL INFLUENCES

THE QUEST FOR affordable housing available to a majority of citizens regardless of race, religion, national origin, or sex has resulted in numerous developments that will be briefly discussed in this chapter.

FEDERAL CIVIL RIGHTS LEGISLATION

The Civil Rights Act of 1866, enacted shortly after the Civil War, states that "all citizens of the United States shall have the same right, in every state and territory, as is enjoyed by white citizens thereof to inherit, purchase, lease, sell, hold and convey real and personal property." This act did not have much effect on real estate for a period of about one hundred years because the federal government was considered to have no authority over "intrastate" or local transactions. A real estate sale or lease was considered to be a private, local transaction that could not be the subject of federal legislation.

The principal means by which citizens "protected" their neighborhood against the perceived evil of intrusion by people of racially different origin was the use of restrictive covenants that prohibited the sale of property to members of minority groups. These covenants, although frequently addressing themselves to race, religion, and national origin were commonly called *Caucasian clauses*. In 1968, the United States Supreme Court, in a landmark decision (*Jones v. Alfred H. Mayer, Co.*), held that these racial covenants were illegal by reason of the Civil Rights Act of 1866; and that the said act applied to individuals as well as to the government. *Test*

In 1947 the U.S. Supreme Court, in a prior landmark decision (*Shelley v. Kraemer*), decided that race restrictions, although valid contracts, could not be enforced by the courts, because such enforcement would be sufficient governmental action to bring the constitutional protections against discrimination into play. While this case decided only the question of race restrictions, it is highly probable that the rationale would be likely to apply to any other form of unreasonable restriction.

FEDERAL FAIR HOUSING LAWS

The need for fair housing is best expressed by the U.S. Commission on Civil Rights in their 1973

publication entitled *Understanding Fair Housing,*
as follows:

> Housing is a key to improvement in a family's
> economic condition. Home ownership is one of
> the important ways in which Americans have
> traditionally acquired financial capital. Tax
> advantages, the accumulation of equity, and
> the increased value of real estate property
> enable homeowners to build economic assets.
> These assets can be used to educate one's
> children, to take advantage of business op-
> portunities, to meet financial emergencies, and
> to provide for retirement. Nearly two of every
> three majority group families are home-
> owners, but less than two of every five non-
> white families own their homes. Consequently,
> the majority of nonwhite families are deprived
> of this advantage.
>
> Housing is essential to securing civil rights in
> other areas. Segregated residential patterns in
> metropolitan areas undermine efforts to
> assure equal opportunity in employment and
> education. While centers of employment have
> moved from the central cities to suburbs and
> outlying parts of metropolitan areas, minority
> group families remain confined to the central
> cities, and because they are confined, they are
> separated from employment opportunities.
> Despite a variety of laws against job discrim-
> ination, lack of access to housing in close
> proximity to available jobs is an effective
> barrier to equal employment.
>
> In addition, lack of equal housing oppor-
> tunity decreases prospects for equal educa-
> tional opportunity. The controversy over
> school busing is closely tied to the residential
> patterns of our cities and metropolitan areas. If
> schools in large urban centers are to be de-
> segregated, transportation must be provided to
> convey children from segregated neighbor-
> hoods to integrated schools.
>
> Finally, if racial divisions are to be bridged,
> equal housing is an essential element. Our
> cities and metropolitan areas consist of sep-
> arate societies increasingly hostile and dis-
> trustful of one another. Because minority and
> majority group families live apart, they are
> strangers to each other. By living as neighbors
> they would have an opportunity to learn to
> understand each other and to redeem the
> promise of America: that of "one Nation
> indivisible."

The Federal Fair Housing Act

The Civil Rights Act of 1968 was enacted 102 years
after the first civil rights act. Title VIII of the 1968
act, which is also known as the *Federal Fair Housing
Act*, made it illegal to discriminate not only on the
basis of race but also on the basis of color, religion,
and national origin. In 1974, the 1968 Act was
amended to make discrimination on the basis of
sex illegal. Specifically, Title VIII of the act means
that no one may refuse to rent, lease, or sell to another for reasons of race, color, national origin, religion, or sex.

To comply with the act, a real estate broker or
salesperson must refuse to accept any listing of
properties that involves discriminatory restrictions.
Furthermore, after a property is listed, the owner
may not refuse to sell to a member of any minority
group protected by the act. It is important that the
broker's clients realize the significance of this act.
Figure 15-1 shows the statement that all brokers
should post in their offices.

Specifically, Title VIII of the Civil Rights Act of
1968 (the Federal Fair Housing Act) prohibits any
owner or his agent (broker or salesperson) from engaging in the following discriminatory practices
(where the discrimination is based upon race, color,
religion, national origin, or sex):

☐ Refusal to rent, lease, sell, or negotiate concerning a property with any individual once the principal has made an offer.
☑ The offering of different terms or conditions for
  the purchase or rental of a property to different
  individuals because of their race, color, religion,
  national origin, or sex.
☐ Advertising that a property is available only to
  certain types of individuals, or indicating in advertising that certain groups are preferred.
☐ Making false statements regarding the availability
  of housing for sale or rent.
☐ Denying someone the use of real estate services
  by a broker or salesperson.

Affirmative Marketing Agreement

One of the consequences of the 1968 federal
legislation is a voluntary program adopted by the
National Association of Realtors® and known as the
Affirmative Marketing Agreement.

The purpose of the agreement, which also involves the Department of Housing and Urban Development, is to comply with the first sentence of

U.S. DEPARTMENT OF HOUSING AND URBAN DEVELOPMENT

Federal Fair Housing Law

(Title VIII of the Civil Rights Act of 1968)

It is Illegal To Discriminate Against Any Person
Because Of Race, Color, Religion,
Or National Origin

- In the sale or rental of housing or
  residential lots

- In advertising the sale or rental of
  housing

- In the financing of housing

- In the provision of real estate brokerage
  services

  Blockbusting is also illegal

*Those who feel they have been discriminated against
should send complaint to*

**U.S. Department of Housing and Urban Development,
Assistant Secretary for Equal Opportunity,
Washington, D.C. 20410**

FIG. 15-1 *All brokers should post this notice of the Federal Fair Housing Law in their offices.*

the 1968 Fair Housing Act. This states that it is the policy of the United States to provide within constitutional limitations fair housing throughout the United States. Pursuant to the agreement, REALTORS® undertake activities designed to inform members of minority groups of equal housing opportunities within a particular community.

This objective is implemented through advertising and educational programs as well as through specific office procedures and techniques.

Each member, Board, or State Association of Realtors must make an individual decision whether to adopt the agreement. In those member boards that adopt it, each REALTOR® must make a voluntary decision to subscribe to the agreements and accept the responsibilities set forth above.

Panic Selling and Blockbusting

The equal housing opportunity logo (Figure 15-2) signifies the compliance of newspapers which carry advertisements for housing for rent, lease, or sale. It must be displayed in every edition carrying real estate advertisements.

In addition to the discriminatory practices listed above, one other very important violation of the act is to call to the attention of a potential seller (in order to persuade him to rent or sell his property) the possibility that a minority group may move into an area and alter property values. This practice, known as *panic selling*, is illegal.

The term *blockbusting* is used to denote a similar but more elaborate practice that the Fair Housing Act has outlawed. In blockbusting unscrupulous brokers and salespersons incite majority-group homeowners to sell at low prices by initiating rumors of an invasion of minority-group owners and then steer minority householders into such transitional neighborhoods. Once the block has been "busted," the unscrupulous brokers can participate in numerous transactions as the racial composition of the neighborhood changes and panic selling occurs.

Discrimination by Lending Institutions

A special part of the Fair Housing Act (Section 805) is directed at banks, savings and loan associations, insurance companies, and any institution whose business is commercial real estate lending. If a person applies to such an institution because he wants to buy, build, improve, or maintain his dwelling, the institution may not discriminate against him by refusing to lend or by altering the amount,

EQUAL HOUSING OPPORTUNITY

All real estate advertised in this newspaper is subject to the Federal Fair Housing Act of 1968, which makes it illegal to advertise "any preference, limitations, or discrimination based on race, color, religion, or national origin, or an intention to make any such preference, limitations, or discrimination."

This newspaper will not knowingly accept any advertising for real estate which is in violation of the law. Our readers are hereby informed that all dwellings advertised in the newspaper are required to be available on an equal opportunity basis.

FIG. 15-2 *The Equal Housing Opportunity logo displayed in all newspapers which carry real estate ads.*

interest rate, term, or any other condition of the loan merely because of the potential borrower's race, color, religion, sex, or national origin.

Exemptions

The Federal Fair Housing Act is supplemented by state and local laws because constitutional questions may arise if the federal act is applied to all types of properties and transactions.

Exempt from the federal act is any single-family house that is sold or rented directly by the owner, provided that the owner's business is not real estate. An exempt owner must be the present or most recent occupant of the house; he may not own, or be committed to purchase, more than three houses at any time. Most important, an exempt owner may not advertise the property for sale or rental in a discriminatory fashion, and he may not use the services of a real estate broker.

The owner of a residence consisting of four or fewer apartments is also included among the exemptions provided he occupies one of the apartments.

Complaint Procedures

One of the Department of Housing and Urban Development's (HUD) most important roles is administration of the Federal Fair Housing Law. HUD has instituted services aimed at clarifying and explaining the law so as to prevent misunderstandings. An aggrieved individual who has been the victim of a discriminatory housing practice may file a complaint with the Secretary of HUD. Actually, under the Civil Rights Act, the complainant may go directly to the federal courts without even filing a complaint with HUD. However, in New York, individuals who feel they have a legitimate complaint have all sorts of local recourse. As we see below, there are state and municipal protections. Individuals may also complain to their local real estate boards. If they are not satisfied after taking such action, they may proceed to a local or state civil rights commisison. Going to the federal courts should probably be the last alternative.

Racial Steering

It is important that a licensee not *steer* a client toward a property for discriminatory reasons. The prospect, not the licensee, must pick the location. To steer the client away from property in a particular neighborhood or to limit the choice of housing based on any of the reasons listed in Title VIII is prohibited. Clients must choose from the properties listed the ones they wish to visit and consider for purchase.

Other Federal Influences on Fair Housing

The Fair Housing Act of 1968 is undoubtedly the principal legislation by the federal government relating to fair housing. Other federal acts and court rulings are however also directed at eliminating discrimination in housing.

The Home Mortgage Disclosure Act of 1975

This act requires most commercial lenders to make public disclosure of the geographical dispersion of their loans on a periodic basis. The purpose of the disclosure is to create pressure on the lenders concerning the geographic distribution of their loans. The act assumes that public opinion and the possibility that savers will withdraw their funds from banks that are not acting in the public interest will affect bank policy.

In passing this act, Congress attempted to minimize or eliminate the practice, known as *redlining*, by which banks automatically refuse to make loans to property owners in certain locations without individual consideration of the merits of each loan. This act does not specifically prohibit redlining and thus cannot be the basis for judicial relief if the practice is encountered. The termination date, without further action by Congress, is October 1, 1985.

Although the 1968 Fair Housing Act, by its own terms, does not apply to certain specified transactions, the Supreme Court in the landmark case of *Jones* vs. *Alfred H. Mayer Co.*, decided in 1968 that the 1866 Civil Rights Act, discussed earlier, bars all racial discrimination, whether private or public. As a practical matter, therefore, racial discrimination in any form is now illegal, including discrimination in housing.

The National Housing Act

This is the act under which HUD operates, in conjunction with the appropriate regulations, to establish minimum construction standards for properties. Since major portions of the national housing inventory have been built and continue to be built with the involvement of a HUD bureau—the Federal Housing Administration (FHA)—HUD construction standards have begun to create a minimum quality level for the construction of housing units.

The Federal Trade Commission

The Federal Trade Commission (FTC) is investigating real estate practices, especially as to multiple listing service access, group boycotts against competitors, group interchange of information to stabilize prices, practices restricting the variety of services consumers may purchase, unfair or deceptive forms, and the nondisclosure of material terms and practices resulting in inadequate representations of buyers' or sellers' interests in real estate transactions. The conduct being investigated is unfair trade practices that are prohibited by various federal laws and could result in enforcement action by the commission. If the FTC were to discover that such activities had occurred, those responsible would be subject to possible penalties for the conduct previously engaged in, as well as to the injunction of future unfair or illegal trade practices. Some of these practices may also be a violation of the antitrust laws.

The Real Estate Settlement and Procedures Act of 1975 (RESPA)

RESPA, as amended, was enacted with four primary objectives. The section of the act dealing with experimental title and recordkeeping systems is intended to explore alternate methods of conveyancing and recordkeeping to minimize the cost involved. Of more practical effect upon the consumer are the three other provisions.

The first of these requires lenders to make disclosures that are intended to enable the consumer to shop more effectively so that market competition reduces settlement cost. Unfortunately, the disclosures that must be made are available so late in the real estate purchase, financing, and settlement process that the consumer's option is illusory.

The second of the consumer protection provisions prohibits sellers or lenders from paying kickbacks, directly or indirectly. It is hoped that this prohibition will reduce costs, with the expectation that such savings will be passed on to the consumer.

Finally, there is a prohibition against the seller requiring the buyer to purchase title insurance from a specific company or agent as a condition of sale.

The Federal Bank Law

The Federal Bank Law prohibits any officer, director, employee, agent, or attorney of any bank which has its deposit insured by the Federal Deposit Insurance Corporation (FDIC) from receiving anything of value in return for the making or modification of a loan. It is also illegal for somebody to obtain such kickbacks for the officer. The Federal Deposit Insurance Corporation insures all national banks and members of the Federal Reserve System. Since most banks belong to the Federal Reserve System, this act applies to almost all banks. Similar laws exist that apply to savings and loan associations.

The Federal Home Loan Bank (FHLB)

The Federal Home Loan Bank has, by regulation, required savings and loan associations to make disclosures of costs incurred for the benefit of the lender but paid by the buyer, itemizing the nature

of the services, the time spent, and the hourly rate charged on all transactions where the charge for such services exceeds $100. The regulation also provides for disclosure of the relationship, if any, between the lender and the purveyor of the services.

The Interstate Land Sales Full Disclosure Act (ILSA)

This act requires land developers who sell in interstate commerce, typically by mail, radio, or periodical advertising, to file with the Secretary of HUD a statement of record which details information about the title to the land, the physical nature thereof, and the availability of roads and utilities. A printed property report must also be furnished any purchaser prior to the signing of a lease or offer to purchase. A failure to furnish timely reports gives the purchaser a right of rescission. This means, simply, that the purchaser can back out of the transaction without being subject to penalty. There are some exemptions from the act for small-scale developers and certain industrial or commercial developments.

The National Flood Insurance Act

This act provides a mechanism that makes available to homeowners casualty insurance against losses resulting from physical damage from flooding. The program is implemented at the market level by the requirement that certain categories of loans made on housing in flood-prone areas must be covered by flood insurance. The designated flood-prone areas appear on maps produced under HUD directive that are now available throughout the country. The act also provides that new construction in flood-prone areas must meet certain performance standards and it prohibits building in certain types of areas.

The Emergency Mortgage Relief Act of 1975

This act gives some help to homeowners who are threatened with foreclosure of their home because unemployment and loss of income makes it impossible for them to meet their mortgage loan payments. The act makes loans available to such owners amounting to $250 a month for two years to assist them in meeting their loan payments. Should this relief prove inadequate, HUD may ask lenders to delay or forego foreclosures in exchange for HUD's guarantee to the lender against ultimate loss.

The Consumer Credit Protection Act of 1969

This law was passed as the result of consumer concern about the quality of home mortgages. Included as part of this act was the Truth-in-Lending Act, which empowered the Federal Reserve Board to implement Regulation Z. The objective of Regulation Z is to let the purchaser of real property know exactly what credit charges are being paid to the lender and the exact terms of the loan. The regulation also covers advertising.

NEW YORK STATE LAW AGAINST DISCRIMINATION

New York State Executive Law (Sections 290-299) provides that it shall be unlawful for anyone who has the right to sell, rent, or lease a housing accommodation, land, or commercial space to refuse to sell, rent, or lease that interest because of the race, creed, color, national origin, age, sex, or marital status of the interested buyer, renter, or lessee.

Who must fulfill the requirements of this law? Obviously, an individual who has the right to sell, rent, or lease. He may be an owner, his assignee, a lessee, or sublessee, or an agent (broker or his salesperson).

What are they enjoined from doing? They cannot offer inferior or discriminatory provisions of sale, rental, or lease. They may not offer inferior furnishings or services to the protected minorities. They cannot prepare an advertisement that refers to their discrimination.

Is anyone exempt? Yes. The owner of a two-family house who lives in one of the two units and wishes to rent the other is exempt from this law. The renter of a room or rooms in a housing accommodation in which he or his family also live, is also exempt.

Does the real estate broker or salesperson have specific responsibilities? Yes. The broker, the real estate salesperson or his employee or his agent are specifically mentioned. They cannot refuse to sell, rent, or lease real property (residential or commercial) to any person or group because of race, creed, color, national origin, age, disability, sex, or marital status. They cannot tell such minority persons that a property is not available for sale, rental, or lease when, in fact, that is not the truth and the untruth is being used for discriminatory purposes. They cannot run an ad or use an application form or create any records that directly or indirectly express a "limitation, specification, or discrimination" related to a potential purchaser's or renter's race, creed, color national origin, or age. The prohibitions against age discrimination in the sale, rental, or leasing of any housing accommodation, land, or communal space shall not apply *exclusively* to persons 55 years of age or older.

Blockbusting

The real estate salesperson or his employer is prohibited from benefiting financially from transactions that we subsume under the name *blockbusting,* the solicitation of business using racial fear techniques. The rules and regulations promulgated by the New York Department of State under Article 12A of the Real Property Law prohibit this practice. (We have already noted that the practice is illegal under the Civil Rights Act of 1968.) Rule 175.17 specifically provides that no broker or salesperson shall solicit a residential property owner to sell, lease, or list property for sale on the grounds that the property may imminently lose its value because of the present or prospective entry into the neighborhood of persons of a particular race, religion, or ethnic origin. Nor shall a broker or salesperson distribute or cause to be distributed material or make statements designed to induce a residential property owner to sell or lease his property because the material persuades him that such change in the neighborhood is imminent.

An example of a typical blockbusting scheme runs as follows: A broker chooses a white neighborhood adjacent to a minority area, or an area in which the first signs of softening in real estate values can be seen, and offers to buy one or two homes from families (often from householders nearing retirement age) at prices well above fair market value. He then sells these homes (often at bargain rates) to minority families. As other homes are put up for sale (sometimes encouraged by the broker who fans fear that the area is "turning"), the broker continues to buy up homes at lower prices and sell them at higher prices to minority families. The domino effect of blockbusting has helped exacerbate racial prejudice and the flight to the suburbs.

Nonsolicitation Orders (Cease and Desist)

New York courts have held that licensed real estate brokers and salespersons have no absolute rights of solicitation. The New York Department of State has continuing responsibilities to set standards of broker's practice and to review broker's compliance with those standards and regulations whenever need for it is indicated.

The Secretary of State may issue a general *nonso-*

licitation order that prohibits all real estate brokers and salespersons from soliciting the listing of property for sale or purchase in a specified area.

The court has upheld action of the Secretary of State that has prohibited solicitation by real estate brokers and salespersons in a specified area as being in accord with the provisions of Article 12A, authorizing the secretary to revoke or suspend licenses for demonstrated unworthiness or incompetency.

However, in one case, the Court of Appeals backed a group of real estate brokers and salespersons who challenged a 1976 order by the Secretary of State that prohibited the solicitation of listings in Brooklyn and Queens by any means other than ads in newspapers of general circulation. The Secretary of State had contended that the nonsolicitation order was necessary because the real estate industry had been using racial blockbusting practices that undermined the stability of these two New York City boroughs. The court held that the particular order was arbitrary and capricious because the state had not established that a real danger existed.

In setting aside the nonsolicitation order, the court said that there was no need to decide about the constitutional validity of the Secretary of State's authority to issue the order or about the need for a prior public hearing before a nonsolicitation order can be promulgated. However, such orders generally must be reasonable in scope. If they are excessive or capricious, judicial review will not uphold them.

Redlining

Redlining is a name given to the alleged policy of certain financial institutions of refusing to make loans in so-called high-risk neighborhoods where the default-to-loan ratio is high. The picturesque phrase entered the language because of the lenders' alleged practice of outlining with a red pencil areas within which they would not make loans. Most lenders deny that they have such a policy. As we indicated, the federal government requires lenders to disclose the location of their mortgage loans by zip code number. The purpose of this disclosure is to enable depositors, and possibly local governments, to withdraw funds and so to punish lenders who do not make loans in certain areas.

New York State also recognizes the problems that may result from the practice of redlining. A New York State statute prohibits banking institutions from refusing to make prudent loans upon the security of real property, or from otherwise discriminating against properties because of their location, if such properties are located within the geographic area that these institutions ordinarily service.

under N.Y.'s Executive Law ag. Discrimination

State Mortgage Insurance

Recognizing that a shortage of mortgage financing has been one of the causes of substandard housing accommodations and deterioration of neighborhoods that threaten the health, safety, welfare, and comfort of the people of the state, the legislature has provided for the insurance of mortgage loans made in certain "blighted" areas. The insurance is administered by an agency known as the State of New York Mortgage Agency. The agency is charged with creating a revolving mortgage insurance fund the monies of which are to be derived primarily from an increase in the state's mortgage recording tax. These monies held in a mortgage insurance fund are used for the payment of the agency's liabilities as they arise from mortgage loan insurance.

Enforcement of Fair Housing Rules

The state law against discrimination is administered by the State Commission for Human Rights. Subject to review of their findings by the courts of New York State, seven commissioners receive, investigate, and pass on any complaints that allege the law was violated. If an individual violates a commission order, he may be fined $500, or imprisoned for not more than one year, or both.

Other violations of fair housing principles may be punished under terms of Section 441 of the Real Property Law. That law permits the Department of State to revoke or suspend a real estate broker's or salesperson's license for "untrustworthiness." (The Real Property Law was discussed in detail in Chapter 12.)

The Department of State considers discrimination to be an act of untrustworthiness prohibited under Article 12A of the Real Property Law. The courts have upheld the Department. In a case involving the suspension of the licenses of three real estate salespersons on the grounds that they had demonstrated untrustworthiness by discriminatory practices, the court indicated that the fact that racial discrimination by real estate brokers and salespersons is the basis of a complaint to the State Commission for Human Rights does not bar the Department of State from additionally disciplining licensees under Article 12A of the Real Property Law. The court indicated that the Department of State's actions do not involve enforcing provisions of the Executive Law but are merely the exercise of the general disciplinary powers that the Department has over real estate brokers and salespersons.

In an early instance, when the court concluded that a real estate practitioner's activities promoted racial segregation and disharmony, it held that the imposition of the 30-day suspension of the practitioner's license, or, in the alternative, a fine of $50 for each of the practitioner's offenses, plus a further and indefinite suspension of the licenses of the corporate licensee and its president did not constitute either excessive punishment or an abuse of discretion by the Department of State. Later cases have provided for substantially increased penalties.

NEW YORK CITY LAW AGAINST DISCRIMINATION

The terms of the New York City law are similar to those of the state law. It applies to the same categories of persons and gives similar exemptions.

Individuals who have been the victims of discrimination may file complaints with the Commission on Intergroup Relations. That commission refers its insoluble problems to the Fair Housing Practices Board which may, in turn, bring equitable proceedings in the State Supreme Court to enforce its recommendations.

ETHICAL STANDARDS FOR REAL ESTATE BROKERS AND SALESPERSONS

The general public views real estate practitioners as business people rather than as professionals. Even though real estate practitioners do not have the same standing as doctors or lawyers, they must nonetheless conduct their clients' business in a responsible, professional manner. Although each broker (and the salesperson responsible to the broker) competes with other brokers for new properties to list and sell, all brokers in a community should work together to establish and maintain ethical standards for dealings with clients, fellow brokers and salespersons, and with the general public.

High standards of ethical conduct are more important in the real estate business than in other businesses in which clients have a better understanding of services they are entitled to receive. In a typical real estate transaction, the broker may be required to perform a number of services with which clients are generally unfamiliar. Clients rely on the broker (or the salesperson) to guide them through the complicated maze of activities involved in buying or selling a home. It is most important therefore that the client be able to have the utmost confidence in the individual performing this critical service. Chapter 12 devotes itself to an analysis of the ethical responsibilities of the real estate broker and salesperson.

While real estate is not a true profession, social policy demands that its members conduct themselves in a professional manner. It is an area demanding great knowledge and specialists are found in the many different areas of the real estate business.

REAL ESTATE ORGANIZATIONS

The real estate industry is organized into several associations that operate on national, state, and local levels. They promote the general interest of the real estate community and they advocate the high standards of ethical conduct desired by those in the industry.

By far the largest of the real estate trade associations is the National Association of Realtors® (NAR®). The NAR® functions at local, state, and national levels. To be eligible to use the designation REALTOR®, a broker must be a member of NAR®.

Most brokers join a local board which is, in turn, affiliated with the state association and with the national association. Brokers and salespersons associated with principal brokers who are members of a local board join the board as associate members for a small additional fee assessed to the principal.

The NAR® has adopted a Code of Ethics and also a Code for Equal Opportunity which all REALTORS® are expected to adhere to (see Figures 15-3 and 15-4).

With respect to the question of discriminatory practices, Article 10 of the National Association of Realtors® Code of Ethics requires that "the REALTOR® shall not deny equal professional services to any person for reasons of race, creed, sex or country of national origin."

The REALTOR® shall also not be a party to any plan or agreement to discriminate against a person or persons on the basis of race, creed, sex, or country of national origin.

Article 10 of the Code of Ethics represents a firm statement of position and philosophy on housing opportunity promulgated by NAR® for all people.

There are many other national associations of real estate professionals; most are related to a real estate specialty. Each offers memberships in both the national organization and in local chapters. Some publish distinguished professional publications or offer specialized training, either through self-study or through organized classes. They usually urge real estate professionals to become candidates for their professional designations and certifications. Since many of these designations cannot be earned merely by the completion of courses and examinations but require an experience com-ponent, new professionals are advised to examine association literature carefully before enrolling in classes.

Appendix D lists the names and addresses of the major national real estate associations. It examines the purpose of each, the designations each confers, and the requirements for earning each designation.

Code of Ethics
of the
NATIONAL ASSOCIATION OF REALTORS®

REVISED AND APPROVED BY THE DELEGATE BODY OF THE ASSOCIATION AT ITS 75TH ANNUAL CONVENTION NOVEMBER 15, 1982

Preamble...

Under all is the land. Upon its wise utilization and widely allocated ownership depend the survival and growth of free institutions and of our civilization. The REALTOR® should recognize that the interests of the nation and its citizens require the highest and best use of the land and the widest distribution of land ownership. They require the creation of adequate housing, the building of functioning cities, the development of productive industries and farms, and the preservation of a healthful environment.

Such interests impose obligations beyond those of ordinary commerce. They impose grave social responsibility and a patriotic duty to which the REALTOR® should dedicate himself, and for which he should be diligent in preparing himself. The REALTOR®, therefore, is zealous to maintain and improve the standards of his calling and shares with his fellow REALTORS® a common responsibility for its integrity and honor. The term REALTOR® has come to connote competency, fairness, and high integrity resulting from adherence to a lofty ideal of moral conduct in business relations. No inducement of profit and no instruction from clients ever can justify departure from this ideal.

In the interpretation of this obligation, a REALTOR® can take no safer guide than that which has been handed down through the centuries, embodied in the Golden Rule, "Whatsoever ye would that men should do to you, do ye even so to them."

Accepting this standard as his own, every REALTOR® pledges himself to observe its spirit in all of his activities and to conduct his business in accordance with the tenets set forth below.

Article 1
The REALTOR® should keep himself informed on matters affecting real estate in his community, the state, and nation so that he may be able to contribute responsibly to public thinking on such matters.

Article 2
In justice to those who place their interests in his care, the REALTOR® should endeavor always to be informed regarding laws, proposed legislation, governmental regulations, public policies, and current market conditions in order to be in a position to advise his clients properly.

Article 3
It is the duty of the REALTOR® to protect the public against fraud, misrepresentation, and unethical practices in real estate transactions. He should endeavor to eliminate in his community any practices which could be damaging to the public or bring discredit to the real estate profession. The REALTOR® should assist the governmental agency charged with regulating the practices of brokers and salesmen in his state.

Article 4
The REALTOR® should seek no unfair advantage over other REALTORS® and should conduct his business so as to avoid controversies with other REALTORS®.

Article 5
In the best interests of society, of his associates, and his own business, the REALTOR® should willingly share with other REALTORS® the lessons of his experience and study for the benefit of the public, and should be loyal to the Board of REALTORS® of his community and active in its work.

Article 6
To prevent dissension and misunderstanding and to assure better service to the owner, the REALTOR® should urge the exclusive listing of property unless contrary to the best interest of the owner.

Article 7
In accepting employment as an agent, the REALTOR® pledges himself to protect and promote the interests of the client. This obligation of absolute fidelity to the client's interests is primary, but it does not relieve the REALTOR® of the obligation to treat fairly all parties to the transaction.

Article 8
The REALTOR® shall not accept compensation from more than one party, even if permitted by law, without the full knowledge of all parties to the transaction.

Article 9
The REALTOR® shall avoid exaggeration, misrepresentation, or concealment of pertinent facts. He has an affirmative obligation to discover adverse factors that a reasonably competent and diligent investigation would disclose.

Article 10
The REALTOR® shall not deny equal professional services to any person for reasons of race, creed, sex, or country of national origin.

FIG. 15-3 The NAR® Code of Ethics.

The REALTOR® shall not be party to any plan or agreement to discriminate against a person or persons on the basis of race, creed, sex, or country of national origin.

Article 11

A REALTOR® is expected to provide a level of competent service in keeping with the standards of practice in those fields in which the REALTOR® customarily engages.

The REALTOR® shall not undertake to provide specialized professional services concerning a type of property or service that is outside his field of competence unless he engages the assistance of one who is competent on such types of property or service, or unless the facts are fully disclosed to the client. Any person engaged to provide such assistance shall be so identified to the client and his contribution to the assignment should be set forth.

The REALTOR® shall refer to the Standards of Practice of the National Association as to the degree of competence that a client has a right to expect the REALTOR® to possess, taking into consideration the complexity of the problem, the availability of expert assistance, and the opportunities for experience available to the REALTOR®.

Article 12

The REALTOR® shall not undertake to provide professional services concerning a property or its value where he has a present or contemplated interest unless such interest is specifically disclosed to all affected parties.

Article 13

The REALTOR® shall not acquire an interest in or buy for himself, any member of his immediate family, his firm or any member thereof, or any entity in which he has a substantial ownership interest, property listed with him, without making the true position known to the listing owner. In selling property owned by himself, or in which he has any interest, the REALTOR® shall reveal the facts of his ownership or interest to the purchaser.

Article 14

In the event of a controversy between REALTORS® associated with different firms, arising out of their relationship as REALTORS®, the REALTORS® shall submit the dispute to arbitration in accordance with the regulations of their board or boards rather than litigate the matter.

Article 15

If a REALTOR® is charged with unethical practice or is asked to present evidence in any disiplinary proceeding or investigation, he shall place all pertinent facts before the proper tribunal of the member board or affiliated institute, society, or council of which he is a member.

Article 16

When acting as agent, the REALTOR® shall not accept any commission, rebate, or profit on expenditures made for his principal-owner, without the principal's knowledge and consent.

Article 17

The REALTOR® shall not engage in activities that constitute the unauthorized practice of law and shall recommend that legal counsel be obtained when the interest of any party to the transaction requires it.

Article 18

The REALTOR® shall keep in a special account in an appropriate financial institution, separated from his own funds, monies coming into his possession in trust for other persons, such as escrows, trust funds, clients' monies, and other like items.

Article 19

The REALTOR® shall be careful at all times to present a true picture in his advertising and representations to the public. He shall neither advertise without disclosing his name nor permit any person associated with him to use individual names or telephone numbers, unless such person's connection with the REALTOR® is obvious in the advertisement.

Article 20

The REALTOR®, for the protection of all parties, shall see that financial obligations and commitments regarding real estate transactions are in writing, expressing the exact agreement of the parties. A copy of each agreement shall be furnished to each party upon his signing such agreement.

Article 21

The REALTOR® shall not engage in any practice or take any action inconsistent with the agency of another REALTOR®.

Article 22

In the sale of property which is exclusively listed with a REALTOR®, the REALTOR® shall utilize the services of other brokers upon mutually agreed upon terms when it is in the best interests of the client.

Negotiations concerning property which is listed exclusively shall be carried on with the listing broker, not with the owner, except with the consent of the listing broker.

Article 23

The REALTOR® shall not publicly disparage the business practice of a competitor nor volunteer an opinion of a competitor's transaction. If his opinion is sought and if the REALTOR® deems it appropriate to respond, such opinion shall be rendered with strict professional integrity and courtesy.

Where the word REALTOR® is used in this Code and Preamble, it shall be deemed to include REALTOR-ASSOCIATE®. Pronouns shall be considered to include REALTORS® and REALTOR-ASSOCIATE®s of both genders.

The Code of Ethics was adopted in 1913. Amended at the Annual Convention in 1924, 1928, 1950, 1951, 1952, 1955, 1956, 1961, 1962, 1974, and 1982.

Standards of Practice
Relating to
Articles of the Code of Ethics
(Adopted through May 10, 1984)

The Standards of Practice relating to the Code of Ethics are "interpretations" of various Articles of the Code of Ethics and are not a part of the Code itself. The proper relationship between the Standards of Practice and the Code of Ethics is set forth in the following advisory opinion by the Professional Standards Committee, which was approved by the Board of Directors of the National Association:

"In filing a charge of an alleged violation of the Code of Ethics by a REALTOR®, the charge shall read as an alleged violation of one or more Articles of the Code. A Standard of Practice may only be cited in support of the charge."

The Standards of Practice are supplementary to, and do not replace, the "numbered cases" found in *Interpretations of the Code of Ethics*. A Standard of Practice is a statement of general principle related to an Article of the Code of Ethics to guide REALTORS® and REALTOR-ASSOCIATE®s as to the professional conduct required in the specific situation described by the Standard of Practice, whereas each of the "numbered cases" in *Interpretations of the Code of Ethics* presents a set of particular facts alleging a violation of the Code of Ethics, and describes the conclusion determined on merit by the Professional Standards Committee as related to the particular facts of the case.

As additional Standards of Practice are adopted, Member Boards and Board Members will be advised of their adoption.

Standard of Practice 4-1

"The REALTOR® shall not misrepresent the availability of access to show or inspect a listed property."

Standard of Practice 7-1

"The REALTOR® shall receive and shall transmit all offers on a specified property to the owner for his decision, whether such offers are received from a prospective purchaser or another broker."

Standard of Practice 7-2

"The REALTOR®, acting as listing broker, shall submit all offers to the seller as quickly as possible."

Standard of Practice 7-3

"The REALTOR®, in attempting to secure a listing, shall not deliberately mislead the owner as to market value."

Standard of Practice 7-4

(Refer to Standard of Practice 22-1, which also relates to Article 7, Code of Ethics.)

Standard of Practice 7-5

(Refer to Standard of Practice 22-2, which also relates to Article 7, Code of Ethics.)

Standard of Practice 7-6

The REALTOR®, when acting as a principal in a real estate transaction, cannot avoid his responsibilities under the Code of Ethics.

Standard of Practice 9-1

"The REALTOR® shall not be a party to the naming of a false consideration in any document, unless it be the naming of an obviously nominal consideration."

Standard of Practice 9-2

(Refer to Standard of Practice 21-3, which also relates to Article 9, Code of Ethics.)

Standard of Practice 9-3

(Refer to Standard of Practice 7-3, which also relates to Article 9, Code of Ethics.)

Standard of Practice 9-4

"The REALTOR® shall not offer a service described as 'free of charge' when the rendering of a service is contingent on the obtaining of a benefit such as a listing or commission."

Standard of Practice 9-5

"The REALTOR® shall, with respect to the subagency of another REALTOR®, timely communicate any change of compensation for subagency services to the other REALTOR® prior to the time such REALTOR® produces a prospective buyer who has signed an offer to purchase the property for which the subagency has been offered through MLS or otherwise by the listing agency."

Standard of Practice 9-6

REALTORS® shall disclose their REALTOR® status when seeking information from another REALTOR® concerning real property for which the other REALTOR® is an agent or subagent.

Standard of Practice 11-1

"Whenever a REALTOR® submits an oral or written opinion of the value of real property for a fee, his opinion shall be supported by a memorandum in his file or an appraisal report, either of which shall include as a minimum the following:
1. Limiting conditions
2. Any existing or contemplated interest
3. Defined value
4. Date applicable
5. The estate appraised
6. A description of the property
7. The basis of the reasoning including applicable market data and/or capitalization computation
" This report or memorandum shall be available to the Professional Standards Committee for a period of at least two years (beginning subsequent to final determination of the court if the appraisal is involved in litigation) to ensure compliance with Article 11 of the Code of Ethics of the NATIONAL ASSOCIATION OF REALTORS®."

Standard of Practice 11-2

"The REALTOR® shall not undertake to make an appraisal when his employment or fee is contingent upon the amount of appraisal."

Standard of Practice 11-3

"REALTORS® engaged in real estate securities and syndications transactions are engaged in an activity subject to regulations beyond those governing real estate transactions generally, and therefore have the affirmative obligation to be informed of applicable federal and state laws, and rules and regulations regarding these types of transactions."

Standard of Practice 12-1

(Refer to standards of Practice 9-4 and 16-1, which also relate to Article 12, Code of Ethics.)

Standard of Practice 15-1

"The REALTOR® shall not be subject to disciplinary proceedings in more than one Board of REALTORS® with respect to alleged violations of the Code of Ethics relating to the same transaction."

Standard of Practice 15-2

"The REALTOR® shall not make any unauthorized disclosure or dissemination of the allegations, findings or decision developed in connection with an ethics hearing or appeal."

Standard of Practice 16-1

"The REALTOR® shall not recommend or suggest to a principal or a customer the use of services of another organization or business entity in which he has a direct interest without disclosing such interest at the time of the recommendation or suggestion."

Standard of Practice 19-1

"The REALTOR® shall not submit or advertise property without authority, and in any offering, 'the price quoted shall not be other than that agreed upon with the owners."

Standard of Practice 19-2

(Refer to Standard of Practice 9-4, which also relates to Article 19, Code of Ethics.)

Standard of Practice 21-1

"Signs giving notice of property for sale, rent, lease, or exchange shall not be placed on property without the consent of the owner."

Standard of Practice 21-2

"The REALTOR® obtaining information from a listing broker about a specific property shall not convey this information to, nor invite the cooperation of a third party broker without the consent of the listing broker."

Standard of Practice 21-3

"The REALTOR® shall not solicit a listing which is currently listed exclusively with another broker. However, if the listing broker, when asked by the REALTOR®, refuses to disclose the expiration date and nature of such listing; i.e., an exclusive right to sell, an exclusive agency, open listing, or other form of contractual agreement between the listing broker and his client, the REALTOR® may contact the owner to secure such information."

Standard of Practice 21-4

"The REALTOR® shall not use information obtained by him from the listing broker, through offers to cooperate received through Multiple Listing Services or other sources authorized by the listing broker, for the purpose of creating a referral prospect to a third broker, or for creating a buyer prospect unless such use is authorized by the listing broker."

Standard of Practice 21-5

"The fact that a property has been listed exclusively with a REALTOR® shall not preclude or inhibit any other REALTOR® from soliciting such listing after its expiration."

Standard of Practice 21-6

"The fact that a property owner has retained a REALTOR® as his exclusive agent in respect of one or more past transactions creates no interest or agency which precludes or inhibits other

REALTORS⁽ᴿ⁾ from seeking such owner's future business."

Standard of Practice 21-7
"The REALTOR⁽ᴿ⁾ shall be free to solicit a listing in respect to any property which is open listed at any time."

Standard of Practice 21-8
"Unless otherwise precluded by law, the REALTOR⁽ᴿ⁾ may discuss with an owner of a property which is exclusively listed with another REALTOR⁽ᴿ⁾ the terms upon which he would accept a future listing upon the expiration of the present listing provided the owner initiates the discussion and provided the REALTOR⁽ᴿ⁾ has not directly or indirectly solicited such discussion."

Standard of Practice 21-9
"In cooperative transactions a REALTOR⁽ᴿ⁾ shall compensate the cooperating REALTOR⁽ᴿ⁾ (principal broker) and shall not compensate nor offer to compensate, directly or indirectly, any of the sales licensees employed by or affiliated with another REALTOR⁽ᴿ⁾ without the prior express knowledge and consent of the cooperating broker."

Standard of Practice 21-10
"Article 21 does not preclude REALTORS⁽ᴿ⁾ from making general announcements to property owners describing their services and the terms of their availability even though some recipients may have exclusively listed their property for sale or lease with another REALTOR⁽ᴿ⁾ A general telephone canvas, general mailing or distribution addressed to all property owners in a given geographical area or in a given profession, business, club, or organization, or other classification or group is deemed 'general' for purposes of this standard.
Article 21 is intended to recognize as unethical two basic types of solicitation:
First, telephone or personal solicitations of property owners who have been identified by a real estate sign, multiple listing compilation, or other information service as having exclusively listed their property with another REALTOR⁽ᴿ⁾; and
Second, mail or other forms of written solicitations of property owners whose properties are exclusively listed with another REALTOR⁽ᴿ⁾ when such solicitations are not part of a general mailing but are directed specifically to property owners identified through compilations of current listings, 'for sale' signs, or other sources of information required by Article 22 and multiple listing service rules to be made available to other REALTORS® under offers of subagency or cooperation."

Standard of Practice 21-11
"The REALTOR®, prior to accepting a listing, has an affirmative obligation to make reasonable efforts to determine whether the property is subject to a current, valid exclusive listing agreement."

Standard of Practice 22-1
"It is the obligation of the selling broker as subagent of the listing broker to disclose immediately all pertinent facts to the listing broker prior to as well as after the contract is executed."

Standard of Practice 22-2
"The REALTOR®, when submitting offers to the seller, shall present each in an objective and unbiased manner."

"The NATIONAL ASSOCIATION OF REALTORS® reserves exclusively unto itself the right to officially comment on and interpret the CODE and particular provisions thereof. For the NATIONAL ASSOCIATION's official interpretations of the CODE, see INTERPRETATIONS OF THE CODE OF ETHICS; NATIONAL ASSOCIATION OF REALTORS®."

REALTOR®

NATIONAL ASSOCIATION OF REALTORS®

Code for Equal Opportunity

(Local Board Name Goes Here)

subscribes to the policy that equal opportunity in the acquisition of housing can best be accomplished through leadership, example, education, and the mutual co-operation of the real estate industry and the public. In the spirit of this endeavor, this board proclaims the following provisions of its Code for Equal Opportunity to which each member is obligated to adhere:

1. In the sale, purchase, exchange, rental, or lease of real property, REALTORS' and their REALTOR ASSOCIATES have the responsibility to offer equal service to all clients and prospects without regard to race, color, religion, or national origin. This encompasses:

    A. Standing ready to enter broker-client relationships or to show property equally to members of all racial, creedal, or ethnic groups.

    B. Receiving all formal written offers and communicating them to the owner.

    C. Exerting their best efforts to conclude all transactions.

    D. Maintaining equal opportunity employment practices.

2. Members, individually and collectively, in performing their agency functions have no right or responsibility to volunteer information regarding the racial, creedal, or ethnic composition of any neighborhood or any part thereof.

3. Members shall not engage in any activity which has the purpose of inducing panic selling.

4. Members shall not print, display, or circulate any statement or advertisement with respect to the sale or rental of a dwelling that indicates any preference, limitations, or discrimination based on race, color, religion, or ethnic background.

5. Members who violate the spirit or any provision of this Code for Equal Opportunity shall be subject to disciplinary action.

Those who feel they have been discriminated against may contact the management of this office or the Board of REALTORS®

FIG. 15-4 The NAR® Code for Equal Opportunity.

REVIEW QUESTIONS

1. The agency which administers the insurance of mortgage loans made in blighted areas is

   (a) State Commission on Human Rights.
   (b) The State of New York Mortgage Agency.
   (c) The Office of the Secretary of State.
   (d) None of the above.

2. Redlining is the alleged practice of certain banks of not lending money secured by mortgages on

   (a) Residential property.
   (b) Commercial property.
   (c) Property in blighted areas.
   (d) None of the above.

3. Blockbusting is the solicitation of the sale, leasing, or listing for sale of residential property on the grounds of

   (a) Appreciation of property values in the area.
   (b) Entry of commercial business into the area.
   (c) Entry into the area of persons of another race, religion or ethnic origins.
   (d) None of the above.

4. The application of a nonsolicitation order by the Secretary of State

   (a) Must be reasonable in scope.
   (b) May be arbitrary and capricious.
   (c) Must last no longer than thirty days.
   (d) All of the above.

5. New York State Executive Law prohibits discrimination based upon considerations of

   (a) Race.
   (b) National origin.
   (c) Both a and b.
   (d) None of the above.

6. Discrimination which is practiced by a broker is considered to be an act of untrustworthiness and is a violation of which article of the Real Property Law?

   (a) Article 9A.
   (b) Article 9B.
   (c) Article 12A.
   (d) None of the above.

7. The agency which enforces antidiscrimination laws is the

   (a) State Commission for Human Rights.
   (b) Secretary of State.
   (c) Both a and b.
   (d) None of the above.

8. The Civil Rights Act of 1866 was not very effective for over 100 years because

   (a) It affected only intrastate transfers.
   (b) Real estate is not in interstate commerce.
   (c) It was believed that real estate was in intrastate commerce.
   (d) None of the above.

9. *Jones v. Alfred H. Mayer* (1968)

   (a) Did not affect the Civil Rights Act of 1866.
   (b) Held that Caucasian clauses were enforceable only by governmental officials.
   (c) Held that the Civil Rights Act of 1866 applied to individuals as well as government.
   (d) None of the above.

10. *Shelley v. Kraemer* (1947)

    (a) Expanded the decision of *Jones v. Alfred H. Mayer.*
    (b) Held race restrictions to be unenforceable.
    (c) Held race restrictions to be illegal.
    (d) None of the above.

11. The need for fair and equal housing opportunities exists because

    (a) It is morally correct and in the interest of the community.
    (b) It raises real estate taxes.
    (c) It creates a larger supply of rental housing.
    (d) None of the above.

12. The Federal Fair Housing Act is

    (a) Title VIII of the Civil Rights Act of 1968.
    (b) Title VIII of the Civil Rights Act of 1866.
    (c) Title VI of the Civil Rights Act of 1968.
    (d) Title VI of the Civil Rights Act of 1866.

13. Under the Federal Fair Housing Act,

    (a) A broker may not accept listings which involve discriminatory practices.

(b) A broker may accept a listing which involves discriminatory practices but must nevertheless show the house to all customers.

(c) A homeowner may not, under any circumstances, discriminate.

(d) None of the above.

14. A homeowner who has listed his house with a broker may, under the Federal Fair Housing Act,

(a) Refuse to sell to a minority owner protected by the act.

(b) Sell under different terms to a minority owner protected by the act.

(c) Must sell on the same terms to a minority owner protected by the act.

(d) None of the above.

15. Under federal law, a salesperson or broker must

A. Show listed real estate to any interested party.

B. Not discriminate in the rental, sale, or lease of property.

(a) A only.   (c) Both A and B.
(b) B only.   (d) Neither A nor B.

16. Title VIII of the Civil Rights Act allows

(a) Racial steering.
(b) Direct complaint procedures.
(c) Panic selling.
(d) Both a and c.

17. Under Title VIII discrimination in housing takes place when individuals are denied housing on the basis of

age isn't considered in this

A. Race, creed, or age.
B. Religion, sex, or national origin.

(a) A only.   (c) Both A and B.
(b) B only.   (d) Neither A nor B.

18. A broker is guilty of racial steering if

A. He steers clients into a particular neighborhood.

B. He steers prospective clients to a broker of their national origin or color.

(a) A only.   (c) Both A and B.
(b) B only.   (d) Neither A nor B.

19. Under the 1968 Federal Fair Housing Act, it is possible to

(a) Complain about discriminatory practices to HUD.

(b) Take complaints directly to court.

(c) Require immediate repayment of expenses caused by discriminatory practices.

(d) Two of the above.

20. The practice of blockbusting is acceptable

(a) When the purchaser and seller agree to it.

(b) When the broker explains to his client that it is being practiced.

(c) When approved by HUD.

(d) Never.

Chapter 16
Land Use Regulations

VOCABULARY

You will find it important to have a complete working knowledge of the following concepts and words found in this chapter:

building codes	exclusionary zoning	restrictive covenant
building permit	merger of covenants	setback ordinance
certificate of occupancy (CO)	mutual covenant	spot zoning
cluster zoning	nonconforming use	subdivision
common scheme restrictions	planned unit development	variance
convenant	protective covenant	zoning
density	racial restriction	zoning district
enabling act		

THE OPENING CHAPTERS of this book indicated that the allodial system of land ownership prevails in this country. Although this system clothes the individual (as opposed to the state) with the ownership of real property, that ownership is nevertheless limited by certain legally recognized restrictions concerning the use of the property.

In recent years, due to increased recognition of the need to control and regulate the environment for the benefit of all, property use has been publicly regulated either through the exercise of the legislative power of eminent domain or through the implementation of zoning laws enacted at the local level of government.

In addition, individual ownership rights may be limited by private agreements. Adjoining property owners may agree to restrict the use to which their lands may be placed. The concepts of restrictive covenants and zoning regulations will be examined in this chapter.

RESTRICTIVE COVENANTS

A *restrictive covenant* is a private agreement, usually arranged between adjoining property owners, that limits the use to which a designated parcel of real property may be placed. The agreement, if properly prepared, is enforceable in a court of law, and, in effect, permits the property owners to write their own law limiting the use of a specific parcel of property. A restrictive covenant may be made to "run with the land" so that it binds not only the parties to the agreement, but the successive owners of the burdened estate. The agreement creating the covenant usually must be executed not only by the interested property owners but by others, such as existing mortgage lenders who have an interest in the burdened property and who might otherwise cancel the agreement by foreclosure.

Restrictive covenants may be used to limit the size, area, and location of buildings which may be erected on the property. They may require that buildings be set back a specified distance from one or more property lines. They may limit the type of occupancy in the property or the business use to which the property may be put.

Restrictive Covenant Distinguished From a Zoning Regulation. A zoning law is a governmentally imposed restriction affecting the use of real property. Zoning laws result from police powers inherent in the states and granted by the states to local municipalities by special laws known as enabling statutes. Although both zoning laws and restrictive covenants limit the use which may be made of real property, the sources of their authority are separate and distinct. Even if a zoning law is imposed by a governmental entity, it does not negate, supersede, or otherwise cancel an incompatible restrictive covenant. For example, if the current zoning law permits properties in a certain area to be developed or used for commercial purposes, a restrictive covenant that prohibits that use on a specific parcel may nevertheless be enforced by the owner of the benefited estate.

Restrictive Covenant Distinguished from Conditional Conveyance. A restrictive covenant must also be distinguished from a conveyance on condition. This type of conveyance was discussed in Chapter 3. That chapter indicated that the two basic types of conditional conveyances are a fee simple subject to a condition subsequent and a fee simple on special limitation. When ownership is the result of either of these conveyances, if the condition is breached or if the event recited in the grant occurs, the title to the property may revert back to the original grantor or to his successors in interest.

By contrast, if a property is sold subject to a covenant, and that covenant is subsequently breached, the violating owner does not forfeit his title. The owner of the property benefited by the covenant may sue the burdened property owner who has violated the covenant for damages suffered, or the benefited party may try to enjoin the activity or use that is prohibited by the covenant. Sometimes, doubt exists as to whether the language in a particular conveyance creates a restrictive covenant or a conveyance upon condition. In those cases the courts are generally inclined to treat the ambiguous clause as a restrictive covenant. This is reasonable. The courts are generally reluctant to impose the penalties of fortfeiture or loss of title that might possibly be required if the grant were deemed a conditional conveyance.

Types of Restrictive Covenants

The various classes or kinds of restrictive covenants generally recognized in New York State have been described by the courts in several significant cases. These cases indicated that there are three basic types of enforceable covenants.

The Uniform Neighborhood Plan

A so called *common scheme* or *uniform neighborhood plan* is usually created by a developer who subdivides property. Either by a declaration of covenant and restrictions or by recitals appearing in all the deeds to all the different lot purchasers, the developer imposes uniform restrictions on the use of the burdened properties.

These covenants are often known as *protective covenants,* because they are designed to upgrade the quality of the neighborhood by imposing a measure of uniformity on the type of structures and on the uses which may be made of the property. Such a common scheme type of covenant is enforceable by any property owner in the subdivision against any other property owner in the same subdivision, on the theory of mutuality of covenants and consideration. Every property owner is deemed to have bought his property in reliance upon the existence and enforceability of the restrictive covenants. The decrease in value which the lot owner may suffer because his use of the land is restricted is offset by the increase in value that arises from the imposition of the same covenants on all the other lots in the development. An example of such a covenant is found in Figure 16-1.

Covenant Benefiting Neighboring Owners

The second basic type of covenant is a covenant for the benefit of land contiguous to or neighboring that of the covenant grantor. If, for example, a property owner sells a portion of his property and retains the balance, he may impose a restriction on the land sold for the benefit of the unsold portion of his property. For instance, he might sell the land with the covenant that no commercial or industrial use be made of the property. Since the covenant benefits his remaining lands, he or any subsequent purchaser of those remaining lands could enforce it. The covenant burdens the land that was originally sold. If the burdened tract were resold and further subdivided, all subsequent owners would be similarly burdened by that covenant.

The courts have refused to enforce covenants that have been imposed on a parcel of land at the time of its transfer if the seller did not retain either abutting land or land in the same neighborhood. They have held that in such cases, the seller had no legally recognized interest in enforcing a restrictive covenant.

Mutual Covenants

The third broad class of covenants recognized by case law are the so-called *mutual covenants* by which adjoining property owners similarly restrict their respective properties for the benefit of each other. The original parties to the agreement as well as all successive parties in interest would normally

HARRY JONES AND MARY JONES, his wife

-to-

ROBERT SMITH AND JANE SMITH, his wife

Dated: 1/4/52   Recorded: 1/8/52   Liber: 1219   Page: 228

Subject to the following restrictions, conditions and covenants which shall run with the title to said lot forever:

(1)   That no business or manufacturing shall ever be conducted on the lands hereby conveyed or any part thereof.

(2)   That no junk or other unsightly, objectionable or offensive material shall ever be stored, kept or maintained on said premises or any part thereof.

(3)   That not more than one dwelling house shall ever be built or maintained on one lot and no lot on which a dwelling house is erected or maintained shall have a street frontage of less than fifty feet.

(4)   That no dwelling house either designed for occupancy by more than two families, or actually occupied by more than two families shall ever be erected or maintained on the lands hereby conveyed or any part thereof.

(5)   That no building designed for use as dwelling, or actually used as a dwelling, which shall occupy less that 500 square feet of ground space, exclusive of porches, shall ever be erected or maintained on said premises.

(6) That no part of any structure shall ever be erected, constructed or maintained on said premises within fifteen feet of the street line abutting the front of said premises, as shown on said map, except such structures as may be wholly below the actual grade of such street.

(7)   That no garage or structure other than a dwelling house shall ever be erected or maintained on said premises within sixty feet of the street line abutting the front of said premises as shown on said map, unless such garage or other structure shall be built in or attached to a dwelling house or shall be made a part thereof.

(8)   That no billboard or sign shall ever be erected or maintained on said premises, nor shall any tight board or metal fence over five feet in height ever be erected or maintained upon or about the lands hereby conveyed, or any part thereof.

(9)   That no outside privy or water closet shall be constructed, used or maintained on said premises.

FIG. 16-1   An example of a common-scheme covenant.

be both benefited and burdened by those covenants and either could enforce them in a court of law.

Effect of Restrictive Covenants on the Land

A restrictive covenant that burdens a parcel of land renders the title to that parcel "unmarketable" because it limits the use that may be made of that particular parcel. It is deemed to be a legal defect, even though it may, in fact, have a beneficial effect and actually enhance the value of the affected property. When he prepares the sales contract, the seller's attorney should set forth any covenant of which he is aware so that the buyer may not reject title upon learning of its existence. When the purchaser's attorney receives a contract reciting such a restrictive covenant, he should analyze it carefully to determine whether it will interfere with the purchaser's contemplated property use. Title insurance companies will usually cooperate with the respective attorneys by providing them with copies of the particular restrictive covenant for their review.

Interpretations of Covenants and Restrictions

Covenants and restrictions are strictly construed by the courts. If there is any ambiguity in the meaning of the covenant, the court's decision is normally against the imposer. In interpreting a covenant, the courts try to ascertain the intention of the parties at the time of the creation of the covenant. However, establishing the intention of the parties after the fact may be difficult if the only guide available to the court is the particular language in the covenant. For example, a covenant that restricts the use of the property to "residential purposes," may have been intended to limit the use to single-family dwellings. However, this is vague language that may also permit the erection of an apartment building.

Duration of Restrictive Covenants

An agreement constituting a covenant running with the land does not abate nor is it affected by the death of either property owner. However, unless the agreement creating the restrictive covenant sets forth an expiration date, the covenant is limited to a reasonable time, given the circumstances and the purpose of its imposition.

In addition to terminating at an expiration date provided in the agreement, a covenant may become ineffective for any of the following reasons:

☐ *Release and cancellation by all affected parties.* A covenant may be terminated (released) by agreement of all of the benefited property owners and their successors in interest. To be effective, such release should be in writing, subscribed (signed) by the interested parties, and properly acknowledged and recorded so as to make the release a matter of public record. However, a single objecting property owner, who has a valid enforcement right, is entitled to relief even though every other owner with a similar right of enforcement has released.

☐ *Merger.* In the event that title to both the benefitted and burdened property is united in the same individual or legal entity, unless otherwise provided a merger of interest results and the covenant expires as a matter of law.

☐ *Lack of purpose.* If the restriction is of no actual or substantial benefit to the person seeking its enforcement, either because the purpose of the restriction has already been accomplished or by reason of changes of conditions, or for any other cause, a court may adjudge that the restriction is unenforceable. It can be completely extinguished if the burdened property owner pays any damages that the person entitled to enforce the restriction may sustain from the extinguishment.

☐ *Changing character of the neighborhood.* If the character and conditions in a neighborhood have so changed as to render the enforcement of a covenant unconscionable, it will not be enforced. However, the change must be radical, extensive, and permanent.

Sometimes a title insurance company is asked to "insure over the enforcement of restrictive covenants." That is, the insurer is asked to insure that the covenants will not be enforced. If investigations and personal inspection persuade the insurer that the character of the affected neighborhood has changed so dramatically that it is apparent that a court will not enforce the covenants, a title company may, for the payment of additional premium, insure against the successful outcome of an action brought to enforce the covenants.

Enforceability of Covenants

A benefited owner attempting to enforce a covenant must, himself, not have violated the covenant that he is attempting to enforce. Unless he comes into court with clean hands, his application for relief will usually be denied.

Racial or ethnic restrictions that prohibit the sale of property to members of a particular racial or ethnic group have been outlawed, and such covenants no longer have any force and effect. In New York, the County Clerk's office may not accept for recordation any instrument which contains a racial restriction. Preexisting restrictive covenants that include racial (or ethnic) restrictions, among other restrictions, are deemed enforceable as to the other restrictions but not as to the racial restrictions.

ZONING AND SUBDIVISION PLANNING

Zoning may be defined as land use regulation by legislation. A governmental entity creates within its boundaries certain districts within which are grouped various phases of communal activity. (For convenience we shall refer to the municipality as the zoning authority, although other government entities also have zoning powers and responsibilities.)

The general purpose of zoning is to control the future growth of an area so that the growth follows a comprehensive, orderly plan. Zoning attempts to control the physical growth of a community so that it does not endanger the health, safety, and general welfare of the inhabitants of the community. Zoning may have aesthetic motivations, or it may attempt to preserve the "quality of life" in a community. Zoning may also have economic motivation and may be a technique for preserving property values.

The creation of and enforcement of zoning laws and regulations stem from the police power that is inherent in each of the 50 states. A state delegates police powers to its local communities by laws known as enabling statutes. The police power having thus been delegated can be exercised by the local community through the promulgation of a comprehensive community plan and zoning ordinances adopted pursuant to the enabling statutes.

Since zoning regulations are based upon the police power, they are justified only to the extent that they promote the public health, safety, welfare, and good order of the community. Zoning regulations that are "arbitrary," "unreasonable," or "confiscatory" have been held invalid by the courts. The burden of establishing the arbitrariness or unreasonableness of a particular zoning ordinance is imposed upon the individual or private entity that attacks it.

Planning Commissions

State law provides for the existence of planning commissions that operate at various levels of state and local government. The purpose of such commissions is to guide development in local communities in order to create or maintain healthy and safe environments in which the residents can lead productive and useful lives. Planning boards generally have the power to prepare and amend comprehensive master plans for the development of their political jurisdictions. The plans may set out, among other things, streets, parks, sites for public buildings and structures, zoning districts, and routes for the location of public utilities. The commissions also have the power to approve or disapprove subdivision plats and to make investigations and issue reports concerning the planning and development of the municipality as are deemed desirable.

The various planning decisions of a community are implemented primarily by statutes known as zoning ordinances.

Zoning Ordinances

In order to protect buildings and their occupants from fire and other hazards, to assure that building occupants have adequate light and air, to guard against excessive concentration of population, and to otherwise promote the public health, safety, and welfare, a municipality may divide itself into a number of zoning districts in accordance with a comprehensive community plan. Large communities usually include a number of residential, business, commercial, and industrial districts. In each type of district there are regulations or restrictions concerning property use, building height, the percentage of a lot that a building may cover, and even population density.

One of the major goals of zoning is to establish a certain degree of homogeneity in each district. However, not all districts of the same type are zoned alike. One district may require that each single-family residential lot have a minimum of 100 front feet, while the minimum in the next single-family residential district may be 50 front feet. A municipality may impose a *basic homogeneity* on an area by designating it for residential use, while permitting variations of residential use within the zone. Homogeneity and variations may be specified for building heights, the number of families in each home, and for other factors limiting the use of the land. In certain instances, overlapping of zone areas may be permitted. For example, a residential zone may permit certain commercial uses within the zone if they are free of nuisances or if they have a beneficial professional nature. Lawyers, doctors, and dentists are often permitted to operate within residential areas.

The control of height and lot area covered is achieved by specifying the following:

☐ The number of permitted stories, or the building height in feet, or both.
☐ Setback distances of buildings from particular property lines.
☐ Percentage of the lot that may be covered by buildings or other structures.

Control of population may be achieved by specifying the following:

☐ Maximum number of families per acre.
☐ Number of families permitted to occupy a given floor area.
☐ Required number of square feet of open space on a lot for each family to be housed.

Control of use may be accomplished by specifying the following:

☐ The particular type of activity for which the property may be used. (e.g., light manufacturing, or heavy manufacturing, or unrestricted use).
☐ The minimum number of square feet in a residence that must be used for residential purposes. (Such a regulation limits and controls the size of professional offices that may be placed in the residence.)

Exclusionary or Snob Zoning

Exclusionary zoning has the purpose or the effect of keeping low- and moderately low-income groups out of certain residential districts. Zoning that requires large minimum lot sizes and floor areas usually prevents the construction of low-income housing. The courts in New York State have indicated that when local communities enact such zoning ordinances, they must give consideration to regional needs and requirements and they must balance the local desire to maintain the existing quality of the community with the greater public interest that regional housing needs be met. To the extent that local zoning laws frustrate the region's overall housing goals, they may be held invalid.

One case which was recently decided in another state and which may proceed up to the Supreme Court of the United States not only has held exclusionary zoning to be illegal, but has imposed an affirmative obligation on the part of local governmental units to encourage mixed housing, including housing that is affordable by lower-income residents. According to the decision, this should be accomplished through the use of tax incentives and subsidies.

Although this decision does not reflect the present law of New York State, it may well point the way in which such law may develop.

Cluster Zoning

Cluster zoning is a technique which controls average population density on a tract of land by modifying the existing zoning law to permit high-density construction in one portion of a tract in return for the dedication of another portion of the tract to the community for park purposes. The number of dwelling units that the existing zoning law permits on the entire tract may, as a result of cluster zoning, be concentrated on a small portion of the tract, while the rest of the tract becomes open space.

Spot Zoning

A change in zoning regulations to accommodate the construction of specific structures that do not satisfy the zoning requirements of the location is known as *spot zoning*. If indulged in extensively, the practice of spot zoning can, of course, ultimately destroy the effectiveness of the general zoning plan of the entire area. Adversely affected property owners can challenge spot zoning in the courts on the grounds that since it is not a part of a comprehensive plan, it is not in the general interest of the community.

An amended zoning ordinance that is enacted within the framework of a comprehensive zoning plan is not spot zoning merely because it singles out and affects one small plot or because it creates areas or districts devoted to special uses. The true test of whether special zoning is spot zoning is whether the ordinance is part of a well-considered and comprehensive plan.

Changes in Zoning

Changes in zoning ordinances may be made only by the legislative body of the community. Such changes are usually the result of problems created by changes in community conditions. A purchaser wishing to purchase a property for a particular type of use in the future should be aware not only of current zoning laws but of proposed changes in the law that may affect the contemplated use.

Special Permits and Variances

A *variance* is the right to improve a particular property in a manner not authorized by the existing zoning ordinance. Zoning ordinances may provide for the issuance of special exemption permits and variances that allow the construction and use of buildings, or the use of unimproved lands, in a manner that varies from requirements of the zoning regulations. Such special exemption permits may be issued only if the zoning ordinance actually specifies that there can be exceptions to the general zoning requirements. The ordinance usually defines the type of building or use that may be permitted under its exemption rules. Local zoning boards of appeal, which have the right to consider petitions for changes and exceptions in the zoning law, may also grant variances (as permitted by the zoning law) that allow certain property owners to avoid the effect of the law. Variances may also be granted if undue hardship is imposed by literal application of the zoning ordinance, or if the owner is faced with a unique situation not contemplated by the law.

Nonconforming Uses

A nonconforming use is a use that conformed to zoning regulations prior to the enactment of the current zoning ordinance but that was made nonconforming by that latter enactment. Nonconforming uses are protected by the constitutional prohibition that prevents a governmental body from depriving anyone of his property without due process. The nonconforming use must be allowed to continue because the owner has a vested right in the particular use. A casual or occasional property use may not be a nonconforming use. Nor is the incidental use of a property for recreational or amusement purposes only. A nonconforming use is permitted to remain only if enforcement of the new ordinance would render a substantial improvement valueless and would cause serious financial harm to the affected property owner.

If an owner decides to alter or expand an existing nonconforming use, the change must conform to current zoning regulations. Suppose a nonconforming use (a hotel in a residential district) has been partially destroyed by fire. The property owner has no vested right to reconstruct it as a nonconforming use (as a hotel). His only remedy is to apply for a variance (on the grounds of hardship) to permit the desired reconstruction.

A nonconforming use of the property may be extinguished by a period of voluntary abandonment. In this circumstance, the owner must have intended to abandon or relinquish the property. If he merely discontinues the use, there is normally not sufficient cause to nullify his rights in the use.

Some zoning ordinances provide for a reasonable and sufficient period of permitted nonconformity for existing uses and further provide that at the end of such period the use must cease. Of course, the owners of such uses may seek compensation for losses imposed by such ordinances.

The Effect of Zoning Ordinances on the Marketability of Title

A zoning ordinance in and of itself is not an encumbrance on real property and therefore does not render a title unmarketable. However, a property owner who violates a zoning ordinance is not only subject to fines and penalties, he is vulnerable to injunctions for the discontinuance of the use. In certain cases, he may have to remove or relocate

the violating structure. He may be responsible to take such action even if the violation was caused by a former property owner.

Thus, there is a difference between taking title subject to zoning ordinances and taking title subject to a violation of zoning ordinances. In the first case, the buyer receives marketable title because every contract is subject to zoning ordinances. In the latter case, the violation may render the title unmarketable. Of course, the buyer may, for appropriate consideration or under appropriate circumstances, take title subject to the violations.

The purchaser is not the only one concerned about zoning violations. The mortgage lender has the same concern as the buyer because it may eventually become the property owner through foreclosure. The security upon which the mortgage loan is based is substantially reduced if the property violates the zoning laws.

How the Zoning Status of Property May Be Ascertained

Before property is purchased, the buyer must make sure that the property does not violate existing ordinances. The amount of investigation obviously varies with the complexity of the purchase. The problems posed by an existing one-family home in an established residential district are less complex than those involved in the purchase of commercial or manufacturing property whose height, bulk, area, and use compliance must be checked. In such a complex purchase, it may be necessary to draw upon the knowledge of a competent engineer or architect who is familiar with local zoning ordinances.

If the purchaser anticipates zoning problems, he is wise to consult with law firms that are expert in this particular field and that have contacts with local zoning officials.

Subdividing Real Property

The term *land subdivision* refers to the division of one or more large tracts of land into smaller sites for purposes of future sales or development. It can refer to the activities of a subdivider who buys undeveloped land and divides it into smaller tracts that he can improve and sell, and to those of a developer who improves the property by building homes on the lots before they are sold.

The subdivider usually must create a map or plat that shows the sections into which he has subdivided the tract. Once the appropriate municipal and county agencies have approved the map, it is filed in the County Clerk's office where the property is located.

Most municipalities strictly control the subdivision of lands within their boundaries. The subdivider usually must make provisions for the installation of utilities and for the grading and paving of streets at his own cost. The map is usually prepared by an engineer, who must take into consideration a large number of complex factors. The size, as well as the location of lots on the subdivision, must reflect the developer's goals. Local zoning laws that, in addition to land use, control the front footage and depth and total area requirements of the lots must be considered. The engineer preparing the subdivision map must obtain the maximum utilization of the land for the subdivider within the framework of all relevant requirements.

Most subdivision maps create both lots and blocks. Areas of land are usually designated as blocks, and each block is divided into lots. The lots on the map are usually numbered consecutively and the dimensions and bearings of the boundary lines are shown on each lot. Streets, easements, utilities, and certain common facilities (e.g., parks and scenic easements) are also shown on the plat or map.

The courts have often held that the owners of lots on a particular subdivision plat have an implied easement for the use of the facilities shown on the map, such as parks, roads, and beach areas, even if such use is not expressly granted by deed to the lot purchasers by the subdivider or developer.

The government plays an important role in making sure that new subdivisions comply with local laws and zoning regulations. The Federal Housing Administration (FHA) may withhold mortgage insurance on homes built in subdivisions that fail to comply with local health and safety standards.

One relatively new form of subdivision is the so-called planned unit development (PUD). The PUD form emerged because of a need for more intensive use of land. It includes nontraditional lot size concepts and variations of land use involving detached single-family homes, townhouse constructions, apartments and condominiums, as well as commercial and industrial tracts. The subdividers of the PUD usually set forth on the plat or map the areas that are reserved for schools, parks, roads, and other forms of recreational areas. PUDs usually involve formal associations of unit owners formed for the purpose of owning, maintaining, and operating common areas within the developments.

BUILDING CODES

A *building code* is promulgated by a local governmental entity (e.g., municipality or county) to regulate building construction. It is designed to protect, preserve, and promote the public health, safety, and welfare and to set certain minimum standards concerning the location, construction, design, quality, use, occupancy, and maintenance of all buildings and structures within the jurisdictional confines of the particular governmental entity.

Like zoning codes, building codes are enacted into law by local governmental authorities under the state's police powers delegated to them pursuant to enabling legislation. The courts will sustain them if they are reasonable exercises of the police power. In areas that have building codes, contractors usually must obtain a building permit before they can proceed with the construction of a building. The building permit evidences a contractor's intention to comply with the building code.

Building codes take two forms. They are either *specification codes* or *performance codes*. Specification codes are by far the more common. A specification code sets forth in detail the minimum construction specifications that the building must follow. *Performance codes* set forth the specific performance requirements that the structure must meet. They leave it up to the builder to choose the building materials and structural specifications by which the code requirements are satisfied. A specification code may call for a water line to be 3/11" copper tubing. A performance code permits any size and material but establishes requirements for the line's durability and capacity. Performance codes demand a high degree of sophistication on the part of the builder and his personnel and are therefore difficult to implement.

Certificate of Occupancy

Building buyers should ascertain if the building conforms to the building code and if its construction and use otherwise comply with legal requirements. Compliance is usually evidenced by the existence of a *certificate of occupancy* (CO) that has been issued for the premises.

A certificate of occupancy is a statement issued by a building inspector who has examined a newly completed building, indicating that the structure complies with the building code and with the appropriate zoning regulations. If the structure does not comply with the zoning law or building codes, the building inspector should not have issued such a certificate.

The need for a certificate of occupancy is applicable to unimproved as well as to improved property; the use of a property as a parking lot, junk yard, or for other similar purpose may also require the issuance of a certificate of occupancy.

The purchaser of a dwelling should obtain a copy of the existing certificate of occupancy at or prior to the closing of title. In addition, the purchaser should have made sure prior to the closing that no structural improvements had been made to the property subsequent to the issuance of the certificate of occupancy. Such improvements would require that an amended certificate of occupancy be issued. The law assumes that the purchaser has made these enquiries; unless otherwise provided in the contract of sale, the fact of whether or not the building does or does not conform to the building code and other ordinances does not affect marketability of the property's title nor does it permit or excuse the rejection of the title by the buyer.

REVIEW QUESTIONS

1. A restrictive covenant is an agreement between adjoining property owners which

   (a) Restricts the use of the burdened premises.
   (b) Renders the burdened premises unmarketable.
   (c) Both a and b.
   (d) None of the above.

2. A zoning ordinance

   (a) Automatically expires at the end of five years.
   (b) Supersedes an inconsistent covenant and restriction.
   (c) Neither a nor b.
   (d) Both a and b.

3. A *common scheme* covenant usually is found in

   (a) Industrial property.
   (b) Commercial property.
   (c) Residential property.
   (d) Only b and c.

4. A covenant is of no force and effect if it

   (a) Restricts the premises only to residential use.
   (b) Restricts the sale of the premises to individuals of a particular racial group.
   (c) Both a and b.
   (d) More than 50 years old.

5. Zoning powers are delegated to municipalities by laws known as

   (a) Enabling statutes.
   (b) Statutes of limitation.
   (c) Both a and b.
   (d) None of the above.

6. A zoning ordinance will not be enforced if it is

   (a) Based on a comprehensive plan.
   (b) Promotes the public health, safety, and welfare.
   (c) Is arbitrary and unreasonable.
   (d) None of the above.

7. A zoning ordinance may

   (a) Control population density.
   (b) Control use of land.
   (c) Both a and b.
   (d) None of the above.

8. A change in zoning to accommodate one or two specific pieces of property is known as

   (a) Spot zoning.
   (b) Cluster zoning.
   (c) Exclusionary zoning.
   (d) None of the above.

9. Zoning laws are usually effective

   (a) For five years.
   (b) Ten years.
   (c) Until repealed.
   (d) None of the above.

10. The violation of a restrictive covenant may result in the benefited party being able to

    (a) Enjoin the violation.
    (b) Sue for damages.
    (c) Neither a nor b.
    (d) Both a and b.

11. A restrictive covenant may be extinguished by the foreclosure of a prior mortgage unless

(a) Consented to at the time of its creation by the mortgagee.
(b) The covenant is recorded in the County Clerk's office.
(c) Neither a nor b.
(d) Both a and b.

12. A covenant may not be enforced in a court of law if

(a) A substantial change has occurred in the affected area rendering of no value the enforcement of the covenant.
(b) If the party seeking enforcement has himself violated the covenant.
(c) Either a or b.
(d) Neither a nor b.

13. A variance may be granted by

(a) The local building inspector.
(b) The local Zoning Board of Appeal.
(c) Neither a nor b.
(d) Either a or b.

14. Additions made to a parcel of land for which a variance has been granted

(a) Need not comply with any zoning law.
(b) Must comply with the present zoning law.
(c) Neither a nor b.
(d) Must comply with future zoning laws.

15. Nonconforming uses are protected on

(a) Constitutional grounds.
(b) Moral grounds.
(c) Neither of the above.
(d) Both of the above.

16. The owner of a nonconforming use which has been totally destroyed by fire may

(a) Rebuild the structure as a matter of right.
(b) Must obtain a variance to rebuild.
(c) Neither a nor b.
(d) Must first get court approval.

17. The document issued by a local municipality which evidences that a completed structure complies with zoning laws and building codes is known as

(a) A building permit.
(b) A certificate of occupancy.
(c) A special use permit.
(d) None of the above.

18. A zoning ordinance extinguishes inconsistent restrictive covenants

(a) Sometimes.
(b) Always.
(c) Never.
(d) By operation of law.

19. A purchaser of vacant real property should be concerned with

(a) The present zoning of the property.
(b) Proposed changes to the existing zoning law.
(c) Both a and b.
(d) Neither a nor b.

20. A subdivision consists of

(a) Lots generally of a size suitable for residential use.
(b) Two or more parcels zoned for different purposes.
(c) Neither a nor b.
(d) Both a and b.

mortgagor is the debtor

Part IV
Testing Yourself

Chapter 17
Real Estate Mathematics

VOCABULARY

You will find it important to have a complete working knowledge of the following words and concepts found in this chapter:

assessed value	expense	lien
assets	income	owner's equity
credit	liabilities	tax liability
debit		

NEW YORK STATE LAW requires that approved real estate salespersons' courses include three hours of mathematics. Unfortunately, the legislators did not specify precisely what level of mathematics. The five math questions that have appeared in recent examinations require the test-taker to solve practical problems using simple multiplication, division, and percentage computations.

HOW TO USE THIS CHAPTER

This chapter contains more material than your instructor will wish to cover in class. We recommend to instructors that they prepare students to solve problems in the section on "The Relationship Between Income and Value," "Profit and Loss," "Commission," and "Settlement Statement Methods."

However, it is possible that some students have forgotten the basic tools of arithmetic, fractions, and decimals. Consequently, the first portions of the chapter are devoted to a review of these manipulations. This review should be done as home study. Most classes should not take time out to review fractions and decimals. As a bonus, the authors have included a section entitled "Geometric Formulas for Real Estate." Geometry is usually not part of the New York State salespersons' exam. But a salesperson who does not know how to measure area and volume is at a competitive disadvantage. The authors recommend that such salesperson candidates devote several hours of home study to the topic.

FRACTIONS

A fraction is a quotient, or ratio, of two numbers. The top number is called the numerator and the bottom is called the denominator. Thus $3 \div 4 = \frac{3}{4}$, where the 3 is the numerator and the 4 the denominator. A fraction in which the numerator is less than the denominator is called a simple fraction and always has a value of less than 1. The values 1/2, 19/32, 52/100, 191/231 are all simple fractions. If the numerator is larger than the denominator, the fraction is an improper fraction. For instance, 4/3 is considered an improper fraction; if the division were completed it would result in a mixed number (a whole number plus a simple fraction) or $1\frac{1}{3}$.

All fractions should be reduced to their lowest possible terms or converted to a mixed number to complete the problem.

Addition and Subtraction of Fractions

If the denominators of two fractions are identical, the two fractions may be added simply by adding their numerators.

$$\frac{1}{3} + \frac{1}{3} = \frac{2}{3} \qquad \frac{1}{8} + \frac{2}{8} = \frac{3}{8}$$

Such fractions may be subtracted from each other by subtracting the numerators.

$$\frac{2}{3} - \frac{1}{3} = \frac{1}{3} \qquad \frac{3}{8} - \frac{1}{8} = \frac{2}{8}$$

If the denominators of two fractions differ, they must be made identical before they can be added or subtracted. To change the denominator of a fraction without changing the value of the fraction, both the denominator and the numerator must be multiplied by the same number. For example:

$$\frac{1}{4} \times \frac{2}{2} = \frac{2}{8}$$

Thus,

$$\frac{1}{4} = \frac{2}{8}$$

Making the denominators of two or more fractions equal is called finding a *common denominator*. Sometimes it is possible to find a common denominator by changing only one fraction. For example:

$$\text{Add } \frac{1}{8} + \frac{1}{4}$$

First, multiply the numerator and denominator of 1/4 by 2:

$$\frac{1}{4} \times \frac{2}{2} = \frac{2}{8}$$

Now we can add

$$\frac{1}{8} + \frac{2}{8} = \frac{3}{8}$$

If the denominators of the two fractions are not "multiples" of one another, both fractions must be multiplied. The numerator and the denominator of one fraction must be multiplied by the denominator of the other fraction. For example:

Find a common denominator for 1/7 + 3/8

$$\frac{1}{7} \times \frac{8}{8} = \frac{8}{56} \qquad \frac{3}{8} \times \frac{7}{7} = \frac{21}{56}$$

The fractions 8/56 and 21/56 may now be added or subtracted.

If more than two fractions are to be added, multiply the numerator and denominator of each fraction by the denominators of the other fractions and then sum the numerators over the common denominator.

$$\frac{1}{4} + \frac{3}{5} + \frac{7}{9} = \text{?}$$

$$\frac{1}{4} \times \frac{5}{5} \times \frac{9}{9} = \frac{45}{180}$$

$$\frac{3}{5} \times \frac{4}{4} \times \frac{9}{9} = \frac{108}{180}$$

$$\frac{7}{9} \times \frac{4}{4} \times \frac{5}{5} = \frac{140}{180}$$

Now add

$$\frac{45}{180} + \frac{108}{180} + \frac{140}{180} = \frac{293}{180} \text{, or } 1\frac{113}{180}$$

Multiplication of Fractions

To multiply two or more fractions, multiply the numerators and multiply the denominators. Then reduce to the lowest terms.

3/4 × 2/3 = ?

$$\frac{3 \times 2}{4 \times 3} = \frac{6}{12} = \frac{1}{2}$$

9/10 × 3/5 × 4/7 = ?

$$\frac{9 \times 3 \times 4}{10 \times 5 \times 7} = \frac{108}{350} = \frac{54}{175}$$

Division of Fractions by Fractions

When one number is divided by another, the number that is divided is called the *dividend*, and the dividing number is called the *divisor*. In order to divide one fraction by another, invert the divisor and then multiply the two fractions. (To invert a fraction, simply turn it upside-down to reverse the positions of the numerator and the denominator.) Invert the fractions

$$\frac{2}{3} , \quad \frac{3}{4} \quad \frac{3}{5} \quad \frac{5}{9}$$

They become

$$\frac{3}{2} \quad \frac{4}{3} \quad \frac{5}{3} \quad \frac{9}{5}$$

Divide 3/4 by 3/2

$$\frac{3}{4} \div \frac{3}{2} = \frac{3}{4} \times \frac{2}{3} = \frac{6}{12} = \frac{1}{2}$$

Multiplying and Dividing a Fraction by a Whole Number

To multiply or divide a fraction by a whole number, simply treat the whole number as if it were a fraction with a denominator of 1. Thus $2 = 2/1$; $22 = 22/1$; $5000 = 5000/1$

Multiply: $1/2 \times 5 = ?$
$1/2 \times 5/1 = 5/2 = 2\ 1/2$

Divide: $1/2 \div 5 = ?$
$1/2 \div 5/1 = 1/2 \times 1/5 = 1/10$

Cancellation Between Fractions

The value of a fraction does not change when both numerator and denominator are multiplied by the same number.

$$\frac{1}{2} \times \frac{50}{50} = \frac{1 \times 50}{2 \times 50} = \frac{50}{100}$$

The value of a fraction does not change when both the numerator and the denominator are divided by the same number.

$$\frac{50}{100} \div \frac{50}{50} = \frac{50/50}{100/50} = \frac{1}{2}$$

When multiplying or dividing fractions, we can take advantage of this fact to reduce the size of the numbers that we must work with.

When two fractions are multiplied together, they may be treated as a single fraction. Thus

$$\frac{3}{5} \times \frac{25}{27} = \frac{3 \times 25}{5 \times 27}$$

We could solve this multiplication problem by simply multiplying the numerators and denominators and arriving at 75/135. But this involves two large multiplications, and we would then have to reduce an awkward fraction to its lowest terms.

Let us try dividing out the common factor from the numerator and denominator of our complex fraction.

Divide $\dfrac{3 \times 25}{5 \times 27}$ by 3

$$\frac{\overset{1}{\cancel{3}} \times 25}{5 \times \underset{9}{\cancel{27}}}$$

Divide the remainder by 5

$$\frac{\overset{1}{\cancel{3}} \times \overset{5}{\cancel{25}}}{\underset{}{\cancel{5}} \times \underset{9}{\cancel{27}}}$$
$$= \frac{1 \times 5}{1 \times 9} = \frac{5}{9}$$

The common factors were 3 and 5.

DECIMALS

A decimal is another way of expressing a fraction. The numerator of the fraction is the number that follows the decimal point; and the denominator is always a multiple of 10; i.e., 10, 100, 1,000, and so on. If the numerator is one place to the right of the decimal point, then the denominator of the fraction is 10; if the numerator is two places to the right of the decimal point, then the denominator is 100; and so on.

$.3 = 3/10 = $ three tenths
$.03 = 3/100 = $ three hundredths
$.003 = 3/1000 = $ three thousandths
$.35 = 35/100 = $ thirty-five hundredths
$.357 = 357/1000 = $ three hundred fifty-seven thousandths

Converting Fractions to Decimals

To change a fraction into a decimal, simply divide the numerator by the denominator.

$$3/5 = 3 \div 5, \quad \text{or} \quad 5\overline{)3.00}^{\ .60} = .6$$

Sometimes when you are dividing, you encounter a series of repeating numbers.

$$1/3 = 3\overline{)1.00000}^{\ .33333 \text{ etc.}}$$
$$2/3 = 3\overline{)2.00000}^{\ .66666 \text{ etc.}}$$

You must decide how much accuracy your problem requires. Round off the last digit and end the decimal. Thus, you may stop at .33 and .67.

Adding or Subtracting Decimals

Place the numbers in the proper columns, paying attention to keeping the decimal points and columns in line, and perform the function.

$$
\begin{array}{r} 1.075 \\ +\ \ .18 \\ \hline 1.255 \end{array}
\quad \text{or} \quad
\begin{array}{r} 1.075 \\ -\ \ .18 \\ \hline .895 \end{array}
$$

Multiplying Decimals

Multiply decimals just as you would multiply whole numbers. The number of decimal places in the product must equal the number of decimal places in the two numbers that you have multiplied.

$$6.3 \text{ (1 decimal place)}$$
$$\times 2.11 \text{ (2 decimal places)}$$
$$\overline{13.293} \text{ (3 decimal places)}$$

$$6.7 \text{ (1 decimal place)}$$
$$\times .002 \text{ (3 decimal places)}$$
$$\overline{.0134} \text{ (4 decimal places)}$$

In the second example above the multiplication produces only three numbers to fill the four places required to the right of the decimal point, so a zero is inserted to the left of the three numbers to fill the spot.

Dividing Decimals

In order to divide decimals, move the decimal point of the divisor to the right until it becomes a whole number. Move the decimal point of the dividend the same number of places to the right. This locates the decimal point in the quotient or answer.

$$.55 \overline{)20.625} \quad \text{becomes} \quad .55.\overline{)20.62.5}$$

Then perform normal division by whole numbers.

$$
\begin{array}{r}
37.5 \\
55 \overline{)2062.5}
\end{array}
$$

PERCENT

Percent indicates that a whole number of quantity has been divided into 100 equal parts, and the percentage represents the number of parts to be used. To convert a percent to a decimal, move the decimal point two places to the left. To convert a decimal to percent, move the decimal point two places to the right and add the percent sign (%).

25% means 25 one-hundredths   or 25/100 or .25
30% = .30
3.5% = .035

PRACTICE PROBLEMS:
FRACTIONS, DECIMALS, PERCENTS

Fractions

Add the following fractions:
1. 1/6 + 1/8 =
2. 3/7 + 4/9 =
3. 19/20 + 3/5 =
4. 1/8 + 5/12 =
5. 3/4 + 1/16 =

Subtract the following fractions:
6. 1/6 − 1/8 =
7. 4/7 − 4/9 =
8. 19/20 − 3/5 =
9. 5/12 − 1/8 =
10. 3/4 − 1/16 =

Multiply the following fractions:
11. 1/8 × 1/4 =
12. 1/9 × 11/12 =
13. 3/4 × 7/16 =
14. 4/5 × 8/9 =
15. 5/12 × 1/5 =

Divide the following fractions:
16. 1/8 ÷ 1/4 =
17. 1/9 ÷ 11/12 =
18. 3/4 ÷ 7/6 =
19. 4/5 ÷ 8/9 =
20. 5/12 ÷ 1/5 =

Decimals and Percents

Add the following decimals:
1. .5 + .075 + .125 =
2. .073 + 1.25 + .93 =
3. .82 + .73 + 2.584 =
4. .0016 + 1.043 + .3 =

Subtract the following decimals:
5. 1.25 − .075 =
6. .073 − .0016 =
7. 1.4874 − .896 =
8. 2.043 − 1.0012 =

Multiply the following decimals:
9. .075 × 1.257 =
10. .342 × .0017 =
11. .7589 × 1.2 =
12. .346 × 3.476 =

Divide the following decimals:
13. .34 ÷ .516 =
14. 1.25 ÷ .07 =
15. .78 ÷ .4 =
16. 1.29 ÷ .432 =

Change the following percents to decimals:
17. 75% =
18. 125% =
19. 27.56% =
20. 43.2% =

Change the following decimals to percents:

21. .0025 =
22. .567 =
23. .493 =
24. 3.475 =

GEOMETRIC FORMULAS FOR REAL ESTATE

Before studying geometric formulas, we must refresh ourselves about concepts like the square and the square root of a number, and the cube and cube root of a number.

Squares and Square Roots

When a number is multiplied by itself it is said to be squared.

Thus, in the equation $3 \times 3 = 9$, the number 9 is said to be 3 squared. The number 3 squared is usually written 3^2.

Thus, $3 \times 3 = 3^2 = 9$ or $5 \times 5 = 5^2 = 25$

Just as 9 can be thought of as 3 squared, 3 is sometimes called the square root of 9. In equations, the concept square root is designated by this symbol $\sqrt{\ }$.

Thus, the square root of 9 is written

$$\sqrt{9} = 3 \quad \text{and} \quad \sqrt{25} = 5$$

We can easily discover the square of a number. We simply multiply the number by itself.

The square roots of numbers are harder to determine. Some we know intuitively. For example,

$$\sqrt{100} = 10 \quad \text{and} \quad \sqrt{81} = 9$$

But what is the square root of 85?

$$\sqrt{85} = ?$$

We know that the answer is a number larger than 9 but smaller than 10. There are mathematical formulas that allow us to compute square roots. But they are cumbersome. If your real estate work requires that you use square roots, you should obtain a table of square roots. Such tables appear in many math books.

Cubes and Cube Roots

When a number is twice multiplied by itself, it is said to be cubed.

Thus $3 \times 3 \times 3 = 27$

Note that 3 cubed may be written 3^3. Similarly, 5 cubed is

$$5^3 = 5 \times 5 \times 5 = 125$$

Just as 125 is 5 cubed, 5 is the cube root of 125 and 3 is the cube root of 27.

We can easily discover the cube of a number by appropriate multiplication. But we should turn to a table if it is necessary to obtain cube roots.

The Measurement of Area

The real estate agent must often determine the area of a flat or plane surface. The area of a particular lot or the total amount of floor space in a house may become an element in the property negotiation. The shapes of lots and other spaces may be infinitely complex, but most spaces can be broken down into three basic shapes for which it is possible to compute areas: quadrilaterals (four-sided shapes), triangles (three-sided shapes), and circles.

Area is expressed in "square" units. We refer to square inches, square feet, and square yards. A square foot is a unit of area that is one foot long, or 12 inches on each side, or its equivalent. A square yard is a unit of area that is one yard, or 36 inches, long on each side, or its equivalent. One square yard is equal to 9 square feet as is readily seen in the following diagram:

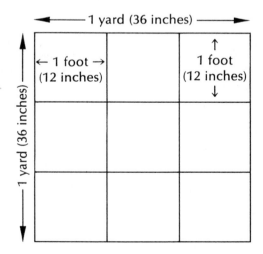

One square foot equals 144 square inches.

Rectangles

The most common form of quadrilateral is a rectangle. The opposite sides of a rectangle are of equal length and the sides of the rectangle are parallel, that is, all the interior angles are equal to 90 degrees. A square is a special form of rectangle, with all four of its sides equal.

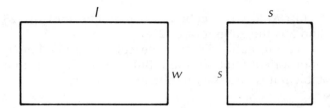

The area of a rectangle may be found by using the formula $A = lw$, where A = area, l = length, or measure of the longer side, and w = width, or measure of the shorter side. By multiplying the length times the width, the area of a rectangle may be found.

If the area of a rectangle is known and the measure of one side is known, the measure of the remaining side may be determined by dividing the area (A) by the measure of the known side.

Example   What is the floor space of a building which has a length of 60 feet and a width of 40 feet?

Solution
Area = length × width
A = lw
A = 60 feet × 40 feet
A = 2,400 square feet

Example   If we know the area of a building is 2,400 square feet and its length is 60 feet, what is the width?

A = 2,400 square feet
l = 60 feet
$w =$?

Solution
A/l   = w
2,400/60 = 40 feet

Squares

Since the square is a special case of the rectangle, with all four sides equal in length, only the measure of one side (s) needs to be known to find the area of the square.

Example
Area = side × side

A = $s \times s$ or s^2
A = 20 feet × 20 feet
A = 400 square feet

Triangles

The area of a triangle is equal to one-half the measure of the base times the height. The height is measured at a right angle from the base to the apex, which is the point where the two sloping sides of the triangle meet.

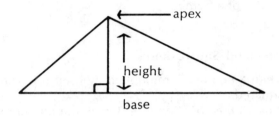

Example   How many square feet are there in a triangle with a base of 40 feet and a height of 10 feet.

Solution
Area = 1/2 base × height
A = 1/2 bh
A = 1/2(40 feet × 10 feet)
A = 1/2 (400)
A = 200 square feet

Right Triangles

The right triangle is unique in that one of the sides is always perpendicular, that is, at right angles to the base of the triangle, so the height is equal to the perpendicular side of the triangle.

Another characteristic of a right triangle is that if the lengths of any two sides are known, the length of the third side may be found. This is based on the Pythagorean theorem, which states that the square of the length of the hypotenuse of a right triangle is equal to the sum of the squares of the length of the other two sides.

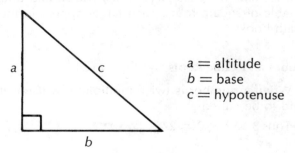

a = altitude
b = base
c = hypotenuse

$c^2 = a^2 + b^2$

The length of side $c = \sqrt{a^2 + b^2}$

The length of side $a = \sqrt{c^2 - b^2}$,

The length of side $b = \sqrt{c^2 - a^2}$

Example If $a = 30$ feet and $b = 40$ feet, what is the length of c?

$c^2 = a^2 + b^2$

$c = \sqrt{a^2 + b^2}$

$c = \sqrt{(30)^2 + (40)^2}$

$c = \sqrt{900 + 1600}$

$c = \sqrt{250}$

$c = 50$

Circles

The circumference of a circle is equal to the distance around the outside of the circle. The diameter is the straight-line distance, passing through the center, between two opposite points on the circumference. The radius is the distance from the center of the circle to a point on the circumference.

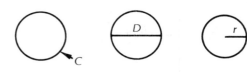

The value of pi (π) is needed to compute various dimensions of a circle. π is equal to the circumference divided by the diameter, so that $\pi = 3.1416$. This value is very close to the fraction 22/7. (For most real estate calculations, the fraction 22/7 will be adequate as a value for π.)

The circumference (C) of a circle is equal to π times the diameter (D), so that $C = \pi D$.

The diameter (D) of a circle is equal to the circumference (C) divided by π, so that $D = C \div \pi$.

The radius (r) is equal to the diameter (D) divided by 2, so that $r = D \div 2$.

Area (A) is equal to π times the radius squared (r^2), so that $A = \pi r^2$.

Example A circular lot has a diameter of 20 feet.

1. What is the circumference of the lot?
   $C = \pi D$
   $C = 3.1416 \times 20$ feet
   $C = 62.832$ feet

2. What is the radius of the circle?
   $r = D \div 2$
   $r = 20$ feet $\div 2$
   $r = 10$ feet

3. What is the area of the circle?
   $A = \pi r^2$
   $A = 3.1416 (10)(10)$
   $A = 314.16$ square feet

Rhomboids

Rhomboids are four-sided shapes (quadrilaterals) in which the opposite sides are parallel (parallelograms) but the internal angles are not right angles. Necessarily, two angles are oblique (more than 90 degrees). A special case of the rhomboid is the rhombus, in which all four sides of the shape are of equal length.

These shapes are shown below

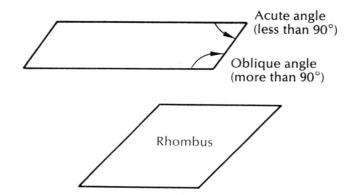

The area of a rhomboid is found by multiplying the length of one of the parallel sides (s) by the vertical distance between the parallel sides (d).

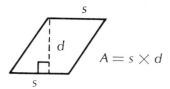

Example What is the area of the following figure?

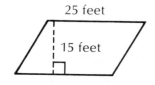

$A = s \times d$
$A = 25$ feet $\times 15$ feet
$A = 375$ square feet

Trapezoid

A quadrilateral that has only two parallel sides is called a trapezoid. Here a is parallel to b, and h equals the vertical distance between sides a and b.

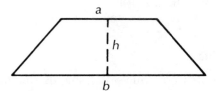

The area of a trapezoid is equal to one-half the sum of the parallel sides times the distance between them.

$$A = \frac{a+b}{2} \times h$$

Example   What is the area of the following figure?

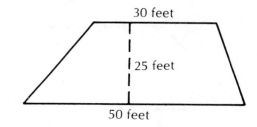

$$A = \frac{a+b}{2} \times h$$

$$A = \frac{30 \text{ feet} + 50 \text{ feet}}{2} \times 25 \text{ feet}$$

$A = 40 \text{ feet} \times 25 \text{ feet}$
$A = 1{,}000 \text{ square feet}$

The Area of Odd-Shaped Figures

Quite often the real estate agent must determine the area of a lot that does not have a regular shape. Usually the lot can be broken down into a series of figures for which area can be determined.

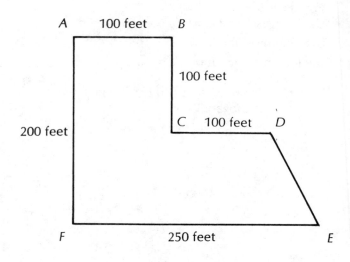

The figure above breaks down into three geometric shapes that are easy to work with:

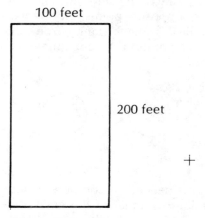

Rectangle
$A = lw$
$A = 200' \times 100'$
$A = 20{,}000 \text{ square feet}$

+

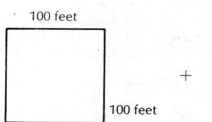

Square
$A = s^2$
$A = 100^2$
$A = 10{,}000 \text{ square feet}$

+

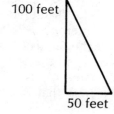

Triangle
$A = 1/2bh$
$A = 1/2(50')(100')$
$A = 2500 \text{ square feet}$

Total area   =   32,500 square feet

Perimeter

Perimeter is the distance around the outside of a one-dimensional figure. The perimeters of figures with straight sides can be computed by adding up the lengths of the sides.

The perimeter of a circle, its circumference, is computed by the following special formula: $P = \pi d$, or 22/7 d.

Examples Compute the perimeters of the following figures:

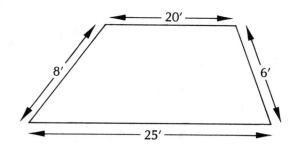

$P = 8 + 20 + 6 + 25 = 59$ feet

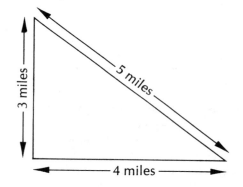

$P = 3 + 5 + 4 = 12$ miles

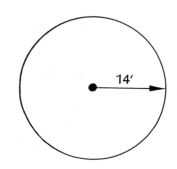

$P = \pi d$
$= \dfrac{22}{7} \times 28 = 88$

Volume

An area problem is concerned with two dimensions, such as length times width. It yields results in square units—square feet, square yards, etc. A volume problem deals in three dimensions—cubic feet, cubic yards, etc.

Rectangular Volume

The volume of a rectangular space, such as the volume of a room, is its length times its width times its height.

$$V = l \times w \times h$$

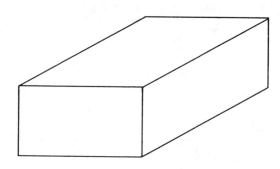

Example Determine the volume of a room that is 15 feet long and 9 feet wide, with an 8 foot ceiling height.

$V = l \times w \times h$
$V = 15 \times 9 \times 8$
$V = 1,080$ cubic feet

Volume of a Triangular Figure

The volume of a triangular area like an attic space may be readily seen if we understand intuitively that the volume is the area of the triangle times the length of the room. Thus in the figure below

$$V = 1/2\,(b \times h \times l)$$

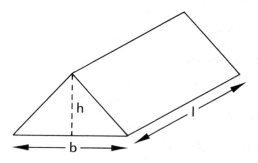

Example: What is the volume of a crawl space 4 feet high at the apex, if the floor area is 15 feet long and 9 feet wide.

$$V = 1/2 \ (b \times h \times l)$$
$$V = 1/2 \ (9 \times 4 \times 15)$$
$$V = 270 \text{ cubic feet}$$

Volume of a Cylinder

The volume of a cylinder is the area of the circular base (πr^2) times the height.

$$V = \pi r^2 \ h$$

Example What is the area of a water tank 14 feet in diameter and 18 feet high.

$$V = \pi r^2 h$$
$$V = \frac{22}{7} \times 7^2 \times 18$$
$$V = 2,772 \text{ cubic feet}$$

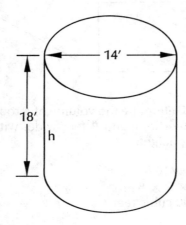

Conversions

The following conversions will be useful to real estate selling personnel involved in land transfers.

Measures of length

7.92 inches = 1 link
25 links = 16 1/2 feet = 1 rod
100 links
    = 66 feet = 22 yards
    = 4 rods = 1 chain
320 rods = 1 mile

Measures of area

144 square inches = 1 square foot
9 square feet = 1 square yard
1 square rod = 272 1/4 square feet
    = 30 1/4 square yards
40 square rods = 1 rood

4 roods = 1 acre
1 acre = 160 square rods
        = 4,840 square yards = 43,560 square feet
640 acres = 1 square mile

Measurements of Volume

1728 cubic inches = 1 cubic foot
27 cubic feet = 1 cubic yard

PRACTICE PROBLEMS: PERIMETER, AREA, VOLUME

1. How many acres in a square mile?
2. How many square feet in an acre?
3. How many square feet in the property below?

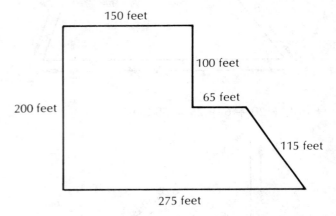

4. What is the price of a rectangular lot measuring 373 X 154 feet at a cost of $1,000 per acre?
5. How many acres are contained in a lot 300 X 450 feet?
6. If concrete costs $16.50 per cubic yard and labor costs are $.20 a square foot, what would be the cost to build a driveway 28 feet long, 9 feet wide, and 6 inches thick?
7. Building restrictions are such that a 20-foot front yard setback, a 15-foot back yard setback, and a side yard setback of 15 feet are required. How much area on the lot is buildable if the dimensions are 120 X 150 feet?

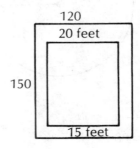

8. Farmer A wants to lease a portion of his farm to Farmer B for cultivation. Farmer B is willing to pay $50 an acre for the tillable land. The area in question has a large pond in the center of it. The dimensions of the area to be leased are 310 X 240 rods. The pond is circular and has a diameter of 90 rods. How many acres is Farmer B leasing, and what is the cost of the lease?

9. How far would a person have to walk to go completely around a circular 1-acre pond with a diameter of 14.28 rods?

10. Compute the cubic content of an industrial warehouse that is 260 X 340 feet and has an average height of 40 feet.

11. A certain lot measures 80 X 135 feet and costs $.63 per square foot. A home is erected on the lot at a cost of $1.85 per cubic foot. The dimensions of the house are 40 X 60 X 10 feet. What is the value of the property?

12. What is the price of a lot measuring 264 feet wide X 660 feet deep at $800 per acre?

13. Compute the proposed cost of the following property:

Land	125' X 100' @ $ 1/square foot
Two-story building	40' X 60' @ $25/square foot
Full basement	40' X 60' @ $ 5/square foot
Driveway	10' X 80' @ $ 4/square foot
Sidewalks	3' X 70' @ $ 3/square foot
Yard improvements	$5,000

Math Problems Frequently Encountered in Real Estate

Students who have mastered basic arithmetic and geometric skills should be capable of solving most of the real estate math problems that they encounter. The following sections discuss the most typical problems and offer problems that enable students to test their skills.

THE RELATIONSHIP BETWEEN INCOME AND VALUE

In the chapter on appraisal we discussed the income approach to value and learned that the rule of thumb capitalization technique was to divide a stabilized income by a capitalization rate. Actually, this is a special case of a simple formula known as the rate formula. *Rate* is a percentage. Two quantities can always be compared by expressing one as a percentage of the other. In the appraisal chapter we wanted to relate income to value. When we

assumed that income was 10 percent of value, we could write:

$$\text{Income} = .10 \times \text{value}$$

But the relationship between income and value changes with many variables. So we write a generalized formula:

$$\text{Income} = \text{rate} \times \text{value}$$

If we know any two variables of this formula, we can compute the third. If we know the value of the property and the rate of return that it produces, we can compute the property's income. If we know the income that a property produces and the rate of return that a potential buyer desires, we can compute its value to him.

Example A man owns a building worth $50,000 and desires a 10 percent return from his property. What income must the property produce to attain this?

$$\text{Income} = \text{rate} \times \text{value}$$
$$\text{Income} = 10\% \times \$50,000$$
$$\text{Income} = .10 \times \$50,000$$
$$\text{Income} = \$5,000 \text{ per year}$$

Using the same information, if the man knew the property's income and his desired rate of return, and he wanted to find the value of the property, he could do so by using the formula.

Example
$$\text{Income} = \text{rate} \times \text{value}$$
$$\frac{\text{Income}}{\text{rate}} = \text{value}$$
$$\frac{\$5000}{.10} = \text{value}$$
$$\$50,000 = \text{value}$$

By dividing the property's income by the rate, we found the property's value. When the rate that we use is the investor's "desired rate of return," that is, his capitalization rate, we have "capitalized" the income to produce a value.

If the same man knew the value of the same property and knew his net income to be the same, using the same components he could find the rate of return on his property by dividing the income by the known value.

$$\text{Income} = \text{rate} \times \text{value}$$
$$\text{Income/value} = \text{rate}$$
$$\$5,000/\$50,000 = \text{rate}$$
$$.10 = \text{rate}$$

Convert to percentage: Rate $= 10\%$

PRACTICE PROBLEMS:
RATE, INCOME, VALUE, INTEREST

1. What is the value of a property that produces $600 of income per month, if similar investments are yielding 8 percent per annum return.
2. The value of a house at the end of six years was estimated to be $7,650. If it was depreciated at a rate of 2½ percent per year, what was the original cost of the house?
3. What is the indicated value of a property producing income of $1,000 per month, with an average annual yield of 13 percent?
4. How long will it take an investor to recapture an initial investment at a rate of 12 percent per year return on his money? (*Hint:* Value = 100 percent)
5. A person has a property that produces a gross income of $325 per month. Monthly expenses average $155. What is the net income per year on the property?
6. A large barn was converted into ten apartments with the following rentals: four at $200 per month, three at $175 per month, and three at $150 per month. The operating expenses were $10,000 and the debt service was $6,000. What is the yield on the owner's equity if $50,000 is invested in the property? Give both the dollar figure and rate.
7. The monthly interest on a $23,000 loan is $300. What is the annual simple interest rate?
8. What is the quarterly interest payment on a loan of $40,000 with an annual interest rate of 9 percent?

PROFIT AND LOSS

A measure of profit or loss compares sales price with the cost of the property. If the cost is less than the sales price, a profit is made. If the cost is greater than the sales price, a loss has been incurred. The amount of profit or loss is often expressed as a percent of the cost.

Example   A seller purchased a property for $8,000 and sold it for a profit of $2,000. What is the percent of profit?

$$\frac{\$2,000}{\$8,000} = 1/4 = .25 = 25\%$$

If you know the sales price and the percentage of profit, you may determine the cost by dividing the sales price by 1 plus the percent of profit.

Example
   Sales price = $10,000

Profit = 25%
Cost = ?

$$C = \frac{SP}{1 + P}$$

$$= \frac{\$10,000}{1 + .25}$$

$$= \frac{\$10,000}{1.25}$$

$$= \$8,000$$

If there has been a loss, you can determine the cost by dividing the sales price by 1 *minus* the rate of loss.

PRACTICE PROBLEMS:
PROFIT AND LOSS

1. A man bought two lots side by side. One measured 50 feet (w) × 100 feet (l) and the other measured 100 feet (w) × 100 feet (l). He paid a total of $4,500 for them. He later divided them into three lots of equal frontage and sold them for $2,000 each. What is the percent of return on his original investment?
2. If a house sold for $35,000 at a loss of 6 percent, what was the original cost of the house?
3. A person buys a lot for $5,000 and sells it at a 15 percent profit. What was the sales price?
4. A person buys a property for $43,500 and sells it for $65,000. What was the percent of profit?
5. A person bought a house for $23,750 and sold it at a $3,400 loss. What was the percent of loss?

COMMISSION

The salesperson's and broker's commissions are generally based on a percentage of the gross sales price of the property.

Example
   Sales price: $30,000
   Commission: 6%
   $30,000 × .06 = $1,800 commission.

PRACTICE PROBLEMS: COMMISSION

1. As a salesperson, you realize that it takes an average of ten showings to sell a house. You calculate that each showing has an average cost of $20. If you are paid one-half of the 8 percent

commission for selling a $50,000 property, what is your net income on this sale?

2. The commission rate for selling an apartment building is 6 percent of the first $10,000 and 5 percent of anything over that. Broker Jones received a commission of $760. What was the sales price of the apartment building?

3. An 80-acre tract was listed for sale at $400 per acre but was sold for $27,500 with the condition that the purchaser pay the broker's commission of 8 percent. What was the net gain for the purchaser?

4. If you are a salesperson for a $95,000 property, the brokerage fee is 8 percent, and you will receive 50 percent of the total fee, what is the dollar amount the brokerage firm will receive from the sale?

5. A broker keeps five-eighths of an 8 percent commission. The salesperson sold the property for $48,500. How much does the salesperson receive for selling the property?

SETTLEMENT STATEMENT MATH METHODS

The following computations should be used in settlement statement calculations.

Mortgage Computations

Following are four basic mortgage relationships:

1. Beginning principal balance $\times$ interest rate = annual interest.
2. Annual interest $\div$ 12 = monthly interest.
3. Constant monthly payment — monthly interest = amount to principal reduction.
4. Beginning principal balance — principal reduction = new principal balance.

Example Compute appropriate balances at the end of the first month for a mortgage with the following terms: 25-year loan, 8 percent interest for $50,000, $475 constant payment.

1. Beginning principal balance $\times$ interest rate = annual interest
   $50,000 \times .08 = $4,000
2. Annual interest $\div$ 12 = monthly interest
   $4,000 \div 12 = $333.33
3. Constant monthly payment — monthly interest = principal reduction
   $475.00 − $333.33 = $141.67
4. Beginning principal balance — principal reduction = new principal balance
   $50,000.00 − $141.67 = $49,858.33

Interest Prorated

In calculating prorated interest, assume that a year consists of 12 months of 30 days each.

1. Compute the annual interest on the mortgage balance by multiplying the rate by the mortgage balance.
2. Divide the annual interest by 12 to obtain the monthly interest.
3. Divide the monthly interest by 30 to obtain the daily interest to the nearest cent.
4. Count the number of days since the last mortgage payment through the closing date.
5. Multiply the number of days by the daily interest figure to obtain the amount being prorated.
6. If the interest is computed in advance, the seller will receive the difference between the prepaid amount of interest and the daily amount used to closing.
7. If the interest is in arrears, the seller will owe for the number of days since the last payment until the closing.

Example A $10,000 mortgage balance after the last payment at 12% interest. There are 15 days between the last payment and the closing.

1. $10,000 $\times$ .12 = $1,200 annual interest
2. $1,200/12 = $100/month
3. $100/30 = $3.33/day
4 and 5. 15 days $\times$ $3.33 = $49.95

15 days is equal to half a month. The difference between one-half the month's interest of $50.00 and the $49.95 computed daily is due to rounding off.

Taxes—Computed and Prorated

For purposes of these examples, taxes are computed annually from January 1 to December 31. Each month is considered to have 30 days, and a year has 360 days. Taxes are computed by multiplying the rate by the assessed value of the land and improvements.

Example
   (Land) $5,000 + (improvements) $12,000
      = (assessed value) $17,000
   Rate = $9.40/$100 of assessed value
   Annual taxes = (land + improvements) $\times$ rate
   Annual taxes $\div$ ($5,000 + $12,000) $\times$
            ($9.40/$100)
   Annual taxes = $17,000 $\times$ ($9.40/$100)
   Annual taxes = $1,598

The rate will be expressed as so many dollars per $100 of assessed value. To prorate taxes for settlement:

1. Compute the amount of time the seller will possess the property in the year of the settlement through the settlement.
2. Compute the annual taxes.
3. Find the monthly amount of the taxes and multiply the amount by the time of settlement to obtain the prorated amount.
4. If taxes were prepaid, subtract the prorated amount from the prepaid taxes to find how much the seller will receive at the settlement. If taxes are paid in arrears, the seller will be charged the prorated share at the settlement.

Example
Assessed value of land ($5,000)
+ improvements ($12,000)
= total assessed value = $17,000
Rate $9.40/$100
Annual taxes = $1,598 due December 31
At closing on June 15:
$1,598/12 = $133.17/month
Seller has held property 5½ months
($133.17)(5½) = $732.44 taxes to be prorated

Insurance Prorated (30-day month)

Most insurance is paid in advance for either one or three years. Therefore, upon cancellation or assignment of the policy in force, the seller desires a refund of the prepaid premiums. This amount represents the unused portion of the seller's premium. In order to compute the unused portion:

1. Compute the time remaining on the policy

Example

	Date	Month	Year
Expiration date	20	8	NY
Date of closing	10	6	TY
Time remaining	10	2	1

2. Multiply the time remaining by the rates.

Example Policy has a premium of $360 per year paid three years in advance

Year = $360
Month = $360/12 = $30/month
Daily = $30/30 = $1/day

Time remaining × rate
  = amount to seller

1 year × 360 =	$360
2 months × $30 =	$60
10 days × $1 =	$10
Amount to seller	$430

Rent Prorated

Rent is usually paid in advance. The purchaser is concerned with obtaining his share of the rent at the settlement when he takes possession of the property.

1. Divide the monthly amount by 30 and round off to the nearest cent to obtain the daily rate.
2. Multiply the daily rate by the number of days the seller has had possession of the property to closing.
3. Subtract this amount from the monthly rent, and the remainder is owed the buyer.

Example The monthly rent of $180 is paid in advance; the closing is on the 20th of the month. Prorate the rent:

$180/30 = $6/day
20 days seller has possession × $6 = $120
$180 − $120 = $60 to buyer

PRACTICE PROBLEMS: MORTGAGE BALANCES, RENT, TAX, INSURANCE, INTEREST PRORATIONS

Mortgage Balances

1. Balance after last payment, $38,500; interest rate, 8 percent; constant payment, $328 per month. What is the balance of the mortgage after the next payment?

2. Balance after May 15, $24,250; interest rate, 7 percent; constant monthly payment, $210. What is the mortgage balance after the July 15 payment?

Rent

3. *D* is purchasing a four-unit apartment building. The building contains two one-bedroom apartments renting for $180 per month; one two-bedroom apartment renting for $210 per month; one three-bedroom apartment renting for $270 per month. All rents are due on the first of the month and are current. The closing is to take place on the 20th. Prorate the rents to determine the total amount owed to *D* at closing.

Taxes

4. A property is assessed at 40 percent of its appraised value. The appraised value is $37,500 and the tax rate is $8.27 per $100. Taxes are due January 1 each year in advance. If the sale of the property closed on July 10th, how much would the buyer owe the seller for the prorated taxes at closing?

Insurance

5. A home is covered by a three-year fire insurance policy which expires July 11, NY. The premium on the policy was $489 and has been paid in full. The home was sold and closing was set for September 23, TY. How much money will be credited the seller at closing if the policy is assumed by the purchaser?

Interest

6. The outstanding mortgage balance after the September 1st payment was $38,500. The monthly constant is $328. The interest is computed in arrears at 8¾ percent. What amount would be debited to the seller if settlement takes place September 20th?

Chapter 18
Sample Examinations

THIS CHAPTER contains two examinations, the first more difficult than the second. The student should practice both.

The first of the following two examinations, "Sample Real Estate Salespersons' Examination," is one of many examinations used by New York University in the 1983—84 academic year. It is typical of exams given by accredited schools pursuant to the requirement that 45 hours of classroom education be completed satisfactorily.

The second examination is a 40-question test modeled after a State of New York test. The questions are similar to actual questions on exams in the last four years. To obtain a salesperson's license, the candidate must pass both the school examination and the state examination. Answers to the problems are found in Appendix A of this book.

SAMPLE REAL ESTATE SALESPERSONS' EXAMINATIONS

MULTIPLE CHOICE: On the ANSWER SHEET, circle the lettered answer that you think is the best response to the question. You may use the back of the answer sheet for mathematical calculations.

1. The most common result of a defaulted mortgage is

    (a) An eviction.
    (b) An injunction.
    (c) A foreclosure sale.
    (d) A reversion.

2. Sam Smith may legally grant his power of attorney to

    (a) His broker.
    (b) His lawyer.
    (c) His wife.
    (d) All of the above.

3. Charging more than the legal rate of interest is called

    (a) Forgery.
    (b) Usury.
    (c) Certiorari.
    (d) Dower.

4. An applicant for a salesperson's license must be at least

    (a) Eighteen.

    (b) Twenty-one.
    (c) Twenty.
    (d) Sixteen.

5. The date upon which the final payment of a loan is due is called the

    I. Impound date
    II. Maturity date

    (a) I only.
    (b) II only.
    (c) Both I and II.
    (d) Neither I nor II.

6. A statement prepared and signed by a lender showing the principal owing on a loan is called a

    I. Certificate of reduction of mortgage
    II. Owner's estoppel certificate

    (a) I only.
    (b) II only.
    (c) Both I and II.
    (d) Neither I nor II.

7. Which of the following does not provide tax shelter?

    I. Depreciation
    II. Mortgage balance reduction

(a) I only.
(b) II only.
(c) Both I and II.
(d) Neither I nor II.

8. A grantor's sister has a possible interest in real estate being conveyed. This is a "cloud on the title." To clear the title, which of the following deeds is commonly used?

(a) A bargain and sale deed.
(b) A quitclaim deed.
(c) Special warranty deed.
(d) Correction deed.

9. The New York Department of State may take the following disciplinary action against a licensed broker.

(a) Revocation of license.
(b) Suspension of license.
(c) Reprimand.
(d) Any of the above.

10. Which of the following statement(s) is (are) true?

   I. Functional obsolescence is the result of factors within the property.
   II. Economic obsolescence is caused by factors outside the property.

(a) I only.
(b) II only.
(c) Both I and II.
(d) Neither I nor II.

11. A person empowered to act on behalf of another is called

(a) A middleman.
(b) An agent.
(c) A principal.
(d) A party.

12. The right of the state to zone land stems from

   I. Eminent domain
   II. Police power

(a) I only.
(b) II only.
(c) Both I and II.
(d) Neither I nor II.

13. No real estate salesperson may operate as a

(a) Part-time employee of a broker.
(b) Solicitor for a broker.

(c) Partner of a broker.
(d) Custodian of real property.

14. When real estate under lease is sold, the lease generally

(a) Expires.
(b) Is broken.
(c) Remains binding upon the new owner.
(d) Must be renewed.

15. A right to real estate or an interest in real estate held by someone other than the owner, diminishing its value, is called a(n)

(a) Bond.
(b) Encumbrance.
(c) Subordination.
(d) Fixture.

16. The type of listing in which the broker is least likely to know the amount of money that will be received as commission for the sale of the property, which is illegal in New York State is a(n)

(a) Open listing.
(b) Exclusive authorization to sell.
(c) Multiple listing.
(d) Net listing.

17. The person who lends the money and to whom the property is pledged as security is known as the

(a) Mortgagee.
(b) Assignor.
(c) Grantee.
(d) Mortgagor.

18. The evidence of the transfer of title to real property is called a(n)

(a) Option.
(b) Deed.
(c) Mortgage.
(d) Lien.

19. Susan Smith listed her home with Bill Brown, a broker. She subsequently sold her home without any assistance whatsoever from broker Brown. Nonetheless, a court ruled that Susan owed broker Brown a full commission on the sale of her home. The logical explanation for the court's action must be that

(a) Brown has an exclusive agency listing.
(b) Brown had an option on the house.
(c) Brown has a contract with an exclusive right-to-sell clause.

(d) Susan was in debt to the broker from a previous transaction.

20. A lease where the tenant pays all expenses (except the mortgage) of the property in addition to his rent is called a(n)

(a) Percentage lease.
(b) Gross lease.
(c) Assigned lease.
(d) Net lease.

21. Which of the following situations require a real estate license?

    I. A property owner selling his own property.
    II. A legal guardian selling on behalf of an incompetent person.

(a) I only.
(b) II only.
(c) Both I and II.
(d) Neither I nor II.

22. If a salesperson takes a listing and also sells the property, the owner pays his commission to the

    I. Salesperson
    II. Broker

(a) I only.
(b) II only.
(c) Both I and II.
(d) Neither I nor II.

23. The original borrower's obligation to repay the promissory note is automatically ended if the buyer

    I. Assumes the loan
    II. Buys subject to the loan

(a) I only.
(b) II only.
(c) Both I and II.
(d) Neither I nor II.

24. A branch real estate office must have a

    I. Branch office license
    II. A licensed broker in charge, or a salesperson who has met certain New York State requirements

(a) I only.
(b) II only.

(c) Both I and II.
(d) Neither I nor II.

25. If a person who owns real estate dies, in order to sell that property

    I. The executor must hold a real estate license
    II. The administrator must hold a real estate license

(a) I only.
(b) II only.
(c) Both I and II.
(d) Neither I nor II.

26. A house valued at $20,000 was insured against fire. The rate was $.60 per $100 for a three (3) year period. How much was the premium for one (1) year?

(a) $40.
(b) $28.
(c) $36.
(d) $32.

27. Tom and Mary Brown bought their home a year ago for $65,800. Property is said to be increasing in value at the rate of 12% annually. If this is true, what is the current market value of the Browns' real estate?

(a) $72,380.
(b) $73,696.
(c) $74,320.
(d) None of the above.

28. Bobbi, Linda, Moira, and Joselyn decided to pool their savings and purchase some commercial real estate for $125,000. Bobbi and Linda each contributed $35,000 and Joselyn contributed $30,000. What percentage of ownership was left for Moira?

(a) 20%.
(b) 24%.
(c) 28%.
(d) 30%.

29. The salesperson's half of a 6% commission of the sale of a $52,500 house would be

(a) $1,575.
(b) $1,260.
(c) $3,150.
(d) None of the above.

30. The buildings on a 150 x 220 foot lot cover 30% of the lot. How many square feet are *not* covered by buildings?

(a) 33,000.
(b) 23,100.
(c) 10,900.
(d) 7,000.

COMPLETION: On the ANSWER SHEET, supply the missing word or words to complete the sentence correctly.

1. In the _____ clause in a mortgage, the borrower agrees that the entire balance of the loan becomes due to the lender if the interest and principal is not paid.

2. *foreclosure* is the legal process by which a property is sold to recover the debt on a mortgage.

3. In a(n) _____ agreement, the person with higher rights agrees to give up priority and assume a lesser position.

4. A deed cannot be recorded unless it is first _____ .

5. A person appointed by the court to administer the estate of a deceased person who left no will is a(n) _____ .

6. The process of reflecting future income in present value is called _____ .

7. The lender (i.e., bank) in a mortgage loan transaction is known as _____ .

8. A _____ description is a legal description of a parcel of land which begins at a well-marked point and follows the boundaries, using direction and distances around the tract, back to the place of beginning.

9. The New York State documentation stamp tax is usually paid by the _____ at closing.

10. A commission is normally earned by a real estate broker when the broker produces a buyer who is _____ to purchase.

11. Ownership of realty by two or more persons who are not married, each of whom has an individual interest with right of survivorship is called _____ .

12. The party representing the principal is the _____ .

13. One who receives a transfer of real property by deed is the _____ .

14. A mortgage that is not insured by a public agency is called a(n) _____ mortgage.

15. When a city or county specifies the type and use to which property may be put, it does so by enacting a(n) _____ ordinance.

16. One appointed by the court to take control and possession of property pending litigation and some final orders by the court is called a(n) _____ .

17. Security pledged for the payment of an obligation is called _____ .

18. A person who dies _____ has prepared his own will indicating the way his property is to be disposed after his death.

19. _____ is a legal process by which a court determines who will inherit the property of a deceased person and what the assets of the estate are.

20. The right of a landowner whose land borders on a river or stream to use that water is called a(n) _____ .

21. A term most frequently applied to a sale of personal property wherein the seller retains the title to the goods or property, though the possession is delivered to the buyer, until the purchase price is paid in full is a(n) _____ sale.

22. Owners of land bordering on rivers, lakes, and other bodies of water may acquire additional land through the process of _____ .

23. The transfer of title made by either gift or sale is a form of _____ alienation.

24. When a person dies intestate and leaves no heirs, the title to his or her real estate passes to the state by operation of law based on the principle of _____ .

25. A right of use that may be exercised by the public or individuals on, over, or through the land of others is known as a(n) _____ .

26. A single mortgage that covers more than one piece of real estate is known as a(n) _____ .

27. The license term for real estate brokers and salespersons is _____ years.

28. A deed which contains a guarantee of the title being transferred is known as a(n) _____ .

29. A mortgage in which repayment of the principal is in one lump sum at the date of maturity is known as a(n) _____ mortgage.

30. Each licensed broker must maintain for a period of _____ years records of transactions involving one- to four-family dwellings.

TRUE OR FALSE: On the ANSWER SHEET, circle TRUE if the statement is true, or FALSE if the statement is FALSE.

1. A deed becomes effective as soon as it is signed.

2. The purpose of the licensing law is to protect the public against the dishonest practices of unscrupulous, and the costly blunderings of incompetent, real estate agents.

3. A license is required for real estate transactions negotiated in New York State even if the property is located in another state.

4. An attorney at law may employ a salesperson without obtaining a license as a real estate broker.

5. Where one of the brokers to an open listing is successful in negotiating a sale of the property, the authority of all the other brokers to the open listing arrangement is automatically terminated.

6. There must be express authority for a broker or salesperson to accept deposits or sign a contract.

7. A broker may be employed by both seller and buyer if both parties consent.

8. An applicant for a broker's license must be at least 21 years old.

9. A rent collector need not be licensed.

10. The revocation of a broker's license to operate suspends the license of all real estate salespersons in the broker's employ.

11. Commission rates are fixed by the local real estate boards.

12. A mortgage serves as evidence of a debt.

13. The laws of the state where the owner of real estate resides govern the details of the deed of conveyance.

14. The Secretary of State can only commence an investigation of a violation of the license law upon a complaint by a third party.

15. When sellers are co-owners, it is necessary for the purchaser to have each of them (and when necessary, their spouses) sign the sales contract.

16. An oral sales contract involving the sale of real estate can be enforced through a court action.

17. The rule against blockbusting prevents a broker from soliciting listings on grounds of loss of value due to the presence of minority groups.

18. A lease for a period of a year or less need not be in writing.

19. A parcel of land may have several highest and best uses at the same time.

20. A parcel of real estate can have only one fair market value at any given point in time.

21. The movement of the real estate market generally reflects current overall economic trends.

22. A real estate broker usually represents a seller; therefore a broker's primary duty is to protect the seller's rights and interests in any real estate transaction.

23. If a maximum FHA and VA loan is given on a house, the buyer can usually be sure that the sales price is fair and reasonable.

24. A salesperson or broker trying to make a sale can make statements about a property without checking the facts.

25. It is the broker or salesperson's duty to establish a selling price for an owner's property.

26. Servicing a listing generally means working with a seller to sell the property once it has been listed.

27. The right of taxation is one of the powers that government has over private ownership of land.

28. Only a husband and wife may hold title to a parcel of real estate as tenants by the entireties.

29. A lien is an encumbrance.

30. The rights of a mechanic's lien claimant can be satisfied, or released, only when the owner of the real estate makes payment on the lien.

MATCHING COLUMN: Select the term that best fits the description listed and write the corresponding letter next to the number on the ANSWER SHEET.

1. Eminent domain

2. Satisfaction

3. Consideration

4. Deed

5. Title

6. Mechanic's lien

7. Right of survivorship

8. Condominium

9. Escheat

10. Tenants in common

a. Joint ownership with right of survivorship.

b. A fee simple title to designated airspace as a unit plus a percentage ownership of common elements and the land.

c. The right to or ownership of land.

d. A lien on property given to a person who has loaned money.

e. The co-owners of a parcel of land whose interest will pass at their deaths to their heirs or by their wills.

f. A written instrument in proper legal form which conveys absolute title to, or an interest in, real estate.

g. That which is given to a seller in return for the deed.

h. A document executed by a creditor and given to a debtor evidencing payment of a debt.

i. The right of governmental bodies to take real estate for public use.

j. The reversion of property to the state because of a lack of heirs or other people legally entitled to hold the property.

k. A lien established by law in favor of those providing labor and materials for the improvement of a parcel of real estate.

l. A lien on real estate to secure payment for specific improvements made by the local community.

m. The power of government to restrict the use of real estate for the good of its citizens.

n. An element of ownership in joint tenancy and tenancy by the entireties.

SAMPLE STATE EXAMINATION FOR SALESPERSONS

Part I
Agency and Real Property Law
(30) questions

1. Salesperson's license applicants must fulfill the following requirements:

    (a) They must have two years experience.
    (b) The applicant must have declared his or her intention of becoming a U.S. citizen if not currently a citizen.
    (c) The applicant must be more than 21 years old.
    (d) The applicant must not have been convicted of a felony within the last five years.

2. If two brokers co-broker a piece of property, but one has lost his license, commission is due and payable to

    (a) Neither.
    (b) Both.
    (c) The licensed broker only, to share as he deems proper.
    (d) The licensed broker, who need not split the commission.

3. The party that owes the real estate salesperson compensation for the salesperson's services is

    (a) The seller.
    (b) The buyer.
    (c) The devisee.
    (d) The broker.

4. If an unlicensed salesperson acts for a broker in a real estate transaction, the broker had committed

    (a) A misdemeanor.
    (b) A felony.
    (c) An unethical act.
    (d) Fraud.

5. A real estate salesperson violate the license law if he makes rebates. The law specifies the following punishment:

    (a) A fine of ten times the rebate.
    (b) A fine of $500
    (c) Suspension or revocation of license.
    (d) Notation of the infraction in the salesperson's pocket card.

6. Jones is managing his wife's property, including preparing the leases and collecting the rent. What kind of license does he require?

    (a) No license.
    (b) A salesperson's license.
    (c) A broker's license.

7. The real estate salesperson is prohibited from entering the following relationship with his broker:

    (a) He may not be a joint tenant.
    (b) He may not be the broker's salaried employee.
    (c) He may not be the broker's partner.
    (d) He may not be the broker's mortgagee.

8. What is the effect on a salesperson when his broker's license is revoked for an illegal act? (The salesperson was not implicated in that act.)

   (a) The salesperson's license is automatically revoked. He must reapply for a license.
   (b) The salesperson's license is not affected. He may continue selling activities.
   (c) The salesperson may not undertake selling activity until the broker's license is restored.
   (d) The salesperson's license is not affected. But he must find a new broker for whom to sell.

9. The licensed real estate salesperson receives both a license and a pocket card. The license is
   (a) Filed in Albany.
   (b) Files with the broker.
   (c) Prominently displayed by the broker.
   (d) Retained by the salesperson and displayed upon request.

10. There is a fiduciary relationship between

    (a) Broker and his salesperson.
    (b) Broker and seller.
    (c) Broker and buyer.
    (d) Buyer and seller.

11. The relationship between real estate brokers and their clients is governed by

    (a) The Law of Agency.
    (b) Article 12A of the Real Property Law.
    (c) Local Law 5.
    (d) Section 421 of the Real Property Tax Law.

12. A broker who receives funds from his client to be held in trust must hold these in a special account. If he places them is a personal bank account, he is guilty of

    (a) Fraud.
    (b) Larceny.
    (c) Commingling.
    (d) Unethical behavior.

13. Enforceable listing agreements must be in writing and signed by the

    (a) Seller.
    (b) Buyer.
    (c) Broker.
    (d) Salesperson.

14. A payment made to validate an agreement concerning the sale of real property is called a

    (a) Note.
    (b) Bond.
    (c) Option.
    (d) Binder.

15. Landlord Brown sells his building to a new owner Green. Units in the building have been leased to five tenants.

    (a) Green must renegotiate each lease.
    (b) The leases are expired and Green may find new tenants.
    (c) The leases are binding upon Green.
    (d) Brown has defaulted under the lease, and the tenants may either renew or not as they wish.

16. Bowery Savings Bank lends money to Jones and receives Jones' pledge of property as security. Bowery is a

    (a) Mortgagee.
    (b) Mortgagor
    (c) Vendee.
    (d) Trust deed holder.

17. ABC Company leases a warehouse from H. Smith. ABC agrees to pay rent, all taxes, utilities, and other operating costs. This lease is

    (a) A gross lease.
    (b) A net lease.
    (c) A percentage lease.
    (d) Illegal.

18. A builder purchases land and accepts a clause in the deed that prohibits him from building a structure higher that ten stories. This clause is a

    (a) Restriction clause.
    (b) Limitation clause.
    (c) Zoning requirement clause.
    (d) Prohibition clause.

19. Regulations in New York City that limit floor area ratios are part of the city's

    (a) Real Property tax code.
    (b) Building code.
    (c) Zoning code.
    (d) Right of eminent domain.

20. Blue borrows $100,000 at interest of 10 percent per annum. His monthly payments to the bank total 11 percent, so that he is making monthly paybacks of the loan principal. These paybacks are called.

    (a) Depreciation.
    (b) Appreciation.
    (c) Economic return.
    (d) Amortization.

21. A deed is

    (a) Evidence of an option to purchase real property.
    (b) Evidence of an offer to purchase real property.
    (c) A binder that commits the buyer to purchase

real property.

(d) Evidence of the transfer of title to real property.

22. In order to be valid, the deed must be signed by

(a) The buyer.
(b) The seller.
(c) The mortgagee.
(d) All of the above.

23. A satisfaction claim deed is

(a) A quitclaim deed.
(b) A special warranty deed.
(c) A bargain and sale deed.
(d) A contingent deed.

24. In a real estate transaction, which of the following instruments must be recorded?

(a) Offer to purchase.
(b) Deed only.
(c) Deed and mortgage.
(d) All of the above.

25. Jones is unable to pay New York City taxes on his home. The delinquent taxes are considered.

(a) Liens.
(b) Judgments.
(c) Attachments.
(d) Easements.

26. Jones builds a bridge across a stream. Although the entire stream is within his property, the bridge's anchorings extend onto another's property. This is known as

(a) Adverse possession.
(b) Encroachment.
(c) Easement.
(d) Generous abandonment.

27. Jones has a right (an interest) in a parcel of property owned by Smith. That interest is known as

(a) Ostensible title.
(b) Subordination.
(c) A judgment.
(d) An encumbrance.

28. A judgment in rem refers to

(a) Chattel.
(b) Real property.
(c) Stocks and bonds.
(d) Personalty.

29. Usury is

(a) The crime of misrepresenting the condition of property that is for sale.
(b) The charging of unconscionable rent.
(c) An illegal extension of secondary finance.

(d) Charging more that the legal interest rate.

30. In a sale of property, title is not conveyed until a deed is

(a) Signed by both seller and buyer.
(b) Recorded.
(c) Signed by the seller and delivered.
(d) Signed and notarized.

Part II
Verbal Analogies
(5 questions)

31. *Giant* is to *dwarf* as *many* is to

(a) Large.
(b) Group.
(c) Size.
(d) Few.

32. *Cat* is to *claw* as *bird* is to

(a) Feather.
(b) Fly.
(c) Seed.
(d) Sing.

33. *Garage* is to *auto* as *stable* is to

(a) Farm.
(b) Hay.
(c) Seed.
(d) Horse.

34. *Beautiful* is to *ugly* as *late* is to

(a) On time.
(b) Tardy.
(c) Early.
(d) Near by.

35. *Pencil* is to *write* as *bell* is to

(a) Awaken.
(b) Ring.
(c) Instrument.
(d) Knock.

Part III
Arithmetic Problems
(5 questions)

36. Smith's house was worth $100,000. He purchased fire insurance for 80 percent of the value. The insurance cost $0.90 per $1,000 for three years of insurance. How much did Smith pay for one year's insurance?

(a) $20

(b) $24.
(c) $72.
(d) $30.

37. A broker retains 60 percent of the commission proceeds from any sale and gives 40 percent to the salesperson. When a $70,000 sale is closed and the commission paid is 6 percent of the selling price, what is the salesperson's share of the commission?

(a) $1,680.
(b) $4,200.
(c) $420.
(d) $2,420.

38. A real estate broker completed a lease transaction involving a one-year lease with a monthly rental of $650. If he received a 5 percent commission, what did he earn?

(a) $340.
(b) $365.

(c) $390.
(d) $415.

39. Green sold his property for $96,000, making 20 percent profit. What did he pay for the house when he first acquired it?

(a) $80,000.
(b) $94,080.
(c) $76,800.
(d) $82,000.

40. Brown owns a small building containing 32 one-bedroom apartments. The gross annual rent is $163,200. What is the monthly rental for each apartment?

(a) $325.
(b) $375.
(c) $400.
(d) $425.

Appendices

Appendices

Appendix A
Answer Key

ANSWERS TO REVIEW QUESTIONS, CHAPTERS 3–16

Chapter 3: Estates and Interests

1. d	11. a
2. c	12. c
3. c	13. d
4. c	14. b
5. b	15. d
6. c	16. c
7. b	17. c
8. d	18. a
9. a	19. c
10. b	20. a

Chapter 4: Forms of Ownership

1. b	11. a
2. c	12. b
3. a	13. b
4. c	14. c
5. b	15. b
6. a	16. c
7. b	17. d
8. a	18. b
9. c	19. b
10. c	20. c

Chapter 5: Real Estate Instruments

1. a	11. b
2. b	12. d
3. c	13. c
4. c	14. c
5. c	15. d
6. c	16. a
7. a	17. d
8. d	18. d
9. a	19. a
10. c	20. c

Chapter 6: Contracts

1. c	3. c
2. a	4. b

5. b	13. b
6. a	14. b
7. b	15. b
8. c	16. b
9. d	17. b
10. b	18. c
11. c	19. c
12. c	20. c

Chapter 7: Mortgages

1. c	11. d
2. d	12. c
3. b	13. d
4. d	14. c
5. b	15. b
6. b	16. a
7. a	17. c
8. c	18. b
9. c	19. a
10. b	20. a

Chapter 8: Real Estate Finance

1. d	11. a
2. c	12. d
3. b	13. a
4. a	14. c
5. d	15. b
6. b	16. a
7. c	17. d
8. c	18. d
9. b	19. c
10. c	20. a

Chapter 9: Evidence of Title and Recording Systems

1. c	11. c
2. c	12. c
3. a	13. d
4. d	14. b
5. c	15. d
6. c	16. a
7. c	17. b
8. b	18. d
9. c	19. c
10. b	20. c

Chapter 10: Closing and Closing Costs

1. c	11. c
2. d	12. b
3. a	13. c
4. d	14. d
5. d	15. d
6. b	16. d
7. b	17. d
8. b	18. d
9. c	19. d
10. c	20. c

Chapter 11: Law of Agency

1. d	11. a
2. c	12. b
3. a	13. a
4. c	14. c
5. d	15. c
6. d	16. a
7. b	17. b
8. a	18. d
9. a	19. d
10. d	20. d

Chapter 12: License Law and Ethics

1. c	11. a
2. d	12. a
3. b	13. b
4. c	14. a
5. b	15. a
6. a	16. c
7. c	17. a
8. b	18. d
9. b	19. b
10. a	20. b

Chapter 13: Real Estate Appraisal

1. b	11. b
2. d	12. d
3. d	13. d
4. c	14. b
5. d	15. d
6. c	16. b
7. d	17. c
8. b	18. d
9. b	19. c
10. d	20. d

Chapter 14: Listing Agreements

1. d	3. b
2. c	4. d

5. c	13. c
6. d	14. d
7. c	15. c
8. c	16. a
9. a	17. d
10. d	18. d
11. c	19. d
12. d	20. d

Chapter 15: Human Rights/Fair Housing

1. b	11. a
2. c	12. a
3. c	13. a
4. a	14. c
5. c	15. c
6. c	16. b
7. c	17. b
8. c	18. a
9. c	19. d
10. b	20. d

Chapter 16: Land Use Regulations

1. c	11. a
2. c	12. c
3. c	13. b
4. b	14. b
5. a	15. a
6. c	16. b
7. c	17. b
8. a	18. c
9. c	19. c
10. d	20. a

SOLUTIONS TO MATH PROBLEMS, CHAPTER 17

Fractions, Decimals, Percents

Fractions

1. $1/6 + 1/8 = 7/24$
2. $3/7 + 4/9 = 55/63$
3. $19/20 + 3/5 = 31/20$ or $1\ 11/20$
4. $1/8 + 5/12 = 13/24$
5. $3/4 + 1/16 = 13/16$
6. $1/6 - 1/8 = 1/24$
7. $4/7 - 4/9 = 8/63$
8. $19/20 - 3/5 = 7/20$
9. $5/12 - 1/8 = 7/24$
10. $3/4 - 1/16 = 11/16$
11. $1/8 \times 1/4 = 1/32$
12. $1/9 \times 11/12 = 11/108$
13. $3/4 \times 7/16 = 21/64$
14. $4/5 \times 8/9 = 32/45$

15. $5/12 \times 1/5 = 5/60 = 1/12$
16. $1/8 \div 1/4 = 4/8 = 1/2$
17. $1/9 \div 11/12 = 12/99 = 4/33$
18. $3/4 \div 7/6 = 18/28 = 9/14$
19. $4/5 \div 8/9 = 36/40 = 9/10$
20. $5/12 \div 1/5 = 25/12 = 2\ 1/12$

Decimals and Percents

1. $.5 + .075 + .125 = .7$
2. $.073 + 1.25 + .93 = 2.253$
3. $.82 + .73 + 2.584 = 4.134$
4. $.0016 + 1.043 + .3 = 1.3446$
5. $1.25 - .075 = 1.175$
6. $.073 - .0016 = .0714$
7. $1.4874 - .896 = .5914$
8. $2.043 - 1.0012 = 1.0418$
9. $.075 \times 1.257 = \sout{.094275}$ .095625
10. $.342 \times .0017 = .0005814$
11. $.7589 \times 1.2 = .91068$
12. $.346 \times 3.476 = 1.202696$
13. $.34 \div .516 = .65891$
14. $1.25 \div .07 = 17.857$
15. $.78 \div .4 = 1.95$
16. $1.29 \div .432 = 2.9861$
17. $75\% = .75$
18. $125\% = 1.25$
19. $27.56\% = .2756$
20. $43.2\% = .432$
21. $.0025 = .25\%$
22. $.567 = 56.7\%$
23. $.493 = 49.3\%$
24. $3.475 = 347.5\%$

Perimeter, Area, Volume

1. 640 acres = 1 sq mile

2. 43,560 sq ft = 1 acre

3.
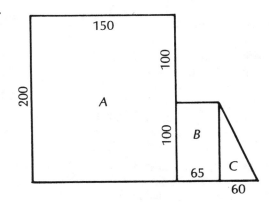

Area $A =$ (150)(200) = 30,000
Area $B =$ (100)(65) = 6,500
Area $C = ½$ (60)(100) = 3,000
Total   39,500 sq ft

4. $A = L \times W$
   $A = 373 \times 154$
   $A = 57,442$ sq ft
   $57,442/43,560 = 1.3187$ acres
   $1.3187\ (\$1,000.00) = \$1,318.70$

5. $A = L \times W$
   $A = 300 \times 450$
   $A = 135,000$ sq ft
   1 acre = 43,560 sq ft
   $135,000/43,560 = 3.1$ acres

6. Labor costs $= 28 \times 9 \times \$.20 = \$50.40$
   Concrete costs $= (28 \times 9 \times .5)/27 \times \$16.50 =$
      $\$77.00$
   $\$50.40 + \$77.00 = \$127.40$

7. $A = L \times W$
   $L = 150 - (20 + 15) = 115$
   $W = 120 - (15 + 15) = 90$
   $A = 115 \times 90 = 10,350$ sq. ft.

8. $A = L \times W$
   $A = 310 \times 240$
   $A = 74,400$ sq rods
   $A = 74,400/160$
   $A = 465$ acres

   $A = \pi r^2$
   $A = 3.1416\ (45)^2$
   $A = 3.1416\ (2025)$
   $A = 6361.74$ sq rods
   $A = 6361.74 \div 160$
   $A = 39.76$ acres

   $\begin{array}{r} 465 \text{ acres} \\ -\ 39.76 \text{ acres} \\ \hline 425.24 \text{ acres} \end{array}$ $\begin{array}{r} 425.24 \\ \times\ \$50.00 \\ \hline \$21,262.00 \end{array}$

9. $C = \pi d$
   $C = (3.1416)(14.28)$
   $C = 44.86$ rods

10. $V = L \times W \times H$
    $V = 340 \times 260 \times 40$
    $V = 3,536,000$ cu ft

11. $A = L \times W$
    $A = 80 \times 135$
    $A = 10,800$

Cost = area × price
Cost = 10,800 × $.63
Cost = $6,804

$V = l \times w \times h$
$V = 40 \times 60 \times 10$
$V = 24,000$ cu ft

Cost = V × price
Cost = 24,000 × $1.85
Cost = $44,400

$$\begin{array}{r} \$44,400 \\ +\;\; 6,804 \\ \hline \$51,204 \end{array}$$

12. 264 × 660   = 174,240 sq ft
    174,240 ÷ 43,560 = 4.0 acres
    4 × $800   = $3,200

13. Land   125 × 100 × $ 1 = $ 12,500
    Two-story
         building   2 × 40 × 60 × $25 = 120,000
    Full basement   40 × 60 × $ 5 =   12,000
    Driveway   10 × 80 × $ 4 =   3,200
    Sidewalks   3 × 70 × $ 3 =   630
    Yard improvements   =   5,000
                                        ─────────
                                        $153,330

Rate, Income, Value, Interest

1. Income = rate × value
   Value = income/rate
          = $600 × 12 months/.08
          = 7,200/.08
          = $90,000

2. 6 × 2½% = 15% depreciation at the end of 6 years
   x = original value of house
   Original value − depreciation = present value
   $x - .15x = \$7,650$
     $.85x = \$7,650$
        $x = \$7,650/.85$
        $x = \$9,000$

3. Value = income/rate
         = $1,000 × 12 months/.13
         = $120,000/.13
         = $92,307.69

4. 12%   = return each year
   100% = total amount invested
   100/12 = 8.33 years

5. Net income per month = $325 − $155 = $170
   $170 × 12 = $2,040

6. Income = 4 × $200 × 12 months = $ 9,600
            3 × $175 × 12 months = $ 6,300
            3 × $150 × 12 months = $ 5,400
                                   ─────────
            Gross income   = $21,300
            Less expenses   = 10,000
            Less debt service   =   6,000
                                   ─────────
            Net income   = $ 5,300

   $ROI = \$5,300/\$50,000$
   $ROI = 10.6\%$

7. Interest = Principal × Rate
   $I = PR$
   $R = I/P$

8. $RP = I$
   $.09(\$40,000) = \$3,600$
   $\$3,600/4 = \$900$ quarterly payment

Profit and Loss

1. 3 × $2,000 = $6,000 total sale price of 3 lots
   $6,000 − original investment = profit
   $6,000 − $4,500 = $1,500 profit
   ROI = profit/original investment
   $ROI = \$1,500/\$4,500$
   $ROI = 33\frac{1}{3}\%$

2. Loss = sales price − cost
   Cost = sales price/(1 − loss)
   Cost = $35,000/(1 − .06)
   Cost = $35,000/.94
   Cost = $37,234.04

3. Profit = sales price − cost
   Sales price = cost + profit
   Sales price = $5,000 + .15 ($5,000)
   Sales price = $5,000 + $750
   Sales price = $5,750

4. Profit = sales price − cost
   Profit = $65,000 − $43,500
   Profit = $21,500
   % Profit = profit/cost
   % Profit = $21,500/$43,500
   % Profit = .494 = 49.4%

5. Percent loss = loss/cost
   % Loss = $3,400/$23,750
   % Loss = .143 or 14.3%

Commission

1. Expenses   = 10 showings at $20 each = $200
   Commission = ½ (.08) ($50,000) = $2,000
   Net income = commission less expenses
   Net income = $2,000 − $200 = $1,800

2. x = selling price
   .06($10,000) + .05(x − $10,000) = $760
   $600 + .05x − 500 = $760
   .05x = $660
   x = $13,200

3. Original offering = 80 acres × $400 = $32,000
   Actual price paid   = 27,500
   Commission paid by purchaser
   .08 × $27,500   = 2,200
   Total paid by purchaser $29,700
   Net gain for purchaser $ 2,300

4. $95,000 × .08 = $7,600
   $7,600/2 = $3,800

5. $SP \times R = C$
   $48,500 × .08 = 3,880
   ⅜ ($3,880) = $1,455 for the salesperson

Mortgage Balances, Rent, Tax, Insurance, Interest Prorations

Mortgage Balances

1. $38,500 × .08 = $3,080.00
   $3,080.00/12 = $256.67/month
   $328.00 − $256.67 = $71.33
   $38,500.00 − $71.33 = $38,428.67 after payment

2. $24,250.00 × .07 = $1,697.50
   $1,697.50/12 = $141.46/month
   $210.00 − $141.46 = $68.54
   $24,250.00 − $68.54 = $24,181.46 after June 15
   payment

   $24,181.46 × .07 = $1,692.70
   $1,692.70/12 = $141.06/month
   $210.00 − $141.06 = $68.94
   $24,181.46 − $68.94 = $24,112.52 after July 15th
   payment

Rent

3. 30 − 20 = 10 days remaining
   1-bedroom (two)
   $180/30 days = $6/day
   $6 × 10 days remaining = $60

2-bedroom (one)
   $210/30 days = $7/day
   7 × 10 days remaining = $70
3-bedroom (one)
   $270/30 days = $9/day
   $9 × 10 days remaining = $90
Total $120 + $70 + $90 = $280 owed to D.

Taxes

4. $37,500
   ×   .4
   $15,000

   $15,000 × $8.27/$100 = $1,240.50 annual taxes
   $1,240.50/12 = $103.375 or $103.38/month
   $103.38 × 6⅓ months = $654.71 charged to
   seller
   $1,240.50 − $654.71 = $585.79 charged to buyer

Insurance

	Day	Month	Year
5. Expires	11	7	82
Close	23	9	81
Remaining	−12	−2	1

One year − 2 months − 12 days = 9 months
   and 18 days
$489/3 = $163/year
$163/12 = $13.58/month
$13.58/30 = $.45/day
18 ($.45) + 9 ($13.58) = $8.10 + $122.22
                       = $130.32 to seller

Interest

6. $38,500.00
   ×   .0875
   $3,368.75/year

   $3,368.75/12 = $280.73/month
   $280.73/30 = $9.36/day
   $9.36 × 20 days = $187.20

SOLUTIONS TO SAMPLE EXAMINATIONS, CHAPTER 18

Sample School Examination

MULTIPLE CHOICE

1. c   4. a
2. d   5. b
3. b   6. a

7. b
8. b
9. d
10. c
11. b
12. b
13. c
14. c
15. b
16. d
17. a
18. b
19. c
20. d
21. d
22. b
23. d
24. c
25. d
26. a
27. b
28. a
29. a
30. b

COMPLETION
1. default or acceleration
2. foreclosure
3. subordination
4. acknowledged
5. administrator
6. capitalization
7. mortgagee
8. metes and bounds
9. seller
10. ready, willing, and able

11. joint tenancy
12. agent
13. grantee
14. conventional
15. zoning
16. receiver
17. collateral
18. testate
19. probate
20. riparian right
21. conditional or installment
22. accretion
23. voluntary
24. escheat
25. easement
26. blanket mortgage
27. two (2)
28. warranty deed
29. term
30. three (3)

TRUE OR FALSE
1. False
2. True
3. True
4. False
5. True
6. True
7. True
8. True
9. False
10. True
11. False
12. False
13. True
14. False
15. True

16. False
17. True
18. True
19. False
20. False
21. False
22. True
23. True
24. False
25. False
26. True
27. True
28. True
29. True

30. False

MATCHING COLUMN
1. i
2. h
3. g
4. f
5. c
6. k
7. n
8. b
9. j
10. e

Sample State Examination for Salespersons
1. b
2. a
3. d
4. a
5. c
6. a
7. c
8. d
9. b
10. b
11. b
12. c
13. a
14. d
15. c
16. a
17. b
18. a
19. c
20. d

21. d
22. b
23. a
24. c
25. a
26. b
27. d
28. b
29. d
30. c
31. d
32. a
33. d
34. c
35. b
36. b
37. a
38. c
39. a
40. d

Appendix B

Real Estate Salespersons' License Law

A message from the Secretary

This publication is part of the Department of State's license law booklet series. It is designed for persons who have applied to take the written examination required for a Real Estate Salespersons' license in New York State.

This booklet contains summaries of relevant laws and includes rules, regulations and other information pertaining to the duties and functions of Real Estate Salespersons.

The series has been designed for ease of reading and can be conveniently inserted in a loose-leaf binder. For further information, please contact the Division of Licensing Services at the above address.

I hope you find this booklet a helpful study aid and general reference.

Gail S. Shaffer
Secretary of State

INTRODUCTION

The business of real estate brokerage is regulated by Article 12-A of the Real Property Law, commonly known as the "Real Estate Brokers' and Salespersons' License Law," which was enacted in 1922 (Ch. 672, L. 1922). All applicants for licenses as real estate brokers or salespersons must establish their competency by passing appropriate written examinations. The statute requires all persons who fail to renew their licenses within two years from expiration to pass a written examination.

Applicants for real estate brokers' licenses must demonstrate that they have adequate knowledge of the English language; a fair understanding of the general purposes and general legal effects of deeds, mortgages, land contracts of sale and leases; a general and fair understanding of the obligations between principal and agent, and of the provisions of the License Law.

Applicants for real estate salespersons' licenses are required by law to pass a written examination that will satisfy the Department of State as to their character and general intelligence. The material contained in this booklet is used as reference material in gauging the applicant's intelligence and ability to absorb information.

The real estate brokers' examinations prescribed by the statute are conducted in New York City, Albany, Binghamton, Buffalo, Hauppauge, Mineola, Newburgh, Plattsburgh, Rochester, Syracuse, Utica and Watertown every month. The real estate salespersons' examinations are conducted every week in New York City, Albany, Buffalo, Hauppauge, Mineola, Rochester and Syracuse; every other week in Binghamton, Newburgh, Utica and Yonkers; and, every other month in Plattsburgh and Watertown. Applicants may appear at the place of examination that is most convenient to them, after applying to the Department of State, Division of Licensing Services, 162 Washington Ave., Albany, NY 12231. Any of the materials contained in this booklet may be the basis for questions on the real estate examination.

Change of Address or Association

Change of Broker The old broker returns the license to the salesperson and at the same time sends in **Termination of Association** form 411201-556 to the Department (no fee required). The salesperson then gives the license to the new broker. The new broker sends to the Department a **Salesperson Change of Association** form 411201-557 with the required $1.00 fee.

After the new broker sends in the required form and fee, the salesperson then makes the necessary changes on his/her own license—crossing out the old broker number, name and address, and in its place printing in the number, name and address of the new broker. The salesperson, in addition thereto, makes the same changes on his/her pocket card.

The new broker retains the license and the salesperson retains the pocket card.

Change of Address Before moving principal or branch office, a broker must secure the Department of State's approval of the new address.

The broker crosses out the old address and places in the new address on his/her own license, as well as on the licenses of all salespersons and, in addition thereto, sends to the Department of State all the necessary 411201-560 **Broker Changes of Address** and 411201-555 **Salesperson Change of Address** forms, each with the required $1.00 fee. After securing the approval, the salesperson then corrects the address on the pocket to reflect the new address.

SUMMARY OF ARTICLE 12-A OF THE REAL PROPERTY LAW

Purpose and effect. This statute was enacted, primarily, for the protection of the public against the dishonest practices of unscrupulous, and the costly blunderings of incompetent real estate agents. The more important effects of its enactment and the efforts that have been made to enforce its provisions efficiently, have been the minimizing of fraud and fraudulent practices in real estate transactions, and the promotion of higher standards of efficiency and trustworthiness in the real estate brokerage business.

Real estate agents must be licensed. This statute forbids anyone who is not a duly licensed real estate broker or salesperson to negotiate any form of real estate transaction, for another and for compensation of any kind, in the State of

New York (§440-a). The provision covers the negotiation of mortgages and the collection of rents, as well as the making of leases of and sale by auction or otherwise of real property (§440). In addition arranging the relocation of commercial or residential tenants for a fee is an activity restricted to real estate brokers. The negotiation of, or attempt to negotiate the sale of a lot or parcel for another under provisions of Article 9-A of the Real Property Law, relating to the sale or lease of subdivided land, requires a real estate broker's license (§440). A licensed broker may not use an unlicensed person to assist in the negotiation of a real estate transaction. If the broker does, the broker forfeits rights to a commission on the transaction, is guilty of a misdemeanor (§442-c) and may have the license revoked (§441-c).

Nonresident brokers. A nonresident of the State of New York may be licensed as a real estate broker in this state upon the same terms as resident brokers, except that a nonresident broker must file a duly executed ''irrevocable consent'' that service of summons, complaints and other legal documents in actions and other proceedings instituted against the broker, in any court in the State of New York may be served upon the Secretary of State, with the same force and effect as if served upon the broker personally. A nonresident who is licensed in another state must demonstrate competency in the prescribed written examination, and must maintain an office in this state, unless in his/her state a New York broker may be licensed without passing the qualifying examination that is there required of resident applicants for real estate brokers licenses, and is not required to maintain an office in that state.

Persons exempt from application of law. The provisions of the statute do not apply to public officers while performing their official duties, to persons acting in any capacity under the judgment or order of a court, or to attorneys at law duly admitted to practice in the courts of New York (§442-f). Where an attorney at law employs a salesperson or salespersons, the attorney at law must obtain a license as real estate broker.

Territorial application of law. The statute is statewide in its application (§440-a).

Eligibility for license. Licenses to act as real estate brokers are granted to citizens of the United States or to persons who are legal resident aliens; persons under the age of 21 years are ineligible.[1] No one may be licensed as a real estate broker unless he/she has actively participated in the general real estate brokerage business as a licensed real estate salesperson under the supervision of a licensed real estate broker for a period of not less than one year, or has had the equivalent experience in general real estate business for a period of at least two years, the nature of which experience shall be established by affidavit duly sworn to under oath and/or other further proof as required by the Department of State; and has attended for at least 90 hours and has successfully completed a real estate course or courses approved by the Secretary of State as to method, content and supervision, and has demonstrated competency to act as a broker by passing the required examination (subd. 1[d], §441).

Applicants for salespersons' licenses are examined only to establish their character and general intelligence. An alien, a person age 18 or over, or a person who has had no experience in real estate brokerage business may be licensed as a real estate salesperson; but must, within one year from the date of issue of his/her license, successfully complete an approved 45-hour course of study.

No person shall be entitled to a license as a real estate broker or real estate salesperson under this article who has been convicted in this State or elsewhere of a felony, and who has not subsequent to such conviction received executive pardon therefor or a certificate of good conduct from the parole board, to remove the disability under this section because of such conviction.

Renewal of license. A person who does not apply for renewal of either a broker's or salesperson's license within two years from expiration of a previously issued license must qualify by passing a written examination (subd. 2, §441).

Application for licenses. Persons wishing to be licensed, either as real estate brokers or salespersons, will be furnished with appropriate forms of applications, instructions, etc., by the Division of Licensing Services, Department of State.

Where the real estate broker desires to be licensed under an assumed name (trade name) the availability of that name must first be cleared with the Division of Licensing Services, Department of State, Albany, NY.

Where a proposed corporation is to be licensed as a real estate broker the availability of the proposed corporate name must first be cleared with both the Division of Licensing Services and the Division of Corporations and State Records of the Department of State, Albany, NY. Expenses should not be incurred for stationery, printing, advertising, etc., until receipt of such clearances from both divisions of the Department of State.

The mere filing of an application for a license does not authorize the applicant to engage in the real estate brokerage business. An applicant for a real estate broker's license may not lawfully act as a real estate agent until the license has actually been issued.

Continuing education. No renewal license will be issued for the licensing period commencing November 1, 1983, or any two-year license period thereafter, unless the licensee meets the continuing education requirement set forth in subd. 3(a), §441. The licensee must submit proof satisfactory to the Department that he/she has attended at least 45 hours of classroom instructions and successfully completed a real estate course or courses approved by the Secretary of State, within the preceding four years. Brokers with more than 15 years full-time experience and attorneys admitted to the bar in New York State are exempted from this requirement.

[1]The age at which a person may become licensed as a broker in New York State has been reduced from 21 to 19 years of age.

Temporary permits. Upon receipt of an application for a real estate salesperson's license, and on express request, a permit will be issued authorizing the applicant to act as a rent collector for a period not exceeding 90 days, pending the written examination. Not more than one such permit shall be issued the same applicant during the same license term. If employment terminates prior to expiration of permit, such permit must be returned by broker to Department of State (subd. 1-A, §441). The statute does not authorize the granting of temporary permits to applicants for brokers' licenses.

Corporations and copartnerships. Each officer of a corporation or member of a copartnership who engages in any form of real estate brokerage, in behalf of the corporation or firm, must be licensed, as its representative, as a real estate broker. Salespersons' licenses are not issued to officers of corporations, nor to members of copartnerships (subd. 2, §441-b).

License fee. The nonrefundable fee for the issuance or renewal of a license authorizing a person, copartnership or corporation to act as a real estate broker is $100 and the fee for issuance or renewal of a salespersons' license is $20. The fee for additional real estate broker's licenses issued to other officers or members of duly licensed corporations or copartnerships other than the initial representative broker, is the same as the fee for the license issued to the corporation or copartnership.

With respect to any real estate broker's or salesperson's license which may be effective for a period of less than two years, the following fee schedule shall apply:
1. Full fees shall be required for any such license which shall be effective for more than one year.
2. Half fees shall be required for any such license which shall be effective only during the second year or part thereof, of any licensing term.

Issue and reissue of license. The license term for real estate brokers and real estate salespersons shall be two years. Licenses for real estate brokers and real estate salespersons issued or renewed for a full term shall be effective on the 1st day of November of an odd-numbered year, the license term, and expire on the 31st day of October, two years later.

Article 12-A of the Real Property Law was amended by Chapter 868 of the Laws of 1977 to the extent that for the first time real estate salesperson applicants, will, beginning as of November 1, 1979, be required to take and pass an approved 45-hour course of study as a prerequisite to licensing. Applicants will be allowed to obtain a conditional license for a period of one year prior to the completion of such a course, if they so desire; but any such conditional license will be cancelled if such course is not completed within the one-year period.

Additional provisions included in these amendments will require all licenses, including salespersons, to accumulate 45 hours of continuing education credits during the period between November 1, 1979 and October 31, 1983, in order that they can renew their licenses at that time. This continuing education provision will be renewed for every four-year period thereafter.

Real estate broker's licenses are issued directly to the licensees named therein.

Where there is a change of association by a salesperson, termination of association as a salesperson, or change of address by a broker, the following procedures must be followed:
1. Change of Association
   a. Sponsoring broker gives license to salesperson. The broker also sends form entitled Salesperson Termination of Association to Department of State. If the broker wishes, he/she may also send a letter giving reason for termination.
   b. Salesperson sends form entitled Salesperson Change of Association Report signed by salesperson and new broker, to Department of State with fee of $1 prior to commencement of the salesperson's activities with the new broker. In addition to the penalties provided, a salesperson who applies for

his/her own broker's license may not receive credit for sales experience unless the Department of State has received notification of such change of broker as described above. Commission unlawfully earned through the efforts of unlicensed salespersons must be returned. Failure to comply with this provision is in violation of Sections 442, 442-b, 442-c and 442-d of the Real Property Law.
   c. Salesperson crosses out name and address of broker number, prints name, address and broker of new broker on front of license. Where this is not the first change of association for the current term, the salesperson prints new information on the back of the license.
2. Termination of Association as Salesperson
When a salesperson terminates association with a broker, the broker must forward to the Department of State, form entitled Salesperson Termination of Association and return the license and pocket card to the salesperson.
3. Broker Change of Address
The broker must secure the prior approval of the Department of State before moving. It should be noted that every office of the Department of State, wherever located, is empowered to approve changes of address on the licenses of real estate brokers. In areas subject to a nonsolicitation order, the Department restricts a broker from opening a new office.

After securing approval, the following steps must be completed within five days after the new premises are occupied:
   a. The broker will complete form entitled Broker Change of Address and send it to the Department of State.
      The broker will cross out the former address on the license, print in the complete new address.
   b. Each salesperson employed by such broker will complete a form entitled Salesperson Change of Address and send same to the Department of State; the address will also be changed on the pocket card.
      The broker will cross out the old address on the license of each of the salespersons and will print in the complete new address on each license.

Application forms to effect any change in broker's or salesperson's license status can be obtained from and must be filed with the Division of Licensing Services, Department of State, Albany, NY.

A fee of $1 is required when a broker changes principal place of business and a $1 fee for each salesperson (subd. 5, §441-a), and when a salesperson changes association (§441-a).

Offices and branch offices. A real estate broker must have and maintain a principal place of business (subd. 3, §441-a). A broker may also maintain branch offices, for which licenses are issued upon payment of separate fee of $100 unless the license will expire in one year or less, in which event the fee is $50. Upon changing business address the broker must promptly apply to the licensing authorities to have the license reissued. Branch offices must be owned, maintained and operated by the broker (Rule 175.20).

Licenses must be displayed. The license of a real estate broker must be conspicuously displayed in the principal place of business at all times. Licenses issued for branch offices must be displayed therein (subd. 4, §441-a). A broker's license should not be laid away in a safe or in a desk drawer. The display of a real estate broker's license, the term whereof has expired, by any person, partnership or corporation not duly licensed as a real estate broker for the current year is prohibited (subd. 4, §441-a). A broker is not required to display his/her salespersons' licenses. They may, and probably should, be filed in some secure place, as a broker is responsible for their safekeeping and must be ready to return them immediately to the licensing authorities, upon the termination of the salespersons' association, as the statute requires (subd. 1, §441-a; §442-b).

Signs. A real estate broker must post a sign, containing his/her name and indicating business (which must be stated as "licensed real estate broker") on the outside of the place of business, unless same is located in an office, apartment or hotel building, in which event, his/her name and the words "licensed real estate broker" must be posted in the space provided for that purpose in the lobby of the building, other than a mail box. In case a sign is posted, it must be of such size and so lettered as to be readable from the sidewalk (subd. 3, §441-a). A similar sign must be posted on each branch office maintained by the licensee. A real estate broker is not exempt from compliance with the statutory sign requirement because the office is maintained in his/her residence located in a district which, under a local zoning regulation, is restricted against business occupancy. In such a case, the broker must move the office to a district that is not restricted against business occupancy or surrender the broker's license for cancellation. A broker will not be allowed to violate the law in order to comply with a city or village ordinance.

Pocket license card. The Department of State issues a pocket license card to each licensee, which must be exhibited on demand (subd. 6, §441-a). Anyone doing business of any kind with a real estate agent should insist that credentials be shown, as by so doing it may be determined whether or not the agent is duly licensed, and, if licensed, in what capacity.

Compensation of salespersons. A real estate salesperson may not demand or receive compensation from any person other than a duly licensed real estate broker with whom he/she is associated. Hence, payment of a commission to a licensed real estate salesperson by the client does not cancel the claim of the employer for the services rendered by the salesperson.

Splitting commissions. No real estate broker may pay any part of a fee, commission or other compensation received by the broker to any person for any service, help or aid rendered by him/her to such broker in the negotiation of any real estate transaction, unless such person is a duly licensed real estate salesperson associated with the broker, or is a licensed real estate broker of this State, or is engaged in the real estate brokerage business in another state (§442) or is exempt from the application of the License Law (§442-f). Further, a real estate broker may not pay or agree to pay any part of a fee, commission, or other compensation received or due, or to become due to the broker to any person who is or is to be a party to the transaction (§442). ("*Kick-back*"—*colloquial*)

Violations and penalties. A violation by any unlicensed person of any provision of Article 12-A of the Real Property Law is a class A misdemeanor (§442-e), which is punishable by a fine of not more than $1,000 (Penal Law, section 80.05, subd. 1), or by imprisonment for not exceeding one year

(Penal Law, section 70.15, subd. 1), or by both such fine and imprisonment (Penal Law, section 60.10, subd. 2[d]). The commission of a single act prohibited by this article constitutes a violation thereof (subd. 1, §442-e). In case the offender shall have received any sum of money, as compensation or profit by, or in consequence of offending, the offender is also liable to a civil penalty up to the sum of four times the amount of money so received by the offender, which may be sued for and recovered by the person aggrieved by the offender's misconduct (subd. 3, §442-e). An unlicensed real estate agent cannot collect compensation for services by resort to the courts, for the agent must allege and prove that he/she is a duly licensed real estate broker in order to be entitled to a judgment (§442-d).

Disciplinary provisions. The license of any real estate broker or salesperson may be suspended pending hearing (§441-e) or may be suspended or revoked by the licensing authorities, after hearing and upon conviction of a violation of any provision of the License Law, or for a material misstatement in the application for the broker's license, or for fraud, fraudulent practice, the use of dishonest or misleading advertising, or demonstrated untrustworthiness to act as a real estate broker or salesperson, as the case may be (§441-c). The revocation of a broker's license operates to suspend the licenses of all real estate salespersons associated with the broker, pending a change of association and the reissuing of their licenses accordingly (§441-d). All brokers' and salespersons' licenses and pocket cards shall be returned to the Department of State within five days after the receipt of notice of such revocation or suspension, or in lieu thereof, the broker or salesperson whose license has been revoked or suspended shall make and file an affidavit in form prescribed by the Department of State, showing that the failure to return such license and pocket card is due either to loss or destruction thereof. Whenever the license of a real estate broker or real estate salesperson is revoked by the Department, such real estate broker or real estate salesperson shall be ineligible to be relicensed either as a real estate broker or real estate salesperson until after the expiration of a period of one year from the date of such revocation (subd. 2, §441-c). The display of a real estate broker's license after the revocation or suspension thereof is prohibited (subd. 3, §441-c).

Drawing of legal documents. While the license as real estate broker gives the right to negotiate real estate transactions, it does not give the right to draw legal documents or give legal advice. The preparation of a legal document may result, in addition to other penalties and damages, in the loss of commissions and the revocation of the license. It is essential that real estate brokers and their salespersons refrain from drawing legal instruments of any character.

Racial discrimination and panic selling. The Executive Law prohibits discrimination because of race, creed, color, national origin or sex by brokers, salespersons, employees or agents thereof in selling or renting housing or commercial space covered by the law, and in advertising the sale or rental of any housing or commercial space.

Moreover, under a rule promulgated by the Secretary of State, licensed real estate brokers and salespersons are prohibited from engaging in the practice of "blockbusting"—the solicitation of the sale or lease of property due to a change in the ethnic structure of a neighborhood.

Upon written petition of property owners revoking the implied invitation to solicitation, the Secretary may issue an order to real estate brokers and salespersons requiring them to cease and desist from such solicitation. Also the Secretary may issue a general "nonsolicitation order" which prohibits all real estate brokers and salespersons from soliciting the listing of property for sale or purchase in a prohibited area. Failure to comply imperils the license of the broker or salesperson, which is then subject to suspension or revocation after hearing.

By the adoption of Rule 175.17 under the licensing statute, the Department has embodied in its rules and regulations the principle that discrimination is against public policy and that licensees, in their activities, must abide by the law of the State.

SUMMARY OF THE LAW OF AGENCY RELATING TO REAL ESTATE BROKERAGE

The law of principal and agent, or agency, governs the relation of real estate brokers and salespersons and their clients.

Authorization—employment. The foundation of an agency is an authorization or contract of employment, the terms of which may be either expressed or implied. An expressed agreement is one the terms of which have been discussed and agreed to by the parties, either verbally or in writing. An implied contract is one which arises from the act of the parties, as where an owner lists his/her property as being for sale or rent with a real estate broker, or sells or leases property to a person introduced to him/her as purchaser or lessee by a broker, or by the appropriation of the labors of the broker. The law of New York does not require that an authorization must be in writing, unless, by its terms, it is not to be performed within one year, in which event a written contract is required to be signed by the party to be bound thereby. Generally, where an owner is interested in disposing of real property, such property is listed for sale with a number of brokers. This form of listing is known as an open listing. Where one of such brokers is successful in negotiating a sale or exchange, the authority of all the other brokers is automatically terminated. Owners may also list their property with one broker, granting to such broker either an exclusive agency or the exclusive right to sell. In granting the exclusive agency, the owner constitutes the broker as sole agent to the exclusion of all other brokers. In the event that the owner succeeds in selling the property without any broker participating in the sale, then there is no liability for commissions to the broker holding the exclusive agency. However, where an owner has granted an exclusive right to sell to a broker, the owner nevertheless becomes obligated to such broker for a commission even though the owner succeeds in effecting a sale of the property and even though there is no broker involved in such sale. The owner in granting the exclusive right to sell, in effect has surrendered such right to the broker and it is for that reason that the obligation to the broker for commission continues. Rule 175.24 which refers to exclusive listings of one-, two- or three-family dwellings states as follows:

(b) In all commission agreements obtained by a broker which provide for an exclusive listing of residential property, the broker shall have attached to the listing or printed on the reverse side of the listing and signed by the homeowner or the homeowner's agent the following explanation in type size of not less than six point.

"EXPLANATION:

An 'exclusive right to sell' listing means that if you, the owner of the property, find a buyer for your house, or if another broker finds a buyer, you must pay the agreed commission to the present broker.

An 'exclusive agency' listing means that if you, the owner of the property find a buyer, you will not have to pay a commission to the broker. However, if another broker finds a buyer, you will owe a commission to both the selling broker and your present broker."

(c) If an exclusive listing of residential property is obtained by a broker who is a member of a multiple listing service,

(1) he shall give to the homeowner a list of the names and addresses of all member broker; and

(2) the listing agreement shall provide that the homeowner shall have the option of having all negotiated offers to purchase the listed residential property submitted either through the listing broker or submitted through the selling broker.

A broker can bind the principal only insofar as the broker has been authorized. The broker's powers or authority are limited to those actually conferred by the principal. Hence, employment to sell or lease is mere authority to find a buyer or lessee and to act as an intermediary between them. There must be express authority to accept deposits or sign a contract.

Duration and termination of broker's employment. The employment of a real estate broker may or may not be for a definite time. Where by agreement between the broker and the principal a fixed time is set for the duration of the broker's authority or agency, the principal is answerable for damages to the broker for the cancellation of the broker's authority prior to the expiration date of the broker's agency. Where no time is fixed for the duration of the broker's authority or agency, either party acting in good faith may terminate the broker's employment at will. To avoid any assumption that the employment of the broker is to continue until a sale is effected, the principal should take some action to notify the broker that the employment is terminated. The notice of termination may be in writing, oral, or implied from circumstances. Where the period of the broker's authority is not fixed, in the absence of any act terminating such authority, it continues for a reasonable time. It should be noted that a principal has the unquestionable power to cancel the authority or agency given to a broker. That power stems from the inalienable right of an owner to dispose or refuse to dispose of property. The only distinction between the authority given to a broker for a fixed time and for an unspecified time is, as above indicated, that where the authority is for a fixed time, the principal is answerable for damages for the cancellation of the broker's authority prior to the expiration date whereas, where the authority is for an unspecified time, the principal, acting in good faith, may cancel the broker's authority at will. Whether the broker's authority is for a specified or unspecified time it is terminable upon the occurrence of any of the following events (a) when the object has not been performed during the specified period or, where the period of authority is unspecified, the object has not been performed or accomplished within a reasonable time (b) death or insanity of a broker or principal (c) bankruptcy of either (d) destruction of the subject matter (e) broker's fraudulent conduct for own benefit, or (f) sale by another broker if the authority is for an unspecified time.

Dual employment. A broker may be employed by both the seller and buyer of real estate, neither of whom can avoid payment of compensation if both knew and consented that the broker also represent the other party.

Interpretation of authorization. The law of the place of the contract governs its enforcement. An authorization made in New York is enforceable in accordance with the provisions of the laws of New York, irrespective of the location of the land the broker is employed to sell or lease.

When commissions are earned. To entitle a broker, to compensation, the broker's services must have been the procuring cause of the sale or lease. A broker is not entitled to a commission until the buyer and seller agree, not only as to the respective price, but as to the terms of the transaction and all other points material thereto. A broker may not be entitled to commission where, although the broker introduced the purchaser to the seller, the broker did not bring them to an agreement and the transaction was subsequently negotiated by another broker.

In the absence of a special agreement, the services rendered by a broker to an owner of real property generally fall into one of two categories, (1) where an owner has given the broker full and complete terms upon which the owner is willing to sell the property and not merely the asking price thereof, (2) where the owner has the property for sale and may or may not have set an asking price thereof, and has not fixed the terms of the transaction, leaving them to be determined thereafter. In the first case, the broker's duty is fulfilled when the broker produces a customer ready, able and willing to comply with all the terms fixed by the owner. In the second case, the broker's commissions may not be earned until the customer produced by the broker reaches an agreement with owner upon the price and terms upon which a sale can be made. This of course, does not mean that a contract in writing must be signed by the parties, but that they are in agreement not only upon price but upon all the terms which they reasonably consider to be essential. The terms essential to effect a meeting of minds are: (1) Price, (2) Amount of Cash, (3) Duration of Mortgages, (4) Rate of Interest, and (5) Amortization. Having rendered the services described in these two transactions, the broker's right to commissions is undisturbed even though the transaction was not consummated by the principals.

Commission rates. The commission or reasonable rate of compensation of a real estate broker is not regulated by statute nor is it legally fixed by the regulations of the real estate board in a particular community, as many suppose. The broker and the employer may agree upon any reasonable rate of compensation, or the method or time of payment thereof, that is mutually acceptable. But, in the absence of such an agreement, the broker is entitled to commissions, or compensation for services, only at the rate customarily paid for similar services in the community in which the broker's services were rendered.

Conflicting commission claims: "procuring cause." Where an owner employs a number of brokers to negotiate a transaction, the broker whose services are the procuring cause of the sale or lease is entitled to compensation. Usually this means the broker who first induces the customer to agree to the owner's terms. The broker who actually negotiates a sale or lease may be entitled to compensation, notwithstanding the fact that the owner has erroneously paid a full commission on the same transaction to another broker.

"Ready, willing and able." The words "ready" and "willing" are synonymously used to mean that the broker's customer is prepared to enter into a contract with the broker's principal on the principal's terms. The word "able" refers to the customer's ability to enter into a contract with the broker's principal on the principal's terms. It refers to financial ability to buy the property offered to the customer and in the event of an exchange it refers to the ownership or right to the property owned by the customer and offered in exchange. If the prospective purchaser is able to tender the sums or deeds required at the time of the execution of a contract such customer is considered "able" to perform the contract. However, the above discussed elements of the broker's customer's ability to buy or exchange must be proved in case where no binding contract has been signed by the principals. Where the principals entered into a written contract they are both treated as being mutually satisfied of each other's ability to perform.

Disclosure of customer. Where the disclosure of the name of the customer is not requested by the broker's employer, a broker may not be bound to disclose to the client the identity of the customer. However, a broker may not be entitled to commissions where the broker did not inform the client of the name of the prospective customer and, after negotiations failed, the purchaser sought out the owner and effected a sale directly. A broker may lose commissions where the broker failed to disclose name of buyer for fear the price would be increased by the seller and later the property is sold to the same buyer. It is obvious that without disclosure of the name of the customer, the employer is unable to investigate the customer.

Commissions payable. Unless otherwise provided in the authorization a broker's commission is due and payable when it has been earned. A broker employed to negotiate a sale of real property, for instance, earns a commission when the broker produces a purchaser who is ready, able and willing to buy on the seller's terms. It is not imperative, however, that a broker shall produce a customer who will buy or lease upon the terms specified in the listing. The broker is entitled to the commission if the broker brings the client and the customer together and, after mutual bargaining, they come to an agreement; even at a price and on terms materially different from those specified in the authorization.

Deferment of payment of commissions. The original commission agreement between a broker and employer may contemplate that the commission will be earned by the broker only if and when title passes to the buyer. Even if such a provision was not in the original commission agreement, the broker may still agree, subsequently, to waive payment of commission unless and until title passes. Notwithstanding the fact that a broker has fulfilled the terms of the broker's employment in effecting a sale of real property, the broker may agree to forego the payment of commissions in the event the sale is not consummated by a transfer of title. Such waiver of the payment of commissions is enforceable against the broker if such agreement of waiver between the broker and the principal is in writing. Sections 5—1103 and 1105 of the General Obligations Law dispenses with the old rule of law that valuable consideration must be paid the broker for such waiver of commissions. However, the courts have refused to enforce such waiver of commission agreements, where the broker's employer was found to be at fault for the nonconsummation of the transaction. It is not uncommon for a broker to agree to waive the payment of commissions where the failure to transfer the title is due for any cause whatsoever, including the fault of the employer. Brokers are therefore cautioned to seek advice of counsel before entering into such waiver of commission agreements.

Default by client. In order to deprive a broker of a commission, a seller cannot, in bad faith, terminate a broker's employment and make a sale or lease directly. A broker is entitled to compensation where the owner refuses to sign a contract of sale on the terms the owner originally proposed, or where, because of some defect, the title to the property is unmarketable, or where the owner is guilty of misrepresentation or mistake as to size of property or is guilty of a misstatement of the amount of rentals. Where an owner of property employs a broker to sell property upon condition that the broker is to receive a commission from the buyer, the owner of the property is liable for damages equal to the commission earned, where the broker finds a buyer ready, able and willing to buy upon the owner's terms and the owner refuses to perform.

Default by customer. A broker is not entitled to a commission unless the customer is ready and able to comply with the terms of the agreement to buy or lease. If however, a contract was entered into between buyer and seller, the broker's right to commission is not affected by the customer's failure to complete the purchase, for refusal or failure to perform. If the purchaser is an irresponsible "dummy," the owner is justified in refusing to enter into a contract or to pay brokerage. When a binder, signed by a prospective customer, provides that the customer will pay the broker's commission the customer is liable for the commission if the customer fails or refuses to consummate the negotiation or fails or refuses to complete the transaction.

Duty to client. A client is the broker's principal or employer, the person from whom the broker expects compensation for services. An agent is bound, not only to good faith, but to reasonable diligence and such skill as is generally possessed by persons of ordinary capacity acting in the same business. A broker may not profit by deceiving the employer. A principal may hold the agent to strict loyalty and require the agent to account fully for the profits of a transaction wherein the employer was defrauded. If a broker submits any offer of purchase to the client, the broker is duty bound to reveal any other better offers that have been made. If a broker fails to do so the broker cannot recover commissions. A broker must disclose higher offers even if the higher offer has less cash. A broker is not entitled to any commission where the broker induced the client to accept less than the asking price after the purchaser has indicated a willingness to pay the asking price. A broker cannot claim commissions where the broker has induced the client to accept less than the asking price knowing the property is of special value to the buyer. A broker is duty bound to reveal any facts in the broker's possession concerning purchaser's intention to resell at an increased price. If client (owner) requests the name of the purchaser, the broker must disclose it or lose commissions. For failure to disclose the name of the purchaser, the broker loses the commissions even if the property is sold to the broker's undisclosed buyer.

A broker cannot take an incompatible position with the broker's clients. Hence, a broker employed to sell cannot purchase for himself/herself without a full disclosure of the broker's interest. A broker cannot sell the client's property to a corporation or partnership in which the broker is interested without similar disclosure.

Duty to a customer. Brokers should guard against inaccuracies in their representations to customers. If a misstatement is made as to a matter of fact by a broker, it may have the most serious consequences, both to the broker and to the employer. Such a misrepresentation, if it is material and intentional, may be fraudulent and may justify a refusal by a purchaser to take title and afford the owner a defense to the broker's claim for a commission. It is not the duty of the broker to verify all representations made by the owner. Nonetheless, if the broker knows or has reason to know that the owner has made misrepresentations, or has failed to disclose material defects, then a broker is under a duty not to perpetuate such misrepresentations.

Deposit money—broker's duty with relations thereto. The real estate broker, by reason of the nature of the broker's work, is in a position to come into possession of funds belonging to others. The question very often arises as to whom such money belongs and what disposition should be made of the funds by the broker. In this discussion, reference is not being made to the real estate broker who is duly authorized to manage real property and therefore authorized to collect rents. With relation to such monies, there is never any question but that the money belongs to the owner and must be kept in a separate bank account and must be duly accounted for to the broker's principal. However, where the real estate broker has been employed by the owner to find a buyer, it is customary for the broker to take a deposit from the prospective buyer, issue a receipt therefor, and have the prospective purchaser execute an offer to buy subject to acceptance by the broker's principal, the owner. The problem is comparatively simple where the owner accepts the offer in writing before there has been notice of revocation of the offer by the buyer and where the broker at the time of the owner's acceptance turns the deposit over in full to the principal. But all situations are not so simple as this. Unfortunately, experience has demonstrated that brokers may become involved in difficulties and may place their licenses in jeopardy where they do not take time to learn their responsibilities with relation to other people's money. Brokers should be throughly familiar with the following rules applicable to deposits to avoid the pitfalls encountered in the handling of funds belonging to third persons.

The real estate broker must at all times remember that he/she occupies the status of agent acting on behalf of others. By reason of this, the License Law in determining an individual's competency as a broker requires that the prospective broker, among other things, have a fair knowledge and understanding of the law of Agency. The broker should at all times be cognizant of his/her obligation as an agent and must have a complete awareness that in dealing with the property of others the broker is held to a very high degree of accountability.

The average real estate broker is an agent of limited authority and must act entirely within the scope of such limited authority. Where a parcel of real estate is listed for sale with a real estate broker, the authority of such broker is limited to finding a purchaser who is ready, willing and able to buy on the terms established and prescribed by the owner. The broker by virtue of the broker's employment by the owner becomes a mere negotiator or intermediary between the owner and the prospective purchaser. The listing of a parcel of real property with a broker does not in and of itself confer upon the broker the authority to accept a deposit from a prospective purchaser. In order for the broker to have authority on behalf of a seller to accept a deposit, the listing agreement or contract of employment must expressly grant such authority. In the absence of such specific grant of authority, if a real estate broker in conjunction with the receipt of an offer of purchase undertakes to accept a deposit from the prospective purchaser, the broker does so on his/her own and the receipt of such deposit by the broker has no binding effect insofar as the owner is concerned.

Keeping in mind that the broker is an agent of very limited authority, and considering that such authority does not include the power to accept deposits, it must, therefore, be concluded that when a broker takes such deposit from a prospective purchaser, the broker is impliedly being employed by the purchaser for the purpose of conveying the offer to the seller and turning such deposit over when the seller does accept the offer. Since the broker becomes the agent of the purchaser for the purpose mentioned, the deposit which is in the broker's possession remains the property of the purchaser until the moment that the seller accepts the offer. The moment the seller accepts the offer the broker has completed his/her agency for the purchaser, the deposit becomes the property of the seller and the broker is no longer responsible to the purchaser to refund the deposit. It must be considered elementary that where the offer made by the purchaser is rejected by the seller, the deposit received by the broker still remains the property of the purchaser and therefore must be refunded to the latter. The offer having been rejected by the seller, the deposit in the possession of the broker is still held by the broker as agent of the purchaser and the broker is, therefore, accountable to the purchaser for such deposit. The same conclusion must be reached where the purchaser has revoked the offer delivered to the broker by due notice to the latter and before the seller has accepted the offer to buy. The offer not having been accepted, the broker still holds the deposit as agent for the purchase. That being the case, the deposit must be returned to the purchaser without any delay.

In the circumstances where the seller accepts the offer made and necessarily becomes aware of the fact that the broker was given a deposit by the prospective buyer, the unauthorized act of the broker in taking the deposit, that is, insofar as the seller is concerned, becomes ratified by the seller upon the seller's acceptance of the offer. For this reason, the seller becomes entitled to the deposit.

There are many transactions negotiated by real estate brokers which require mortgage financing by the purchaser in order to complete the purchase. In practically all of these cases, the broker is fully aware that the purchaser does not have sufficient cash and therefore provision is made in the binder or contract that the transaction is conditioned on a mortgage loan being obtained and further providing an escape from the contract by the purchaser and for a refund of the deposit to the purchaser in the event the mortgage loan is not obtainable. The pattern of these transactions has demonstrated that the broker induces the buyer to make the deposit in the first instance by the assurance that the deposit will be returned in the event the mortgage loan is not obtained and incorporates such assurance in the form of an escape clause. A similar situation may also exist where the

purchase of one property is made conditional upon the sale by the purchaser of a property the purchaser already owns. The problem that often arises in these situations is the one relating to the deposit paid by the purchaser to the broker who retains such deposit. As discussed earlier, we found that where the seller has accepted the offer to purchase, the deposit becomes the property of the seller and the broker's obligation with relation to the purchaser ceases. The next question is—does the conditional type of transaction affect the situation? Where the mortgage loan is not obtainable or the prior sale by the purchaser is not made, the seller, by virtue of the condition in the contract becomes obligated to return the deposit to the purchaser. The seller, however, does not have the deposit; it has been retained by the broker. The broker is required in such instance to return the deposit the broker holds to the purchaser when the condition does not take place. There is no gainsaying the right of the purchaser to the return of the deposit. Regardless of the rights of the broker with relation to the seller, the purchaser would not have made the deposit in the first place unless the broker had induced the transaction through the employment of the condition or contingency. The broker having used such inducement would be considered most unethical and guilty of improper conduct if the broker were to insist on retaining the deposit after the condition had failed to eventuate. In the final analysis, the conditional transaction differs from the ordinary one which involves no condition in that essentially the latter type is a fully completed contract with a purchaser accepted as ready, willing and able, whereas the former does not actually ripen into an enforceable contract until the contingency occurs or the condition is fulfilled, thus rendering the purchaser able to perform.

The situation is immediately altered where the failure of the contingency or condition to take place is due to the fault of the buyer because of the buyer's arbitrary refusal to accept the loan or sell the property. That being the case, there would be no expectation of the broker returning the deposit to the defaulter. Where the buyer, however, is not at fault, the broker holding the deposit and refusing to return it to the innocent purchaser would be considered as having demonstrated untrustworthiness of sufficient gravity to warrant action under the disciplinary provisions of the License Law.

Situations do arise in which it is not possible or appropriate for the broker to make an evaluation as to who is at fault, the buyer or the seller, and who is entitled to the moneys held in escrow. In such cases the broker would be wise to consult legal counsel. There are legal mechanisms that may be employed to resolve conflicting claims on an escrow account.

The real estate broker in carrying out the broker's functions must always realize that the broker represents the interest of others. The broker must at all times consider those interests before the broker's own.

In handling of deposits, there should be a constant consciousness that the monies placed in the broker's hands are trust funds and that with relation to such monies the broker is a trustee and fiduciary. Of course, the monies cannot be commingled with the broker's personal funds and must be kept in a separate, special bank account.

CONTRACTS FOR THE SALE OR LEASE OF REAL PROPERTY

Essentials. 1. A contract for the leasing for a longer period than one year, or for the sale of any real property, or an interest therein, is void, unless the contract, or some note or memorandum thereof, expressing the considerations, is in writing, subscribed by the party to be charged, or by the party's lawful agent thereunto authorized by writing (§5-703, General Obligations Law). The other essentials of a valid contract for the sale of real property are:

2. Competent parties (sane adults);

3. An expression of their agreement to sell and to buy;

4. An understanding and adequate description of the premises that are the subject of the transaction;

5. The consideration for the contemplated conveyance (price and terms of payment);

6. Agreement of grantor to convey title (although it is not essential, the contract should usually specify the form of the deed to be delivered to the grantee).

7. Place and date of closing (again, this item may not be required to make the contract enforceable, but it is usually prudent to include this item).

The contract speaks for itself. Care should be taken that the written contract includes all special terms and covenants that were verbally agreed upon by the parties. It should always be kept in mind that:

"A covenant is not implied in a conveyance of real property, whether the conveyance contains any special covenant or not." (§251, Real Property Law.)

This applies as well to real property contracts as it does to conveyances. For instance, if such a contract does not specifically provide that the grantor shall deliver a full covenant and warranty deed, the grantor may require the grantee to accept a bargain and sale deed; for the latter form of conveyance passes whatever title the grantor has as effectively as does the former, even if it does not warrant the grantee's ownership against encumbrances and other obstacles to the grantee's complete enjoyment of the property. Under a contract providing that the seller shall deliver "a good and sufficient deed," the seller cannot be required to turn over a deed containing full covenants, for even a bargain and sale deed, without covenant against the grantor, is "a good and sufficient deed." A marketable title is one that a court will compel a buyer to accept in any action for specific performance of a contract.

Incumbrances. Where there are encumbrances, or other flaws in the title to the property that is the subject of the contract, it is imperative that the contract shall express the agreement of the parties respecting them. Incumbrance is a right or interest in property held by a third party, which often limits the use and diminishes the value of the property, but usually does not prevent the transferring of title. The more common forms of incumbrances are:

1. Taxes, water rents and assessments for local improvements that have become liens upon the property to which a contract or conveyance relates;

2. Mortgages, upon such property;

3. Lease of property or any part thereof;

4. Judgments against the grantor, duly recorded in the county in which the property is located;

5. Mechanics' liens for work or labor done or material furnished for use upon such property;

6. *Lis pendens* (a legal document, filed in the office of the county clerk, giving notice that an action or proceeding is pending in the courts affecting the title to the property);

7. Encroachments of a building, or other structure on the property, upon a street or other public place, or upon land of an adjoining owner*;

*In this sense, a party wall is an incumbrance, because it is a wall built along the line separating two properties, partly on each, which wall either the owner, the owner's heirs and assigns has the right to use; such right constituting an easement over so much of the adjoining owner's land as is covered by the wall.

8. Easements (rights that may be exercised by the public or individuals on, over or through the lands of others; such as rights-of-way, rights to erect poles and string wires or cables overhead, or rights to construct and maintain conduits, pipes or mains underground);

9. Restrictive covenants (limitations upon the use of property, contained in these or other written instruments in the chain of title thereto, providing that the property shall not be used for specified purposes, or that buildings thereon must be set back from the property line for a given distance, or shall not be constructed of certain materials, etc.; zoning regulations, however, are not restrictions that, in a legal sense, are incumbrances);

10. Strictly speaking, violations are not considered incumbrances, although they may diminish the value of the property. Violations are written notices from State or municipal officers, addressed to the owners, lessees or occupants of specified real property, requiring compliance with definitely stated provisions of laws or ordinances relating to such property, which it is the duty of such officers to enforce.

"Time is of the essence of this contract." This clause is frequently found in real property contracts. It is useful where a quick "turn-over" is contemplated by the purchaser, or the seller has a special reason for closing title upon the date specified in the contract. Its legal effect is to require the seller to be able to deliver the required deed and the purchaser to be prepared to make payment of the agreed purchase price, upon the exact closing date fixed in the contract. If, then, either party is unprepared, the contract is breached and the delinquent is at a serious disadvantage and may suffer substantial financial loss. Obviously, neither party to a real property contract should bind himself/herself by such a provision, unless reasonably certain that the party can make good his/her part of the agreement precisely on the closing date specified therein.

Mortgage clauses. Contracts for the sale of real property frequently contain provisions relating to existing or contemplated mortgages upon the properties to which such contracts relate. It is particularly important for the purchaser to know whether he/she is to take the property "subject to" an existing mortgage, or is assuming payment of the mortgage indebtedness; for, in the latter case, in the event of the foreclosure of the mortgage, the purchaser will be liable for the deficiency, if the property sells for less than the mortgage debt.

Again, in the purchase of land intended for subdivision into building lots, it is usually to the interest of the purchaser to have the sale contract provide that a "release clause" shall be included in the mortgage to be given by the purchaser as security for the payment of a part of the purchase price. The purpose of such a provision is to enable the purchaser to give clear title to lots in the subdivision, which is possible only upon their release from the lien of the "blanket" mortgage, by a document which the usual release clause requires the mortgagee to execute and deliver, upon the payment to the mortgagee of an agreed sum in reduction of the principal of the mortgage debt.

Sometimes, what is known as a "mortgage subordination clause" is included in a contract for the sale of realty. The ordinary purpose of such a provision is to subordinate the mortgage to be taken by the seller, as a part of the purchase price, to a contemplated mortgage to secure a loan required to defray the cost of erecting a new building or altering an existing building upon the property. But, not infrequently, a contract is foisted upon an ignorant or inexperienced property owner binding the property owner to accept a purchase money mortgage containing a clause providing that such mortgage shall be subordinate to another mortgage which the purchaser may place upon the property, but making no provision for the disposition of the money borrowed by the purchaser and secured by the mortgage to which the purchase money mortgage will be subordinated. For this reason, a sale contract should be carefully scrutinized and, if a mortgage subordination clause is included therein, the property owner should defer signing the contract until the property owner has had the advice thereon of a competent lawyer of his/her own selection.

Action for specific performance. This is a court action to compel defaulting principal to comply with provisions of contract.

Recording land contracts. Contracts for the sale or purchase of real property are usually not recorded, for, as a rule, they are not acknowledged by the parties thereto. They are recordable, if duly acknowledged pursuant to subd. 1 of §294 of the Real Property Law which reads as follows:

§294. Recording executory contracts and powers of attorney. 1. An executory contract for the sale, purchase or exchange of real property, or an instrument canceling such a contract, or an instrument containing a power to convey real property, as the agent or attorney for the owner of the property, acknowledged or proved, and certified, in the manner to entitle a conveyance to be recorded, may be recorded in the office of the recording officer of any county in which any of the real property to which it relates is situated, and such recording officer shall, upon the request of any party, on tender of the lawful fees thereof, record the same in his said office.

DEEDS

Ordinarily, a "deed" is understood to be an instrument in writing duly executed and delivered, that conveys title to real property. A deed is "duly executed" when it is signed and acknowledged by the maker thereof, who is usually termed the "grantor."

Essentials of a valid deed. They are as follows:
1. It must be in writing;
2. The grantor thereto must be competent (sane adult);
3. It must contain an adequate expression of intent to convey real property;
4. There must be a definite description of the real property conveyed;
5. It must include an "habendum" clause ("to have and to hold the above granted premises unto the party of the second part . . . his heirs and assigns forever");

6. It must be signed by the grantor;
7. There must be an acknowledgement of its execution by grantor (see Acknowledgments);
8. It must be delivered to the grantee (purchaser).

Kinds of deeds. The forms of deeds in general use in the State of New York are: (a) deed with full covenants; (b) bargain and sale deed, without covenant against grantor; (c) bargain and sale deed with covenant against grantor; (d) quitclaim deed; (e) executor's deed; and (f) referee's deed. Short forms of all the foregoing conveyances are prescribed by section 258 of the Real Property Law.

Deed with full covenants. This form of conveyance is usually styled a "full covenant and warranty deed" and is most advantageous to the purchaser of real property, because it must contain, at least, the five covenants prescribed in the statutory short form of such a deed. A purchaser of real property is not entitled to a deed with full covenants unless a provision to that effect is included in the contract for the sale of the property described in the deed. In case a sale contract does not set forth the form of deed to be delivered to the purchaser, the purchaser may be required to accept a bargain and sale deed, without even a covenant therein that the grantor "has not done or suffered anything whereby the said premises have been incumbered in any way."

The following are the five covenants found in the full covenant and warranty deed:

First. That said . . . is seized of said premises in fee simple, and has good right to convey the same;
Second, that the party of the second part shall quietly enjoy the said premises;
Third. That the said premises are free from incumbrances;
Fourth. That the party of the first part will execute or procure any further necessary assurance of the title to said premises;
Fifth. That said . . . will forever warrant the title to said premises.

Bargain and sale deed, without covenant against grantor. This is the simplest form of a deed. It is generally used when the purpose is to convey all the right, title and interest of the owner of record in the real property described in the document, and the grantor is not under contract to deliver a deed containing specified covenants.

Bargain and sale deed with covenant against the grantor. This form of deed contains the following covenant by the grantor: "And the party of the first part covenants that he has not done or suffered anything, whereby the said premises have been incumbered in any way whatever." In all other respects the statutory short form thereof is identical with the short form of a bargain and sale deed, without covenant against the grantor, as prescribed by the statute and quoted above.

Quitclaim deed. The usual purpose of this form of deed is to remove a cloud from the title to real property. Its statutory short form is practically identical with the short form of a bargain and sale deed, without covenant against the grantor, as prescribed by the statute and hereinbefore quoted, the only difference being the use of the word "quitclaim" in the conveying clause of the deed so named.

Executor's deed. This form of deed is used to convey title to a decedent's real property. It will be noted that the statutory short form of such a deed, contains only the covenant against incumbrances that is included in the form of bargain and sale deed with covenant against grantor, prescribed by the statute.

Referee's deed. This form of deed is used for the conveyance of real property sold pursuant to a judicial order, in an action for the foreclosure of a mortgage or for partition. This deed does not contain any covenants.

MORTGAGES

The term "mortgage" means an instrument in writing, duly executed and delivered, that creates a lien, upon the real property described therein, as security for the payment of a specified debt, which may be in the form of a bond or note. The essentials of a valid mortgage are:

1. It must be in writing;
2. The parties thereto must be competent (sane adults);
3. Its purpose must be stated (to secure payment of a specified bond or obligation);
4. There must be an appropriate mortgaging clause (the mortgagor hereby mortgages to the mortgagee");
5. The description of the property mortgaged must be stated definitely;
6. It must be signed by the mortgagor;
7. It must be acknowledged by the mortgagor;
8. It must be delivered to the mortgagee.

The statutory short form of mortgage contains the following covenants:

1. That the mortgagor will pay the indebtedness as hereinbefore provided.
2. That the mortgagor will keep buildings on the premises insured against loss by fire for the benefit of the mortgagee.
3. That no building on the premises shall be removed or demolished without the consent of the mortgagee.
4. That the whole of said principal sum shall become due after default in the payment of any installment of principal or of interest for . . . days, or after default in the payment of any tax, water rate of assessment for . . . days after notice and demand.
5. That the holder of this mortgage in any action to foreclose it, shall be entitled to the appointment of a receiver.
6. That the mortgagor will pay all taxes, assessments or water rates, and in default thereof, the mortgagee may pay the same.
7. That the mortgagor within . . . days upon request in person or within . . . days upon request by mail will furnish a statement of the amount due on this mortgage.
8. That notice and demand or request may be in writing and may be served in person or by mail.
9. That the mortgagor warrants the title to the premises.

Bond. A bond is evidence of the debt which creates the obligation for repayment of a loan, while a mortgage is the security for the debt with specific property as a pledge.

In addition to a statutory short form of mortgage, there is also a statutory short form of bond and mortgage. This includes all of the provisions enumerated in the short form of mortgage, as well as an acknowledgment of indebtedness by the mortgagor.

Priority of lien. Mortgages are frequently referred to as first, second and third mortgages, as the case may be. This reference indicates their relative priority in lien upon the mortgaged premises. The lien of the first mortgage has priority over the liens of subsequently recorded mortgages, which means that in case of the sale of the mortgaged premises, by court order (in an action to foreclose a mortgage, for instance), the indebtedness secured by the first mortgage must be paid, whether or not there is any money left to apply on the second or third mortgage debt.

"Blanket," "purchase money" and "open" mortgages. A "blanket" mortgage is one that is a lien upon several parcels of property, or upon property that has been subdivided into lots or plots.

A "purchase money" mortgage is one given by a purchaser on the real property bought by the purchaser, on account of a balance due of the purchaser price thereof.

A "open" mortgage is one that is security for the payment of an indebtedness that has matured or is overdue and, therefore, is "open" to foreclosure at any time.

Assignment of mortgage. A mortgage may be sold by the holder thereof, in which case it is customary for the holder to execute and deliver to the purchaser a document known as an assignment of mortgage, in which it is advisable for the assignee (purchaser) to require that there shall be included a covenant, setting forth the amounts due of principal and interest on account of the mortgage debt.

Amortization of mortgage. Amortization is the periodical payments of a stipulated sum of money for the purpose of reducing the principal amount of the mortgage.

Extension agreement. When a property on which there is a mortgage has been sold and the mortgage falls due, the new owner may wish its terms extended. Frequently the reason for the request is the new owner's inability to refinance the property. This extension agreement makes the new owner personally liable for the debt, whatever the former owner's previous status. The former owner cannot be held—without the former owner's consent—except for the part of the debt which may exceed the value of the property at the time the extension is granted. Furthermore, the former owner does not involuntarily assume responsibility for any future depreciation in value.

Estoppel certificate. Usually the purchaser of a mortgage upon real property requires that the mortgagee shall furnish a certificate, duly executed by the mortgagor, substantially providing that the mortgage is a valid lien, that a certain amount of principal and interest is due and that there are no defenses or offsets to the mortgage. This acknowledgment by the mortgagor of the validity of the mortgage lien and of the amount of the debt precludes the mortgagor from asserting contrary claims thereafter.

Satisfaction or assignment of mortgage. When the owner of property incumbered by a mortgage pays the mortgage debt, the owner should not only require the holder of the mortgage to return the mortgage and the bond or other obligation secured by it, but should insist that the mortgagee deliver to the owner a duly executed and acknowledged "satisfaction piece," which will authorize the mortgage to be discharged of record. Alternatively, the owner usually may require the mortgage holder to execute an assignment of the mortgage to a third party, without recourse against the mortgage holder.

Mortgage foreclosure. One of the mortgagee's remedies for the failure of the mortgagor to pay interest upon or installments of the principal of the mortgage debt, as agreed, or for the violation of any other of the mortgagor's covenants, is by way of an action for the foreclosure of the lien of the mortgage. Such an action usually culminates in a judgment directing the sale of the property covered by the mortgage, and the application of the proceeds of the sale toward the payment of the mortgage debt.

LEASES

A lease is a contract whereby, for a consideration, usually termed rent, one who is entitled to the possession of real property grants such right to another for life, for a term of years, or at will.

Essentials of a valid lease. These are:

1. Competent parties (sane adults);

2. A definite demising clause, whereby the lessor (landlord) leases and the lessee (tenant) takes the property leased;

3. A reasonably definite description of the property leased;

4. A clear statement of the term (duration) of the letting;

5. Specification of the rent payable and how it is to be paid;

6. If the term of the lease is for more than one year it must be in writing, signed by all parties thereto and duly delivered.

Generally. There is no limitation upon the length of the term for which property may be leased. It is not necessary that the wife of the lessor join him in executing a lease even if its term is for 99 years, or longer.

A net lease is one that provides that the tenant, in addition to paying the agreed rent, shall defray the expense of all repairs, taxes, water rents, insurance, premiums, and such other items of the carrying charges upon the leased property, as may be specified.

Leases usually include numerous covenants, conditions of limitations, collateral to the letting and containing such provisions as the parties may agree upon as necessary to define their respective rights and responsibilities. Many of such collateral agreements are incorporated in all leases. Others are used only in connection with the letting of a particular class of property, such as apartments, lofts or offices.

All clauses or conditions contained in a lease are binding on the parties thereto because they are part of the contract entered into between the landlord and tenant. However, one of the exceptions to this rule of law exists with relation to the clause which is known as the "automatic renewal clause." Section 5-905 of the General Obligations Law reads as follows: "No provision of a lease of any real property or premises which states that the term thereof shall be deemed renewed for a specified additional period of time unless the tenant gives notice to the lessor of his intention to quit the premises at the expiration of such term shall be operative unless the lessor, at least fifteen days and not more than thirty days previous to the time specified for the furnishing of such notice to him, shall give to the tenant written notice, served personally or by registered or certified mail, calling the attention of the tenant to the existence of such provision in the lease."

The results that may flow from the omission of a necessary or desirable covenant or condition are often annoying and, sometimes, may prove serious to the landlord or the tenant, as the case may be. For instance, rent is not payable in advance unless the lease so provides. So, too, a landlord has no right to send the landlord's mechanics into leased premises, to make alterations or to install new equipment, unless the lease authorizes the landlord to do so. On the other hand, the tenant should carefully consider the negative covenants the lease contains. A negative covenant binds the tenant not to do specified acts, such as assigning the lease, subletting, or using the premises for other than a specified purpose, etc. The tenant should also bear in mind that, unless the lease provides that the landlord shall make all repairs, or such of them as the landlord has agreed to make, the tenant must bear the cost of even the most necessary repairs to the leased premises. Under section 226-b of the Real Property Law, a tenant of a residence of four or more units is given the right to sublet the premises or to assign his or her lease, such subletting or assignment being subject to the landlord's prior approval. If, however, the landlord unreasonably withholds consent, the landlord upon request must release the tenant from the lease. These provisions are applicable to all leases or renewals of leases now entered into. Every residential lease is also deemed to contain a covenant by the landlord that the premises are fit for human habitation and for the uses for which they were reasonably intended by the parties. The tenant's rights under this covenant cannot be waived.

Form. There is no statutory form of lease. The law does require, however, that a residential lease be written in a clear and coherent manner, using words with every day meaning—that is, in plain language.

Recording leases. A lease is not recordable unless it is for a term of three years, or more, and has been duly signed and acknowledged by the parties thereto.

ACKNOWLEDGMENTS

Technically, the term "acknowledgment" means both the act and the evidence thereof made by the officer taking the acknowledgment. Practically, an acknowledgment is the certificate of an officer, duly empowered to take an acknowledgment or proof of the conveyance of real property, that on a specified date "before me came . . . , to be known to be the individual described in, and who executed the foregoing instrument and acknowledged that he executed the same."

Concerning acknowledgments and authentication of acknowledgments, the Real Property Law provides:

§298. Acknowledgments and proofs within the state.

The acknowledgment of proof, within this state, of a conveyance of real property situate in this state may be made:

1. At any place within the state, before (a) a justice of the supreme court; (b) an official examiner of title; (c) an official referee; or (d) a notary public.

2. Within the district wherein such officer is authorized to perform official duties, before (a) a judge or clerk of any court of record; (b) a commissioner of deeds outside of the city of New York, or a commission of deeds of the city of New York within the five counties comprising the city of New York; (c) the mayor or recorder of a city; (d) a surrogate, special surrogate, or special county judge; or (e) the county clerk or other recording officer of a county.

3. Before a justice of the peace, town councilman, village police justice or a judge of any court of inferior local jurisdiction, anywhere within the county containing the town, village or city in which he is authorized to perform official duties.

A certificate of authentication of an acknowledgment made anywhere in the State as to the execution of a conveyance, is no longer required to entitle a conveyance to be recorded when acknowledged or proved before any officer designated in section 298 of the Real Property Law, except a commissioner of deeds, justice of the peace, town councilman or village police justice.

The usual form of acknowledgment by an individual is as follows:

STATE OF NEW YORK,

ss.:

County of _____

On this _____ day of _____,

before me came _____ ,to me known to be the individual described in, and who executed the foregoing instrument, and acknowledged that he executed the same.

_____
Notary Public,

_____County, No. _____

The form of acknowledgment by a corporation is set forth in section 309 of the Real Property Law.

When a certificate of acknowledgment on a conveyance is made by a notary public in another state, it is acceptable for recording without further authentication. A certificate of acknowledgment or proof of conveyance made by a notary public in a foreign country other than Canada requires a certificate of authentication in accordance with the provisions of subdivision 2 of section 311 of the Real Property Law.

In addition to providing a conveyance by acknowledgment pursuant to the above section, a conveyance may also be proved by a subscribing witness. However, this is not the usual and ordinary method of proof.

RECORDING CONVEYANCES, ETC.

The statute provides that to be recordable, the document must be a conveyance of real property within the State of New York, duly acknowledged, or otherwise proved as authorized by law. The courts have held that not only deeds and mortgages, but leases for more than three years, trust agreements, releases, extensions, assignments and discharges of mortgages, are conveyances of real property eligible for recording, and this list is not exhaustive. There is a particular statutory provision (§294, Real Property Law) that authorizes the recording of executory contracts for the sale or purchase of real property (and powers of attorney for its conveyance). Prior to the amendments enacted in 1961 (Ch. 956, L. 1961) it was held that the recording of such a contract does not give constructive notice.

Recording conveyances serves two purposes: Preservation of a record of the instrument in a public office for convenient reference, and to give general notice of the rights created or conveyed under it.

The latter result is, of course, exceedingly important, and is completely governed by the provisions of Article 9 of the Real Property Law, frequently referred to as the Recording Act. If the instrument is of the kind which the law permits to be recorded, and it is recorded in a county clerk's office (or register's office, in New York, Kings, Bronx and Queens counties) as provided by the statute, subsequent purchasers, from the same common source of title, acquire no greater right than as though they, in fact, knew of the instrument so recorded at the time of their purchase. If the instrument is of the kind which may be recorded, and is not recorded, it is void as against any subsequent purchaser of the same property or any portion thereof in good faith and for a valuable consideration, from the same vendor, the vendor's distributees or devisees (§291, Real Property Law) and whose conveyance is first duly recorded.

The statute creates the presumption that the subsequent good faith purchaser did not know that a previous unrecorded conveyance had been made. If it is shown that he did—as by the fact that the prior purchaser was in possession of the property—then the presumption may be lost.

RULES AND REGULATIONS

Under Article 12-A of the Real Property Law Promulgated by the Department of State

Section numbers conform to the numbering system in Title 19 of the Official Compilation of Codes, Rules and Regulations of the State of New York (NYCRR)

Section 175.1 Commingling money of principal. A real estate broker shall not commingle the money or other property of his principal with his own and shall at all times maintain a separate, special bank account to be used exclusively for the deposit of said monies and which deposit shall be made as promptly as practicable. Said monies shall not be placed in any depository, fund or investment other than a federally insured bank account. Accrued interest, if any, shall not be retained by, or for the benefit of, the broker except to the extent that it is applied to, and deducted from, earned commission, with the consent of all parties.

175.2 Rendering account for client. A real estate broker shall, within a reasonable time, render an account to his client and remit to him, any monies collected for his client, and unexpended for his account.

175.3 Managing property for client. When acting as an agent in the management of property, a real estate broker shall not accept any commission, rebate or profit on expenditures made for his client without his full knowledge and consent.

(b) A person, firm or corporation licensed or acting as a real estate broker, and having on deposit or otherwise in custody or control any money furnished as security by a tenant of real property, shall treat, handle and dispose of such money (including any required interest thereon) in compliance with the requirements of section 7-103 of the General Obligations Law. Failure to so comply, including failure to pay, apply or credit any required interest, shall constitute grounds for disciplinary or other appropriate action by the Secretary of State.

175.4 Broker's purchase of property listed with him. A real estate broker shall not directly or indirectly buy for himself property listed with him, nor shall he acquire any interest therein without first making his true position clearly known to the listing owner.

175.5 Disclosure of interest to client. Before a real estate broker buys property for a client in the ownership of which the broker has an interest, he shall disclose his interest to all parties to the transaction.

175.6 Broker's sale of property in which he owns an interest. Before a real estate broker sells property in which he owns an interest, he shall make such interest known to the purchaser.

175.7 Compensation. A real estate broker shall make it clear for which party he is acting and he shall not receive compensation from more than one party except with the full knowledge and consent of all parties.

175.8 Negotiating with party to exclusive listing contract. No real estate broker shall negotiate the sale, exchange or lease of any property directly with an owner or lessor if he knows that such owner, or lessor, has an existing written contract granting exclusive authority in connection with such property with another broker.

175.9 Inducing breach of contract of sale or lease. No real estate broker shall induce any party to a contract of sale or lease to break such contract for the purpose of substituting in lieu thereof a new contract with another principal.

175.10 Broker's offering property for sale must be authorized. A real estate broker shall never offer a property for sale or lease without the authorization of the owner.

175.11 Sign on property. No sign shall ever be placed on any property by a real estate broker without the consent of the owner.

175.12 Delivering duplicate original of instrument. A real estate broker shall immediately deliver a duplicate original of any instrument to any party or parties executing the same, where such instrument has been prepared by such broker or under his supervision and where such instrument relates to the employment of the broker or to any matters pertaining to the consummation of a lease, or the purchase, sale or exchange of real property or any other type of real estate transaction in which he may participate as a broker.

175.13 Accepting services of another broker's employee. A real estate broker shall not accept the services of any salesman or employee in the organization of another real estate broker without the knowledge of the broker and no real estate broker should give or permit to be given or directly offer to give anything of value for the purpose of influencing or rewarding the actions of any salesman or employee of another real estate broker in relation to the business of such broker or the client of such broker without the knowledge of such broker.

175.14 Termination of salesman's association with broker. A real estate salesman shall, upon termination of his association with a real estate broker, forthwith turn over to such broker any and all listing information obtained during his association whether such information was originally given to him by the broker or copied from the records of such broker or acquired by the salesman during his association.

175.15 Automatic continuation of exclusive listing contract. No real estate broker shall be a party to an exclusive listing contract which shall contain an automatic continuation of the period of such listing beyond the fixed termination date set forth therein.

175.16 Obsolete.

175.17 Prohibitions in relation to solicitation. (a) No broker or salesperson shall induce or attempt to induce an owner to sell or lease any residential property or to list same for sale or lease by making any representations regarding the entry or prospective entry into the neighborhood of a person or persons of a particular race, color, religion or national origin.

(b) No broker or salesperson shall solicit the sale, lease or the listing for sale or lease of residential property after such licensee has received notice from the owner thereof, or from the department, that such owner does not desire to sell or lease such residential property or does not desire to be solic-

ited to sell, lease, or list for sale or lease, such property. A notice from the department under this section shall be in writing and shall be issued when the department has received written notification from the owner of the residential property that he or she does not desire to sell or lease such property, or does not desire to be solicited to list to sell or lease the same, and requests the department to so notify a particular broker or brokers, or brokers in general.

175.18 Use of trade or corporate name. No licensed real estate broker or applicant applying for a real estate broker's license, may use a trade or corporate name which, in the opinion of the Department of State, is so similar to the trade name or corporate name of any licensed real estate broker that confusion to the public will result therefrom.

175.19 Net listing agreements. (a) The term *net listing* as used herein shall mean an agency or other agreement whereby a prospective seller of real property or an interest therein, lists such property or interest for sale with a licensed real estate broker authorizing the sale thereof at a specified net amount to be paid to the seller and authorizing the broker to retain as commission, compensation, or otherwise, the difference between the price at which the property or interest is sold and the specified net amount to be received by the seller.

(b) No real estate broker shall make or enter into a "net listing" contract for the sale of real property or any interest therein.

175.20 Branch offices. (a) Every branch office shall be owned, maintained and operated only by the licensed broker to whom the license for such office is issued. A branch office shall not be conducted, maintained and operated under an arrangement whereby a licensed salesman or employee of the broker shall pay, or be responsible for, any expense or obligation created or incurred in its conduct, maintenance or operation, or under any other arrangement, the purpose, intent or effect of which shall permit a licensed salesman or employee to carry on the business of real estate broker for his own benefit, directly, or indirectly, in whole or in part.

(b) Every branch office shall be under the direct supervision of the broker to whom the license is issued, or a representative broker of a corporation or partnership holding such license. A salesman licensed as such for a period of not less than two years and who has successfully completed a course of study in real estate approved by the Secretary of State, may be permitted to operate such a branch office only under the direct supervision of the broker provided the names of such salesman and supervising broker shall have been filed and recorded in the division of licenses of the Department of State.

(c) Supervision of such a licensed salesman shall in addition to the requirements of subdivision (a) of section 175.21 of this Part, include guidance, oversight, management, orientation, instruction and supervision in the management and operation of the branch office and the business of real estate broker conducted therein.

(d) No broker shall relocate his principal office or any branch office without prior approval of the department.

175.21 Supervision of salesman by broker. (a) The supervision of a real estate salesman by a licensed real estate broker, required by subdivision 1(d) of section 441 of the Real Property Law, shall consist of regular, frequent and consistent personal guidance, instruction, oversight and superintendence by the real estate broker with respect to the general real estate brokerage business conducted by the broker, and all matters relating thereto.

(b) The broker and salesman shall keep written records of all real estate listings obtained by the salesman, and of all sales and other transactions effected by, and with the aid and assistance of, the salesman, during the period of his association, which records shall be sufficient to clearly identify the transactions and shall indicate the dates thereof. Such records must be submitted by the salesman to the Department of State with his application for a broker's license.

(c) Participation in the general real estate brokerage business as a licensed real estate salesman shall consist of active service under the supervision of a licensed real estate broker for at least 35 hours per week for 50 weeks in each year required for qualification under the law.

175.22 Ownership of voting stock by salesmen prohibited. [Additional statutory authority: Real Property Law, art. 12-A] No licensed real estate salesman may own, either singly or jointly, directly or indirectly, any voting shares of stock in any licensed real estate brokerage corporation with which he is associated.

175.23 Records of transactions to be maintained. (a) Each licensed broker shall keep and maintain for a period of three years records of each transaction effected through his office concerning the sale or mortgage of one to four family dwellings. Such records shall contain the names and addresses of the seller, the buyer, mortgagee, if any, the purchase price and the resale price, if any, amount of deposit paid on contract, amount of commission paid to broker, or gross profit realized by the broker if purchased by him for resale, expenses of procuring the mortgage loan, if any, the net commission or net profit realized by the broker, showing the disposition of all payments made by the broker. In lieu thereof each broker shall keep and maintain, in connection with each such transaction a copy of (a) contract of sale, (2) commission agreement, (3) closing statement, (4) statements showing disposition of proceeds of mortgage loan.

(b) Each licensed broker engaged in the business of soliciting and granting mortgage loans to purchasers of one to four family dwellings shall keep and maintain for a period of three years, a record of the name of the applicant, the amount of the mortgage loan, the closing statement with the disposition of the mortgage proceeds, a copy of the verification of employment and financial status of the applicant, a copy of the inspection and compliance report with the Baker Law requirements of FHA with the name of the inspector. Such records shall be available to the Department of State at all times upon request.

175.24 Exclusive listings—residential property. (a) Residential property as used in this section shall not include condominiums or cooperatives but shall be limited to one-, two- or three-family dwellings.

(b) In all commission agreements obtained by a broker which provide for an exclusive listing of residential property, the broker shall have attached to the listing or printed on the reverse side of the listing and signed by the homeowner or the homeowner's agent the following explanation in type size of not less than six point:

"EXPLANATION:

An 'exclusive right to sell' listing means that if you, the owner of the property, find a buyer for your house, or if another broker finds a buyer, you must pay the agreed commission to the present broker.

An 'exclusive agency' listing means that if you, the owner of the property find a buyer, you will not have to pay a commission to the broker. However, if another broker finds a buyer, you will owe a commission to both the selling broker and your present broker."

(c) If an exclusive listing of residential property is obtained by a broker who is a member of a multiple listing service,

(1) he shall give to the homeowner a list of the names and addresses of all member brokers; and

(2) the listing agreement shall provide that the homeowner shall have the option of having all negotiated offers to purchase the listed residential property submitted either through the listing broker or submitted through the selling broker.

175.25 Advertising. (a) All advertisements placed by a broker must indicate that the advertiser is a broker or give the name of the broker and his telephone number.

(b) All advertisements placed by a broker which state that property is in the vicinity of a geographical area or territorial subdivision must include as part of such advertisement the name of the geographical area or territorial subdivision in which such property is actually located.

175.26 Disclaimer. Nothing in this Part is intended to be, or should be construed as, an indication that a salesperson is either an independent contractor or employee of a broker.

176.15 College degree major in real estate. Evidence satisfactory to the department of the successful completion of a course of study at any accredited college or university in the United States of America, approved by the Commissioner of Education of the State of New York or by a regional accrediting agency, accepted by said Commissioner of Education, which has a program leading to a recognized collegiate degree, which includes therein a major in real estate, may be deemed acceptable for the educational credit under sections 176.3 and 176.4 of this Part, provided attendance at such real estate course is not less than 90 hours in the case of an applicant for licensure as a real estate broker, and 45 hours in the case of an applicant for licensure as a real estate salesperson, and the applicant presents evidence of the issuance of a bachelor's degree and that he has passed the required course in real estate.

176.3 Subjects for study—real estate salesperson. (a) The following are the required subjects to be included in the course of study in real estate for licensure as a real estate salesperson, and the required minimum number of hours to be devoted to each such subject:

Subject	Hours
Real estate instruments	6
Law of agency	5
Real estate financing	5
Valuation and listing procedures	5
Law of contracts	5
License law and ethics	5
Human rights—fair housing	4
Closing and closing costs	4
Land use regulations	3
Real estate mathematics	3

* * *

176.4 Subjects for study—real estate broker. (a) The following are the required subjects to be included in a course of study in real estate for licensure as a real estate broker and the required minimum number of hours to be devoted to each such subject:

Subject	Hours
Operation of a real estate broker's office	10
General business law	5
Construction	3
Subdivision and development	3
Leases and agreements	3
Liens and easements	3
Taxes and assessments	3
Investment property	3
Voluntary and involuntary alienation	3
Property management	2
Condominiums and cooperatives	2
Appraisal	2
Advertising	2
Rent regulations	1

(b) The course provided for by section 176.3 of this Part shall be successfully completed before the course provided for by this section is taken.

GLOSSARY OF REAL ESTATE TERMS

A

Abstract of Title—A summary of all of the recorded instruments and proceedings which affect the title to property, arranged in the order in which they were recorded.

Accretion—The addition of land through processes of nature, as by water or wind.

Accrued Interest—Accrue: to grow; to be added to. Accrued interest is interest that has been earned but not due and payable.

Acknowledgment—A formal declaration before a duly authorized officer by a person who has executed an instrument that such execution is the person's act and deed.

Acquisition—An act or process by which a person procures property.

Acre—A measure of land equaling 43,560 feet.

Adjacent—Lying near to but not necessarily in actual contact with.

Adjoining—Contiguous; attaching, in actual contact with.

Administrator—A person appointed by court to administer the estate of a deceased person who left no will; i.e., who died intestate.

Ad Valorem—According to valuation.

Adverse Possession—A means of acquiring title where an occupant has been in actual, open, notorious, exclusive, and continuous occupancy of property under a claim of right for the required statutory period.

Affidavit—A statement or declaration reduced to writing, and sworn to or affirmed before some officer who is authorized to administer an oath or affirmation.

Affirm—To confirm, to ratify, to verify.

Agency—That relationship between principal and agent which arises out of a contract either expressed or implied, written or oral, wherein an agent is employed by a person to do certain acts on the person's behalf in dealing with a third party.

Agent—One who undertakes to transact some business or to manage some affair for another by authority of the latter.

Agreement of Sale—A written agreement between seller and purchaser in which the purchaser agrees to buy certain real estate and the seller agrees to sell upon terms and conditions set forth therein.

Air Rights—Rights in real property to use the space above the surface of the land.

Alienation—A transferring of property to another; the transfer of property and possession of lands, or other things, from one person to another.

Alienation Clause—Allows lender to require the balance of a loan to be paid in full if the collateral is sold (also known as a "die on sale" clause).

Amortization—A gradual paying off of a debt by periodical installments.

Annuity—An amount of money or its equivalent which represents one of a series of periodic payments.

Apportionment—Adjustment of the income, expenses or carrying charges of real estate usually computed to the date of closing of title so that the seller pays all expenses to that date. The buyer assumes all expenses commencing the date the deed is conveyed to the buyer.

Appraisal—An estimate of a property's valuation by an appraiser who is usually presumed to be expert in this work.

Appraisal by Capitalization—An estimate of value by capitalization of productivity and income.

Appraisal by Comparison—Comparability with the price of other similar properties.

Appraisal by Summation—Adding together all parts of a property separately appraised to form a whole: e.g., value of the land considered as vacant added to the cost of reproduction of the building, less depreciation.

Appartenance—Something which is outside the property itself but belongs to the land and adds to its greater enjoyment such as a right-of-way or a barn or a dwelling.

Arbitration Clause—Sometimes appears in a long-term lease or other contract requiring a third party referee's decision in the event of a dispute.

Assessed Valuation—A valuation placed upon property by a public officer or a board, as a basis for taxation.

Assessment—A charge against real estate made by a unit of government to cover a proportionate cost of an improvement such as a street or sewer.

Assessor—An official who has the responsibility of determining assessed values.

Assignee—The person to whom an agreement or contract is assigned.

Assignment—The method or manner by which a right or contract is transferred from one person to another.

Assignor—A party who assigns or transfers an agreement or contract to another.

Assumption Mortgage—The taking of title to property by a grantee, wherein the grantee assumes liability for payment of an existing note or bond secured by a mortgage against a property and becomes personally liable for the payment of such mortgage debt.

Attest—To witness to; to witness by observation and signature.

Avulsion—The removal of land from one owner to another, when a stream suddenly changes its channel.

Axial Growth—City growth which moves out along main transportation routes, taking the form of fingerlike extensions.

B

Balloon Mortgage Payment—A large payment during the term of a mortgage, often at the end.

Bearer of the Note—Lender in whose hands the note remains until it is paid in full.

Beneficiary—The person who receives or is to receive the benefits resulting from certain acts.

Bequeath—To give or hand down by will; to leave by will.

Bequest—That which is given by the terms of a will.

Betterment—A property improvement which increases the property value.

Bill of Sale—A written instrument given to pass title of personal property from vendor to vendee.

Binder—An agreement to cover the down payment for the purchase of real estate as evidence of good faith on the part of the purchases.

Blanket Mortgage—The underlying mortgage on a parcel of land in favor of an original mortgagee which covers various tracts of a subdivision.

Bona Fide—In good faith, without fraud.

Bond—The evidence of a personal debt which is secured by a mortgagee or other lien on real estate.

Building Codes—Regulations established by local governments stating fully the structural requirements for building.

Building Line—A line fixed at a certain distance from the front and/or sides of a lot, beyond which no building can project.

Building Loan Agreement—An agreement whereby the lender advances money to an owner with provisional payments at certain stages of construction.

C

Cancellation Clause—A provision in a lease or other contract which confers upon one or more or all of the parties to the lease the right to terminate the party's or parties' obligations thereunder upon the occurrence of the condition or contingency set forth in the said clause.

Capital Appreciation—The appreciation accruing to the benefit of the capital improvement to real estate.

Capital Asset—Any asset of a permanent nature used for the production of income.

Capital Gain—Income that results from the sale of an asset not in the usual course of business. (Capital gains may be taxed at a lower rate than ordinary income.)

Capital Improvement—Any structure erected as a permanent improvement to real estate, usually extending the useful life and value of a property. (The replacement of a roof would be considered a capital improvement.)

Capital Loss—A loss from the sale of an asset not in the usual course of business.

Capital Recapture—The manner in which the investment in a property is to be returned to investors; normally stated as a rate or dollar amount per unit of time.

Caveat Emptor—Let the buyer beware. The buyer must examine the goods or property and buy at the buyer's own risk.

Cease and Desist Order—An order executed by the Secretary of State directing broker recipients to cease and desist from all solicitation of homeowners whose names and addresses appear on the list(s) forwarded with such order. The order acknowledges petition filings by homeowners listed evidencing their premises are not for sale, thereby revoking the implied invitation to solicit. The issuance of a cease and desist order does not prevent an owner from selling or listing his premises for sale. It prohibits soliciting by licensees served with such order and subjects violators to penalties of suspension or revocation of their license as provided in section 441-c of the Real Property Law.

Cease and Desist Petition—A statement filed by a homeowner showing address of premises owned which notifies the Department of State that such premises are not for sale and does not wish to be solicited. In so doing, petitioner revokes the implied invitation to be solicited by any means and with respect thereto, by licensed real estate brokers and salespersons.

Certiorari—A proceeding to review in a competent court the action of an inferior tribunal board or officer exercising judicial functions.

Chain of Title—A history of conveyances and encumbrances affecting a title from the time the original patent was granted, or as far back as records are available.

Chattel—Personal property, such as household goods or fixtures.

Chattel Mortgage—A mortgage on personal property.

Client—The one by whom a broker is employed and by whom the broker will be compensated on completion of the purpose of the agency.

Closing Date—The date upon which the buyer takes over the property.

Cloud on the Title—An outstanding claim or encumbrance which, if valid, would affect or impair the owner's title.

Codicil—Some addition to or amendment of one's last will and testament.

Collateral—Additional security pledged for the payment of an obligation.

Color of Title—That which appears to be good title, but which is not title in fact.

Commission—A sum due a real estate broker for services in that capacity.

Commitment—A pledge or a promise or affirmation agreement.

Condemnation—Taking private property for public use, with fair compensation to the owner; exercising the right of eminent domain.

Conditional Sales Contract—A contract for the sale of property stating that delivery is to be made to the buyer, title to remain vested in the seller until the conditions of the contract have been fulfilled.

Consideration—Anything given to induce entering into a contract such as, money, personal services. Any contracts, lease, obligation or mortgage may be modified without consideration provided it is in writing and signed by the party charged or his agent. (General Obligations Law §5-1103.)

Constructive Notice—Information or knowledge of a fact imputed by law to a person because the person could have discovered the fact by proper diligence and inquiry; (public records).

Contract—An agreement between competent parties to do or not to do certain things which is legally enforceable, whereby each party acquires a right.

Conversion—Change from one character or use to another.

Conveyance—The transfer of the title of land from one to another. The means or medium by which title or real estate is transferred.

Correlation—The final stage in the appraisal process where the appraiser reviews the data and estimates the subject property's value.

County Clerk's Certificate—When an acknowledgment is taken by an officer not authorized in the state or county where the document is to be recorded, the instrument which must be attached to the acknowledgment is called a county clerk's certificate. It is given by the clerk of the county where the officer obtained his/her authority and certifies to the officer's signature and powers.

Covenants—Agreements written into deeds and other instruments promising performance or nonperformance of certain acts, or stipulating certain uses or nonuses of the property.

Cul-de-sac—A blind alley; a street with only one outlet.

Current Value—The value usually sought to be estimated in an appraisal.

D

Damages—The indemnity recoverable by a person who has sustained an injury, either to his/her person, property, or relative rights, through the act or default of another.

Debit—The amount charged as due or owing.

Debt Capital—Money borrowed for a particular business purpose.

Debt Service—Annual amount to be paid by a debtor on an obligation to repay borrowed money.

Decedent—One who is dead.

Decree—Order issued by one in authority; an edict or law; a judicial decision.

Dedication—A grant and appropriation of land by its owner for some public use, accepted for such use, by an authorized public official on behalf of the public.

Deed—An instrument in writing duly executed and delivered, that conveys title to real property.

Deed Restriction—An imposed restriction in a deed for the purpose of limiting the use of the land such as:
1. A restriction against the sale of liquor thereon.
2. A restriction as to the size, type, value or placement of improvements that may be erected thereon.

DeFacto—In fact or reality.

Default—Failure to fulfill a duty or promise, or to discharge an obligation; omission or failure to perform any acts.

Defeasance Clause—The clause in a mortgage that permits the mortgagor to redeem his or her property upon the payment of the obligations to the mortgagee.

Defendant—The party sued or called to answer in any suit, civil or criminal, at law or in equity.

Deficiency Judgment—A judgment given when the security for a loan does not entirely satisfy the debt upon its default.

Delivery—The transfer of the possession of a thing from one person to another.

Demand Note—A note which is payable on demand of the holder.

Demising Clause—A clause found in a lease whereby the landlord (lessor) leases and the tenant (lessee) takes the property.

Depreciation—Loss of value in real property brought about by age, physical deterioration, or functional or economic obsolescence.

Descent—When an owner of real estate dies intestate, the owner's property descends, by operation of law, to the owner's distributees.

Desist and Refrain Order—An order issued by a real estate commissioner to stop an action in violation of the real estate law.

Devise—A gift of real estate by will or last testament.

Devisee—One who receives a bequest of real estate made by will.

Devisor—One who bequeaths real estate by will.

Directional Growth—The location or direction toward which the residential sections of a city are destined or determined to grow.

Dispossess Proceedings—Summary process by a landlord to oust a tenant and regain possession of the premises for non-payment of rent or other breach of conditions of the lease or occupancy.

Distributee—Person receiving or entitled to receive land as representative of the former owner.

Documentary Evidence—Evidence in the form of written or printed papers.

Domicile—A place where a person lives or has his home; in a legal sense, the place where he has his true, fixed, permanent home and principal establishment, and to which place he has, whenever he is absent, the intention of returning.

Duress—Unlawful constraint exercised upon a person whereby the person is forced to do some act against the person's will.

E

Earnest Money—Down payment made by a purchaser of real estate as evidence of good faith.

Easement—A right that may be exercised by the public or individuals on, over or through the lands of others.

Economic Life—The period over which a property will yield the investor a return on the investment.

Economic Obsolescence—Lessened desirability or useful life arising from economic forces, such as changes in optimum land use, legislative enactments which restrict or impair property rights, and changes in supply-demand ratios.

Economic Rent—The base rent payable for the right of occupancy of vacant land.

Egress—A way out; an outlet.

Ejectment—A form of action to regain possession of real property, with damages for the unlawful retention; used when there is no relationship of landlord and tenant.

Eminent Domain—A right of the government to acquire property for necessary public use by condemnation; the owner must be fairly compensated.

Encroachment—A building, part of a building, or obstruction which intrudes upon or invades a highway or sidewalk or trespasses upon the property of another.

Encumbrance—Any right to or interest in the land interfering with its use or transfer, or subjecting it to an obligation. (Also Incumbrance)

Endorsement—An act of signing one's name on the back of a check or note, with or without further qualifications.

Equity—The interest or value which the owner has in real estate over and above the liens against it.

Equity Cushion—The amount of equity required before a lender will make a loan.

Equity Loan—Junior loan based on a percentage of the equity.

Equity of Redemption—A right of the owner to reclaim property before it is sold through foreclosure proceedings, by the payment of the debt, interest and costs.

Erosion—The wearing away of land through processes of nature, as by water and winds.

Escheat—The reversion to the state of property in event the owner thereof abandons it or dies, without leaving a will and has no distributees to whom the property may pass by lawful descent.

Escrow—A written agreement between two or more parties providing that certain instruments or property be placed with a third party to be delivered to a designated person upon the fulfillment or performance of some act or condition. (See rule 175.1

Estate—The degree, quantity, nature and extent of interest which a person has in real property.

Estate for Life—An estate or interest held during the terms of some certain person's life.

Estate in Reversion—The residue of an estate left for the grantor to commence in possession after the termination of some particular estate granted by the grantor.

Estate at Will—The occupation of lands and tenements by a tenant for an indefinite period, terminable by one or both parties at will.

Estoppel Certificate—An instrument executed by the mortgagee setting forth the present status and the balance due on the mortgage as of the date of the execution of the certificate.

Eviction—A legal proceeding by a lessor landlord to recover possession of real property.

Eviction, Actual—Where one is either by force or by process of law, actually put out of possession.

Eviction, Constructive—Any disturbance of the tenant's possessions by the landlord whereby the premises are rendered unfit or unsuitable for the purpose for which they were leased.

Eviction, Partial—Where the possessor of the premises is deprived of a portion thereof.

Exclusive Agency—An agreement of employment of a broker to the exclusion of all other brokers; if sale is made by any other broker during term of employment, broker holding exclusive agency is entitled to commissions in addition to the commissions payable to the broker who effected the transaction. (See rule 175.24).

Exclusive Right to Sell—An agreement of employment by a broker under which the exclusive right to sell for a specified period is granted to the broker; if a sale during the term of the agreement is made by the owner or by any other broker, the broker holding such exclusive right to sell is nevertheless entitled to compensation. (See rule 175.24).

Executor—A male person or a corporate entity or any other type of organization named or designated in a will to carry out its provisions as to the disposition of the estate of a deceased person.

Executrix—A woman appointed to perform the same duties as an executor.

Extension Agreement—An agreement which extends the life of a mortgage to a later date.

F

Fee; Fee Simple; Fee Absolute—Absolute ownership of real property; a person has this type of estate where the person is entitled to the entire property with unconditional power of disposition during the person's life and descending to the person's distributees and legal representatives upon the person's death intestate.

Fiduciary—A person who on behalf of or for the benefit of another transacts business or handles money on property not the person's own; such relationship implies great confidence and trust.

Fixtures—Personal property so attached to the land or improvements as to become part of the real property.

Foreclosure—A procedure whereby property pledged as security for a debt is sold to pay the debt in the event of default in payments or terms.

Forfeiture—Loss of money or anything of value, by way of penalty due to failure to perform.

Freehold—An interest in real estate, not less than an estate for life. (Use of this term discontinued Sept. 1, 1967.)

Front Foot—Property measurement for sale or valuation purposes; the property measures by the "front foot" on its street line, each "front foot" extending the depth of the lot.

G

Grace Period—Additional time allowed to perform an act or make a payment before a default occurs.

Graduated Leases—A lease which provides for a graduated change at stated intervals in the amount of the rent to be paid; used largely in long term leases.

Grant—A technical term used in deeds of conveyance of lands to indicate a transfer.

Grantee—The party to whom the title to real property is conveyed.

Grantor—The person who conveys real estate by deed; the seller.

Gross Income—Total income from property before any expenses are deducted.

Gross Lease—A lease of property whereby the lessor is to meet all property charges regularly incurred through ownership.

Ground Rent—Earnings of improved property credited to earning of the ground itself after allowance made for earnings of improvements.

Guardian's Deed—Issued to the person responsible for the estate of a minor or incompetent.

H

Habendum Clause —The "To Have and To Hold" clause which defines or limits the quantity of the estate granted in the premises of the deed.

Hereditaments—The largest classification of property; including lands, tenements and incorporeal property, such as rights-of-way.

Holdover Tenant—A tenant who remains in possession of leased property after the expiration of the lease term.

Hypothecate—To give a thing as security without the necessity of giving up possession of it.

I

Incompetent—A person who is unable to manage his/her own affairs by reason of insanity, imbecility or feeble-mindedness.

Incumbrance—(See Encumbrance).

Ingress—A place or means of entering; entrance.

Injunction—A writ or order issued by a court to restrain one or more parties from doing an act which is deemed to be inequitable or unjust in regard to the rights of some other party or parties.

In Rem—A proceeding against the realty directly; as distinguished from a proceeding against a person. (Used in taking land for nonpayment of taxes, etc.)

Installments—Parts of the same debt, payable at successive periods as agreed; payments made to reduce a mortgage.

Instrument—A written legal document; created to effect the rights of the parties.

Interest Rate—The percentage of a sum of money charged for its use.

Intestate—A person who dies having made no will, or leaves one which is defective in form, in which case the person's estate descends to the person's distributees in the manner prescribed by law.

Involuntary Lien—A lien imposed against property without consent of the owners, e.g., taxes, special assessments.

Irrevocable—Incapable of being recalled or revoked; unchangeable; unalterable.

J

Jeopardy—To have one's property or liberty subjected to a possible adverse decree of a court or agency.

Joint Tenancy—Ownership of realty by two or more persons, each of whom has an undivided interest with the "right of survivorship."

Judgment—Decree of a court declaring that one individual is indebted to another, and fixing the amount of such indebtedness.

Junior Mortgage—A mortgage second in lien to a previous mortgage.

Jurat—The clause written at the bottom of an affidavit stating when, where, and before whom such affidavit was sworn.

L

Laches—Delay or negligence in asserting one's legal rights.

Land, Tenements and Hereditaments—A phrase used in the early English Law, to express all sorts of property of the immovable class.

Landlord—One who rents property to another.

Lease—A contract whereby, for a consideration, usually termed rent, one who is entitled to the possession of real property transfers such rights to another for life, for a term of years, or at will.

Leasehold—The interest or estate which a lessee of real estate has therein by virtue of the lessee's lease.

Lessee—A person to whom property is rented under a lease.

Lessor—One who rents property to another under a lease.

Lien—A legal right or claim upon a specific property which attaches to the property until a debt is satisfied.

Life Estate—The conveyance of title to property for the duration of the life of the grantee.

Life Tenant—The holder of a life estate.

Lis Pendems—A legal document, filed in the office of the county clerk giving notice that an action or proceeding is pending in the courts affecting the title to the property. (Not applicable in commission disputes.)

Listing—An employment contract between principal and agent, authorizing the agent to perform services for the principal involving the latter's property.

Litigation—The act of carrying on a lawsuit.

M

Mandatory—Requiring strict conformity or obedience.

Marginal Land—Land which has returns that barely meet the costs of operation.

Marginal Revenue—An additional amount of revenue resulting from a given business decision.

Marginal Satisfaction—An alteration in the level of satisfaction derived from the occurrence of a given event.

Marginal Utility—The worth of one additional unit of a good or a service that is produced.

Market Value—The highest price which a buyer, willing but not compelled to buy, would pay, at the lowest a seller, willing but not compelled to sell, would accept.

Marketable Title—A title which a court of equity considers to be so free from defect that it will enforce its acceptance by a purchaser.

Mechanic's Lien—A lien given by law upon a building or other improvement upon land, and upon the land itself, to secure the price of labor done upon, and materials furnished for, the improvement.

Meetings of the Minds—Whenever all parties to a contract agree to the exact terms thereof.

Metes and Bounds—A term used in describing the boundary lines of land, setting forth all the boundary lines together with their terminal points and angles.

Minor—A person under an age specified by law; usually under 18 years of age.

Monument—A fixed object and point established by surveyors to establish land locations.

Moratorium—An emergency act by a legislative body to suspend the legal enforcement of contractual obligations.

Mortgage—An instrument in writing, duly executed and delivered, that creates a lien upon real estate as security for the payment of a specified debt, which is usually in the form of a bond.

Mortgage Commitment—A formal indication, by a lending institution that it will grant a mortgage loan on property, in a certain specified amount and on certain specified terms.

Mortgage Reduction Certificate—An instrument executed by the mortgagee, setting forth the present status and the balance due on the mortgage as of the date of the execution of the instrument.

Mortgagee—The party who lends money and takes a mortgage to secure the payment thereof.

Mortgagor—A person who borrows money and gives a mortgage on the person's property as security for the payment of the debt.

Multiple Listing—An arrangement among Real Estate Board of Exchange Members, whereby each broker presents the broker's listings to the attention of the other members so that if a sale results, the commission is divided between the broker bringing the listing and the broker making the sale. (See rule 175.24).

N

Net Listing—A price below which an owner will not sell the property, and at which price a broker will not receive a commission; the broker receives the excess over and above the net listing as the broker's commission. (See rule 175.19).

Notary Public—A public officer who is authorized to take acknowledgments to certain classes of documents, such as deeds, contracts, mortgages, and before whom affidavits may be sworn.

O

Obligee—The person in whose favor an obligation is entered into.

Obligor—The person who binds himself/herself to another; one who has engaged to perform some obligation; one who makes a bond.

Obsolescence—Loss in value due to reduced desirability and usefulness of a structure because its design and construction become obsolete; loss because of becoming old-fashioned, and not in keeping with modern means, with consequent loss of income.

Open Listing—A listing given to any number of brokers without liability to compensate any except the one who first secures a buyer ready, willing and able to meet the terms of the listing, or secures the acceptance by the seller of a satisfactory offer; the sale of the property automatically terminates the listing.

Open Mortgage—A mortgage that has matured or is overdue and, therefore, is "open" to foreclosure at any time.

Option—A right given for a consideration to purchase or lease a property upon specified terms within a specified time; if the right is not exercised the option holder is not subject to liability for damages; if exercised, the grantor of option must perform.

P

Partition—The division which is made of real property between those who own it in undivided shares.

Party Wall—A party wall is a wall built along the line separating two properties, partly on each, which wall either owner, the owner's heirs and assigns has the right to use; such right constituting an easement over so much of the adjoining owner's land as is covered by the wall.

Percentage Lease—A lease of property in which the rental is based upon the percentage of the volume of sales made upon the leased premises, usually provides for minimum rental.

Performance Bond—A bond used to guarantee the specific completion of an endeavor in accordance with a contract.

Personal Property—Any property which is not real property.

Plat Book—A public record containing maps of land showing the division of such land into streets, blocks and lots and indicating the measurements of the individual parcels.

Plottage—Increment in unity value of a plot of land created by assembling smaller ownerships into one ownership.

Points—Discount charges imposed by lenders to raise the yields on their loans.

Police Power—The right of any political body to enact laws and enforce them, for the order, safety, health, morals and general welfare of the public.

Power of Attorney—A written instrument duly signed and executed by an owner of property, which authorizes an agent to act on behalf of the owner to the extent indicated in the instrument.

Premises—Lands and tenements; an estate; the subject matter of a conveyance.

Prepayment Clause—A clause in a mortgage which gives a mortgagor the privilege of paying the mortgage indebtedness before it becomes due.

Principal—The employer of an agent or broker; the broker's or agent's client.

Probate—To establish the will of a deceased person.

Proration—Allocation of closing costs and credits to buyers and sellers.

Purchase Money Mortgage—A mortgage given by a grantee in part payment of the purchase price of real estate.

Q

Quiet Enjoyment—The right of an owner or a person legally in possession to the use of property without interference of possession.

Quiet Title Suit—A suit in court to remove a defect, cloud or suspicion regarding legal rights of an owner to a certain parcel of real property.

Quitclaim Deed—A deed which conveys simply the grantor's rights or interest in real estate, without any agreement or covenant as to the nature or extent of that interest, or any other covenants; usually used to remove a cloud from the title.

R

Racial Steering—The unlawful practice of influencing a person's housing choice based on his race.

Real Estate Board—An organization whose members consist primarily of real estate brokers and salespersons.

Real Estate Syndicate—A partnership formed for participation in a real estate venture. Partners may be limited or unlimited in their liability.

Real Property—Land, and generally whatever is erected upon or affixed thereto.

Realization of Gain—The taking of the gain or profit from the sale of property.

Realtor—A coined word which may only be used by an active member of a local real estate board, affiliated with the National Association of Real Estate Boards.

Recording—The act of writing or entering in a book of public record instruments affecting the title to real property.

Recourse—The right to a claim against a prior owner of a property or note.

Red Lining—The refusal to lend money within a specific area for various reasons. This practice is illegal.

Redemption—The right of a mortgagor to redeem the property by paying a debt after the expiration date and before sale at foreclosure:—the right of an owner to reclaim the owner's property after the sale for taxes.

Release—The act or writing by which some claim or interest is surrendered to another.

Release Clause—A clause found in a blanket mortgage which gives the owner of the property the privilege of paying off a portion of the mortgage indebtedness, and thus freeing a portion of the property from the mortgage.

Rem—(See In Rem)

Remainder—An estate which takes effect after the termination of a prior estate, such as a life estate.

Remainderman—The person who is to receive the property after the termination of the prior estate.

Rent—The compensation paid for the use of real estate.

Reproduction Cost—Normal cost of exact duplication of a property as of a certain date.

Restriction—A limitation placed upon the use of property contained in the deed or other written instrument in the chain of title.

Reversionary Interest—The interest which a grantor has in lands or other property upon the termination of the preceding estate.

Revocation—An act of recalling a power of authority conferred, as the revocation of a power of attorney, a license, an agency, etc.

Right of Survivorship—Right of the surviving joint owner to succeed to the interests of the deceased joint owner, distinguishing feature of a joint tenancy or tenancy by the entirety.

Right-of-Way—The right to pass over another's land pursuant to an easement or license.

Riparian Grant—The transmittal of riparian rights.

Riparian Owner—One who owns land bounding upon a river or watercourse.

Riparian Rights—The right of a landowner to water on, under, or adjacent to the landowner's land.

S

Sales Contract—A contract by which the buyer and seller agree to terms of sale.

Satisfaction Piece—An instrument for recording and acknowledging payment of an indebtedness secured by a mortgage.

Second Mortgage—A mortgage made by a home buyer in addition to an existing first mortgage.

Seizin—The possession of land by one who claims to own at least an estate for life therein.

Setback—The distance from the curb or other established line, within which no buildings may be erected.

Situs—The location of a property.

Special Assessment—An assessment made against a property to pay for a public improvement by which the assessed property is supposed to be especially benefited.

Specific Performance—A remedy in a court of equity compelling a defendant to carry out the terms of an agreement or contract.

Statute—A law established by an act of the Legislature.

Statute of Frauds—State law which provides that certain contracts must be in writing in order to be enforceable at law.

Statute of Limitations—A statute barring all right of action after a certain period of time from the time when a cause of action first arises.

Stipulations—The terms within a written contract.

Straight Line Depreciation—A definite sum set aside annually from income to pay costs of replacing improvements, without reference to the interest it earns.

Subdivision—A tract of land divided into lots or plots.

Subletting—A leasing by a tenant to another, who holds

under the tenant.

Subordination Clause—A clause which permits the placing of a mortgage at a later date which takes priority over an existing mortgage.

Subscribing Witness—One who writes his/her name as witness to the execution of an instrument.

Sui Juris—Having legal ability to handle one's own affairs; not under any legal disability.

Surety—One who guarantees the performance of another; guarantor.

Surrender—The cancellation of a lease by mutual consent of the lessor and the lessee.

Surrogate's Court (Probate Court)—A court having jurisdiction over the proof of wills, the settling of estates and of citations.

Survey—The process by which a parcel of land is measured and its area ascertained; also the blueprint showing the measurements, boundaries and area.

T

Tax Sale—Sale of property after a period of nonpayment of taxes.

Tenancy in Common—An ownership of realty by two or more persons, each of whom has an undivided interest, without the "right of survivorship."

Tenancy by the Entirety—An estate which exists only between husband and wife with equal right of possession and enjoyment during their joint lives and the "right of survivorship."

Tenancy at Will—A license to use or occupy lands and tenements at the will of the owner.

Tenant—One who is given possession of real estate for a fixed period or at will.

Tenant at Sufferance—One who comes into possession of lands by lawful title and keeps it afterwards without any title at all.

Testate—Where a person dies leaving a valid will.

Title—Evidence that owner of land is in lawful possession thereof; evidence of ownership.

Title Insurance—A policy of insurance which indemnifies the holder for any loss sustained by reason of defects in the title.

Title Search—An examination of the public records to determine the ownership and encumbrances affecting real property.

Torrens Title—System of title records provided by state law; it is a system for the registration of land titles whereby the state of the title, showing ownership and encumbrances, can be readily ascertained from an inspection of the "register of titles" without the necessity of a search of the public records.

Tort—A wrongful act, wrong, injury; violation of a legal right.

Transfer Tax—A tax charged under certain conditions on the property belonging to an estate.

U

Unearned Increment—An increase in value of real estate due to no effort on the part of the owner; often due to increase in population.

Urban Property—City property; closely settled property.

Usury—On a loan, claiming a rate of interest greater than that permitted by law.

V

Valid—Having force, or binding force; legally sufficient and authorized by law.

Valuation—Estimated worth or price. The act of valuing by appraisal.

Variance—The authorization to improve or develop a particular property in a manner not authorized by zoning.

Vendee's Lien—A lien against property under contract of sale to secure deposit paid by a purchaser.

Verification—Sworn statements before a duly qualified officer to the correctness of the contents of an instrument.

Violations—Act, deed or conditions contrary to law or permissible use of real property.

Void—To have no force or effect; that which is unenforceable.

Voidable—That which is capable of being adjudged void, but is not void unless action is taken to make it so.

W

Waiver—The renunciation, abandonment, or surrender of some claim, right or privilege.

Warranty Deed—A conveyance of land in which the grantor warrants the title to the grantee.

Will—The disposition of one's property to take effect after death.

Without Recourse—Words used in endorsing a note or bill to denote that the future holder is not to look to the endorser in case of nonpayment.

Wraparound Loan—A new loan encompassing any existing loans.

Z

Zone—An area set off by the proper authorities for specific use; subject to certain restrictions or restraints.

Zoning Ordinance—Act of city or county or other authorities specifying type and use to which property may be put in specific areas.

Appendix C
Summary of the Law of Agency Relating to Real Estate Brokerage

The law of principal and agent, or agency, governs the relation of real estate brokers and salespersons and their clients.

Authorization—employment. The foundation of an agency is an authorization or contract of employment, the terms of which may be either expressed or implied. An expressed agreement is one the terms of which have been discussed and agreed to by the parties, either verbally or in writing. An implied contract is one which arises from the act of the parties, as where an owner lists his/her property as being for sale or rent with a real estate broker, or sells or leases property to a person introduced to him/her as a purchaser or lessee by a broker, or by the appropriation of the labors of the broker. The law of New York does not require that an authorization must be in writing, unless, by its terms, it is not to be performed within one year, in which even a written contract is required to be signed by the party to be found thereby. Generally, where an owner is interested in disposing of real property, such property is listed for sale with a number of brokers. This form of listing is known as an open listing. Where one of such brokers is successful in negotiating a sale or exchange, the authority of all the other brokers is automatically terminated. Owners may also list their property with one broker, granting to such broker either an exclusive agency or the exclusive right to sell. In granting the exclusive agency, the owner constitutes the broker as sole agent to the exclusion of all other brokers. In the event that the owner succeeds in selling the property without any broker participating in the sale, then there is no liability for commissions to the broker holding the exclusive agency. However, where an owner has granted an exclusive right to sell to a broker, the owner nevertheless becomes obligated to such broker for a commission even though the owner succeeds in effecting a sale of the property and even though there is no broker involved in such sale. The owner in granting the exclusive right to sell, in effect has surrendered such right to the broker and it is for that reason that the obligation to the broker for commission continues.

Rule 175.24 which refers to exclusive listings of one- two- or three-family dwellings states as follows:

(b) In all commission agreements obtained by a broker which provide for an exclusive listing of residential property, the broker shall have attached to the listing or printed on the reverse side of the listing and signed by the homeowner or the homeowner's agent the following explanations in type size of not less than six points:

"EXPLANATION:

An "exclusive right to sell" listing means that if you, the owner of the property, find a buyer for your house, or if another broker finds a buyer, you must pay the agreed commission to the present broker.

An "exclusive agency" listing means that if you, the owner of the property find a buyer, you will not have to pay a commission to the broker. However, if another broker finds a buyer, you will owe a commission to both the selling broker and your present broker."

(c) If an exclusive listing of residential property is obtained by a broker who is a member of a multiple listing service,
(1) he shall give to the homeowner a list of the names and addresses of all member brokers; and
(2) the listing agreement shall provide that the homeowner shall have the option of having all negotiated offers to purchase the listed residential property submitted either through the listing broker or submitted through the selling broker.

A broker can bind his/her principal only insofar as the broker has been authorized. The broker's powers or authority are limited to those actually conferred by the principal. Hence employment to sell or lease is mere authority to find a buyer or lessee and to act as an intermediary between them. There must be express authority to accept deposits or sign a contract.

Duration and termination of broker's employment. The employment of a real estate broker may or may not be for a definite time. Where by agreement between the broker and the principal a fixed time is set for the duration of the broker's authority or agency, the principal is answerable for damages to the broker for the cancellation of the broker's authority prior to the expiration date of the broker's agency. Where no time is fixed for the duration of the broker's authority or agency, either party acting in good faith may terminate the broker's employment at will. To avoid any assumption that the employment of the broker is to continue until a sale is effected, the principal should take some action to notify the broker that employment is terminated. The notice of termination may be in writing, oral or implied from circumstances. Where the period of the broker's authority is not fixed, in the absence of any act terminating such authority, it continues for a reasonable time. It should be noted that a principal has the unquestionable power to cancel the authority or agency given by the principal to a broker. That power stems from the inalienable right of an owner to dispose or refuse to dispose of his/her property. The only distinction between the authority given to a broker for a fixed time and for an unspecified time is, as above indicated, that where the authority is for a fixed time, the principal is answerable for damages for the cancellation

SOURCE: *License Law for Brokers,* Division of Licensing Services, Department of State, Albany, New York.

of the broker's authority prior to the expiration date whereas where the authority is for an unspecified time, the principal acting in good faith, may cancel the broker's authority at will. Whether the broker's authority is for a specified or unspecified time it is terminable upon the occurrence of any of the following events: (a) when the object has not been performed during the specified period or, where the period of authority is unspecified, the object has not been performed or accomplished within a reasonable time, (b) death or insanity of a broker or principal, (c) bankruptcy of either, (d) destruction of the subject matter, (e) broker's fraudulent conduct for own benefit, or (f) sale by another broker if the authority is for an unspecified time.

Dual employment. A broker may be employed by both the seller and buyer of real estate, neither of whom can avoid payment of compensation if either knew and consented that the broker also represent the other party.

Interpretation of authorization. The law of the place of the contract governs its enforcement. An authorization made in New York is enforceable in accordance with the provisions of the laws of New York, irrespective of the location of the land the broker is employed to sell or lease.

When commissions are earned. To entitle a broker to compensation, the broker's services must have been the procuring cause of the sale or lease. A broker is not entitled to a commission until the minds of the buyer and seller meet, not only as to the respective price, but as to the terms of the transaction and all other points material thereto. A broker is not entitled to commission where, although the broker introduced the purchaser to the seller, the broker did not bring them to an agreement and the transaction was subsequently negotiated by another broker.

In the absence of a special agreement, the services rendered by a broker to an owner of real property generally fall into one of two categories: (1) where an owner has given the broker full and complete terms upon which the owner is willing to sell the property and not merely the asking price thereof; (2) where the owner has the property for sale and may or may not have set an asking price thereof, and has not fixed the terms of the transaction, leaving them to be determined thereafter. In the first case, the broker's duty is fulfilled when the broker produces a customer ready, able and willing to comply with all the terms fixed by the owner. In the second case, the broker's commissions are not earned until the customer produced by the broker reaches an agreement with the owner upon the price and terms upon which a sale can be made. This of course, does not mean that a contract in writing must be signed by the parties, but that their minds must meet not only upon price but upon the essential terms of the agreement to purchase. The terms essential to effect a meeting of minds are: (1) Price; (2) Amount of Cash; (3) Duration of Mortgages; (4) Rate of Interest; and (5) Amortization. Having rendered the services described in these two transactions, the broker's right to the commissions is undisturbed even though the transaction was not consummated by the principals.

Commission rates. The commission or compensation of a real estate broker is not regulated by statute; nor is it legally fixed by the regulations of the real estate board in a particular community, as many suppose. The broker and the employer may agree upon any rate of compensation, or the method or time of payment thereof, that is mutually acceptable. But, in the absence of such an agreement, the broker is entitled to commissions, or compensation for services, only at the rate customarily paid for similar services in the community in which the broker's services were rendered. The commission rates adopted by a real estate board merely govern the members of the board in their charges for their services; the community may follow or disregard the board's regulations, as it sees fit. But the public's general acceptance of a schedule of commissions, adopted by a real estate board, creates prevailing or customary rates of compensation, which the courts will require the employers of a real estate broker to pay in the absence of a specific agreement between the parties as to the rate of commission to be paid.

Conflicting commission claims: "procuring cause." Where an owner employs a number of brokers to negotiate a transaction, independently of each other, only the broker whose services are the procuring cause of the sale or lease is entitled to compensation. The broker who first induces the customer to agree to the owner's terms is entitled to the commission. The broker who actually negotiates a sale or lease is entitled to compensation, notwithstanding the fact that the owner has erroneously paid a full commission on the same transaction to another broker.

"Ready, willing and able." The words "ready" and "willing" are synonymously used to mean that the broker's customer is prepared to enter into a contract with the broker's principal on his/her terms. The word "able" refers to the customer's ability to enter into a contract with the broker's principal on his/her terms. It refers to financial ability to buy the property offered to the customer and in the event of an exchange it refers to the ownership or right to the property owned by the customer and offered in exchange. If the prospective purchaser is able to tender the sums or deeds required at the time of the execution of a contract such customer is considered "able" to perform the contract. However, the above discussed elements of the broker's customer's ability to buy or exchange must be proved in a case where no binding contract has been signed by the principals. Where the principals entered into a written contract they are both treated as being mutually satisfied of each other's ability to perform.

Disclosure of customer. Where the disclosure of the name of the customer is not requested by the broker's employer, a broker is not bound to disclose to the client the identity of the customer. However, a broker is not entitled to commissions where the broker did not inform the client of the name of the prospective customer and, after negotiations failed, the purchaser sought out the owner and effected a sale directly. A broker loses commissions where the broker failed to disclose the name of the buyer for fear the price would be increased by the seller and later the property is sold to the same buyer. It is obvious that without disclosure of the name of the customer, the employer is unable to investigate the customer.

Commissions payable. Unless otherwise provided in the authorization, a broker's commission is due and payable when it has been earned. A broker employed to negotiate a sale of real property, for instance, earns a commission when the broker produces a purchaser who is ready, able and willing to buy on the seller's terms. It is not imperative, however, that a broker shall produce a customer who will buy or lease upon the terms specified in the listing. The broker is entitled to a commission if the broker brings the client and the customer together and, after mutual bargaining, they come to an agreement; even at a price and on terms materially different from those specified in the authorization.

Deferment of payment of commissions. Notwithstanding the fact that a broker has fulfilled the terms of the broker's employment in effecting a sale of real property, the broker may agree to forego the payment of commissions in the event the sale is not consummated by a transfer of title. Such waiver of the payment of commissions is enforceable against the broker if such agreement of waiver between the broker and the principal is in writing. Section 5–1103 and 1105 of the General Obligations Law dispense with the old rule of law that valuable consideration must be paid the broker for such waiver of commission. However, the courts have refused to enforce such waiver of commission agreements, where the broker's employer was found to be at fault for the nonconsummation of the transaction. It is not uncommon for a broker to agree to waive the payment of commissions where the failure to effect transfer of title is due to any cause whatsoever, including the fault of the employer. Brokers are therefore cautioned to seek advice of counsel before entering into such waiver of commission agreements.

Default by client. In order to deprive a broker of a commission, a seller cannot, in bad faith, terminate a broker's employment and make a sale or lease directly. A broker is entitled to compensation where the owner refuses to sign a contract of sale on the terms the owner originally proposed, or where, because of some defect, the title to the property is unmarketable, or where the owner is guilty of misrepresentation or mistake as to size of property or is guilty of a misstatement of the amount of rentals. Where an owner of property employs a broker to sell the property upon condition that the broker is to receive a commission from the buyer, the owner of the property is liable for damages equal to the commission earned, where the broker finds a buyer ready, able and willing to buy upon the owner's terms and the owner refuses to perform. A broker is not entitled to a commission where the purchaser refuses to take title because of ordinary street encroachments, but if the sale is prevented by encroachments upon abutting owners the broker is entitled to compensation for services.

Default by customer. A broker is not entitled to a commission unless the customer is ready and able to comply with the terms of the agreement to buy or lease. If however, a contract was entered into between buyer and seller, the broker's right to commission is not affected by the customer's failure to complete the purchase, for inability, refusal or failure to perform. If the purchaser is an irresponsible "dummy," the owner is justified in refusing to enter into a contract or to pay brokerage. When a binder, signed by a prospective customer, provides that the customer will pay the broker's commission the customer is liable for the commission if the customer fails or refuses to consummate the negotiation or fails or refuses to complete the transaction. In such instance the customer is also liable for commission even though the transaction is not closed because the seller's title is defective.

Duty to client. A broker's client is the broker's principal or employer, the person from whom the broker expects compensation for services. An agent is bound, not only to good faith, but to reasonable diligence and such skill as is generally possessed by persons of ordinary capacity acting in the same business. A broker may not profit by deceiving the employer. A principal may hold the agent to strict loyalty and require the agent to account fully for the profits of a transaction wherein the employer was defrauded. If a broker submits any offer of purchase to the client, the broker is duty bound to reveal any other better offers that have been made. If the broker fails to do so a broker cannot recover commissions. A broker must disclose higher offers even if the higher offer has less cash. A broker is not entitled to any commission where the broker induced the client to accept less than the asking price after the purchaser has indicated a willingness to pay the asking price. A broker cannot claim commissions where the broker has induced the client to accept less than the asking price knowing the property is of special value to the buyer. A broker is duty bound to reveal any facts in the broker's possession concerning purchaser's intention to resell at an increased price. If client (owner) requests the name of the purchaser, the broker must disclose it or lose commissions. For failure to disclose the name of the purchaser, the broker loses the commissions even if the property is sold to the broker's undisclosed buyer.

A broker cannot take an incompatible position with his/her clients. Hence a broker employed to sell cannot purchase for himself/herself without a full disclosure of the broker's interest. A broker cannot sell the client's property to a corporation or partnership in which the broker is interested without similar disclosure.

Duty to a customer. Brokers should guard against inaccuracies in their representations to customers. If a misstatement is made as to a matter of fact by a broker, it may have the most serious consequences, both to the broker and to the employer. In law, such a misrepresentation is a fraud, which justifies the refusal by a purchaser to take title and affords the owner a good defense to the broker's claim for commission.

Deposit money—broker's duty with relation thereto. The real estate broker, by reason of the nature of the broker's work, is in a position to come into possession of funds belonging to others. The question very often arises as to whom such money belongs and what disposition should be made of the funds by the broker. In this discussion, reference is not being made to the real estate broker who is duly authorized to manage real property and therefore authorized to collect rents. With relation to such monies, there is never any question but that the money belongs to the owner and must be kept in a separate bank account and must be duly accounted for to the broker's principal. However, where the real estate broker has been employed by the owner to find a buyer, it is customary for the broker to take a deposit from the prospective buyer, issue a receipt therefor, and have the prospective purchaser execute an offer to buy subject to acceptance by the broker's principal, the owner. The problem is comparatively simple where the owner accepts the offer in writing before there has been notice of revocation of the offer by the buyer and where the broker at the time of the owner's acceptance turns the deposit over in full to the principal. But all situations are not so simple as this. Unfortunately, experience has demonstrated that brokers may become involved in difficulties and may place their licenses in jeopardy where they do not take time to learn their responsibilities with relation to other people's money. Brokers should be thoroughly familiar with the following rules applicable to deposits to avoid the pitfalls encountered in the handling of funds belonging to third persons.

The real estate broker must at all times remember that he/she occupies the status of agent acting on behalf of others. By reason of this, the License Law in determining an individual's competency as a broker requires that the prospective broker, among other things, have a fair knowledge and understanding of the law of Agency. The broker should at all times be cognizant of his/her obligation as an agent and must have a complete awareness that in dealing with the property of others the broker is held to a very high degree of accountability.

The average real estate broker is an agent of limited authority and must act entirely within the scope of such limited authority. Where a parcel of real estate is listed for sale with a real estate broker, the authority of such broker is limited to finding a purchaser who is ready, willing and able to buy on the terms established and prescribed by the owner. The broker by virtue of the broker's employment by the owner becomes a mere negotiator or intermediary between the owner and the prospective purchaser. The listing of a parcel of real property with a broker does not in and of itself confer upon the broker the authority to accept a deposit from a prospective purchaser. In order for the broker to have authority on behalf of a seller to accept a deposit, the listing agreement or contract of employment must expressly grant such authority. In the absence of such specific grant of authority, if a real estate broker in conjunction with the receipt of an offer of purchase undertakes to accept a deposit from the prospective purchaser, the broker does so on his/her own and the receipt of such deposit by the broker has no binding effect insofar as the owner is concerned.

Keeping in mind that the broker is an agent of very limited authority, and considering that such authority does not include the power to accept deposits, it must, therefore, be concluded that when a broker takes such deposit from a prospective purchaser, the broker is impliedly being employed by the purchaser for the purpose of conveying the offer to the seller and turning such deposit over when the seller does accept the offer. Since the broker becomes the agent of the purchaser for the pur-

pose mentioned, the deposit which is in the broker's possession remains the property of the purchaser until the moment that the seller accepts the offer. The moment the seller accepts the offer the broker has completed the broker's agency for the purchaser, the deposit becomes the property of the seller and the broker is no longer responsible to the purchaser to refund the deposit. It must be considered elementary that where the offer made by the purchaser is rejected by the seller, the deposit received by the broker still remains the property of the purchaser and therefore must be refunded to the latter. The offer having been rejected by the seller, the deposit in the possession of the broker is still held by the broker as agent of the purchaser and the broker is, therefore, accountable to the purchaser for such deposit. The same conclusion must be reached where the purchaser has revoked the offer delivered to the broker by due notice to the latter and before the seller has accepted the offer to buy. The offer not having been accepted, the broker still holds the deposit as agent for the purchaser. That being the case, the deposit must be returned to the purchaser without any delay.

In the circumstances where the seller accepts the offer made and necessarily becomes aware of the fact that the broker was given a deposit by the prospective buyer, the unauthorized act of the broker in taking the deposit, that is, insofar as the seller is concerned, becomes ratified by the seller upon the seller's acceptance of the offer. For this reason, the seller becomes entitled to the deposit.

There are many transactions negotiated by real estate brokers which require mortgage financing by the purchaser in order to complete the purchase. In practically all of these cases, the broker is fully aware that purchaser does not have sufficient cash and therefore provision is made in the binder or contract that the transaction is conditioned on a mortgage loan being obtained and further providing an escape from the contract by the purchaser and for a refund of the deposit to the purchaser in the event the mortgage loan is not obtainable. The pattern of these transactions had demonstrated that the broker induces the buyer to make the deposit in the first instance by the assurance that the deposit will be returned in the event the mortgage loan is not obtained and incorporates such assurance in the form of an escape clause. A similar situation may also exist where the purchase of one property is made conditional upon the sale by the purchaser of a property the purchaser already owns. The problem that often arises in these situations is the one relating to the deposit paid by the purchaser to the broker who retains such deposit. As discussed earlier, we found that where the seller has accepted the offer to purchase, the deposit becomes the property of the seller and the broker's obligation with relation to the purchaser ceases. The next question is—does the conditional type of transaction affect the situation? Where the mortgage loan is not obtainable or the prior sale by the purchaser is not made, the seller, by virtue of the condition in the contract becomes obligated to return the deposit to the purchaser. The seller, however, does not have the deposit; it has been retained by the broker. The broker is required in such instance to return the deposit the broker holds to the purchaser when the condition does not take place. There is no gainsaying the right of the purchaser to the return of the deposit. Regardless of the rights of the broker with relation to the seller, the purchaser would not have made the deposit in the first place unless the broker had induced the transaction through the. employment of the condition or contingency. The broker having used such inducement would be considered most unethical and guilty of improper conduct if the broker were to insist on retaining the deposit after the condition had failed to eventuate. In the final analysis, the conditional transaction differs from the ordinary one which involves no condition in that essentially the latter type is a fully completed contract with a purchaser accepted as ready, willing and able, whereas the former does not actually ripen into an enforceable contract until the contingency occurs or the condition is fulfilled thus rendering the purchaser able to perform.

The situation is immediately altered where the failure of the contingency or condition to take place is due to the fault of the buyer because of the buyer's arbitrary refusal to accept the loan or sell the property. That being the case, there would be no expectation of the broker returning the deposit to the defaulter. Where the buyer,

however, is not at fault, the broker holding the deposit and refusing to return it to the innocent purchaser would be considered as having demonstrated untrustworthiness of sufficient gravity to warrant action under the disciplinary provisions of the license law.

The real estate broker in carrying out the broker's functions must always realize that he/she represents the interests of others. The broker must at all times consider those interests before the broker's own.

In handling of deposits, there should be a constant consciousness that the monies placed in the broker's hands are trust funds and that with relation to such monies the broker is a trustee and fiduciary. Of course, the monies cannot be commingled with the broker's personal funds and must be kept in a separate, special bank account.

Accrued interest, is any, shall not be retained for the benefit of the broker except to the extent that it is applied to and deducted from earned commissions with the consent of all parties.

Appendix D
Major National Real Estate Associations

A number of prominent professional or trade associations serve the real estate industry. Indeed, as real estate persons have attempted to make their industry more professional, these organizations have proliferated. There are organizations that disseminate information, promulgate standards of ethical conduct, engage in poltical activity, and publish journals.

Local Chapters

The new real estate salesperson may find membership in a national association to be most useful. Most of the national associations operate through local chapters. Membership in a local chapter puts the new real estate person in contact with his peers, and many benefits are to be obtained from these contacts and meetings.

Professional Designations

In the drive for professionalization, almost every national real estate organization offers professional designations, based on a combination of experience, courses, and examinations, that its members may earn. Some of these designations are exceedingly prestigious; others are less meaningful.

Every new salesperson receives solicitations to enroll in (relatively expensive) courses that are "the first step" toward professional designations. But the wise salesperson carefully studies all the requirements for a designation before enrolling in a beginning course to be sure that all of the sometimes complex steps required to earn the designation can be completed. Often, local real estate boards, adult education courses, or college courses offer more immediate benefits and prestige.

National Organizations

The largest real estate association in the country is the *National Association of Realtors®* (NAR). NAR is an umbrella for two types of organizations. First, it functions largely through local and state chapters. Second, it is the parent of a large number of affiliates. You can join a special purpose affiliate (like the Institute of Real Estate Managers) and thus become a member of NAR, or you can join a local chapter which, in turn, is affiliated with the state and national associations.

Other large national associations tend to be directed toward specific segments of the industry. Examples are the National Association of Home Builders and the Building Owners and Managers Association.

Descriptions of selected national organizations follow. The list is not meant to be comprehensive. National organizations that are not popular in New York are omitted, farm land organizations are omitted, and organizations that invite to membership only senior industry members are omitted.

NATIONAL UMBRELLA ORGANIZATIONS

National Association of Realtors® (NAR)
430 North Michigan Avenue
Chicago, Illinois 60611

Purpose
This is a membership organization. Membership is achieved by joining a local or state board. (To become a member of an affiliate, the real estate professional must join that affiliate separately.) NAR defines a REALTOR® as a professional who subscribes to a strict code of ethics.

Affiliation
This is the parent body. Listed below are the affiliates:
American Institute of Real Estate Appraisers (AIREA)
American Society of Real Estate Counsellors (ASREC)
Farm and Land Institute (FLI)
Institute of Real Estate Management (IREM)
Real Estate Securities and Syndication Institute (RESSI)
Realtors National Marketing Institute (RMMI)
Society of Industrial Realtors (SIR)

Designations
REALTOR®; REALTOR® Associate
These designations may be used by all members.
Graduate, Realtors® Institute (GRI)
Designation is earned by those who complete three 30-hour courses.

National Association of Home Builders (NAHB)
15th and M Streets, N.W.
Washington, D.C. 20005

Purpose

This is a multipurpose membership organization. Its members are single family and apartment builders, brokers, and managers, NAHB disseminates information, holds national conventions and meetings, and offers two professional designations.

Designations

Residential Apartment Manager (RAM)

RAM candidates earn required points by attending NAHB-RAM courses. Points are also awarded for experience, real estate licenses, and college degrees. Candidates must successfully complete a national RAM examination.

Member of the Institute of Residential Marketing (MIRM)

MIRM candidates with high school degrees must complete four Institute of Residential Marketing courses and earn elective credits from experience and otherwise.

MARKETING ORGANIZATIONS

Realtors® National Marketing Institute (RNMI)
430 North Michigan Avenue
Chicago, Illinois 60611

Purpose

To promote the professional standing of REALTORS® by providing practical education and advocating sound and ethical practices.

Affiliation
  NAR

Designation

Certified Real Estate Brokerage Manager (CRB)
Certified Residential Salesman (CRS)
Certified Commercial Investment Member (CCIM)

Designations are available to individuals with high school education and modest real estate experience who complete certain required courses that RNMI offers and who fulfill certain other requirements.

National Association of Home Builders (NAHB)
See description under national umbrella organizations.

MANAGEMENT ORGANIZATIONS

Institute of Real Estate Management (IREM)
430 North Michigan Avenue
Chicago, Illinois 60611

Purpose

To serve the professional needs of property managers, to disseminate useful property management information, and to issue three types of certifications.

Affiliation
  NAR

Designations

Certified Property Manager (CPM)

To earn the CPM, a candidate must have a college degree, five years of appropriate experience, and must have completed required IREM courses.

Accredited Resident Manager (ARM)

The ARM is an intermediate designation for those who complete a single course enroute to the prestigious CPM.

Accredited Management Organization (AMO)

The AMO is a designation for firms, not individuals.

Building Owners and Managers Association (BOMA)
1221 Massachusetts Ave., N.W.
Washington, D.C. 20005

Purpose

A national membership organization for managers of commercial property. (Functions through local chapters in major cities.) Designed to increase professionalism and disseminate information. Sponsors its certification affiliate, *Building Owners and Managers Institute International.*

Designation

Real Property Administrator (RPA)

Designation is earned by those over 21 who successfully complete seven rigorous courses and national examinations. Courses may be self-study, or they are offered at major universities like New York University. Unlike other organizations offering management certifications, the RPA does not permit experience to be substituted for the successful completion of examinations.

National Association of Home Builders (NAHB)
See description under national umbrella organizations.

APPRAISAL ORGANIZATIONS

American Institute of Real Estate Appraisers (AIREA)
430 North Michigan Avenue
Chicago, Illinois 60611

Purpose

To establish standards of professionalism and competence in appraisal activity; to train and test professional appraisers.

Affiliation
NAR

Designations
Member, Appraisal Institute (MAI)
Residential Member (RM)

The MAI is one of the best known and most respected professional real estate designations. The RM is a designation of more recent vintage. The MAI may be earned by candidates with five years of appraisal experience through the successful completion of various required examinations and demonstration appraisals. AIREA offers a large battery of courses that prepare candidates for the examinations. Requirements for earning the RM are similar but less comprehensive.

Society of Real Estate Appraisers
7 South Dearborn Street
Chicago, Illinois

Purpose

A large membership organization established to promote professionalism and education for real estate appraisers and analysts. It establishes standards of performance and ethical conduct and offers courses and designations.

Designations
Senior Residential Appraiser (SRA)
Senior Real Property Appraiser (SRPA)
Senior Real Estate Analyst (SREA)

The society offers its own courses and examinations, but allows candidates to substitute courses and examinations of the American Institute of Real Estate Appraisers. Upgrading its standards, the society will require SRA and SPRA candidates born after December 31, 1979 to have a college degree. SRA and SRPA candidates must complete two courses successfully, pass national exams, and produce a demonstration report. SREA candidates must previously have earned the SRPA designation. Requirements for the SREA designation are a combination of experience, courses, and an oral examination.

SPECIAL INTEREST ORGANIZATIONS

International Council of Shopping Centers (ICSC)
665 Fifth Avenue
New York, N.Y. 10022

Purpose

A membership organization for shopping center developers, marketers, managers, and other shopping center professionals. Engages in wide-ranging educational activities for members, disseminates information, and the products of its own research. Sponsors conventions, conferences, "colleges," and meetings.

Designations
Accredited Shopping Center Promotion Director (ASPD)

ASPD candidates who have three years of shopping center experience must pass ICSC courses and examinations.

Certified Shopping Center Manager (CSM)

CSM candidates with four years management experience must pass appropriate examinations. ICSC or college courses may substitute for required experience.

National Association of Corporate Real Estate Executives (NACORE)
7799 Southwest 62nd Avenue
South Miami, Florida 44143

Purpose

A national membership organization for corporate real estate officers. Disseminates information and offers numerous seminars and conferences.

Designations
Three designations are now being developed.

Mortgage Bankers Associations of America (MBA)
1125 15th Street, N.W.
Washington, D.C. 20005

Purpose

A national membership organization that includes mortgage bankers and brokers as well as many institutional lenders. Operates through local chapters organized in cities throughout the country. Designed to improve professionalism in real estate finance. Engages in research and political activity in its members' interests. Publishes a national monthly, *The Mortgage Banker*.

Designation
Certified Mortgage Bankers (CMB)
   Designation based on complicated system of points that may be earned by experience, MBA activities, attendance at courses, and seminars.

Real Estate Securities and Syndication Institute
   (RESSI)
430 North Michigan Avenue
Chicago, Illinois 60611

Purpose
   To establish professional standards of practice, to offer educational courses and the designation CRSS.

Affiliation
   NAR

Designation
Certified Real Estate Securities Sponsors (CRSS)
   Designations are available to those with high school education and modest real estate or securities brokerage experience who complete special courses and fulfill other requirements.

Society of Industrial Realtors® of the
National Association of Realtors® (SIR)

Purpose
   To unite those REALTORS® who buy, sell, or lease land or buildings to industry; to foster knowledge, education, integrity, and quality workmanship in industry real estate; to exchange information and listings; and to offer certain certifications.

Affiliation
   NAR

Designations
SIR, Active
SIR, Salesman Affiliate
SIR, Associate
SIR, International Associate
   The primary qualifications that a candidate must demonstrate for one of these designations are specific experience and reputation. Certain education (graduate professional school or SIR courses) may substitute for a portion of the required experience.

Appendix E

Federal Income Taxation of Income-Producing Real Estate

THE FEDERAL TAX TREATMENT of investments in income property is complex and has become more difficult for the layman to understand as a consequence of revisions in the tax code which occurred in 1981 and 1982. This article attempts to cut through the jargon and give the real estate investor who is not a tax expert a simplified interpretation of the key elements of the tax code that influence the decisionmaker. The explanation is not intended to substitute for the advice of tax advisers, but such expert advice cannot take the place of a basic understanding of how the system works.

PRELIMINARY DEFINITIONS

The analysis focuses on the taxation of an existing income-producing property that is to be held for a period of time and then sold.

Depreciation Categories

Such properties may be comprised of three types of depreciable physical assets. These asset categories are:

- The building or building shell
- Rehabilitation improvements undertaken at the time the property is placed in service
- Personal property

The initial value of the property (excluding the proportion allocated to land) must be allocated among one or more of these categories.

Each of these asset categories is subject to different depreciation or cost recovery rules. (In this article, the terms "depreciation" and "cost recovery" are used interchangeably. The terms represent the "reasonable" allowance or deduction from income that reflects the wear and tear of property held for the production of income.)

Rehabilitation expenditures are expenditures on the improvement of buildings at least thirty years old or on "certified historic structures." For the moment, we will ignore this type of depreciation category. Personal property includes mechanical equipment such as refrigerators or stoves (in the case of residential income property) or removable tenant improvements (in the

EXHIBIT 1

DIAGRAM DEPICTING HOLDING PERIOD
AND RELEVANT TERMINOLOGY

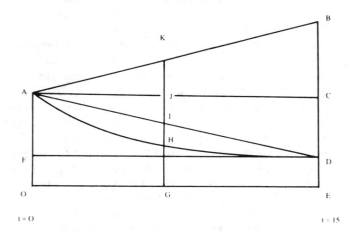

case of commercial property). We will also ignore this category initially.

Life Cycle

We indicated that the investor is purchasing the property to hold it for a period of time and then to sell. There are, therefore, three points or periods in time at or during which we must examine the tax implications. They are:

- The time of acquisition
- The holding period
- The time of disposition or sale

Exhibit 1 depicts these points and periods of time. The horizontal axis depicts the passage of time. The point of acquisition is t = 0 (the left edge of the figure or

This article was written by Professor David Dale-Johnson of the University of Southern California, Los Angeles.

It was originally published in the Summer 1984 issue of *Real Estate Review*, a publication of Warren, Gorham & Lamont Inc., Boston, Massachusetts.

point 0). The figure assumes that the property is held for fifteen years, so the holding period is the line OE that runs from t = 0 to t = 15. The time (point) of disposition is t = 15 (the right edge of the figure or point E).

THE TIME OF ACQUISITION

For existing income properties, the time of acquisition is the time at which the property is "placed in service," that is, the time at which the property is ready for use in the production of income or in a personal activity.

From a tax perspective, the time of acquisition is important simply to identify some values which will be used to determine tax liability during the holding period and at the time of disposition. The "initial basis" of the property is the purchase price plus any costs of acquisition. The purchase price consists of the down payment or equity, the value of any new loans used to finance the acquisition, and the value of any existing loans assumed. Costs of acquisition include items such as a finder's fee or price paid for an option to buy the property. In Exhibit 1, the initial basis at the time of acquisition (t = 0) is represented by the line OA.

The initial basis must be allocated between land and improvements (the building). The allocation is typically based on the relative values of the land and building as determined by the property tax assessor, by an independent appraiser or by an arm's-length agreement between the buyer and seller. The allocation is important because it establishes the basis that is eligible for cost recovery. In the simple example upon which we focus, the basis is the value of the building. In Exhibit 1, the line OF represents the allocation of basis to land, while the line FA represents the basis eligible for cost recovery. (For the moment we are ignoring the possibility that rehabilitation expenditures may have been incurred or that the acquisition includes personal property.)

For the purpose of computing a measure of return on the investment, the investor must determine the cash flow at the time of acquisition. At the moment of acquisition, the cash flow is typically a negative figure (an outflow). It is the investor's expenditure for the purchase price *plus* the costs of acquisition *minus* the amount of total loans that the investor receives.

THE HOLDING PERIOD

Exhibit 1 assumes that the property that it depicts appreciates in value during the holding period. As a consequence, the net selling price of the property during the holding period is represented by the positively sloped line, AB, that runs from t = 0 to t = 15.

During the holding period, the basis eligible for cost recovery can be depreciated or written off. Depreciation is an expense of ownership, albeit a noncash expense, that annually reduces the investor's taxable income. When computing the return on his investment, the real estate investor typically looks at after-tax cash flows. After-tax cash flows are increased (indeed, negative pretax cash flows may be made positive) when the taxable income from the property is negative as a consequence of noncash expenses like depreciation.

The 1981 revisions to the federal tax code created significant after-tax benefits for investors in real estate by reducing the period of time over which buildings can be depreciated and allowing accelerated rather than straight-line depreciation over that shorter time period. The methods of depreciation made available as a result of the 1981 changes are broadly termed the "accelerated cost recovery system" (ACRS).

Types of ACRS Depreciation

For buildings that were placed in service after 1980 (not rehabilitation expenditure or personal property), the methods of depreciation or cost recovery available include the following:

- 175 percent of the fifteen-year, straight-line rate applied to the declining balance;
- 200 percent of the fifteen-year, straight-line rate applied to the declining balance;
- fifteen-year straight line;
- thirty-five-year straight line; and
- forty-five-year straight line.

For each of the first two options the Internal Revenue Service provides a table which the taxpayer must follow in determining the percentage of the basis eligible for cost recovery that can be recovered in a particular year. The percentage depends on the month of acquisition, and the table reflects a change from declining balance depreciation to straight line when the switch maximizes the deduction. The second option (200 percent of declining balances) is available only for qualified low-income housing projects. The investor or taxpayer is free to choose among the remaining options. However, the taxpayer must formally "elect" one of the stright-line options, and once he has done so he may not switch to other options for depreciation of the building in subsequent tax years.

Exhibit 1 depicts the "adjusted basis" of the property during the holding period under two different cost recovery methods. The adjusted basis is the initial basis less total cost recovery accumulated using the chosen cost recovery method. (Note that the cost recovery is computed as a proportion of the basis eligible for cost recovery, i.e., a proportion of the initial basis allocated to the building.) The straight line AD (or AID) depicts the path of the adjusted basis if the investor elects straight-line cost recovery. If the investor chooses accelerated cost recovery, the curved line AD (AHD) depicts the path of the adjusted basis. The line GK is drawn at a random point during the fifteen-year holding period. On this line, the segment GI is the adjusted basis assuming straight-line cost recovery was chosen. The segment GH is the adjusted basis assuming accelerated cost recovery was chosen, and the segments IJ and HJ are total, accumulated cost recovery for the respective cases.

During the holding period, the investor may make expenditures on improvements that he capitalizes in order to create a new cost recovery account or depreciable asset pool. Unless the expenditures are "substantial," the investor must write off the new account (using the same cost recovery option that he is using for the building). This is not the case if the improvements are substantial. In order to be considered substantial, improvements over a two-year period must amount to at least 25 percent of the basis of the building as of the first day of the period. The improvements must be made at least three years after the property was placed in service. If the improvements are substantial, they are treated like a separate building and the investor again may choose whichever cost recovery technique he prefers.

THE TIME OF DISPOSITION OR SALE

It is at the time of disposition that the federal tax treatment of income properties becomes most complicated. The main reason for the complexity is that the method of computation of the tax liability at disposition depends on three factors: (1) the type of investor (individual or corporate); (2) the type of property (residential or nonresidential); and (3) the type of cost recovery that has previously been elected (accelerated or straight line). For simplicity, we will assume that the holding period has been *more than one year* and therefore the investor may be eligible for capital gains treatment of some or all of the "gain" at disposition.

Disposition Definitions

Again it is necessary to define some terminology. "Disposition" occurs at the time of sale or foreclosure of the property, and the "gain" is the selling price less selling expenses less the "adjusted basis." In Exhibit 1, the positively sloped line AB, which depicts property value, also depicts the net selling price that would be garnered at any point during the holding period. In

Exhibit 1, if the holding period were fifteen years, the vertical line EB where t = 15 would represent the net selling price. The gain is the net selling price minus the adjusted basis and, therefore, the line BCD is the gain. Note that since we are assuming that the property was held for the full fifteen years, the building is fully depreciated and the adjusted basis of the property is equal to the original allocation to land (the line ED = 0F).

Eight Alternative Treatments at Disposition

For every type of investor, every type of income property, and every cost recovery choice, gain is computed in the same fashion. However, the portion of the gain that is treated as ordinary income and the portion that is treated as capital gain depend on those three factors. For both individual and corporate investors, capital gains may be taxed at a lower rate than ordinary income.

Exhibit 2 is identical to Exhibit 1 with two exceptions. Eight vertical lines are added to represent the allocation of the gain between ordinary income and capital gain in each of eight alternatives. In Exhibit 1, two lines (curves) AID and AHD represented two alternative depreciation options. In Exhibit 2, an additional line, AL, is added above the line AD. The distance between straight line AD and line AL is 15 percent of the accumulated, straight-line cost recovery at each point during the holding period. This measure is necessary for computing the tax liability of corporate investors.

The eight alternative treatments are based on the following factors:

- Individual ownership of:
  1. Residential property that used straight-line cost recovery
  2. Residential property that used accelerated cost recovery
  3. Nonresidential property that used straight-line cost recovery
  4. Nonresidential property that used accelerated cost recovery

- Corporate ownership of:
  5. Residential property that used straight-line cost recovery
  6. Residential property that used accelerated cost recovery
  7. Nonresidential property that used straight-line cost recovery
  8. Nonresidential property that used accelerated cost recovery

In Exhibit 2, the eight vertical lines are numbered to correspond to the eight alternative tax categories listed above. Six of these lines are divided into two seg-

E X H I B I T   2
TAX TREATMENT AT DISPOSITION

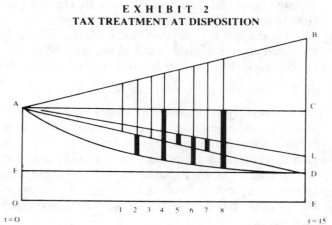

ments. The wide, lower portion of the line is the part of the gain that is taxed as ordinary income. The narrow, upper portion of the line is the part of the gain that is taxed as capital gain. The formulas for computing tax liability at disposition for each of the eight ownership and depreciation alternatives are given in Exhibit 3.

As Exhibits 2 and 3 indicate, properties that were held by noncorporate owners and that used straight-line depreciation are subject to capital gain tax only. Investments in residential income properties (lines 1, 2, 5, and 6) are also given preferential tax treatment at disposition.

What differs among the various options is the portion of the gain that is viewed as "recapture." Recapture is income that has been expensed during the holding period that is now "recaptured" at disposition and taxed as income. Thus, for example, in alternative 1, when straight-line depreciation is used, all of the gain is treated as capital gain. In alternative 2, when accelerated depreciation is used, the portion of the gain that represents the difference between the sale price and the basis that would have existed if straight-line depreciation had been used, is treated as capital gain. The rest of the gain is treated as "excess cost recovery." Excess cost recovery is recaptured, i.e., it is taxed at income tax rates.

In order to compute a property's return as an investment, it is necessary to compute its cash flow after-tax at disposition. The cash flow from disposition consists of the net selling price minus the outstanding loan amount minus the tax liability. For individual investors, the tax liability is equivalent to the investor's marginal rate *times* that portion of his net cash receipts that is considered to be ordinary income *plus* the investor's marginal rate *times* 40 percent of the cash flow that is

EXHIBIT   3

FORMULAS FOR COMPUTING TAX LIABILITY AT DISPOSITION*

Individual Ownership of

1. Residential property that used straight-line cost recovery
    Tax liability = tax rate × 40% × gain
2. Residential property that used accelerated cost recovery
    Tax liability = tax rate × (lesser of gain or excess cost recovery[b]) + tax rate × 40% × excess of gain over excess cost recovery
3. Nonresidential property that used straight-line cost recovery
    Tax liability = tax rate × 40% × gain
4. Nonresidential property that used accelerated cost recovery
    Tax liability = tax rate × (lesser of gain or excess cost recovery) + tax rate × 40% × excess of gain over excess recovery

Corporate Ownership of

5. Residential property that used straight-line cost recovery
    Tax liability = tax rate × (lesser of gain or 15% of S/L cost recovery) + alternate rate *or* tax rate × excess of gain over 15% of S/L cost recovery
6. Residential property that used accelerated cost recovery
    Tax liability = tax rate × (lesser of gain or (excess cost recovery + 15% of S/L cost recovery)) + alternate rate *or* tax rate × (excess of gain over (excess cost recovery + 15% of S/L cost recovery))
7. Nonresidential property that used straight-line cost recovery
    Tax liability = tax rate × (lesser of gain or 15% of S/L cost recovery) + alternate rate *or* tax rate × excess of gain over 15% of S/L cost recovery
8. Nonresidential property that used accelerated cost recovery
    Tax liability = tax rate × (lesser of gain or cost recovery) + alternate rate *or* tax rate × excess of gain over cost recovery

---

a These formulas are relevant only for the building or building shell, and rehabilitation expenditures. For personal property, all recapture of cost recovery at disposition is taxed as ordinary income.

b Excess cost recovery is the cost recovery taken in excess of straight-line cost recovery. In Exhibit 2, it is the amount represented by the height of the lines between curved line AD and straight line AD.

treated as capital gain. As Exhibit 2 indicates, only noncorporate investors who use straight-line depreciation can avoid having any part of their gain treated as ordinary income. Corporate investors are limited to two choices: (1) treating the capital gain as ordinary income and computing the tax liability accordingly or (2) using a preferential rate of 28 percent to compute the tax liability on the capital gain. Note that the excess of cost recovery over straight-line depreciation is classified as a "tax preference" item and may have the effect of influencing the investor's marginal rate both during the holding period and at disposition.

TAXATION OF PERSONAL PROPERTY AND REHABILITATION EXPENDITURE

There are two major categories of assets other than the building that the investor in income-producing real estate must consider. These classes are "personal property" and "rehabilitation expenditure." The tax code classifies personal property according to the number of years over which it can be depreciated. Virtually

EXHIBIT 4

ASSET CLASSES AND COST RECOVERY OPTIONS

Personal Property	Rehabilitation Expenditure	Building or Building Shell
5-year ACRS[a]	15-year S/L	15-Year ACRS[a]
5-year S/L[b]	35-year S/L	15-year S/L[b]
12-year S/L[b]	45-year S/L	35-year S/L[b]
25-year S/L[b]		45-year S/L[b]

[a] Use ACRS Tables
[b] Election required

all personal property associated with a real estate investment (e.g., the kitchen appliances in an apartment building) is "five year" personal property.

There are also two categories of rehabilitation expenditure:

- Improvements to nonresidential income property that is at least thirty years old; or
- Improvements to "certified historic structures" (both residential and nonresidential income properties).

Expenditures for either of these purposes *at the time a property is placed in service* create assets that have unique cost recovery treatment. Furthermore, both categories of assets establish associated tax credits. Exhibit 4 illustrates the possible classes into which the three major categories of assets may be divided and enumerates the cost recovery options that are available to each.

Personal Property

Examples of personal property that are relevant for real estate investors include removable tenant improvements in commercial property and mechanical equipment, such as refrigerators and stoves, in residential property. Investors in transient residential income properties (hotels and motels) can include furnishings in the category of personal property.

Personal property that qualifies as five-year property can be depreciated in four ways: (1) 150 percent of the five-year, straight-line rate applied to the declining balance; (2) five-year, straight line; (3) twelve-year straight line; and (4) twenty-five-year straight line. The straight-line options must be formally elected. Investment in personal property as part of an income-producing venture makes available a dollar-for-dollar reduction in the investor's tax liability equal to 10 percent of the expenditure on qualified personal property. The "basis" of the personal property (the original cost, all of which is subject to cost recovery) must be reduced by one half the amount of the tax credit that the

investor takes. (If the cost of the personal property is $1,000, the tax credit is $100, and the investor who takes the credit reports the basis as $950.) However, if the investor elects to reduce the tax credit by 2 percent, he need not reduce the basis of the asset. Basis reduction imposes a penalty on the taxpayer by reducing the dollar value against which cost recovery percentages are applied. It is usually beneficial to take the maximum tax credit.

The investor in personal property may elect not to use one of the straight-line depreciation options. He may use instead the statutory ACRS percentages that reflect 150 percent declining balance depreciation with a switch to straight line at such time as the switch maximizes the deduction.

In the calculation of personal property depreciation, a half-year convention is followed no matter which depreciation system is used. Essentially, this convention allows only one half of the cost recovery to be claimed in the year the property is placed in service. The remaining one half is claimed in the year following the end of the recovery period (the sixth year) if straight-line cost recovery is elected. The ACRS table percentages are adjusted so as to incorporate the half-year convention for the first year but allow total cost recovery over five years. Generally, no recovery deduction is allowed in the year of disposition of personal property.

For tax and investment analysis purposes, the investor must look at personal property as an asset class that has acquisition, holding period, and disposition implications just as the building itself does. The amount of the initial basis establishes the cost recovery amounts to which the investor is entitled during the holding period. These noncash deductions affect the periodic after-tax cash flows of the property. At disposition, the difference between the value (sale price) of the asset class and the adjusted basis is the gain, and the amount of gain affects the tax liability and the after-tax cash flow. What is unique about personal property is that in all cases, all cost recovery is recaptured and is taxed as ordinary income. Only the portion of the gain above the cost recovery taken is taxed as capital gain (assuming that the property has been held for at least one year).

Rehabilitation Expenditure

All types of qualified rehabilitation expenditure must be depreciated using straight-line cost recovery over fifteen, thirty-five or forty-five years *if* a tax credit is claimed at the time the expenditure is incurred. The amount of the investment tax credit (and the amount of a required basis reduction) depends on the nature of the rehabilitation expenditure. Specifically, expenditure on rehabilitating a certified historic structure entitles the investor to a tax credit amounting to 25 percent of the expenditure; the investor must reduce the basis of the asset class by 50 percent of the tax credit. Expenditure on the rehabilitation of nonresidential buildings at least thirty years old but less than forty years old entitles the investor to a 15 percent tax credit, and expenditures on buildings at least forty years old creates a 20 percent tax credit. In both cases of nonresidential rehabilitation, the basis of the asset class must be reduced by 100 percent of the tax credit. If the investor chooses not to take the tax credit, he may depreciate the rehabilitation expenditures along with the building shell.

Again, for tax and investment analysis purposes, the investor must look upon rehabilitation expenditure as having acquisition, holding period, and disposition implications just like the building itself. The amount of the initial basis determines the periodic cost recovery during the holding period, which affects the property's after-tax cash flows. At disposition, the difference between the value of the rehabilitation expenditures and the adjusted basis is the gain, which affects the tax liability and, consequently, the after-tax cash flow. Unlike personal property, at disposition rehabilitation expenditures are treated for tax purposes in the same way as the building or building shell.

We must add one general rule concerning tax credits that applies to both personal property and rehabilitation expenditure. The maximum amount of the tax credit that can be used to reduce tax liability is $25,000 plus 85 percent of the tax liability in excess of $25,000. Unused tax credits can be carried back three years and forward fifteen years.

Early Disposition and Tax Credits

If an investor takes tax credits as a consequence of expenditure on personal property or rehabilitation and subsequently disposes of the property within five years, he must pay back (or allow to be recaptured) a portion of the tax credit that he took and he must readjust the basis of the asset class. In this case, recapture refers to previously forgiven taxes which must be repaid due to early disposition.

The following schedule applies. If disposition is within one year, recapture and basis readjustment is 100 percent. That is, the investor must repay 100 percent of the tax credit, and he increases the basis of the asset class by 100 percent of the original basis reduction. Each year the percentage of the adjustment declines 20 percentage points, until in the fifth year, 20 percent of the tax credit must be repaid and the basis of the asset class increased by 20 percent of the original reduction. If the disposition is made after five years, there is no recapture of the tax credit or readjustment of the basis.

THE ALTERNATIVE MINIMUM TAX AND THE CORPORATE MINIMUM TAX

In general, taxpayers who take advantage of certain tax shelter opportunities or "tax preference items" are prevented from avoiding a minimum tax liability because of the existence of two tax computation requirements: the alternative minimum tax, which applies to individuals, and the corporate minimum tax, which applies to corporations. The individual taxpayer must pay a tax of at least 20 percent of his adjusted gross income plus tax preference items less certain allowable deductions less an exemption amount. The corporate taxpayer must add on a minimum tax of 15 percent of total tax preference items less the greater of $10,000 or the previously computed tax liability. A key tax preference item for real estate investors is the excess of accelerated cost recovery over straight-line cost recovery for fifteen-year real property (buildings). So, when trying to determine after-tax cash flows, the investor must consider carefully how the dollar value of tax preference items affects the effective tax rate.

Appendix F
Forms

Standard N Y B T. U. Form 8041 •   —Contract of Sale

CONSULT YOUR LAWYER BEFORE SIGNING THIS INSTRUMENT—THIS INSTRUMENT SHOULD BE USED BY LAWYERS ONLY.

NOTE: FIRE LOSSES. This form of contract contains no express provision as to risk of loss by fire or other casualty before delivery of the deed. Unless express provision is made, the provisions of Section 5-1311 of the General Obligations Law will apply. This section also places risk of loss upon purchaser if title or possession is transferred prior to closing.

THIS AGREEMENT, made the   day of   , nineteen hundred and
BETWEEN

hereinafter described as the seller, and

hereinafter described as the purchaser,

WITNESSETH, that the seller agrees to sell and convey, and the purchaser agrees to purchase, all that certain plot, piece or parcel of land, with the buildings and improvements thereon erected, situate, lying and being in the

1.   This sale includes all right, title and interest, if any, of the seller in and to any land lying in the bed of any street, road or avenue opened or proposed, in front of or adjoining said premises, to the center line thereof, and all right, title and interest of the seller in and to any award made or to be made in lieu thereof and in and to any unpaid award for damage to said premises by reason of change of grade of any street; and the seller will execute and deliver to the purchaser, on closing of title, or thereafter, on demand, all proper instruments for the conveyance of such title and the assignment and collection of any such award.

Contract of Sale (page 1 of 4)

2. The price is

                                                                        Dollars, payable as follows:

                                                                                Dollars,

on the signing of this contract, by check subject to collection, the receipt of which is hereby acknowledged;

                                                                                Dollars,

in cash or good certified check to the order of the seller on the delivery of the deed as hereinafter provided;

                                                                                Dollars,

by taking title subject to a   mortgage now a lien on said premises in that amount, bearing interest at the rate of   per cent per annum, the principal being due and payable

                                                                                Dollars,

by the purchaser or assigns executing, acknowledging and delivering to the seller a bond or, at the option of the seller, a note secured by a purchase money   mortgage on the above premises, in that amount, payable

                                                        together with interest at the rate of   per cent per annum payable

3. Any bond or note and mortgage to be given hereunder shall be drawn on the standard forms of New York Board of Title Underwriters for mortgages of like lien; and shall be drawn by the attorney for the seller at the expense of the purchaser, who shall also pay the mortgage recording tax and recording fees.

4. If such purchase money mortgage is to be a subordinate mortgage on the premises it shall provide that it shall be subject and subordinate to the lien of the existing   mortgage of $, any extensions thereof and to any mortgage or consolidated mortgage which may be placed on the premises in lieu thereof, and to any extensions thereof provided (a) that the interest rate thereof shall not be greater than   per cent per annum and (b) that, if the principal amount thereof shall exceed the amount of principal owing and unpaid on said existing mortgage at the time of placing such new mortgage or consolidated mortgage, the excess be paid to the holder of such purchase money mortgage in reduction of the principal thereof. Such purchase money mortgage shall also provide that such payment to the holder thereof shall not alter or affect the regular installments, if any, of principal payable thereunder and shall further provide that the holder thereof will, on demand and without charge therefor, execute, acknowledge and deliver any agreement or agreements further to effectuate such subordination.

5. If there be a mortgage on the premises the seller agrees to deliver to the purchaser at the time of delivery of the deed a proper certificate executed and acknowledged by the holder of such mortgage and in form for recording, certifying as to the amount of the unpaid principal and interest thereon, date of maturity thereof and rate of interest thereon, and the seller shall pay the fees for recording such certificate. Should the mortgagee be a bank or other institution as defined in Section 274-a, Real Property Law, the mortgagee may, in lieu of the said certificate, furnish a letter signed by a duly authorized officer, or employee, or agent, containing the information required to be set forth in said certificate. Seller represents that such mortgage will not be in default at or as a result of the delivery of the deed hereunder and that neither said mortgage, nor any modification thereof contains any provision to accelerate payment, or to change any of the other terms or provisions thereof by reason of the delivery of the deed hereunder.

6. Said premises are sold and are to be conveyed subject to:

a. Zoning regulations and ordinances of the city, town or village in which the premises lie which are not violated by existing structures.

b. Consents by the seller or any former owner of premises for the erection of any structure or structures on, under or above any street or streets on which said premises may abut.

c. Encroachments of stoops, areas, cellar steps, trim and cornices, if any, upon any street or highway.

7. All notes or notices of violations of law or municipal ordinances, orders or requirements noted in or issued by the Departments of Housing and Buildings, Fire, Labor, Health, or other State or Municipal Department having jurisdiction, against or affecting the premises at the date hereof, shall be complied with by the seller and the premises shall be conveyed free of the same, and this provision of this contract shall survive delivery of the deed hereunder. The seller shall furnish the purchaser with an authorization to make the necessary searches therefor.

Omit Clause 8 if the property is not in the City of New York. 8. All obligations affecting the premises incurred under the Emergency Repairs provisions of the Administrative Code of the City of New York (Sections 564-18.0, etc.) prior to the delivery of the deed shall be paid and discharged by the seller upon the delivery of the deed. This provision shall survive the delivery of the deed.

Clause 9 is usually omitted if the property is not in the City of New York. 9. If, at the time of the delivery of the deed, the premises or any part thereof shall be or shall have been affected by an assessment or assessments which are or may become payable in annual installments, of which the first installment is then a charge or lien, or has been paid, then for the purposes of this contract all the unpaid installments of any such assessment, including those which are to become due and payable after the delivery of the deed, shall be deemed to be due and payable and to be liens upon the premises affected thereby and shall be paid and discharged by the seller, upon the delivery of the deed.

10. The following are to be apportioned:

(a) Rents as and when collected. (b) Interest on mortgages. (c) Premiums on existing transferable insurance policies or renewals of those expiring prior to the closing. (d) Taxes and sewer rents, if any, on the basis of the fiscal year for which assessed. (e) Water charges on the basis of the calendar year. (f) Fuel, if any.

Contract of Sale (page 2 of 4)

11. If the closing of the title shall occur before the tax rate is fixed, the apportionment of taxes shall be upon the basis of the tax rate for the next preceding year applied to the latest assessed valuation.

12. If there be a water meter on the premises, the seller shall furnish a reading to a date not more than thirty days prior to the time herein set for closing title, and the unfixed meter charge and the unfixed sewer rent, if any, based thereon for the intervening time shall be apportioned on the basis of such last reading.

13. The deed shall be the usual

deed in proper statutory short form for record and shall be duly executed and acknowledged so as to convey to the purchaser the fee simple of the said premises, free of all encumbrances, except as herein stated, and shall contain the covenant required by subdivision 5 of Section 13 of the Lien Law.

If the seller is a corporation, it will deliver to the purchaser at the time of the delivery of the deed hereunder a resolution of its Board of Directors authorizing the sale and delivery of the deed, and a certificate by the Secretary or Assistant Secretary of the corporation certifying such resolution and setting forth facts showing that the conveyance is in conformity with the requirements of Section 909 of the Business Corporation Law. The deed in such case shall contain a recital sufficient to establish compliance with said section.

14. At the closing of the title the seller shall deliver to the purchaser a certified check to the order of the recording officer of the county in which the deed is to be recorded for the amount of the documentary stamps to be affixed thereto in accordance with Article 31 of the Tax Law, and a certified check to the order of the appropriate officer for any other tax payable by reason of the delivery of the deed, and a return, if any be required, duly signed and sworn to by the seller; and the purchaser also agrees to sign and swear to the return and to cause the check and the return to be delivered to the appropriate officer promptly after the closing of title.

Omit Clause 15 if the property is not in the City of New York.

15. In addition, the seller shall at the same time deliver to the purchaser a certified check to the order of the Finance Administrator for the amount of the Real Property Transfer Tax imposed by Title II of Chapter 46 of the Administrative Code of the City of New York and will also deliver to the purchaser the return required by the said statute and the regulations issued pursuant to the authority thereof, duly signed and sworn to by the seller; the purchaser agrees to sign and swear to the return and to cause the check and the return to be delivered to the City Register promptly after the closing of the title.

16. The seller shall give and the purchaser shall accept a title such as
a Member of the New York Board of Title Underwriters, will approve and insure.

17. All sums paid on account of this contract, and the reasonable expenses of the examination of the title to said premises and of the survey, if any, made in connection therewith are hereby made liens on said premises, but such liens shall not continue after default by the purchaser under this contract.

18. All fixtures and articles of personal property attached or appurtenant to or used in connection with said premises are represented to be owned by the seller, free from all liens and encumbrances except as herein stated, and are included in this sale; without limiting the generality of the foregoing, such fixtures and articles of personal property include plumbing, heating, lighting and cooking fixtures, air conditioning fixtures and units, ranges, refrigerators, radio and television aerials, bathroom and kitchen cabinets, mantels, door mirrors, venetian blinds, shades, screens, awnings, storm windows, window boxes, storm doors, mail boxes, weather vanes, flagpoles, pumps, shrubbery and outdoor statuary.

19. The amount of any unpaid taxes, assessments, water charges and sewer rents which the seller is obligated to pay and discharge, with the interest and penalties thereon to a date not less than two business days after the date of closing title, may at the option of the seller be allowed to the purchaser out of the balance of the purchase price, provided official bills therefor with interest and penalties thereon figured to said date are furnished by the seller at the closing.

20. If at the date of closing there may be any other liens or encumbrances which the seller is obligated to pay and discharge, the seller may use any portion of the balance of the purchase price to satisfy the same, provided the seller shall simultaneously either deliver to the purchaser at the closing of title instruments in recordable form and sufficient to satisfy such liens and encumbrances of record together with the cost of recording or filing said instruments; or, provided that the seller has made arrangements with the title company employed by the purchaser in advance of closing, seller will deposit with said company sufficient monies, acceptable to and required by it to insure obtaining and the recording of such satisfactions and the issuance of title insurance to the purchaser either free of any such liens and encumbrances, or with insurance against enforcement of same out of the insured premises. The purchaser, if request is made within a reasonable time prior to the date of closing of title, agrees to provide at the closing separate certified checks as requested, aggregating the amount of the balance of the purchase price, to facilitate the satisfaction of any such liens or encumbrances. The existence of any such taxes or other liens and encumbrances shall not be deemed objections to title if the seller shall comply with the foregoing requirements.

21. If a search of the title discloses judgments, bankruptcies or other returns against other persons having names the same as or similar to that of the seller, the seller will on request deliver to the purchaser an affidavit showing that such judgments, bankruptcies or other returns are not against the seller.

22. In the event that the seller is unable to convey title in accordance with the terms of this contract, the sole liability of the seller will be to refund to the purchaser the amount paid on account of the purchase price and to pay the net cost of examining the title, which cost is not to exceed the charges fixed by the New York Board of Title Underwriters, and the net cost of any survey made in connection therewith incurred by the purchaser, and upon such refund and payment being made this contract shall be considered canceled.

23. The deed shall be delivered upon the receipt of said payments at the office of

at   o'clock on   19

24. The parties agree that   is the broker who brought about this sale and the seller agrees to pay any commission earned thereby.

25. It is understood and agreed that all understandings and agreements heretofore had between the parties hereto are merged in this contract, which alone fully and completely expresses their agreement, and that the same is entered into after full investigation, neither party relying upon any statement or representation, not embodied in this contract, made by the other. The purchaser has inspected the buildings standing on said premises and is thoroughly acquainted with their condition and agrees to take title "as is" and in their present condition and subject to reasonable use, wear, tear, and natural deterioration between the date thereof and the closing of title.

26. This agreement may not be changed or terminated orally. The stipulations aforesaid are to apply to and bind the heirs, executors, administrators, successors and assigns of the respective parties.

27. If two or more persons constitute either the seller or the purchaser, the word "seller" or the word "purchaser" shall be construed as if it read "sellers" or "purchasers" whenever the sense of this agreement so requires.

IN WITNESS WHEREOF, this agreement has been duly executed by the parties hereto.

In presence of:

Contract of Sale (page 3 of 4)

STATE OF NEW YORK, COUNTY OF   **ss:**

On the   day of   19   , before me
personally came

to me known to be the individual   described in and who executed
the foregoing instrument, and acknowledged that
executed the same.

STATE OF NEW YORK, COUNTY OF   **ss:**

On the   day of   19   , before me
personally came

to me known to be the individual   described in and who executed
the foregoing instrument, and acknowledged that
executed the same.

STATE OF NEW YORK, COUNTY OF   **ss:**

On the   day of   19   , before me
personally came
to me known, who, being by me duly sworn, did depose and say
that   he resides at No.

that   he is the
of
                     , the corporation described
in and which executed the foregoing instrument; that   he knows
the seal of said corporation; that the seal affixed to said instrument
is such corporate seal; that it was so affixed by order of the board
of directors of said corporation, and that   he signed h   name
thereto by like order.

STATE OF NEW YORK, COUNTY OF   **ss:**

On the   day of   19   , before me
personally came
to me known and known to me to be a partner in

a partnership, and known to me to be the person described in and
who executed the foregoing instrument in the partnership name, and
said   duly
acknowledged that he executed the foregoing instrument for and
on behalf of said partnership.

Closing of title under the within contract is hereby adjourned to   19   , at
o'clock, at   ; title to be closed and all adjustments to be made
as of   19
Dated,   19
For value received, the within contract and all the right, title and interest of the purchaser thereunder are hereby assigned,
transferred and set over unto
and said assignee hereby assumes all obligations of the purchaser thereunder.
Dated,   19

                                                        Purchaser

                                               Assignee of Purchaser

---

Contract of Sale

TITLE No. _____

                     TO

> **STANDARD FORM OF NEW YORK BOARD OF TITLE UNDERWRITERS**
> *Distributed by*
>
> **CHICAGO TITLE
> INSURANCE COMPANY**

PREMISES

Section
Block
Lot
County or Town
Street Numbered Address

Recorded At Request of

       RETURN BY MAIL TO:

                                         Zip No.

THE OBSERVANCE OF THE FOLLOWING SUGGESTIONS WILL SAVE TIME AND TROUBLE AT THE CLOSING OF THIS TITLE

The **SELLER** should bring with him all insurance policies and duplicates, receipted bills for taxes, assessments and water rates, and any leases, deeds or agreements affecting the property.

When there is a water meter on the premises, he should order it read, and bring bills therefor to the closing.

If there are mortgages on the property, he should promptly arrange to obtain the evidence required under Paragraph 5 of this contract.

He should furnish to the purchaser a full list of tenants, giving the names, rent paid by each, and date to which the rent has been paid.

The **PURCHASER** should be prepared with cash or certified check drawn to the order of the seller. The check may be certified for an approximate amount and cash may be provided for the balance of the settlement.

Contract of Sale (page 4 of 4)

Standard N.Y.B.T.U. Form 8041 *-01 Rev. 11/78   - Contract of Sale

WARNING: NO REPRESENTATION IS MADE THAT THIS FORM OF CONTRACT FOR THE SALE AND PURCHASE OF REAL ESTATE COMPLIES WITH SECTION 5-702 OF THE GENERAL OBLIGATIONS LAW ("PLAIN ENGLISH").

CONSULT YOUR LAWYER BEFORE SIGNING IT.

NOTE: FIRE AND CASUALTY LOSSES: This contract form does not provide for what happens in the event of fire or casualty loss before the title closing. Unless different provision is made in this contract, Section 5-1311 of the General Obligations Law will apply. One part of that law makes a purchaser responsible for fire and casualty loss upon taking of title to or possession of the premises.

Date:
Parties:

CONTRACT OF SALE made as of the   day of   , 19
BETWEEN

Address:

hereinafter called "SELLER", who agrees to sell, and

Address:

hereinafter called "PURCHASER", who agrees to buy:

Premises:

The property, including all buildings and improvements thereon (the "PREMISES") (more fully described on a separate page marked "Schedule A") and also known as:

Street Address.

Tax Map Designation:

Together with SELLER'S interest, if any, in streets and unpaid awards as set forth in Paragraph 9.

Personal
Property:

The sale also includes all fixtures and articles of personal property attached to or used in connection with the PREMISES, unless specifically excluded below. SELLER states that they are paid for and owned by SELLER free and clear of any lien other than the EXISTING MORTGAGE(S). They include but are not limited to plumbing. heating, lighting and cooking fixtures, bathroom and kitchen cabinets. mantels, door mirrors, venetian blinds, shades, screens, awnings, storm windows, window boxes, storm doors, mail boxes, weather vanes, flagpoles, pumps, shrubbery, fencing, outdoor statuary, tool sheds, dishwashers, washing machines. clothes dryers, garbage disposal units. ranges. refrigerators, freezers, air conditioning equipment and installations, and wall to wall carpeting.

Excluded from this sale are:
    Furniture and household furnishings,

Purchase
Price:

1. **a.** The purchase price is $
payable as follows:

On the signing of this contract, by check subject to collection: $

By allowance for the principal amount still unpaid on EXISTING MORTGAGE(S): $

By a Purchase Money Note and Mortgage from PURCHASER (or assigns) to SELLER: $

BALANCE AT CLOSING: $

Contract of Sale—Plain English (page 1 of 5)

b. If this sale is subject to an EXISTING MORTGAGE, the Purchase Money Note and Mortgage will also provide that it will remain subject to the prior lien of any EXISTING MORTGAGE even though the EXISTING MORTGAGE is extended or modified in good faith. The Purchase Money Note and Mortgage shall be drawn on the standard form of New York Board of Title Underwriters by the attorney for SELLER. PURCHASER shall pay the mortgage recording tax, recording fees and the attorney's fee in the amount of $ for its preparation.

c. If any required payments are made on an EXISTING MORTGAGE between now and CLOSING which reduce the unpaid principal amount of an EXISTING MORTGAGE below the amount shown in Paragraph 2, then the balance of the price payable at CLOSING will be adjusted. SELLER agrees that the amount shown in Paragraph 2 is reasonably correct and that only payments required by the EXISTING MORTGAGE will be made.

d. If there is a mortgage escrow account that is maintained for the purpose of paying taxes or insurance, etc., SELLER shall assign it to PURCHASER, if it can be assigned. In that event PURCHASER shall pay the amount in the escrow account to SELLER at CLOSING.

Existing Mortgage(s):

2. The PREMISES will be conveyed subject to the continuing lien of "EXISTING MORTGAGE(S)" as follows:

Mortgage now in the unpaid principal amount of $ and interest at the rate of
                        per cent per year, presently payable   in installments of $
which include principal, interest,
and with any balance of principal being due and payable on

SELLER hereby states that no EXISTING MORTGAGE contains any provision that permits the holder of the mortgage to require its immediate payment in full or to change any other term thereof by reason of the fact of CLOSING.

Acceptable Funds:

3. All money payable under this contract, unless otherwise specified, shall be either:

a. Cash, but not over one thousand ($1,000.00) Dollars,

b. Good certified check of PURCHASER, or official check of any bank, savings bank, trust company, or savings and loan association having a banking office in the State of New York, payable to the order of SELLER, or to the order of PURCHASER and duly endorsed by PURCHASER (if an individual) to the order of SELLER in the presence of SELLER or SELLER'S attorney.

c. Money other than the purchase price, payable to SELLER at CLOSING, may be by check of PURCHASER up to the amount of   ($) dollars, or

d. As otherwise agreed to in writing by SELLER or SELLER'S attorney.

"Subject to" Provisions:

4. The PREMISES are to be transferred subject to:

a. Laws and governmental regulations that affect the use and maintenance of the PREMISES, provided that they are not violated by the buildings and improvements erected on the PREMISES.

b. Consents for the erection of any structures on, under or above any streets on which the PREMISES abut.

c. Encroachments of stoops, areas, cellar steps, trim and cornices, if any, upon any street or highway.

Title Company Approval:

5. SELLER shall give and PURCHASER shall accept such title as
a member of The New York Board of Title Underwriters, will be willing to approve and insure in accordance with their standard form of title policy, subject only to the matters provided for in this contract.

Closing Defined and Form of Deed:

6. "CLOSING" means the settlement of the obligations of SELLER and PURCHASER to each other under this contract, including the payment of the purchase price to SELLER, and the delivery to PURCHASER of a
                                                                deed in proper statutory form for recording
so as to transfer full ownership (fee simple title) to the PREMISES, free of all encumbrances except as herein stated. The deed will contain a covenant by SELLER as required by Section 13 of the Lien Law.

If SELLER is a corporation, it will deliver to PURCHASER at the time of CLOSING (a) a resolution of its Board of Directors authorizing the sale and delivery of the deed, and (b) a certificate by the Secretary or Assistant Secretary of the corporation certifying such resolution and setting forth facts showing that the transfer is in conformity with the requirements of Section 909 of the Business Corporation Law. The deed in such case shall contain a recital sufficient to establish compliance with that section.

Closing Date and Place:

7. CLOSING will take place at the office of

at   o'clock on   , 19

Broker:

8. PURCHASER hereby states that PURCHASER has not dealt with any broker in connection with this sale other than

and SELLER agrees to pay the broker the commission earned thereby (pursuant to separate agreement).

Streets and Assignment of Unpaid Awards:

9. This sale includes all of SELLER'S ownership and rights, if any, in any land lying in the bed of any street or highway, opened or proposed, in front of or adjoining the PREMISES to the center line thereof. It also includes any right of SELLER to any unpaid award by reason of any taking by condemnation and/or for any damage to the PREMISES by reason of change of grade of any street or highway. SELLER will deliver at no additional cost to PURCHASER, at CLOSING, or thereafter, on demand, any documents which PURCHASER may require to collect the award and damages.

Mortgagee's Certificate or Letter as to Existing Mortgage(s):

10. SELLER agrees to deliver to PURCHASER at CLOSING a certificate dated not more than thirty (30) days before CLOSING signed by the holder of each EXISTING MORTGAGE, in form for recording, certifying the amount of the unpaid principal and interest, date of maturity, and rate of interest. SELLER shall pay the fees for recording such certificate. If the holder of a mortgage is a bank or other institution as defined in Section 274-a, Real Property Law, it may, instead of the certificate, furnish an unqualified letter dated not more than thirty (30) days before CLOSING containing the same information. SELLER hereby states that any EXISTING MORTGAGE will not be in default at the time of CLOSING.

Compliance with State and Municipal Department Violations and Orders:

Omit if the Property is Not In the City of New York:

11. a. SELLER will comply with all notes or notices of violations of law or municipal ordinances, orders or requirements noted in or issued by any governmental department having authority as to lands, housing, buildings, fire, health and labor conditions affecting the PREMISES at the date hereof. The PREMISES shall be transferred free of them at CLOSING and this provision shall survive CLOSING. SELLER shall furnish PURCHASER with any authorizations necessary to make the searches that could disclose these matters.

b. All obligations affecting the PREMISES, incurred pursuant to the Administrative Code of the City of New York prior to CLOSING and payable in money shall be discharged by SELLER at CLOSING. This provision shall survive CLOSING.

Installment Assessments:

12. If at the time of CLOSING the PREMISES are affected by an assessment which is or may become payable in annual installments, and the first installment is then a lien, or has been paid, then for the purposes of this contract all the unpaid installments shall be considered due and are to be paid by SELLER at CLOSING.

Apportionments:

13. The following are to be apportioned as of midnight of the day before CLOSING:

(a) Rents as and when collected. (b) Interest on EXISTING MORTGAGE(S). (c) Premiums on existing transferable insurance policies and renewals of those expiring prior to CLOSING. (d) Taxes, water charges and sewer rents. on the basis of the fiscal period for which assessed. (e) Fuel, if any. (f) Vault charges, if any.

If CLOSING shall occur before a new tax rate is fixed, the apportionment of taxes shall be upon the basis of the old tax rate for the preceding period applied to the latest assessed valuation.

Any errors or omissions in computing apportionments at CLOSING shall be corrected. This provision shall survive CLOSING.

Water Meter Readings:

14. If there be a water meter on the PREMISES, SELLER shall furnish a reading to a date not more than thirty (30) days before CLOSING date and the unfixed meter charge and sewer rent, if any, shall be apportioned on the basis of such last reading.

Allowance for Unpaid Taxes, Etc.:

15. SELLER has the option to credit PURCHASER as an adjustment of the purchase price with the amount of any unpaid taxes, assessments, water charges and sewer rents, together with any interest and penalties thereon to a date not less than five(5) business days after CLOSING, provided that official bills therefor computed to said date are produced at CLOSING.

Use of Purchase Price to Pay Encumbrances:

16. If there is anything else affecting the sale which SELLER is obligated to pay and discharge at CLOSING, SELLER may use any portion of the balance of the purchase price to discharge it. As an alternative SELLER may deposit money with the title insurance company employed by PURCHASER and required by it to assure its discharge; but only if the title insurance company will insure PURCHASER'S title clear of the matter or insure against its enforcement out of the PREMISES. Upon request, made within a reasonable time before CLOSING, the PURCHASER agrees to provide separate certified checks as requested to assist in clearing up these matters.

Affidavit as to Judgments, Bankruptcies Etc.:

17. If a title examination discloses judgments, bankruptcies or other returns against persons having names the same as or similar to that of SELLER, SELLER shall deliver a satisfactory detailed affidavit at CLOSING showing that they are not against SELLER.

Deed Transfer and Recording Taxes:

18. At CLOSING, SELLER shall deliver a certified check payable to the order of the appropriate State, City or County officer in the amount of any applicable transfer and/or recording tax payable by reason of the delivery or recording of the deed, together with any required tax return. PURCHASER agrees to duly complete the tax return and to cause the check(s) and the tax return to be delivered to the appropriate officer promptly after CLOSING.

Purchaser's Lien:

19. All money paid on account of this contract, and the reasonable expenses of examination of the title to the PREMISES and of any survey and survey inspection charges are hereby made liens on the PREMISES and collectable out of the PREMISES. Such liens shall not continue after default in performance of the contract by PURCHASER.

Seller's Inability to Convey Limitation of Liability:

20. If SELLER is unable to transfer title to PURCHASER in accordance with this contract, SELLER's sole liability shall be to refund all money paid on account of this contract, plus all charges made for: (i) examining the title, (ii) any appropriate additional searches made in accordance with this contract, and (iii) survey and survey inspection charges. Upon such refund and payment this contract shall be considered cancelled, and neither SELLER nor PURCHASER shall have any further rights against the other.

Condition of Property:

21. PURCHASER has inspected the buildings on the PREMISES and the personal property included in this sale and is thoroughly acquainted with their condition. PURCHASER agrees to purchase them "as is" and in their present condition subject to reasonable use, wear, tear, and natural deterioration between now and CLOSING. PURCHASER shall have the right, after reasonable notice to SELLER, to inspect them before CLOSING.

Entire Agreement:

22. All prior understandings and agreements between SELLER and PURCHASER are merged in this contract. It completely expresses their full agreement. It has been entered into after full investigation, neither party relying upon any statements made by anyone else that is not set forth in this contract.

Contract of Sale—Plain English (page 3 of 5)

Rider* which may be used with Standard NYBTU Form 8041, rev. 11/78

SCHEDULE A
(Description of Premises)

All that certain plot, piece or parcel of land, with the buildings and improvements thereon erected, situate, lying and being in the

Distributed by
**CHICAGO TITLE
INSURANCE COMPANY**

Contract of Sale—Plain English (page 4 of 5)

Changes Must be in Writing: 23. This contract may not be changed or cancelled except in writing. The contract shall also apply to and bind the distributees, heirs, executors, administrators, successors and assigns of the respective parties. Each of the parties hereby authorize their attorneys to agree in writing to any changes in dates and time periods provided for in this contract.

Singular Also Means Plural: 24. Any singular word or term herein shall also be read as in the plural whenever the sense of this contract may require it.

In Presence Of:

Closing of title under the within contract is hereby adjourned to   19   , at
o'clock, at   ; title to be closed and all adjustments to be made
as of   19
Dated,   19
For value received, the within contract and all the right, title and interest of the purchaser thereunder are hereby assigned, transferred and set over unto
and said assignee hereby assumes all obligations of the purchaser thereunder.
Dated,   19

....

Purchaser

....

Assignee of Purchaser

Contract of Sale

Title No.

TO

PREMISES

Section
Block
Lot
County or Town
Street Numbered Address

Recorded At Request of

RETURN BY MAIL TO:

Zip No.

STANDARD FORM OF NEW YORK BOARD OF TITLE UNDERWRITERS
Distributed by

**CHICAGO TITLE
INSURANCE COMPANY**

Contract of Sale—Plain English (page 5 of 5)

Standard N.Y.B.T.U. Form 8003—   —   —Warranty Deed With Full Covenants—Individual or Corporation (single sheet)

CONSULT YOUR LAWYER BEFORE SIGNING THIS INSTRUMENT - THIS INSTRUMENT SHOULD BE USED BY LAWYERS ONLY

THIS INDENTURE, made the   day of   , nineteen hundred and

BETWEEN

party of the first part, and

party of the second part,

WITNESSETH, that the party of the first part, in consideration of ten dollars and other valuable consideration paid by the party of the second part, does hereby grant and release unto the party of the second part, the heirs or successors and assigns of the party of the second part forever,

ALL that certain plot, piece or parcel of land, with the buildings and improvements thereon erected, situate, lying and being in the

TOGETHER with all right, title and interest, if any, of the party of the first part in and to any streets and roads abutting the above described premises to the center lines thereof; TOGETHER with the appurtenances and all the estate and rights of the party of the first part in and to said premises; TO HAVE AND TO HOLD the premises herein granted unto the party of the second part, the heirs or successors and assigns of the party of the second part forever.

AND the party of the first part, in compliance with Section 13 of the Lien Law, covenants that the party of the first part will receive the consideration for this conveyance and will hold the right to receive such consideration as a trust fund to be applied first for the purpose of paying the cost of the improvement and will apply the same first to the payment of the cost of the improvement before using any part of the total of the same for any other purpose.

AND the party of the first part covenants as follows: that said party of the first part is seized of the said premises in fee simple, and has good right to convey the same; that the party of the second part shall quietly enjoy the said premises; that the said premises are free from incumbrances, except as aforesaid; that the party of the first part will execute or procure any further necessary assurance of the title to said premises; and that said party of the first part will forever warrant the title to said premises.

The word "party" shall be construed as if it read "parties" whenever the sense of this indenture so requires.

IN WITNESS WHEREOF, the party of the first part has duly executed this deed the day and year first above written.

IN PRESENCE OF:

Warranty Deed with Full Covenants (page 1 of 2)

STATE OF NEW YORK, COUNTY OF   **SS:**

On the   day of   19   , before me
personally came

to me known to be the individual   described in and who
executed the foregoing instrument, and acknowledged that
executed the same.

STATE OF NEW YORK, COUNTY OF   **SS:**

On the   day of   19   , before me
personally came

to me known to be the individual   described in and who
executed the foregoing instrument, and acknowledged that
executed the same.

STATE OF NEW YORK, COUNTY OF   **SS:**

On the   day of   19   , before me
personally came
to me known, who, being by me duly sworn, did depose and
say that   he resides at No.
                                                          ;
that   he is the
of
                                , the corporation described
in and which executed the foregoing instrument; that   he
knows the seal of said corporation; that the seal affixed
to said instrument is such corporate seal; that it was so
affixed by order of the board of directors of said corporation, and that   he signed h   name thereto by like order.

STATE OF NEW YORK, COUNTY OF   **SS:**

On the   day of   19   , before me
personally came
the subscribing witness to the foregoing instrument, with
whom I am personally acquainted, who, being by me duly
sworn, did depose and say that   he resides at No.
                                                          ;
that   he knows

                                to be the individual
described in and who executed the foregoing instrument;
that   he, said subscribing witness, was present and saw
          execute the same; and that   he, said witness,
at the same time subscribed h   name as witness thereto.

𝔚𝔞𝔯𝔯𝔞𝔫𝔱𝔶 𝔇𝔢𝔢𝔡
WITH FULL COVENANTS

TITLE NO.

TO

| STANDARD FORM OF NEW YORK BOARD OF TITLE UNDERWRITERS |
| *Distributed by* |
| **CHICAGO TITLE INSURANCE COMPANY** |

SECTION

BLOCK

LOT

COUNTY OR TOWN

Recorded at Request of
CHICAGO TITLE INSURANCE COMPANY

Return by Mail to

Zip No.

RESERVE THIS SPACE FOR USE OF RECORDING OFFICE

Warranty Deed with Full Covenants (page 2 of 2)

Standard N.Y.B.T.U. Form 8002–20M   —Bargain and Sale Deed, with Covenants against Grantor's Acts–Individual or Corporation. (single sheet)

CONSULT YOUR LAWYER BEFORE SIGNING THIS INSTRUMENT - THIS INSTRUMENT SHOULD BE USED BY LAWYERS ONLY

THIS INDENTURE, made the   day of   , nineteen hundred and

BETWEEN

party of the first part, and

party of the second part,

WITNESSETH, that the party of the first part, in consideration of ten dollars and other valuable consideration paid by the party of the second part, does hereby grant and release unto the party of the second part, the heirs or successors and assigns of the party of the second part forever,

ALL that certain plot, piece or parcel of land, with the buildings and improvements thereon erected, situate, lying and being in the

TOGETHER with all right, title and interest, if any, of the party of the first part in and to any streets and roads abutting the above described premises to the center lines thereof; TOGETHER with the appurtenances and all the estate and rights of the party of the first part in and to said premises; TO HAVE AND TO HOLD the premises herein granted unto the party of the second part, the heirs or successors and assigns of the party of the second part forever.

AND the party of the first part covenants that the party of the first part has not done or suffered anything whereby the said premises have been encumbered in any way whatever, except as aforesaid.

AND the party of the first part, in compliance with Section 13 of the Lien Law, covenants that the party of the first part will receive the consideration for this conveyance and will hold the right to receive such consideration as a trust fund to be applied first for the purpose of paying the cost of the improvement and will apply the same first to the payment of the cost of the improvement before using any part of the total of the same for any other purpose.

The word "party" shall be construed as if it read "parties" whenever the sense of this indenture so requires.

IN WITNESS WHEREOF, the party of the first part has duly executed this deed the day and year first above written.

IN PRESENCE OF :

Bargain and Sale Deed with Covenant Against Grantor's Acts (page 1 of 2)

STATE OF NEW YORK, COUNTY OF   SS:

On the   day of   19   , before me
personally came

to me known to be the individual   described in and who
executed the foregoing instrument, and acknowledged that
executed the same.

STATE OF NEW YORK, COUNTY OF   SS:

On the   day of   19   , before me
personally came

to me known to be the individual   described in and who
executed the foregoing instrument, and acknowledged that
executed the same.

STATE OF NEW YORK, COUNTY OF   SS:

On the   day of   19   , before me
personally came
to me known, who, being by me duly sworn, did depose and
say that   he resides at No.   ;

that   he is the
of
                              , the corporation described
in and which executed the foregoing instrument; that   he
knows the seal of said corporation; that the seal affixed
to said instrument is such corporate seal; that it was so
affixed by order of the board of directors of said corporation, and that   he signed h   name thereto by like order.

STATE OF NEW YORK, COUNTY OF   SS:

On the   day of   19   , before me
personally came
the subscribing witness to the foregoing instrument, with
whom I am personally acquainted, who, being by me duly
sworn, did depose and say that   he resides at No.
                                                     ;

that   he knows

                                        to be the individual
described in and who executed the foregoing instrument;
that   he, said subscribing witness, was present and saw
            execute the same; and that   he, said witness,
at the same time subscribed h   name as witness thereto.

Bargain and Sale Deed
WITH COVENANT AGAINST GRANTOR'S ACTS

TITLE NO.

SECTION

BLOCK

LOT

COUNTY OR TOWN

TO

Recorded at Request of
CHICAGO TITLE INSURANCE COMPANY

Return by Mail to

STANDARD FORM OF NEW YORK BOARD OF TITLE UNDERWRITERS

Distributed by

CHICAGO TITLE
INSURANCE COMPANY

Zip No.

RESERVE THIS SPACE FOR USE OF RECORDING OFFICE

Bargain and Sale Deed with Covenant Against Grantor's Acts (page 2 of 2)

Standard N.Y.B.T.U. Form 8001 —   Bargain and Sale Deed, without Covenants against Grantor's Acts—Individual or Corporation. (single sheet)

CONSULT YOUR LAWYER BEFORE SIGNING THIS INSTRUMENT - THIS INSTRUMENT SHOULD BE USED BY LAWYERS ONLY

THIS INDENTURE, made the   day of   , nineteen hundred and

BETWEEN

party of the first part, and

party of the second part,

WITNESSETH, that the party of the first part, in consideration of ten dollars and other valuable consideration paid by the party of the second part, does hereby grant and release unto the party of the second part, the heirs or successors and assigns of the party of the second part forever,

ALL that certain plot, piece or parcel of land, with the buildings and improvements thereon erected, situate, lying and being in the

TOGETHER with all right, title and interest, if any, of the party of the first part, in and to any streets and roads abutting the above-described premises to the center lines thereof; TOGETHER with the appurtenances and all the estate and rights of the party of the first part in and to said premises; TO HAVE AND TO HOLD the premises herein granted unto the party of the second part, the heirs or successors and assigns of the party of the second part forever.

AND the party of the first part, in compliance with Section 13 of the Lien Law, covenants that the party of the first part will receive the consideration for this conveyance and will hold the right to receive such consideration as a trust fund to be applied first for the purpose of paying the cost of the improvement and will apply the same first to the payment of the cost of the improvement before using any part of the total of the same for any other purpose.

The word "party" shall be construed as if it read "parties" whenever the sense of this indenture so requires.

IN WITNESS WHEREOF, the party of the first part has duly executed this deed the day and year first above written.

IN PRESENCE OF:

Bargain and Sale Deed without Covenant Against Grantor's Acts (page 1 of 2)

STATE OF NEW YORK, COUNTY OF   SS:

On the   day of   19   , before me
personally came

to me known to be the individual   described in and who
executed the foregoing instrument, and acknowledged that
          executed the same.

STATE OF NEW YORK, COUNTY OF   SS:

On the   day of   19   , before me
personally came

to me known to be the individual   described in and who
executed the foregoing instrument, and acknowledged that
          executed the same.

STATE OF NEW YORK, COUNTY OF   SS:

On the   day of   19   , before me
personally came
to me known, who, being by me duly sworn, did depose and
say that   he resides at No.
                                                                 ;

that   he is the
of
                                            , the corporation described
in and which executed the foregoing instrument; that   he
knows the seal of said corporation; that the seal affixed
to said instrument is such corporate seal; that it was so
affixed by order of the board of directors of said corporation, and that   he signed h   name thereto by like order.

STATE OF NEW YORK, COUNTY OF   SS:

On the   day of   19   , before me
personally came
the subscribing witness to the foregoing instrument, with
whom I am personally acquainted, who, being by me duly
sworn, did depose and say that   he resides at No.
                                                                 ;

that   he knows

                                            to be the individual
described in and who executed the foregoing instrument;
that   he, said subscribing witness, was present and saw
            execute the same; and that   he, said witness,
at the same time subscribed h   name as witness thereto.

Bargain and Sale Deed
WITHOUT COVENANT AGAINST GRANTOR'S ACTS
TITLE NO.

                        TO

| STANDARD FORM OF NEW YORK BOARD OF TITLE UNDERWRITERS |
| Distributed by |
| CHICAGO TITLE |
| INSURANCE COMPANY |

SECTION

BLOCK

LOT

COUNTY OR TOWN

Recorded at Request of
CHICAGO TITLE INSURANCE COMPANY

Return by Mail to

                                        Zip No.

RESERVE THIS SPACE FOR USE OF RECORDING OFFICE

Bargain and Sale Deed without Covenant Against Grantor's Acts (page 2 of 2)

Standard N.Y.B.T.U. Form 8004   Quitclaim Deed—Individual or Corporation (Single Sheet)

CONSULT YOUR LAWYER BEFORE SIGNING THIS INSTRUMENT — THIS INSTRUMENT SHOULD BE USED BY LAWYERS ONLY

THIS INDENTURE, made the   day of   , nineteen hundred and
BETWEEN

party of the first part, and

party of the second part,

WITNESSETH, that the party of the first part, in consideration of ten dollars paid by the party of the second part, does hereby remise, release and quitclaim unto the party of the second part, the heirs or successors and assigns of the party of the second part forever,

ALL that certain plot, piece or parcel of land, with the buildings and improvements thereon erected, situate, lying and being in the

TOGETHER with all right, title and interest, if any, of the party of the first part of, in and to any streets and roads abutting the above-described premises to the center lines thereof; TOGETHER with the appurtenances and all the estate and rights of the party of the first part in and to said premises; TO HAVE AND TO HOLD the premises herein granted unto the party of the second part, the heirs or successors and assigns of the party of the second part forever.

AND the party of the first part, in compliance with Section 13 of the Lien Law, hereby covenants that the party of the first part will receive the consideration for this conveyance and will hold the right to receive such consideration as a trust fund to be applied first for the purpose of paying the cost of the improvement and will apply the same first to the payment of the cost of the improvement before using any part of the total of the same for any other purpose.

The word "party" shall be construed as if it read "parties" whenever the sense of this indenture so requires.

IN WITNESS WHEREOF, the party of the first part has duly executed this deed the day and year first above written.

IN PRESENCE OF:

Quitclaim Deed (page 1 of 2)

STATE OF NEW YORK, COUNTY OF   SS:

On the   day of   19 , before me
personally came

to me known to be the individual described in and who
executed the foregoing instrument, and acknowledged that
    executed the same.

STATE OF NEW YORK, COUNTY OF   SS:

On the   day of   19 , before me
personally came

to me known to be the individual described in and who
executed the foregoing instrument, and acknowledged that
    executed the same.

STATE OF NEW YORK, COUNTY OF   SS:

On the   day of   19 , before me
personally came
to me known, who, being by me duly sworn, did depose and
say that he resides at No.
                  ;
that he is the
of
         , the corporation described
in and which executed the foregoing instrument; that he
knows the seal of said corporation; that the seal affixed
to said instrument is such corporate seal; that it was so
affixed by order of the board of directors of said corporation, and that he signed h name thereto by like order.

STATE OF NEW YORK, COUNTY OF   SS:

On the   day of   '19 , before me
personally came
the subscribing witness to the foregoing instrument, with
whom I am personally acquainted, who, being by me duly
sworn, did depose and say that he resides at No.
                  ;
that he knows

            to be the individual
described in and who executed the foregoing instrument;
that he, said subscribing witness, was present and saw
      execute the same; and that he, said witness,
at the same time subscribed h name as witness thereto.

𝔔uitclaim 𝔇eed

TITLE NO. _____

TO

| STANDARD FORM OF NEW YORK BOARD OF TITLE UNDERWRITERS |
| *Distributed by* |
| **CHICAGO TITLE INSURANCE COMPANY** |

SECTION

BLOCK

LOT

COUNTY OR TOWN

Recorded at Request of
CHICAGO TITLE INSURANCE COMPANY

Return by Mail to

Zip No.

RESERVE THIS SPACE FOR USE OF RECORDING OFFICE

Quitclaim Deed (page 2 of 2)

Standard N. Y. B. T. U. Form 8005-A • 12-70-6M—Executor's Deed—Individual or Corporation (Single Sheet)

CONSULT YOUR LAWYER BEFORE SIGNING THIS INSTRUMENT—THIS INSTRUMENT SHOULD BE USED BY LAWYERS ONLY.

THIS INDENTURE, made the   day of   , nineteen hundred and

BETWEEN

as executor   of   the last will and testament of
                                                                              , late of

who died on the   day of   , nineteen hundred and
party of the first part, and

party of the second part,

WITNESSETH, that whereas letters testamentary were issued to the party of the first part by the Surrogate's
Court,   County, New York, on   and by virtue
of the power and authority given in and by said last will and testament, and/or by Article 11 of the Estates,
Powers and Trusts Law, and in consideration of
                                                                              dollars,
                              paid by the party of the second part, does hereby grant and
release unto the party of the second part, the distributees or successors and assigns of the party of the second
part forever,

ALL that certain plot, piece or parcel of land, with the buildings and improvements thereon erected, situate,
lying and being in the

TOGETHER with all right, title and interest, if any, of the party of the first part in and to any streets and
roads abutting the above described premises to the center lines thereof; TOGETHER with the appurtenances,
and also all the estate which the said decedent had at the time of decedent's death in said premises, and also
the estate therein, which the party of the first part has or has power to convey or dispose of, whether individually, or by virtue of said will or otherwise; TO HAVE AND TO HOLD the premises herein granted unto
the party of the second part, the distributees or successors and assigns of the party of the second part forever.

AND the party of the first part covenants that the party of the first part has not done or suffered anything
whereby the said premises have been incumbered in any way whatever, except as aforesaid.
Subject to the trust fund provisions of section thirteen of the Lien Law.
The word "party" shall be construed as if it read "parties" whenever the sense of this indenture so requires.

IN WITNESS WHEREOF, the party of the first part has duly executed this deed the day and year first above
written.

IN PRESENCE OF:

Executor's Deed (page 1 of 2)

STATE OF NEW YORK, COUNTY OF   **ss:**

On the   day of   19   , before me
personally came

to me known to be the individual   described in and who
executed the foregoing instrument, and acknowledged that
executed the same.

STATE OF NEW YORK, COUNTY OF   **ss:**

On the   day of   19   , before me
personally came

to me known to be the individual   described in and who
executed the foregoing instrument, and acknowledged that
executed the same.

STATE OF NEW YORK, COUNTY OF   **ss:**

On the   day of   19   , before me
personally came
to me known, who, being by me duly sworn, did depose and
say that   he resides at No.
                                                                            ;
that   he is the
of
                                         , the corporation described
in and which executed the foregoing instrument; that   he
knows the seal of said corporation; that the seal affixed
to said instrument is such corporate seal; that it was so
affixed by order of the board of directors of said corporation, and that   he signed h   name thereto by like order.

STATE OF NEW YORK, COUNTY OF   **ss:**

On the   day of   19   , before me
personally came
the subscribing witness to the foregoing instrument, with
whom I am personally acquainted, who, being by me duly
sworn, did depose and say that   he resides at No.
                                                                            ;
that   he knows
                                                      to be the individual
described in and who executed the foregoing instrument;
that   he, said subscribing witness, was present and saw
                             execute the same; and that   he, said witness,
at the same time subscribed h   name as witness thereto.

Executor's Deed

TITLE NO. _____

                          TO

| SECTION |
| BLOCK |
| LOT |
| COUNTY OR TOWN |
| STREET ADDRESS |

STANDARD FORM OF NEW YORK BOARD OF TITLE UNDERWRITERS
Distributed by
**CHICAGO TITLE
INSURANCE COMPANY**

Recorded at Request of
CHICAGO TITLE INSURANCE COMPANY

Return by Mail to

                                                              Zip No.

REVERSE THIS SPACE FOR USE OF RECORDING OFFICE

Executor's Deed (page 2 of 2)

Standard N.Y.B.T.U. Form 8011-**10M**   Mortgage Note. Individual or Corporation. (Straight or Instalment.)
CONSULT YOUR LAWYER BEFORE SIGNING THIS INSTRUMENT — THIS INSTRUMENT SHOULD BE USED BY LAWYERS ONLY

MORTGAGE NOTE

$ New York,   19

FOR VALUE RECEIVED,

promise   to pay to

or order, at

or at such other place as may be designated in writing by the holder of this note, the principal sum of

Dollars on

with interest thereon to be computed from the date hereof, at the rate of   per centum per annum
and to be paid on the   day of   19   , next ensuing and

IT IS HEREBY EXPRESSLY AGREED, that the said principal sum secured by this note shall become due at the option of the holder thereof on the happening of any default or event by which, under the terms of the mortgage securing this note, said principal sum may or shall become due and payable; also, that all of the covenants, conditions and agreements contained in said mortgage are hereby made part of this instrument.

Presentment for payment, notice of dishonor, protest and notice of protest are hereby waived.

This note is secured by a mortgage made by the maker to the payee of even date herewith, on property situate in the

This note may not be changed or terminated orally.

_____

Mortgage Note (page 1 of 2)

STATE OF NEW YORK, COUNTY OF   **SS:**

On the   day of   19 , before me
personally came

to me known to be the individual   described in and who
executed the foregoing instrument, and acknowledged that
executed the same.

STATE OF NEW YORK, COUNTY OF   **SS:**

On the   day of   19 , before me
personally came

to me known to be the individual   described in and who
executed the foregoing instrument, and acknowledged that
executed the same.

STATE OF NEW YORK, COUNTY OF   **SS:**

On the   day of   19 , before me
personally came
to me known, who, being by me duly sworn, did depose and
say that   he resides at No.   ;

that   he is the
of
                    , the corporation described
in and which executed the foregoing instrument; that   he
knows the seal of said corporation; that the seal affixed
to said instrument is such corporate seal; that it was so
affixed by order of the board of directors of said corporation, and that   he signed h   name thereto by like order

STATE OF NEW YORK, COUNTY OF   **SS:**

On the   day of   19 , before me
personally came
the subscribing witness to the foregoing instrument, with
whom I am personally acquainted, who, being by me duly
sworn, did depose and say that   he resides at No.   ;

that   he knows

                     to be the individual
described in and who executed the foregoing instrument;
that   he, said subscribing witness, was present and saw
           execute the same; and that   he, said witness,
at the same time subscribed h   name as witness thereto.

Mortgage Note

TITLE NO.

WITH

SECTION

BLOCK

LOT

COUNTY OR TOWN

Recorded at Request of
CHICAGO TITLE INSURANCE COMPANY

Return by Mail to

Zip No.

STANDARD FORM OF NEW YORK BOARD OF TITLE UNDERWRITERS

Distributed by

**CHICAGO TITLE
INSURANCE COMPANY**

Mortgage Note (page 2 of 2)

Standard N.Y.B.T.U. Form 8011—20M— First Mortgage—Individual or Corporation.

CONSULT YOUR LAWYER BEFORE SIGNING THIS INSTRUMENT - THIS INSTRUMENT SHOULD BE USED BY LAWYERS ONLY

THIS MORTGAGE, made the   day of   , nineteen hundred and

BETWEEN

, the mortgagor,

and

the mortgagee,

WITNESSETH, that to secure the payment of an indebtedness in the sum of

dollars,

lawful money of the United States, to be paid

with interest thereon to be computed from the date hereof, at the rate of   per centum
per annum, and to be paid on the   day of   19   , next ensuing and
                        thereafter,

according to a certain bond,
note or obligation bearing even date herewith, the mortgagor hereby mortgages to the mortgagee

ALL that certain plot, piece or parcel of land, with the buildings and improvements thereon erected, situate,
lying and being in the

Mortgage (page 1 of 4)

TOGETHER with all right, title and interest of the mortgagor in and to the land lying in the streets and roads in front of and adjoining said premises;

TOGETHER with all fixtures, chattels and articles of personal property now or hereafter attached to or used in connection with said premises, including but not limited to furnaces, boilers, oil burners, radiators and piping, coal stokers, plumbing and bathroom fixtures, refrigeration, air conditioning and sprinkler systems, wash tubs, sinks, gas and electric fixtures, stoves, ranges, awnings, screens, window shades, elevators, motors, dynamos, refrigerators, kitchen cabinets, incinerators, plants and shrubbery and all other equipment and machinery, appliances, fittings, and fixtures of every kind in or used in the operation of the buildings standing on said premises, together with any and all replacements thereof and additions thereto;

TOGETHER with all awards heretofore and hereafter made to the mortgagor for taking by eminent domain the whole or any part of said premises or any easement therein, including any awards for changes of grade of streets, which said awards are hereby assigned to the mortgagee, who is hereby authorized to collect and receive the proceeds of such awards and to give proper receipts and acquittances therefor, and to apply the same toward the payment of the mortgage debt, notwithstanding the fact that the amount owing thereon may not then be due and payable; and the said mortgagor hereby agrees, upon request, to make, execute and deliver any and all assignments and other instruments sufficient for the purpose of assigning said awards to the mortgagee, free, clear and discharged of any encumbrances of any kind or nature whatsoever.

AND the mortgagor covenants with the mortgagee as follows:

1. That the mortgagor will pay the indebtedness as hereinbefore provided.

2. That the mortgagor will keep the buildings on the premises insured against loss by fire for the benefit of the mortgagee; that he will assign and deliver the policies to the mortgagee; and that he will reimburse the mortgagee for any premiums paid for insurance made by the mortgagee on the mortgagor's default in so insuring the buildings or in so assigning and delivering the policies.

3. That no building on the premises shall be altered, removed or demolished without the consent of the mortgagee.

4. That the whole of said principal sum and interest shall become due at the option of the mortgagee: after default in the payment of any instalment of principal or of interest for fifteen days; or after default in the payment of any tax, water rate, sewer rent or assessment for thirty days after notice and demand; or after default after notice and demand either in assigning and delivering the policies insuring the buildings against loss by fire or in reimbursing the mortgagee for premiums paid on such insurance, as hereinbefore provided; or after default upon request in furnishing a statement of the amount due on the mortgage and whether any offsets or defenses exist against the mortgage debt, as hereinafter provided. An assessment which has been made payable in instalments at the application of the mortgagor or lessee of the premises shall nevertheless, for the purpose of this paragraph, be deemed due and payable in its entirety on the day the first instalment becomes due or payable or a lien.

5. That the holder of this mortgage, in any action to foreclose it, shall be entitled to the appointment of a receiver.

6. That the mortgagor will pay all taxes, assessments, sewer rents or water rates, and in default thereof, the mortgagee may pay the same.

7. That the mortgagor within five days upon request in person or within ten days upon request by mail will furnish a written statement duly acknowledged of the amount due on this mortgage and whether any offsets or defenses exist against the mortgage debt.

8. That notice and demand or request may be in writing and may be served in person or by mail.

9. That the mortgagor warrants the title to the premises.

10. That the fire insurance policies required by paragraph No. 2 above shall contain the usual extended coverage endorsement; that in addition thereto the mortgagor, within thirty days after notice and demand, will keep the premises insured against war risk and any other hazard that may reasonably be required by the mortgagee. All of the provisions of paragraphs No. 2 and No. 4 above relating to fire insurance and the provisions of Section 254 of the Real Property Law construing the same shall apply to the additional insurance required by this paragraph.

11. That in case of a foreclosure sale, said premises, or so much thereof as may be affected by this mortgage, may be sold in one parcel.

12. That if any action or proceeding be commenced (except an action to foreclose this mortgage or to collect the debt secured thereby), to which action or proceeding the mortgagee is made a party, or in which it becomes necessary to defend or uphold the lien of this mortgage, all sums paid by the mortgagee for the expense of any litigation to prosecute or defend the rights and lien created by this mortgage (including reasonable counsel fees), shall be paid by the mortgagor, together with interest thereon at the rate of six per cent. per annum, and any such sum and the interest thereon shall be a lien on said premises, prior to any right, or title to, interest in or claim upon said premises attaching or accruing subsequent to the lien of this mortgage, and shall be deemed to be secured by this mortgage. In any action or proceeding to foreclose this mortgage, or to recover or collect the debt secured thereby, the provisions of law respecting the recovering of costs, disbursements and allowances shall prevail unaffected by this covenant.

Mortgage (page 2 of 4)

13.   That the mortgagor hereby assigns to the mortgagee the rents, issues and profits of the premises as further security for the payment of said indebtedness, and the mortgagor grants to the mortgagee the right to enter upon and take possession of the premises for the purpose of collecting the same and to let the premises or any part thereof, and to apply the rents, issues and profits, after payment of all necessary charges and expenses, on account of said indebtedness. This assignment and grant shall continue in effect until this mortgage is paid. The mortgagee hereby waives the right to enter upon and take possession of said premises for the purpose of collecting said rents, issues and profits, and the mortgagor shall be entitled to collect and receive said rents, issues and profits until default under any of the covenants, conditions or agreements contained in this mortgage, and agrees to use such rents, issues and profits in payment of principal and interest becoming due on this mortgage and in payment of taxes, assessments, sewer rents, water rates and carrying charges becoming due against said premises, but such right of the mortgagor may be revoked by the mortgagee upon any default, on five days' written notice. The mortgagor will not, without the written consent of the mortgagee, receive or collect rent from any tenant of said premises or any part thereof for a period of more than one month in advance, and in the event of any default under this mortgage will pay monthly in advance to the mortgagee, or to any receiver appointed to collect said rents, issues and profits, the fair and reasonable rental value for the use and occupation of said premises or of such part thereof as may be in the possession of the mortgagor, and upon default in any such payment will vacate and surrender the possession of said premises to the mortgagee or to such receiver, and in default thereof may be evicted by summary proceedings.

14.   That the whole of said principal sum and the interest shall become due at the option of the mortgagee: (a) after failure to exhibit to the mortgagee, within ten days after demand, receipts showing payment of all taxes, water rates, sewer rents and assessments; or (b) after the actual or threatened alteration, demolition or removal of any building on the premises without the written consent of the mortgagee; or (c) after the assignment of the rents of the premises or any part thereof without the written consent of the mortgagee; or (d) if the buildings on said premises are not maintained in reasonably good repair; or (e) after failure to comply with any requirement or order or notice of violation of law or ordinance issued by any governmental department claiming jurisdiction over the premises within three months from the issuance thereof; or (f) if on application of the mortgagee two or more fire insurance companies lawfully doing business in the State of New York refuse to issue policies insuring the buildings on the premises; or (g) in the event of the removal, demolition or destruction in whole or in part of any of the fixtures, chattels or articles of personal property covered hereby, unless the same are promptly replaced by similar fixtures, chattels and articles of personal property at least equal in quality and condition to those replaced, free from chattel mortgages or other encumbrances thereon and free from any reservation of title thereto; or (h) after thirty days' notice to the mortgagor, in the event of the passage of any law deducting from the value of land for the purpose of taxation any lien thereon, or changing in any way the taxation of mortgages or debts secured thereby for state or local purposes; or (i) if the mortgagor fails to keep, observe and perform any of the other covenants, conditions or agreements contained in this mortgage.

15.   That the mortgagor will, in compliance with Section 13 of the Lien Law, receive the advances secured hereby and will hold the right to receive such advances as a trust fund to be applied first for the purpose of paying the cost of the improvement and will apply the same first to the payment of the cost of the improvement before using any part of the total of the same for any other purpose.

16.   That the execution of this mortgage has been duly authorized by the board of directors of the mortgagor.

This mortgage may not be changed or terminated orally. The covenants contained in this mortgage shall run with the land and bind the mortgagor, the heirs, personal representatives, successors and assigns of the mortgagor and all subsequent owners, encumbrancers, tenants and subtenants of the premises, and shall enure to the benefit of the mortgagee, the personal representatives, successors and assigns of the mortgagee and all subsequent holders of this mortgage. The word "mortgagor" shall be construed as if it read "mortgagors" and the word "mortgagee" shall be construed as if it read "mortgagees" whenever the sense of this mortgage so requires.

IN WITNESS WHEREOF, this mortgage has been duly executed by the mortgagor.

IN PRESENCE OF:

Mortgage (page 3 of 4)

STATE OF NEW YORK, COUNTY OF   SS: | **STATE OF NEW YORK, COUNTY OF**   SS:

On the   day of   19   , before me | On the   day of   19   , before me
personally came | personally came

to me known to be the individual   described in and who | to me known to be the individual   described in and who
executed the foregoing instrument, and acknowledged that | executed the foregoing instrument, and acknowledged that
    executed the same. | executed the same.

STATE OF NEW YORK, COUNTY OF   SS: | **STATE OF NEW YORK, COUNTY OF**   SS:

On the   day of   19   , before me | On the   day of   19   , before me
personally came | personally came
to me known, who, being by me duly sworn, did depose and | the subscribing witness to the foregoing instrument, with
say that   he resides at No. | whom I am personally acquainted, who, being by me duly
                                                      ; | sworn, did depose and say that   he resides at No.
that   he is the | ;
of | that   he knows
                         , the corporation described |
in and which executed the foregoing instrument; that   he | to be the individual
knows the seal of said corporation; that the seal affixed | described in and who executed the foregoing instrument;
to said instrument is such corporate seal; that it was so | that   he, said subscribing witness, was present and saw
affixed by order of the board of directors of said corpora-| execute the same; and that   he, said witness,
tion, and that   he signed h   name thereto by like order.| at the same time subscribed h   name as witness thereto.

𝔐𝔬𝔯𝔱𝔤𝔞𝔤𝔢

TITLE NO.   **SECTION**

                                                           BLOCK

                                                           LOT

                    TO   **COUNTY OR TOWN**

                                                           Recorded at Request of
                                                           CHICAGO TITLE INSURANCE COMPANY

STANDARD FORM OF NEW YORK BOARD OF TITLE UNDERWRITERS   Return by Mail to
Distributed by
**CHICAGO TITLE
INSURANCE COMPANY**

                                                           Zip No.

RESERVE THIS SPACE FOR USE OF RECORDING OFFICE

Mortgage (page 4 of 4)

Standard N.Y.B.T.U. Form 8035—   Satisfaction of Mortgage—Individual or Corporation

CONSULT YOUR LAWYER BEFORE SIGNING THIS INSTRUMENT · THIS INSTRUMENT SHOULD BE USED BY LAWYERS ONLY

KNOW ALL MEN BY THESE PRESENTS,

Insert residence, if in-dividual or principal office, if corporation, giving street and street number.

that

DO   HEREBY CERTIFY that the following Mortgage   **IS PAID,** and do   hereby consent that the same be discharged of record.

Mortgage dated the   day of   , 19   , made by

to

in the principal sum of \$ and recorded on the   day of
19   , in Liber   of Section   of Mortgages, page   , in the office of the
    of the

Insert "further" when required.

which mortgage   has not been   assigned of record

Dated the   day of   , 19

IN PRESENCE OF:

Section 321 of the *Real Property Law* expressly provides who must execute the certificate of discharge in specific cases and also provides, among other things, that (1) no certificate shall purport to discharge more than one mortgage, (except that mortgages affected by instruments of consolidation, spreader, modification or correction may be included in one certificate if the instruments are set forth in detail in separate paragraphs); (2) if the mortgage has been assigned, in whole or in part, the certificate shall set forth; (a) the date of each assignment in the chain of title of the person or persons signing the certificate, (b) the names of the assignor and assignee, (c) the interest assigned, and (d) if the assignment has been recorded, the book and page where it has been recorded or the serial number of such record, or (e) if the assignment is being recorded simultaneously with the certificate of discharge, the certificate of discharge shall so state, and (f) if the mortgage has not been assigned of record, the certificate shall so state; (3) if the mortgage is held by any fiduciary, including an executor or administrator, the certificate of discharge shall recite the name of the court and the venue of the proceedings in which his appointment was made or in which the order or decree vesting him with such title or authority was entered.

Satisfaction of Mortgage (page 1 of 2)

STATE OF NEW YORK, COUNTY OF   SS:

On the   day of   19   , before me
personally came

to me known to be the individual   described in and who
executed the foregoing instrument, and acknowledged that
executed the same.

STATE OF NEW YORK, COUNTY OF   SS:

On the   day of   19   , before me
personally came

to me known to be the individual   described in and who
executed the foregoing instrument, and acknowledged that
executed the same.

STATE OF NEW YORK, COUNTY OF   SS:

On the   day of   19   , before me
personally came
to me known, who, being by me duly sworn, did depose and
say that   he resides at No.
                                                            ;
that   he is the
of
                                  , the corporation described
in and which executed the foregoing instrument; that   he
knows the seal of said corporation; that the seal affixed
to said instrument is such corporate seal; that it was so
affixed by order of the board of directors of said corporation, and that   he signed h   name thereto by like order.

STATE OF NEW YORK, COUNTY OF   SS:

On the   day of   19   , before me
personally came
the subscribing witness to the foregoing instrument, with
whom I am personally acquainted, who, being by me duly
sworn, did depose and say that   he resides at No.
                                                            ;
that   he knows

                                         to be the individual
described in and who executed the foregoing instrument;
that   he, said subscribing witness, was present and saw
             execute the same; and that   he, said witness,
at the same time subscribed h   name as witness thereto.

𝕾𝖆𝖙𝖎𝖘𝖋𝖆𝖈𝖙𝖎𝖔𝖓 𝖔𝖋 𝕸𝖔𝖗𝖙𝖌𝖆𝖌𝖊

TITLE NO.

SECTION

BLOCK

LOT

COUNTY OR TOWN

TO

Recorded at Request of
CHICAGO TITLE INSURANCE COMPANY

Return by Mail to

| STANDARD FORM OF NEW YORK BOARD OF TITLE UNDERWRITERS |
| *Distributed by* |
| **CHICAGO TITLE INSURANCE COMPANY** |

Zip No.

RESERVE THIS SPACE FOR USE OF RECORDING OFFICE

Satisfaction of Mortgage (page 2 of 2)

The City of New York DEPARTMENT OF HOUSING PRESERVATION & DEVELOPMENT OFFICE OF RENT AND HOUSING MAINTENANCE

Princ. House No.	Street Name	Boro

MULTIPLE DWELLING REGISTRATION APPLICATION

Registration is Due —

FOR DEPARTMENT USE ONLY

RHM FORM 513 (Rev. 10/81)   — DO NOT SEPARATE CARDS — FOLD HERE FOR RETURN —   Card 1A

RHM FORM 513 (Rev. 10/81)   **MULTIPLE DWELLING REGISTRATION APPLICATION**   Card 2A

Princ. House No.	Street Name	Street Code	Boro	SC	Reg. No.	Expiration Date	Amt. Due ▼

Have You Registered This Building Before? Yes ☐ No ☐	This Registration By: Owner ☐ Lessee ☐	Redesignation of Managing Agent? Yes ☐ No ☐
OWNER NAME		Check One: Partnership ☐ Corp. ☐ Indiv. ☐ Other ☐

	STREET	TOWN/COUNTY STATE	ZIP	Area Code	Tele. No.
BUS. ADDRESS: HOUSE NO.					
HOME ADDRESS: HOUSE NO.	STREET	TOWN/COUNTY STATE	ZIP	Area Code	Tele. No.

MANAGING AGENT (INDIVIDUAL ONLY, MUST LIVE IN OR HAVE OFFICE IN NEW YORK CITY)

NAME — Age 21 or Over

	STREET	TOWN/COUNTY STATE	ZIP	Area Code	Tele. No
BUS. ADDRESS: HOUSE NO.					
HOME ADDRESS: HOUSE NO.	STREET	TOWN/COUNTY STATE	ZIP	Area Code	Tele. No.

I CONSENT TO THE DESIGNATION AS MANAGING AGENT OF THE ABOVE PREMISES

SIGNATURE OF MANAGING AGENT	DATE / /

Multiple Dwelling Registration Application (page 1 of 2)

RHM FORM 513
(Rev. 10/81)

N.Y.C. H.P.D. Office of Rent and Housing Maintenance Division of Code Enforcement   Card 1B

MULTIPLE DWELLING EMERGENCY CONFIDENTIAL 24 HOUR TELEPHONE NUMBER

INSERT
24 Hr. Tel. No.(s) ➡️

Area Code	Local Number

Area Code	Local Number

Multiple dwelling owner/managing agent must file with the Department a confidential telephone number where they can reasonably be expected to be reached at all times for emergencies. Phone must be within 50 mile radius of New York City limits.

Failure to produce receipt is prima facie evidence of a failure to comply with registration.

INSURANCE – Fire Casualty and/or Liability ☐ YES   ☐ NO   (If yes, complete the following)

NAME OF CO. (FIRE CASUALTY)	POLICY NO.

ADDRESS: HOUSE NO.	STREET	TOWN/COUNTY STATE	ZIP	EXPIR. DATE / /

NAME OF CO. (LIABILITY)	POLICY NO.

ADDRESS: HOUSE NO.	STREET	TOWN/COUNTY STATE	ZIP	EXPIR. DATE / /

RHM FORM 513 (Rev. 10/81)   **OFFICERS OF CORPORATION FILING THIS REGISTRATION**   Card 2B

NAME	ADDRESS		PHONE NO.
President	Bus.		
	Home		
Vice-president	Bus.		
	Home		
Secretary	Bus.		
	Home		

TO OWNER REGISTERING: If this whole building is leased, give Lessee's Name and Address (If corporation, give Corporation's Name and Address)

Lessee (**Lessee must also file separately**)

Lessee - Receiver

BUS. ADDRESS: HOUSE NO.	STREET	TOWN/COUNTY STATE	ZIP	Area Code	Tele. No.

HOME ADDRESS: HOUSE NO.	STREET	TOWN/COUNTY STATE	ZIP	Area Code	Tele. No.

I CERTIFY THAT ALL STATEMENTS MADE HEREIN ARE TRUE AND CORRECT.

Date / /

Personal signature of owner, officer of corporation, or lessee of entire building

False statements are punishable under Section D26–40.11, Housing Maintenance Code.

Multiple Dwelling Registration Application (page 2 of 2)

DEPARTMENT OF HOUSING PRESERVATION AND DEVELOPMENT

AFFIDAVIT IN LIEU OF

REGISTRATION STATEMENT

COUNTY OF   )

                    ss.:

STATE OF NEW YORK)

_____, being duly sworn, deposes and says:

1. I am personally familiar with the real property known by the street address of (insert street address):_____

_____Block_____,Lot_____,

and make this affidavit as (describe capacity in which affidavit is made)_____

_____in connection with a deed/lease/memorandum of lease(delete inapplicable description) which transfers an interest in the above real property, is

dated_____, and is between (insert name)_____,

as (insert capacity)_____ and (insert name)_____

_____as (insert capacity)_____.

2. The statements made in this affidavit are true of my own knowledge and I submit this affidavit in order that this Instrument be accepted for recording without being accompanied by a registration statement, as such is defined by article forty-one of title D of chapter twenty-six of the Administrative Code of the City of New York.

3. Exemption from registration is claimed because the Instrument does not affect an entire multiple dwelling as such term is defined by Section D26-1.07(a)(7) of the Administrative Code of the City of New York and Section 4(7) of the Multiple Dwelling Law. The Instrument does not affect a dwelling which is or is to be occupied as the residence of three or more families because it affects the following (check applicable item):

      ( ) commercial building

      ( ) one or two-family dwelling

      ( ) condominium unit in a multiple dwelling

      ( )cooperative corporation shares relating to a single residential unit in a multiple dwelling

      ( ) lease of commercial space in a multiple dwelling

      ( ) mineral, gas, water, air or other similar rights not affecting a multiple dwelling

      ( ) vacant land

4. I am aware that this affidavit is required by law to be submitted in order that the Instrument be recorded or accepted for record without being accompanied by registration statements. I am aware that false statements made in this affidavit may be punishable as a felony or misdemeanor under Article 210 of the Penal Law or as an offense under Section 1151-9.0 of the Administrative Code of the State of New York.

Sworn To Before Me

this_____day of_____,198___

_____

            Notary Public

_____

                 Signature

Address:

Telephone No.(   )

Affidavit as to Non-Multiple Dwelling

Schedule of Property Recording Fees and Taxes for New York City

(January 1, 1984)

Real Property Fees

1. Recording Instruments:
   a. $10.00 plus $1.00 per page or part thereof ($12.00 minimum).
   b. Where the page exceeds 9″ × 14″ and the page is set up in double columns—$10.00 per page or part thereof.
   c. Where the point size is less than 8 points (ordinary newsprint)—$10.00 plus $2.00 per page or part thereof.
   d. Additional Blocks—$2.00 for each block in excess of one.

2. Assignments of Mortgage—$10.00 plus $1.00 per page or part thereof. An additional $2.00 is charged for every mortgage recited in an Assignment of Mortgage in excess of one.

3. Satisfactions of Mortgage—$10.00 plus $1.00 per page or part thereof. However, if the satisfaction involves a consolidated mortgage, the total recording charge must be multiplied by the number of mortgages included in the consolidated mortgage. (A spreader agreement is treated as a separate mortgage.)

4. Certificate of Record—$2.00 each.

NOTE: All instruments to be recorded must be clear and legible. It is suggested that signatures and notarial stamps be in black ink and capable of reproduction on microfilm. Authentication certificates, riders and legal backs are considered extra pages.

Uniform Commercial Code Fees

	On Standard Form (Approved by New York Secretary of State)	Other Form
1. Financing Statement (UCC-1)	$3.00	$4.50
2. Each additional debtor	.75	.75
3. Indexing against real property—per block	2.00	2.00
4. Fixture filings	2.50	2.50
—each additional block	2.00	2.00
5. Continuation, Release, Assignment	3.00	4.50
6. Each additional debtor	.75	.75
7. Terminations (UCC-3)	1.50	3.00
8. Personal Property Search (UCC-11)	4.50	7.50
9. Issuing a separate receipt for UCC filing—$1.00 each		
10. Copy Request (UCC-11)	1.50 per page	1.50 per page

New York State Real Property Transfer Gains Tax Fees

For filing New York State Gains Tax forms TP-582, TP-584, TP-585 or supplements thereto—$1.00 per form.

For information regarding the New York State Real Property Transfer Gains Tax, contact the New York State Department of Taxation and Finance at (518) 457-3496.

Bad Check Fee

A fee of $10.00 will be imposed for processing checks in payment of any tax, recording fee or other charge which are returned unpaid by a bank for any reason other than verified bank error.

Taxes

1. Mortgage Tax:
   A. Real property securing a principal debt or obligation of less than $500,000: $1.50 for each $100.00 or major fraction thereof of principal amount secured.* Where property covered is a 1 or 2 family dwelling, individual cooperative apartment or individual residential condominium unit (and mortgage so recites): $1.25 for each $100.00 on the first $10,000.00 of principal debt.
   B. Where the real property is a 1, 2 or 3 family house, individual cooperative apartment or individual residential condominium unit securing a principal debt or obligation of $500,000 or more: $1.625 for each $100.00 or major fraction thereof of principal amount secured.* Where property covered is a 1 or 2 family dwelling, individual cooperative apartment or individual residential condominium unit (and mortgage so recites): $1.375 for each $100.00 on the first $10,000.00 of principal debt.
   C. All other real property: $2.25 for each $100.00 or major fraction thereof of principal amount secured.*
   *If an exemption is claimed, the appropriate tax affidavit must be filed in DUPLICATE ORIGINAL. No fee for filing affidavits in New York City.

2. New York State Real Property Transfer Tax (State Stamp Tax): $2.00 for each $500.00 or any fraction thereof of consideration paid, if said consideration is in excess of $100.00. Deductions for continuing liens may be taken where the consideration is less than $500,000. Deductions for continuing liens where consideration is $500,000 or more may *only* be taken in the case of a 1, 2, or 3 family house or individual condominium unit.

3. New York City Real Property Transfer Tax:
   A. 1% of the consideration with respect to conveyances made on or after July 1, 1982 of a 1, 2 or 3 family house or individual residential condominium unit.
   B. 1% of the consideration with respect to other conveyances made on or after July 1, 1982 where the consideration is less than $500,000 (other than grants, assignments or surrenders of leasehold interests in real property taxable as hereafter provided).
   C. (i) 1% of the consideration with respect to a grant, assignment or surrender, made on or after July 1, 1982, of a leasehold interest in a 1, 2, or 3 family house or an individual dwelling unit, in a dwelling which is to be occupied or is ocupied as the residence or home of four or more families living independently of each other,
   (ii) 1% of the consideration with respect to grants, assignments or surrenders of leasehold interests in real property made on or after July 1, 1982, where the consideration is less than $500,000, or
   (iii) 2% of the consideration with respect to grants, assignments or surrenders of leasehold interests in real property made on or after July 1, 1982 where the consideration is $500,000 or more,
   (iv) provided, however, that for purpose of subparagraphs (i), (ii) and (iii) of this paragraph (C.), the amount subject to tax in the case of a grant of a leasehold interest shall be only such amount as is not considered rent for purposes of the Commercial Rent Tax.
   D. 2% of the consideration with respect to all other conveyances made on or after July 1, 1982.
   The tax is applicable to any conveyance or transfer of real property or interest therein where the real property is located in New York City, regardless of where transactions, negotiations, transfer of deeds or other actions with regard to the transfer or conveyance take place. Tax does not apply where consideration is $25,000 or less.

A tax return (Form RPT) must be filed with every deed as well as any assignment or surrender of a leasehold interest within New York City. A return may not be required for the granting of a leasehold interest where there is no consideration and no tax is due. The Register is authorized to reject a return which states that there was no consideration for the deed unless there is attached to such form a statement setting forth the grounds upon which it is claimed is based. For purposes of this tax, consideration means the price paid or required to be paid but does not include anything defined as rent under New York City Commercial Rent and Occupancy statutes.

Land Title Registration (Torrens System)

1. Filing a deed or transfer of title of registered land. $6.00
2. Filing a mortgage. 4.00
3. Filing any modification or satisfaction of a mortgage. 4.00
4. Registration copy of any instrument. 1.00
   per page
5. Filing any other lien pending or subsequent to registration, or any discharge of a lien or a certification of title. 4.00
6. Filing a notice of petition. 5.00
7. Filing a survey, map or plan of registered land. 2.00
8. Recording a certified copy of the final order and judgment of registration and issuing the certificate of title. 6.00

Services

1. Issuing a Certified Copy.
   $2.00 per page. The City Register does not certify parts of instruments.
2. Satisfaction Certificate of Mortgage: $2.00
3. Satisfaction Certificate of Federal Tax Lien: $2.00
4. Certification of copy of Filed map: $5.00

NOTE: Costs incurred for private reproduction of map are assumed by requesting party.

Miscellaneous

1. Filing a Federal Tax Lien or a Release—$4.50
2. Issuing Certificate of Federal Tax Lien search—$4.50 .
3. Filing a Certificate of the Appointment of a Commissioner of Deeds for the State of New York—$10.00
4. Filing a Map—$10.00 plus $1.00 for each square foot of map or fraction thereof.

A deed or lease or memorandum thereof, cannot be accepted for recording unless a Multiple Dwelling Registration card, Emergency Confidential 24 hour Telephone Number card and a check for $6.00 payable to: City of New York-H.P.D. is filed with the instrument. If not a Multiple Dwelling, an affidavit to that effect is required instead.

All fees and taxes are due at the time of recording or requesting service.

The City Register reserves the right to require payment by certified check.

Instruments must be recorded in the County Office where the property in the transaction is located.

Recording Hours: 9 A.M.-4 P.M.

Checks for Recording Fees, Mortgage Tax and State Stamp Tax should be made payable to: Office of the City Register. Checks for City Real Property Tax should be made payable to:
Commissioner of Finance.

(page 2 of 2)

RPT

**Department of Finance
Bureau of Tax Operations**

Real Property Transfer Tax Return
Pursuant to Chapter 46, Title II,
NYC Administrative Code

For Departmental Use Only
● Return Number
● Deed Serial Number
N.Y.S. Real Estate Transfer Tax Paid

TYPE OR PRINT LEGIBLY. If the grantor or grantee is a business entity, the name and address of an owner, partner, officer or other individual who will be responsible for responding to any audit inquiries must be provided.

● Grantor: _____
       Business name, if applicable

● _____
       Individual name

● _____
       Permanent mailing address, after transfer

_____
Federal Employer Identification Number   Social Security Number

● Grantee: _____
       Business name, if applicable

● _____
       Individual name

● _____
       Permanent mailing address, after transfer

● _____
       Federal Employer Identification Number / Social Security Number

Grantor's attorney: _____
       Name

_____
       Address

Grantee's attorney: _____
       Name

_____
       Address

● Property Use (Check One)

___ 1-3 Family House
___ Residential Condominium
___ Apartment Building
___ Office Building
___ Industrial Building
___ Utility
___ Individual dwelling unit in a 1-3-family house or in an apartment building with 4 or more units
___ Other (Describe) _____

● **LOCATION OF REAL PROPERTY** (List each lot separately.)

Address	County	Block	Lot

Current Assessed Value
of Property
$_____

● Type of Interest Transferred ___ Fee ___ Leasehold Grant ___ Leasehold Assignment or Surrender
(Check one)
     ___ Other (Describe) _____

● Date of Delivery to Grantee _____   ● Percentage of Interest Transferred _____ %
     Month   Day   Year

● CONDITION OF TRANSFER

Check the condition or conditions which apply and fill out the appropriate schedule on Page 3 or 4 of this return, if required.

a. ___ Arms Length Transfer

b. ___ Transfer in Exercise of Option to Purchase

c. ___ Transfer from Co-op Sponsor to Co-op Corporation

d. ___ Transfer by Referee or Receiver (Complete Schedule A, Page 3)

e. ___ Deed in Lieu of Foreclosure (Complete Schedule B, Page 3)

f. ___ Transfer Pursuant to Marital Settlement Agreement (Complete Schedule C, Page 3)

g. ___ Transfer Pursuant to Corporate Liquidation (Complete Schedule D, Page 3)

h. ___ Transfer to Business Entity Related to Grantor (Complete Schedule E, Page 4)

i. ___ Transfer Without Consideration to or from Agent Dummy or Conduit (Complete Schedule F, Page 4)

j. ___ Transfer Pursuant to Trust Agreement or Will

k. ___ Gift Transfer

l. ___ Transfer to a Governmental Body

m. ___ Correction Deed

n. ___ Transfer by or to a Tax Exempt Organization (Complete Schedule G, Page 4)

o. ___ Transfer of Property Partly Within and Partly Without New York City

p. ___ Other (Describe) _____
_____
_____

Complete the appropriate tax computation schedule on page 2 of this return. If you are reporting a transfer with a consideration of $25,000 or less, no tax is due; however, you must complete Schedule 1 on Page 2, and file a return.

THIS RETURN, INCLUDING ALL REQUIRED SCHEDULES, MUST BE COMPLETELY FILLED OUT AND FILED WITH ALL NECESSARY ATTACHMENTS BEFORE THE REPORTED TRANSFER WILL BE RECORDED.

New York City Real Property Transfer Tax Return (page 1 of 6)

Schedules 1 and 2 apply to transfers made on or after July 1, 1982 and not made in performance of contracts executed before February 1, 1982. Schedule 1 also applies to certain leasehold grants, assignments and surrenders occurring between February 1, 1982 and July 1, 1982. If the transfer reported is not covered by Schedules 1 or 2, complete Form RPT-ATT. See the instructions for further information. IF THE CONSIDERATION ON LINE 1 OF SCHEDULE 1 OR 2 IS $1,000,000 OR MORE, COPIES OF THE CLOSING STATEMENT OR THE CONTRACT OF SALE MUST BE ATTACHED TO THIS RETURN.

SCHEDULE 1: COMPUTATION OF TAX FOR TRANSFERS TAXED AT 1% RATE

Use this schedule for the following transfers: 1. Conveyances (other than grants, assignments or surrenders of leasehold interests) made on or after July 1, 1982, where: a. The consideration is less than $500,000, or b. The property transferred is a 1-, 2- or 3-family house or an individual residential condominium unit. 2. *Grants, assignments or surrenders, made on or after July 1, 1982, of leasehold interests where: a. The consideration is less than $500,000, or b. The leasehold interest is in a 1-, 2- or 3-family house or an individual dwelling unit in a dwelling which is occupied or is to be occupied as the residence of 4 or more families living independently of each other. 3. *Grants, assignments or surrenders of leasehold interests in real property made on or after February 1, 1982 and before July 1, 1982, where the consideration is $500,000 or more, and where the leasehold interest is not in a 1, 2- or 3-family house or individual dwelling unit. The tax rate is 1% of the consideration with respect to these transfers. Pre-existing mortgages and liens may not be deducted.

1. Consideration paid or required to be paid	● $	
2. Tax due: 1% of Line 1	●	
3. Penalty (See instructions)		
4. Interest (See instructions)		
5. TOTAL DUE: Add Lines 2, 3, and 4	● $	

SCHEDULE 2: COMPUTATION OF TAX FOR TRANSFERS TAXED AT 2% RATE

Use this schedule for the following transfers: 1. Conveyances of real property (other than grants, assignments and surrenders of leasehold interests) made on or after July 1, 1982, for a consideration of $500,000 or more, where the real property transferred is not a 1-, 2- or 3-family house or individual residential condominium unit and where the transfer is not made in performance of a contract executed before February 1, 1982. 2. *Grants, assignments or surrenders of leasehold interests in real property made on or after July 1, 1982, where the consideration is $500,000 or more and where the leasehold interest is not in a 1-, 2- or 3-family house or an individual dwelling unit. The tax rate is 2% of the consideration with respect to these transfers. Pre-existing mortgages and liens may not be deducted.

1. Consideration paid or required to be paid	● $	
2. Tax due: 2% of Line 1	●	
3. Penalty (See instructions)		
4. Interest (See instructions)		
5. TOTAL DUE: Add Lines 2, 3, and 4	● $	

MAKE CERTIFIED CHECK OR MONEY ORDER PAYABLE TO THE ORDER OF THE COMMISSIONER OF FINANCE

*The amount subject to tax in the case of a grant or assignment of a leasehold interest in real property shall be only such amount as is not considered rent for the purposes of the Commercial Rent or Occupancy Tax imposed by Title L, Chapter 46 of the Administrative Code of the City of New York. (See instructions.)

SCHEDULE 3: DETAILS OF CONSIDERATION

Complete Schedule 3 for all transfers. Enter zero on Line 15 if the transfer reported was without consideration.

6. Cash	● $_____
7. Purchase money mortgage	● $_____
8. Unpaid principal on pre-existing mortgages	● $_____
9. Accrued interest on pre-existing mortgages	● $_____
10. Accrued real estate taxes	● $_____
11. Amounts of other liens on property	● $_____
12. Value of shares of stock or of partnership interest received	● $_____
13. Value of real property exchanged	● $_____
14. Other (Describe)	● $_____
15. TOTAL CONSIDERATION: Add Lines 6 through 14 (Must equal amount entered on Page 2, Line 1 of Schedule 1 or 2.)	$_____

I swear or affirm that this return, including the accompanying schedules, affidavits and attachments, has been examined by me and is, to the best of my knowledge, a true and complete return made in good faith, pursuant to Chapter 46, Title II of the Administrative Code and the regulations issued thereunder.

Sworn to and subscribed to me before

this .... day of

............................, 19 ....

Name of Grantor

Signature

Sworn to and subscribed to me before

this .... day of

............................, 19 ....

Name of Grantee

Signature

New York City Real Property Transfer Tax Return (page 2 of 6)

Schedule A   TRANSFER BY REFEREE OR RECEIVER

If condition "d" was checked on Page 1, complete Schedule A below:

NOTE: The consideration for a transfer by a referee or receiver under foreclosure or execution is the amount bid for the property and costs paid by the purchaser, plus the amount of any pre-existing mortgages, liens or other encumbrances remaining on the property after the transfer, whether or not the underlying indebtedness is assumed.

1. Was this transfer the result of a court-ordered sale pursuant to foreclosure or execution? _____ Yes _____ No

    If yes, complete Lines "a" through "f" below:

    a. Status of grantee: _____ Plaintiff in foreclosure action _____ Assignee of plaintiff

           _____ Nominee of plaintiff   _____ Other (Describe) _____

    b. Priority of mortgage foreclosed upon: _____ 1st _____ 2nd _____ 3rd or other

    c. Amount of foreclosure judgment .... $_____

    d. Price bid by grantee .... $_____

    e. Costs paid by grantee .... $_____

    f. Amount of mortgages, liens or other encumbrances .... $_____

2. If the answer to Line 1 above is no, state the reason for this transfer _____

_____

Schedule B   DEED IN LIEU OF FORECLOSURE

If condition "e" was checked on Page 1, complete Schedule B below:

NOTE: A conveyance by a defaulting mortgagor to the mortgagee (or to a nominee or assignee of the mortgagee) in consideration of the cancellation of the mortgage debt is taxable. The consideration is the amount of the unpaid mortgage debt and unpaid accrued interest, plus the amount of any other mortgages, liens or encumbrances remaining on the property after the transfer, whether or not the underlying indebtedness is assumed.

1. Status of grantee: _____ Mortgagee   _____ Nominee of mortgagee

           _____ Assignee of mortgagee   _____ Other (Describe) _____

2. Priority of mortgage in default: _____ 1st _____ 2nd _____ 3rd or other

3. Amount of debt owed by grantor to mortgagee at time of transfer:

    a. Outstanding principal .... $_____

    b. Accrued interest .... $_____

4. Amount of mortgages, liens or other encumbrances .... $_____

Schedule C   TRANSFER PURSUANT TO MARITAL SETTLEMENT AGREEMENT

If condition "f" was checked on Page 1, complete Schedule C below:
NOTE: Consideration for a transfer pursuant to a marital settlement agreement includes the value of any marital rights exchanged for the property plus any money paid by the grantee for the transfer. The consideration is presumed to equal the fair market value of the property in proportion to the interest transferred unless otherwise shown.

Does the consideration listed on Page 2, Line 1 of Schedule 1 or 2 represent the fair market value of the property in proportion to the interest transferred? _____ Yes _____ No

If the answer is no, ATTACH AN AFFIDAVIT fully explaining why, along with a copy of the marital settlement agreement.

Schedule D   TRANSFER PURSUANT TO CORPORATE LIQUIDATION

If condition "g" was checked on Page 1, complete Schedule D below and ATTACH A BALANCE SHEET reflecting the grantor's assets and liabilities at the time of the liquidation.

NOTE: The consideration for a transfer pursuant to a corporate liquidation is measured by the liabilities assumed and the debts cancelled and forgiven by the grantee, except that the consideration also includes the amounts of any mortgages, liens or other encumbrances remaining on the property after the transfer, whether or not the underlying indebtedness is assumed. Where only real estate, and no personal property, is distributed, complete question 1 below, omit questions 2-10, enter the total of the amount of liabilities assumed, debts cancelled or forgiven, and mortgages and liens remaining on the property on Line 1 of Schedule 1 or 2, and follow the instructions to calculate the tax due. Where both real property and personal property are distributed by the corporation, complete questions 1 through 10 of this schedule, enter the amount on Line 10 of this schedule on Line 1 of Schedule 1 or 2 and follow the instructions to calculate the tax due.

1. Is this transfer pursuant to a liquidation of a subsidiary by a parent occurring not more than two years after the acquisition of control by the parent through stock purchases over a period of not more than 12 months? _____ Yes _____ No

2. Present fair market value of real property .... $_____

3. Amount of mortgages and other liens .... $_____

4. Equity in real property (Line 2 less Line 3) .... $_____

5. Present fair market value of personal property (less any continuing liens) .... $_____

6. Total value of property (Add Line 4 and Line 5) .... $_____

7. Amount of accounts payable and other liabilities
   (other than continuing liens on real or personal property) .... $_____

8. Apportionment of consideration:

   $$\frac{\text{Line 4 (Schedule D): _____}}{\text{Line 6 (Schedule D): _____}} \times \text{Line 7 (Schedule D) _____} = \$_____$$

9. Amount of mortgages, liens or other encumbrances on the real property .... $_____

10. TOTAL CONSIDERATION (Add Line 8 and Line 9. Enter on Page 2, Line 1,
    Schedule 1 or 2) .... $_____

New York City Real Property Transfer Tax Return (page 3 of 6)

Schedule E   TRANSFER TO BUSINESS ENTITY RELATED TO GRANTOR

If condition "h" was checked on Page 1. complete Schedule E below.

NOTE: A transfer of real property to a corporation in exchange for shares of its capital stock is taxable, even where there is no simultaneous exchange of shares of stock for the real property, so long as the transfer is part of a plan to form a corporation for the purpose of holding title to the property. A transfer to a partnership as a contribution of partnership assets is similarly taxable. The tax is computed on the fair market value of the common stock or partnership interest received in exchange for the real property. The fair market value of the stock or partnership interest is presumed to equal the fair market value of the real property. The consideration includes the amount of any mortgages, liens or other encumbrances remaining on the property after the transfer, whether or not the underlying indebtedness is assumed.

1. Relationship of grantee to grantor(s) immediately after the transfer:

____ Corporation wholly owned by grantor(s)   ____ Partnership consisting wholly of grantors   ____ Limited partnership consisting wholly of grantors

____ Corporation owned by grantor(s) and other(s)   ____ Partnership consisting of grantor(s) and other(s)   ____ Limited partnership consisting of grantor(s) and other(s)

____ Other (Describe) _____   _____

2. If this transfer has more than one grantor, state the percentage of interest transferred by each grantor (If the grantor is a partnership or limited partnership, state the percentage of interest transferred by each individual partner or limited partner.):

Name	Percentage of Interest

3. If the grantee is a partnership or limited partnership consisting wholly of the grantors, state the percentage of interest immediately after the transfer, of each partner or limited partner, in the partnership:

Name of Partner	Percentage of Interest

4. (a) Date of formation of grantee business: _____

   (b) Date of formation of grantor business (if applicable): _____

5. (a) Fair market value of real property at time of transfer: $_____

   (b) Fair market value of stock or partnership interest transferred: $_____

   (c) If (a) and (b) above are different, explain why: _____

   _____

6. Amount of basis used for depreciation of the property on Federal tax returns by the grantor before this transfer: $_____

7. Amount of basis to be used for depreciation of the property on Federal tax returns by the grantee after this transfer: $_____

Schedule F   TRANSFER FROM AN AGENT, DUMMY, STRAWMAN OR CONDUIT TO A PRINCIPAL OR FROM A PRINCIPAL TO AN AGENT, DUMMY, STRAWMAN OR CONDUIT

If condition "i" was checked on Page 1, complete Schedule F below:

NOTE: A deed from an agent, dummy, strawman or conduit to a principal or from a principal to an agent, dummy, strawman or conduit, is exempt from the Real Property Transfer Tax. Complete questions 1 through 6 below to establish the claim of exemption.

1. Name and address of party from whom property was acquired by grantor: _____

   _____

2. Date of acquisition _____ Recording date: _____

   Reel number: _____ Page number: _____

3. Amount of Real Property Transfer Tax paid upon acquisition by grantor: $_____

4. Is this transfer part of a transfer to and from a corporation for the sole purpose of acquiring mortgage financing?   ____ Yes ____ No

5. Is this transfer part of a transfer to and from a corporation during a construction period?   ____ Yes ____ No

6. If the answers to both questions 4 and 5 above are no, describe the relationship of the grantor and the grantee and the purpose of the transfer: _____

   _____

   _____

Schedule G   TRANSFER BY OR TO A TAX EXEMPT ORGANIZATION

If condition "n" was checked on Page 1, complete Schedule G below:

NOTE: A deed by or to any organization operated exclusively for religious, charitable or educational purposes will be exempt from taxation, if proof of the organization's tax exempt status is given to the Department of Finance. If such status is claimed, answer questions 1 and 2 below and ATTACH AN AFFIDAVIT to this return stating the purposes and activities of the organization, the sources and disposition of its income, whether any of its income may be credited to surplus or passed on to any private stockholder or individual and any other facts relevant to the organization's tax exempt status. The affidavit should further state that exempt status still applies when IRS letters are attached.

Is the grantee or grantor an organization exempt from taxation pursuant to Internal Revenue Code Section 501(c)(3)? ____ Yes ____ No If yes, attach a copy of the letter from the U.S. Treasury Department granting tax exempt status.

Has the grantor or grantee received an exemption from Sales Tax from the NYS Department of Taxation and Finance? ____ Yes ____ No If yes, attach a copy of the letter granting such exemption.

New York City Real Property Transfer Tax Return (page 4 of 6)

THE CITY OF NEW YORK—DEPARTMENT OF FINANCE—BUREAU OF TAX OPERATIONS

Instructions for Preparation
of Real Property Transfer Tax Return

Contact the Bureau of Tax Operations, Tax Review Division, Room 601, 139 Centre Street, New York, NY 10013, Telephone 566-3003, for assistance in preparing the return or information about this tax.

The return must be complete in all details.

The contract of sale, title report, records showing the amounts of liens and encumbrances and the closing statement used in the preparation of the return must be retained and made available for inspection upon demand by the Commissioner of Finance.

COPIES OF THE CONTRACT OF SALE OR CLOSING STATEMENT MUST BE ATTACHED TO THE RETURN FOR ANY TRANSFER WITH A CONSIDERATION OF $1,000,000 OR MORE.

DEFINITIONS OF TERMS:

1. "Deed". Any document, instrument or writing (other than a will), regardless of where made, executed or delivered, whereby any real property or interest therein is created, vested, granted, bargained, sold, transferred, assigned or otherwise conveyed, including any such document, instrument or writing whereby any leasehold interest in real property is granted, assigned, or surrendered.

2. "Real property or interest therein". Every estate or right, legal or equitable, present or future, vested or contingent, in lands, tenements or hereditaments, which are located in whole or in part within the City of New York. It shall not include a mortgage or a release of mortgage. It shall not include rights to sepulture.

3. "Consideration". The price actually paid or required to be paid fo the real property or interest therein, without deduction for mortgages, liens or encumbrances, whether or not expressed in the deed and whether paid or required to be paid by money, property, or any other thing of value. It shall include the cancellation or discharge of an indebtedness or obligation. It shall also include the amount of mortgage, lien or other encumbrance, whether or not the underlying indebtedness is assumed.

4. "Net consideration". Any consideration, exclusive of any mortgage or other lien or encumbrance on the real property or interest therein which existed before the delivery of the deed and remains thereon after the delivery of the deed.

5. "Grantor". The person making, executing or delivering the deed.

6. "Grantee". The person accepting the deed or who obtains any of the real property which is the subject of the deed or any interest therein.

IMPOSITION OF THE TAX

A tax is imposed on each deed at the time of delivery by a grantor to a grantee when the consideration for the real property and any improvement on the real property (whether or not included in the same deed) exceeds $25,000. The tax rates are as follows:

The Real Property Transfer Tax is *1% of the consideration*, with no deduction for pre-existing mortgages or liens, for the following transfers:

1. A conveyance made on or after July 1, 1982, of a 1-, 2- or 3-family house or an individual residential condominium unit,

2. A conveyance made on or after July 1, 1982, where the consideration is less than $500,000,

3. A grant, assignment or surrender, made on or after July 1, 1982, of a leasehold interest:

  a. In a 1-, 2- or 3-family house or an individual dwelling unit in a dwelling which is occupied or is to be occupied as the residence of four or more families living independently of each other, or

  b. In real property where the consideration is less than $500,000.

4. A grant, assignment or surrender of a leasehold interest in real property (where the leasehold is not in a 1-, 2- or 3-family house or an individual dwelling unit) made on or after February 1, 1982 and before July 1, 1982, where the consideration is $500,000 or more.

The tax is *2% of the consideration*, with no deductions for pre-existing mortgages or liens, for the following conveyances:

1. A grant, assignment or surrender of a leasehold interest in real property (where the leasehold interest is not in a 1-, 2- or 3-family house or an individual dwelling unit) made on or after July 1, 1982, where the consideration is $500,000 or more.

2. A conveyance of real property other than a 1-, 2- or 3-family house, or individual residential condominium unit, made on or after July 1, 1982 for a consideration of $500,000 or more. where the transfer is not made in performance of a contract executed before February 1, 1982.

The tax is *1% of the net consideration* with respect to the following non-leasehold transfers:

1. A conveyance made before February 1, 1982.

2. A conveyance made on or after February 1, 1982. in performance of a contract executed before February 1, 1982,

3. A conveyance made before July 1, 1982 of a 1-, 2- or 3-family house or an individual residential condominium unit,

4. A conveyance made before July 1, 1982 where the consideration is less than $500,000.

The tax is *2% of the net consideration and 1% of the amount of any pre-existing mortgages or liens* for any non-leasehold conveyance made on or after February 1, 1982, and before July 1, 1982, where the consideration is $500,000 or more and the property transferred is other than a 1-, 2- or 3-family house or an individual residential condominium unit.

The tax applies to any transfer of an interest in real property located in New York City, regardless of where the delivery of the deed or other actions concerning the transfer occur.

CONSIDERATION FOR TRANSFERS OF LEASES

Grants, assignments and surrenders of leases are taxable based on the consideration received by the party transferring the interest. However, nothing included in the definition of "rent" contained in the Commercial Rent and Occupancy Tax statutes (Title L of Chapter 46 of the New York City Administrative Code) is consideration for the purpose of taxing leasehold transfers under the Real Property Transfer Tax statutes. Rent is defined as:

"The consideration paid or required to be paid by a tenant for the use or occupancy of premises, valued in money, whether received in money or otherwise, including all credits and property or services of any kind and including any payment required to be made by him on behalf of his landlord for real estate taxes, water rents or charges, sewer rents or any other expenses (including insurance) normally payable by a landlord who owns the realty other than expenses for the improvement, repair or maintenance of the tenant's premises." §L46-1.0(6) New York City Administrative Code.

FILING OF RETURN AND PAYMENT OF TAX

A notarized joint return must be filed by the grantor and grantee for any non-leasehold transfer of an interest in real property and for any assignment and surrender of a lease for real property located in the City of New York, whether or not any tax is due. A return need not be filed for a new lease except where transfer tax is owed.

If the deed or lease is to be recorded, the return must be filed and any tax due paid at the City Register of the county where the property is located (or at the County Clerk of Richmond County if the property is located there). If the deed or lease is not recorded, the return must be filed and the tax paid, by mail or in person, at the NYC Finance Department, Tax Review Division, 139 Centre Street, Room 601, New York, New York, 10013.

The return must be filed and any tax due paid within 30 days of the delivery of the deed by the grantor to the grantee and before the transfer is recorded. If the tax due is not paid by the grantor, the grantee is liable for payment. The tax applies to all deeds except for those which are exempt. (Exemptions are listed below.)

New York City Real Property Transfer Tax Return (page 5 of 6)

The tax may be paid in cash, or by certified check or money order made payable to the Commissioner of Finance.

Section 1201(b)(i) of the State Tax Law states:

"The payment of, and the filing of a return relating to any ... [Real Property Transfer] taxes may be required as a condition precedent:

(1) to the recording or filing of a deed, lease, assignment or surrender of lease or other instrument,

(2) to the commencement of any action or proceeding in any court of this state in which any conveyance, transfer or lease described herein is in issue, directly or indirectly, or

(3) to the receipt in evidence of such deed, lease, assignment or surrender of lease or other instrument in any such court."

The City Register borough offices and the Richmond County Clerk are located at:

MANHATTAN (New York County)
31 Chambers Street
New York, New York 10007
(212) 566-3734

BRONX
1960 Benedict Avenue
Bronx, New York 10462
(212) 823-7800

BROOKLYN (Kings County)
Municipal Building
Brooklyn, New York 11201
(212) 643-4095

QUEENS
90-27 Sutphin Boulevard
Jamaica, New York 11435
(212) 658-4600

STATEN ISLAND (Richmond County)
Richmond County Clerk
County Court House
Staten Island, N.Y. 10301
(212) 390-5393

Real Property Transfer Tax returns are available at City Register offices, the office of the County Clerk of Richmond County, the Finance Department Tax Review Division (139 Centre Street, Room 601, N.Y., N.Y. 10013) or the borough offices of the City Collector, listed below:

MANHATTAN (New York County)
Municipal Building
1 Centre Street
New York, New York 10013

BRONX
Tremont & Arthur Avenues
Bronx, New York 10457

BROOKLYN (Kings County)
Municipal Building, Room 1
Brooklyn, New York 11201

QUEENS
90-15 Sutphin Boulevard
Jamaica, New York 11435

STATEN ISLAND (Richmond County)
350 St. Marks Place, Room 200
St. George, Staten Island, N.Y. 10301

APPORTIONMENT OF CONSIDERATION FOR PROPERTY LOCATED PARTLY WITHIN AND PARTLY WITHOUT THE BOUNDARIES OF THE CITY

The consideration for a transfer of real property situated partly within and partly without the boundaries of the City of New York is taxed in proportion to the amount of the property located within the boundaries of the City. To determine the tax due on a transfer of such property, calculate the percentage ratio which the assessed valuation of the property situated within the City bears to the total assessed valuation of the property and then multiply the consideration for the transfer by that percentage ratio to arrive at the amount of consideration subject to tax. That amount should be entered on Page 2, Line 1 of Schedule 1 or 2, whichever is applicable, and a rider showing the calculations should be attached to the return.

Use the assessed valuations in effect at the time of the transfer. Instead of the assessed valuations, the equalized valuations based on the state equalization tables may be used, provided that they are applied to the property both within and without the City.

EXEMPTIONS FROM THE TAX:

a. The following parties are exempt from the payment of the tax and from filing a return:

1. The State of New York, its agencies, instrumentalities, public corporations (including a public corporation created pursuant to agreement or compact with another state or the Dominion of Canada), or political subdivisions.

New York City Real Property Transfer Tax Return (page 6 of 6)

2. The United States of America and its agencies and instrumentalities, insofar as they are immune from taxation.

The exemption of such governmental bodies does not relieve a grantee from them of liability for the tax or from filing a return.

b. The tax imposed does not apply to any of the following deeds:

1. A deed by or to the United Nations or other world-wide international organization of which the United States is a member.

2. A deed by or to any corporation, or association, or trust, or community chest, fund or foundation, organized and operated exclusively for religious, charitable, or educational purposes, or for the prevention of cruelty to children or animals, and no part of the net earnings of which inures to the benefit of any private shareholder or individual and no substantial part of the activities of which is carrying on propaganda, or otherwise attempting to influence legislation, provided, however, that nothing in this paragraph shall include an organization operated for the primary purpose of carrying on a trade or business for profit, whether or not all of its profits are payable to one or more organizations described in this paragraph.

3. A deed to any governmental body listed in "a" above.

4. A deed given solely as security for a debt, provided that the Mortgage Recording Tax imposed by Article 11 of the Tax Law is paid for such deed, or a deed given solely for the purpose of returning such security.

5. A deed from a mere agent, dummy, straw man or conduit to his principal, or a deed from the principal to his agent, dummy, straw man or conduit.

Where a tax does not apply to any deed, neither the grantor nor the grantee is required to pay the tax. However, a return relating to the deed must be filed.

PENALTIES AND INTEREST

A penalty of 5% per month, up to a maximum of 25% will be charged on the tax due to anyone who fails to file a return or to pay the tax due within 30 days after delivery of the deed unless it is shown that the failure is due to reasonable cause and not due to willful neglect. Interest will be charged by a rate setting formula based upon the average prime rate, and will be determined by the Commissioner of Finance. The rate will be charged on the tax due for each month or fraction of a month of delay, beginning 30 days after the delivery of the deed

FORM RPT

Specific instructions for completing Form RPT are incorporated into the return itself. Contact the NYC Department of Finance, Tax Review Division at 566-8933 or 566-3003 for assistance in completing the return.

FORM RPT-ATT

Form RPT-ATT is an attachment to Form RPT to be used when Schedules 1 and 2 of Form RPT do not apply to the transfer reported. Form RPT-ATT applies only to non-leasehold transfers made before July 1, 1982 and to non-leasehold transfers made after that date but in performance of contracts executed before February 1, 1982. Page 1 of Form RPT, Schedule 3 on Page 2 and all other relevant schedules of that form (except for Schedules 1 and 2) must be completed and filed along with Form RPT-ATT.

A FOR COUNTY USE ONLY

1. Swis Code

2. Date Deed Recorded

3. Book   4. Page

STATE OF NEW YORK
STATE BOARD OF EQUALIZATION AND ASSESSMENT
REAL PROPERTY TRANSFER REPORT

EA-5217
Rev. 6/84

CONTROL NUMBER 5363030

B IDENTIFICATION INFORMATION

1. Property Location

City or Town

Village

Street Number   Street Name   Zip Code

2. Buyer Name

Last Name   First Name

3. Buyer Address

Buyer Address

4. Buyer's Attorney

Name   (   ) Telephone Number

5. Seller Name

Last Name   First Name

6. Tax Billing Address

☐ Same as Buyer Address   ☐ Same as Property Location   ☐ Other (Specify Below)

Street Name and Number   City or Town   State   Zip Code

7. Deed Property Size

Dimensions or Acres

8. School District Name

(Data should be taken from the latest final assessment roll)

1. Enter the year of the assessment roll from which the information was taken.

2. Check the box indicating the number of parcels which sold.

☐ One Parcel   ☐ More Than One Parcel (Specify)   ☐ Only Part of a Parcel

3. Enter the total assessed value (of all parcels in the sale).

4. Enter the tax map identifier of the parcel. (If more than one, list on a separate sheet)

Section   Block   Lot

5. Enter the roll identifier if different than tax map identifier.

1. Check the box in the Property Use Table which most accurately describes the use of the property at the time of sale.

2. Is the sale of a condominium or a cooperative?

☐ Yes ☐ No

Property Use Table

1 ☐	Agricultural			6 ☐	Community Service
2 ☐	1, 2, 3 Family Residential	4A ☐	Commercial	7 ☐	Industrial
3A ☐	Residential Vacant Land	4B ☐	Apartment	8 ☐	Public Service
3B ☐	Non-Residential Vacant Land	5 ☐	Recreation/Entertainment	9 ☐	Forest

1. Date of Sale

2. **State the Full Sales Price.** $

(Full Sales Price is the total amount paid for the property, including personal property. This payment may be in the form of cash, other property or goods, or the assumption of mortgages or other obligations.)

3. Was there personal property in excess of $500 included in this sale? ☐ Yes ☐ No

4. If yes, indicate the value of the personal property included in the sale. $

5. Is this an arm's length sale? ☐ Yes ☐ No

6. Check all of the conditions below that apply to this sale.

A ☐ Sale Between Relatives
B ☐ Sale Between Related Companies or Partners in Business
C ☐ Land Contract Sale (Specify Contract Date)
U ☐ Sale Contract executed more than one year prior to the Date of Sale
F ☐ Buyer or Seller is a Government Agency or a Lending Institution
R ☐ Deed Type is not Warranty or Bargain and Sale (Specify Deed Type)
T ☐ Interest conveyed is not a fee (Specify Interest)
G ☐ Other unusual factors affecting sale price (Specify)

F CERTIFICATION

I certify that all the items of information entered on this transfer form are true and correct (to the best of my knowledge and belief) and I understand that the making of any willful false statement of material fact herein will subject me to the provisions of the penal law relative to the making and filing of false instruments.

Name (Print or Type)

Signature

Telephone Number (   )

Date

SBEA COPY

REAL PROPERTY TRANSFER REPORT-EA-5217

FILING INSTRUCTIONS

1. Before completing this form, read the detailed instructions on the reverse side.

2. A deed may not be accepted for recording unless this form is legible and complete. All entries must be typed or clearly printed in black ballpoint pen. Please press hard. Four copies are being made.

3. This form must be completed by the buyer or the seller or an agent with personal knowledge of the transaction.

New York State Board of Equalization and Assessment Report (page 1 of 2)

DETAILED INSTRUCTIONS FOR INFORMATION REQUIRED
ON REAL PROPERTY TRANSFER REPORT EA-5217

Section 333 (1-e) of the Real Property Law provides that "A recording officer shall not record or accept for record any conveyance of real property affecting land in New York State unless accompanied by a transfer report form prescribed by the State Board of Equalization and Assessment which shall contain such information as required by such board including the tax billing address of the new owner, the appropriate tax map designation, if any, and a statement of the full sales price relating thereto".

IMPORTANT

Pursuant to section 574 (5) of the Real Property Tax Law, "Forms or reports filed pursuant to this section or section three hundred thirty-three of the Real Property Law shall not be made available for public inspection or copying except for purposes of administrative or judicial review of assessments".

This form should be completed by the buyer or the seller or an agent with knowledge of the transaction. All entries should be typed or clearly printed. All entries must be completed. One EA-5217 form should be filed for each deed being recorded.

The following instructions explain each item of information required on Real Property Transfer Report EA-5217. The code in parenthesis indicates the location of each data item on the form.

SECTION B — IDENTIFICATION INFORMATION

(B1) Property Location - Enter the complete address of the property being transferred.

(B2) Buyer Name - Enter the name or names of the buyer(s) of the property being transferred. Enter last name first.

(B3) Buyer Address - Enter the mailing address of the buyer.

(B4) Buyer's Attorney - Enter the name and telephone number of the attorney representing the buyer. If the buyer does not have an attorney, enter "none".

(B5) Seller Name - Enter the name or names of the person(s) selling the property, last name first.

(B6) Tax Billing Address - If the real property tax billing address is the same as the property location or buyer address, check the appropriate box. Otherwise, enter the mailing address which should be used for real property tax billing purposes.

(B7) Deeded Property Size - Enter the property size as specified on the deed. In most cases, where the property is under an acre, dimensions will be listed. If the property is over an acre, the size will be listed in acres. Either entry is sufficient; do not enter both.

(B8) School District Name - Enter the legal name of the school district in which the property lies. This is not necessarily the popular name by which the local school or district is known.

SECTION C — ASSESSMENT INFORMATION

This information should be taken from the latest final city or town assessment roll except in Nassau County where the county roll should be used. The local County Office of Real Property Tax Services can be of assistance in obtaining this information.

(C1) Assessment Roll Year - Enter the year of the last final assessment roll at the time of sale.

(C2) Number of Parcels - Indicate the number of assessment roll parcels transferred on the deed by checking the appropriate box and indicating the number, if greater than one.

(C3) Assessed Value, Total - Enter the total assessed value (before deduction for any exemptions) for all parcels from the latest final assessment roll as of the sale date. If only a part of a parcel is transferred, enter the assessed value of the whole assessment parcel.

(C4) Tax Map Identifier - This is the number consisting of section, block and lot which distinguishes the parcel from all others. Enter the tax map number in the box provided. If the property consists of more than one parcel, enter the tax map numbers of all parcels. Attach a separate sheet, if necessary, referencing the tax map number with the EA-5217 control number.

(C5) Roll Identifier - This is the number on the assessment roll which distinguishes each assessment parcel from all others. In most cases, that number is the tax map number. Enter the roll identifier in C5 only if it is different from the tax map identifier, otherwise enter N/A (not applicable).

SECTION D — PROPERTY USE INFORMATION

(D1) Property Use Table
1. Agricultural - used for production of crops or livestock;
2. 1,2,3 Family Residential - used for human habitation; three dwelling units or less;
3A. Residential Vacant Land - a vacant lot or acreage located in a residential area or suitable for residential development;
3B. Non-Residential Vacant Land - any other vacant lots or acreage except residential, agricultural or forest land;
4A. Commercial - used for the sale of goods or services, e.g., restaurant, bank, car wash, etc.;
4B. Apartment - used for human habitation; four or more dwelling units;
5. Recreation/Entertainment - used for the gathering of groups, e.g., sports stadium, theatre, etc.;
6. Community Service - used for the well being of the community, e.g., hospital, school, cultural center, etc.;
7. Industrial - used for the production of goods;
8. Public Service - used to provide services such as water, gas or electric;
9. Forest - tracts of forested land.

(D2) Condominium or Cooperative Sale - Check the Yes box if the sale is of individual ownership of a unit in a multi-unit structure or property.

SECTION E — SALE INFORMATION

(E1) Date of Sale - Enter the date on which the seller conveyed the title of the real property to the buyer. Generally, this will be the date of the closing or, if there is no formal closing, the date on the deed.

(E2) Full Sales Price - Enter the total amount paid for the property. This is the price actually paid in money, property, or any other thing of value, including the cancellation of an indebtedness or the assumption of an encumbrance on the real property. Full sales price also includes the value of any personal property received by the buyer as part of the sale. Typical components of the Full Sales Price would include:

cash consideration - include the total amount of cash transferred from the buyer to the seller. This includes any standard purchase money mortgages and second or third mortgages.

assumed mortgages and other liens or obligations - include the principal amount of any existing mortgages, liens, or encumbrances on the property assumed or taken subject to by the buyer and the amount of any other indebtedness or obligation assumed, cancelled or discharged by the buyer as part of the consideration.

property received by the seller - include the fair market value of any other property or thing of value received by the seller as part of the full sales price.

(E3) / (E4) Personal Property - If property other than real estate, with a value in excess of $500, was included in the property transferred and in the amount of Full Sales Price, check the box marked Yes and then estimate the value of such personal property and enter it on the line provided.

(E5) Arm's-Length Sale - Check the box marked Yes if the sale has taken place in the open market, between an informed and willing buyer and seller where neither is under any compulsion to participate in the transaction, unaffected by any unusual conditions indicating a reasonable possibility that the full sales price is not equal to the fair market value of the property. Otherwise, check the box marked No.

(E6) Conditions That Apply to the Sale - Review the conditions listed and check any that apply to this sale.
A. Sale Between Relatives - Buyer and seller are related by blood or marriage.
B. Sale Between Related Companies or Partners in Business - Buyer and seller hold interest in the same business or are controlled by the same person or corporation.
C. Land Contract Sale - This is a sale of real property where pursuant to contract the buyer pays the full sales price in installments and the seller retains title to the property until payment of the final installment at which time the seller delivers a conveyance to the buyer. In many instances the buyer is in possession of the real property while making the payments.
U. Sale Contract executed more than one year prior to the Date of Sale - Check this box if the date of sale is more than one year later than the date that the contract for sale was signed or the full sales price established.
F. Buyer or Seller is a Government Agency or Lending Institution - Local, state or federal government or a bank is a party to the transfer.
R. Deed Type is not Warranty or Bargain and Sale - If the deed conveying the property is other than a Warranty Deed or a Bargain and Sale Deed, check this box and indicate in the space provided the deed type.
T. Interest Conveyed is not a Fee - If a fee or all undivided interest in real estate is not being conveyed, check the box and in the space provided indicate the interest conveyed.
G. Other - Check the box and describe in the space provided any unusual facts or circumstances that related to the sale that may affect the sale price or terms of the sales agreement.

SECTION F — CERTIFICATION

Certification - Enter the name, phone number, signature and the date of signature of the person completing the form.

NEW YORK BOARD OF TITLE UNDERWRITERS FORM 100D

CHICAGO TITLE INSURANCE COMPANY

in consideration of the payment of its charges for the examination of title and its premium for insurance, insures the within named insured against all loss or damage not exceeding the amount of insurance stated herein and in addition the costs and expenses of defending the title, estate or interest insured, which the insured shall sustain by reason of any defect or defects of title affecting the premises described in Schedule A or affecting the interest of the insured therein as herein set forth, or by reason of unmarketability of the title of the insured to or in the premises, or by reason of liens or encumbrances affecting title at the date hereof, or by reason of any statutory lien for labor or material furnished prior to the date hereof which has now gained or which may hereafter gain priority over the interest insured hereby, or by reason of a lack of access to and from the premises, excepting all loss and damage by reason of the estates, interests, defects, objections, liens, encumbrances and other matters set forth in Schedule B, or by the conditions of this policy hereby incorporated into this contract, the loss and the amount to be ascertained in the manner provided in said conditions and to be payable upon compliance by the insured with the stipulations of said conditions, and not otherwise.

In Witness Whereof, CHICAGO TITLE INSURANCE COMPANY has caused this policy to be signed and sealed as of the date of policy shown in Schedule A, the policy to become valid when countersigned by an authorized signatory.

CHICAGO TITLE INSURANCE COMPANY

By: _____

President.

Issued by:
EASTERN REGION
Main Office
233 Broadway
New York, New York 10007
(212) 285-4000

ATTEST:

_____

Secretary.

New York Board of Title Underwriters Form 100D (page 1 of 4)

CONDITIONS OF THIS POLICY

1. Definitions

(a) Wherever the term "insured" is used in this policy it includes those who succeed to the interest of the insured by operation of law including, without limitation, heirs, distributees, devisees, survivors, personal representatives, next of kin or corporate successors, as the case may be, and those to whom the insured has assigned this policy where such assignment is permitted by the terms hereof, and whenever the term "insured" is used in the conditions of this policy it also includes the attorneys and agents of the "insured."

(b) Wherever the term "this company" is used in this policy it means Chicago Title Insurance Company.

(c) Wherever the term "final determination" or "finally determined" is used in this policy, it means the final determination of a court of competent jurisdiction after disposition of all appeals or after the time to appeal has expired.

(d) Wherever the term "the premises" is used in this policy, it means the property insured herein as described in Schedule A of this policy, including such buildings and improvements thereon which by law constitute real property.

(e) Wherever the term "recorded" is used in this policy it means, unless otherwise indicated, recorded in the office of the recording officer of the county in which property insured herein lies.

2. Defense and Prosecution of Suits

(a) This company will, at its own cost, defend the insured in all actions or proceedings founded on a claim of title or encumbrances not excepted in this policy.

(b) This company shall have the right and may, at its own cost, maintain or defend any action or proceeding relating to the title or interest hereby insured, or upon or under any convenant or contract relating thereto which it considers desirable to prevent or reduce loss hereunder.

(c) In all cases where this policy requires or permits this company to prosecute or defend, the insured shall secure to it the right and opportunity to maintain or defend the action or proceeding, and all appeals from any determination therein, and give it all reasonable aid therein, and hereby permits it to use therein, at its option, its own name or the name of the insured.

(d) The provisions of this section shall survive payment by this company of any specific loss or payment of the entire amount of this policy to the extent that this company shall deem it necessary in recovering the loss from those who may be liable therefor to the insured or to this company.

3. Cases Where Liability Arises

No claim for damages shall arise or be maintainable under this policy except in the following cases:

(a) Where there has been a final determination under which the insured may be dispossessed, evicted or ejected from the premises or from some part or undivided share or interest therein.

(b) Where there has been a final determination adverse to the title upon a lien or encumbrance not excepted in this policy.

(c) Where the insured shall have contracted in good faith in writing to sell the insured estate or interest, or where the insured estate has been sold for the benefit of the insured pursuant to the judgment or order of a court and the title has been rejected because of a defect or encumbrance not excepted in this policy and there has been a final determination sustaining the objection to the title.

(d) Where the insurance is upon the interest of a mortgagee and the mortgage has been adjudged by a final determination to be invalid or ineffectual to charge the insured's estate or interest in the premises, or subject to a prior lien or encumbrance not excepted in this policy; or where a recording officer has refused to accept from the insured a satisfaction of the insured mortgage and there has been a final determination sustaining the refusal because of a defect in the title to the said mortgage.

(e) Where the insured shall have negotiated a loan to be made on the security of a mortgage on the insured's estate or interest in the premises and the title shall have been rejected by the proposed lender and it shall have been finally determined that the rejection of the title was justified because of a defect or encumbrance not excepted in this policy.

(f) Where the insured shall have transferred the title insured by an instrument containing covenants in regard to title or warranty thereof and there shall have been a final determination on any of such covenants or warranty, against the insured, because of a defect or encumbrance not excepted in this policy.

(g) Where the insured estate or interest or a part thereof has been taken by condemnation and it has been finally determined that the insured is not entitled to a full award for the estate or interest taken because of a defect or encumbrance not excepted in this policy.

No claim for damages shall arise or be maintainable under this policy (1) if this company, after having received notice of an alleged defect or encumbrance, removes such defect or encumbrance within thirty days after receipt of such notice; or (2) for liability voluntarily assumed by the insured in settling any claim or suit without the written consent of this company.

4. Notice of Claim

In case a purchaser or proposed mortgage lender raises any question as to the sufficiency of the title hereby insured, or in case actual knowledge shall come to the insured of any claim adverse to the title insured hereby, or in case of the service on or receipt by the insured of any paper, or of any notice, summons, process of pleading in any action or proceeding, the object or effect of which shall or may be to impugn, attack or call in question the validity of the title hereby insured, the insured shall promptly notify this company thereof in writing at its New York office and forward to this company such paper or such notice, summons, process or pleading. Delay in giving this notice and delay in forwarding such paper or such notice, summons, process or pleading shall not affect this company's liability if such failure has not prejudiced and cannot in the future prejudice this company.

5. Payment of Loss

(a) This company will pay, in addition to the loss, all statutory costs and allowances imposed on the insured in litigation carried on by this company for the insured under the terms of this policy. This company shall not be liable for and will not pay the fees of any counsel or attorney employed by the insured.

(b) In every case where claim is made for loss or damage this company (1) reserves the right to settle, at its own cost, any claim or suit which may involve liability under this policy; or (2) may terminate its liability hereunder by paying or tendering the full amount of this policy; or (3) may, without conceding liability, demand a valuation of the insured estate or interest, to be made by three arbitrators or any two of them, one to be chosen by the insured and one by this company, and the two thus chosen selecting an umpire. Such valuation, less the amount of any encumbrances on said insured estate and interest not hereby insured against, shall be the extent of this company's liability for such claim and no right of action shall accrue hereunder for the recovery thereof until thirty days after notice of such valuation shall have been served upon this company, and the insured shall have tendered a conveyance or assignment of the insured estate or interest to this company or its designee at such valuation, diminished as aforesaid. The foregoing option to fix a valuation by arbitration shall not apply to a policy insuring a mortgage or leasehold interest.

(c) Liability to any collateral holder of this policy shall not exceed the amount of the pecuniary interest of such collateral holder in the premises.

(d) All payments made by this company under this policy shall reduce the amount hereof *pro tanto* except (1) payments made for counsel fees and disbursements in defending or prosecuting actions or proceedings in behalf of the insured and for statutory costs and allowances imposed on the insured in such actions and proceedings, and (2) if the insured is a mortgagee, payments made to satisfy or subordinate prior liens or encumbrances not set forth in Schedule B.

(e) When liability has been definitely fixed in accordance with the conditions of this policy, the loss or damage shall be payable within thirty days thereafter.

CONDITIONS OF THIS POLICY (CONTINUED)

6. Co-insurance and Apportionment

(a) In the event that a partial loss occurs after the insured makes an improvement subsequent to the date of this policy, and only in that event, the insured becomes a co-insurer to the extent hereinafter set forth.

If the cost of the improvement exceeds twenty per centum of the amount of this policy, such proportion only of any partial loss established shall be borne by the company as one hundred twenty per centum of the amount of this policy bears to the sum of the amount of this policy and the amount expended for the improvement. The foregoing provisions shall not apply to costs and attorneys' fees incurred by the company in prosecuting or providing for the defense of actions or proceedings in behalf of the insured pursuant to the terms of this policy or to costs imposed on the insured in such actions or proceedings, and shall apply only to that portion of losses which exceed in the aggregate ten per cent of the face of the policy.

Provided, however, that the foregoing co-insurance provisions shall not apply to any loss arising out of a lien or encumbrance for a liquidated amount which existed on the date of this policy and was not shown in Schedule B; and provided further, such co-insurance provisions shall not apply to any loss if, at the time of the occurrence of such loss, the then value of the premises, as so improved, does not exceed one hundred twenty per centum of the amount of this policy.

(b) If the premises are divisible into separate, independent parcels, and a loss is established affecting one or more but not all of said parcels, the loss shall be computed and settled on a *pro rata* basis as if this policy were divided *pro rata* as to value of said separate, independent parcels, exclusive of improvements made subsequent to the date of this policy.

(c) Clauses "(a)" and "(b)" of this section apply to mortgage policies only after the insured shall have acquired the interest of the mortgagor.

(d) If, at the time liability for any loss shall have been fixed pursuant to the conditions of this policy, the insured holds another policy of insurance covering the same loss issued by another company, this company shall not be liable to the insured for a greater proportion of the loss than the amount that this policy bears to the whole amount of insurance held by the insured, unless another method of apportioning the loss shall have been provided by agreement between this company and the other insurer or insurers.

7. Assignment of Policy

If the interest insured by this policy is that of mortgagee, this policy may be assigned to and shall enure to the benefit of successive assignees of the mortgage without consent of this company or its endorsement of this policy. Provision is made in the rate manual of New York Board of Title Underwriters filed with the Super-

intendent of Insurance of the State of New York on behalf of this and other member companies for continuation of liability to grantees of the insured in certain specific circumstances only. In no circumstance provided for in this section shall this company be deemed to have insured the sufficiency of the form of the assignment or other instrument of transfer or conveyance or to have assumed any liability for the sufficiency of any proceedings after date of this policy.

8. Subrogation

(a) This company shall, to the extent of any payment by it of loss under this policy, be subrogated to all rights of the insured with respect thereto. The insured shall execute such instruments as may be requested to transfer such rights to this company. The rights so transferred shall be subordinate to any remaining interest of the insured.

(b) If the insured is a mortgagee, this company's right of subrogation shall not prevent the insured from releasing the personal liability of the obligor or guarantor or from releasing a portion of the premises from the lien of the mortgage or from increasing or otherwise modifying the insured mortgage provided such acts do not affect the validity or priority of the lien of the mortgage insured. However, the liability of this company under this policy shall in no event be increased by any such act of the insured.

9. Misrepresentation

Any untrue statement made by the insured with respect to any material fact, or any suppression of or failure to disclose any material fact, or any untrue answer by the insured to material inquiries before the issuance of this policy shall void this policy.

10. No Waiver of Conditions

This company may take any appropriate action under the terms of this policy whether or not it shall be liable hereunder and shall not thereby concede liability or waive any provision of this policy.

11. Policy Entire Contract

All actions or proceedings against this company must be based on the provisions of this policy. Any other action or actions or rights of action that the insured may have or may bring against this company in respect of other services rendered in connection with the issuance of this policy, shall be deemed to have merged in and be restricted to its terms and conditions.

12. Validation and Modification

This policy is valid only when duly signed by a va..dating officer or agent. Changes may be effected only by written endorsement. If the recording date of the instruments creating the insured interest is later than the policy date, such policy shall also cover intervening liens or encumbrances, except real estate taxes, assessments, water charges and sewer rents.

New York Board of Title Underwriters Form 100D (page 3 of 4)

F-3415R 10-77

Number	Date of Issue	Amount of Insurance

Name of Insured:

The estate or interest insured by this policy is   vested in the insured by means of

SCHEDULE A

The premises in which the insured has the estate or interest covered by this policy is described on the description sheet annexed.

SCHEDULE B

The following estates, interests, defects, objections to title, liens, and incumbrances and other matters are excepted from the coverage of this policy.

1. Defects and incumbrances arising or becoming a lien after the date of this policy, except as herein provided.

2. Consequences of the exercise and enforcement or attempted enforcement of any governmental, war or police powers over the premises.

3. Any laws, regulations or ordinances (including, but not limited to zoning, building, and environmental protection) as to the use, occupancy, subdivision or improvement of the premises adopted or imposed by any governmental body, or the effect of any noncompliance with or any violation thereof.

4. Judgments against the insured or estates, interests, defects, objections, liens or incumbrances created, suffered, assumed or agreed to by or with the privity of the insured.

5. Title to any property beyond the lines of the premises, or title to areas within or rights or easements in any abutting streets, roads, avenues, lanes, ways or waterways, or the right to maintain therein vaults, tunnels, ramps or any other structure or improvement, unless this policy specifically provides that such titles, rights, or easements are insured. Notwithstanding any provisions in this paragraph to the contrary, this policy, unless otherwise excepted, insures the ordinary rights of access and egress belonging to abutting owners.

6. Title to any personal property, whether the same be attached to or used in connection with said premises or otherwise.

Countersigned

_____
Authorized Signatory

NOTE: ATTACHED HERETO   ADDED PAGES.

New York Board of Title Underwriters Form 100D (page 4 of 4)

Form **2119**

Department of the Treasury
Internal Revenue Service (O)

Sale or Exchange of Principal Residence

▶ See instructions on back.

▶ **Attach to Form 1040 for year of sale (see instruction B).**

OMB No. 1545-0072

1984
21

Do not include expenses that you deduct as moving expenses.

Name(s) as shown on Form 1040.

Your social security number

1 (a) Date former residence sold ▶

(b) Enter the face amount of any mortgage, note (for example, second trust), or other financial instrument on which you will receive periodic payments of principal or interest from this sale ▶

2 (a) If you bought or built a new residence, enter date you occupied it; otherwise enter "none"

(b) Are any rooms in either residence rented out or used for business for which a deduction is allowed? ☐ Yes ☐ No
(If "Yes" do not include gain in line 7 from the rented or business part; instead include in income on Form 4797.)

Part I Gain and Adjusted Sales Price

3	Selling price of residence. (Do not include selling price of personal property items.)	**3**
4	Commissions and other expenses of sale not deducted as moving expenses	**4**
5	Amount realized (subtract line 4 from line 3)	**5**
6	Basis of residence sold	**6**
7	Gain on sale (subtract line 6 from line 5). If zero or less, enter zero and do not complete the rest of form. Enter the gain from this line on Schedule D, line 2 or 10*, unless you bought another principal residence or elect the exclusion in Part III.	**7**

If you haven't replaced your residence, do you plan to do so within the replacement period? ☐ Yes ☐ No
(If "Yes" see instruction B.)

8	Fixing-up expenses (see instructions for time limits.)	**8**
9	Adjusted sales price (subtract line 8 from line 5).	**9**

Part II Gain to be Postponed and Adjusted Basis of New Residence

Do not complete this part if you check "Yes" to 14(d) to elect the Age 55 or over Exclusion in Part III.

10	Cost of new residence	**10**
11	Gain taxable this year. (subtract line 10 from line 9). If result is zero or less, enter zero. Do not enter more than line 7. Enter the gain from this line on Schedule D, line 2 or 10.*	**11**
12	Gain to be postponed (subtract line 11 from line 7).	**12**
13	Adjusted basis of new residence (subtract line 12 from line 10)	**13**

Part III 55 or over Exclusion, Gain to be Reported, and Adjusted Basis of New Residence

		Yes	No
14 (a)	Were you 55 or over on date of sale?		
(b)	Was your spouse 55 or over on date of sale? (If you answered "No" to 14(a) and (b), do not complete this part.)		
(c)	Did the one who answered "Yes" to 14(a) or (b) own and use the property sold as his or her principal residence for a total of at least 3 years (except for short absences) of the 5-year period before the sale? (If "No," see Part II.)		
(d)	If you answered "Yes" to 14(c), do you elect to take the once in a lifetime exclusion of the gain on the sale? (If "Yes," complete the rest of Part III. If "No," see Part II.)		
(e)	At time of sale, was the residence owned by: ☐ you, ☐ your spouse, ☐ both of you?		
(f)	Social security number of spouse, at time of sale, if different from number on Form 1040 ▶ (Enter "none" if you were not married at time of sale.)		

Do not complete rest of Part III if you did not check "Yes" to line 14(d).

15	Enter the smaller of line 7 or $125,000 ($62,500, if married filing separate return)	**15**
16	Part of gain included (subtract line 15 from line 7)(If the result is zero, do not complete the rest of form.)	**16**
17	Cost of new residence. If you did not buy a new principal residence, enter "None." Then enter the gain from line 16 on Schedule D, line 10,* and do not complete the rest of form	**17**
18	Gain taxable this year. (subtract line 15 plus line 17 from line 9). If result is zero or less, enter zero. Do not enter more than line 16. Enter the gain from this line on Schedule D, line 10.*	**18**
19	Gain to be postponed (subtract line 18 from line 16)	**19**
20	Adjusted basis of new residence (subtract line 19 from line 17)	**20**

*Caution: If you completed Form 6252 for the residence in 1(a), do not enter your taxable gain from Form 2119 on Schedule D.

For Paperwork Reduction Act Notice, see back of form.

Form **2119** (1984)

Instructions

Paperwork Reduction Act Notice.—We ask for this information to carry out the Internal Revenue laws of the United States. We need it to ensure that taxpayers are complying with these laws and to allow us to figure and collect the right amount of tax. You are required to give us this information.

A. Purpose of Form.—Use Form 2119 to report gain from selling your principal residence, whether or not you buy another. A loss is not deductible. Use this form to postpone gain and make the one-time election to exclude it from your income.

If you sold your residence on the installment method, complete **Form 6252,** Computation of Installment Sale Income, in addition to Form 2119.

For more information, see **Publication 523,** Tax Information on Selling Your Home.

Principal Residence.—Postponement or exclusion of gain applies only to the sale of your principal residence. Usually, the home where you live is your principal residence. It can be for example, a house, houseboat, housetrailer, cooperative apartment, or condominium. If you have more than one residence, your principal residence is the one you physically occupy most of the time.

B. When to File.—File Form 2119 for the year of sale whether or not you replaced your principal residence.

In the following cases file 2 Forms 2119:

If you plan to replace your residence but have not done so by the time you file your return, and the replacement period has not expired, attach Form 2119 to Form 1040 for the year of sale, but complete lines 1 through 7 only. In that case, do not include the gain on Schedule D. If you replace it after you file your return, within the replacement period, and the new residence costs as much as the adjusted sales price of your old residence, write to notify the Director of the Internal Revenue Service Center where you filed your return. Attach a new Form 2119 for the year of sale.

If you replace your residence after you file your return, within the replacement period, and the new one costs less than the adjusted sales price of the old one, or you do not replace it within the replacement period, file **Form 1040X,** Amended U.S. Individual Income Tax Return, with a Schedule D and a new Form 2119 for the year of sale. Show the gain then. Interest will be charged on the additional tax due.

If you paid tax on the gain from selling your old residence and then buy a new one within the replacement period, file Form 1040X with Form 2119 to claim a refund.

C. Excluding Gain from Income.—You can elect to exclude from your income part or all of the gain from the sale of your principal residence if you meet the following tests:

1. You were 55 or over on the date of the sale.

2. Neither you nor your spouse has already elected this exclusion after July 26, 1978.

3. You owned and occupied your residence for periods totaling at least 3 years within the 5 years ending on the date of sale.

The exclusion election is a once-in-a-life-time election, so you may choose not to make it now.

The gain excluded from your income is never taxed. The rest of your gain is taxed in the year of sale, unless you replace the residence and postpone that part of the gain. Generally, you can make or revoke the exclusion election within 3 years from the date the return for the year you sold the residence was due, including extensions. Use Form 1040X to amend your return.

Married Taxpayers.—If you and your spouse own the property jointly and file a joint return, only one of you must meet the age, ownership, and use tests for electing the exclusion. If you do not own the property jointly, only the owner must meet these tests, regardless of your filing status on Form 1040.

If you are married at the time of sale, both you and your spouse must make the election to exclude the gain. If you do not file a joint return with that spouse, that spouse must consent to the election by writing in the bottom margin of Form 2119 or on an attached statement, "I consent to Part III election," and signing.

The election does not apply separately to you and your spouse. If you and your spouse make an election during marriage and later divorce, no further elections are available to either of you or to your new spouse if you remarry.

D. Postponing Gain on Sale of Principal Residence.— You may have to postpone gain if you buy or build, and occupy another principal residence within 2 years before or after the sale.

If, after you sell your old residence, you are on active duty in the U.S. Armed Forces for more than 90 days, or you live and work outside the U.S., see Publication 523 for a longer replacement period.

If you sell the new residence in a later year and do not replace it, the postponed gain will be taxed then. If you do replace it, you may continue to postpone the gain. If you change your principal residence more than once during the replacement period, only the last residence you bought qualifies as your new residence for postponing gain, unless you sold the residence because of a job relocation and are allowed a moving expense deduction.

E. Applying Separate Gain to Basis of New Residence.—If you own the old residence separately, but you and your spouse own the new residence jointly (or vice versa) you and your spouse may elect to divide the gain and the adjusted basis if both of you:

1. use the old and new residences as your principal residence; and

2. sign a consent that says, "We consent to reduce the basis of the new residence by the gain from selling the old residence." Write this statement in the bottom margin of Form 2119 or on an attached sheet, and sign it. If you both do not sign the consent, determine the recognition of gain in the regular way with no division.

Line-By-Line Instructions

Use Parts I and II to figure the gain that must be postponed. Complete Parts I and III if you elect the one-time exclusion.

Line 3. Selling Price of Residence.— Enter the amount of money you received, the amount of all notes, mortgages, or other liabilities to which the property was subject, and the fair market value of any other property you received.

Note: *Report interest from a note as income for the tax year in which the interest is received.*

Line 4. Commissions and Other Expenses of Sale.—This includes sales commissions, advertising expenses, attorney and legal fees, etc., incurred in order to sell the old residence. Loan charges, such as "loan placement fees" or "points" charged the seller are selling expenses.

Line 6. Basis of Residence Sold.—Include the original cost of the property, commissions, and other expenses incurred in buying it, plus the cost of improvements. Subtract any depreciation allowed or allowable, any casualty loss or energy credit you took on the residence, and the postponed gain on the sale or exchange of a previous principal residence. For more information, see **Publication 551,** Basis of Assets.

Line 8. Fixing-up Expenses.—These are decorating and repair expenses incurred only to help sell the old property. You must have incurred them for work performed within 90 days before the contract to sell was signed, and paid for within 30 days after the sale. Do not include capital expenditures for permanent improvements or replacements that are added to the basis of the property sold.

Lines 10 and 17. Cost of New Residence.—The cost of your new residence includes one or more of the following:

(a) cash payments;
(b) the amount of any mortgage or other debt on the new residence;
(c) commissions and other purchase expenses you paid that were not deducted as moving expenses;
(d) construction costs (when you build your own residence) made within 2 years before and 2 years after the sale of the old residence;
(e) if you buy rather than build your new residence, all capital expenditures made within 2 years before and 2 years after the sale of the old residence.

TP-584 (7/84)

New York State
Department of
TAXATION
and FINANCE

REAL PROPERTY TRANSFER GAINS TAX
AFFIDAVIT OF INDIVIDUALS

STATE OF   )
) SS:
COUNTY OF   )

I (we) _____ , being duly sworn, depose(s) and say(s) under penalty of perjury that (I am) (we are) the (transferor(s)) (transferee(s)) of real property located at _____ , _____ ,
                          Street   City
New York; that property has been, or is being transferred to/from _____ _____ , for a consideration of _____ ; that it is true to the knowledge of the affiant(s) that the transfer of such real property is exempt from the Tax on Gains Derived From Certain Real Property Transfers imposed by Article 31-B of the Tax Law by reason that: (Check Appropriate Box)

    1. [ ] the transfer of real property consists of the execution of a contract to sell real property without the use or occupancy of such property or the granting of an option to purchase real property without the use or occupancy of such property.

    2. [ ] the transfer is a transfer of real property where the consideration is less than five hundred thousand dollars and which is neither (A) pursuant to a cooperative or condominium plan, nor (B) a partial or successive transfer pursuant to an agreement or plan to effectuate by partial or successive transfers a transfer which would otherwise be included in the coverage of Article thirty-one-B of the Tax Law.

    3. [ ] the transfer is a transfer of real property by tenants in common, joint tenants or tenants by the entirety where the aggregate consideration is less than five hundred thousand dollars. (All such transferors must sign this form.)

    4. [ ] the conveyance is not a transfer of real property within the meaning of subdivision seven of section fourteen hundred forty of Article thirty-one-B of the Tax Law. (Attach documents supporting such claim.)

    5. [ ] the transfer of real property consists of premises wholly occupied and used by the transferor exclusively as his residence, including a cooperative apartment or condominium occupied by the transferor exclusively as a residence. (See footnote.) (A TRANSFEREE MAY NOT CHECK THIS BOX.)

_____
Transferor's or Transferee's Signature

_____
Transferor's or Transferee's
Social Security Number

_____

_____

_____

_____

Subscribed and sworn before me this _____ day of _____ , 19____ .

_____
NOTARY PUBLIC
COUNTY OF _____

STATE OF_____

These statements are made with the knowledge that a willfully false representation is unlawful and is punishable as the crime of perjury under Article 210 of the Penal Law.

This affidavit must be filed on the date of transfer with the recording officer of the county wherein the real property transferred is located or if the transfer is not recorded, directly with: New York State Department of Taxation and Finance, P.O. Box 5045, Albany, NY 12205.

*If only part of the premises was actually occupied and used for residential purposes and if the consideration for the entire real property is $500,000 or more, Form TP-580, New York State Real Property Transfer Gains Tax, Questionnaire - Transferor and Form TP-581, New York State Real Property Transfer Gains Tax, Questionnaire - Transferee, must be completed. See instructions, Form TP-580-I and TP-581-I.

Real Property Transfer Gains Tax Affidavit—Individual

TP-584-C   (7/84)

New York State
Department of
TAXATION
and FINANCE

REAL PROPERTY TRANSFER GAINS TAX
AFFIDAVIT
CORPORATION, PARTNERSHIP, ESTATE OR TRUST

STATE OF   )
) SS:
COUNTY OF   )

I _____, being duly sworn, depose and say under penalty of perjury
that I am the _____ of _____
                      Title   Corporation, Partnership, Estate or Trust
the (transferor) (transferee) of real property located at _____,
                                                                   Street
_____, New York; that property has been, or is being transferred
          City
to/from _____, for a consideration of
_____; that it is true to the knowledge of the affiant that
the transfer of such real property is exempt from the Tax on Gains Derived From
Certain Real Property Transfers imposed by Article 31-B of the Tax Law by reason
that: (Check Appropriate Box)

1. [ ]   the transfer of real property consists of the execution of a
           contract to sell real property without the use or occupancy of
           such property or the granting of an option to purchase real
           property without the use or occupancy of such property.

2. [ ]   the transfer is a transfer of real property where the consid-
           eration is less than five hundred thousand dollars and which
           is neither (A) pursuant to a cooperative or condominium plan,
           nor (B) a partial or successive transfer pursuant to an
           agreement or plan to effectuate by partial or successive
           transfers a transfer which would otherwise be included in the
           coverage of Article thirty-one-B of the Tax Law.

3. [ ]   the transfer is a transfer of real property by tenants in
           common, joint tenants or tenants by the entirety where the
           aggregate consideration is less than five hundred thousand
           dollars. (All such transferors must sign this form.)

4. [ ]   the conveyance is not a transfer of real property within the
           meaning of subdivision seven of section fourteen hundred forty
           of Article thirty-one-B of the Tax Law. (Attach documents
           supporting such claim.)

5. [ ]   the transfer of real property consists of premises wholly
           occupied and used by the transferor exclusively as his
           residence, including a cooperative apartment or condominium
           occupied by the transferor exclusively as a residence. (See
           footnote.) *This exemption may only be claimed by an estate
           or trust which is a transferor.

_____   _____
     Transferor or Transferee   Transferor's or Transferee's
                                                 Federal Employer I.D. Number

By _____
          (Title)

Subscribed and sworn before me this _____ day of _____, 19____.

_____
NOTARY PUBLIC
COUNTY OF _____

STATE OF_____

These statements are made with the knowledge that a willfully false representation
is unlawful and is punishable as the crime of perjury under Article 210 of the Penal
Law.

This affidavit must be filed on the date of transfer with the recording officer of
the county wherein the real property transferred is located or if the transfer is
not recorded, directly with: New York State Department of Taxation and Finance,
P.O. Box 5045, Albany, NY 12205.

*If only part of the premises was actually occupied and used for residential
purposes and if the consideration for the entire real property is $500,000 or more,
Form TP-580, New York State Real Property Transfer Gains Tax Questionnaire -
Transferor and Form TP-581, New York State Real Property Transfer Gains Tax
Questionnaire - Transferee, must be completed. See instructions, Form TP-580-I and
TP-581-I.

Real Property Transfer Gains Tax Affidavit—Corporation, Partnership, Estate or Trust

Glossary of Real Estate Terms

Abandonment: The voluntary surrender, relinquishment, disclaimer, or cession of property or rights.

Abatement: Termination; end; reduction of amount otherwise due.

Abatement of nuisance: Termination of a nuisance.

Abrogate: To repeal; to make void; to annul.

Absolute fee simple: Complete ownership and control without condition or limitation.

Abstract of judgment: A summation of the essentials of a court judgment.

Abstract of title: A summary of the conveyances, transfers, and other facts relied on as evidence of title, together with all such facts appearing on record which may impair the validity. It should contain a brief but complete history of the title.

Accelerated depreciation: A method of depreciation used in the computation of income taxes, which speeds up the write-off of the value of the property at a rate greater than normal depreciation.

Acceleration clause: A clause giving the lender the right to call all sums owed him immediately due and payable upon the occurrence of a specified event, such as default, sale, etc.

Acceptance: Acceptance is determined by the seller's or his agent's agreement to the terms of the agreement of sale; approval of the negotiation on the part of the agent.

Acceptance of deed: The physical taking of the deed by the grantee recognizing the vesting of title in the grantee. Upon due execution and recording of a deed, acceptance is generally presumed.

Accessibility: Ease or difficulty of approach to real property, either via public land or by private property maintained for public use.

Accession: In its legal meaning, generally used to signify the acquisition of property by incorporation or union with other property.

Access right: The right of an owner to have ingress and egress to and from his or her real property.

Accretion: The act of growing; usually applied to the gradual and imperceptible accumulation of land through natural causes, as out of the sea or a river.

Accrued depreciation: The difference between the cost of replacement at the date of the original appraisal and the present appraised value.

Accrued interest: Accrue is to grow, to be added to. Accrued interest is interest which has been earned but which is not yet due and payable.

Acknowledgment: A formal declaration of one's signing of an instrument before a duly authorized public official.

Acknowledgment of a deed: A form of authenticating instruments conveying property or otherwise conferring rights. It is a public declaration by the grantor that the act evidenced by the instrument is his or her act or deed.

Acquisition: Making property one's own; obtaining the ownership of or an interest in property.

Acre: A unit of land measure equal to 43,560 square feet.

Actual age: The number of years a structure has actually existed.

Adjacent: Usually used to designate property which is in the neighborhood of other property but which does not actually touch such property; sometimes used to mean touching or contiguous, e.g., immediately adjacent.

Adjoining: Touching or contiguous, as distinguished from lying near or adjacent.

Adjustments: Those items which should be prorated or apportioned between the purchaser and seller of a real estate transaction, i.e., taxes, rents, fuel.

Administration: The management of a business, activity, or resource.

Administration of real estate resources: The efficient utilization of real estate resources to achieve desired results.

Administrator: A person to whom letters of administration, that is, authority to administer the estate of a deceased person who died intestate, have been granted by the proper court.

Administrator's deed: A deed used to convey the property of one who has died intestate (leaving no will).

Ad valorem tax: A tax according to a fixed percentage of value.

Advance: In regard to a construction loan, a periodic transfer of funds from the lender to the borrower during the construction process.

Advance fee: A fee paid in advance of service rendered in the sale of property or in obtaining a loan.

Advancement: A gift from a parent to a child in anticipation of the share the child will eventually inherit from the parent's estate, which is intended to be deducted therefrom.

Adverse possession: A method of acquiring title to real property by occupying it actually, openly, notoriously, exclusively, and continuously under a claim of right for the required statutory period of time.

Advertising real estate: The act of informing the public in order to produce action regarding real estate; public announcements to aid in the sale of real property.

Affiant: Any person who has made an affidavit.

Affidavit: A statement or declaration reduced to writing and sworn to or affirmed before a public official who has authority to administer an oath or affirmation.

Affirm: To confirm or verify.

Affirmation: The confirmation of a former judgment or court order; the confirmation by a principal of an agent's acts.

Affirmative action program: A detailed plan used to overcome the causes and effects of discriminatory policies in the hiring, employment and/or training of minority group members; the program also investigates complaints made to HUD concerning housing.

Affirmative easement: An easement giving the owner of the dominant estate the right to use the servient estate or tenement for certain purposes. For example, a right of way over the servient tenement to a main highway and a right to install water or sewer pipes through the servient estate are affirmative easements.

We gratefully acknowledge permission to use materials from Alvin L. Arnold and Jack Kusnet, *The Arnold Encyclopedia of Real Estate*, published by Warren, Gorham & Lamont.

After-acquired property: Property acquired after a particular date or event, e.g., the execution of a mortgage to property not yet owned.

Agency: The relationship between principal and agent, arising from a contract wherein the agent is employed by the principal to perform certain acts dealing with third parties.

Agent: One who represents another, who is known as the principal.

Agreement: A coming together of minds; in contract law, a meeting of the minds.

Agreement of sale: A written agreement whereby the purchaser agrees to buy specific real estate and the seller agrees to sell upon specific terms and conditions set forth in the contract.

AIREA: See American Institute of Real Estate Appraisers.

Air rights: Rights in real property to use the space above the surface of the land.

Alienation: The voluntary act or acts by which one person transfers his or her own property to another. There can be involuntary alienation as in the event of unpaid taxes, bankruptcy, etc.

Alienation clause: Provision in a mortgage that permits the mortgagee to accelerate the loan (demand immediate payment) upon a transfer of title to the property securing the loan. Also known as a due on sale clause.

Allodial land: Land held in absolute independence, without being subject to any rent, service, or acknowledgment to a superior; opposed to "feud."

Allodial ownership: A system of free individual ownership of real property under which ownership may be complete except for government-held rights.

Alluvion: Soil deposited by natural accretion, i.e., an increase of earth on a shore or river bank.

Amenities, amenity return: Satisfactions received through using rights in real property and not in monetary form.

American Bankers' Association (ABA): A trade association of commercial bankers.

American Institute of Real Estate Appraisers (AIREA): A trade association of real estate appraisers, which conducts educational programs, publishes materials, and promotes research on real estate appraisal. Confers MAI (Member, Appraisal Institute) and RM (Residential Member).

American Society of Appraisers (ASA): The national professional and trade association for appraisers and their firms.

American Society of Real Estate Counselors (ASREC): A national professional and trade association of developers, consultants, and experienced advisors on all real estate matters. Confers CRE (Counselor on Real Estate).

Amortization: The process of paying an obligation through a series of payments over time. Generally the payments are made in equal amounts, including principal and interest, and at uniform time intervals.

Amortized mortgage: A mortgage in which repayment is made according to a plan requiring the payment of certain amounts at specified times so that all the debt is repaid at the end of the term.

Annuity: An amount of money or its equivalent which represents one of a series of periodic payments.

Apportionment: Adjustment of the income, expenses, or carrying charges of real estate usually computed to the date of closing of title so that the seller pays all the expenses to that date. The buyer assumes all expenses commencing at the date the deed is conveyed to the buyer.

Appraisal: An opinion or estimate of value of property. Also refers to the report setting forth the estimate and conclusion of value.

Appraisal inventory: A compilation of all separate items comprising property included in an appraisal report and valued by the appraiser.

Appraisal process: The method of making an estimate of value; the art of judging the market value of property, either real or personal, i.e., the price at which the property would be sold by a willing and knowledgeable seller after bargaining with a willing and knowledgeable buyer.

Appraisal report: A report of the appraised value, together with pertinent information concerning the property appraised and the evidence and analysis leading to the reported value estimate.

Appraiser: One who is in the business of making appraisals on the basis of a fee or salary in conjunction with some compensated employment.

Appreciation: An increased value in property

Appurtenance: Property that is an accessory to other property to which it is annexed.

Arterial highway: A major route into a prime traffic area.

Artisan's lien: A lien given under common law to one skilled in some kind of mechanical craft or art for the reasonable charges for his or her work.

ASREC: See American Society of Real Estate Counselors.

Assemblage: The act of bringing together two individuals or things to form a new whole; specifically, the cost of assembling parcels of land under a single ownership. See plottage.

Asssessed valuation: The process by which a value is placed upon property by a public official or officials as a basis for taxation.

Assessed value: The value placed on property for the purpose of taxation.

Assessment: A levy or tax imposed on real estate for improvements or taxes.

Assessor: An official whose responsibility is to determine assessed values for taxation.

Assets: Property of any kind under ownership.

Assignee: A person to whom an assignment is made; a successor in interest to the rights of a party to a contract.

Assignment: A transfer or setting over of property, or some right or interest therein, from one person to another. In its ordinary application, the word is limited to the transfer of choses in action, e.g., the assignment of a contract.

Assignor: A person who makes an assignment of interest in a contract.

Assumed name: A name other than one's own under which a person engages in a business venture.

Assumption agreement: The undertaking of a debt or obligation of another by contract.

Assumption of a mortgage: The undertaking of a mortgage, by the buyer, which is currently held against the real estate the buyer is purchasing.

Attachment: A writ issued in the course of a lawsuit, directing the sheriff or law officer to attach the property of the defendant to satisfy the demands of the plaintiff.

Attachment of property: Taking property into the legal custody of an officer by virtue of the directions contained in a writ of attachment; a seizure under a writ of debtor's property.

Attest: To affirm a statement or document to be genuine or accurate.

Attestation: The act of witnessing the execution of a paper and subscribing the name of the witness in testimony of such fact.

Attorney in fact: One who is authorized to perform certain acts for another under a power of attorney.

Auction: A public sale of property to the highest bidder.

Authentication: Such official attestation of a written instrument as will render it legally admissible as evidence in a law court.

Avulsion: The removal of land from one owner to another when a stream, etc., suddenly changes its course.

Axial growth: City growth which moves out along main transportation routes, taking the form of fingerlike extensions.

Backfill: The replacement of excavated earth against a structure or to fill a hole.

Balloon mortgage payment: A large payment during the term of a mortgage, often at the end.

Balustrade: A supporting column for a handrail.

Bargain and sale deed with covenant: A deed which conveys the real property described and which contains a covenant by the grantor warranting title against his acts only. The warranty is thus generally limited to claims held by, through or under the grantor arising out of the period of grantor's ownership.

Bargain and sale deed without covenant: A deed which conveys the real property described but which contains no covenant warranting title.

Barter: The exchange of goods or commodities for other goods or commodities.

Base and meridian: Imaginary lines used by surveyors as a reference to find and describe land location. (Base lines run east and west, meridian lines run north and south.)

Baseboard heating: A system of heating in which the radiators or convectors are located in or on the wall, replacing the baseboard itself.

Base line: A part of the rectangular survey system; a parallel which serves as a reference for other parallels.

Base molding: Molding used at the top of a baseboard.

Base shoe: Molding used at the junction of a baseboard and the floor; more commonly known as a carpet strip.

Basic employment, urban growth employment: Employment in establishments that receive their income from outside the community.

Basic income: Income received from outside the community.

Batten: Narrow strips of wood or metal used to cover joints; may be used for a decorative effect.

Beam: A horizontal load-supporting member.

Bedroom community: A suburban community in which a large number of a major city's workers reside.

Beltline highway: A limited-access highway which surrounds a city.

Bench mark: Permanent markers placed by surveyors at important points, upon which local surveys are based.

Beneficiary: A person having the enjoyment of property of which a trustee, executor, etc., has the legal possession; the person to whom a policy of insurance is payable.

Benefit-cost ratio: A measure of social benefits to dollar cost.

Bequeath: Commonly used to denote a testamentary gift; synonymous with "to devise."

Bequest: That which is given according to the terms of a will.

Betterment: A property improvement which increases the property value.

Bilateral contract: A contract under which two parties exchange promises for the performance of certain acts; for example, A promises to buy B's house, and B promises to sell it to A.

Bill of sale: A written instrument which evidences the transfer of title to personal property from seller to buyer.

Binder: A preliminary agreement in writing as evidence of good faith by the offerer; the memorandum of an agreement for insurance, intended to give temporary protection pending investigation of the risk and issuance of a formal policy. See title insurance.

Blacktop: Asphalt paving.

Blanket mortgage: A mortgage that has two or more properties pledged or conveyed as security for a debt.

Blight: Decay, as in the case of a neighborhood.

Blockbusting: The illegal practice of introducing a nonconforming user or use into a neighborhood for the purpose of causing an abnormally high turnover of property ownership in the area.

Board foot: A unit of measurement for lumber; 144 cubic inches; 1 foot wide, 1 foot long, 1 inch thick.

Bona fide: Good faith.

Bona fide mortgagee: One who acquires an interest in property for a valuable consideration, in good faith and without knowledge of rights of others or infirmities in the seller's or mortgagor's title.

Bona fide purchaser: A purchaser who, for a valuable consideration paid in the belief that the vendor had a right to sell, purchases a particular property.

Bond: An instrument used as evidence of a debt; also a guarantee of performance.

Borough: A land division of a city having its own charter.

Bracing: Lumber nailed at an angle in order to provide rigidity.

Breach: The breaking or violation of a law, right, or duty, either by commission or omission; failure to meet a contractual obligation.

Breakeven point: The amount of income needed to just meet the total amount of expenses for a project.

Breezeway: A covered passage, open on two sides, connecting a house with a garage or other parts of the house.

Bridging: Small wood or metal pieces used to brace floor joists.

Broker: An agent who negotiates for the sale, leasing, management, or financing of a property or of property rights on a commission basis.

Brokerage: The business of a broker; the selling of products or assets of others.

BTU: British thermal unit; the amount of heat required to raise the temperature of 1 pound of water. 1°F.

Budget mortgage: A type of amortizing mortgage which includes in the monthly payments of principal and interest other costs such as taxes and fire insurance; referred to as a PITI monthly payment.

Builder: One who improves land by erecting structures.

Building codes: Rules promulgated by a local government entity (e.g., municipal or county) regulating building and construction standards designed to preserve, protect, and promote the public health, safety, and welfare.

Building line: A setback line; a line set by law or deed restriction a certain distance from a street in front of which an owner cannot build.

Building loan agreement: An agreement whereby the lender obligates himself to advance money to an owner with provisional payments at certain stages of construction.

Building paper: A heavy, waterproof paper used as sheathing in wall or roof construction.

Building permit: Authorization by a local government for the erection, alteration, or remodeling of improvements within its jurisdiction.

Building restrictions: Limitations on the use of property established by legislation or by covenants or limitations in deeds.

Built in: Such features built as part of the house, e.g., cabinets, etc.

Bundle of rights: The definition of ownership based on the concept of combining all possible interests in land into a whole.

Business broker: A person, firm, or corporation that negotiates the sale of business establishments.

Business-government relations: The framework of laws, codes, regulations, and contracts between business and government within which business operates.

Business risk: Anticipation of losses caused by internal operating inefficiencies and external factors.

Buyer's market: A market characterized by many available properties and few potential users demanding them at prevailing prices.

Buying, assuming, and agreeing to pay: Undertaking and promising to pay the seller's personal liability for a debt at the time of purchase.

Buying subject to: Phrase meaning no personal liability is assumed in regard to a mortgage debt which exists against real estate at the time of purchase.

By-laws: In reference to condominiums, the day-to-day rules and regulations for operation of the project. They usually appear as an appendix to the master deed and are recorded. Generally, self-imposed rules adopted by a corporation or other group.

California ranch house: A one-story house having a style similar to that of a ranch.

Cancellation clause: A provision in a lease that confers upon one or more or all of the parties to the lease the right to terminate the party's or parties' obligations thereunder upon the occurrence of the condition or contingency set forth in the said clause.

Cape Cod architecture: A style featuring a steeply sloped gable roof, dormer windows for second-story rooms, windows with shutters, a square chimney, and usually having Early American decor.

Capital: The store of produced goods (money) used for the production of income.

Capital asset: Any asset of a permanent nature used for the production of income (land, buildings, machinery, equipment, etc.).

Capital gain: Income that results from the sale of an asset and not from the usual course of business. (Capital gains are taxed at a lower rate than ordinary income.)

Capital recapture: The manner in which the investment in a property is to be returned to investors; normally stated as a rate or dollar amount per unit of time.

Capitalism: An economic system based on the principles of ownership of private property, equality, and personal rights.

Capitalization: The process of reflecting future income in present value; capitalization in perpetuity is capitalization without a time limit.

Capitalization rate: A percentage made up of the interest rate (return on the investment) plus the recapture rate (return of the original investment).

Carport: A roof over part of a driveway, usually extending from the side of a house.

Carrying charges: Charges for holding property, such as tax expense on idle property or property under construction.

Casement windows: Windows with frames of wood or metal which swing outward.

Cash flow: The net income from a property before depreciation and other noncash expenses.

Caveat emptor: Let the buyer beware. The maxim expresses the general idea that the buyer purchases at his or her peril, and that no warranties, either express or implied, are made by the seller.

Caucasian clause: A restriction in a conveyance which restricts the use or occupancy of the affected premises only to members of the white race; a clause which prohibits the use and occupancy of premises by individuals of a particular race, religion, or nationality.

CCIM: Certified Commercial and Investment Member. A designation conferred by RNMI.

Cease and desist order: An order executed by the Secretary of State directing broker recipients to cease and desist from all solicitation of homeowners whose names and addresses appear on the list forwarded with such order.

Central business district: The downtown shopping and office area of a city.

Central city: The downtown area of a city; also, a city that is the center of a geographic trade area for which it performs certain market and service functions.

Certificate of acknowledgment: A certificate of a notary or other duly authorized public official stating that a particular individual appeared before the officer who acknowledged the execution of an instrument.

Certificate of compliance: A document issued by a municipality that proves compliance by the recipient of certain conditions referred to in previously issued building or alteration permits.

Certificate of occupancy (CO): A document issued by a zoning board, building department, or other municipal agency to indicate that a structure complies with building code requirements and may be legally occupied.

Certificate of no defense: An instrument executed by the mortgagor, upon the sale of the mortgage, to the assignee as to the validity of the full mortgage debt. See estoppel certificate.

Certificate of sale: A document issued to the highest bidder at a foreclosure sale to indicate ownership.

Certificate of title: A certificate issued by a person who has examined the record of title of real estate as to the state of the title of such real estate.

Certificates of beneficial interest: The ownership shares in a trust or mutual fund.

Certified Residential Broker (CRB): Designation granted by NIREB.

Certiorari: An appellate proceeding for reexamination of the action of an inferior tribunal, or an auxiliary process to enable the appellate court to obtain further information in a pending case.

Cestui que use: One who has the right to receive the profits and benefits of the lands or tenements, the legal title and possession of which are held by another person as trustee.

Chain measures: A series of 100 interconnected wire links each of which is 1 foot in length. A chain 66 feet in length, composed of interconnected wire links each of which is 7.92 inches long. (10 square chains of land equal 1 acre.)

Chain of title: Successive conveyances, or other forms of alienation, affecting a particular parcel of land, arranged consecutively, from the government or original source of title down to the present holder.

Chancellor: The name given in some states to the judge of a court of chancery (equity).

Chancery: A court of equity; the system of jurisdiction administered in courts of equity.

Change: The appraisal principle which describes existence in three states: integration, equilibrium, and degeneration; holds that it is the future not the past which is of prime importance in estimating value.

Chattel mortgage: A mortgage of personal property to secure a debt. See security interest.

Chattel personal: An object of movable personal property.

Chattel real: An item usually considered personal property which is annexed to or attached to real estate.

Chattels: Items of personal property.

Chose in action: A right of action for recovery of a debt.

Circuit breaker: The electrical instrument which automatically breaks an electric circuit when an overload occurs.

Circulating fireplace: A type of fireplace which is built around

a metal form, containing air ducts to distribute heat by convection.

Civil action: Any lawsuit between private parties.

Clapboard: The boards used for siding, which are usually thicker at one edge.

Clear title: A title free of any encumbrances or defects.

Client: The one by whom a broker is employed and by whom the broker will be compensated on completion of the purpose of the agency.

Close: A parcel of land, enclosed by a fence, hedge, or visual enclosure; in surveying it has several meanings and could easily be confused with "closing." Close also refers to completing a transaction; when real estate formally changes ownership.

Closing costs: The costs of the settlement in the transfer of property ownership, such as recording fees, attorney fees, title insurance premium, etc.

Closing date: The date upon which title is transferred and the buyer takes over the property; usually between 30 and 60 days after the signing of the contract.

Closing statement: A listing of the debits and credits of the buyer and seller in a real estate transaction for the final financial settlement of the transaction.

Cloud on the title: An outstanding claim or condition which affects the title to property and which cannot be removed without a quitclaim deed or court action.

Cluster housing: A housing arrangement in which units are placed close together to allow for large recreational or common areas.

Cluster zoning: Zoning laws which permit units to be placed close together so as to allow for large recreational or common areas.

Code of ethics: The standards adopted by NAR and the various real estate boards for the business conduct of members.

Codicil: Some addition to or amendment of one's last will and testament.

Cognovit clause: The borrower confesses judgment or gives written authority to the lender to secure a judgment that can be attached to the borrower's property as a lien; a waiver of any defense to the claim.

Cognovit note: A note which authorizes a confession of judgment and admission of the validity of a claim for money.

Collar beam: The beam that joins together the pairs of opposite roof rafters above the attic floor.

Collateral: Anything of value that a borrower pledges as security.

Collateral security: An additional obligation to guarantee performance of a contract.

Collusion: A secret combination, conspiracy, or concert of action between two or more persons for fraudulent or deceitful purposes.

Colonial architecture: The traditional design, usually using the characteristics of New England homes; usually two-story houses with balanced openings along the main facade, windows constructed with small panes, shutters and dormer windows on the third floor, with attention to small detail.

Color of title: A writing upon the face of a document professing to pass title but which does not, either through want of title in the grantor or a defective mode of conveyance; that which appears to be good title, but as a matter of fact, is not good title.

Combed plywood: A grooved building plywood used mainly for interior finish.

Combination door: A permanent door that employs a screen panel for summer and glass panel for winter.

Commercial acre: The remnant of an acre of newly subdivided land after the land devoted to streets, sidewalks, etc., has been deducted.

Commercial banks: National or state chartered banks which operate on a basis of stock ownership. The dividends are distributed to the shareholders. The depositors have no share in the management.

Commercial easement in gross: An easement in gross which is not appurtenant to any estate or tenement; unlike other easements in gross it is assignable and runs with the land. Examples include railroad rights of way and general utility easements.

Commercial paper: Bills of exchange or other debt instruments used in place of money.

Commercial properties: Properties intended for use in business areas.

Commercial structures: Structures intended for use in business.

Commingle: To mix, as to deposit a client's funds in the broker's personal account.

Commission: An agent's compensation for the performance of his duties; in real estate, a percentage of the selling price of property or percentage of rentals.

Commitment: For a mortgage, a statement by the lender of the conditions and terms under which he or she will lend. A conditional commitment is a statement that mortgage funds will be provided if certain conditions are met which permit an owner or developer to begin construction. A firm commitment is a written notification that a financial institution will lend money and on what terms it will do so.

Commitment (or binder) to insure: The form of preliminary title evidence issued by a title insurer which indicates the conditions under which it will issue its title policy.

Common law: Rules developed by usage; judge-made law.

Common property: Land considered to be public property; also, a legal term denoting an incorporeal hereditament consisting of a right of one person in the land of another.

Common scheme restrictions: Uniform restrictions imposed by a developer who subdivides property in all the deeds to the different lots concerning the use of the burdened property.

Common wall: The wall which serves two dwellings simultaneously.

Community Associations Institute (CAI): A national association of homeowners' associations.

Community property: In certain states, the property owned by the "community" or marriage of husband and wife; property owned by the marriage and not in shares.

Compaction: The act of compressing soil added as fill to a lot so that it will bear the weight of buildings without the danger of their settling, tilting, or cracking.

Comparables: Properties of like nature which might be compared to one another through careful study, thereby allowing a value to be determined for one of them.

Compensatory damages: Are such as will simply make good or replace the loss caused by wrong or injury and nothing more.

Competence: Under the law of evidence, being of such form as to be admissible in court for use as evidence.

Competent: Legally qualified and mentally capable to transact business.

Complainant: The party who instigates a legal action.

Compound interest: The interest paid on the original principal and on the accrued interest from the time it became due.

Concentric circle hypothesis: Transportation is assumed to be the central force in community growth. Therefore the land values are highest where mobility is greatest.

Concentric circles: Ring growth around the nucleus of an urban area.

Conclusive evidence: Incontrovertible evidence.

Condemnation: The process by which property of a private owner is taken for public use without the owner's consent but with the owner's awareness and with payment of just compensation. The exercise of the right of eminent domain.

Condition: A future and uncertain event upon the happening of which is made to depend the existence of an obligation, or that which subordinates the existence of liability under a contract to a certain future event.

Conditional fee: See fee simple conditional.

Conditional sale: A term most frequently applied to a sale wherein the seller reserves the title to the goods, though the possession is delivered to the buyer, until the purchase price is paid in full.

Conditional sales contract: A contract for the sale of property specifying that delivery is to be made to the buyer with the title to remain vested in the seller until the conditions of the contract have been fulfilled.

Conditional vendee: The buyer under a conditional sales contract.

Conditional vendor: The seller under a conditional sales contract.

Condominium: The individual ownership of a single unit in a multiunit structure, together with an interest in the common land areas and the underlying ground.

Condominium conversion: A process by which rental units are turned into individually owned units.

Conduit: A metal pipe through which electrical wiring is installed.

Confession of judgment: An entry of judgment upon the debtor's voluntary admission without defense in a legal proceeding. See cognovit note.

Confirmation: The ratification of a transaction known to be voidable.

Confirmation of sale: A court approval of the sale of property by an executor, administrator, guardian, or conservator of an estate.

Confiscation: The seizure of property without compensation.

Conformity: The blending of the use of real estate and

improvements upon it with the surroundings so as to appear harmonious.

Consequential damage: The impairment of value which arises as an indirect result of an act.

Conservation: The process of saving resources or of using them in such a way that they will not be depleted.

Consideration: Anything of value given or given up by both parties to a contract and necessary to the enforcement of the contract.

Constant: The percentage of the unpaid balance of a loan which is represented by the sum of the principal and interest payment for the following year, which is needed to fully amortize the loan.

Constant payment: A regular, periodic payment which does not fluctuate in amount and which includes both interest and amortization.

Constant-payment mortgage: A loan reduction plan whereby the borrower pays a fixed amount each month, part to be applied to repayment of the principal and the remainder to payment of interest.

Construction loan: A loan to finance the improvement of real estate, generally short-term or interim financing pending completion of improvements.

Constructive eviction: Inability of a tenant to retain possession by reason of a condition making occupancy hazardous or unfit for its intended use.

Constructive notice: Not actual notice, but the notice the law charges one with as imparted from the public records, an inspection of the premises, and the possession thereof.

Constructive trustee: One who is a trustee by operation of law resulting from unlawful possession of property of another.

Consultant: An advisor on matters who receives a fee for his or her services and advice.

Consumer goods: Goods used or purchased primarily for personal, family, or household purposes.

Contemporary architecture: Modern design, as differentiated from the traditional; functional design.

Contiguous: Adjacent; touching or adjoining.

Contingencies: Possible future events which are uncertain.

Contingent fees: Payment to be made upon future occurrences, conclusions, or results of services to be performed.

Contract: A written or oral agreement to perform or not to perform certain obligations.

Contract for deed: See conditional sales contract.

Contract rent: Rent stipulated in a lease agreement.

Contractor: One who has the responsibility for and supervises the improvement of land.

Contribution: A payment by each, or by any; of several having a common interest or liability of his or her share in the loss suffered, or in the money necessarily paid by one of the parties in behalf of the others.

Control data: The means of using the transactions of real properties to adjust the market data utilized in the comparative approach to valuation. Such control data is necessary in order to segregate certain influences which have caused changes in real estate values, either generally or specifically.

Convenience factor: The commonly recognized and easily understood quality offering advantages and values to a particular parcel of real property over that of other properties.

Conventional home: A home that is constructed totally at the site. It is the opposite of a factory-built or mobile home.

Conventional loan: A mortgage loan made by a financial institution, conforming to its own standards, modified within legal bounds by mutual consent of the parties involved, and without insurance or guarantee by the FHA or VA.

Conventional mortgage: A mortgage that is not insured by a public agency.

Conversion: A change in the use of real estate by altering improvements but without destroying them; legally, the unlawful taking of possession of the property of another.

Conversion value: Value created by converting from one state or use to another.

Conveyance: In its common use, refers to a written instrument transferring the title to land or some interest therein from one person to another. Transfer of title or ownership to real estate from one party to another.

Cooperative: Ownership form in which a single property is subdivided into several use portions, with each user owning stock in the corporation that owns the property and occupying a portion of it.

Cooperative apartment: An apartment complex owned by a corporation or a trust, in which each owner purchases stock to the value of his or her apartment and is given a proprietary lease.

Cooperative ownership: Usually a form of apartment ownership in which an occupant acquires ownership by purchasing shares in a corporation. The cooperative property is owned in severalty. The cooperative plan is permitted to place extensive restraints on the alienation of the units as well as their use and improvements.

Co-ownership: Ownership of the same property by two or more persons.

Corner influence: The effect of street intersections upon the adjoining property.

Corner influence table: A statistical table which attempts to reflect the additional value accorded a lot with a corner location.

Corporation: An artificial person that is a distinct legal entity created by law. It is separate and distinct from its owners or shareholders, may hold title in its own name, and conducts its business through its board of directors and officers.

Corporeal rights: Possessory rights in real property.

Correction deed: A written instrument which corrects an error in a recorded deed.

Correction line: The line every 24 miles that runs due north and south from the base line in order to compensate for the narrowing of the earth in the rectangular method of survey.

Cost: That which must be given up to obtain property. The replacement cost is the cost of replacing real estate improvements with an alternative of like utility. Reproduction cost is the cost of replacing real estate improvements with an exact replica.

Cost approach to value: Valuation reached by estimating the cost of providing a substitute for that which is being valued. Depreciation must be deducted in making the valuation.

Cost of capital: The amount that must be paid to attract money into an investment project.

Cost of reproduction: The normal cost of duplication of a property.

Counselor: One who assists clients with advice regarding use and management of assets.

Counterflashing: Flashing used on chimneys at the roof line to cover the shingle flashing and to prevent moisture from entering.

County: A civil division of a territory organized for political and judicial purposes.

County clerk's certificate: A certificate given by the clerk of the county where a notary public or officer has obtained his or her authority to take acknowledgments and which certifies to interested parties as to the officer's signature and powers.

Covenant: Used in contracts as synonymous with promise; in deeds, it may be a positive or negative undertaking by one or both parties.

Covenant for benefit of grantors remaining lands: One which is designed to protect and benefit lands of the grantor while burdening or restricting the parcel conveyed.

Covenant for further assurance: An undertaking, in the form of a covenant, on the part of the vendor of real estate to perform such further acts for the purpose of perfecting the purchaser's title as the latter may reasonably require.

Covenant running with the land: One which binds the successive owners of real property.

CPM: Certified property manager; a member of IREM of NAREB.

CRB (certified residential broker): A designation conferred by RNMI.

CRE (counselor on real estate): A designation conferred by ASREC.

CRS (certified residential specialist): A designation conferred by RNMI.

Credit: The power of an individual to secure money, or obtain goods on time, in consequence of the favorable opinion held by the community, or by the particular lender, as to his or her solvency and reliability; a debt considered from the creditor's standpoint, or that which is to be incoming or due to one.

Crossroad development: Pattern of city growth characterized by fingerlike extensions moving out along the main transportation routes.

Cubical content: The actual space within the outer surfaces of outside walls and contained between the outer surfaces of the roof and the finished surface of the lowest basement or cellar floor; the actual space that lies within the interior dimensions of a structure.

Cul-de-sac: A deadend street with a widened, circular area at the end to enable a car to make a U-turn.

Curable depreciation: Any deficiency that can be cured.

Curable penalty: Element of depreciation whose cost of repair or correction is offset by the increase in value of the property caused by the repair or correction. Incurable penalty occurs when the cost of repair adds less than its cost to the property's value.

Current assets: Liquid assets such as cash, accounts receivable, and merchandise inventories.

Current liabilities: Short-term debts, generally debts due within one year's time.

Curtesy: The right a husband has in a wife's real estate at her death.

Custodian: One who is responsible for the care of something entrusted to him or her; e.g., a custodian of a public building.

Custom-built house: A house sold before construction begins and built to the owner's specifications.

Customer: The person dealing with the agent. Typically, in a real estate transaction, the potential buyer or tenant; the party with whom the broker or salesperson deals who is *not* the principal.

Cyclical fluctuation: Variations around a trend in activity that recur from time to time; fluctuations remaining after removal of trend and seasonal factors that recur regularly.

Damages: Indemnity to the person who suffers a loss or harm from an injury; a sum recoverable as amends from a wrong; an adequate compensation for the loss suffered or the injury sustained.

Data assembly: Gathering, analyzing, and classifying data pertaining to a subject property.

Data plant: A collection of information about real properties maintained usually by an appraiser, mortgage lender, and the like.

Datum: The horizontal plane from which heights and depths are measured.

De facto: In fact or in reality.

Dealer-builder: A builder who constructs structures from prefabricated components, usually as the local representative of a prefabricated house manufacturer.

Debit: The amount charged as due or owing.

Debt: Something which must be repaid or a duty owed, such as a loan.

Debt capital: Money borrowed for a particular business purpose.

Debt service: Annual amount to be paid by a debtor to retire an obligation to repay borrowed money.

Debt service coverage: The requirement that earnings be a percentage or dollar sum higher than debt service.

Debtor: The party who owes money to another.

Decedent: A deceased person.

Decedent's estate: The interest of a decedent in property of all kinds.

Decentralization: Dispersion from a center point or figure.

Deciduous trees: Trees which do not keep their leaves through the autumn and winter.

Decree: The final determination of the rights of the parties to a suit.

Decree of foreclosure: The decree by a court for the sale of property to pay an obligation found to be due and owing.

Dedication: An offer of land to some public use, made by an owner and accepted for such use by or on behalf of the public.

Deed: An instrument conveying title to real property.

Deed covenants: The warranties made by a seller of property to protect the buyer against items such as liens, encumbrances, or title defects.

Deed of trust: An instrument in use in many states, taking the place and serving the uses of a common-law mortgage, by which the legal title to real property is placed in one or more trustees to secure the repayment of a sum of money or the performance of other conditions.

Deed money escrow: An agreement where money is retained by a third party to be delivered to a seller of real estate upon the receipt of the deed to the property sold.

Deed restrictions: Limitations placed upon the use of real property in the deed to that property.

Default: Failure to fulfill a duty or to discharge an obligation.

Defeasance clause: The clause in a mortgage that permits the mortgagor to redeem his or her property upon the payment of the obligations to the mortgagee.

Defective title: A title which would be impaired were an outstanding claim proved to be valid.

Defects in title: Imperfections that cast a reasonable doubt on the marketability of title.

Defendant: A party sued in a legal action.

Deferred maintenance: An existing but unfulfilled need for repairs and rehabilitation.

Deferred payments: Money payments which are to be made at some date in the future.

Deficiency judgment: A judgment for that part of a secured debt that was not liquidated by the proceeds from the sale of foreclosed real property.

Delegation of authority: A transfer of authority by one person to another.

Delinquency: A financial obligation which is in default, such as an overdue loan.

Delivery: The transfer from one person to another of an item, or a right or interest therein, which means more than physical transfer of possession. However, in the popular sense, in the case of a contract or lease or the like, it implies a transfer of the actual contract or document to the possession of the other party.

Demand: The amount of a good or service which will be bought at various prices (and under varying conditions).

Demand note: A note which is payable on demand of the holder.

Demise: The transfer of interest or conveyance of an estate primarily by lease.

Demising clause: A clause found in a lease whereby the landlord (lessor) leases and the tenant (lessee) leases the property.

Demographic: Pertaining to population structure.

Demographic characteristics: Political, social, and economic characteristics of a population of people.

Density: The number of units present per unit of area such as dwellings per acre or persons per square mile.

Department of Housing and Urban Development (HUD): A cabinet-level federal department actively engaged in national housing programs, including urban renewal, urban planning assistance, college housing, senior citizens housing programs, model cities, and rehabilitation loans.

Deposit: A sum of money or other consideration tendered in conjunction with an offer to purchase rights in real property as evidence of good faith. (*See also* earnest money)

Depositary: The party receiving a deposit. The obligation on the part of the depositary to keep the item with reasonable care and, upon request, restore it to the depositor, or otherwise deliver it, according to the original agreement.

Depreciation: Loss in property value. Accelerated depreciation is a method of reflecting depreciation that enables the owner of an asset to take more of the depreciation during the early years of the asset's life. Contingent depreciation is a loss in property value because of expectations of a decline in property services. Depletion is the exhaustion of a resource such as the removal of a mineral deposit. Economic obsolescence is a loss in property value from events outside the property that unfavorably affect income or income potential. Functional obsolescence is a loss in property value because of a loss in the ability of the physical property to provide services as compared with alternatives. Physical depreciation is a loss in property value due to wearing away or deterioration.

Depreciation accrued: The actual amount of depreciation existing in a property at a given date.

Depreciation allowance: The amounts to be claimed or allowed for depreciation.

Depreciation base: Cost of an asset that is to be depreciated.

Depreciation methods: The methods used to measure decreases in the value of an improvement through depreciation. In appraising, the methods generally used are annuity, sinking fund, and straight-line. In accounting, it relates to various methods by which capital impairment is computed. In addition to the three methods used in appraising, accountants also use declining balance (and variations thereof), weighted rate, and accelerated.

Depreciation rate: The periodic amount or percentage at which the usefulness of a property is used up, especially the percentage at which amounts are computed to be set aside as an accrual for future depreciation.

Depreciation, straight line: An accounting term showing the reduction of the cost or other basis of property, less estimated salvage value, in equal amounts over the estimated useful life of the property.

Depreciation, sum of the years' digits: Annual depreciation computed by applying changing fractions to the cost or other basis of property reduced by estimated salvage. The numerators of the fraction change each year to the estimated remaining useful life of the asset, and the constant denominator is the sum of all the years' digits corresponding to the estimated useful life of the asset. For example, the fraction for the first year's depreciation on a 5-year asset is 5/15. The 5 is the estimated useful life remaining, and 15 is computed by adding together each year's remaining useful life, i.e., $5+4+3+2+1=15$.

Depth table: A technique for real estate appraisal using statistical tables based on the theory that added depth increases the value of land.

Descent: The process by which the property of a decedent passes to his or her legal heirs.

Desist and refrain order: An order issued by a real estate commissioner to stop an action in violation of the real estate law (also known as cease and desist order).

Deterioration: A worsening of the condition of a property.

Determinable fee: An estate which may last forever is a "fee," but if it may end on the happening of a merely possible event, it is a "determinable," or "qualified fee."

Developer: One who prepares land for income production, the making of improvements, and the sale of completed properties.

Devise: A testamentary disposition of land or realty. Leaving real property through a will.

Devisee: The person to whom lands or other real property are devised or given by will.

Direct reduction mortgage: A mortgage which is to be repaid by periodic fixed amounts plus interest on the unpaid balance.

Directional growth: The direction in which the residential sections of a city are destined to expand.

Disability: The lack of legal capacity to perform an act.

Disaffirm: To repudiate; to revoke a consent once given; to disclaim the intention of being bound by an antecedent transaction.

Discharge: The release or performance of a contract or other obligation.

Disclosure acts: Statutes which require the revelation of certain basic facts involved in particular transactions.

Discount rate: The correlation between dollars transmitted from a lender to a borrower and dollars that must be repaid by the borrower. If a lender advances $960 and the borrower must repay $1,000, the discount rate is

$$\frac{\$40}{\$1,000} = 4\%$$

Discounting: A means of converting any cash flow in to present value at a selected rate of return; based upon the premise that one would pay less than $1 today for the right to receive $1 at a future date.

Discretion: Power or privilege of a fiduciary to act unhampered by legal restrictions or limitations on his normal authority.

Discrimination: Distinguishing in favor of or against one person or thing as compared with others.

Disintermediation: An outflow of funds from savings institutions by investors to reinvest their monies elsewhere where the rates of return are expected to be higher.

Disposable income: The income left to a household after taxes.

Disposable field: A drainage area, not close to the water supply, where refuse from the septic tank is dispersed, being drained into the ground through tile and gravel filtration.

Dispossess: To put one out of possession of real estate.

Distress: The act of distraining; assuming possession of a tenant's chattels by a landlord in order to satisfy, in whole or in part, a claim for rent in arrears. Another common word for this is "distrain."

Distributee: One who receives part of the property of a person who dies intestate.

Distribution: The division and transfer of the property of a decedent.

District: A city area with a land use different from that of adjacent areas, e.g., commercial, industrial, or residential.

Documentary evidence: Evidence supplied by written instruments such as contracts, deeds, etc.

Documentary stamp: The revenue stamp issued for payment of a tax on documents such as deeds.

Documents: Written records; in real estate, contracts, deeds, leases, mortgages, etc.

Domicile: A place where a person lives or has his home; in a strict legal sense, the place where he has his true, fixed, permanent home and principal establishment, and to which place he has, whenever he is absent, the intention of returning.

Dominant tenement or estate: That to which a servitude or easement is due, or for the benefit of which it exists. For example, land which includes the right to the use of a right of way over other land.

Donee: A person who receives a gift.

Donor: The one who makes a gift to another.

Double, duplex: Two dwelling units under one roof. A double usually denotes two dwellings side by side, a duplex, one dwelling above the other.

Doubling up: The occupation of a dwelling unit by two or more families.

Dower: The legal rights a widow possesses to her deceased husband's real estate.

Down payment: Initial partial payment of the total selling price.

Downzoning: A public action by which the local government reduces the allowable density for subsequent development (e.g., fewer housing units, fewer stores, etc.) or allowable use from a high to low use (e.g., multifamily to single-family).

Drainage: The running off of water from the surface of land.

Due on sale clause: Provision in a mortgage that permits the mortgagee to accelerate the loan (demand immediate payment) upon a transfer of title to the property securing the loan. Also known as an alienation clause.

Duress: Unlawful pressure placed upon a person to coerce him to perform some act against his will.

Dutch Colonial: The style of architecture that features a gambrel roof, exterior walls of masonry or wood, and porches at the side; especially adapted to flat sites and difficult to fit into a steep slope.

Earnest money: Money paid to evidence good faith when an offer of purchase is submitted to a property owner by a prospective purchaser.

Easement: The right which the owner of one parcel of land has to use or control the use of another parcel of land owned by another; such rights and obligations run with the land itself and are not mere personal rights of an individual.

Easement appurtenant: An easement which is attached to, benefits, and passes with the conveyance of the dominant estate. Such an easement runs with the land for the benefit of the dominant estate and continued to burden the servient estate, though such estates may be conveyed to new owners.

Easement in gross: An easement which is not attached or appurtenant to any particular estate and therefore does not run with the land and is not transferred through the conveyance of the title. (See, however, commercial easement in gross.)

"Easy" money: A financial situation that occurs when lenders have an abundance of funds available for lending. The terms of the loans are favorable to borrowers.

Eaves: The lower part of a roof that protrudes over the wall.

Economic base: The major economic support of a community.

Economic base analysis: A technique for analyzing the major economic supports of a community; analysis as a means of predicting population, income, or other variables having an effect on real estate value or land utilization.

Economic goods: Goods that have scarcity and utility; goods that provide desired services but are not in sufficient abundance to be free.

Economic life: The period over which a property will yield the investor a return on the investment over and above the economic or ground rent due to land.

Economic obsolescence: Lessened desirability or useful life arising from economic forces, such as changes in optimum land use, legislative enactments which restrict or impair property rights, and changes in supply-demand relationships. Loss in the use and value of property arising from the factors of economic obsolescence is to be distinguished from loss in value from physical deterioration and functional obsolescence.

Economic rent: The base rent payable for the right of occupancy of vacant land. ~~buyer~~

Economics: Allocation of scarce resources.

Economy: The efficient use of resources with an eye to productivity.

Effective age: A statement regarding the amount of depreciation that has occurred on a property. The amount is stated in terms of the number of years that would ordinarily be associated with the degree of depreciation.

Effective demand: Desire for property backed by the ability to purchase.

Effective gross revenue: A method to determine income less allowance for vacancies, contingencies, and sometimes collection losses, but before deductions for any operating expenses.

Egress: A way out; exit; an outlet.

Ejectment: Legal action brought to regain possesion of property.

Elasticity: Ability of the supply of real estate to respond to price increases over a short period of time.

Emancipate (a child): To release a child from parental control for purposes of legal capacity or competency.

Embezzlement: A statutory offense consisting of the fraudulent coversion of another's personal property by one to whom it has been entrusted, with the intention of depriving the owner thereof, the gist of the offense being usually the violation of relations of fiduciary character.

Emblements: Crops growing on the property which require annual care and usually are the possession of the tenant.

Eminent domain: The right of the government to take private property for public use, with just compensation.

Enabling act: A state statute used to provide a legal base for zoning codes or other local governmental action.

Encroachment: An improvement which intrudes upon property adjacent to that on which it was meant to be constructed.

Encumbrance: Any claim, right, or interest in land held by someone other than the owner which interest lessens the value of the owner's estate. Examples are covenants, restrictions, liens, mortgages, and easements.

Endorsement: An act of signing one's name on the back of a check or note with or without further qualification.

English architecture: The design using the characteristics of Elizabethan, Tudor Cotswold, and other English styles; frequently large stone houses with slate shingles on gabled roofs, mullioned casement windows, and wainscotted interiors. Exposed timbers constitute the structural frame of authentic Elizabethan houses, although in modern adaptations the half-timbering is purely decorative. Between the half-timbers there usually is plaster, although in the original types the spaces were filled with brick nogging.

Entrepreneur: One who organizes, manages, and assumes responsibility for a business.

Equality of economic opportunity: A state of affairs in which all people have equal chances for the same jobs at equal pay, regardless of race, creed, color, or sex.

Equitable title: The right that exists in equity to obtain absolute ownership to property when title is held in another name. Also, an interest in land that may not amount to fee simple ownership, but is such that a court will take notice of the rights of the holder of such interest.
   The beneficiary of a trust and the contract purchaser or vendee have equitable title, respectively, to the trust and the property being sold.

Equity: Justice. Also, in finance, the value of the interest of an owner of property exclusive of the encumbrances on that property.

Equity funds: Capital invested to gain a residual ownership interest in property.

Equity interest: The amount of the value or total combined worth of a property minus any debts outstanding against it. The amount of the interest may be established through: (1) cash originally put into the property (down payment), (2) the amortization of any debt against the property, (3) any appreciation in the value of the property.

Equity participation: That percentage of the income or other return on the investment required by a lender in excess of the normal interest received for financing a real estate project.

Equity of redemption: The right to redeem property during the foreclosure period.

Erosion: The wearing away of the ground surface.

Escalator clause: A clause in a contract providing for the upward or downward adjustment of specific terms to cover certain contingencies, e.g., right to increase interest rates on a loan under specified conditions.

Escheat: The reversion of private property to the state.

Escrow: The arrangement for the handling of instruments or money not to be delivered until specified conditions are met.

Escrow closing: A closing in which the title instruments, related documents, and consideration are not simultaneously and effectively exchanged, but instead are placed in escrow.

Escrow holder: The third party who receives a deed or item from a grantor to be held until the performance of a condition by the grantee or until the occurrence of a contingency, then to be delivered to the grantee.

Estate at will: The occupation of lands and tenements by a tenant for an unspecified period terminable by one or both parties.

Estate for years: A leasehold interest in lands by virtue of a contract for the possession for a specified period of time.

Estate (in land): The degree of interest a person has in land with respect to the nature of the right, its duration, or its relation to the rights of others. *Estate in expectancy* is a classification of estates by time of enjoyment when possession will be at some future time. An *estate in possession* is a classification of estates by time of enjoyment when possession is present. *Estate in severalty* is the ownership in a single individual; a classification of estates by number of owners where the number is one. A *freehold estate* is a nonleasehold estate such as a fee simple estate, fee tail estate, or life estate. *Fee simple estates* are the most complete form of estate ownership; the "totality of rights" in real property. A *fee tail estate* is an estate or a limited estate in which transfer of the property is restricted in that the property must pass to the descendants of the owner. Originally used to insure the passing of land in a direct ancestral line. A *life estate* is an estate that has a duration of the life of an individual.

Estate in possession: An estate that entitles the owner to the immediate possession, use, and enjoyment of the property.

Estate in reversion: The remnant of an estate left in the grantor, to commence in possession after the termination of some lesser estate granted by him or her to another.

Estate of inheritance: An estate which may be passed on to heirs. All freehold estates are estates of inheritance, except estates for life.

Estoppel: A legal doctrine under which one is precluded and forbidden to deny his own act or deed.

Estoppel certificate: The certificate which shows the unpaid principal of a mortgage and the interest thereon, if the principal or interest notes are not produced or if the seller asserts that the amount due under the mortgage which the purchaser is to assume is less than shown on record. The certificate is usually executed by the mortgagor.

Et al.: And others.

Et ux.: And wife.

Ethics: The moral principles, such as those owed by a member of a profession or craft to the public, to clients, and to professional associates.

Eviction: The ouster from possession of real property of one in possession under a valid lease.

Eviction notice: A notice to a tenant to vacate premises because of nonpayment of rent or other violation of the lease agreement.

Evidence: That which tends to prove or disprove any matter in question, or to influence the belief respecting it.

Ex officio: By virtue of the office; without any other warrant or appointment than that resulting from the holding of a particular office.

Ex parte: One side only, or done in behalf of only one person.

Exception: An objection; a reservation; a contradiction.

Excess rent: The monetary difference between contract rent and economic rent.

Exchange: The process of trading an equity in a piece of property for the equity in another piece of property.

Exchange brokerage: The process of bringing two parties together in transactions involving trading of properties.

Exchangor: The broker or salesperson who accomplishes the exchange.

Exclusionary zoning: The effect, whether intentional or not, of excluding racial minorities and low income persons from a community.

Exclusive agency listing: A listing contract providing that the agent shall receive a commission if the property is sold as a result of the efforts of that agent or any other agent, but not as a result of the efforts of the principal; the contract further provides that the agent will receive a commission if a buyer is secured under the terms of the contract.

Exclusive authorization (right) to sell listing: A contract between owner and agent giving agent the right to collect a commission if the property is sold by anyone during the term of the agreement.

Exclusive listing: The contract to market property as an agent, according to the terms of which the agent is given the exclusive right to sell the property or is made the exclusive agent for its sale. The term is also applied to the property which is listed.

Exculpatory clause: A clause often included in leases that clears or relieves the landlord of liability for personal injury to tenants as well as for property damages.

Execute: To complete; to perform.

Execution: The act of performing the final judgment or decree of a court; the formal action, usually signing, taken to complete a legal document and make it binding.

Executor: The person who is designated in a will as one who is to administer the estate of the testator. (Executrix, *f.*)

Executor's (or fiduciary) deed: A deed given by an executor or other fiduciary which conveys the real property described and generally contains a covenant by the fiduciary warranting title against his acts.

Exempt: To release, discharge, waive, relieve from liability.

Existing mortgage: The debt contract in which the seller of real estate is the mortgagor, which is to be assumed by the purchaser.

Exoneration (in suretyship): The right which a surety has, on payment of the principal debtor's obligation, to look to the principal debtor for reimbursement.

Expansible house: A home created for future additions.

Expansion joint: A bituminous fiber strip used to separate units of concrete to prevent cracking because of expansion as a result of temperature changes.

Express contract: One expressed in words, either written or oral.

Expropriation: The act or process whereby private property is acquired for public use, or the rights therein modified by a sovereignty or any entity vested with the necessary legal authority; e.g., where property is taken under eminent domain.

Extended coverage endorsement: An addition to a fire insurance policy which extends the coverage to include losses caused by windstorm, hail, explosion, riot, aircraft, vehicle, and smoke damage.

Extensive margin: Extra benefits derived from adding increasing amounts of land to a productive state.

Extinguishment: The destruction or cancellation of a right, power, contract, or estate.

Extra use: Use (or activity) level in excess of a real or normal level of use.

Facade: The front or face of a building.

Factor: A commercial agent who sells goods consigned to him, for a principal, but uses his own name.

Fair value: Reasonable value, consistent with all known facts, at which the purchaser is willing to pay the price and the seller is willing to sell at the price.

Fannie Mae: Federal National Mortgage Association.

Farm and Land Institute: Brings together specialists in the sale, development, planning, management, and syndication of land to establish professional standards through educational programs for members. Confers AFLM (Accredited Farm and Land Member).

Feasibility survey: The analysis of the cost/benefit ratio of an economic endeavor prior to its undertaking.

Fed: Federal Reserve Board.

Federal Deposit Insurance Corporation (FDIC): Federal agency that insures deposits at commercial banks and savings banks.

Federal Home Loan Bank: A district bank of the Federal Home Loan Bank System that lends only to member financial institutions such as savings and loan associations.

Federal Home Loan Bank Board: The administrative agency that charters federal savings and loan associations and exercises regulatory authority over members of the Federal Home Loan Bank System.

Federal Home Loan Bank System: The network of Federal Home Loan Banks and member financial institutions.

Federal Housing Administration (FHA): A federal agency that insures mortgage loans.

Federal National Mortgage Association: Federal agency that buys and sells FHA-insured and VA-guaranteed mortgage loans. Popularly known as "Fannie Mae."

Federal savings and loan association: A savings and loan association with a federal charter issued by the Federal Home Loan Bank Board. A federally chartered savings and loan association is in contrast to a state-chartered savings and loan association.

Federal Savings and Loan Insurance Corporation: Federal agency which insures savers' accounts at savings and loan associations.

Fee: An estate of inheritance in real property; compensation for a particular act.

Fee on condition: A fee simple estate which may be terminated upon the occurrence of a specified event, the time of which is uncertain and/or where the event itself may or may not ever occur. The breach of the condition does not automatically terminate the estate. The grantor, his heirs, or designee must act to terminate the estate.

Fee on limitation: A fee simple estate which is automatically terminated upon the occurrence of a specified event, the time of which is uncertain and/or where the event itself may or may not ever occur.

Fee simple: In modern estates, the terms "fee" and "fee simple" are substantially synonymous. The term "fee" is of Old English derivation.

Fee simple absolute: An estate in real property by which the owner has the greatest power over the title which it is possible to have; an absolute estate. It expressly establishes the title of real property in the owner, without any limitation or end. He or she may dispose of it by sale, trade, or will, as desired.

Fee simple conditional: A fee that may terminate upon the occurrence of a specific event, the time of which is uncertain and/or the event itself may or may not ever occur.

Fee simple determinable: See fee simple conditional.

Fee simple limited: See fee simple conditional.

Fee tail: A freehold estate of inheritance limited so as to descend to a particular class of heirs of the person to whom it is granted.

Felony: A crime graver than those termed "misdemeanor"; the word is defined by several of the statutes and codes of the United States and includes crimes punishable by death or imprisonment in a penitentiary or state prison.

Feudal system: A political and social system which prevailed throughout Europe during the eleventh, twelfth, and thirteenth centuries under which ownership of land was vested in the monarch and subjects had only privileges of its use as opposed to private or allodial ownership.

Feudal tenure: See feudal system.

Feuds: Grants of land.

FHA: See Federal Housing Administration.

FHA loan: A loan insured by the Federal Housing Administration against loss by reason of default in payments.

FHLMC: Federal Home Loan Mortgage Corporation.

Fidelity bond: A bond posted as security for the discharge of an obligation of personal services.

Fiduciary: One who holds title to property for the benefit of another; or one who holds a position of trust and confidence.

Filtering: Upward mobility of people of one income group into homes that have recently dropped in price and that were previously occupied by persons in the next higher income group.

Filtering down: In housing, the process of passing the use of real estate to successively lower-income groups as the real estate produces less income.

Financial institutions: Organizations that deal in money or claims to money and serve the function of channeling money from those who wish to lend to those who wish to borrow. Such organizations include commercial banks, savings and loan associations, savings banks, and insurance companies.

Financial intermediary: A financial institution which acts as an intermediary between savers and borrowers by selling its own obligations for money and, in turn, lending the accumulated funds to borrowers. This type of institution includes savings associations, mutual savings banks, life insurance companies, credit unions, and investment companies.

Financial risk: Possibility of losses created by the amount of and legal provisions concerning borrowed funds.

Finder: A person who brings parties together for a deal which the parties themselves then negotiate.

Finish floor: Finish floor is the final covering on the subflooring; wood, linoleum, cork, tile, or carpet.

Fire stop: A solid, tight closure of a concealed space, built to prevent the spread of fire and smoke through such a space.

Firm commitment: A commitment assumed by the FHA to insure a mortgage of a specified mortgagor; an unqualified promise to make a loan under specified conditions.

First mortgage: The mortgage which prevails as a lien over all other mortgages.

Fiscal controls: Efforts to control the level of economic activity by manipulation of the amount of federal tax and spending programs and the amount of surplus or deficit.

Fixity of location: The characteristic which subjects real estate to the influence of its surroundings and prevents it from escaping such influence.

Fixture: A chattel permanently attached to real estate, and becoming accessory to it, and part and parcel of it.

Flashing: Sheet metal or other material used to protect a building from water seepage.

Flexible payment mortgage: A mortgage loan in which the amount of individual payments may vary from time to time under ascertainable circumstances; not legal in New York on residential mortgages unless made under certain federal laws.

FLI: See Farm Land Institute.

Flood-prone area: Area having a 1 percent annual chance of flooding, i.e., a flood may be anticipated once every one hundred years.

Floor load: The weight-supporting capabilities of a floor, measured in pounds per square foot; the weight, stated in pounds per square foot, which may be safely placed upon the floor of a building if it is uniformly distributed.

Flow of funds: An accounting method (used primarily by the Federal Reserve) to describe the sources and uses of the nation's funds in a given period of time.

FNMA: Federal National Mortgage Association, the secondary market agency for FHA and VA loans.

Footing: The base of a foundation wall or column.

Forced sale: The act of selling property under compulsion as to time; frequently the result of legal proceedings ordering the sale.

Forced sale value: The price realized at the forced sale.

Foreclosure: The legal process by which a mortgagee, after default by the mortgagor, forces sale of the property mortgaged in order to recover his or her loan.

Forfeiture: Deprivation or destruction of a right in consequence of the nonperformance of some obligation or condition.

Forgery: The legal offense of imitating or counterfeiting documents or signatures in an effort to deceive.

Forthwith: At once; promptly.

Foundation: The supporting portion of a structure below the first floor construction, including the footings.

Foundation wall: The masonry wall below ground which supports the building.

Franchise: A specific privilege conferred by government or contractually by a business firm.

Fraud: Intentional deception or trickery used to gain an unfair advantage over another.

Free and clear: Title to property which is unencumbered by mortgages or other liens.

Freehold estate: An estate in real property with no measurable length of time or termination date.

French architecture: Any of several styles originating in France; very common in smaller houses and the perfectly balanced, rectangular formal house with a steep roof, hipped at the ends, its plaster walls one story high, with dormer windows provided for second-floor rooms. The French farmhouse style is informal, of stone, painted brick, or plaster, sometimes with half-timbering used as an accent. Norman French architecture is large in scale, usually distinguished by a round tower.

Front foot: A measure (1 foot in length) of the width of lots taken along their frontage upon a street.

Front foot cost: Cost of a piece of real estate expressed in terms of front foot units.

Frostline: The depth to which frost will penetrate the soil. Footings should be placed below this depth to prevent movement.

Full covenant and warranty deed: A deed conveying the real property described in which the grantor generally warrants the title making the five covenants of seisen, quiet enjoyment, against encumbrances, further assurances, and warranty or defense.

Full face rate of interest: Rate of interest stated in the debt.

Functional obsolescence: Defects in the plan or design of a structure that detract from its marketability and value.

Functional plan: The special arrangement of real estate improvements as it relates to property services.

Functional utility: The total of a property's attractiveness and usefulness.

Funds: Cash or any other resource having value which may be sold in order to buy some other asset.

Furring: The strips of wood or metal applied behind a wall or other surface to even it, to form an air space, or to give the wall an appearance of greater thickness.

Future estate: An estate that is presently owned but the use, possession, and enjoyment of which is postponed to some future time.

Gable roof: A steeply pitched roof with sloping sides.

Gambrel roof: A curb roof having a flatter upper slope and a steep lower slope.

General agency: The relationship wherein the agent acts for the principal in a number of transactions over a period of time in a broad area. For example, a branch manager acting for the owner of a business.

General Assembly: State Senate and House of Representatives.

General mortgage bond: A document representing an obligation secured by a mortgage.

General warranty: A provision that guarantees the quality of title to property conveyed and undertakes to defend that title and to pay damages if the title is defective.

GI loan: A mortgage loan granted veterans, which is guaranteed by the VA subject to their restrictions.

Gift deed: A deed given without consideration.

Ginnie Mae: Government National Mortgage Association (GNMA).

Girder: A large beam used to support smaller beams, joists, and partitions.

GNMA (Government National Mortgage Corporation): A federal agency of HUD, created in 1968 out of the Federal National Mortgage Association, whose purpose is to carry on supportive mortgage activities which cannot be carried out economically by the private sector. Also known as Ginnie Mae.

GNP: Gross national product.

Good faith: An honest intention to abstain from taking conscious advantage of another.

Governmental survey: The process adopted in 1785, also known as the rectangular survey, used for describing land and establishing boundaries. It is used to describe both large and small tracts of land in legal descriptions.

Grace period: Period of time, usually measured in days, during which the borrower under a mortgage or other debt instrument may cure a default without penalty and without triggering the right of the creditor to foreclose or exercise other remedies.

Grade: The ground level taken at the foundation.

Grading: The process of plowing and raking a lot to give it a desired contour and drainage.

Graduated lease: A lease that provides for a variable rental rate, often based upon future determination; sometimes rent is based upon the result of periodic appraisals; used largely in long-term leases.

Graduate Realtors Institute (GRI): Educational program for REALTORS® sponsored by NAR. Awards GRI (Graduate Realtors Institute).

Grand jury: A group of persons who inquire as to the commission of offenses, hearing evidence only against the accused, and in proper cases return indictments or accusations against such accused.

Grant: A transfer of real property by a written instrument. A private grant is the transfer of real property from one person to another. A public grant is a government transfer of ownership of real property to a private party.

Grantee: One who receives a transfer of real property by deed.

Granting clause: A clause in a deed which indicates the quantity of the estate conveyed.

Grantor: One who transfers real property by deed.

GRI: Graduate Realtors Institute, and that program's designation.

Grid: A chart used for the purpose of rating the borrower risk, property, and neighborhood.

Gridiron pattern: A layout of streets that resembles a gridiron; a system of subdivision with blocks of uniform length and width and streets that intersect at right angles.

GRM: Gross rent multiplier.

Gross earnings: The total revenue from operations, before deduction of the expenses incurred in gaining such revenues.

Gross income: The total income from property before any expenses are deducted.

Gross income multiplier: A technique for estimating real estate value based on some factor (multiplier) times the gross income derived from the property in the past. See gross rent multiplier.

Gross lease: A lease of property under the terms of which the lessor is to assume all property charges regularly incurred as the result of property ownership, e.g., taxes, maintenance, etc.

Gross national product: The total value of all goods and services produced in the economy in any given period; also, the accounting method used to list the major income and expenditure (product) accounts of the nation.

Gross profits: Total profits computed before the deduction of general expenses.

Gross rent multiplier (GRM): A factor used in arriving at an estimate of real estate value. The factor is obtained by dividing known sales prices of comparable properties by the rental income of those properties. It is usually the average quotient arrived at from the above division (sales price by rental income) of several comparable properties. The gross rental income of a particular property is then multiplied by this factor.

Gross revenue: Total revenue from all sources before subtraction of expenses incurred in gaining such revenue.

Gross sales: The total amount of sales as shown by invoices, before deducting returns, allowances, etc.

Ground lease: A lease for the use of the land only.

Ground rent: The earnings of improved property proportionally credited to earnings of the ground itself after allowance is made for earnings of improvements; often called "economic rent."

Guaranteed mortgage: A mortgage in which a party other than the borrower assures payment in the event of default by a mortgagor, e.g., VA-guaranteed mortgages.

Guaranteed sale: The written commitment by a broker that within a specified period of time he or she will, in absence of a sale, purchase a given piece of property at a specified sum.

Guide meridian: A correction line which runs due north and south to compensate for the narrowing of the earth. Used in rectangular survey.

Habendum: The second part of a deed following that part which names the grantee. It describes the estate conveyed and to what use.

Habendum clause: The "have and to hold" clause which defines or limits the quantity of the estate granted in the premises of the deed. Not essential today per leading authorities unless the estate being granted is a limited one.

Haec verba: In the exact words.

Half-timbering: A means of construction of house walls with the timber frame exposed, the space between timbers being filled with masonry or plaster on laths; also simulated half-timbering, with boards applied on plaster walls as decoration.

Header: One beam which is placed prependicular to joists and to which joists are nailed in framing for a chimney, stairway, or other opening.

Height density: A zoning regulation designed to control the use or occupancy within a certain area by designating the maximum height of the structures.

Heirs: Persons appointed by law to succeed to the real estate of a decedent, in case of intestacy.

Hereditaments: A larger and more comprehensive word than either "land" or "tenements," and meaning anything capable of being inherited, whether it be corporeal, incorporeal, real, personal, or mixed.

High-rise apartment building: An indefinite term used to describe the modern elevator apartment building.

Highest and best use: The utilization of real property to its greatest economic advantage; the use that provides the highest land value; the use of land that provides a net income stream to the land that when capitalized provides the highest land value.

Hip roof: A pitched roof that features sloping sides and ends.

Holdover tenant: A person who remains in possession of leased property after expiration of the leased term.

Holographic will: A will written entirely by the testator with his own hand.

Homeowners Loan Corporation: A federal agency that refinanced mortgages in default in the early 1930s.

Homestead: A dwelling with its land and buildings; a dwelling with its land and buildings protected by a homestead law.

Homestead exemption: The interest of the head of a family in his or her owned residence that is exempt from the claims of creditors.

Horizontal Property Act: The laws enacted by the various states, which permit creation of the condominium form of real property ownership.

Housing stock: The total inventory of dwelling units. This includes forms both owned and rented.

Housing starts: Newly constructed housing units. This includes both single-family and multifamily domiciles.

HUD (Housing and Urban Development): A federal department created in 1965 to solve the complex housing problems of the American city by utilization of the vast resources of the federal government in coordination with the various state and local governments. Administrations under HUD include FNMA, FHA, Public Housing, Urban Renewal, and Community Facilities.

Hundred percent location: A city retail business location which is considered the best for attracting business.

Hypothecate: To pledge something without delivering possession of it to the pledgee.

Hypothesis of median location: A theory stating that there is the tendency for businesses and other entities to locate at their lowest time and cost point.

Identity of interest: The system whereby the builder and sponsor of a housing project subsidized by the government have ownership interests in each other.

Illegal contract: An agreement entered into for an illegal purpose is unenforceable in a court of law.

Illegality: That which is contrary to principles of law. (See also illegal contract.)

Implied: Contained in substance or essence or by fair inference but not actually expressed; deductible by inference or implication.

Implied contract: One implied by the acts and/or conduct of the parties involved.

Impossibility of performance: A contract which for one reason or another is impossible of performance by the party so charged.

Improper improvement: Out-of-place improvement; improvement which does not conform to the best use of the site.

Improved value: The difference between the income-producing ability of a property and the amount required to pay a return on the investment in the property.

Improvement: That which is erected or constructed upon land to release the income-earning potential of the land; buildings or appurtenances on land. An overimprovement is an improvement of real estate in excess of that justifiable to release the earning power of land. An underimprovement is an improvement insufficient to release the earning power of the land.

Improvements to land: Publicly owned additions such as curbs, sidewalks, street lighting system, and sewers, constructed so as to permit the development of privately owned land for utilization. (As opposed to improvements on land, which are usually privately owned.)

In personam: Against the person. Applied to actions in which the court is to impose upon the defendant a personal obligation to obey the order, judgment, or decree.

Incentive: Payment or reward for taking a certain action, usually in excess of fixed compensation and based upon better performance than required by agreement.

Inchoate dower: A wife's interest in the real estate of her husband during his life, which may become a right of dower upon his death.

Income: A stream of financial benefits generally measured in terms of money as of a certain time; a flow of service. It is the origin of value.

Income approach to value: The most important of the three approaches when income properties are appraised. Here the appraiser or investor is asking the present value of the future flow of income that can be expected from the property.

Income method: A method of appraising real property basing the value of the property upon the net amount of income produced by it.

Income/price ratio: Net income compared to the selling price of the property.

Income property: A property in which the income is generated by means of commercial rentals or in which the returns attributable to the real estate can be so segregated as to permit direct estimation. The income may come from several sources; e.g., commercial rents, business profits attributable to real estate other than rents, etc.

Incompetent: One who is mentally incapable; any person who, though not insane, is not considered legally competent enough to properly manage and take care of self or property and therefore could easily be taken advantage of by designing persons.

Incorporeal rights: Nonpossessory rights in real estate.

Increment: An increase. Used in reference to the increases in land values that accompany population growth and increasing wealth in the community.

Incremental income tax: The additional income tax caused by a given investment.

Incurable depreciation: A defect which cannot be removed or which it is impractical to remove. A defect in the "bone structure" of a building. It is measured by age-life tables or life expectancy.

Indenture: Any contract by which two or more parties enter into reciprocal obligations.

Independent contractor: A self-employed person, or one

employed by another who has no right of control over the employee except as to final results.

Indirect lighting: Light that is reflected from the ceiling or other object external to the source.

Industrial districts: Areas in which the primary or major improvements to land are in the nature of factory, warehouse, or related property.

Industrial park: An area in which the land is developed specifically for use for industrial purposes.

Industrial property: In a broad sense, all the tangible and intangible assets pertinent to the conducting of an enterprise for the manufacturing, processing, and assembling of finished products from raw or fabricated materials. Also, in a limited sense, the land, fixed improvements, machinery, and all equipment (fixed or movable) comprising the facilities devoted to such enterprise.

Infant: A person not of full age; a minor lacking legal capacity to enter into contracts other than for necessities.

Infiltration: Displacement by persons of a lower economic status.

Inflation: An economic circumstance that occurs when real purchasing is decreased as a result of rate price increases being greater than the advances in productivity.

Infrastructure: The network of public facilities located within the community (e.g., roads, schools, sewers, parks, utilities, etc.).

Ingress: A place or means of entering; entrance.

Inheritance: An estate in lands or tenements or other things so great that it is infinite and therefore inheritable; an estate of inheritance is the maximum degree of ownership recognized.

Injunction: An order of the court to restrain one or more parties to a suit or proceeding from performing an act which is deemed unjust in regard to the rights of some other party in the suit or proceeding or compelling positive action.

Input-output analysis: A technique for analysis of an economy through description of the production and purchases of specific sectors of the economy.

In rem: A proceeding against the realty directly; as distinguished from a proceeding against a person. (Used in taking land for nonpayment of taxes.)

Installment contract: An agreement providing for the payment of a specified amount in periodic installments by the buyer as a condition precedent to the performance by the seller.

Installment note: A note which provides that payments of a certain sum be paid periodically on the dates specified in the instrument.

Institute of Real Estate Management (IREM): National organization to professionalize members who are involved in all elements of property management through standards of practice, ethical considerations, and educational programs. Confers CPM (Certified Property Manager), AMO (Accredited Management Organization), ARM (Accredited Resident Manager).

Institutional advertising: Advertising intended to popularize a particular company as opposed to the promotion of its products or services.

Institutional lender: A mortgagee who is a bank, insurance company, pension fund, savings and loan association, etc.

Instrument: Any formal legal document, such as a contract, deed, or grant.

Insulation: A heat-retarding material applied in outside walls, top-floor ceilings, or roofs to prevent the passage of heat or cold into or out of the house.

Insurable interest: An ownership interest which an insurer will recognize as a property right, the loss of which will result in true loss of money value to the insured party.

Insurable value: The value at which an insurer will recognize any loss.

Insurance coverage: The total amount of insurance carried.

Insurance rate: The ratio of the insurance premium to the total amount of insurance carried thereby—usually expressed in dollars per $100 or per $1,000—sometimes in percent.

Insurance risk: A general or relative term denoting the hazard involved in the insuring of property. The premium or cost of insurance is determined by the relative risk or hazard considered to be involved.

Insured mortgage: A mortgage in which a party other than the borrower, in return for the payment of a premium, assures payment in the event of default by a mortgagor, e.g., FHA-insured mortgages, PMI (private mortgage insurance).

Intangible assets: The elements of property in an enterprise that are represented in the established organization—doing business, good will, and other rights incident to the enterprise—as distinguished from the physical items comprising the plant facilities and working capital.

Intangible value: An asset's worth which is not immediately available in dollars but which may be of significant value. An example of this is good will.

Intensive margin: Extra benefits derived from adding increasing amounts of labor and capital to land.

Interchange: A system of underpasses and overpasses for routing traffic on and off highways without interfering with through traffic and for linking two or more highways.

Interest rate: The percentage of a sum of money charged for its use.

Interest rate risk: The risk of loss due to changes in the interest rate. Earnings, or the value of a property, may be affected as a result of changes in prevailing interest rates in the money market. When interest rates go up or down, properties are generally capitalized at higher or lower rates.

Interim financing: A temporary or short-term loan secured by a mortgage, which is generally paid off from the proceeds of permanent financing. See construction loan.

Internal rate of return: The predetermined earning rate requirement for a project; usually established by comparison with other return opportunities available to the investor.

International Real Estate Federation, American Chapter: Promotes understanding of real estate among those involved in the real estate business throughout the world.

Interpret: To construe; to seek out the meaning of language; legally, to determine the intent of an agreement between parties.

Interurbia: A contiguous urban development larger than a city or metropolitan area.

Intestate: A person who has died without leaving a valid will disposing of his or her property and estate.

Intrastate transaction: One occurring or transacted within the boundaries of a particular state.

Inventory: A detailed list of articles, giving the code number, quantity, and value of each; a formal list of the property of a person or estate; a complete listing of stock on hand made each year by a business.

Inversely related cost: Cost that declines as volume of activity to which it relates increases.

Investment: Monies placed in a property with the expectation of producing a profit, assuming a reasonable degree of safety and ultimate recovery of principal; especially permanent use, as opposed to speculation.

Investment calculation: Estimation of value for a particular investor or user.

Investment property: The property which is within itself a business enterprise consisting of all tangible and intangible assets considered integral with the property, assembled and developed as a single unit of utility for lease or rental (in whole or in part) to others for profit.

Investor: An individual, group of individuals, or institution that exchanges cash or other consideration for an ownership interest in real estate or for an equity interest in an organization or entity which in turn will own an interest in real estate.
  Distinguished from a lender, who loans cash with the expectation of receiving a fixed interest return plus repayment of the loan at a future date. An investor also may be distinguished form a speculator, with the former intending to hold real estate for a relatively long period of time rather than intending to make a resale for profit in the near future.

Involuntary lien: A lien imposed against property without consent of an owner, e.g., taxes, special assessments, and federal income tax.

IREF: See International Real Estate Federation.

IREM: See Institute of Real Estate Management.

Irrevocable: Incapable of being revoked, modified, withdrawn, or changed.

Irrigation districts: Quasi-political districts created under special laws to provide for water services to property owners in the district, an operation governed to a great extent by law.

Italian architecture: A style which varies from a completely balanced design to an informal composition with formal treatment and openings. Typical details include completely framed window openings, circular heads over exterior openings, high windows and doors, and S-shaped red tile on the roof.

Jamb: The side post or lining of a doorway, window, or other such opening.

Joint: The space between the adjacent surfaces of two components connected by nails, glue, cement, or mortar.

Joint and several: A duty against two or more, which may be enforced against all jointly or against each individually.

Joint note: A note signed by two or more persons who share equal liability for repayment.

Joint tenancy: Joint ownership with right of survivorship. All joint tenants have equal rights in the property with the right to automatic succession to title of the whole upon the death of one tenant.

Joint venture: An arrangement under which two or more individuals or businesses participate in a single project as partners.

Joist: One of the series of parallel beams to which the boards of a floor and ceiling laths are fixed and which in turn are supported by larger beams, girders, or bearing walls.

Judgment: The final verdict of a court of competent jurisdiction on a matter presented to it. Money judgments provide for the payment of claims presented to the court.

Judgment creditor: The person who has received a decree or judgment of the court against his debtor for money due him for any cause.

Judgment debtor: The person against whom a judgment has been issued by the court for monies owed.

Judgment lien: The statutory lien upon the real and personal property of a judgment debtor, which is created by the judgment itself.

Judicial action and sale: Foreclosure carried out by the institution of a lawsuit and resulting in a sale under the supervision of a court.

Judicial notice: The doctrine that a court will, of its own knowledge, assume certain facts to be true without the production of evidence in support of them. It is said that the court takes judicial notice of such facts because they are common knowledge.

Judicial sale: A court action which serves to enforce the judgment lien; the property is sold under judicial process to pay the debt.

Junior lien: A lien granted after the granting of an earlier lien on a different debt against the same property.

Junior mortgage: A mortgage having claim ranking below that of another mortgage which preceded it in time.

Jurat: The clause written at the foot of an affidavit stating when, where, and before whom such affidavit was sworn.

Jurisdiction: A political subdivision with power to govern its own affairs; in law, the power of a court to try specific suits.

Key lot: A lot in such a position that one side is adjacent to the rear of other lots. It is considered to be the least desirable of the lots in a subdivision.

Kickback: Payments made for referrals of clients, customers, or businesses.

Kiln-dried lumber: Lumber that was dried in a large ovenlike chamber for a period of time dependent upon its thickness and grade. This reduces the moisture content.

Knob-and-tube wiring: A method of wiring whereby the wires are attached to the house frame with porcelain knob insulators and porcelain tubes. Not used very frequently any more.

Laches: The established doctrine of equity under which, apart from any questions of statutory limitation, courts will discourage delay and sloth in the enforcements of rights and will decline to try suits not brought within a reasonable time.

Land: In a physical sense, the earth's surface; in a legal sense, ground and everything annexed to it, whether by nature or by humans.

Land contract: A written agreement by which real estate is sold to a buyer who pays a portion of the purchase price when the contract is signed and completes payment in installments made over a specified period of years, with the title remaining with the seller until the total purchase price or a stipulated portion of the purchase price is paid.

Land economics: That branch of economics which deals with utilization of land resources in the attainment of objectives set by society.

Land grant: A gift of government land to a university, public utility, or railroad, or for a purpose that would be in the best interest and benefit of the general public; also, the original granting of land from the public sector to the private sector commonly used in the early history of the United States.

Land improvements: Physical alterations in, or construction of a more-or-less permanent nature attached to or appurtenant to, land, of such character as to increase its utility and/or value.

Land planning: The designing of land area uses, road networks, and layout for utilities to achieve efficient utilization of real estate resources.

Land, tenements, hereditaments: A phrase used in early English law to express various types of property of the immovable class.

Land trust certificate: An instrument used in financing larger real estate transactions. The investor receives a trust certificate as evidence of his or her share in the trust which is used as the investment vehicle.

Landlord: The owner of real estate which is leased to others.

Landmarks: A monument or erection set up on the boundary line of two adjoining parcels to fix such boundary.

Landscaping: The utilization of a lawn and plantings to improve the appearance of a lot.

Latent defects: Physical weaknesses or construction defects not noticeable after a reasonable inspection of the property.

Lateral and subjacent support: The right to have land supported by the adjoining land or the soil beneath by the owner of the adjoining property who excavates to the boundary line between the two properties.

Law: In a legal sense, an established rule or standard of conduct or action that is enforceable by government. A license law is a law that regulates the practices of real estate brokers and salespersons. Real estate law is the body of laws relating to real estate; generally evolved from the English common law but now including regulations such as zoning, building codes, etc.

Layout: The design or floor plans for the arranging of rooms in an apartment or an office.

Lease: A transfer of possession and the right to use property to a tenant for a stipulated period, during which the tenant pays rent to the owner; the contract containing the terms and conditions of such an agreement. A graded or step-up lease is a lease with a rental payment that increases over specified periods of time. A ground lease is a lease for vacent land upon which the tenant may erect improvements. An index lease is a lease in which the rental payment varies in accordance with variation in an agreed upon index of prices or costs. A lease with option to purchase is a lease in which the lessee has the right to purchase the real property for a stipulated price at or within a stipulated time. A leasehold is an estate held under lease. A net lease is a lease in which the tenant pays certain agreed upon property expenses such as taxes or maintenance. A percentage lease is a lease in which the rental is based upon a percentage of the lessee's sales income. A tax participation clause (in a lease) is an agreement in a lease whereby the lessee agrees to pay all or a stated portion of any increase in real estate taxes.

Lease-purchase agreement: An arrangement whereby a portion of the rent is applied toward a down payment. Upon payment of the down payment the tenant, using borrowed funds, purchases the property and becomes the owner outright rather than a mere lessee.

Leased fee: A property held in fee whereby a lease conveys the right of use and occupancy to others. A property which has the right to receive ground rentals over a period of time, and consisting of the further right of ultimate repossession at the termination of the lease.

Leasehold estate: An estate in real property that transfers possession to the tenant for a fixed period of time.

Leasehold policy: A form of title insurance taken out by the lessee in order to protect his or her interest in the property. It is commonly used in insuring commercial property because of the value of the fixtures and equipment which are added.

Legal capacity: One's capability, power, or fitness to enter into a contractual agreement as determined by law.

Legal description: A means of identifying the exact boundaries of land by metes and bounds, by a plat, or by township and range survey system. Metes refer to measures; bounds refer to direction. Metes and bounds descriptions are means of describing land by measurement and direction from a known point or marker on land. A plat is a recorded map of land that identifies a parcel by a number or other designation in a subdivision. A township and range survey system is a system of legal description of land with a township as the basic unit of measurement. A base line is a parallel that serves as a reference for other parallels. Meridians are the north-south lines of survey, 6 miles apart. Parallels are the east-west lines of survey, 6 miles apart. A principal meridian is a meridian that serves as a reference for other meridians. A range is a north-south row of townships; the 6-mile strip of land between meridians. A section is a 1-mile square in a township. A tier is an east-west row of townships; the 6-mile strip of land between parallels. A township is a 6-mile square of land bounded by parallels and meridians and composed of 36 sections.

Legality: The quality or condition of being legal or in conformity with the law.

Legality of objects: An essential element of every contract is that it be for a legal purpose. If not so, the contract is automatically void.

Legal rate of interest: The maximum rate of interest that may be charged in accordance with state law.

Lessee: The party who possesses the right to possession of real estate for a limited time under a lease. The lessee is commonly referred to as the tenant.

Lessor: The landlord under a lease; one who conveyed a right or estate in realty to another under a lease.

Leverage: A financial method applied with the anticipation that the property acquired will increase in return so that the investor will realize a profit not only on his or her own investment but also on the borrowed funds, with the borrowed funds being predominant.

Levy: A seizure of property to satisfy a judgment; the imposition of a tax.

LHA: Local Housing Authority.

Liability: Any debt or obligation; an obligation or duty that must be performed.

License: A personal privilege to perform some act or series of acts upon the land of another without possessing any estate therein; a permit or authorization to do what, without a license, would be unlawful.

License term: A term beginning November 1 of odd number years and ending October 31 two years thereafter.

License year: The period of time for which a license retains its validity. Usually specified in the licensing act, it generally differs from a calendar year.

Licensee: A person to whom a license is granted.

Lien: A charge or claim upon property which encumbers it until the obligation is satisfied.

Lien theory: The state law providing a lender a lien against real estate as collateral for a loan. This is less protective to lenders than title theory.

Lien theory of mortgage: The mortgage theory under which title to mortgaged property vests in the borrower, with the lender having a lien against the real estate.

Life estate: An estate in land held during the term of a certain person's life. The estate terminates upon the death of the holder. The estate may be held by more than one person. The balance of the estate resides in the remainderman who will succeed to the title upon termination of the life estate.

Life tenant: The holder of a life estate, which lasts as long as the measuring life continues.

Limited-access highway: A highway designed for the constant flow of traffic. The entrance and exit opportunities have been predetermined and set at specific intervals.

Limited partnership: A partnership in which some partners make only specified contributions and in return have only limited liabilities.

Lintel: The horizontal board over a door or window that supports the load.

Liquidated damages: The amount agreed upon as payment for a breach of contract by the parties themselves and in advance.

Liquidity: Measurement of the ability one has to sell his or her property quickly.

Lis pendens: A pending suit. The doctrine of lis pendens creates a notice against the property of a defendant in a lawsuit pending its final resolution.

Listing contract: A written agreement or contract between a principal and an agent providing that the agent will receive a commission for finding a buyer who is ready, willing, and able to purchase a particular property under terms specified in the agreement. A multiple listing is a listing that, in addition to employing the agent, provides for the services of other agents who have agreed among themselves that they will cooperate in finding a purchaser for the property. An open listing contract provides that the agent shall receive a commission if the property is sold as a result of the efforts of that agent or if the agent produces a buyer under the terms of the contract before the property is sold.

Litigation: A contest in a court of justice for the purpose of enforcing a right; a lawsuit.

Load-bearing wall: An integral part of the house, which helps support the floors or roof and is relatively permanent in structure.

Load center: The electrical distribution center for the structure, either the main center or a branch center. The center is equipped with circuit breaks instead of a main switch and fuse box.

Loan discount: The amount withheld by a lender from the loan proceeds given to the borrower, representing interest paid in advance or, more accurately, interest paid at the beginning of a loan based upon the sum to be repaid at its maturity. (*See also* points.)

The Federal Housing Administration and the Veterans Administration do not permit the buyer of a home insured by either agency to be charged with points. Consequently, if the mortgage lender in such transactions requires a discount, the seller rather than the buyer must absorb it by a reduction in the sale price.

Loan fee: The service charge made by the lender for the granting of a loan in addition to required interest.

Loan maturity: The life of the loan. The amount of time the loan will remain in existence until the debt is retired. A 20-year loan has a maturity of 20 years.

Loan value: The basic value which determines amount a lending institution will lend on a property.

Loan/value ratio: The amount of mortgage debt and the market or appraisal value of the property for debt purposes, usually expressed as a percentage. For example, an 80% loan/value ratio on a $100,000 property means a mortgage of up to $80,000 may be obtained. The greater the loan/value ratio, the greater the financial leverage available to the purchaser.

Local Housing Authority (LHA): The local body whose major concern is public housing.

Localization of income: Income production at fixed locations; e.g., from real estate, which has a fixed and unique location.

Location: Position of land and improvements in relation to other land and improvements and to local or general economic activity.

Location quotient: An analytic technique using proportionality comparisons, for example, the comparison of the percentage of an activity in a city with the percentage of the same activity in the nation.

Locked-in period: A period of time during which the borrower of a mortgage may not repay any of the principal. This is written into the contract.

Lot: A specific plot of land.

Louver: An opening filled with a series of horizontal slats set at an angle to permit ventilation without admitting rain, sunlight, or vision.

MAI: A designation for a person who is a member of the American Institute of Appraisers, a group associated with NAR.

Maintenance: The keeping up or the expenditures necessary to keep a property in condition to perform the services for which it is designed.

Maintenance reserve: The sum of money allotted to cover the costs of maintenance.

Majority age: The age at which an individual is capable of entering into a binding contract; sometimes referred to as "legal age" or "adulthood."

Malfeasance: The performance of an act that is unlawful or wholly wrong.

Management contract: An agreement used to define the rights and duties of the contracting parties. It enumerates in detail the method of payment and the rates of compensation of the agent for renting of space and maintaining another's property.

Management process: A set of guidelines for action, for the implementation of decisions; an orderly means for the accomplishment of objectives.

Mandatory: Continuing a command; imperative.

Map: A representation of some feature on the earth's surface such as physical features or boundary lines, and the like.

Margin of security: The dollar differential between the amount of the mortgage loan(s) and the appraised value of a property.

Marginal land: Land which has returns that barely meet the costs of operation.

Marginal revenue: An additional amount of revenue resulting from a given business decision.

Marginal satisfaction: An alteration in the level of satisfaction derived from the occurrence of a given event.

Marginal utility: The worth of one additional unit of a good or a service that is produced.

Market: A set of arrangements for bringing buyers and sellers together through the price mechanism. A buyer's market is a market in which buyers can fulfill their desires at lower prices and on more advantageous terms than those prevailing earlier. It is a market characterized by many properties available and few potential users demanding them at prevailing prices. A capital market is comprised of the activities of all lenders and borrowers of equity and long-term debt funds. A money market is a market for borrowed funds, generally short-term. A seller's market is a market in which potential sellers can sell at prices higher than those prevailing in an immediately preceding period. It is a market characterized by very few properties available and a large number of users and potential users demanding them at prevailing prices.

Marketable title: A title which is so free from defect that a purchaser, mortgagee, or lessee cannot legally reject the tender of such title.

Market analysis: An estimate of value developed for the purpose of arriving at a selling or market price.

Market comparison (market approach): The approach to real property appraisal which compares a certain property to equivalent properties which have sold recently to develop a value.

Market indicators: Sign posts or indexes of market activity.

Market price: The price paid for an object regardless of external influences.

Market rent: The amount charged for rent; established by pricing the rent at a level near that of similar properties in the market area.

Market value: The price property would command in the market.

Marketing function: The determination of how land will be put to use after the limits are set by zoning and other restrictions both public and private.

Marketing myopia: A failure to match the needs with the people who have needs.

Master deed: The title document used in condominium projects, which creates both the fee units and the common interests involved in the projects.

Master/servant relationship: The relationship between employer and employee (as distinguished from principal and agent); typically identified by employer's control over employee.

Master switch: An electrical wall switch which controls several fixtures or outlets in a room.

Maximum rent: The greatest amount of rent that may be charged as set down in a rent regulation or order.

Mechanic's lien: A claim created by law for the purpose of securing a priority of payment of the price or value of work performed and materials furnished in erecting or repairing a building or other structure, and as such it attaches to the land as well as to the buildings erected thereon. It is enforceable by foreclosure proceedings.

Meeting of the minds: Whenever all parties to a contract agree to the material terms thereof.

Megalopolis: An urban area of great size.

Merger: In real estate law, the doctrine that a lesser interest is absorbed by a greater estate when both are owned by the same person. E.g., when a tenant buys the fee simple, and leasehold is absorbed into the fee and he is then the owner and no longer a tenant.

Merger of covenant: Involves the acquisition of title to both the burdened and benefited parcel by one individual, thus resulting in the extinguishment of the covenant.

Meridians: The imaginary north-south lines that intersect base lines to form a point of origin for the measurement of land.

Messuage: The residence and all the adjacent buildings and the land around it.

Metes and bounds: The boundary lines of land, with their terminal points and angles.

MGIC: Mortgage Guarantee Insurance Corporation.

Microeconomics: The science of economic functions from the viewpoint of the individual firm or decision maker.

Mill: In taxes, equals one-tenth of 1 cent; a measure used to state the property tax rate; a tax rate of 1 mill on the dollar is the same as a rate of one-tenth of 1% of the assessed value of the property.

Minor: An infant or person who is under the age of legal competence, which in New York is generally established by statute to be under 18 years of age.

Misdemeanor: A criminal offense of a lesser grade than that of a felony usually punishable by a fine and/or a short jail sentence.

Misrepresentation: Transmitting an untruth from one person to another via words or other conduct. Presenting something not in accordance with the facts.

Mission architecture: The architectural style employing the characteristics of early California missions, generally Spanish in style.

Mistake of fact: Errors which do not state the true conditions of the contract. If curable, these errors of fact do not generally void the contract.

Mistake of law: Occurs when a party to a contract having full knowledge of the facts comes to an erroneous conclusion as to their legal effect. The party may not void the contract under a mistake of law based on the erroneous conclusion.

Mobile home: A manufactured standardized home which is entirely constructed in a factory and then transported to the site. It is the opposite of a conventionally built home.

Model house: A house used for exhibition in order to sell other houses.

Modern architecture: The architectural style that employs the principles of contemporary, functional design, intended to combine esthetic quality and utility in a home.

Modern English architecture: An architectural design consisting of many elements of the Elizabethan and Tudor styles, but called modern because it is of more recent vintage. Prominent characteristics are the rough plaster or stucco exterior, the steep roof slopes with variegated and graduated slate or red tile, and having no cornices or eaves.

Modernization: A process involving the restoration of a structure to its maximum attractiveness and productivity without altering any of its property functions.

Modular construction: Prefabrication in three dimensions; i.e., entire rooms of houses or apartments are built in the factory and shipped to their eventual location where very little on-site labor is required.

Modular planning: The designing of structures using a designated minimum dimension of length and width such as 4 feet.

Moisture barrier: A material used to stop or slow down the flow of moisture into walls.

Monetary controls: Efforts by the Federal Reserve to influence the level of economic activity by regulating the availability of money and the rate of interest.

Monopoly: An economic condition attained when one party controls the entire market.

Monument: Visible mark or indications left on natural or other objects indicating the lines and boundaries of a survey.

Moral turpitude: Conduct contrary to the social duty owed by one person to another, criminal in nature.

Moratorium: A temporary suspension, often by statute, of enforcement of the liability for a financial obligation.

Mortgage: An instrument in writing, duly executed and delivered, that creates a lien upon real estate as security for the payment of a specified debt.

Mortgage bank correspondents: The various mortgage bankers who serve as agents of lenders for the purpose of placing and servicing mortgage loans in a local community.

Mortgage banker: A firm which primarily originates real estate loans and either holds them in its own portfolio or sells them to institutional lenders and other investors; also known as a mortgage company.

Mortgage bond: A formal written promise by a borrower to pay to a lender a specified sum of money at a fixed future day or days with the promise secured by a pledge of security.

Mortgage brokerage: The business of bringing together the lender and borrower, with additional services such as aiding in the closing of a loan.

Mortgage commitment: A notice in writing from the lending institution promising the mortgage loan in the future and also specifying the terms and conditions of the loan.

Mortgage company: The private corporation whose principal function is to originate and service mortgage loans sold to financial institutions.

Mortgage constant: The percentage of an original loan balance represented by a constant annual mortgage payment required to retire the debt on schedule.

Mortgage correspondent: A representative of a lender of money on the security of real property; a representative of a potential mortgagee.

Mortgage guaranty insurance: The insurance issued against financial loss. It is available to mortgage lenders from MGIC, a private company organized in 1956, and others who have since entered the field.

Mortgage insurance premium: The amount the borrower pays for the insurance on a loan by the FHA.

Mortgage note: A promissory note executed by a borrower which is payable to the order of the lender and which is secured by a mortgage on the borrower's property.

Mortgagee: The creditor or lender under a mortgage.

Mortgagee reduction certificate: An instrument executed by the mortgagee setting forth the present status and the balance due on a particular mortgage as of a specified date.

Mortgagor: The debtor or borrower under a mortgage.

Motivation research: Analysis of consumers in an attempt to determine why prospective buyers react as they do to products or services or to advertisements used in attempting to sell them.

Mud entrance: A vestibule or small room designed for entrance from a play yard or alley.

Multifamily structure: A dwelling for (usually) five or more household units.

Multiple exchange: Three or more principals involved in the exchanging of various pieces of property.

Multiple listing: A cooperative listing arrangement whereby listings are taken and distributed to the other brokers so that they will have an opportunity to sell the property.

Multiple nuclei: A theory of urban growth emphasizing separate nuclei and differentiated districts occurring in clusters.

Municipal improvements: Improvements, such as streets, sidewalks, sewers, etc., made by a local governmental body for the benefit of all property owners in a specific area. The costs of such improvements are charged or assessed in the nature of real estate taxes against the benefited owners.

Mutual covenants: One which both benefits and burdens the parcel being sold as well as the parcel being retained.

Mutual savings bank: A financial institution in which the depositors are the owners. Mutual savings banks are a primary source of home mortgage funds.

Mutual water company: A water company created by or for water users in a specific area with the object of securing an ample water supply at a more reasonable rate; stock is issued to users.

NAR: National Association of Realtors®.

National Association of Real Estate License Law Officials (NARELLO): An association composed of real estate commissioners and other officers and officials charged with the responsibility of enforcing the license laws of the various states, provinces, etc.

National Association of Realtors® (NAR)®: An association formally known as the National Association of Real Estate Boards, made up of some 500,000 members and, as such, the largest organization representing the real estate industry in the country and probably the largest and most prestigious real estate organization in the world. The membership of NAR® consists of Realtors® and Realtor® Associates and includes among its members real estate brokers, property managers, appraisers, and salespersons working in all areas of the real estate industry.

National Savings and Loan League: The national professional and trade association for individual savings and loan associations.

Necessaries: An economic term referring to the essentials required for existence, such as food and shelter.

Negative easement: An easement whereby the owner of the servient estate is prohibited from doing something, otherwise lawful, upon his own propery because of the effect this activity would have on the dominant estate, e.g., an easement which prevents a property owner from building on his own property because the structure would interrupt the passage of light and air to the dominant estate is a negative easement.

Negative fraud: The act of not disclosing to the buyer a material fact, thereby inducing him to enter into a contractual situation causing him damage or loss.

Net income: That amount of money which remains after expenses are subtracted from income, also termed "profit."

Net lease: An arrangement between the lessee and lessor whereby the lessee pays the charges against the property and the lessor nets the rental payments received.

Net listing: A listing of real estate which specifies the amount which the owner must receive from a sale, with any excess being retained by the broker as his commission.

Net worth: The value remaining after all debts and obligations are removed.

Nominal interest rate: The rate of interest in the contract.

Nonbearing wall: A wall used as a divider and not to carry any load.

Nonconforming use: A use that conformed with zoning regulations prior to the enactment of the current zoning ordinance and which, though nonconforming as to present zoning laws, may continue.

Nonresident: One who does not reside within the state or is not from that particular state.

Nonresident broker: One who lives in another state and does not maintain an office in the State of New York.

Nonsolicitation order: Order issued by the Secretary of State of New York prohibiting the seeking of listings in geographic areas determined to be the subject of panic selling or excessive solicitation.

Nonzoning: Not placing any restriction on the use of the land via regulations, etc.

Notary public: A public officer who is authorized to take acknowledgments and before whom affidavits may be sworn.

Note: An acknowledgment and promise to pay a debt. It must be in writing and signed.

Novation: The substitution of a new obligation for an old one, e.g., where parties to an agreement accept a new debtor in the place of an old one.

Nuisance: Conduct or activity which results in actual physical interference with another person's reasonable use or enjoyment of his or her property for any lawful purpose.

Obligee: One to whom a debt is owed.

Obligor: One who is bound by debt.

Obsolescence: Loss in property value because of the existence of a less costly alternative that provides comparable or more desirable property services.

Occupancy: Physical possession.

Offer: To present a set of terms intended to result in a contract subject to another's acceptance. This is not a contract until accepted by the other party.

Offeree: The one who receives an offer, such as when the owner of property for sale receives an offer from a potential buyer based on certain terms subject to the seller's acceptance.

Offeror: The one making the offer.

OILSR: Officer of Interstate Land Sales Regulation.

Oligopoly: Control of a market by a limited number of participants.

Open-end clause: A clause in a mortgage which provides a method of advancing additional funds against a note after partial payment. To meet new obligations the debt can be quickly restored to its original amount.

Open-end mortgage: A mortgage given to secure future loans made from time to time, usually back up to the original balance after partial repayment has been made.

Open house: A house that is available for inspection by potential purchasers without appointments.

Open listing: An authorization given by a property owner to a real estate agent wherein said agent is given the nonexclusive right to secure a purchaser; open listings may be given to any number of agents without liability to compensate any except the one who first secures a buyer ready, willing, and able to meet the terms of the listing, or secures the acceptance by the seller of a satisfactory offer. The seller retains the right to sell directly without payment of any commission.

Operating expense: Generally any expense occurring periodically which is necessary to produce net income before depreciation.

Operating expense ratio: The relationship between operating expenses and project gross income.

Operating profit: Profit arising from the regular operation of a firm engaged in performing physical services (public utilities, etc.), excluding income from other sources and expenses other than those of direct operation.

Operation of law: A legal conclusion or determination which occurs automatically and which is mandated by a certain principle of law.

Opinion of title: Legal opinion stating that title to the property is clear and merchantable or pointing out defects which must be cured.

Option (to purchase real estate): The right to purchase property at a stipulated price and under stipulated terms within a period of time; the instrument that is evidence of such a right.

Optionee: The one who receives an option, such as the potential purchaser of real estate.

Optionor: The one who gives the option, such as the owner of the real estate.

Oral contract: A verbal agreement; one which is not placed in writing.

Ordinance: A public regulation (usually local laws).

Orientation: The position of a structure on a site and its general relationship to its surroundings.

Original cost: The initial cost; the amount paid to build on or acquire the property.

Outdoor living: Referring to the use of porches, patios, terraces, lawns, gardens, and rooms opening into the yard, or which have extensive glass areas which tend to "bring in the outdoors."

Overall interest rate: The rate that includes interest on the land, interest on the building, and a recapture of capital.

Overbuilding: The building of more structures of a particular type than can be absorbed by the market at prevailing prices.

Overhang: The part of the roof extending beyond the walls, used to shade buildings and cover walks.

Owner's policy: A title insurance policy taken out to protect the owner's interest in the real estate.

Ownership of real property: The holding of rights or interests in real estate.

Package mortgage: A form of mortgage used with new residential sales. Included in the debt is the cost of certain mechanical or electrical equipment. Interest, principal, and equipment are all paid for by means of one equal monthly payment.

Panel heating: A means of radiant heating, with pipes or ducts built into walls, floor, or ceiling, which serve as heating panels.

Panic selling: The illegal practice of inducing fear among property owners in a particular neighborhood that an abnormally high turnover might occur as the result of the introduction of a nonconforming use or user into the area.

Parapet: A low protective wall or barrier built around the edge of a balcony, roof, bridge, or the like.

Parcel of real estate: A particular piece of land and its improvements.

Parity: Equality; often used to refer to an equivalence between farmers' current purchasing power and their purchasing power at a selected base period, maintained by government support of commodity prices.

Parking lot: A parcel of real estate used for the storage of automobiles. Usually about 300 square feet per auto is required for parking space and aisles.

Parol evidence: Oral or verbal evidence.

Parquet floor: Hardwood flooring laid in squares or patterns instead of being laid in strips.

Partially amortized mortgage: A combination of an amortized mortgage and a term mortgage (straight term mortgage).

Participation loan: A mortgage loan made by one lender with other lenders purchasing interests in the loan.

Participation mortgage: A loan in which the lender receives debt repayment plus a share of the profits from ownership.

Partition: A division of real or personal property among co-owners of real estate through a legal proceeding brought for that purpose.

Partition action: Court proceedings in which co-owners seek to divide the property into individual shares.

Partition proceedings: A legal procedure by which an estate held by tenants in common is divided and title in severalty to a designated portion given to each of the previous tenants in common.

Partnership: A contractual union of two or more parties who share in risks and profits of a business venture.

Party wall: A wall built partly on the land of one owner and partly on the land of another, for the common benefit of both, on supporting timbers used in the construction of contiguous buildings.

Pass-through securities program: A GNMA mortgage-backed security program wherein the principal and interest on the mortgages purchased by the investors are passed through to them as they are collected.

Patent: A conveyance from the federal government to a private buyer.

Payback period: Period of time necessary for the cash flow from a project to equal the amount of money invested.

Pennsylvania farmhouse: An architectural style that employs a Colonial residential type of design with stone walls, sometimes pargeted with plaster and whitewashed, characteristically informal.

Per capita: By the head; according to the number of individuals.

Percentage lease: A lease under which the lessee pays rent according to the amount of business he or she does, usually a percentage of the gross from the business. There is usually a provision for a minimum rent payment.

Performance bond: A bond used to guarantee the specific completion of an endeavor in accordance with a contract, such as that supplied by a contractor guaranteeing the completion of a building or a road.

Perimeter heating: Any system in which the heat registers are located along the outside dimensions of a room, especially under the windows.

Periodic tenancy: A tenancy that continues for successive periods (such as month to month) and continues until terminated by notice of one of the parties.

Permanent loan: Long-term financing through a mortgage loan or deed of trust.

Perpetual easement: An easement without a time limit.

Perpetuity: Without limitation as to time; theoretically, forever.

Personal liability: The obligation of a person (individual or business entity) to satisfy a debt, to the extent of the person's entire assets if necessary.

Personal property: The exclusive right to exercise control over personalty; all property objects other than real estate.

Personalty: All property other than realty; chattels.

Physical depreciation: Physical deterioration inherent in the property, which impairs its use.

Pier: A column of masonry, used to support other structural members.

Pitch: The incline of a roof.

PITI: Stands for principal, interest, taxes, insurance when they are all included in one mortgage payment.

Plaintiff: The party who originates an action at law.

Planned unit development: A design for an area which provides for intensive use of land often through a combination of private and common areas with arrangements for sharing responsibilities for the common areas. Typically, zoning boards consider the entire development and allow its arrangements to be substituted for traditional subdivisions. An example is a residential cluster development.

Planning: The process of formulating a program in advance to achieve desired results. Long-range planning is planning for a period of years in the future. This type of planning is used as a framework for shorter-range planning.

Plat, plat map: A map that shows boundary lines of parcels of real estate, usually of an area that has been subdivided into a number of lots.

Plat book: A book containing a series of plat maps.

Plat book designation: The location of the recorded subdivision of a tract of land. It has a distinguishing name or number so that it can be readily located in the public records.

Plenum: The chamber in a warm-air furnace where the air is heated and from which the ducts carry the warm air to the registers.

Plottage: The extent to which value is increased when two or more lots are combined in a single ownership or use.

Plottage increment: The appreciation in unit value attained by joining smaller ownerships into a large single ownership.

Plottage value: Increased value to land created by joining small parcels into large tracts.

Plywood: Laminated wood made up in several layers; several thicknesses of wood glued together with the grain at different angles for strength.

PMI: Private mortgage insurance.

Pocket cards: Cards issued by the Department of State which identify the holder as being either a licensed salesperson or licensed broker.

Points: A charge assessed by a lending institution to increase the yield of a mortgage loan so that it is competitive with other investments. Sometimes the loan origination fee is referred to in terms of points.

Police powers: The right of the state to enact laws and enforce them for the order, safety, health, morals, and general welfare of the public.

Portico: A roof supported by columns. It may be part of a building or by itself.

Possibility of reverter: A future estate which is left in the creator or his successors in interest upon the simultaneous creation of an estate that will terminate automatically upon the occurrence of a specified event. The estate retained by the grantor upon the conveyance of a fee on limitation.

Power of attorney: A written authorization to an agent to perform specified acts on behalf of his principal.

Prefabricated house: A house with components that are prebuilt and sometimes partly assembled prior to delivery to the building site.

Prefabrication: The process of manufacturing component parts of a structure in a factory for later assembly on-site.

Premises: Land and tenements, an estate, the subject matter of conveyance.

Prepayment clause: A clause in the mortgage which gives a mortgagor the privilege of paying the mortgage indebtedness before it becomes due.

Prepayment penalty: The penalty levied on the mortgagor or trustor for early payment of the obligation.

Prepayment privilege: A mortgage contract clause permitting the borrower to pay loan payments in advance of their due date.

Prepayment yield: The sum that may be realized by paying a debt prior to the date due.

Prerogative: A sovereign power.

Prescription: The name given to a mode of acquiring property rights in land of another by continuous use, without claiming ownership.

Present value: The value today, computed by measuring all future benefits of an investment and converting those benefits into terms of today's dollars.

Price: The amount of money at which property is offered for sale or is exchanged for at a sale; value in terms of money.

Price level: A relative position on the scale of prices as determined by a comparison of prices (of labor, materials, capital, etc.) at one time with prices at other times.

Prima facie: Presumptive evidence of fact which is legally sufficient to establish that fact unless rebutted by evidence to the contrary.

Principal: One who has another act for him; one who is represented by an agent; also, the amount of a debt.

Principal meridian: Part of the rectangular method of survey. It is a meridian which serves as a reference for the other meridians.

Priority: When two persons have similar rights in respect to the same subject matter, but one is entitled to exercise his right to the exclusion of the other, he is said to have priority.

Priority (of mortgages): In mortgage finance, the priority of the loan determines its rank in connection with the distribution of assets of a foreclosed or bankrupt debtor. Other things being equal, first in time is first in priority. However, a claim later in time that is recorded prior to an earlier claim will take priority provided the later claimant does not have notice of the earlier claim. A later claimant may also obtain priority as a result of an agreement by which the earlier claimant subordinates his position.

Private sector: The portion of the economy which produces goods and services consumed, in contrast to the portion containing governmental bodies.

Probate: A word originally meaning merely "relating to the proofs of wills," in American law it is now a general name or term used to include all matters over which probate courts have jurisdiction, which in many states are the estates of deceased persons and of persons under guardianship as well as trusts and trustees.

Procuring cause: The activity of a broker which actually brings about a sale of real property.

Profit à prendre: A right to take part of the soil or produce of the land of another.

Promisee: One to whom a promise is made.

Promissory note: A written promise by one person to pay a certain sum of money to another individual at some future specified time. In real property financing, it serves as evidence of a debt for which a mortgage on the property is held as security.

Property: The exclusive right to exercise control over an economic good.

Property brief: A folder that presents pertinent information about a property.

Property management: The operation of real property, including the leasing of space, collection of rents, selection of tenants, and the repair and renovation of the buildings and grounds.

Property manager: An agent for the owner of real estate in all matters pertaining to the operation of the property or properties which are under his or her direction, who is paid a commission for his or her services.

Property owners association: An organization with the purpose of administering private regulations affecting residential land uses.

Property services: The benefits accruing from the use of property.

Proposition: An offer to do something; in real estate, an offer to purchase.

Proprietorship: A business run by its owner as an individual rather than as a corporation.

Proration: The allocation of costs or revenues due between the buyer and the seller of real property.

Proration of taxes: The division of taxes equally or proportionately in accordance with time of use.

Prospectus: A printed document describing the characteristics of a specific property.

Protective covenant: One designed by its restrictions to upgrade and enhance the value of property in the area affected by the covenant.

Public domain: That land to which title is held by the federal government.

Public housing: Housing owned by a governmental body.

Public Housing Administration: A unit of the HUD, which administers legislation providing for loans and subsidies to local housing authorities to encourage the development of low-rental dwelling units.

Public property: A property, the title to which is vested in the community.

Public sector: That portion of the economy which is most affected by governmental bodies and which contains governmental bodies themselves.

Public trustee: The public official in each county whose office has been created by law and to whom title to real property is conveyed by trust deed to protect the interests of beneficiaries.

Punitive damages: The fine assessed to the wrongdoer in excess of damages actually suffered.

Purchase and lease back: A method whereby an investor becomes the actual owner of property through purchase for cash from the original owner-occupant, who continues to occupy and use the property under a long-term lease from the new owner.

Purchase money mortgage: A mortgage given concurrently with a conveyance of land, by the vendee to the vendor, on the same land, to secure the unpaid balance of the purchase price.

Purchase on contract: The purchase of property on installments with title remaining with the seller.

Purchasing power risk: Risk that the value of an investment will decline as a result of inflation (decline in the purchasing power of the dollar).

Purpose of appraisal: To estimate the dollar value of the future utility of a parcel of real property for a specific purpose.

Qualities of value: Scarcity, desire, ability to buy, and utility.

Quantity survey: A means of determining building replacement costs in which all elements of labor, materials, and overhead are priced and totaled to obtain the building cost.

Quarter round: A molding that presents a profile of a quarter-circle.

Quasi: Corresponding to, or similar to; having a limited legal status.

Quasi-contract: An obligation similar to a contract, which is implied by law.

Quiet enjoyment: The right of an owner to use property without interference by others.

Quiet title action: Legal action to remove a defect, cloud, or questionable claim against the title to property.

Quitclaim deed: A deed conveying only the right, title, and interest of the grantor in the property described, as distinguished from a deed which guarantees that actual ownership is being transferred.

Racial restrictions: Those designed to exclude members of a particular race, nationality, or religion from acquiring real property in a given area.

Racial steering: The unlawful practice of influencing a minority person's housing choice.

Radiant heat: A form of heating which transmits hot water or air through ducts embedded in the walls, ceiling, or floors; panel heating.

Radiator: A configuration of metal tubes, usually cast iron, heated by steam or hot water from the boiler. Heat is transferred to the objects in a room by radiation, and to the air by convection.

Rafters: The sloping wood components of a roof.

Ranch style: A one-story home design, usually with a rambling plan and without a basement.

Range: A part of the rectangular system of survey; a north-south row of townships; the 6-mile strip of land between meridians.

Ratification: The approval or adoption of an act performed on behalf of a person without previous authorization.

Real estate: Land and all things permanently attached to it, including buildings, structures, improvements, and fixtures.

Real estate broker: A person, firm, or corporation who acting for another and for a valuable consideration buys, sells, or exchanges real estate, or attempts to collect rent for the use of real estate, or who negotiates or attempts to negotiate loans to be secured by real estate.

Real estate business: A form of business that deals in rights to land and improvements.

Real estate developing: Preparing land for use, constructing buildings and other improvements, and making the completed properties available for use.

Real estate financing: The channeling of monies into the production and use of real estate; facilitating the production and use of real estate through borrowed or equity funds.

Real estate investment corporation: A corporation that sells its securities to the public and has a special interest in real estate or is a builder or developer of real estate.

Real estate investment trust: A trust designed in a form similar to that of an investment or mutual fund for the purpose of allowing investors to channel funds into the real estate investment market. Special federal law permits pooled investments in real estate and mortgages without exposure to corporate income taxes.

Real estate market function: The process of placing real properties and their services into the hands of consumers.

Real estate marketing: The process of putting real properties and their services into the hands of consumers. Brokerage and property management are the two main subdivisions of real estate marketing.

Real estate operator: Any individual engaged in the real estate business acting for himself rather than as an agent.

Real estate salesperson: Any person who for a compensation or valuable consideration has contracted with a real estate broker to sell or offer to sell or negotiate the sale or exchange of real estate, or to lease, rent, or offer for rent any real estate, or to negotiate leases thereof, or of the improvement thereon, as a whole or partial vocation.

Real Estate Securities and Syndication Institute (RESSI): Provides educational opportunities in the field of marketing securities and syndication of real estate.

Real Estate Settlement Procedures Act (RESPA): A federal act which regulates the settlement or closing of real estate transactions involving purchase money mortgages on one- to four-family residences.

Real estate syndicate: A partnership formed for participation in a real estate venture. Partners may be limited or unlimited in their liability.

Real estate tax: A money charge levied upon real property for support of local government and for public services.

Real estate transfer tax: A tax imposed by the state and some local governments upon the conveyance of real estate.

Real property: Real estate and the rights of ownership thereto.

REALTOR®: A broker who is affiliated with a local real estate board that is a member of NAR.

Realtors National Marketing Institute (RNMI): Provides educational programs for REALTORS® in the area of commercial and investment properties, residential sales, and real estate office administration. Confers CCIM (Certified Commercial and Investment Member) and CREBM (Certified Real Estate Brokerage Manager).

Realty: Land and all fixtures permanently attached to it.

Reappraisal lease: A lease having a clause calling for the periodic revaluation of rents.

Recapture: A provision for predicting the return of investment. It may be accomplished by inclusion in the capitalization rate in the income approach to valuation.

Recapture rate: The rate of interest necessary to provide for the return of the initial investment. Not to be confused with interest rate, which is the rate of interest on an investment.

Receiver: One appointed by the courts to take control and possession of property pending litigation and some final order by the court.

Receiver clause: A clause in the mortgage to prevent dissipation of the value of the asset that secures a loan. This clause provides for the orderly appointment of a receiver to take over residential property abandoned by the mortgagor. The receiver rents, manages, and thus conserves the value of the property.

Reciprocity: The mutual exchange of privileges between groups or states. In the case of real estate it is the automatic recognition of the license of one state in another. Many states do not have reciprocity agreements.

Recital of consideration: That part of an instrument which states the consideration or value given for the interest conveyed.

Reconstructed operating statement: Operating revenue and expense figures put into a standard format which permits comparisons with similar properties.

Recording: The process of entering or recording a copy of certain legal instruments or documents, such as a deed, in a government office provided for this purpose, thus making a public record of the document for the protection of all concerned and giving constructive notice to the public at large.

Recording acts, registry laws: Laws providing for the recording of instruments affecting title as a matter of public record to preserve such evidence and give notice of their existence and content; laws providing that the recording of an instrument informs all who deal in real property of the transaction and that, unless the instrument is recorded, a prospective purchaser without actual notice of its existence is protected against it.

Record plat: A recorded map of land showing the subdivision of such land into blocks, lots, and streets, and indicating the measurements of individual parcels.

Recording system: The particular system utilized by a state, county, or other governmental subdivision for the recording of documents which affect real property.

Recourse: The right to a claim against a prior owner of a property or note.

Rectangular, or governmental, grid: The system of land description established by the federal government which utilizes identifiable north and south lines (meridians) and east and west lines (parallels or base lines).

Redemption: The regaining of title to real property after a foreclosure sale. An equity of redemption is the interest of the mortgagor in real property prior to foreclosure. A statutory right of redemption is the right under law of the mortgagor to redeem title to real property before a foreclosure sale for a limited period of time.

Redevelopment: The process of clearance and reconstruction of blighted areas.

Redlining: The refusal to lend money within a specific area for various reasons. This practice is now illegal.

Referee's deed: A deed given by a referee or public officer pursuant to a court order conveying the real property described and containing no covenants of title.

Refinancing: The negotiation of a new mortgage loan to replace and pay off the unpaid balances of existing mortgages.

Reformation: An action to correct an error in a deed or other document.

Regime: A listing of the system of rules or regulations affecting the owners of a condominium project.

Regional analysis: A process applied to real estate, pertaining mainly to local economies and the surrounding area; for other purposes, the area of a "region" may be defined more broadly.

Registrar of deeds, recorder: The government officer in charge of a land records office.

Registration: Recording; inserting in an official register.

Regression: The appraisal principle that maintains that the value of high-quality properties will be adversely affected by the presence of low-quality properties.

Regulation Z: Regulations regarding credit disclosure issued by the Board of Governors of the Federal Reserve System to aid in implementation of the Truth-in-Lending Act.

Regulations: A set of rules for controlling activities or procedures. Coercive regulations are regulations which provide penalties for noncompliance. An inducive regulation is a regulation which provides incentive for compliance.

Rehabilitate: The process of removing blight by repairing and renovating rather than by destroying improvements.

Release: The giving up of a right and claim by the person in whom it exists to the person against whom it might have been enforced.

Release clause: The stipulation that, upon payment of a specific amount of money to the holder of a trust deed or mortgage, the lien of the instrument as to a specific described lot or area shall be removed, e.g., from the blanket lien on the whole area involved.

Remainder: The right of a person to an estate in land that matures at the end of another estate; a classification of estates by time of enjoyment. A contingent remainder is an interest that will become a remainder only if some condition is fulfilled.

Remainderman: One who is entitled to the remainder of the estate after a particular estate carved out of it has expired.

Remodel: To make physical alterations other than keeping the property in repair.

Renewal: The process of redevelopment or rehabilitation in urban areas; often used in relation to rebuilding or restoration of blighted areas.

Rent: The return on land or real property; the price paid for the use of real property belonging to another.

Rent controls: The legal regulation of the maximum rental payment for the use of real property.

Rent multiplier: A number used to estimate value by multiplying it by the rent. A rent multiplier may be either a gross rent multiplier or a net rent multiplier. See gross rent multiplier.

Rent schedule: A plan to estimate the rents to be paid; also, records kept of rentals actually paid in a specific period.

Rental value: The value for a stated period of the right to use and occupy property; the amount a prospective tenant is warranted in paying for a stated period of time, e.g., a month, a year, etc., for the right to use and occupy real property under certain prescribed or assumed conditions.

Replace: To restore to a former plan or condition.

Replacement cost: The estimated cost of building a substantially similar structure as of a certain time utilizing modern materials at present costs and having equal utility.

Replacement reserves: Funds allotted for replacement of building components, equipment, etc.

Replevin: An action to regain possession of goods.

Representation: The principle upon which the issue of a deceased person takes or inherits the share of an estate his or her immediate ancestor would have taken or inherited if living.

Reproduction cost: The cost to duplicate at current prices an asset as closely as possible as of a certain time not knowing for corrective measures.

Rescission: The cancellation of an agreement, either by mutual consent of the parties, a judgment, or a decree of court or an arbitrator.

Research and development: The process of creating new products or new methods.

Reservation: A clause in a deed or other instrument of conveyance by which the grantor reserves some estate, interest, or profit in the real estate conveyed.

Reserve fund: For multifamily properties, an amount budgeted from income to replace short-lived items such as furniture and equipment; the distinctive feature of a budget mortgage loan on residential property; the monthly payments on such a loan including certain sums which are impounded or reserved to pay taxes and insurance when due; a mortgagee's escrow account.

Reserves: Portions of earnings allotted to take care of possible losses in the conduct of business; listed on the balance sheet as a liability item.

Residence: The property in which one actually lives as his or her home.

Residual: That which remains; an appraisal technique to estimate the amount of net annual income derived from property; that which is left after deduction; the remainder of the income.

Residual techniques: Allocation of a portion of income to part of an asset, with the remainder (or residual) flowing automatically to the rest of the asset. Also, the allocation of part of the income to cover debt payments with the balance accruing to the equity being built up in the property.

Residuary: Pertaining to the residue.

RESPA (Real Estate Settlement Procedures Act): A federal act passed in 1975 to force disclosure of all aspects of financing to potential borrowers.

Respondeat superior: The legal theory under which the employer is responsible in damages for his employees' acts which are related to the employment.

RESSI: See Real Estate Securities and Syndication Institute.

Restriction: The term as used in relation to real property means the owner of real property is restrained or prohibited from doing certain things relating to the property, or using the property for certain purposes. For instance, the requirement in a deed that a lot may be used for the construction of not more than a single-family dwelling costing not less than $10,000 is termed a restriction. Also, a legislative ordinance affecting all properties in a given area, requiring that improvements on property shall not be constructed any closer to the street curb than 25 feet is a restriction by operation of law

Restrictive covenant: A clause in a deed in which there is an agreement between the seller and the purchaser in regard to certain restraints as to the use of the property, and which is binding on all subsequent owners.

Return on investment: The percentage correlation between the price an investor pays and the stream of income dollars he or she obtains from the investment.

Revenue stamps: Stamps issued by the state government, which must be purchased and affixed in the amounts provided by law to documents or instruments representing original issues, sales and transfers of deeds of conveyance, stocks, and bonds; these stamps are evidence that transfer taxes have been paid.

Reversion: A right to future possession retained by an owner at the time of transfer of some limited interest in real property.

Reversion value: The estimated value of a reversion as of a given date determined actuarially.

Reversionary right: The right of a person to receive possession and use of property upon the termination and defeat of an existing limited estate carrying the rights of possession and use and vested in another person.

Reversioner: A person who is entitled to a reversion.

Reverter: That portion of an estate which returns or goes back to an owner (or reverts) or his or her heirs after the end or termination of an estate such as a leasehold or a life estate.

Revocation: A withdrawal; a recall; a repudiation; the taking back of a power or authority that has been previously conferred, such as the revoking of a license; the withdrawal of an offer prior to its acceptance.

Ridge: A horizontal line at the joining of the top edges of two sloping roof surfaces. The rafters for both slopes are nailed at the ridge.

Ridge board: A board placed on its edge at the ridge of the roof so as to support the upper ends of the rafters; also called a roof tree, ridge piece, ridge plate, or ridge pole.

Right of reacquisition: A future estate, retained by the grantor upon the conveyance of a fee on condition subsequent.

Right of occupancy: The privilege to occupy and use property for a specified period of time under the terms of some contract such as a lease or other formal agreement.

Right of redemption: The privilege, limited in time, of a property owner to reacquire foreclosed property by paying the mortgage debt or real estate taxes after the final payment date.

Right of rescission: The privilege of cancelling an agreement or transaction.

Right of survivorship: The distinguishing feature of any joint tenancy. It is the automatic succession to the interest of a deceased joint owner.

Right of way: A grant serving as an easement upon land, whereby the owner by agreement gives to another the right of passage over his or her land to construct a roadway, or use as a roadway, a specific part of his or her land, or the right to construct through and over his or her land, telephone, telegraph, or electric power lines; or the right to place underground water mains, gas mains, or sewer mains.

Riparian: Belonging or relating to the banks of a river, stream, waterway, etc.

Riparian grant: The transmittal of riparian rights.

Riparian lease: The document defining the terms, conditions, and date of expiration of the rights to use lands lying between the high water mark and the low water mark.

Riparian owner: One who owns land adjoining a watercourse.

Riparian rights: The rights of a landowner to water on, under, or immediately adjacent to his or her land and its uses.

Riser: An upright board at the rear of each step of a stairway. In heating, a riser is a duct slanted upward to carry hot air from the furnace to the room above.

Risk: The degree of danger of future loss of capital or income.

Risk rating: The method by which various risks are evaluated, usually employing grids to develop precise and relative figures for the purpose of determining the overall soundness of a loan.

RNMI: See Realtors National Marketing Institute.

Rod: The unit of linear measure equal to a length of 5½ yards.

Roman brick: A form of thin brick with slimmer proportions than the standard building brick.

Row houses: A series of individual houses having identical architectural features and the presence of a common wall between two units.

Rules of thumb: The cost indicators sometimes used to assist in estimating the value of a property. Examples are price per front foot, gross rent multiplier, price per square foot, cost per room, and cost per apartment unit. These are usually guidelines or averages based on experience in the same vicinity.

Running with the land: A covenant is said to run with the land when either the liability to perform it or the right to take advantage of it passes to the subsequent grantees of that land.

Safe rate: The rate of interest on government bonds, utility bonds, or bank savings.

Sale-lease back: A plan that allows for the simultaneous transfer of ownership and execution of the lease—the grantor becomes the lessee and the grantee the lessor.

Sales contract: The contract by which the buyer and the seller agree to terms of a sale of property.

Sales expenses: Costs incurred in the sale of real property. Broker's commissions, advertising costs, and costs incurred in the preparation of the property for sale are examples of common expenses.

Salesperson: One acting under the employment and direction of a broker to perform any of the acts which a broker could perform with respect to real estate.

Salvage value: The estimated worth of an item after it is fully depreciated.

Sanborn insurance maps: A series of maps showing locations of individual structures in many cities; developed for underwriting insurance.

Sandwich lease: A leasehold interest which is present between the primary lease and the operating lease. In subleasing property, when the holder of a sublease in turn sublets to another, his or her position is that of being sandwiched between the original lessee and the second sublessee.

Sash: Wood or metal frames containing one or more window panes.

Satisfaction of mortgage: The written acknowledgment of the release of a mortgage or trust deed lien on the records upon payment of the secured debt.

Satisfaction piece: An instrument acknowledging payment of indebtedness secured by a mortgage.

Savings and loan association: A state or federally chartered thrift institution that specializes in making residential mortgages.

Savings bank: A type of bank which receives savings in the form of the deposits in mortgages and other securities allowed by law. The banks, with the exception of a few in New Hampshire, are mutual institutions and are governed by self-perpetuating boards of trustees.

Scarcity: The amount of limitation of real estate facilities in relation to their demand.

Scribing: The fitting of woodwork to an irregular surface.

Seal: A particular sign, made to attest in the most formal manner, the execution of an instrument.

Seasonal fluctuations: Variations in economic activity that recur at about the same time each year.

Seasoned mortgage: A mortgage in which periodic payments have been made for a long period of time and the borrower's payment pattern is well established.

Secondary financing: The loan secured by a second trust deed or a mortgage on real property.

Second mortgage: A mortgage made by a home buyer to generate enough capital for the down payment required under the first mortgage. (FHA does not permit this on loans it insures for first mortgages.) Such mortgages are also used to secure borrowings for home improvements or other related purposes.

Secret interest: Interest hidden or concealed from third-party knowledge.

Section (of land): A portion of land 1 mile square containing 640 acres, into which the public lands of the United States were originally divided; one thirty-sixth part of a township.

Section VIII: A federal program for leasing housing to lower-income families; sponsored through HUD.

Sector hypothesis: A theory stating that sectors of land use arise whereby the highest-priced homes are in the most attractive locations, medium-priced homes follow traffic arteries, and lower-priced homes are near places of employment.

Sectors: Wedge-shaped areas pointing to the center of the urban area; a recognized pattern of urban growth and development.

Sector theory: A theory of city growth that considers the city as a circle with wedge-shaped sectors pointing into the center of the urban area.

Secured party: The party having a security interest in property owned by the debtor. Thus the pledgee, the conditional seller, or the mortgagee are all now referred to as secured parties.

Security: Something of value deposited to make certain the fulfillment of an obligation or the payment of a debt.

Security agreement: The agreement created between the secured party and the debtor that creates the security interest.

Security deposits: The funds placed as collateral by a tenant so that the leased property may be restored to its original condition if need be at the termination of the lease.

Security interest: The interest of the creditor in the property of the debtor in all types of credit transactions. It thus replaces such terms as chattel mortgage, pledge, trust receipt, chattel trust, equipment trust, conditional sale, and inventory lien.

Seed money: The money needed to begin a project, such as the funds needed for acquiring or controlling a site, obtaining zoning, making feasibility studies, etc.

Seised: Possessed of an estate in fee.

Seisin: In the legal sense, possession of premises with the intention of asserting a claim to a freehold estate therein; practically, the same as ownership.

Self-liquidating mortgage: A mortgage which, by means of constant periodic payments, will be fully paid off at the end of its term.

Self-regulating: A system of controls over the conduct of a group, all of whom voluntarily submit to such rules, e.g., the code of ethics adopted by NAR.

Seller's market: An economic market in which sellers can sell at prices higher than those prevailing in an immediately preceding period; a market in which a limited number of properties is available and there is a large number of users and potential users demanding them at prevailing prices.

Senior mortgage: The mortgage having a claim preferential to that of another mortgage.

Separate property: Property owned by a husband or wife which is not jointly owned property; property acquired by either spouse prior to the marriage or by gift or devise after the marriage.

Septic tank: As underground receptacle in which sewage from the house is reduced to liquid by bacterial action and then drained off.

Service property: A property devoted to or available for utilization for a special purpose, but which has no independent marketability in the generally recognized acceptance of the term, such as a church property, a public museum, or a school.

Servicing: The collection of payments on a mortgage. Servicing by the lender also consists of operational procedures covering accounting, bookkeeping, insurance, tax record, loan payment follow-up, delinquent loan follow-up, and loan analysis.

Servient tenement: Property subject to an easement which benefits another property, called the "dominant tenement."

Setback: The distance from curb or other established line, within which no buildings may be erected.

Setback ordinance: An ordinance prohibiting the erection of a building or structure in the area between the curb and the setback line.

Set-off: A counterclaim or cross-demand charged by a defendant against the claim of a plaintiff in an action seeking money damages.

Settlement: The process at the closing of a sale of real estate negotiated by a real estate broker whereby the broker accounts to his or her principal for the earnest money deposit and deducts commission and advances by use of a form of settlement statement.

Severalty: Ownership by a person in his or her own right.

Severalty ownership: Owned by only one person; sole ownership.

Severance damage: The reduction in value caused by separation. Commonly, the damage resulting from the taking of a fraction of the whole property, reflected in a lowered utility and value in the land remaining and brought about by reason of the fractional taking.

Shake: A hand-split shingle, usually edge-grained.

Sheathing: The structural covering, usually consisting of boards, plywood, or wallboards, placed over exterior studding or rafters of a house.

Shed roof: A single-pitch roof that slopes from front to back or back to front.

Sheriff's deed: A deed executed by the sheriff pursuant to a court order in connection with the sale of property to satisfy a judgment.

Sheriff's sale: A sale of property, conducted by a sheriff, or sheriff's deputy, by virtue of his or her authority as an officer pursuant to a court ordered sale.

Shopping center: A planned area for shopping, usually in an outlying location. Typically, stores are surrounded by a parking area. A mall-type shopping center is a shopping center in which the stores face inward toward an enclosed walkway rather than fronting on the parking lot, so that the shoppers can stay inside one building while they visit various stores.

Sill: The lowest part of the frame of a house, resting on the foundation and supporting the uprights of the frame. The board or metal forming the bottom side of an opening, as a door sill, window sill, etc.

Simple interest: The interest computed on the original principal alone.

Simulation: The use of a controlled environment in which to test the effects of a decision.

Single-family home: A dwelling designed for occupancy by one household only.

Sinking fund: A fund set aside from the income of a property which, with accrued interest, will pay for replacement of the improvements as they wear out.

SIR: See Society of Industrial Realtors.

Site: A parcel of real estate that is suitable for improvement.

Siting: The placement and orientation of a house in reference to its lot.

Situs: Location.

Skylease: A long-term lease on the space above a parcel of real estate; the upper stories of a building to be erected by the tenant.

Slander of title: A false and malicious statement, oral or written, made in disparagement of a person's title to real property, causing him special damage.

Slum area: A heavily populated area marked by blight, squalor, or wretched living conditions.

Slum clearance: The removal of blighted improvements by destruction of the improvements.

Society of Industrial Realtors (SIR): Provides educational opportunities to REALTORS® working with industrial property transactions. Confers SIR designation.

Society of Real Estate Appraisers (SREA): A trade association of residential real estate appraisers. Awards SRA, SREA, and SRPA designations.

Social class: A group of people of common social and economic characteristics.

Social overhead capital: The investments by the government for public betterments such as bridges, roads, schools, and parks.

Soil pipe: The pipe which conveys waste from the house to the main sewer line.

Soil pipe and soil stack: The house sewer transporting waste from the house, and the vertical pipe ending in a vent in the roof, which transports vapors from the plumbing system.

Sole or sole plate: The piece, usually a 2 × 4, on which wall and partition studs rest.

Southern Colonial: An architectural design that combines both Georgian and New England Colonial, usually characterized by the use of two-story columns forming a porch across the long facade or at the side of the house.

Sovereign consumer: The theory that the consumer is the decision maker who determines what goods and services are to be provided within the society.

Span: A measure of the distance between structural supports such as walls, columns, piers, beams, girders, and trusses.

Special agency: The relationship wherein the agent acts for the principal for a single transaction or only for a limited, often related, number of transactions. For example, a person closing a real estate transaction under a power of attorney.

Special assessment: A legal charge against real estate levied by a public authority to fund the cost of public improvements such as street lights, sidewalks, street improvements, etc.

Special warranty: A covenant of warranty in a deed, by which the grantor guarantees the title against the claims of persons claiming "by, through, or under" the grantor only.

Special warranty deed: A guarantee only against the acts of the grantor herself and all persons claiming by, through, or under the grantor.

Specific performance: The requirement that a party must perform as agreed under a contract, in contrast to compensation or damages in lieu of performance; the arrangement whereby courts may force either party to a real estate contract to carry out an agreement exactly in accordance with its terms.

Specification: As used in the law relating to patents and machinery, and in building contracts, a particular or detailed statement of the various elements required to define the end product and to which it is to conform.

Specimen tree: A tree of special interest because of its shape or species, placed in a position of prominence in the yard; often a silver spruce, weeping birch, magnolia, or other unique ornamental tree.

Split rate interest: The interest rate paid on property when the rate determined for the buildings differs from the rate determined for the land.

Spot zoning: The allowance of a nonconforming use in an area zoned for a specific purpose.

Spouse: One's wife or husband.

Spouse's right of election: The right of a surviving spouse to elect against the provisions of the will of the deceased spouse and to take the general equivalent of an intestate share.

Square-foot method: A means of estimating construction, reproduction, or replacement costs of a building by multiplying the square-foot floor area by the appropriate square-foot construction cost figure.

Squatters' rights: The rights to occupancy of land created through long and undisturbed use but with no legal title or arrangement.

SRA: Senior Residential Appraiser.

SREA: Senior Real Estate Analyst.

SRPA: Senior Real Property Appraiser.

Stability of income: The constant annual net income reasonably anticipated over the entire economic life of the property.

Stagflation: An economic condition in which there is no economic growth (stagnation) or rapid or large price increases (inflation).

Stand-by commitment: An agreement by the lender to make funds available at a future date upon specified terms.

Standard depth: The depth chosen as normal, usually the one most common in the neighborhood.

Standard metropolitan area: Defined by the Bureau of Census as a county, or a group of contiguous counties, containing a city of 50,000 population or more.

Standing mortgage: A mortgage that provides for interest payments only, with the entire principal falling due in one payment at maturity of the mortgage.

State association: The association of real estate boards that copes with matters which vitally affect the business of its members within its own state.

State vet's loan: A loan made at 4% interest to eligible war veterans upon security of real property located in any state for the acquisition of homes and farms. The program is administered by the State Department of Veterans' Affairs.

Statement of consideration: Statement in a deed or other sales contract that confirms the fact that the purchaser actually gave something of value for the property.

Status: Standing, state, or condition.

Statute: A particular law enacted and established by the legislative department of the government.

Statute of Frauds: Legislation providing that all agreements affecting title to real estate must be in writing to be enforceable.

Statute of limitations: A statute barring all right of action after a certain period of time from the time when a cause of action first arises.

Statutory foreclosure: Foreclosure of a mortgage or lien on real estate by public notice and sale pursuant to statute, but without the need to commence a lawsuit.

Statutory lien: A lien granted to a party by the operation of a statute, e.g., the lien of real estate taxes.

Statutory redemption period: The time allowed to a delinquent borrower to cure his deficiencies before his property is taken permanently from him.

Statutory warranty deed: A warranty deed form outlined by state statutes.

Step-up lease: A lease that permits increasing rentals at specified times during the lease period.

Stockholder (or shareholder): The legal owner of one or more shares of stock in a corporation.

Straight-line capital recapture: The amount of dollar investment recovery in each year that is constant throughout the life of the investment.

Straight-line depreciation: See depreciation, straight line.

Straight-term mortgage: A mortgage in which repayment of the principal is in one lump sum at maturity.

Strict foreclosure: The action taken by a court which, after determination that sufficient time has elapsed for a mortgagor to pay a mortgage past due, terminates all right and interest of the mortgagor in the real property. A forced sale of the property is then ordered for the benefit of the creditors secured by the mortgage.

String, stringer: A timber or other support for cross-members. In stairs, the support on which the stair treads rest.

Studs, studding: The vertical supporting timbers in walls and partitions.

Subcontractor: A contractor employed by a general contractor. A subcontractor usually is concerned only with one particular part of the improvement of real estate, such as plumbing, masonry, carpentry, and the like.

Subdividing: Division of a large parcel of land into smaller parcels.

Subdivision: An area of land divided into parcels or lots generally of a size suitable for residential use.

Subject to and agreeing to pay: The purchaser takes title to the real estate and is also obligated to pay the debt along with the original maker of the note.

Subject to mortgage: The purchaser takes title to the property but is not obligated to pay the mortgage. If foreclosure occurs, the purchaser loses his equity and the original mortgagor is responsible for the debt.

Subjective value: A value created in the mind. It is the amount people will pay regardless of cost. In appraising, it is used in the income and market data approaches.

Sublease: One executed by the lessee of an estate to a third person, conveying the same estate for a shorter term than that for which the lessee holds it.

Subordinate: To make subject to, junior to, or inferior to, usually with respect to security.

Subordination clause: The clause in a junior or a second lien which permits retention of priority for prior liens. A subordination clause may also be used in a first deed of trust, permitting it to be subordinated to subsequent liens, for example, the liens of construction loans.

Subrogation: The substitution of one person in the place of another with reference to a lawful claim, demand, or right by virtue of having paid a claim under an insurance contract.

Subscribing witness: One who writes his name as witness to the execution of an instrument.

Subsidized housing: Housing for low- and moderate-income families in which rentals are paid in part by the government or in which the government pays a portion of the developer's loan interest costs so that he or she can charge lower rentals.

Subsidy (two types): In real estate, a grant by government that eases the financial burden of holding, using, or improving real property. A direct subsidy is a subsidy which is of direct, visible benefit to the recipient, such as a cash grant. An indirect subsidy is a subsidy whose benefit is felt indirectly, such as tariffs of farm price supports which may affect the land values in a particular area.

Suburb: A development of real estate in areas peripheral to the central area of a city.

Succession: The legal act or right of acquiring property by descent; succeeding to an asset by will or inheritance.

Sufficient description: The real estate which is to be conveyed by the deed can be identified; will stand up in court.

Sui juris: Having legal ability to handle one's own affairs; not under any legal disability.

Summation: An appraisal method for determining an interest rate; an indicated value derived by estimating the reproduction cost, subtracting depreciation, and adding the value of the land; one method of the cost approach.

Summons: A writ directed to the sheriff or other proper officer which requires him to notify the person named in the writ that an action has been brought against him and that he is required to appear, on a day named, and answer the complaint in such action.

Sump pump: An automatic electric pump installed in a basement for the purpose of emptying the sump, a pit serving as a drain for basement water accumulations.

Supermarket: A 20,000- to 40,000- square-foot grocery store that is often free-standing.

Supersession costs: Costs incurred in scrapping existing improvements in order to make possible new land uses.

Supply: Amount available for sale.

Supply and demand, law of: A theory that price or value varies directly, depending upon the quantity of units available and quantity of units desired or demanded by the buying public.

Surcharge: An additional charge added to the usual charge.

Surety: One who undertakes to pay money or to perform any other act in the event that his or her principal fails to do so.

Surplus productivity: An appraisal theory whereby net income remains after the costs of labor, coordination, and capital have been paid. This appraisal tends to fix the value of the land.

Surrender: The process of cancellation of a lease by mutual consent of lessor and lessee.

Surrogates court: A court having jurisdiction over the proof of wills and the settling of decedents' estates.

Survey: The process by which a parcel of land is measured and its boundaries ascertained.

Survivorship: See joint tenancy.

Sustained-yield management: Selective harvesting of slow-growing crops such as trees to provide for a relatively stable yield every year rather than periodic large yields at irregular times.

Swing loan: A short-term loan enabling the purchaser of a new property to purchase that property before having been paid for the equity from the property he or she is presently selling.

Sweat equity: Labor or services put into improving real property to gain possession and title in lieu of money.

Syndicate: A group of individuals, corporations, or trusts who pool money to undertake economic endeavors. The syndicate can assume the structure of a corporation, a trust, a partnership, a tenancy in common, or any other legal ownership form.

Syndication: The process of combining persons or firms to accomplish a joint venture which is of mutual interest.

Tacking: The adding together of successive periods of adverse possession of persons in privity with each other in order to create one continuous adverse possession for the time required by statute to establish title.

Tandem plan: A secondary mortgage market arrangement whereby GNMA purchases certain original mortgages for resale to FNMA or other investors.

Tangible property: Property that, by its nature, may be perceived by the senses. In general, the land, its fixed improvement, furnishings, merchandise, cash, etc.

Tax: A charge or burden, usually monetary in nature, levied upon persons or property for public purposes; a forced contribution of wealth to aid in meeting the public needs of a government.

Tax abatement: The amount of decrease or deduction of a tax improperly levied.

Tax base: The sum of the taxable property values which determines the financial capability of the government to raise funds through taxation.

Tax deed: A deed given upon a sale of lands made for the nonpayment of taxes.

Tax lien: A claim against property arising out of nonpayment of taxes; the claim may be sold by the taxing authority.

Tax penalty: The amount to be paid due to nonpayment of the taxes. Usually expressed as a percent of the unpaid balance.

Tax roll: The list describing the persons and properties subject to a particular tax.

Tax sale: A sale of land for unpaid taxes.

Tax sale certificate: A certificate given to the purchaser of land at a tax sale which transfers the lien but not the title to the purchaser.

Tax shelter: An investment motivated primarily to obtain an income tax deduction to apply against taxable income earned from other sources.

Tax title: The title transferred through a tax sale.

Taxable value: The value upon which the taxes are computed when tax rates have been determined.

Taxation (several types): The right of government to payment for the support of activities in which it engages. A double tax in real estate is the taxation of the property as an asset and the taxation of the property income the owner receives. Estate taxation is the tax imposed by government on property passed by will or descent. A personal property tax is a tax imposed upon owners of personal property. A real property tax is a tax imposed upon the owners of real property.

Taxing district: The geographical area over which a taxing authority levies taxes.

Taxpayer: One who pays a tax.

Temporary rent collector: One authorized by permit to act as a rent collector for a period not exceeding 90 days.

Tenancy: An interest in real property; the right to possession and use of real property.

Tenancy at sufferance: The wrongful holding over by a tenant whose lease has terminated.

Tenancy at will: Holding possession of premises by permission of the owner or landlord, but without a fixed term.

Tenancy by the entirety: An estate held by a husband and wife, in which both are viewed as one person under common law which thus provides for ownership by the marriage itself and not by the two parties in shares. Each has an undivided and equal right of possession and enjoyment during their joint lives, with the right of survivorship of the other spouse.

Tenancy in common: An ownership of realty by two or more persons, each of whom has an undivided fractional interest in the whole of the property, without the right of survivorship.

Tenancy in partnership: The co-ownership interest of partners in real property held in the partnership name. It is not a separate and distinct interest in partnership property, but represents a partner's general rights with respect to partnership property.

Tenant: One who has the temporary use and occupation of real property owned by another.

Tenant per autre vie: One who holds lands for the period of another's life.

Tenant selection: A process used by property managers to choose rental prospects.

Tenement: Everything of permanent nature, such as land and buildings, which may be owned; in a more restrictive sense, a house or dwelling.

Tentative map: A map of the subdivision submitted to a local planning commission for study and approval.

Tenure: In accordance with the American concept of real estate ownership, this means that all right and title in and to the land rest with the owner.

Tenure in land: The conditions under which an individual holds an estate in lands.

Termites: Antlike insects which feed on wood.

Termite shield: A shield of noncorrodible metal located on top of the foundation wall or around pipes to prevent the entrance of terminites.

Term mortgage: A specific type of mortgage loan having a stipulated duration, normally under 5 years, on which only interest is paid. At the expiration of the term the entire principal is paid.

Terms: The conditions spelled out in an arrangement or agreement such as a mortgage or a contract.

Testament: A will.

Testamentary: After death; e.g., a devise of real estate by a will is a testamentary transfer because the will is not operative until after death.

Testate: A person who dies leaving a valid will disposing of his property (testator). *Also* leaving a will.

Testator: The person who makes or has made a will.

Time-interval maps: A series of maps that show land use or some other feature as of different dates.

Title (several types): Proof or evidence of ownership or ownership rights. A search of title is a study of the history of the title to a property. A title by descent is a title acquired by the laws of succession; title acquired by an heir in the absence of a will. A title by devise is a title received through a will.

Title company: A corporation whose primary function is to insure titles to real property.

Title guarantee policy: The title insurance provided by the owner in lieu of an abstract of title.

Title insurance: An insurance policy which indemnifies the insured for actual loss sustained by reason of defects, infirmities, or encumbrances of title within the coverage of and not excepted to in the policy. Such a policy also obligates the insurer to defend the title at its expense against all attacks not excepted to.

Title report: A report, prepared prior to the issuance of title insurance, which states the condition of the title.

Title search: The process of checking the public records and legal proceedings to disclose the current state of a real property's ownership.

Title theory: A state statute allowing lenders or lending institutions to secure the title to property as collateral for a loan.

Title theory of mortgage: The mortgage arrangement whereby title to mortgaged real property vests in the lender.

Topographical map: A map that shows the slope and contour of land; a map of the physical features of a parcel of real estate or an area of land.

Topography: The contour and slope of land and such things as gullies, streams, knolls, and ravines.

Torrens certificate: A document issued by the registrar, in accordance with the Torrens law, which identifies the party who holds the title to property.

Torrens system: A system of land title registration in which the state insures the quality of title against certain defects.

Tort: A private or civil wrong or injury.

Township: A territorial subdivision in the quadrangular survey method 6 miles long, 6 miles wide, and containing 36 sections, each 1 mile square.

Trade area: The geographical area from which purchasers of particular goods and services are ordinarily drawn.

Trade association: A voluntary organization of individuals or firms in a common area of economic activity; the organization has for its purpose the promotion of certain aspects of that common area of activity.

Trade fixtures: Articles of personal property which have been annexed to the freehold and which are necessary to the carrying on of a trade and which may be removed.

Trade-in: A method of guaranteeing an owner a minimum amount of cash on sale of his present property to permit him to purchase another. If the property is not sold within a specified time at the listed price, the broker agrees to arrange financing to purchase the property at an agreed upon discount.

Trades: Used synonymously with "exchange." A transaction in which owners convey the rights in a particular property for rights in another.

Traditional design: The home styling incorporating the ideas of the past, reminiscent of Cape Cod, Colonial, Georgian, and similar architectures.

Transcript: A written record of a proceeding which may have been verbal, such as a record of testimony in a trial.

Transfer book: A book in which all transfers of real estate within the county are kept. Such books are kept by the county recorder and, usually, the auditor.

Transfer tax: The tax required by state law to be paid when real estate is sold.

Transition: Change.

Traverse rod: An instrument for hanging draperies or window curtains on a rod fitted with slides, pulleys, and cords, by means of which draperies may be drawn.

Treads: The horizontal boards forming the stairway.

Trend: A prevailing tendency of behavior of some observable phenomenon, such as economic activity, over a long period of time despite intermittent fluctuations.

Trespass: Any unauthorized entry on another's property; any person who makes such an entry is a trespasser.

Trim: Finish materials such as moldings applied around openings or at the floor and ceiling such as baseboards, cornices, or picture moldings.

Trust: A fiduciary relationship in which an independent party (trustee) holds legal title to property for the beneficiaries of the trust who hold the equitable title during the life of the trust. The trustee may not deal with the property as his own but must deal with it in the best interests of the beneficiaries.

Trust account: A bank account held separate from a broker's personal funds, in which a broker is required by state law to deposit all monies collected for clients. (Also see "escrow account.")

Trust deed: An instrument which may be used instead of a mortgage to give security in real estate. The trust deed has the same purpose as a mortgage—that is, to act as security for a debt. However, whereas a mortgage is a two-party instrument which in form conveys title to the property to the mortgagee subject to its return to the mortgagor when the debt is paid, the trust deed conveys the property to a third party (the trustee) who holds it for the benefit of the creditor (called the beneficiary). When the debt is repaid, the trustee is obligated to reconvey the property back to the debtor. In the event of a default under the terms of the trust deed, the trustee normally is given a power of sale to sell the real estate and apply so much of the proceeds as is necessary to discharge the debt, with the balance being given to the debtor. Also often referred to as a deed of trust.

Trust indenture: A document showing the trust agreement.

Trust res: Any property which is the subject of a trust.

Trustee: One who holds legal title to trust assets for the benefit of those holding equitable title. See trust.

Trustor: The one who conveys title of his property to the trustee to be held as security until he has performed his obligation to a lender under the terms of a deed of trust, or for other purposes, such as management.

Truth-in-Lending Act: That portion of Public Law 90-231 (the Consumer Credit Protection Act) which requires that the borrower be informed of true credit costs being charged.

Turnkey: A form of housing for low-income families that was originally built by private sponsors to be sold to local housing authorities.

Ultra vires: Beyond the power. Applied to the acts of a corporation beyond the powers granted in its charter.

Unbalanced improvement: An improvement which does not serve the highest best use for the site on which it is placed.

Underimprovement: An improvement which does not serve

the highest best use for the site on which it is placed by reason of being smaller in size or less in cost than a building which would bring the site to its highest and best use.

Undisclosed principal: One of the parties to a transaction who is unidentified. This might occur when a broker is instructed to keep the identity of his client a secret.

Undivided interest: Fractional ownership but without physical division into shares.

Undue influence: Taking any fraudulent advantage of another's weakness of mind, distress, or necessity.

Unearned increment: An increase in the value of real estate as a result of no effort on the part of the owner; often due to an increase in population.

Unenforceable contract: One that is a good contract but for some reason cannot be enforced under the law, e.g., an unwritten contract for the sale of real estate which is unenforceable because of the Statute of Frauds.

Uniform Commercial Code: Applicable after January 1, 1965, it establishes a unified and comprehensive scheme for the regulation of security transactions in personal property, superseding the existing statutes on chattel mortgages, conditional sales, trust receipts, assignment of accounts receivable, and others in this field.

Unilateral contract: A contract under which one party promises to do something upon the completed act of another.

Unimproved: As relating to land, vacant, returned to nature, or lacking in essential appurtenant improvements required to serve a useful purpose.

United States governmental survey system: A means of describing or locating real property by reference to the governmental survey; often referred to as the rectangular survey.

United States Savings and Loan League: A trade association of savings and loan associations.

Unities of title: The particular characteristic of an estate held by several in joint tenancy and which contains the unities of interest, title, time, and possession; i.e., all joint tenants have one and the same interest accruing through the same conveyance commencing at one time and held by each through an undivided possession of the whole property.

Unit-in-place costs: A means of estimating building replacement cost in which quantities of materials are costed on an in-place rather than purchased basis and summarized to obtain a building cost.

Universal agency: The relationship wherein the agent may act for the principal in every way, without limitation. A very unusual and rarely used form of agency.

Urban plan: The community facilities that enable the community to function as a unit, e.g., the system of streets, sewers, water mains, parks, playgrounds, and the like.

Urban property: City property; densely settled property.

Urban renewal: The controlled method of redevelopment within urban areas. Although often used to refer to Title I and other public projects, it also encompasses private redevelopment efforts.

Urban renewal area: A slum area; a blighted, deteriorated, or deteriorating area; an open land area which is approved by HUD as necessary for an urban renewal project.

Urban renewal project: The term applied to the specific activities undertaken by a local public agency in an urban renewal area to prevent and eliminate slum and blight. The activities may involve slum clearance and redevelopment, rehabilitation, or conservation, or a combination thereof.

Urban size rachet: The theory that, once a town reaches a certain size, it will continue to grow of its own accord.

Urban sprawl: Expansion of a municipality over a large geographical area.

Usage: Uniform practice or course of conduct followed in certain businesses or professions or some procedure or phase thereof.

Use: A beneficial interest in land under a trust.

Use density: The number of buildings having a specific use per unit of area; sometimes calculated by a percentage of land coverage or density of coverage.

Use districts: Areas in a city which have land uses that differ from adjacent land uses, e.g., commercial, industrial, and residential.

Use map: Map of the municipal area showing important types of land uses.

User of real estate: One who has the use of property rights, whether it be through ownership, lease, easement, or license.

Usury: The practice of lending money at a rate of interest above the legal rate. This is an illegal practice.

Utility: Ability of real estate to provide useful services; usefulness of real property.

VA: Veterans' Administration of the federal government.

VA-guaranteed mortgage: Veteran's mortgage guaranteed by the VA for an amount not in excess of VA's appraised value of the property.

VA loan: A loan guaranteed by the VA.

Valid: Having force or binding force; legally sufficient, authorized by law, or incapable of being set aside.

Valid contract: One recognized by the law as being legally enforceable.

Valley: The internal angle formed as a result of the junction between the two sloping sides of a roof.

Valuation: Estimated worth or price; the act of valuing a property by appraisal.

Value analysis: Estimation of the present worth of the future benefits to be derived from a property investment.

Value calculation: The estimation of the value to be recognized by buyers, sellers, lenders, and renters in the marketplace.

Value figure: A figure used to determine how much capital to invest in the property under consideration.

Value for a purpose: The theory that in real estate emphasis must be placed on different value factors depending upon the purpose of the valuation; the use for which the property is being considered.

Value in exchange: The price an investment asset is predicted to bring based upon comparable market transactions.

Value in use: The price an investor would pay based upon his or her personal opinion of the investment asset's merit.

Value of property: The usefulness of the property relative to its scarcity.

Variable payment mortgage: *See* flexible payment mortgage.

Variable rate mortgage: A mortgage which carries an interest rate which may move either up or down, depending on the movements of the standard to which the interest rate is tied.

Variance: The authorization to improve or develop a particular property in a manner not authorized by the zoning ordinance; generally granted by a Board of Zoning Appeals.

Vendee: A purchaser of property. The word is more commonly applied to a purchaser of real property.

Vendee's lien: A lien against property under contract to secure the down payment paid by a purchaser.

Vendor: A person who sells property to a vendee. The word is more commonly applied to a seller of real estate.

Vendor's lien: A lien implied to belong to a vendor for the unpaid purchase price of property, when he has not taken any other lien or security beyond the personal obligation of the purchaser.

Veneer: Thin sheets of wood of excellent quality glued over wood of lesser quality.

Vent: A pipe installed to provide a flow of air to or from a drainage system or to provide for the circulation of air within such a system to protect trap seals from siphonage and backpressure.

Venue: Locality; also, the heading of a legal document showing the state and county to which it refers. Legally, the appropriate forum for filing a lawsuit.

Verbal: By word of mouth; spoken; oral; parol.

Verification: A confirmation of correctness, truth, or authenticity by affidavit, oath, or deposition.

Verified: Confirmed or substantiated by an oath.

Vested: Placed in possession and control; given or committed to another.

Veterans Administration: An agency of the federal government that, among other activities, guarantees loans made to veterans.

Void: That which is entirely null. A void act is one which is not binding on either party and which is not susceptible of ratification.

Voidable: Capable of being made void; not utterly null and void; hence may be either voided or confirmed.

Voluntary lien: A lien placed on property with the consent of, or as a result of, the voluntary act of the owner.

Wainscotting: Wood lining of an interior wall; also the lower part of a wall when finished differently from the upper wall.

Waiver: The intentional relinquishment of a known right. It is a voluntary act and implies an election by the party to dispense with something of value or to forego some advantage or right.

Wall: A bearing wall is one that supports any vertical load in addition to its own weight. A cavity wall is a thin, non-load-bearing wall supported by the structure. A foundation wall is below or partly below ground, providing support for the exterior or other structural parts of the building. A masonry wall is a bearing or non-bearing wall of hollow or solid masonry units.

Warrant: To guarantee or promise that a certain fact or state of facts, in relation to the subject matter of a transaction, is or shall be as it is represented to be.

Warranted value: A term often erroneously used in place of "warranted price."

Warranty deed: One which contains a general guarantee of the quality of title being conveyed.

Waste: An abuse or destructive use of property by one in rightful possession.

Water rights: An aggregate right consisting of the rights to a water supply; guarantee of access to nearby body of water.

Water softener: A mechanical device for treating hard water by circulating it through a chemical solution.

Water table: Distance from surface of ground to a depth where natural groundwater can be found.

Waterpower rights: A property containing the rights to the use of water as a source of power, developed or undeveloped.

WCR: See Women's Council of Realtors.

Will: A written instrument executed with the formalities of law, whereby a person makes a disposition of property to take effect after death.

Will-cut cruise: The estimated volume of lumber that can be sawed from the timber in a given area. It is obtained by deducting from the stand cruise an allowance for breakage and other waste (To cruise is to inspect land to determine possible lumber yield.)

Without recourse: An endorser without recourse specially declines to assume any responsibility to subsequent holders for payment of a debt instrument which is transferred by endorsement.

Women's Council of Realtors: Provides educational programs and publications for women REALTORS® whose primary interest is in residential brokerage.

Words of conveyance: The statement that follows the statement of consideration in a deed to show the intent on the part of the grantor to transfer the property.

Working capital: Properly, the readily convertible capital required in a business to allow the regular functioning of operations free from financial embarrassment. In accounting, the excess of current assets less the current liabilities as of any date.

Working drawing: A sketch of a part or a whole structure, drawn to scale and in such detail as to dimensions and instructions as is needed to guide the work on a construction job.

Wraparound mortgage: A form of junior mortgage which incorporates the full amount of the loan desired with a higher repayment to retire the existing debt. It is used when it is not feasible or desirable to retire the first mortgage.

Writ of execution: An order to carry out the judgment or decree of a court.

X-bracing: Cross-bracing of a partition or floor joist.

Yield: Income of a property—the ratio of the annual net income from the property to the cost or market value of the property.

Zone: The area described by the proper authorities for a specific use, subject to certain restrictions or restraints.

Zoning: Governmental regulation of land use; regulation by local government under police powers of such matters as height, bulk, and use of buildings and use of land. The enabling act is a state statute necessary to provide a legal base for zoning codes. Snob zoning is zoning regulations that require large lots, etc., as a method of excluding those in low-income groups.

Zoning district: The area within a given community which is affected by a zoning ordinance or a portion of such ordinance.

Zoning map: A map showing the various sections of the community and the division of the sections into zones of permitted land uses under the zoning ordinance.

Zoning ordinance: The use of police powers by the governing body to regulate and control the use of real estate for the health, morals, safety, and welfare of the general public.

Index